SERVIN<

GW01454147

SERVING HUMANITY

COMPILED BY A STUDENT WHO HAS
IMPOSED HIS OWN PUNCTUATION
ON THE TEXT

From the Writings of
Alice A. Bailey
and
The Tibetan Master, Djwhal Khul

LUCIS PUBLISHING COMPANY
113 University Place
11th Floor
New York, NY 10003

LUCIS PRESS LTD.
Suite 54
3 Whitehall Court
London SW1A 2EF

First Printing, 1972

Fourth Printing, 1987 (Paperback Edition)

ISBN No. 0-85330-133-6

MANUFACTURED IN THE UNITED STATES OF AMERICA
By FORT ORANGE PRESS, INC., ALBANY, N.Y.

REFERENCE INDEX

Books by The Tibetan (Djwhal Khul), through Alice A. Bailey

Book Ref. No.	Title	First Edition	Reference Edition	Pages
1.	*Initiation, Human and Solar*	1922	8th 1967	225
2.	*Letters on Occult Meditation*	1922	8th 1966	360
3.	*A Treatise on Cosmic Fire*	1925	6th 1964	1 283
4.	*A Treatise on White Magic*	1934	8th 1967	640
5.	*Discipleship in the New Age—Vol. I*	1944	6th 1966	790
6.	*Discipleship in the New Age—Vol. II*	1955	2nd 1955	768
7.	*The Problems of Humanity*	1947	3rd 1964	181
8.	*The Reappearance of The Christ*	1948	3rd 1960	189
9.	*The Destiny of Nations*	1949	2nd 1960	152
10.	*Glamour: A World Problem*	1950	3rd 1967	272
11.	*Telepathy and the Etheric Vehicle*	1950	3rd 1963	197
12.	*Education in the New Age*	1954	1st 1954	153
13.	*The Externalisation of the Hierarchy*	1957	2nd 1958	701
	A Treatise on the Seven Rays			
14.	Vol. I: *Esoteric Psychology I*	1936	5th 1967	430
15.	Vol. II: *Esoteric Psychology II*	1942	2nd 1960	751
16.	Vol. III: *Esoteric Astrology*	1951	5th 1965	695
17.	Vol. IV: *Esoteric Healing*	1953	4th 1967	715
18.	Vol. V: *The Rays and the Initiations*	1960	2nd 1965	769

BOOKS BY ALICE A. BAILEY

The Consciousness of the Atom
The Soul and its Mechanism
From Intellect to Intuition
From Bethlehem to Calvary
The Light of The Soul
The Unfinished Autobiography

NOTE

Reference Example: A reference number, such as for instance (12–135/6) at the end of a quotation, would refer to a quotation taken from *Education in the New Age* (12) starting on page 135, and continued on page 136.

CONTENTS

1.	The True Server	1
2.	A Challenge	1
3.	A Call to Service	3
4.	The Inertia of the Average Spiritually-minded Man	9
5.	The Law of Service	11
6.	The Need for Servers	14
7.	What is Service?	17
8.	The Urge to Serve	19
9.	Characteristics of the Server	20
10.	Learning to Serve	21
11.	Serving Humanity	24
12.	Divine Inspiration	27
13.	Forces of Enlightenment	28
14.	Mystical Perception	29
15.	Preparing for the Reappearance of the Christ	30
16.	Overshadowing by the Avatar	33
17.	The Plan for Human Evolution	35
	(a) The Plan	35
	(b) The Plan Created by Meditation	38
	(c) Sensing the Plan	40
	(d) Problems of the Masters in Transmitting the Plan	42
	(e) Dangers to which Workers are Subject	44
	(f) Materialising the Plan	45
18.	Humanity	49
19.	Human Relationships	54
	(a) Love	54
	(b) Brotherhood	62
	(c) Goodwill	65
	(d) World Goodwill	68
	(e) Right Human Relations	71
	(f) Christ and Right Human Relations	74
	(g) Racial Relations	78
	(h) The New World Order	79
	(i) World Citizenship	84
	(j) World Unity	87
20.	Control of Speech	91
21.	Criticism	95
22.	The Service Rendered by Humanity	97
23.	Energy	101
	(a) Cyclic Nature of Energy Impulses	104
	(b) Energy in Service	107
	(c) The Etheric Vehicle (The Vital Body)	109
	(d) The Awakening of the Centres	113

	(e) The Aura	116
	(f) Radiation	121
24.	Telepathy	122
	(a) Telepathic Communication	122
	(b) Telepathic Rapport	123
	(c) Telepathic Sensitivity	124
25.	Impression	126
26.	Occult Blindness	132
27.	Revelation	133
28.	Illumination	140
29.	The Intuition	142
30.	Soul Awareness	145
31.	Meditation	146
	(a) What is Meditation?	146
	(b) Meditation: Occidental and Oriental	147
	(c) Dangers of Meditation	147
	(d) Visualisation	149
	(e) Realisations Resulting from Meditation	150
	(f) Meditation and Service	152
32.	Discipleship	153
33.	Requirements needed by Aspirants	156
34.	What is a Disciple?	162
35.	Status of Disciples	164
36.	Requirements of the Disciple	164
	(a) Sincerity	172
	(b) Sensitivity	172
	(c) Psychic Powers	174
	(d) Astral Polarisation	178
	(e) Mental Polarisation	179
	(f) Detachment	180
	(g) Impersonality	182
	(h) Divine Indifference	184
	(i) Serenity	186
	(j) Humility	188
	(k) Esoteric Sense	189
	(l) Perseverance	190
	(m) Courage	191
	(n) Capacity to Give	191
37.	Equipping for Service	192
38.	Control of the Mind	193
39.	Purification of the Vehicles for Service	194
40.	Care of the Physical Body	200
41.	Diet	203
42.	The Power to Heal	204
43.	Healing Work	205

44.	The Evolving Form	209
45.	The Life Span	212
46.	Death	213
47.	The Unfolding Disciple	215
48.	Dual Life of the Disciple	220
49.	Choice of Path	221
50.	Right Decision	222
51.	The Probationary Path	225
52.	The Treading of the Way	226
53.	The Immediate Goal for Disciples	232
54.	Working under Existing Conditions	233
55.	Standing Alone	233
56.	Loneliness	236
57.	Accepted Disciple	238
58.	Sonship to the Master	241
59.	Masters and Disciples	243
60.	Occult Obedience	250
61.	Free Will	253
62.	Freedom	255
63.	Age of the Disciple	258
64.	The Sannyasin	259
65.	Old Age and Service	262
66.	The New Group of World Servers (N.G.W.S.)	265
	(a) Classification of Humanity	265
	(b) Historical Background	268
	(c) Birth of the N.G.W.S.	276
	(d) Organisation of the N.G.W.S.	279
	(e) Characteristics of the N.G.W.S.	281
	(f) Requirements for Membership	284
	(g) Membership	288
	(h) The Group Symbol	291
	(i) Uniting the Men of Goodwill	292
	(j) Their Mission	294
	(k) Activities and Techniques	298
	(l) Dangers to be Avoided by the Group	303
	(m) Training of Servers	304
	(n) The Present Situation	308
	(o) Ushering in the New Age	311
	(p) The Future of the Group	311
	(q) Creative Work	313
	(r) Cyclic Rhythm of the New Group Work	313
	(s) The Plan for Humanity	314
	(t) Impressing the Plan	317
	(u) Expressing of Group Love	319
	(v) Stage of Development of the Disciple	320

	(w) The Externalisation of the Hierarchy	322
	(x) Preparing for the Reappearance of the Christ	324
	(y) Conclusion	328
67.	The Serving Hierarchy	330
68.	Externalisation of the Hierarchy	338
69.	A Master's Ashram	342
70.	Disciples Preparing for the New Age	349
71.	Service as Approach to the Great Ones	353
72.	Channels for Service	354
73.	Light Bearers	355
74.	The Joy of Service	356
75.	The Life of Service	359
76.	Dangers in the Life of Service	366
77.	Service to Individuals	368
78.	Motives for Service	369
79.	Loving Service	370
80.	Selfless Service	371
81.	Scope of Service	373
82.	Money in Service	376
83.	Creative Service	385
84.	Limitations	386
85.	Irritation	388
86.	Points of Tension	389
87.	Points of Crisis	391
88.	Losing Time for Service	394
89.	Master of Time	395
90.	The Future	395
91.	The Law of Rebirth	397
92.	Factors Governing Incarnations for Service	399
93.	Incarnating Souls Affecting Civilisation	400
94.	Karma	401
95.	Knowledge	403
96.	Responsibility	405
97.	Sacrifice	407
98.	Pain and Suffering	409
99.	Glamour and Illusion	412
	(a) Glamour	412
	(b) The Glamour of Materiality	415
	(c) The Glamour of Idealism	416
	(d) The Illusion of Power	417
	(e) Overcoming the Dweller	418
100.	Success	419
101.	Failure	420
102.	Recognition	422
103.	Relaxation and Recreation	425

104.	Consciousness	426
	(a) The Indwelling Consciousness	426
	(b) Expanding Consciousness	428
	(c) Continuity of Consciousness	430
	(d) Limitation and Imprisonment	431
	(e) Serving by Releasing the Prisoners	432
105.	Training	434
	(a) Training of Disciples	434
	(b) Training of Students	437
	(c) Rules of Life for the Young Aspirant	438
106.	Teaching	439
107.	Transmission of Teachings	443
108.	Esoteric Studies	451
109.	Education	452
110.	Group Aspects	458
	(a) The Law of Group Life	458
	(b) Choosing the Right Workers	458
	(c) Group Training	460
	(d) Group Integrity	460
	(e) Bonds of Service	462
	(f) Growth Through Sharing	463
	(g) Disciple and Group Relationships	464
	(h) Group Consciousness	467
	(i) Telepathic Sensitivity	467
	(j) Group Work	470
	(k) Leadership	473
	(l) New Age Groups	475
	(m) The Kingdom of God on Earth	476
111.	Initiation	478
	(a) Rules for Applicants for Initiation	478
	(b) Preparing for Initiation	479
	(c) Initiation	481
	(d) Group Initiation	483
	(e) The Initiate	485
	(f) First Initiation	489
	(g) Second Initiation	491
	(h) Third Initiation	493
	(i) Fourth Initiation	495
112.	Dark Forces	496
113.	The White Magician	501
114.	Mantrams	502
115.	The Pilgrim	504
116.	An Esoterical Catechism	505
117.	Some Words of Cheer	507
118.	Conclusion	509

COMMENTS BY THE COMPILER

This is to a certain extent a continuation of the compilations commenced in a previous book *Ponder on This*.

Readers of *Ponder on This* will find that there is some overlapping between the latter book and the present volume, with regard to certain of the extracts that have been used. The re-inclusion of such quotations has been done deliberately for the sake of rounding off the present book. In this connection The Tibetan states "This covers familiar ground for you, but in the effort to achieve a vision of the whole, constant repetition has its place" (16-614), or again "It is only through constant reiteration that men learn, and these things must be said again and again" (15-668). Furthermore, those who have learnt to appreciate D.K.'s writings, can read his beautiful words and thoughts over and over again, gradually penetrating into deeper meanings that remained hidden or unnoticed with the first perusals.

This is a book of quotations, so let me commence on the proper footing:

That your vision may expand, and your power to think and reflect abstractly, may grow, is my hope and wish for you.   (18-207)

Those who read and study these ideas, are occupied with concepts and thoughts totally unrealised, and wholly inexplicable and sometimes even senseless, to the ordinary everyday businessman in the street. (18-363)

Pretoria,   A Student
June 1972

EXTRACT FROM A STATEMENT BY THE TIBETAN

August 1934

Suffice it to say, that I am a Tibetan disciple of a certain degree, and this tells you but little, for all are disciples, from the humblest aspirant up to, and beyond, the Christ Himself. I live in a physical body like other men, on the borders of Tibet, and at times (from the exoteric standpoint) preside over a large group of Tibetan lamas, when my other duties permit. It is this fact that has caused it to be reported that I am an abbot of this particular lamasery. Those associated with me in the work of the Hierarchy (and all true disciples are associated in this work) know me by still another name and office. A.A.B. knows who I am and recognises me by two of my names.

I am a brother of yours, who has travelled a little longer upon the Path than has the average student, and has therefore incurred greater responsibilities. I am one who has wrestled and fought his way into a greater measure of light than the aspirant who will read this article, and I must therefore act as a transmitter of the light, no matter what the cost. I am not an old man, as age counts among the teachers, yet I am not young or inexperienced. My work is to teach and spread the knowledge of the Ageless Wisdom wherever I can find a response, and I have been doing this for many years. I seek also to help the Master M. and the Master K.H. whenever opportunity offers, for I have been long connected with Them and with Their work. In all the above, I have told you much; yet at the same time I have told you nothing which would lead you to offer me that blind obedience and the foolish devotion which the emotional aspirant offers to the Guru and Master Whom he is as yet unable to contact. Nor will he make that desired contact until he has transmuted emotional devotion into unselfish *service to humanity*—not to the Master.

The books I have written are sent out with no claim for their acceptance. They may, or may not, be correct, true and useful. It is for you to ascertain their truth by right practice and by the exercise of the intuition. Neither I nor A.A.B. is the least interested in having them acclaimed as inspired writings, or in having anyone speak of them (with bated breath) as being the work of one of the Masters. If they present truth in such a way that it follows sequentially upon that already offered in the world teachings, if the information given raises the aspiration and the will-to-serve from the plane of the emotions to that of the mind (the plane whereon the Masters *can* be found), then they will have served their purpose. If the teaching conveyed calls forth a response from the illumined mind of the worker in the world, and brings a flashing forth of his intuition, then let that teaching be accepted. But not otherwise. If the statements meet with eventual corroboration, or are deemed true under the test of the Law of Correspondences, then that is well and good. But should this not be so, let not the student accept what is said.

Training for new age

discipleship is provided

by the *Arcane School*.

The principles of the

Ageless Wisdom are

presented through esoteric

meditation, study and

service as a *way of life*.

*Write to the publishers
for information.*

THE GREAT INVOCATION

From the point of Light within the Mind of God
  Let light stream forth into the minds of men.
    Let Light descend on Earth.

From the point of Love within the Heart of God
  Let love stream forth into the hearts of men.
    May Christ return to Earth.

From the centre where the Will of God is known
  Let purpose guide the little wills of men—
    The purpose which the Masters know and serve.

From the centre which we call the race of men
  Let the Plan of Love and Light work out
    And may it seal the door where evil dwells.

Let Light and Love and Power restore the Plan on Earth.

The above Invocation or Prayer does not belong to any person or group, but to all Humanity. The beauty and the strength of this Invocation lies in its simplicity, and in its expression of certain central truths which all men, innately and normally, accept—the truth of the existence of a basic Intelligence to Whom we vaguely give the name of God; the truth that behind all outer seeming, the motivating power of the universe is Love; the truth that a great Individuality came to earth, called by Christians, the Christ, and embodied that love so that we could understand; the truth that both love and intelligence are effects of what is called the Will of God; and finally the self-evident truth that only through *humanity* itself can the Divine Plan work out.

Alice A. Bailey

1. THE TRUE SERVER

The Master looks not at a worker's worldly force or status, not at the numbers of people who are gathered around his personality, but at the motives which prompt his activity and at the effect of his influence upon his fellow men. True service is the spontaneous outflow of a loving heart and an intelligent mind; it is the result of being in the right place and staying there; it is produced by the inevitable inflow of spiritual force and not by strenuous physical plane activity; it is the effect of a man's being what he truly is, a divine Son of God, and not by the studied effect of his words or deeds. A true server gathers around him those who it is his duty to serve and aid by the force of his life and his spiritualised personality, and not by his claims or loud speaking. In self-forgetfulness he serves; in self-abnegation he walks the earth, and he gives no thought to the magnitude or the reverse of his accomplishment, and has no preconceived ideas as to his own value or usefulness. He lives, serves, works and influences, asking nothing for the separated self.   (4-188/9)

2. A CHALLENGE

I challenge the thinkers of the world to drop their sectarianism, their nationalism, and their partisanships, and in the spirit of brotherhood to work in their particular nation, regarding it as an integral part of a great federation of nations—a federation that now exists on the inner side, but waits for the activity of world thinkers to bring it to materialisation on the outer side. I charge them to work in the cause of religion and in the field of that particular religion in which they, by an accident of birth or by choice, are interested, regarding each religion as part of the great world religion. They must look upon the activities of their group, society or organisation as demanding their help, just in so far, and only so far, as the principles upon which they are founded, and the techniques which they employ, serve the general good and develop the realisation of Brotherhood.

I ask you to drop your antagonisms and your antipathies, your hatreds

1

and your racial differences, and attempt to think in terms of the one family, the one life, and the one humanity. I ask for no sentimental or devotional response to this challenge. I would remind you that hatred and separateness have brought humanity to the present sad condition. I would add to that reminder, however, the fact that there is in the world today a large enough number of liberated men to produce a change in the attitudes of mankind and in public opinion, if they measure up by an act of the will to what they know and believe.

I challenge you also to make sacrifices; to give yourself and your time and your money and your interest, to carry these ideas to those around you in your own environment and to the group in which you find yourself, thus awakening your associates. I call you to a united effort to inculcate anew the ideas of brotherhood and of unity. I ask you to recognise your fellow workers in all the groups and to strengthen their hands. I ask you to seal your lips to words of hatred and of criticism, and to talk in terms of brotherhood and of group relationships. I beg of you to see to it that every day is for you a new day, in which you face new opportunity. Lose sight of your own affairs, your petty sorrows, worries and suspicions, in the urgency of the task to be done, and spread the cult of unity, of love and of harmlessness.

I ask you also to sever your connection with all groups which are seeking to destroy and to attack, no matter how sincere their motive. Range yourself on the side of the workers for constructive ends, who are fighting no other groups or organisations, and who have eliminated the word "anti" out of their vocabulary. Stand on the side of those who are silently and steadily building for the new order—an order which is founded on love, which builds under the impulse of brotherhood, and which possesses a realisation of a brotherhood which is based on the knowledge that we are each and all, no matter what our race, the children of the One Father, and who have come to the realisation that the old ways of working must go, and the newer methods must be given a chance.

If you cannot yourself teach or preach or write, give of your thought and of your money so that others can. Give of your hours and minutes of leisure so as to set others free to serve the Plan; give of your money so that the work of those associated with the New Group of World Servers may go forward with rapidity. Much time you waste on non-essentials. Many of you give little or nothing of time. The same is the case with money. Give as never before, and so make the physical aspects of the work possible. Some give of their very need, and the power they thereby release is great. Those on the inner side are grateful for the giving by those who can give only at great personal cost. Others give of what they can spare and only when it needs no sacrifice to give. Let that condition also end, and give to the limit, with justice and understanding, so that the age of love and light may be more rapidly ushered in. I care not where or to whom you give, only that you give—little if you have but little of time or money, much if you have much. Work and give, love and think, and aid those groups who are building and not destroying, loving and not attacking, lifting and not tearing down. Be not taken in by the specious argument that destruction is needed. It has been needed, no doubt; but the cycle of destruction is practically over, could you but realise it, and the builders must now get busy.

I challenge you above all to a deeper life, and I implore you for the sake of your fellow men to strengthen your contact with your own soul, so that you will have done your share in making revelation possible; so that you will have served your part in bringing in the light, and will therefore be in a position to take advantage of that new light and new information, and so be better able to point the way and clear the path for the bewildered seeker at that time. Those who are not ready for the coming events will be blinded by the emerging light, and bewildered by the revealing wonder; they will be swept by the living breath of God, and it is to you that we look to fit them for the event. (14-187/9)

3. A CALL TO SERVICE

1. World Unity, brotherhood in its true sense, the growth of telepathic interplay, the elimination of the non-essentials which serve to separate the thoughts of men and bring about separateness on the physical plane, and the laying of a true emphasis upon the fundamentals of the Ageless Wisdom, the manifestation of a true understanding, the bringing about of at-one-ment with the soul, the recognition of those who belong to the group of world Saviours—this is the immediate work to be done, and this must engross your attention.

This, and this alone, warrants the expenditure of all that any of you have to give—love and life, time and money.

This, and this alone, justifies your existence and calls forth from all of you who respond to the vision, that utter self-sacrifice which is so rare and so far-reaching in its effects. The casting of all that one has at the

feet of the Lord of Life, in order that the work of world salvage may go
forward, the elimination out of one's life of all that can possibly hinder,
the giving of all that one has until it hurts to give, the ruling of one's life
on the basis of surrender, asking oneself all the time : What can I relinquish in order that I may help more adequately?—that and more than
that lies ahead of all of you who hear the call and respond to the need
and opportunity.   (4-428)

2. Every time there is a tendency towards synthesis and understanding in
the world, every time the lesser is merged in the greater and the unit is
blended in the whole, every time great and universal concepts make their
impact upon the minds of the masses, there is a subsequent disaster and
cataclysm and breaking down of the form aspect, and of that which might
allow those concepts becoming physical plane facts. This is therefore the
problem of the hierarchical workers : how to avert the dreaded suffering
and carry man along, whilst the tidal wave of the spiritual realisation
sweeps over the world and does its needed work. Hence the present *call
to service* which is sounding like a trumpet in the ear of all attentive disciples.

This call to service usually meets with a response, but that response is
coloured by the personality of the aspirant and tinctured with his pride
and his ambition. Need is truly realised. The desire to meet the need is
genuine and sincere; the longing to serve and lift is real. Steps are taken
which are intended by the aspirant to enable him to fit in with the Plan.
But the trouble with which we on the inner side have perforce to deal is
that, though there is no question as to willingness and desire to serve, the
characters and temperaments are such that well nigh insuperable difficulties are presented. Through these aspirants we have to work, and the
material they present gives us much trouble frequently.

Latent Characteristics

These latent characteristics often do not make their appearance until
after the service has been undertaken. That they are there, the watching
guides may suspect, but even they have not the right to withhold opportunity. When there is this delayed appearance, the tragedy is that many
others suffer besides the aspirant concerned. As the human fabric makes
itself felt, and stands out of the mist of idealism, of lovely plans and much
talk and arranging, many are in the meantime attracted by synchronous
idealism, and gather around the server. When the hidden weaknesses
appear, they suffer as well as he. The method of the Great Ones, which

is to seek out those who have trained themselves somewhat in sensitive response, and to work through them, carries with it certain dangers. The ordinary well-meaning aspirant is not in such danger as the more advanced and active disciple. He is in danger in three directions, and can be swept off his feet in three ways :

i. His whole nature is under undue stimulation on account of his inner contacts, and the spiritual forces with which he is in touch, and this carries with it real danger, for he hardly knows as yet how to handle himself, and is scarcely aware of the risk entailed.

ii. The people with whom he is working, in their turn, make his problem. Their greed, their adulation and praise, and their criticism, tend to becloud his way. Because he is not sufficiently detached and spiritually advanced, he walks bemused in a cloud of thought-forms, and knows it not. Thus he loses his way and wanders from his original intent, and again he knows it not.

iii. His latent weaknesses must emerge under the pressure of work, and inevitably he will show signs of cracking at times, if I may use such a word. The personality faults become strengthened as he seeks to carry his particular form of service to the world. I refer to that service which is self-sought, and formulated on a background of personal ambition and love of power, even if only partially recognised or not recognised at all. He is under strain naturally, and—like a man carrying a heavy load up a steep hill—he discovers points of strain, and evinces a tendency to break down physically, or to lower his ideal so as to conform to weaknesses.

To all this must be added the strain of the period itself, and the general condition of unhappy humanity. This subconsciously has its effect on all disciples, and upon all who are now working in the world. Some are showing signs of physical pressure, though the inner life remains poised and normal, sane and rightly oriented. Others are breaking up emotionally and this produces two effects according to the point of development of the aspirant to service. He is either, through the strain, learning detachment, and this curiously enough is what might be called the "defense mechanism" of the soul in this present period of world unfoldment, or he is becoming increasingly nervous, and is on the way to become a neurotic. Others again are feeling the pressure in the mental body. They become bewildered in some cases, and no clear truth appears. They then work on without inspiration, and because they know it to be right, and they also have the rhythm of the work. Others are grasping opportunity as they

see it and, to do so, fall back on innate self-assertion (which is the outstanding fault of the mental types) and build up a structure around their
service, and construct a form which in reality embodies what they desire,
what they think to be right, but which is separative and the child of their
minds and not the child of their souls. Some, in their turn, more potent
and more co-ordinated, feel the pressure of the entire personality; the versatile psychic nature responds both to need and to the theory of the plan;
they realise their truly valuable assets, and know they have somewhat to
contribute. They are still, however, so full of what is called *personality*,
that their service is gradually and steadily stepped down to the level of
that personality, and is consequently coloured by their personality reactions, their likes and dislikes, and their individual life tendencies and
habits. These eventually assert themselves, and there is then a worker,
doing good work, but spoiling it all by his unrealised separateness and
individual methods. This means that such a worker gathers to himself
only those whom he can subordinate and govern. His group is not
coloured by the impulses of the New Age, but by the separative instincts
of the worker at the centre. The danger here is so subtle that much care
must be taken by a disciple in self-analysis. It is so easy to be glamoured
by the beauty of one's own ideals and vision, and by the supposed recti-
tude of one's own position, and yet all the time to be influenced subjectively by love of personal power, individual ambition, jealousy of other
workers, and the many traps which catch the feet of the unwary disciple.

But if true impersonality is cultivated, if the power to stand steady is
developed, if every situation is handled in a spirit of love, and if there is
a refusal to take hasty action and to permit separation to creep in, then
there will be the growth of a group of true servers, and the gathering
out of those who can materialise the Plan, and bring to birth the New
Age and its attendant wonders.   (4-622/5)

3. I seek to do two things:

i. Indicate the immediate goal for students in this century, and summarise the steps that they must take.

ii. Indicate the things which must be eliminated and overcome, and the
penalties which overtake the probationer and the disciple when mistakes are made and faults condoned.

The Immediate Goal

. . . The immediate goal must be well recognised, if lost effort is to be
avoided and real progress achieved. Many well-intentioned aspirants are

prone to give undue time to their registered aspirations, and to the formulation of their plans for service. The world aspiration is now so strong, and humanity is now so potently orienting itself towards the Path, that sensitive people everywhere are being swept into a vortex of spiritual desire, and ardently long for the life of liberation, of spiritual undertakings, and of recorded soul consciousness. Their recognition of their own latent possibilities is now so strong, that they over-estimate themselves; they give much time to picturing themselves as the ideal mystic, or in deploring their lack of spiritual achievement, of their failure to achieve a sphere of service. Thus they become lost, on the one hand in the vague and misty realms of a beautiful idealism, of colourful hypotheses and of delightful theories; on the other hand, they become engulfed in a dramatisation of themselves as centres of power in a field of fruitful service; they draw up, mentally, plans for world endeavour, to see themselves as the pivotal point around which that service will move; they frequently make an effort to work out these plans and produce an organisation, for instance on the physical plane, which is potentially valuable but equally potentially useless, even if not dangerous. They fail to realise that the motivating impulse is primarily due to what the Hindu teachers call a "sense of I-ness", and that their work is founded on a subjective egoism which must—and will—be eliminated before true service can be rendered. (4-618/9)

4. The mobilisation of every disciple is demanded at this time, and when I say "this time" I refer to the present time (about 1930—comp.) and the next fifty years. This mobilisation involves the focussing of the disciple's energies, his time and his resources on behalf of humanity; it requires a new dedication to service, a consecration of the thought-life (do you realise what that would mean, my brothers?) and a forgetfulness of self, which would rule out all moods and feelings, all personality desires, resentments, grievances, and all pettiness in your relations with your fellow men. On the physical plane, it would mean the conditioning of all active, outer living so that the whole of life becomes one focussed, active service. I would ask you to study the above phrasing, using it as a light of revelation so that you may know wherein you are lacking, and what you have to do.

. . . Today make a new beginning—not for your own sake, but for the helping of a needy world. Forget yourselves. (5-98/9)

5. One of the first lessons which those in training for initiation have to master, is that difficult dual attitude, which permits right personality acti-

vity and real interest in personality affairs, and yet at the same time permits nothing personal to interfere with the subjective spiritual life, with service and with the training given in preparation for initiation. (5-99)

6. The service you can render is to you of more value than the service that can be rendered to you. (5-301)

7. The world today offers opportunity to all disciples to become world disciples, close to the Master's heart, and to pass rapidly through the earlier stages of discipleship. It offers opportunity to world disciples to begin their approach to the Heart of the Hierarchy, to Christ. It is with this first possibility that you should be concerned, for—as you come closer to your group—you can begin to get that training which will develop in you *world* usefulness. Are the majority of you too old to achieve this? That is for you to say. The soul knows no age and can use its instrument if it makes itself into a suitable and available instrument. Are you too set and too preoccupied with yourselves to achieve the detachment needed for world service? That is for you to find out and to prove to yourselves. . . . Are you too depressed (which is a synonym for selfishness) and too sensitive to render service to humanity in a larger way than hitherto? That can be overcome *if you care enough*. Is your awareness a constant group-awareness? Or is it a constant self-awareness which comes consistently between you and your fellowmen? That is for you to discover. Have you the deep humility—based on a realisation of the Plan and the glory of the goal—and not a sense of self-depreciation over which you gloat and regard as an indication of spiritual humility? You need to re-interpret this theme of humility, as well as all your terms, in the light of the esoteric and spiritual values. Can you do this? (5-768/9)

8. Upon your understanding response to the collective need will depend the rapidity with which you will be enabled to achieve the next expansion of consciousness or initiation which may be, for you as an individual, possible. You have, therefore, to consider your individual response to the demands of your own soul and your collective response to the collective need. It is the initiate in you, the Christ in you, which is now called to this collective service and the radiation today of the Christ spirit, actively present in the hearts of all disciples, is the one thing which can salvage mankind, enable humanity to move forward on to the Path of Discipleship and thus evoke that new spirit which can and will build the new world. (6-244)

4. THE INERTIA OF THE AVERAGE SPIRITUALLY-MINDED MAN

The average spiritually-minded person, man of goodwill, or disciple, is constantly aware of the challenge of the times and the opportunity which spiritual events may offer. The desire to do good and to accomplish spiritual ends is ceaselessly gnawing away within his consciousness. No one who loves his fellow men, who has a dream of seeing the Kingdom of God materialise on earth, or who is conscious of the awakening—slow though it may be—of the masses to the higher spiritual values, but is thoroughly dissatisfied. He realises that what he contributed of help to these desirable objectives is little indeed. He knows that his spiritual life is a side issue; it is something which he keeps carefully to himself and which he is frequently afraid to mention to his nearest and dearest; he tries to dovetail his spiritual efforts into his ordinary, outer life, struggling to find time and opportunity for it in a gentle, futile and innocent manner. He finds himself helpless before the task of organising and rearranging his affairs so that the spiritual way of living may dominate; he searches for alibis for himself and eventually rationalises himself so successfully, that he ends by deciding that he is doing the best he can in the given circumstances. The truth is that he is doing so little that probably one hour out of twenty-four (or perhaps two) would cover the time given to the Master's work; he hides behind the alibi that his home obligations prevent his doing more, and does not realise that—given tact and loving understanding—his home environment can and must be the field in which he triumphs; he forgets that *there exist no circumstances in which the spirit of man can be defeated,* or in which the aspirant cannot meditate, think, talk and prepare the way for the coming of the Christ, provided he cares enough and knows the meaning of sacrifice and silence. *Circumstances and environment offer no true obstacle to the spiritual life.*

Perhaps he hides behind the alibi of poor health, and frequently behind that of imaginary ills. He gives so much time to the care of himself that the hours which could be given to the Master's work are directly and seriously curtailed; he is so preoccupied with feeling tired, or tending a cold, or with fancied heart difficulties, that his "body consciousness" steadily develops until it eventually dominates his life; it is then too late to do anything. This is particularly the case with people who have reached their fiftieth year or over. It is an alibi which it is hard not to use, for many feel tired and ailing, and this, as the years go by, is apt to get worse.

9

The only cure for this creeping inertia, is to ignore the body and take your joy in the livingness of service. I speak here not of definite disease or of serious physical liabilities; to these right care and attention must be duly given; I speak to the thousands of ailing men and women who are preoccupied with taking care of themselves, and so waste hours of the time which could be given to the service of humanity. Those who are seeking to tread the Path of Discipleship, should release those many hours spent in needless self-care into the service of the Hierarchy.

Still another alibi, leading to inertia, is *the fear* people have of speaking about the things of the Kingdom of God to others; they are afraid of being rebuffed, or of being thought peculiar, or of intruding. They therefore preserve silence, lose opportunity and never discover how ready people are for the discussion of realities, for the comfort and hope which the thought of Christ's return can bring, or for the sharing of spiritual light. This is essentially a form of spiritual cowardice, but is so widespread that it is responsible for the loss of millions of hours of world service.

There are other alibis, but those above noted are the most common; the release of the majority of people from these hindering conditions would bring to the service of the Christ so many hours and so much overtime endeavour that the task of those who admit no alibis would be greatly enlightened, and the coming of the Christ would be much nearer than it is today. To the rhythm of life under which the Christ and the spiritual Hierarchy operate, and which vibrates in harmony with human need and spiritual response, we are not called. We are, however, called to demonstrate the quality of spiritual activity and to refuse to hide behind alibis. It is essential that all spiritual people recognise that in the place where they now are, among the people who are their associates and with the psychological and physical equipment with which they are endowed, they *can and must work.* There is no possible coercion or undue pressure exerted in the service of the Hierarchy. The situation is clear and simple. (8-166/9), (13-619/23)

5. THE LAW OF SERVICE

1. The Law of Service . . . is the governing law of the future . . . In past ages, it was the service of one's own soul (with the emphasis upon one's own individual salvation) which engrossed the attention of the aspirant. Naught else was considered. Then came the period wherein the service of the Master and also of one's own soul was considered of dominant interest; the Master was served and duty to Him emphasised, because thereby the salvation of the individual was aided. Now a new note is sounding forth—the note of growth through the service of the race, and through a cultivated self-forgetfulness.   (5-551)

2. You will awaken some day to the realisation that the *Science of Service* is of greater importance than the Science of Meditation, because it is the effort and the strenuous activity of the serving disciple which evokes the soul powers, makes meditation an essential requirement, and is the mode —ahead of all others—which invokes the Spiritual Triad, brings about the intensification of the spiritual life, forces the building of the antah-karana, and leads in a graded series of renunciations to the Great Renunciation, which sets the disciple free for all eternity.   (6-59)

3. The third Law of the Soul is intended to govern all soul activity. It is the Law of Service. Before we elaborate this theme, there are three things which I seek to say and which merit our careful attention:

First, is the fact that the result of all contact achieved in meditation and the measure of our success, will be determined by the ensuing service to the race. If there is right understanding, there will necessarily be right action.

. . . The three great sciences which will come to the fore in the New Age, and which will lead humanity from the unreal to the real, and from aspiration to realisation, are:

i. The science of Meditation, the coming science of the mind.

ii. The science of Antahkarana, or the science of the bridging which must take place between the higher and lower mind.

iii. The science of Service, which is a definite technique of at-one-ment.

Secondly, this Law of Service is something which may not be escaped. Evasion brings its penalties, if that evasion is conscious. Ability to serve marks a definite stage of advance upon the Path, and until that stage is reached, spontaneous service, rendered in love and guided by wisdom,

11

cannot be given. What is found up to that time is good intention, mixed
motives, and oft fanaticism. . . .

Thirdly, this Law of Service was expressed for the first time fully by
the Christ, two thousand years ago. . . . The Piscean age slowly, very
slowly, prepared the way for the divine expression of service, which will
be the glory of the coming centuries. Today, we have a world which is
steadily coming to the realisation that "no man liveth unto himself", and
that only as love, about which so much has been written and spoken,
finds its outlet in service, can man begin to measure up to his innate
capacity. . . . It is not easy to serve. Man is today only beginning to
learn how to serve. . . .

Service is usually interpreted as exceedingly desirable, and it is seldom
realised how very difficult service essentially is. It involves so much sacrifice of time and of interest and of one's own ideas, it requires exceedingly
hard work, because it necessitates deliberate effort, conscious wisdom,
and the ability to work without attachment. These qualities are not easy
of attainment by the average aspirant, and yet today the tendency to
serve is an attitude which is true of a vast majority of the people in the
world. Such has been the success of the evolutionary process.

Service is frequently regarded as an endeavour to bring people around
to the point of view of the one who serves, because what the would-be
server has found to be good and true and useful, must necessarily be good
and true and useful for all. Service is viewed as something we render to
the poor, the afflicted, the diseased and the unhappy, because we think we
want to help them, little realising that primarily this help is offered because
we ourselves are made uncomfortable by distressing conditions, and must
therefore endeavour to ameliorate those conditions in order ourselves to
be comfortable again. The act of thus helping releases us from our misery,
even if we fail to release or relieve the sufferers.

Service is frequently an indication of a busy and over-active temperament, or of a self-satisfied disposition, which leads its possessor to a
strenuous effort to change situations, and make them what he feels they
should be, thus forcing people to conform to that which the server feels
should be done.

Or again, service can grow out of a fanatical desire to tread in the
footsteps of the Christ, that great Son of God Who "went about doing
good", leaving an example that we should follow in His footsteps.
People, therefore, serve from a sense of obedience, and not from a spontaneous outgoing towards the needy. The essential quality for service is,
therefore, lacking, and from the start they fail to do more than make cer-

tain gestures. Service can likewise be rendered from a deep seated desire
for spiritual perfection. It is regarded as one of the necessary qualifications for discipleship and, therefore, if one is to be a disciple, one must
serve. This theory is correct, but the living substance of service is lacking.
The ideal is right and true and meritorious, but the motive behind it all is
entirely wrong. Service can also be rendered because it is becoming
increasingly the fashion and the custom to be occupied with some form of
service. The tide is on. Everybody is actively serving in welfare movements, in philanthropic endeavours, in Red Cross work, in educational
uplifts, and in the task of ameliorating distressing world conditions. It is
fashionable to serve in some way. Service gives a sense of power; brings
one friends; service is a form of group activity, and frequently brings far
more to the server (in a worldly sense) than to the served.

And yet, in spite of all this, which indicates wrong motives and false
aspiration, service of a kind is constantly and readily being rendered.
Humanity is on its way to a right understanding of services. . . .
(15-118/23)

4. When the personal lower self is subordinated to the higher rhythms and
obedient to the new Law of Service, then the life of the soul will begin to
flow through the man to the others, and the effect in a man's immediate
family and group will be to demonstrate a real understanding and a true
helpfulness. As the flow of life becomes stronger through use, the effect
will spread out from the small surrounding family group to the neighbour-
hood. A wider range of contacts becomes possible, until eventually (if
several lives have been thus spent under the influence of the Law of Service) the effect of the outpouring life may become nationwide and worldwide. But it will not be planned, nor will it be fought for, as an end in
itself. It will be a natural expression of the soul's life, taking form and
direction according to a man's ray and past life expression; it will be
coloured and ordered by environing conditions—by time, by period, by
race and age. It will be a living flow, and a spontaneous giving forth, and
the life, power and love demonstrated, being sent forth from soul levels,
will have a potent, attractive force upon the group units with which the
disciple may come in contact in the three worlds of soul expression. There
are no other worlds wherein the soul may at this time thus express itself.
Nothing can stop or arrest the potency of this life of natural, loving service, except in those cases wherein the personality gets in the way. Then
service, as the Teachers on the inner side of life understand it, gets distorted and altered into busy-ness. It becomes changed into ambition, into

an effort to make others serve as we think service should be rendered, and into a love of power which hinders true service, instead of into love of our fellow men. There is a point of danger in every life when the theory of service is grasped, and the higher law is recognised; then the imitative quality of the personality, its monkey nature, and the eagerness of a high grade aspiration, can easily mistake theory for reality, and the outer gestures of a life of service for the natural, spontaneous flow of soul life through its mechanism of expression.   (15-128/9)

6.   THE NEED FOR SERVERS

1. The need of the world today has never been so great, nor the responsibility resting upon those who are treading the Path of Discipleship so deep, real and urgent. We need all who are working upon this Path and who are aspiring towards release. We need those who are seeking close contact with their souls and with Us Who are seeking to guide the race today. We need co-operators of dedication and selflessness as never before in the history of the race.

   . . . These are days when the unit either counts for very little, and simply has a normal collective value in the presence of the pressure in the world and the current turmoil, or else he can count for a very great deal.   (5-652/3)

2. The world today is going through a preparation period and an interlude of adjustment to the new world and the new order which is coming into being. This new world is verily a new creation, and with its activities the Masters are today engaged, working as always through the medium of Their disciples. In this preparatory period, the Masters are today occupied, among other things, with preparing disciples for constructive work for service and eventually for initiation. They are consequently occupied with forming new groups of disciples, who can gradually be integrated into existent groups and be available for world service. It is planned to do this on a large scale because of world need, and the willingness of the world aspirants to take the personal risks, incident to this preparatory work.   (5-680)

3. Nothing matters these days (when the bulk of humanity is in such dire distress) except to aid in its liberation at any personal sacrifice. The

temptation of many people these times is oft to evade the issue and find
in the daily task and karmic responsibilities, as well as in a type of satisfaction with their emotional reactions, a way of escape from direct and
practical action on behalf of humanity.

. . . What do you do of a practical nature to add your burden-bearing
capacity to the group of world workers everywhere, who are attempting
to absorb the world's sorrow? . . . There is a symbol which flashes out
from the heart of all who serve their fellow men, for which we look at
times; when found, it indicates a world server.

. . . The problem of all disciples today is to achieve successful activity
in their chosen task of competent citizenship and life occupation and
yet, at the same time, to add to that *at any cost* a practical life of service.   (6-570/2)

4. The demand is . . . for knowers and for those whose minds and hearts
are open; who are free from preconceived ideas, fanatically held, and
from ancient idealisms which must be recognised as only partial indications of great unrealised truths—truths which can be realised in great
measure and for the first time IF the lessons of the present world situation
and the catastrophe of the war are duly learned, and the sacrificial will
is called into play.   (10-170)

5. It is essential that servers everywhere—the intelligent men and women
of goodwill—get a grasp, fresh and clear, of the work to be done, and
that they become "relaying channels and not delaying points of selfish
interest" in the divine flow. This takes vision and courage. It takes courage
to adjust their lives—daily and in all relations—to the need of the hour
and to the service of mankind; it takes courage to attack life problems on
behalf of others and to obliterate one's own personal wishes in the emergency and need, and to do so consistently and persistently. However,
there is much to encourage the server. Humanity has now reached a point
in development where there is a definite grasp of the Plan of the Hierarchy
—call it brotherhood, sharing, internationalism, unity or what you will.
This is a growing and factual apprehension, and is a general recognition
by the thinkers and esotericists of the world, by the religious people of
enlightenment, by broad minded statesmen, by industrialists and businessmen of inclusive vision and humanitarian insight, and even today by the
man in the street. There is also a more definite recognition of emerging
spiritual values, and a greater readiness to relinquish hindrances to service.
The plans of the Christ for humanity's release, are more matured, for
they had to wait until such time that the trend of human aspiration became

more clearly emphatic; and the new era, with its latent possibilities, can now be seen upon the horizon, stripped of the veils of glamour and wishful thinking which obscured it ten years ago. All of this is a challenge to the disciple. What is it that he must do?

The disciple has to take himself as he is, at any time, with any given equipment, and under any given circumstances; he then proceeds to subordinate himself, his affairs and his time to the need of the hour—particularly during the phase of group, national or world crisis. When he does this within his own consciousness and is, therefore, thinking along lines of the true values, he will discover that his own private affairs are taken care of, his capacities are increased, and his limitations are forgotten. He takes his place with those who perceive the needs of the coming cycle— a cycle wherein the new ideas and ideals must be stressed, and for which a fight must be made, wherein the wider plans for the good of the whole must be understood, endorsed and preached, the new and clearer vision for human living must be grasped and finally brought into being, and a cycle wherein the effort of all members of the New Group of World Servers must be given to the lifting of humanity's load.   (11-195/7)

6. You are all adult souls and progress by defined service, not by being helped. Your task is to aid the work which the Hierarchy plans to do, to find the ways and means whereby that service can be wisely rendered, to discover the manner in which world need (not your group need) can be met, to finance that share in the work of the Brotherhood to which you have been assigned by your soul, and to do your part in developing those human attitudes which are needed if true peace is to be found in the world by 1975. If this work is soundly done, then a world unity can be established which will produce right human relations, a sound world politic, a united spiritual effort, and an economic "sharing" which will bring to an end all competition and the present uneven distribution of the necessities of life.   (13-325)

7. The searchlight of the Hierarchy is sweeping the planet at this time singling out men and women here and there, from the mass of men. They indicate esoteric possibility, and in their lives love of humanity and love of the Christ is a basic and fundamental factor.

The ordinary devoted person, who constantly pledges and dedicates himself to the Christ or to the Masters in a spirit of adoration, will *not* be chosen for this specific training. Their own attitudes and development come violently between them and their objective. The man who forgets about himself, and who is more interested in helping unhappy human beings, but who is nevertheless staunchly convinced of the factor of the unseen worlds, is the man for whom search is at this time being made. (13-695/6)

8. Until those who know, and who have the way out presented to them, consecrate themselves and all that they have without reservation to the helping of the world in its hour of need, the work will not be done, and the plans of the Hierarchy cannot then materialise. Should that not eventuate within the near future, then new and perhaps more drastic ways will have to be found.   (15-735)

9. The need for the service of men and women, free from illusion and glamour, has never been so dramatically present as it is today, and it is for these potential servers of a desperate necessity, that I have written.

That the Angel of the PRESENCE may make His nearness felt, and inspire you to pass courageously through the fires of the burning ground, is my earnest prayer; that the *fact* of the PRESENCE may be sensed by you and lead you to greater activity—once the burning ground is passed—is my deepest wish for you; and that the light may shine upon your way, and bring a certain and assured consummation of all the travail and struggle which has characterised your way of life, is my heart's desire for you. To more active and steady enterprise I call you.   (10-271/2)

7.   WHAT IS SERVICE?

1. Service can be briefly defined as the spontaneous effect of soul contact. This contact is so definite and fixed that the life of the soul can pour through into the instrument which the soul must perforce use upon the physical plane. It is the manner whereby the nature of that soul can demonstrate in the world of human affairs. Service is not a quality or a performance; it is not an activity towards which people must strenuously strive, nor is it a method of world salvage. This distinction must be clearly grasped, or else our whole attitude to this momentous demonstration of the success of the evolutionary process in humanity will be at fault. Service is a life demonstration. It is a soul urge, and is as much an evolutionary impetus of the soul as the urge to self-preservation or the reproduction of the species is a demonstration of the animal soul. This is a statement of importance. It is a soul instinct, if we may use such an inade-

quate expression and is, therefore, innate and peculiar to soul unfoldment. It is the outstanding characteristic of the soul, just as *desire* is the outstanding characteristic of the lower nature. It is group desire, just as in the lower nature it is personality desire. It is the urge to group good. It cannot, therefore, be taught or imposed upon a person as a desirable evidence of aspiration, functioning from without and based upon a theory of service. It is simply the first real effect, evidenced upon the physical plane, of the fact that the soul is beginning to express itself in outer manifestation.

Neither theory nor aspiration will or can make a man a real server. How then is it that there is so much activity in service demonstrating in the world today?

Simply because the life, words and deeds of the world's first Great Server, of the One Who came to make clear to us what service essentially is, has necessarily had an effect, and men today are earnestly attempting to imitate His example, little realising that imitation does not net them the true results, but only indicates to them a growing possibility.

. . . Today we have much running after service, and much philanthropic effort. All of it is, however, deeply covered by personality, and it often produces much harm, for people seek to impose their ideas of service and their personal techniques upon other aspirants. They may have become sensitive to impression, but they oft-times misinterpret the truth and are biassed by personality ends. They must learn to lay the emphasis upon soul contact and upon an active familiarity with the egoic life, and not upon the form side of service. May I beg those of you who respond to these ideas, and are sensitive to soul impression (oft-times misinterpreting the truth, being biassed by personality ends) to lay the emphasis upon soul contact and not upon the form side of service. Activity of the form side lays stress upon personality ambition, veiling them with the glamour of service. If care over the essential of service—soul contact—is taken, then the service rendered will flow with spontaneity along the right lines, and bear much fruit. Of this, the selfless service and the deep flow of spiritual life, which have been demonstrated in the world work of late, is a hopeful indication.   (15-124/6)

2. There are those who have so much theory about service and its expression, that they fail to serve, and also fail to comprehend with understanding the period of pain which ever precedes enlarged service. Their theories block the way to true expression, and shut the door on real comprehension. The mind element is too active.   (15-128)

8. THE URGE TO SERVE

When in terms of the occult science we are told to serve and obey, we are not interested. Yet service is the mode, *par excellence*, for awakening the heart centre, and obedience is equally potent in evoking the response of the two head centres to the impact of the soul force, and unifying them into one field of soul recognition. So little do men understand the potency of their urges! *If the urge to satisfy desire is the basic urge of the form life of man, the urge to serve is an equally basic urge of the soul of man.* This is one of the most important statements in this section. It is as yet seldom satisfied. Indications of its presence are ever to be found, nevertheless, even in the most undesirable types of human beings; it is evoked in moments of high destiny, or immediate urgency, and of supreme difficulty. The heart of man is sound, but oft asleep.

Serve and obey (the soul)! These are the watchwords of the disciple's life. They have been distorted into terms of fanatical propaganda, and have thus produced the formulas of philosophy and of religious theology; but these formulas do, at the same time, veil a truth. They have been presented to the consideration of man in terms of personality devotions and of obedience to Masters and leaders, instead of service of, and obedience to the soul in all. The truth is, however, steadily emerging, and must inevitably triumph. Once the aspirant upon the Probationary Path has a vision of this (no matter how slight it may be), then the law of desire which has governed him for ages, will slowly and surely give place to the Law of Repulse, which will, in time, free him from the thraldom of not-self. It will lead him to those discriminations and that dispassionate attitude which is the hallmark of the man who is on his way to liberation. Let us remember, however, that a discrimination which is based upon a determination to be free, and a dispassion which is the indication of a hard heart, will land the aspirant in the prison of a crystallised shell, which is far harder to break than the normal prison of the life of the average selfish man. This selfish spiritual desire is oft the major sin of so-called esotericists, and must be carefully avoided. Therefore, he who is wise will apply himself to serve and obey. (15-158/9)

19

9. CHARACTERISTICS OF THE SERVER

These characteristics can be easily and briefly noted. They are not exactly what one may have been led to believe. I am not here speaking of the qualifications required for the treading of the Path of Discipleship or the Probationary Path. These are well known. They are the platitudes of the spiritual life, and constitute the battleground . . . of most aspirants. We are here concerned with those qualities which will emerge when a man is working under the impulse of the Law of Service. They will appear when he is a real channel for the life of the soul. His major characteristics will then be three in number:

1. He will be distinguished, as might be expected, by the quality of *harmlessness,* and by an active refraining from those acts and that speech which might hurt or cause any misunderstanding. By no word, suggestion, implication, innuendo or voiced dissatisfaction, will he hurt his group. You will note that I do not say "will not hurt any individual". Those working under the Law of Service need no reminder not to hurt any individual. They often need, under the exuberance of spiritual stimulation and the intensity of their aspiration, to be reminded to demonstrate group harmlessness.

2. The second characteristic is *a willingness to let others serve as seems best to them,* knowing that the life flowing through the individual server must find its own channels and outlets, and that direction of these currents can be dangerous and prevent the rendering of the intended service. The server's efforts will be turned in two directions:

i. To the task of helping others to "stand in spiritual being", as he himself is learning to stand.

ii. To aiding the individual to express his service in his chosen field as he desires to express it, and not as the onlooking helper deems that he should do it.

One point might here be made clear. The task of those who are working under the Law of Service, is not exerted primarily with that group in the world today which is working under the effect of that general response to which we earlier referred (workers for the relief of the poor, etc.). These effects are easily shepherded into those activities which, en masse, work out as philanthropic endeavour, as educational experiments, or social efforts in the life of the community. The name of those who thus respond is legion, and the will to serve in this particular way needs no impetus. The remarkable response to the many recent campaigns to goodwill, definitely evidenced this. But the work of the new type of server is directed towards those who are establishing soul contact, and who can therefore work under the new incoming Aquarian Law. This centres around the capacity to stand, not only in spiritual being, but *together with* others, working with them subjectively, telepathically, and synthetically. This distinction merits attention, for one can easily waste effort by entering fields already well handled from the point of view of the attainment of the units in that field.

3. The third characteristic of the new server is *joyfulness.* This takes the place of criticism (that dire creator of misery) and is *the silence that sounds.*

It would be well to ponder on these last words, for their true meaning cannot be conveyed in words, but only through a life dedicated to the newer rhythms, and to the service of the whole. Then that "sounding joy" and that "joyful sounding" can make its true meaning felt. (15-131/3)

10. LEARNING TO SERVE

The first effect of the inflowing force of the soul, which is the major factor leading to demonstrated service, is to integrate the personality, and to bring all the three lower aspects of the man into one serving whole. This is a difficult and elementary stage from the angle of the student in the Hall of Wisdom. The man becomes aware of his power and capacity, and, having pledged himself to service, he begins furiously to serve; he creates this, that and the other channel for the expression of the force which is driving him; he tears down and destroys just as fast as he creates. He temporarily becomes a serious problem to the other servers with whom he may be associated, for he sees no vision but his own, and the aura of criticism which surrounds him, and the strenuous push of the assertive force within him, produces the stumbling of the "little ones", and there has to be constant repair work undertaken (on his behalf) by older, more experienced disciples. He becomes the victim, for the time, of his own aspiration to serve, and of the force which is flowing through him. This stage will in some cases fan into flame the latent seeds of ambition. This ambition is, in the last analysis, only the personality urge towards betterment, and in its right place and time is a divine asset, but it has to be rooted out when the personality becomes the instrument of the soul. In other cases, the server will come into a wider and more loving vision, and, taking his eyes off his own accomplishment, will go to work in silent unison with the groups of all true servers. He will submerge his personality tendencies, his ideas and his ambitions, in the greater good of the whole, and self will be lost to sight. Perhaps no better suggestion can be made to the man or woman who seeks to function as a true server, than to ask them to repeat daily, with their whole hearts and minds behind the words, the dedication at the conclusion of the Esoteric Catechism, which is included at the end of *Initiation, Human and Solar*. I would remind such servers that if they revolt or are dismayed by the ideas embodied in the words, that is perhaps an indication of how much they need the impression of this life objective upon their consciousness. That pledge runs as follows:

> I play my part with stern resolve; with earnest aspiration; I look above, I help below; I dream not, nor I rest; I toil; I serve; I reap; I pray; I am the Cross; I am the Way; I tread upon the work I do, I mount upon my slain self; I kill desire, and I strive, forgetting all reward. I forego peace; I forfeit rest and, in the stress of pain, I lose myself and find Myself and enter into peace. To all this I solemnly pledge myself, invoking my Higher Self.

As the work of learning to serve proceeds, and the inner contact becomes more sure, the next thing which will occur will be a deepening of the life of meditation, and a more frequent illumining of the mind by the light of the soul. Thereby the Plan is revealed. This will not be the shedding of that light upon the plans of the server, either for his own life or upon his chosen field of service. This must be clearly grasped. That might only indicate (if it seems to occur) the mental agility of the server to find means for the justification of his own ambition. It will be the recognition, in the mind, of the Plan of God for the world at the particular time in which the server is existing, and the part that he may play in furthering the ends of those who are responsible for the carrying forward of that Plan. He then becomes willing to be a tiny part of a greater Whole, and this attitude never varies, even when the disciple has become a Master of the Wisdom. He is then in contact with a still vaster concept of the Plan, and His humility and his sense of proportion remain unchanged.

An integrated, intelligent personality is adequate to deal with the working out of the server's part in the active work of the world, provided his vision is not blurred by personal ambition, nor his activity such that it degenerates into a sense of rush and a display of busy feverishness. It takes the soul itself to reveal to the poised and peaceful mind the next step to be taken in the work of world evolution, through the impartation of ideas. Such is the Plan for humanity.

As the force pours through the personality and gives to the server this necessary vision and the sense of power which will enable him to co-operate, it finds its way into the emotional or astral body. Here again the effect will be dual, owing to the condition of the server's astral body and his inner orientation. It may enhance the glamour and deepen the illusion, swinging the server into the psychic illusory effects there to be found. When this happens, he will emerge upon the physical plane glamoured by the idea, for instance, of his amazing personal contacts, whereas he has only contacted some group thought-form of the Great Ones. He will be under the illusion that he is a chosen vessel or mouthpiece for the Hierarchy, when the truth is that he is deceived by the many voices, because the Voice of Silence has been dimmed by the clamour of the astral plane; he will be deluded by the idea that there is no other way but his way. Such an illusion and deception is common among teachers and workers everywhere today, because so many are definitely making a contact with their souls, and are being swept then into the desire for service; they are not yet free, however, from ambition, and their orientation is still basically towards personality expression, and not to the merging of themselves in the Group of World Servers. If however they can avoid glamour, and can discriminate between the Real and the unreal, then the inflowing force will flood their lives with effective unselfish love and with devotion to the Plan, to those whom the Plan serves, and to Those Who serve the Plan. Note the sequence of these attitudes, and govern yourselves accordingly. There will then be no room for self-interest, self-assertiveness, or selfish ambition. All that is considered is the need as it demonstrates before the server's eyes.   (15-134/7)

11. SERVING HUMANITY

1. Those of you who are seeking to serve humanity and to join in the hierarchical effort to bring healing to a world of pain, must learn to penetrate behind appearances, behind the methods and schemes, the results and effects on the physical plane, and endeavour to contact the forces of Shamballa or of the Hierarchy, plus the human need which has produced these modes of expression, and thus see them for what they are—not worn out systems and childish efforts at improvement, but embryonic plans whereby, eventually, may come release and the culture and civilisation of the New Age. If you are seeking to bring illumination into the dark places of the earth (which means into the minds of men), then you must yourselves see clearly and relate the abstract and the concrete in such a manner that, in your own lives, a working idealism may be seen; only so can a working idealism of a national, racial and human nature also be seen. The head as well as the heart must be used, and this many earnest people are apt to forget. . . .

It is in the recognition of what is happening to *mankind as a whole* and behind the scenes, that the thinkers of the world and the New Group of World Servers can best serve; it is the unfoldment of the human consciousness in response to the presented conditions in any country or countries that is of moment; the "human state of mind" is just beginning to focus itself on the things that matter and to express itself in a living fashion. The thinkers and servers must learn to concentrate upon the awakening consciousness, and not upon the superficial movements. This awakening goes on apace and, my brothers, satisfactorily. The form or forms may suffer, but the intrinsic awareness of man is becoming, during this century, expressively divine.   (13-73/4)

2. If it is hard to arouse aspirants, such as yourselves, to urgent service and a full sense of responsibility; if men and women with all the information that you possess cannot be aroused to sacrificing effort, you can gain some idea of the magnitude of the task with which the Hierarchy is confronted at this time. You can realise, perhaps, the sense almost of frustration which could sweep over me (if I were limited by any time concept) when, for instance, those to whom I look for co-operation, are preoccupied with their own affairs, have no sense of immediacy, and prefer to concentrate upon their own development, their own families, their own problems, rather than achieve the larger world view which would lead to

full co-operation. The averting of a world debacle is the aim of our effort, and towards this aim I have asked your help.   (Jan. 1939), (13-79)

3. There is some confusion arising out of the basic idealism which underlies the activities of many peoples in many countries. It is the importance of the somewhat new ideal of the good of the state as a whole versus the good of the individual and the good of humanity. The state becomes almost a divine entity in the consciousness of the idealist. This is necessarily part of the evolutionary plan, but in so far as it constitutes a problem, is too big for the individual to solve alone and unaided. Of one fundamental truth I can, however, assure you. When men everywhere—within the boundaries of their particular state, and whilst upholding its authority and its civilisation—begin to think in terms of mankind, then public opinion will become so potent and so right in its inclusiveness, that state policies must inevitably conform to the larger ideal, and the sacrifice of the individual and of humanity in large numbers to the individual state, will no longer be possible. The part will be seen in its proper relation to the larger whole. It is this arousing of public opinion to world rights, to inclusive human interests and to international co-operation, that is the true goal of all present spiritual endeavour.   (13-219)

4. What can the individual do to aid the cause of humanity and arrest the tide of evil? If he is fighting already upon the side of the Forces of Light . . . he knows his destiny and service. But what of those who question what they can do, and yet are eager to see clearly and to play their part when right vision is theirs? To them I would say the following things:

i. Eliminate prejudice, national pride, and religious antipathies out of your consciousness. . . . The unhappy past of all nations is today used as an alibi by those who do not choose to shoulder responsibility, or to sacrifice anything for the cause of humanity. A recognition of our shortcomings and a spirit of tolerance and forgiveness are needed by all today.

ii. Refuse to be afraid of any results of right and positive action. Fear lies behind much of the dissenting attitudes today, and fear kills truth, hides the vision and arrests right action. The Great Leader of this Christian era has warned us not to be afraid of those who kill the body, but to fear only those who seek to kill the soul. . . .

iii. Having sensed the vision, recognised the hindrances, and dealt with innate prejudice and fear, it will then become apparent to you what . . . you must do. It is not for me to tell you what it is. The details are for you to decide; the methods which you must employ will become clear to you; you will then range yourself on the side of the Forces of Light, and will uphold the hands of those who are *fighting* for world peace and security, preparatory to the inauguration of the new world order. This you will do with no thought of self. You will face life truly and sincerely, with a fully dedicated sacrifice of time, self, money and, if need be, of life. You will realise dynamically that the attitude of the passive onlooker is not that of the agent of the Forces of Light or of a lover of humanity.

iv. You will also learn to keep your mind free from hate, refusing to hate the deluded sinner, even when imposing upon him the penalty of his sin. Hate and separation must cease, and they *will* cease as the individual aspirant stamps them out in his own life. The great error of the neutrally minded and of the pacifist, is his refusal to identify himself constructively with human pain. Even when he reacts with violent emotion over the suffering, for instance, of little children . . . and of the defenceless refugee, he does not truly care enough to do anything about the situation, involving as it does sacrifice. This sounds harsh, but is a needed statement of fact. *Sympathy which does not produce positive action of some kind, becomes a festering sore.*

Thus by thought and word and deed, the lover of humanity will enter the battle against evil; with complete self-forgetfulness he will take up the cause of humanity, hiding not behind the sense of futility and seeking no alibi in a misinterpreted idealism. He will face the facts of the present situation in the light which streams from the vision itself. He will then press forward into the age of right human relations, of spiritual unity and shared resources with complete confidence, because his sense of values is adjusted. He knows that humanity has a divine mission which must be carried out on the wings of love, through understanding action, selfless service, and the willingness to die in battle if that is the only way in which his brother can be served and freed.   (13-244/6)

5. Any student who thinks clearly and applies the teaching to his daily life, is contributing most valuably to the group awareness.

Oft an aspirant says to himself: "Of what real use am I? How can I, in my small sphere, be of service to the world?" Let me reply to these questions by pointing out that by thinking this book into the minds of the public, by expressing before your fellow men the teaching it imparts, and by a life lived in conformity with its teaching, your service is very real.

This will necessarily involve a pledging of the entire personality to the helping of humanity, and the promise to the Higher Self that endeavour will be made to lose sight of self in service—a service to be rendered in the place and under the circumstances which a man's destiny and duty have imposed upon him. I mean a renewal of the effort to bring about the purification of all the bodies, so that the entire lower man may be a pure channel and instrument through which spiritual force may flow unimpeded. I mean the attaining of an attitude wherein the aspirant desires nothing for the separated self, and in which he regards all that he has as something which he can lay upon the altar of sacrifice for the aiding of his brethren. Could all who read this book see the results of such a united effort, there would emerge a group activity, intelligently undertaken, which would achieve great things. So many people run hither and thither after this individual or that, or this piece of work or that, and, working with lack of intelligent co-ordination, achieve nothing and no group results. But united group effort would eventuate in an inspired reorganisation of the entire world, and the elimination of hindrances; there would be the making of real sacrifices and the giving up of personal wishes and desires in order that group purposes may be served. (14-xix/xx)

12. DIVINE INSPIRATION

1. Divine inspiration or that "divine obsession" which is the privilege of all advanced souls, will be understood in the coming years as never before, and will be definitely one of the methods used by the coming Lord and His Great Ones for the helping of the world.

The thing to be remembered is that in the case of wrong obsession the man is at the mercy of the obsessing entity, and is unconsciously or unwillingly a partner in the transaction. In divine obsession the man *consciously* and willingly co-operates with the One Who seeks to inspire, or to occupy or employ his lower vehicles. The motive is ever the greater helping of the race. The obsession is then not the result of a negative condition, but of a positive collaboration and proceeds under law and for a specific period. . . . As more and more of the race develop continuity of consciousness between the physical and the emotional, and later the mental, this act of transference of the vehicles will be more frequent and more understood.   (2-123)

2. The stimulation of certain people to phenomenal action, and the instigation of others to emerge as dynamic and inspired leaders, is also another way in which divine intervention might find expression. Oft, down the ages, men have been overshadowed by divinity and inspired by God to accept positive leadership, and so make divine purpose a fact in conditioning world affairs. Had they not so responded to the influencing impression, and had they not accepted the responsibility imposed upon them, the course of world affairs and world events might have been very different. I refer not here specifically to spiritual leaders, but also to leaders in other departments of human living—to such expressions of the divine will as Moses the Law Giver, Akbar the warrior and student, Leonardo da Vinci the inspired artist, and to other great and outstanding figures who have determined the basic trends of human civilisation; I refer also to the constructive forces which have guided mankind into the increasing light of knowledge and understanding.   (13-260)

13.   FORCES OF ENLIGHTENMENT

These Forces of Englightenment are always present on Earth on a small scale, influencing the minds of the New Group of World Servers, the selfless workers for humanity, and the thinkers in every school of thought, working in every field of human betterment; they work upon and through all who truly love their fellowmen. They are unable to influence the minds of the closed ego-centric person; they can do little with the separative isolationist; they are ineffectual where the theologian of all groups— political, religious or social—is concerned, and they can do little with the type of mind that is concentrated upon personal or group problems (*their* group, expressing *their* ideas and working *their* way) and who fail to see themselves or the group in relation to the whole of humanity.

. . . The organiser of these Forces at this time is the Buddha. He is the symbol of enlightenment or of illumination. Countless millions down the ages have recognised Him as a Lightbearer from on high. His *Four Noble Truths* exposed the causes of human trouble and pointed to the cure. His message can be paraphrased in the following words : Cease to identify yourselves with material things; gain a proper sense of the spiritual values; cease regarding possessions and earthly existence as of major importance; follow the *Noble Eightfold Path,* which is the path of right relations—right relations to God and to each other—and thus be happy. The steps on this Path are:

Right Values	Right Aspiration
Right Speech	Right Conduct
Right Mode of Living	Right Effort
Right Thinking	Right Rapture or True Happiness.

His ancient message is as new today as it was when He spoke His words on earth; a recognition of its truth and value is desperately needed, and the following of the "eight right ways of living" will enable humanity to find liberation. It is on the foundation of His teaching that the Christ raised the superstructure of the brotherhood of man to form an expression of the Love of God. Today, as it views the crumbling, devastated world, mankind has a fresh opportunity to reject selfish, materialistic motives and philosophy, and to begin those processes which will—steadily and gradually—bring about its liberation. It will then be possible for men to tread the Lighted Way which leads back to the divine Source of light and love. (13-462/3)

14. MYSTICAL PERCEPTION

There is a peculiar quality in every human being—an innate, inherent characteristic which is inevitably present—to which one might give the name of "mystical perception". I use this term in a far wider sense than is usually the case, and would have you regard this quality of mystical perception as inclusive of:

1. The mystical vision of the soul, of God and the universe.

2. The power to contact and appreciate the world of meaning, the subjective world of the emerging reality.

3. The power to love and to go out to that which is other than the self.

4. The capacity to grasp and to intuit ideas.

5. The ability to sense the unknown, the desirable and the desired.

The consequent determination and persistence which enable man to seek, search for and demand that unknown reality. It is the mystical tendency which has produced the great mystics of world renown, the large number of explorers, discoverers and inventors.

6. The power to sense, register and record the good, the beautiful and the true. It is this that has produced the writer, the poet, the artist and the architect.

7. The urge to discover and to penetrate to the secrets of God and of nature. It is this which produced the scientist, and the religious man.

From a study of these definitions you will see how inclusive the term "mystical perception" is. It is no more and no less than the power, innate in man, to reach out and to grasp that which is greater and better than himself, and which has driven him on, through progressively developing cultures and civilisations, until today he stands on the verge of a new kingdom in nature. It is the power to appreciate and to strive after the apparently unattainable good.   (12-113/4)

15.   PREPARING FOR THE REAPPEARANCE OF THE CHRIST

1. If the general premise and theme of all that has been here written is accepted, the question necessarily arises: What should be done to hasten this reappearance of the Christ? and also: Is there anything that the individual can do, in the place where he is and with the equipment, opportunities and assets of which he stands possessed? The opportunity is so great, and the need for definite and explicit spiritual help is so demanding, that—whether we like it or not—we are faced with a challenge. We are confronted with the choice of acceptance and consequent responsibility, or with rejection of the idea and the consequent realisation that we are not concerned. What we decide, however, in this time and period, will definitely affect the remainder of our life activity, for we shall either throw what weight or aid we can on the side of the invocation of the Christ and in preparation for His return, or we shall join the ranks of those who regard the whole proposition as an appeal to the gullible and the credulous, and possibly work to prevent men being deceived and taken in by what we

have decided is a fraud. Herein lies our challenge. It will take all that we have of a sense of values, and all that we can give to a specialised intuitive research to meet it. We may then realise that this promised reappearance is in line with the general religious belief and the major hope left in the minds of men which can bring true relief to suffering humanity.

To those who accept the possibility of His reappearance and who are willing to admit that history can again repeat itself, there are three questions which can be asked—the answers to which are strictly individual. These are:

i. How can I personally meet this challenge?

ii. What can I specifically *do*?

iii. What are the steps which I should take and where are those who will take them with me?

What is written here and in the following pages, is essentially for those who accept the fact of the Christ, recognise the continuity of revelation, and are willing to admit the possibility of His return.

The complexities and the difficulties of this post-war period are very great. The closer a man may be to the source of spiritual light and power, the more difficult his problem, for human affairs at this time seem so far away from this divine possibility. He will need all that he has of patience, understanding and goodwill. At the same time, the clearer will be his recognition of the facts. There are inner and outer problems which must be solved; there are inner and outer possibilities which can be made factual. As the spiritually-minded man faces both these inner and outer possibilities and events, it is easy to register a sense of complete frustration; he longs to help but knows not what to do; his grasp of the menacing difficulties, his analysis of his resources and of those with whom he will have to work, and his clarity of perception as to the forces ranged against him (and on a much larger scale against the Christ) will make him inclined to ask: "What is the use of any effort which I can make? Why not let the forces of good and evil fight it out alone? Why not permit the pressure of the evolutionary current—eventually and at long last—to bring cessation to the world fight and usher in the triumph of the good? Why attempt anything *now*?"

These are natural and wholesome reactions. The poverty and starvation of the millions in Europe and elsewhere, . . . the greed of the capitalistic forces of the world, the selfishness of labour, . . . the desperation of the little man in every country who sees no security or hope anywhere,

the work of the churches as they endeavour to restore the old order and
rule which (over the centuries) has saved the world from little, and the
lack of any clear voice or leadership in any country—all these things
make the average man feel the futility of all effort. The problem seems
too big, too terrible, and he himself seems too small and helpless.

Nevertheless, the mass of straight goodness and vision in the world is
enormous, and the amount of clear, humanitarian thinking is unbounded;
it is in the hands of the masses of good little men and the millions of
right thinking people in every land that the salvation of the world lies,
and by them the preparatory work for the coming of the Christ will be
done. Numerically, they are adequate to the task and need only reassur-
ance and wise co-ordination to prepare them for the service required,
before the reappearance of the Christ becomes possible. The problems
confronting us should be faced with courage, with truth and understanding, as well as with the willingness to speak factually, with simplicity and
with love, in the effort to expose the truth and clarify the problems which
must be solved. The opposing forces of entrenched evil must be routed
before He for Whom all men wait, the Christ, can come.

. . . Another very vital question arises : For what period of time must
we endure, struggle and fight? The reply comes with clarity : He will come
unfailingly when a measure of peace has been restored, when the principle of sharing is at least in process of controlling economic affairs, and
when churches and political groups have begun to clean house. Then He
can and will come; then the Kingdom of God will be publicly recognised
and will no longer be a thing of dreams and of wishful thinking and
orthodox hope.   (8-160/3)

2. When the people are told the truth and when they can freely judge and
decide for themselves, we shall then see a much better world.

It is not essential or necessary that all these desirable objectives should
be accomplished facts upon Earth before the Christ again moves amongst
us. It is, however, necessary that this attitude to religion and politics is
generally regarded as desirable, and that steps have been successfully
taken in the direction of right human relations. It is along these lines that
the New Group of World Servers and all men of goodwill are working,
and their first effort must be to offset the widespread sense of frustration
and individual futility.   (8-165)

3. It is for this coming forth to outer active service that (the "Sons of
God Who are the Sons of Men") are already—one by one—entering into
outer activity upon the physical plane. They are not recognised for what

They are, but They go about the Father's business, demonstrating good-will, seeking to enlarge the horizon of humanity, and thus prepare the way for the One Whom They serve, the Christ, the Master of all the Masters, and the Teacher alike of angels and of men.   (8-170)

16.   OVERSHADOWING BY THE AVATAR

The appearance of the Great Lord on the astral plane (whether followed by His physical incarnation or not) will date from a certain Wesak festi-val at which a mantram (known only to those attaining the seventh Initia-tion) will be pronounced by the Buddha, thus setting loose force, and enabling His great Brother to fulfil His mission. Hence the gradual recog-nition of the Wesak festival, and its true significance in the occident is desirable, and opportunity will be offered to all who are willing to place themselves in the line of this force, and thus become vitalised by it, and consequently available for service. The reaction mentioned above, will also become possible through the pressure brought to bear by the present children, many of whom are chelas and some initiates. They have come in to prepare the way for the coming of His Feet.

When the hour strikes (five years prior to the date of His descent) they will be in the full flower of their service, and will have recognised their work, even though they may not be conscious of that which the future holds hid.

When the hour has come (and already a few cases are to be found), many cases of *overshadowing* will be seen and will demonstrate in a threefold manner. In all countries, in the orient and the occident, pre-pared disciples and highly evolved men and women, will be found who will be doing the work along the lines intended, and who will be occupy-ing places of prominence which will make them available for the reach-ing of the many; their bodies also will be sufficiently pure to permit of the overshadowing. It will only be possible in the case of those who have been consecrated since childhood, who have been servers of the race all their lives, or who, in previous lives have acquired the right by karma. This threefold overshadowing will manifest as:

First. An impression upon the physical brain of the man or woman, of thoughts, plans for work, ideals and intentions which (emanating from the Avatar) will yet be unrecognised by him as being other than his own;

he will proceed to put them into action, unconsciously helped by the force flowing in. This is literally a form of higher mental telepathy working out on physical levels.

Second. The overshadowing of the chela during his work (such as lecturing, writing, or teaching), and his illumination for service. He will be conscious of this, though perhaps unable to explain it, and will seek more and more to be available for use, rendering himself up in utter selflessness to the inspiration of His Lord. This is effected via the chela's Ego, the force flowing through his astral permanent atom; and it is only possible when the fifth petal is unfolded.

Third. The conscious co-operation of the chela is necessitated in the third method of overshadowing. In this case he will (with full knowledge of the laws of his being and nature) surrender himself and step out of his physical body, handing it over for the use of the Great Lord or one of His Masters. This is only possible in the case of a chela who has brought all the three lower bodies into alignment, and necessitates the unfolding of the sixth petal. By an act of conscious will, he renders up his body, and stands aside for a specific length of time.

These methods of overshadowing will be largely the ones used by the Great Lord and His Masters at the end of the century, and for this reason They are sending into incarnation, in every country, disciples who have the opportunity offered them to respond to the need of humanity. Hence the need of training men and women to recognise the higher psychism, and the true inspiration and mediumship, and to do this scientifically. In fifty years time (written about 1923), the need for true psychics and conscious mediums (such as H.P.B. for instance) will be very great if the Master's plans are to be carried to fruition, and the movement must be set on foot in preparation for the coming of Him for Whom all nations wait. In this work many have their share, provided they demonstrate the necessary endurance.

Naturally, the first group will be the largest, for it does not necessitate so much knowledge, but more risk is entailed with them than with the others—the risk of a perversion of the plans, and of disaster to the unit involved. The second group will be less numerous, and the last group will involve only a handful, or two or three in certain countries. In this case, it will be verily true that, through sacrifice, the Son of Man will again tread the highways of men, and His physical incarnation be a fact. Very few will be thus available for His use, as the force He carries requires a peculiarly resilient instrument, but due preparation is being made. (3-756/8)

17. THE PLAN FOR HUMAN EVOLUTION

(a) THE PLAN

1. The Plan is as much of the divine Purpose as can be brought into expression upon the planet . . . at any one time or particular epoch in time and space.   (6-371/2)

2. Of what use is all this information to men and to the aspirant who is trying to serve? The one thing which humanity needs today is the realisation that there *IS* a Plan which is definitely working out through all world happenings, and that all that has occurred in man's historical past, and all that has happened lately, is assuredly in line with that Plan. Necessarily also, if such a Plan exists, it presupposes Those Who are responsible for the originating of the Plan and for its successful carrying forward. From the standpoint of average humanity, who think in terms of earthly happiness, the Plan should be something joyful and something which would make material life easier. To the spiritual Hierarchy, the Plan involves those arrangements or circumstances which will raise and expand the consciousness of mankind and enable them, therefore, to discover the spiritual values *for themselves* and to make the needed changes *of their own free will,* and thus produce the demanded betterment of the environment, consistent with the unfolding spiritual recognition. (13-670)

3. The wonder and the immensity of the drama unfolding in the universe is a proof of its reality, and the grasp of man, small though it may appear to be, is a guarantee of his divinity. Stage by stage we slowly make our approach to the goal of conscious and intelligent awareness. Step by step we are mastering matter and making more adequate the mechanism of awareness and of contact. Little by little we (and by that I mean the human family, as a whole) are approaching the "place of recognition", and are preparing to climb the mountain of vision. If aspirants but realised the wonders of that revelation, and if they grasped the magnificence of the reward given to their efforts, we would have less failure, more courage, a greater and steadier achievement, and consequently a more rapidly illumined world.

. . . The vision cannot be appropriated. It is ever on ahead, but if the entire life is given to vision, and if the serving of one's fellow man is overlooked, the vision profits not. I have sought to convey the magnitude of the Plan and the steps upon the evolutionary stairway which lie

ahead of every aspirant and of every member of the Hierarchy.
(14-156/7)

4. This (new) Plan was tentatively formulated in 1900, at one of the
quarterly meetings of the Hierarchy. In 1925, at the next great meeting
of co-operation, the new Plan was discussed in greater detail, certain
necessary changes (growing out of the results of the World War) were
negotiated, and the members of that important Council determined two
things:

First, that there should be a united effort by the collective members of
the planetary Hierarchy, over a period of several years (that is until 1950),
to bring about certain definite results, and that during that time the attention of the Great Ones should be turned towards a definite attempt to
expand the consciousness of humanity and to institute a sort of forcing
process, so that men's horizon of thought would be tremendously enlarged,
and their faith, assurance and knowledge be equally increased and
strengthened. It was decided that certain areas of doubt should be cleared
up.

Secondly, it was determined to link more closely and subjectively the
senior disciples, aspirants and workers in the world. To this end, all the
Masters put Their personal groups of disciples in touch with each other,
subjectively, intuitively, and sometimes telepathically. Thus the New
Group of World Servers came into being.   (14-170/1)

5. Roughly speaking, the Plan fell into three divisions in the minds of its
organisers:

First, Political

The objective of the work here planned was the development and the
establishment of an international consciousness. . . . It is needless to
point out that material stress and strain and the wrecking of old political
parties and trade relations had to play their part. It was determined to
demonstrate the necessity of establishing a spirit of international dependence and interrelation, so that the nations would be forced to realise politi-
cally that isolation, separativeness, and the cultivation of a national egoism must go, and that a national spirit, coloured by a sense of superiority, by class hatreds and racial antagonisms, constitutes a barrier to the
true development of humanity. The people must be taught that the longing to increase possessions is a deterrent to real expansion. Thus plans
were laid whereby the Brotherhood of Nations, based on mutual need,

mutual understanding, and mutual helpfulness, should gradually come into being. (14-172/3)

The originators of these various national movements are often ignorant of the impulses which lie back of their work, and are frequently unable to explain the ideals toward which they are working, except in terms of human ambition and power. Nevertheless, unknown to themselves, they are really sensitive to the great ideas thrown into their minds by the Minds behind the scenes. They respond to the idea of general good, of human equality, of the superman, of universal trade requirements, and of the distribution of wealth, but—and here is the important point—because the inner synthesis of effort is not emphasised, because there is no general knowledge as to the source of the great concepts, and no understanding of the inner Brotherhood which is guiding humanity towards an outer Brotherhood, these great principles are being widely distorted, selfishly applied, and separately utilised. The fires of class hatreds, of racial antagonisms, and of national pride, are burning intensely strong. (14-175)

Second, Religious

The aim before this department is to establish a universal understanding of the nature of reality, and to foster the growth of the spiritual consciousness. Though in some ways religious differences are the hardest to bridge or heal, yet real progress has been made in this phase of the hierarchical work. There is today in the world a very large number of those who fundamentally believe in the brotherhood of religions. Though the unintelligent masses everywhere have little or no idea of things spiritual, they can be more easily brought to believe in the one God and to the idea of a universal faith, than to any other idea. Many thousands of them are frankly agnostic or believe in nothing, whilst many other thousands are restive under the control of theological authority. They have nevertheless within them that germ of the spirit of love which is normally inclusive and intuitive.

. . . During the next ten years the work of the Fellowship of Religions (of which the outer organisations are an externalisation) will greatly increase. Soon we shall have the inner structure of a world-faith so clearly defined in the minds of many thousands, that its outer structure will inevitably make its appearance before the end of the century.

The inner structure of the World Federation of Nations will eventually be equally well organised, with its outer form taking rapid shape by 2025. Do not infer from this that we shall have a perfected world religion and a complete community of nations. Not so rapidly does nature move; but the concept and the idea will be universally recognised, universally desired, and generally worked for, and when these conditions exist, nothing can stop the appearance of the ultimate physical form for that cycle. (14-176/7)

Third, Scientific

The workers along this line have definitely set themselves the goal of expanding man's consciousness, and so widening his horizon that a synthesis of the tangible and the intangible will take place. This will bring about the entrance of mankind into a new and subjective realm, and his apprehension of new states of awareness. These developments will be brought about by the workers in the fields of education, of science, and of psychology. Great things are on the way at this time, and the activities of workers on the third and fifth rays have never been so well directed nor so potent as today.

. . . The energies of the aspirants and disciples on the third and fifth rays are turned to the work of expanding the human consciousness, of bringing to light the hidden wonders of the universe, and of hastening the unfoldment of the latent powers in mankind. These powers, when awakened, will be extensions of many of the present senses, and will admit man into that world which lies behind the veil of ignorance and matter. (14-177/8)

(b) THE PLAN CREATED BY MEDITATION

1. The entire universe has been created, and its evolution processed, through the power of thought, which is only another word for controlled meditation. This covers the combined meditation of numerous subjective, spiritual and mental groups; the laws of this meditative work are the result of certain mental determinations, which embody the will of the planetary Logos, and are imposed upon all lesser groups of lives by Those Whose task it is to wield the divine laws and enforce them. Freedom of the will is here to be noted in relation to the *Time* concept but not in relation to the final and inevitable divine results at the end of the immense world period. The major thought-form of the spiritual Hierarchy, created by joint ashramic meditation, is called by us the *Plan*. The basic purpose of Sanat Kumara is revealed from cycle to cycle by His Agents in Shamballa, and is by Them impressed upon the minds of the senior Members of the Hierarchy. They, in Their turn, make this

impression the subject of Their ashramic meditation, adapting its various concepts and the outlined purpose to a most carefully formulated Plan, presenting—as far as humanity is concerned—seven aspects or phases of evolutionary development and endeavour, according to the work desired of any Ray Ashram implicated at any particular time. Each Ashram thus undertakes meditation upon the general Plan and thus (if you could but realise it) each initiate and disciple finds his place and sphere of activity and service—from the very highest initiate to the least important disciple.

. . . Have you ever stopped to think that the meditation of a Master upon the Plan of which He is custodian, and His formulation of what He can do along the line of effective co-operation, is of no service or usefulness to the illiterate inhabitants of our great cities and agricultural areas? The need of these unthinking masses must be met by disciples of less spiritual development, and probably their greatest appeal is through the application of economic help; the task of these lesser disciples is to prove to the ignorant masses that—as the centuries slip away—spiritual living and true spiritual understanding include every aspect of physical plane expression, and not simply the religious or the philosophic modes of thought. The meditation, therefore, of every grade of disciple and initiate has its use, for by their meditation (carried forward on their own level) they can adapt the Plan to the widely differing masses and thus the hierarchical Plan can reach from the Masters of the Hierarchy, through the Ashrams, to the New Group of World Servers, and thus to the whole of the human family. I would like you to grasp the true simplicity of this picture, if you can, for you can have a share also in this great meditative task.

One of the things which I set myself to achieve when I undertook this work of making the Plan clearer to the minds of men, and thus preparing the way for the Master of all the Masters, was to prove not only that the Plan was based upon planetary meditation but that, in its progress towards expression, it met the need of all possible groups and grades of human beings; and that—more important still—it could be proved that the word "spiritual" covered every phase of living experience. Ponder on this statement. That is spiritual which lies beyond the point of present achievement; it is that which embodies the vision and which urges the man on towards a goal higher than the one attained. The ecclesiastics of the world have made a great line of demarcation between what is human and what is spiritual, between what is material and what is not; in so doing they have created sin and greatly complicated human living and understanding. They have given a selfish import to human aspiration; they have not taught mankind that meditation and prayer were simply phases of co-operation with the divine Plan. Individualism was fostered and group understanding was lost. Maybe—owing to the work of the Brothers of Darkness—there was no way to avoid this dangerous sidetracking of human intent and truth. But the time has now come when the great rhythm of meditation, ranging from desire, through prayer, to worship, and from thence to meditation and invocation, can be imposed by men upon their own thinking.

This is the immediate task of the New Group of World Servers, co-operating everywhere with the men of goodwill; each member of the New Group has to ascertain for himself where he stands, where his meditative responsibility lies, and in what field destiny indicates his service to the race of men must be found. This is no easy task . . . Men are frequently so spiritually ambitious and waste their time in doing that which is not their destined task, because in so doing they satisfy their spiritual pride.   (6-233/5)

2. *Meditation* clarifies the mind as to the fact and nature of the Plan, *understanding* brings that Plan into the world of desire, and *love* releases the form which will make the Plan materialise upon the physical plane. To these three expressions of your soul I call you. All of you without exception, can serve in these three ways, if you so desire.   (13-23)

(c) SENSING THE PLAN

1. In all great movements you have some thought or aggregation of thoughts cast into the minds of the so-called idealists by the Great White Brotherhood. The idea is sounded forth by Them. They choose a man or a group of men and cast into their minds some idea. There it germinates and is embodied by them in other thoughts, not so pure or so wise, but necessarily coloured by the individuality of the thinker. These thought-forms are, in their turn, picked up by the concrete thinkers of the world who—grasping the main outline of the idea—crystallise it and build it into more definite shape, into one more easily apprehended by the general public. It has therefore now reached the lower levels of the mental plane, and a further development becomes possible. It is then seized upon as desirable by those who are focussed upon the astral plane; to them it makes an emotional appeal, becoming public opinion. It is now practically ready to take shape upon the physical plane, and we have the practical adaptation of an ideal to the needs of the physical life. It has been stepped down; it has lost much

of its original beauty; it is not as pure and as lovely as when first conceived, and it is distorted from its original shape, but it is, nevertheless, more adapted to public use and can be employed as a stepping-stone to higher things.   (4-130/1)

2. The Plan exists in four states of consciousness:

i. As it is visioned and known by the Members of the Hierarchy, such as the accepted disciples of the world.

ii. As it exists in the consciousness of the members of the New Group of World Servers, stepped down into their minds and desires.

iii. As it exists in the consciousness of the men of goodwill.

iv. As its faint outlines are found in the minds of the average intelligent God-accepting men of the world at this time.   (5-377)

3. Humanity has now reached a point of development where there is a definite grasp of the Plan of the Hierarchy—call it brotherhood, sharing, internationalism, unity or what you will. This is a growing and factual apprehension, and is a general recognition by the thinkers and esotericists of the world, by the religious people of enlightenment, by broad minded statesmen, and even today by the man in the street; divine purpose, however, implemented or engineered by the divine will, eludes as yet the most advanced.   (6-136/7)

4. The apprehension of this Plan by the disciple will necessarily vary according to the disciple's point in evolution. In the very early stages of discipleship, his capacity to "modify, qualify and adapt" is small indeed, but each expansion of consciousness fits him increasingly to do this. . . . Each stage (when it is a factual experience) enables the disciple to see the Plan from the angle of the Ashram and of the Master with increasing clarity; finally, there comes the time when the disciple arrives at the very heart of things and is so close to the heart of the Master that the hierarchical planning becomes something in which he shares and to which he contributes.   (6-390)

5. I would have you realise that the work which you do is planned by us, and that your task is to render yourself sensitive to our "impression". This developed sensitivity is ever a difficult task for the first ray person. They prefer to stand alone and to generate within themselves the plans which they consider fitted for the type of service which they seek to render. But today disciples are learning that a fused and organ-

ised and blended plan or scheme of worldwide service is required, and
that a master Plan of the Hierarchy must be carried out, and that into
this Plan all disciples . . . must endeavour to fit.   (6-498)

6. The Plan, as it is sensed by the world disciples, in the attempt to
work and co-operate with it, is only the sensing of that portion of it
which concerns the human consciousness. We have not yet been able to
catch even a glimmer of the vastness of the synthetic Plan for evolutions
other than human, both superhuman and subhuman; nor can we grasp
the fabric of God's ideal as it underlies the sum total of the manifested
processes, even upon our little planet. All we really know is the fact
of the Plan, and that it is very good; that we are enfolded within it,
and subject to it.   (15-28/9)

(d) PROBLEMS OF THE MASTERS IN TRANSMITTING THE PLAN

1. The Masters have to contend with problems and difficulties as They
seek to further the Plans of evolution through the medium of the sons
of men. In conclave wise They make Their plans; with judgment, after
due discussion, They apportion the tasks; then, to those who offer themselves for service and who have some measure of soul contact, They
seek to transmit as much of the Plan as possible. They impress the
Plan and some suggestion as to its scope upon the mind of some man
or some woman upon the physical plane. If that mind is unstable or
oversatisfied, if it is filled with pride, with despair, or with self-depreciation, the vision does not come through with clarity of outline; if the
emotional body is vibrating violently with some rhythm set up by the
personality, or if the physical vehicle is ailing, and concentrated attention is therefore prevented, what will happen? The Master will turn
sadly away, distressed to think of the opportunity for service that the
worker has lost through his own fault, and He will seek someone else to
fill the need—someone perhaps not so fundamentally suitable, but the
only one available on account of the failure of the first one approached.

It might incidentally be of value here to remind aspirants to service
that much work done by many is the result of over-zealousness and is
not a carrying forward of the Master's work. With wise discrimination
He apportions the work and never lays upon one human being more
than he can adequately accomplish. He can and does train His disciple
so that it appears to the onlooking world as if he accomplishes miracles,
but forget not that the vast amount of work accomplished by one useful
disciple, only becomes possible when the control of all his three bodies

is co-ordinated and his alignment accomplished. He who has a stable mental body that is strongly positive in reception from above, whilst negative to lower vibrations, he who has an astral body that is clear, uncoloured and still, he who also has a physical body with steady nerves and stable rhythm (it will be like a casket, beautiful, yet strong as steel) will serve as a vessel meet for the Master's use, a channel through which He can unhindered pour His blessing upon the world.

It should be noted that even the Great Ones Themselves have to lay Their plans largely allowing for the lack of perception of those on the physical plane through whom They have to work. They are handicapped and dependent upon Their physical plane instruments and Their main trouble concerns the point of evolution reached by the mass of men in the Occident.

Remember that this point is indicative of the success of the evolutionary process and not its failure but, because much yet remains to be done, the work of the Lodge is often hindered. The point reached at this time might be expressed as a swinging from the rank materialism of the past into a growing and profound realisation of the unseen worlds, without the balance that comes from self-acquired knowledge. The forces that have been set in motion by the thinkers—the scientists of the world, the truly advanced religious men, the Spiritualists, the Christian Scientists, the New Thought workers, the Theosophists and the modern Philosophers and workers in other fields of human thought— are gradually and steadily affecting the subtler bodies of humanity and are bringing them to a point where they are beginning to realise three things :

(a) The reality of the unseen worlds.

(b) The terrific power of thought.

(c) The need for scientific knowledge on these two matters   (4-132/4)

2. A Master . . . searches for those minds which are sensitive to this Plan. He is not primarily occupied in looking for people who are good —so-called. Self-forgetfulness and straight kindness means ever harmlessness, and that connotes the utmost good. He seeks for those types of people who can respond in unison to that aspect of the Plan for which the Master is responsible, and for those who can be taught to subordinate their personalities to its requirements. They have no selfish purposes, and desire nothing but only to aid the Master and those senior disciples who may be working under His supervision at some

aspect of the Plan. This involves, as I have pointed out, their training in adaptation, in the recognition of true values, in fluidity of ideas, and selfless work for their fellow men.   (5-683)

3. Just as the mass of men do not know, recognise or respond to the Hierarchy, so—within the Hierarchy itself—you have a group analogous to this mass of men. There are many lesser members of the Hierarchy, and many, very many disciples who do not know, recognise or as yet respond to the influence or the potency of Shamballa.

Within the Hierarchy, the Science of Impression conditions the relation between senior and junior members in the various Ashrams. All do not respond in the same way, for in its higher aspects it is a science in process of mastering. It might be said, in order that you may understand more easily, that "impression" governs and conditions all those within the Hierarchy whose abstract mind is highly developed. It is not fully developed in the case of many disciples in the Ashram, and hence only certain Members of the Hierarchy (the Masters, the Adepts and the Initiates of the third degree) are permitted to know the details of the Plan; these are protected by means of this very Science of Impression. The remaining members of the Hierarchy take their orders from their seniors.   (11-70/1)

(e) DANGERS TO WHICH WORKERS ARE SUBJECT

Certain dangers which aspirants must watch as they seek to be of use, should be mentioned :

They must guard against over-emphasising one aspect at the expense of another part of the Plan or vision.

They must avoid unequal concentration of thought upon that part of the Plan which appeals the most to them personally.

They must recognise the inability of the workers to continue to bring through the Plans and to work together peacefully and steadily. Friction is oft unavoidable.

They must watch for the creeping in of self-interest and of ambition. They must guard against fatigue, due to long effort in materialising the Plan, and the strain incident upon high endeavour.

They must develop the capacity to recognise those who are sent to help them in the work.

They must above all watch against failure to keep in touch with the higher self and with the Master.   (4-134/5)

(f) MATERIALISING THE PLAN

1. In the sensing of the Plan and its later materialisation, human units are involved and men have perforce to be employed. A vision is given of tremendous possibilities and indications are also granted of the manner in which these possibilities may become facts, but beyond that the Great Ones do not go. The detail and the method of concretising the ideal and the necessary work is left to the sons of men. To the disciple who is an organiser and transmitter of the Plan, falls the work of filling in the details and of taking the necessary action. At this point it is wise for him to remember that he comes (with his little plans) under the same law as do the Great Ones in Their large endeavours, and it is in his dealings with people and his manipulation of the human equation that the difficulties arise.

Units for work fall into three groups:

i. Those who can sense the Plan and are commissioned to work it out.

ii. Those who can be used but who are blind to the greater issues.

iii. Those who can sense nothing except those things which concern their own selfish interests.

The first group the Masters can contact. They work with these units of the human family and expect fair promise of average success. These both hear the sound, and vision the Plan. The second group have to be utilised as best may be, by the disciples of the world. The final group are frequently to be offset from the energy standpoint, and only used when necessary.

One of the primary conditions that a disciple has to cultivate, in order to sense the Plan and be used by the Master, is *Solitude*. In solitude the rose of the soul flourishes; in solitude the divine self can speak; in solitude the faculties and the graces of the higher self can take root and blossom in the personality. In solitude also the Master can approach and impress upon the quiescent soul the knowledge that He seeks to impart, the lesson that must be learnt, the method and plan for work that the disciple must grasp. In solitude the sound is heard. The Great Ones have to work through human instruments and the Plan and vision are much handicapped by failure on the part of these instruments. (4-131/2)

2. Little by little, the picture of the possibilities and of the Plan will unfold before you as your minds increase in sensitivity, and your brains become more responsive to mental impulses. Little by little, the disciple of the world will work at the reproduction—on the physical plane—of that which exists subjectively. Little by little, there will appear all over the earth, groups of illumined souls who can co-operate with the Masters with perfect freedom of intercourse because their responsiveness has been scientifically trained and developed. Their power to work in tune with or in unison with the Hierarchy, to co-operate with the group life of many other groups of disciples, and to communicate light and revelation to the world of men, will later be an accomplished fact and is already much more actively present and potent than you think. A little vision, brother of mine, makes the way of the disciple easier, and hence I have enlarged somewhat upon the possibilities which we, with our prevision, regard as already facts in manifestation. Nothing can stop the eventual success of the Plan; it is simply a question of time.   (5-29)

3. The difficulty of the spiritual builders and the architects of the Plan only really begins when that which they are constructing becomes public property and subject, therefore, to criticism and outer help. Then the task of preserving the original purity of idea and of purpose becomes onerous.

Be prepared for expansion of the work. But expand according to plan, and not according to emergency, for you are building in collaboration with the inner Builders, and the two structures must be counterparts. Ponder on this, yet be not rigid on non-essentials.   (5-162/3)

4. (The disciple) grasps eventually that in relation to humanity, the planning of the Hierarchy falls into certain definite phases of activity—all of them related and all of them tending towards the externalisation of the Plan in any particular century, cycle or world period. These phases are:

i. The phase of *Purpose,* originating in Shamballa and registered by the senior Members of the Hierarchy.

ii. The stage of hierarchical *Planning.* This is the formulation of the purpose in terms of possibility, immediacy, appropriateness and the availability of the disciples, plus the energies to implement the Plan.

iii. Next comes *Programme,* wherein the Plan is taken up by the particular Ashram involved in its implementation, and is then reduced to the formative stages of human impression and direction, the conditions necessary to bring about its emergence, and the two phases of this conditioning. These are usually in two parts; i.e. the destruction of all hindrances, and the presentation of the Plan.

iv. The emergence of the hierarchical *Pattern* (based upon the recognition of purpose, careful planning and a detailed and carefully thought-out programme, both in the minds of the disciples in the Ashram, who are involved in the implementation of the Plan, and among the intelligentsia on Earth. These two groups have the task— the first group consciously, and the other unconsciously—of bringing the pattern of things to be into the mass consciousness, by no means an easy task, as the present state of world affairs demonstrates.

v. Then comes the final phase of *Precipitation,* when all the subjective work has been done on the basis of possibility, and when the pattern and a part of the programme are recognised by the world thinkers in every nation, either favourably or with antagonism. The planning, having reached this final stage, then proceeds under its own momentum.

. . . According to his development and his point in evolution, so will be (the disciple's) emphasis; some disciples can aid the Master in the planning process because they are becoming sensitive to impression by Shamballa; others are engrossed in the formulation of the programme, and in imparting some of its features to more limited disciples, thus setting them to work. A group of carefully chosen disciples are always held in the Hierarchy to work solely with the pattern; this is a most important phase of the work, requiring a spirit of synthesis and an ability to hold streams of hierarchical energy under control. Disciples who are not so advanced, and who are therefore closer to human thinking at the particular moment in history, undertake to supervise the precipitation of the Plan. Their work is necessarily far more exoteric, but is most responsible, because it is when the Plan has reached the stage of human implementation that error is apt to arise and mistakes can occur.

In every Ashram are to be found those disciples whose task it is to make the needed adjustments of the pattern, and the demanded changes in the programme as the process of precipitation goes forward. It is a law that human freedom may not be infringed. The staging of the Plan and its working out is, in the last analysis an entirely human affair, once it has reached the stage of precipitation. It is dependent upon the responsiveness of human brains, and their recognition of need and its sources. This is a point which should be remembered. (6-361/2)

5. There are . . . three types of hierarchical workers:

i. Souls; i.e. those initiates who have taken the fourth Initiation of Renunciation and in whom the soul body, the causal body, has been destroyed. They are the Custodians of the Plan.

ii. Soul-infused personalities; these are the disciples and the initiates of the first three initiations, through whom the "souls" work in the carrying out of the Plan.

iii. Intelligent aspirants who are not yet soul-infused personalities, but who recognise the necessity of the Plan and who seek the welfare of their fellow men.

The highest group formulates the Plan; the second group "modifies, qualifies and adapts" the Plan to contemporary human requirements, and thus ensures the gradual and steady continuity of the Plan; the third group are the agents who carry this Plan to mankind and seek to make it workable, guided by spiritual compromise—the compromise evidenced by the second group.

Disciples, as they grasp the Plan and are spiritually informed as to the steps to be taken to modify the Plan upon the mental plane, so that its acceptance by humanity is intelligently progressive and is not dynamically imposed, with consequent disastrous effects, are the primary agents. They accept the responsibility for the needed compromise, for it is *their* responsibility and not the responsibility of the Masters. The various aspects of the Plan—as presented to them in the Ashram —are then modified and rearranged so that the Plan becomes a series of sequential steps and is not the violent impact of an unrealised idea. It might be said that the spiritual compromise of the disciple (working with the Plan) transforms the basic idea (through mental modification) into an acceptable ideal.

When the process of modification is completed, the idea—in the form of an ideal—descends to the astral plane, the plane of the emotions. There it becomes tinctured with the quality which the working disciple believes will make the best appeal to the masses of men with whom he may be working, and particularly to the aspiring intelligentsia. (6-391/2)

18. HUMANITY

1. Humanity constitutes a centre of energy within the cosmos, capable of three activities:

i. First of all, humanity is responsive to the inflow of spiritual energy. This pours into it from the cosmos, and speaking symbolically, these energies are basically three in number:

(a) Spiritual energy, as we inadequately term it. This emanates from God the Father and reaches humanity from the level of what is technically called the monadic plane, from the archetypal sphere, the highest source of which a man can become conscious. . . .

(b) Sentient energy—the energy which makes man a soul. It is the principle of awareness, the faculty of consciousness, that something, inherent in matter (when brought into relation with spirit), which awakens responsiveness to an outer and far-reaching field of contacts. . . .

(c) Pranic energy, or vitality. This is that vital force, inherent in matter itself and in which all forms are immersed, as they constitute functioning parts of the greater form. . . .

Humanity is intended to be the medium wherein certain activities can be instituted. It is in reality the brain of the planetary Deity, its many units being analogous to the brain cells in the human apparatus. Just as the human brain, made up of an infinite number of sentient responsive cells, can be suitably impressed when quiescence has been achieved, and can become the medium of expression for the plans and purposes of the soul, transmitting its ideas via the mind, so the planetary Deity, working under the inspiration of the Universal Mind, can impress humanity with the purposes of God and produce consequent effects in the world of phenomena.

The Members of the Hierarchy represent those who have achieved peace and quiescence, and can be impressed; aspirants and disciples represent those brain cells which are beginning to fall into the larger divine rhythm. They are learning the nature of responsiveness. The mass of men are like the millions of unused brain cells which the psychologists and scientists tell us we possess but do not employ. This analogy you can think out in greater detail for yourself, but even superficially it will be apparent to you that when this point is grasped, the purpose for which humanity exists, the objective before the group of world mystics and workers, and the ideal set before the individual aspirant, are the same as in the individual meditation; the achieving of that focussed attention and mental quiet wherein reality can be contacted, the true and the beautiful can be registered, divine purpose can be recorded, and it becomes possible to transmit to the phenomenal form, upon the physical plane, the needed energy whereby the subjective realisation can be materialised. The aspirant does this in connection with his own soul purpose if he is successful in his endeavour; the disciple is learning to do this in relation to group purpose, and the initiate co-operates with the planetary purpose. These constitute the inner group of vitally alive brain cells in the planetary brain, the entire human group, and it is evident that the more powerful their united vibration, and the clearer the light which they reflect and transmit, the more rapidly will the present inert mass of human cells be brought into activity. The occult Hierarchy is to the planetary Life what the light in the head is to the average awakened disciple, only on so much vaster a scale, and with such an adequate inner alignment that students such as those who read these Instructions cannot understand the true significance of the words. The point to be grasped is that through humanity on the physical plane, the nature of reality will be revealed; the true and the beautiful will be manifested; the divine Plan will eventually work out, and that energy be transmitted to all forms in nature which will enable the inner spiritual reality to emerge.

ii. The second type of activity of which man is capable, is an intense progressive and spiral development within the human ring-pass-not. This sentence covers the mode of development and the entire procedure of unfoldment of all the evolving units that we call men. With this I seek not here to deal. The history of the human structural growth, the entire field of the unfolding human consciousness, and the history of all races and peoples that have lived or are living upon our planet, can be dealt with under this heading. It concerns the use humanity has made of all the energies available within the natural world of which it is a part, inherent in the fourth kingdom itself, and coming to it also from the world of spiritual realities.

iii. The third type of activity which should occupy the attention of humanity, and one yet little understood, is that it should act as a transmitting centre of spiritual forces—soul force and spiritual energy united and combined—to the prisoners of the planet and to the lives, held in embodied existence in the other kingdoms of nature. Human beings are apt to be primarily concerned with their higher group relations, with their return to the Father's home, and with the trend which we call "upwards" and away from the phenomenal world. They are principally occupied with the finding of the centre within the form aspect, that which we call the soul, and, having found it, with the work then of acquainting themselves with that soul and thus finding peace. This is right and in line with divine intention, but it is *not* all of the Plan for man, and when this remains the prime objective, a man is dangerously near falling into the snare of spiritual selfishness and separateness.

When the centre is found by any human being, and he becomes at-one with, and enters into relation with his soul, then he automatically shifts his position in the human family, and—again speaking in symbols—finds himself part of the centre of light and understanding which we call, esoterically, the occult Hierarchy, the cloud of witnesses, the disciples of the Christ, and other names according to the trend of the disciple's convictions. This Hierarchy is also attempting to externalise itself in the form of the group of World Workers, and when a man has found his soul, and the principle of unity is sufficiently revealed to him, he shifts also into this more exoteric group. All who find the centre do not as yet link up with both the interior and exterior groups. Then he is pledged to the magical work, to the salvaging of souls, to the releasing of the prisoners of the planet. This is the goal for humanity as a whole, and when all the sons of men have attained the objective, these prisoners will be released. (4-525/9)

2. We could take the nations, one by one, and observe how this nationalistic, separative or isolationist spirit, emerging out of an historical past, out of racial complexes, out of territorial position, out of revolt and out of possession of material resources, has brought about the present (1942) world crisis and cleavage, and this global clash of interests and ideals. But it would profit not. The intelligent student of history (who has no nationalistic bias) knows well the facts and is deeply concerned today with the processes which must be brought to bear to end the world strife. He knows that the efforts to attain national aggrandisement, a place in the sun, "lebensraum", financial supremacy, economic control and power must end. At the same time he realises that if humanity is to get rid of these evil products of selfishness, certain basic values must be preserved.

Past and present cultures and civilisations are of great value; the peculiar genius of each nation must be evoked for the enriching of the entire human family; the new civilisation must have its roots in and emerge out of the past; new ideals must come forth and be recognised, and for that the events and education of the past will have prepared the people. *Humanity itself must be the goal of interest and effort, and not any particular nation or empire.* All this has to be wrought out in a practical, realistic manner, divorced from visionary, mystical and impractical dreams, and all that is done must be founded on one basic recognition —human brotherhood, expressing itself in right human relations.

The revolt so widely prevalent against the "vague visionings" of humanitarian dreamers, is based upon the fact that out of the welter of words and the plethora of plans, little of practical value has emerged, and nothing sufficiently potent to end the old and horrid ways of life. Nothing really effective had been done, prior to the war, to offset the visible and shrieking evils. Palliative measures have been tried and compromises made for the sake of peace, but the basic evils of national ambition, economic disparity, and virulent class distinctions (hereditary or financial) still remained. Religious differences were rampant, racial hatreds widespread, and the economic and political orders remained corrupt, fostering party, social and national strife.

. . . People everywhere are waking up and beginning to think, and never again can they sink back into the negative condition of the past. There is faith on every hand that a new and better world order is possible, and that it is even probable.

How can we simply and clearly express the goal of this hoped-for new world order, and word briefly the objective which each person and nation should hold before itself . . .? It is surely that every nation, great and small (with the minorities given equal and proportionate rights) should pursue its own individual culture and work out its own salvation as seems best to it, but that each and all should develop the realisation that they are organic parts of one corporate whole, and that they must contribute to that whole all they have and are. This concept is already present in the hearts of countless thousands and carries with it great responsibility. These realisations, when intelligently developed and wisely handled, will lead to right human relations, economic stability (based on the spirit of sharing) and to a fresh orientation of man to man, of nation to nation, and of all to that supreme power to which we give the name "GOD". (13-375/7)

3.   I ask you to drop your antagonisms and your antipathies, your
      hatreds and your racial differences, and attempt to think in terms
      of the one family, the one Life and the one humanity.   (13-468)

4. Certain great concepts are firmly grasped by man. Certain great hopes
are taking form and will become the pattern of man's living. Certain
great speculations will become experimental theories, and later prove demonstrated facts. Behind all this, two things are happening: Men are being
stimulated and brought to that point of necessary tension which (as a result of a crisis) must precede a great moving forward upon the Path of
Evolution. Secondly, a process of reorientation is going on which will
eventually enable the mass of men to present a united front upon views
hitherto regarded as the vague visions of intelligent and optimistic
dreamers. A great stirring and moving is going on. The world of men is
seething in response to the inflow of spiritual energy. This energy has been
evoked by the unrealised and inaudible cry of humanity itself. Humanity
has become—for the first time in its history—spiritually invocative.
(18-78)

5. Man is a living entity, a conscious son of God (a soul) occupying an
animal body. Here lies the point. He is therefore in the nature of a link,
and a far from missing link. He unifies in himself the results of the
evolutionary process as it has been carried on during the past ages, and he
brings into contact with that evolutionary result a new factor, that of an
individual self-sustaining, self-knowing aspect. It is the presence of this factor and of this aspect which produces in humanity a consciousness of immortality, a self-awareness and a self-centredness which make man truly
to appear in the image of God. It is this innate and hidden power which
gives man the capacity to suffer, which no animal possesses, but which
also confers on him the ability to reap the benefits of this experience in
the realm of the intellect. This same capacity, in embryo, works out in
the animal kingdom in the realm of the instincts. It is this peculiar property of humanity which confers upon it the power to sense ideals, to
register beauty, to react sensuously to music, and to enjoy colour and harmony. It is this divine something which makes of mankind the prodigal
son, torn between desire for the worldly life, for possessions and experience, and the attractive power of that centre, or home, from which he
has come.

    Man stands midway between heaven and earth, with his feet deep in
the mud of material life, and his head in heaven. In the majority of cases
his eyes are closed, and he sees not the beauty of the heavenly vision, or

they are open but fixed upon the mud and slime with which his feet are covered. But when his open eyes are lifted for a brief moment, and see the world of reality and of spiritual values, then the torn and distracted life of the aspirant begins.

Humanity is the custodian of the hidden mystery, and the difficulty consists in the fact that that which man conceals from the world is also hidden from himself. He knows not the wonder of that which he preserves and nourishes. Humanity is the treasure-house of God . . . for only in the human kingdom, as esotericists have long pointed out, are the three divine qualities found in their full flower and *together.* In man, God the Father has hidden the secret of life; in man, God the Son has secreted the treasures of wisdom and of love; in man, God the Holy Spirit has implanted the mystery of manifestation. Humanity, and humanity alone, can reveal the nature of the Godhead and the eternal life. To man is given the privilege of revealing the nature of the divine consciousness, and of portraying before the eyes of the assembled sons of God (at the final conclave before the dissolution) what has lain hidden in the Mind of God. Hence the injunction before us today (in the words of the great Christian Teacher) to possess in ourselves "the mind of Christ". This mind must dwell in us and reveal itself in the human race in ever greater fullness. To man is given the task of raising matter up into heaven, and of glorifying rightly the form side of life through his conscious manifestation of divine powers.　(14-311/3)

19.　HUMAN RELATIONSHIPS

(a) LOVE

1. LOVE

> The sons of men are one, and I am one with them.
> I seek to love, not hate;
> I seek to serve and not exact due service;
> I seek to heal, not hurt.

Let pain bring due reward of light and love.
Let the soul control the outer form,
And life, and all events,
And bring to light the Love
That underlies the happenings of the time.

Let vision come and insight.
Let the future stand revealed.
Let inner union demonstrate and outer cleavages be gone.
Let love prevail.
Let all men love.   (5-790)

2. *Divine Love*

Love is not making the object of the love feel comfortable superficially. If I induced that reaction in you, I would not merit your confidence and trust, and in the long run I would not thus hold your respect. Love is far-seeing wisdom which seeks to keep alive in the object of that love those sensitivities which will guarantee safe progress. Love is, therefore, guarding, stimulating and protective. But it is not a personal matter. It is a positive protection, but does not lead to a negative attitude of being cared for on the part of the one who is the recipient of the love and protection. It is the stimulating power of divine love which I seek to pour out upon you and upon all whom I serve as Master and Teacher. This will lead you wisely to protect yourself from glamour, illusion and personality reactions, also from error and prejudice in order the better to serve both Humanity and the Hierarchy. Ponder on this.   (6-683)

3. *Impersonal Love*

It is not easy to love as do the Great Ones, with a pure love which requires nothing back; with an impersonal love that rejoices where there is response, but looks not for it, and loves steadily, quietly, and deeply through all apparent divergences, knowing that when each has found his own way home, he will find that home to be the place of at-one-ment. (1-76)

4. When the heart is full of love and the head is full of wisdom, nothing then is ever done that can cause distress to others in the long run. . . . The man who is fearless, wise and loving, can do anything and the effects will be harmless and good producing.   (5-143/4)

5. *Glamour of Sentiment*

The glamour of sentiment holds the good people of the world in thrall, and in a dense fog of emotional reactions. The race has reached a point wherein the men of good intention, of some real understanding, and owning a measure of freedom from the love of gold (symbolic way of speaking of the glamour of materiality) are turning their desire to their duty, their responsibilities, their effects upon others, and to their sentimental understanding of the nature of love. Love, for many people, for the majority indeed, is not really love, but a mixture of the desire to love and the desire to be loved, plus a willingness to do anything to show and evoke this sentiment, and consequently to be more comfortable in one's own interior life. The selfishness of the people who are desirous of being unselfish is great. So many contributing sentiments gather around the sentiment or desire to show those amiable and pleasant characteristics which will evoke a corresponding reciprocation towards the would-be lover or server who is still completely surrounded by the glamour of sentiment.

It is this pseudo-love, based primarily on a theory of love and service, which characterises so many human relationships such as those existing, for instance, between husband and wife, parents and their children. Glamoured by their sentiment for them and knowing little of the love of the soul, which is free itself and leaves others free also, they wander in a dense fog, often dragging with them the ones they desire to serve, in order to draw forth a responsive affection. Study the word "affection", my brother, and see its true meaning. Affection is not love. It is that desire which we express through an exertion of the astral body, and this activity affects our contacts; it is not the spontaneous desirelessness of the soul which asks nothing for the separated self. This glamour of sentiment imprisons and bewilders all the nice people in the world, imposing upon them obligations which do not exist, and producing a glamour which must eventually be dissipated by the pouring in of true and selfless love. (10-76/7)

6. *The Law of Love*

It is not easy, in this brief digest, to approach the tremendous problem of the place love plays in the evolving scheme of things as understood by three-dimensional man. . . .

This term "The Law of Love", is after all too generic a term to apply to one law governing one plane, but will have to suffice for the present, as it conveys the type of idea that is needed, to our minds. The Law of

Love is in reality but the law of the system in demonstration on all planes. Love was the impelling motive for manifestation, and love it is that keeps all in ordered sequence; love bears all on the path of return to the Father's bosom, and love eventually perfects all that is. It is love that builds the forms that cradle temporarily the inner hidden life, and love is the cause of the disruption of those forms, and their utter shattering, so that the life may further progress. Love manifests on each plane as the urge that drives the evolving Monad onwards to its goal, and love is the key to the deva kingdom, and the reason of the blending of the two kingdoms eventually into the divine Hermaphrodite. Love works through the concrete rays in the building of the system, and in the rearing of the structure that shelters the Spirit, and love works through the abstract rays for the full and potent development of that inherent divinity. Love demonstrates, through the concrete rays, the aspects of divinity, forming the *persona* that hides the one Self; love demonstrates through the abstract rays in developing the attributes of divinity, in evolving to fullest measure the Kingdom of God within. Love in the concrete rays leads to the path of occultism; love in the abstract rays leads to that of the mystic. Love forms the sheath and inspires the life; love causes the logoic vibration to surge forward, carrying all on its way, and bringing all to perfected manifestation.

. . . On the astral plane, the home of the desires, originate those feelings which we call personal love; in the lowest type of human being this shows itself as animal passion; as evolution proceeds, it shows itself as a gradual expansion of the love faculty, passing through the stages of love of mate, love of family, love of surrounding associates, to love of one's entire environment; patriotism gives place later to love of humanity, often humanity as exemplified in one of the Great Ones. The astral plane is, at the present time, the most important for us, for in desire—not corrected or transmuted—lies the difference between the personal consciousness and that of the Ego.   (3-593/5)

7. The . . . basic postulate was enunciated for us by Christ when he told us to "love our neighbour as ourselves". To this we have paid, as yet, but little attention. We have loved ourselves and have sought to love those we like. But to love universally and because our neighbour is a soul as we are, with a nature essentially perfect and an infinite destiny, this has always been regarded as a beautiful dream to be consummated in a future so distant, and in a heaven so far away, that we may well forget it. Two thousand years have gone since the greatest expression of God's

love walked on earth and bade us love each other. Yet still we fight and
hate and use our powers for selfish ends, our bodies and our appetites for
material pleasures, and our efforts at living are, in the mass, primarily
directed towards personal selfishness. Have you ever considered what the
world would today be if man had listened to the Christ and had sought to
obey His command? We should have eliminated much disease (for the
diseases originating in the misuse of the sex function, underlie a large
percentage of our physical ills, and devastate our modern civilisation), we
should have made war impossible, we should have reduced crime to a
minimum, and our modern life would be an exemplification of a manifesting divinity. But this has not been the case, and hence our modern world
conditions.

But the new law must, and will, be enunciated. This law can be summed up in the words: Let a man so live that his life is harmless. Then no
evil to the group can grow out of his thoughts, his actions or his words.
This is not negative harmlessness, but of a difficult and positive activity.
If the above practical paraphrase of the words of Christ were universally
promulgated and practically applied, we should have order growing out
of chaos, group love superseding personal selfishness, religious unity taking the place of fanatical intolerance, and regulated appetites instead of
licence.   (14-301/2)

8. The Power of Love

In service (man) learns the power of love in its occult significance. He
spends and consequently receives; he lives the life of renunciation and
the wealth of the heavens pours in on him; he gives all and is full to com-
pleteness; he asks nothing for himself, and is the richest man on earth.
(4-117)

9. By the pure light of love for each other, you can draw nearer to me and
to the teachers on the subjective side of life, and arrive more rapidly at
that Gate which opens on the lighted Way. You have the opportunity to
demonstrate to each other the scientific value and power of love, regarded
as a force in nature. Make this demonstration your endeavour. You will
thus release for each other all that is needed to bring about potent and
vital changes in the life patterns and purpose of the group members. Love
is not a sentiment or an emotion, nor is it desire or a selfish motive for
right action in daily life. Love is the wielding of the force which guides
the worlds, and which leads to the integration, unity and inclusiveness
which impels Deity itself to action. Love is a hard thing to cultivate—
such is the inherent selfishness of human nature; it is a difficult thing to

apply to all conditions of life, and its expression will demand of you the utmost you have to give, and the stamping out of your selfish personal activities.

Disciples in the group of a Master have to love each other with intelligence and an abiding strength, and thus release that light and power which will eventually make the group of effective value in the world. (5-10)

10. Give to each other real love in the times that lie ahead, for it is the fusing and illuminating element in the life of the disciple. Let not your love remain theoretical, but give that true understanding which ignores mistakes, recognises no barriers, refuses all separating thoughts, and surrounds each other with that protecting wall of love that meets all need wherever possible—physical, emotional and mental.   (6-4)

11. Disciples and aspirants must on every hand live harmoniously and *love*. The violent vibrations of our surroundings must be stilled by a strong counter vibration of love, remembering ever that as we work on the side of evolution, the power of the Godhead itself is with us, available for use. Naught can withstand the steady pressures of love and harmony when they are applied long enough. It is not spasmodic efforts that count. It is the long-sustained, unvarying pressure which eventually breaks down opposition and the walls of separativeness.   (13-516)

12. *Love in Healing*

All who stand in the world as magnetic centres must proceed, according to the light that is in them, to work with people, in order to help them, to heal them, and to aid them in making needed adjustments. Nothing should stop your service along this line, not even the realisation of limitation and ignorance. Do all you can to encourage and to sympathise, to point out undesirable attitudes, to end wrong ways of living, and change poor modes of psychological expression as far as you see them, and to the best of your ability. Remember, nevertheless, that your best way may be far short of your future capacities, and remain ready ever to change your point of view when a higher and better way is presented to you. Above everything else in life, give to all who seek your aid the fullest measure of *love*, for love releases, love adjusts and interprets, and love heals, on all three planes.   (17-353)

13. Love is the life expression of God Himself; love is the coherent force which makes all things whole (I would have you ponder upon this phrase), and love is all that *is*. The main characteristic of the distinction

between soul energy and personality force, as applied to healing, lies in the region of the application and the expression of love. Personality force is emotional, full of feeling, and—when in use—the personality is ever conscious of itself as the healer, and is the dramatic centre of the stage upon which are two players, the healer and the one to be healed. Soul energy functions unconsciously and is wielded by those who are in contact with their souls and who are consequently decentralised; they are "off the stage" themselves, if I might use that expression, and they are completely occupied with group love, group activity, and group purpose. . . . So let true love, silent, uncomplaining, non-critical and steadfast, be your goal and the quality of your group life. Then, when there is some definite work to do, you will work as a unit, with hearts and minds as one.   (17-356/8)

14. *Love of Humanity*

When love for all beings, irrespective of who they may be, is beginning to be a realised fact in the heart of a disciple, and yet nevertheless love for himself exists not, then comes the indication that he is nearing the Portal of Initiation, and may make the necessary preliminary pledges. These are necessitated before his Master hands in his name as a candidate for initiation. If he cares not for the suffering and pain of the lower self, if it is immaterial to him whether happiness comes his way or not, if the sole purpose of his life is to serve and save the world, and if his brother's need is for him of greater moment than his own, then is the fire of love irradiating his being, and the world can warm itself at his feet. This love has to be a practical, tested manifestation, and not just a theory, nor simply an impractical ideal and a pleasing sentiment. It is something that has grown in the trials and tests of life, so that the primary impulse of the life is towards self-sacrifice and the immolation of the lower nature. (1-192/3)

15. In the New Age . . . the keynote of the aspirant's progress will be *love of humanity*; this will indicate the awakening of the heart centre. In the past and up until the last few years, the keynote has been *service*, because (if selflessly rendered) it embodied a technique which automatically brought the heart centre into activity. It is love of humanity which is the major lack in the character of many disciples today. They love those with whom they may be associated, or they love the work connected with the group endeavour, or they love their own nation; they may also love an ideal or theoretical assumption, but they do not really love humanity as

a whole. There are limits to their capacity to love and it is the transcending of those limits which constitutes their main problem at this time; they have to learn that it is humanity which calls for their allegiance, their loyalty and service. I would ask you all to ponder deeply on the above statements, for they embody the task ahead for you also, as you seek to fit yourselves for the first or the second initiation.   (5-88)

16. Love, which is not emotion or sentiment, and which is not related to feeling (which is a distortion of true love), but is the fixed determination to do what is best for the whole of humanity, or for the group (if the larger concept is not possible to you), and to do this at any personal cost and by means of the uttermost sacrifice. Only those who truly love their fellow men can see the issues clear, and can grasp the inevitability of the things which must be done to end the present rule of terror, and so usher in the new rule of peace. Peace is *not* the goal for our race or time, no matter what many men think. This is a cycle of steadily growing activity, with the aim in view of establishing right human relations, intelligently carried forward. Such activity and intense change is not consonant with what is usually understood as peace. Peace has relation to the emotional side of life, and was the goal in Atlantean days, where peace was a great spiritual issue. But peace and the love of peace can be a deadening soporific, and are so at this time. It is usually selfish in purpose, and people long for peace because they want to be happy. Happiness and peace will come when there are right human relations. Peace and war are not a true pair of opposites. Peace and change, peace and movement, are the real ones. War is but an aspect of change, and has its roots deep in matter. The peace usually desired and discussed, concerns material peace, and in every case is related to the personality, whether it is the individual personality or that of humanity as a whole. Therefore I deal not with peace, but am concerned with love, which oft disturbs the equilibrium of matter and material circumstance, and can consequently work against so-called peace.

. . . Love, true spiritual love as the soul knows it, can ever be trusted with power and opportunity and will never betray that trust. It will bring all things into line with soul vision.   (13-277/9)

17. The hold of the materialistic values over man is steadily becoming weaker. So far has man progressed that there are enough people in the world today to turn the tide *if* they can be aroused from their apathy.

. . . Aspirants are preoccupied with their own little affairs and with their own small efforts, instead of relinquishing everything in an endeavour to unite on the needed appeal and activity. They are contending for their own interpretations of truth, and for their pet ideals of peace, living or work, and—like Nero—they "fiddle whilst Rome burns". All their lives they have fought for an ideal and a dream, and they love that more than they love humanity. Yet—all that is needed is such a deep love of humanity, that it works out on all levels of activity and all life effort. If the idealists of the world would realise the situation *as it is,* they would relinquish all that they hold dear and come to the rescue of humanity, and thus snatch the helpless masses back from slavery and death. They would battle for the freedom of the human soul with every weapon in the armory of mankind. They would hold back the forces of aggression by force itself if need be. They would aim at clear thinking, and thus clear the channel for the inflow of spiritual force. The major prerequisites today for true world service, are an overwhelming love of humanity and a sense of proportion.   (13-310/1)

18. *Universal love*

Be not unduly disturbed. There is no light or dark to the soul, but only existence and love. Rest back on that. There is no separation but only identification with the heart of all love; the more you love, the more love can reach out through you to others. The chains of love unite the world of men and the world of forms, and they constitute the great chain of Hierarchy. The spiritual effort you are asked to make is that of developing youself into a vibrant and powerful centre of that fundamental, universal *Love.*   (6-30)

(b)   BROTHERHOOD

1. If men carried the concept of brotherhood, with all its implications, into the life and work of every day, into all intercourse, whether between the capitalist and the labourer, the politician and the people, between nation and nation, or between race and race, there would emerge that peace on earth which nothing could upset or overturn. So simple a rule, and yet utterly beyond the mental grasp of the majority!   (4-303/4)

2. Astral energies emanate from the new sign of the zodiac into which we are now entering, the sign of Aquarius. . . . It will (through the effect of its potent force) stimulate the astral bodies of men into a new coherency, into a brotherhood of humanity which will ignore all racial and national differences, and will carry the life of men forward into synthesis and unity. This means a tide of unifying life of such power that one

cannot now vision it, but which—in a thousand years—will have welded all mankind into a perfect brotherhood. Its emotional effect will be to "purify" the astral bodies of men so that the material world ceases to hold such potent allure, and may in its later stages bring about a state of exaggeration as potent in the line of sentiency as that which we have undergone in the line of materiality. (4-313/4)

3. When we come to the consideration of other basic trends in the world of current thought, it becomes apparent that one of the most dominant is the increasing emphasis laid upon group consciousness, or environal awareness. This has been recognised by the man in the street as a sense of responsibility, and indicates in the individual an egoic vibration. It is one of the first signs that the soul is beginning to use its mechanism. No longer does the man live in the interests of the separated self, but he begins to realise the need for adjustment to and in the condition of his neighbour. He assumes the duty of being in a very real sense his brother's keeper, and realises that in reality progress, contentment, peace of mind and prosperity, do not exist for him apart from that of his brother. This realisation is steadily expanding from the individual to the state and nation, from the family unit to the world, and hence the big organisations, fraternities, clubs, leagues and movements which have for their objective the uplift and welfare of men everywhere. The necessity of giving instead of getting is growing in the racial consciousness, and the recognition of certain of the basic concepts connected with brotherhood is steadily growing. Brotherhood as a fact in nature is as yet largely a theory, but brotherhood as an ideal is now fashioned in the racial consciousness. (4-338/9)

4. Much has been written, preached and talked about brotherhood. So much has been said and so little brotherhood practised that the word has fallen somewhat into disrepute. Yet the word *is* a statement of the underlying origin and goal of humanity and is the keynote of the fourth kingdom in nature, the human.

Brotherhood is a great natural fact; all men are brothers; under the divergences of colour, creed, cultures and civilisations, there is only *one* humanity, without distinction or differences in its essential nature, in its origin, its spiritual and mental objectives, its capacities, its qualities and its mode of development and of evolutionary unfoldment. In these divine attributes (for that is what they are) all men are equal; it is only in relation to time and in the extent to which progress has been made in the revelation of innate divinity in all its fullness, that temporary differences become apparent. It is the temporary differences and the sins which ignorance and inexperience betray, which have engrossed the attention of the churches to the exclusion of the penetrating, piercing vision of the divine in every man. It is the fact of brotherhood which the churches must begin to teach—not from the angle of a transcendent God, an external unknowable Father—but from the angle of the divine life, eternally present in every human heart, and eternally struggling to express itself through individuals, nations and races.

The true expression of this realised brotherhood must inevitably come through the establishing of right human relations and the cultivation of goodwill. Churchmen have forgotten the sequence in the angel's song: "Glory to God in the highest, on earth peace, goodwill towards men." They have failed to realise and, therefore, to teach that only as goodwill is manifested in the daily lives of men are right human relations thereby established, and peace on earth can come; they have failed also to realise that there is no glory to God until there *is* peace on earth through goodwill among men. The churches have forgotten that all men are sons of the Father and, therefore, brothers; that all men are divine; that some men are already God-conscious and expressing divinity, and that some are not; they have overlooked the fact that because of their point in evolution some men know Christ, because the Christ in them is active, while others are only struggling to bring the Christ life into activity; still others are entirely unaware of the divine Being hidden deep within their hearts. There is only difference in degree of consciousness; there is no difference in nature. (7-147/8)

5. For some years now, the spiritual Hierarchy of our planet has been drawing nearer to humanity, and its approach is responsible for the great concepts of freedom which are so close to the hearts of men everywhere. The dream of brotherhood, of fellowship, of world co-operation and of a peace, based on right human relations, is becoming clearer in our minds. We are also visioning a new and vital world religion, a universal faith which will have its roots in the past, but which will make clear the new dawning beauty and the coming vital revelation. (7-152)

6. The sense of comradeship is surely known by each and all of you, but needs the deepening of service shared. Shew this and draw it forth. The comradeship of burdens shared, the sense to deep response to need, the comradeship of service rendered, the urge to sacrifice—teach these to those who seek to work within the Master's Plan, and show all three yourself. (5-167)

(c) GOODWILL

1. The time will come when you are personally so decentralised that automatically the sense of "others" is far stronger in you than the sense of personality or of the lower self. Let your imagination run wild for a moment, picturing the condition of the world when the majority of human beings are occupied with the good of others, and not with their own selfish goals. Such a play of imaginative thought is good and constructive, and will aid in bringing out into manifestation that new world and that new type of humanity which the future will inevitably demonstrate. On this I shall not enlarge; the practice of goodwill will lay the foundation for this new type of sensitivity.   (6-297/8)

2. Goodwill is today a dream, a theory, a negative force. It should be developed into a fact, a functioning ideal, and a positive energy. That is our work, and we are definitely called to co-operate in bringing it about. (15-732)

3. The Potency of Goodwill

Much will depend upon what you and all men of goodwill and disciples think and what they do. I would like to remind you of another most encouraging thing, and that is that the power wielded by those who are seeking to live as souls and in touch with the soul and the world of spiritual realities, is out of all proportion to their registered sense of power and usefulness. You are, as you endeavour to wield spiritual force constructively and selflessly, far more potent than you realise. If you add to this realisation the recognition that you are not alone in this, but that people with a vision similar to yours, and with the same ideals and spiritual aspiration, are to be found in every country, without exception of any kind, in every religion, group and organisation, then indeed you can go forward in unison with our brothers everywhere, conscious of opportunity, of strength, of responsibility and of the joy of service.

As regards some of the things which you can do, I would suggest the following. Refuse to allow yourselves to be swept by any fear psychosis, or to be stampeded into any attitude through which the anxiety and unrest and distress in the world can overwhelm you. Strive to stand in spiritual being. Each morning, in your meditation, seek to take that attitude with a new and fresh definiteness and to hold it during the hours of service which lie ahead each day. This will not be an easy thing to do, but it can be done if you can get quiet enough for five minutes each morning—com-

pletely and interiorly quiet—and if you fill your days with vital occupation
and true service, guarding with care all thought and speech.   (13-81/2)

4. Goodwill is the simplest expression of true love and the one most easily
understood. The use of goodwill in connection with the problems with
which humanity is faced, releases the intelligence along constructive lines;
where goodwill is present, the walls of separation and of misunderstanding fall.

Love and understanding will eventually follow upon a practical expression of goodwill as a factor in every type of human relation, and as a
mode of contact between groups, between nations and their minorities,
between nation and nation, and also in the field of international politics
and religions. The expression of true love as a factor in the life of our
planet may lie very far ahead, but goodwill is a present possibility and the
organising of goodwill an outstanding necessity.   (7-118)

5. *Lack of Unity between the Men of Goodwill*

We live in an era of extremes—of extreme riches and extreme poverty;
of extreme ignorance and extreme learning; of extreme discontent and the
extreme satisfaction of personal ambitions; of extreme selfishness and extreme self-sacrifice. . . . In every country in the world today, men of goodwill and of true understanding are to be found. Many thousands of them
are known. They are, however, either ridden by fear or by a feeling
of futility, and by the realisation that the work to be done is so stupendous, that their little isolated efforts are utterly useless to break down
the barriers of hate and separation everywhere to be found. They realise
that there is apparently no systematised spread of the principles which
seem to hold the solution of the world problem; they have no conception
of the numerical strength of those who may be thinking as they do, and
they are consequently rendered impotent through their loneliness, their
lack of unity, and the dead weight of the surrounding inertia.   (15-
670/1)

6. How can the economic situation be stabilised, and the world be
brought to a condition where there is a just and right sufficiency for all?
How can national differences be healed, and racial hatreds be ended? How
can the many religious groups pursue their work of leading men to an
expression of their divinity along the lines of individual heritage, and yet
at the same time exist in harmony and present a united front to the world?
How can wars be ended and peace be brought about on earth? How can a
true prosperity be established, which shall be the result of unity, peace
and plenty?

Only in one way. *By the united action of the men and women of good-will and understanding in every country and in every nation.* Steadily and quietly, with no sense of hurry, must they do three things:

First, they must discover each other and be in touch with each other. Thus the sense of weakness and of futility will be offset. This is the first duty and task of the New Group of World Servers.

Secondly, they must clarify and elucidate those basic principles of right living, goodwill and harmony, which are recognised, but not applied, by all right thinking people today. These principles must be formulated in the simplest terms and made practical in action.

Thirdly, the general public must be educated in these principles. Steadily, regularly and systematically, they must be taught the principles of brotherhood, of an internationalism which is based on goodwill and love of all men, of religious unity and of co-operative interdependence. The individual in every nation and group must be taught to play his important part with goodwill and understanding; the group must shoulder its responsibility to other groups, and the responsibility of nation to nation, and of all nations to the world of nations, must be explained and emphasised.

This is no idle or mystical, impractical program. *It undermines and attacks no authority or government. It is not interested in the overthrow of rulers or the downfall of any political or national party.* It calls for intelligent and practical effort. It will call for the co-operation of many types of mind and many trained executives. The men of goodwill in every country must be discovered, and all who respond to these ideals must be gathered together through mailing lists. Their co-operation must be sought and systematised. This program will call, eventually, for the assistance of many lecturers and writers, who will work along the same idealistic lines, but with differing methods. Through their knowledge of their own country, and of the best way to bring these basic truths home to their own nationals, they must be left free to work as they see best for their particular nation. They, and all men and women of goodwill constitute the New Group of World Servers. A central group, chosen from among them, should synthesise this work and co-ordinate it, whilst giving the widest latitude to individual servers and workers. (15-672/3)

7. The main hierarchical need today (apart from its need for workers), is the forming everywhere of such groups as yours, the relating of group with group within the range of influence of that super group, the Hierarchy. Such groups are forming now in their thousands, and are to be

found in every land, and they will eventually blend and fuse together into one great movement of goodwill, which is spirit in actual expression. Aspirants everywhere . . . must contact these groups, bringing them together on one point only, and that is *Goodwill*. Each group must necessarily be left free to proceed with its own destiny and mode of work. Unity is a necessary ideal, and is the reverse side of Goodwill. Unitedly, when the right time comes, these groups must issue a great manifesto to the world—identical manifestos being issued in each country by all the groups who stand for world unity and goodwill. Thus they will make the word "goodwill" carry power throughout the planet, whilst the disciples and aspirants will, through their thought, make the word "unity" carry hidden power. Thus a vast band of men of goodwill will be working unitedly, yet independently, and there will be made available— in moments of world crisis—an organised, ready, and world-wide public opinion of such strength and organisation that it cannot be ignored. (6-457)

8. Seek not to link groups with your group, but recognise your group and all similar groups, as parts of a *worldwide spiritual movement* which (when it reaches momentum) results in unity for all. A super-organisation which emphasises unity, is the last thing to be desired; a multiplicity of living organisms, held loosely together by co-operation, constant communication, and possessing identity of goal and purpose, is what the world needs today.   (6-458)

(d) WORLD GOODWILL

1. With goodwill to all, with a staunch belief in the divine possibilities of human beings, and in the future resurrection of humanity, with an exalted recognition of God, with an acknowledgement of the fundamental values of Christ's teaching, and with a joyful determination to go forward with the work of reconstruction, I call upon those who respond to this vision, immediately to set to work.

I call you to no organisational loyalties, but only to love your fellow men, be they German, American, Jewish, British, French, Negro or Asiatic. I call you from your dreams of vague beauty, impossible Utopias, and wishful thinking, *to face life as it is today*; and then to begin, in the place where you are, to make it better. I call you to the experiment of right human relations, beginning with your own personal relations to your family and friends, and then to the task of educating those you contact so that they also start a similar work. It is the work of attaining right

individual relations, right group relations, right inter-group relations, right
national relations and right international relations. I call you to the realisation that in this work no one is futile or useless, but that all have a place of
practical value. I call you to recognise that goodwill is a dynamic energy
which can bring about world changes of a fundamental kind, and that
its mode of expression is through the activity of the individual man and
woman, and through their massed intent. The massed power of goodwill,
the dynamic effect of intelligent and active understanding, and the potency of a trained and alive public opinion, which desires the greatest good
of the greatest number, are beyond belief. This dynamic power has never
been employed. It can today save the world.   (13-210/1)

2. It is hard to admit that none of the nations (including our own) has clean
hands, and that all are guilty of greed and theft, of separativeness, of pride
and prejudice, as well as national and racial hatreds. All nations have
much interior house cleaning to do, and this they must carry forward
along with their outer efforts to bring about a better and more habitable
world. It must be a world consciousness, motivated by the idea of the
general good, one in which higher values than individual and national
gain are emphasised, and one in which people are trained in right national
citizenship upon the one hand, and on the other in the responsibility for
world citizenship.

Is this too idealistic a picture? The guarantee of its possibility lies in
the fact that thousands today are thinking along these idealistic lines;
thousands are occupied with planning a better world and thousands are
talking about the possibility. All ideas which emanate from the divine
in man and nature, eventually become ideals (even though somewhat distorted in the process) and these ideals finally become the governing principles of the masses.   (7-14)

3. In spite of war and separation, of cruelty and of passions and selfishness running wild, there is nevertheless today more understanding, more
goodwill and more outgoing love than at any previous time in the history
of the race. I say this with deliberation and because I have the hierarchical
knowledge available to my hand. Be not deceived, therefore, by the outer
clamour of war. I tell you that men's hearts everywhere are full of compassion, both for themselves and for all other men; the wide scope and
the vast extent of the conflict is indicative of an inner unity and a subjective interrelation of which all are somewhat conscious and which the
conflict itself does not negate.   (13-105/6)

4. Promote ceaselessly the work of World Goodwill, so that every nation may have its group of men and women dedicated to the establishing of right human relations. You have the nucleus, and expansion must be undertaken. You have the principle of goodwill present throughout the world; the task will be heavy indeed, but far from impossible.   (13-641)

5. There is today much talk about goodwill, and a constant use of the word; there is a real intention to employ it in every field of human thought and in relation to every problem; there is evidence that there is a real effort at this time to make goodwill an effective agent in negotiating world peace and understanding, and in bringing about right human relations.

The major need is an immediate campaign, carried forward by all men of goodwill everywhere throughout the world, to interpret the meaning of goodwill, to emphasise the practical nature of its expression, to gather together into an effective and active world group all men and women of goodwill and to do this, not in order to create a super-organisation, but to convince the unhappy, the distressed and the abused, of the magnitude of the intelligent aid which stands ready to assist them. They must also demonstrate their ability to strengthen the hands of all workers who are struggling to bring about right human relations and prove to them the potency of the force of an educated and alive public opinion (educated by the men of goodwill) upon which they can draw. Thus there will be established in every nation, in every city and village, men of goodwill—with trained understanding, practical commonsense, a knowledge of world problems and a willingness to spread goodwill and find the men of like mind in their environment.

The work of the men of goodwill is an educational one. They hold and advocate no miraculous solution of world problems, but they *know* that a spirit of goodwill, particularly if trained and implemented by knowledge, can produce *an atmosphere* and *an attitude* which will make the solving of problems possible. When men of goodwill meet, no matter what their political party, nation or religion, there is no problem which they cannot eventually solve, and solve to the satisfaction of the various parties involved. *It is the production of this atmosphere and the evocation of this attitude which is the principal work of the men of goodwill, and not the presentation of some cut and dried solution.* This spirit of goodwill can be present even where there is fundamental disagreement between parties.   (7-118/9)

(e) RIGHT HUMAN RELATIONS

1. The immediate spiritual problem with which all are faced, is the problem of gradually offsetting hate and initiating the new technique of trained, imaginative, creative and practical goodwill.

Goodwill is man's first attempt to express the love of God. Its results on earth will be peace. It is so simple and practical that people fail to appreciate its potency or its scientific and dynamic effect. One person sincerely practising goodwill in a family, can completely change its attitudes. Goodwill really practised among groups in any nation, by political and religious parties in any nation, and among the nations of the world, can revolutionise the world. (7-6/7)

2. All nations have a vast house cleaning to do, and the difficulty at this time is that they must do it alongside of the strict fulfilling of their international relationships. No nation can live unto itself today. If it attempts to do so it treads the way to death, and that is the true horror of the isolationist position. Factually today we have one world and this sums up *the psychological problem of humanity.* The goal is right human relations; nations will stand or fall just in so far as they measure up to that vision. The era ahead of us—under evolutionary law and the will of God—is to see the establishment of right human relations.

We are entering a vast experimental period of discovery; we shall discover just exactly what we are—as nations, in our group relationships, through our expression of religion and in our mode of governments. It will be an intensely difficult era and will be only successfully lived through if each nation will recognise its own internal defects and will handle them with vision and deliberate humanitarian purpose. This means for each nation the overcoming of pride and the attainment of interior unity. Each country today is divided within itself by warring groups—idealists and realists; political parties and far-sighted statesmanship; religious groups, fanatically occupied with their own ideas; capital and labour; isolationists and internationalists; people violently against certain groups or nations, and others working on behalf of them. The only factor which can eventually and in due time bring harmony and the end of these chaotic conditions, is right human relations. (7-27/8)

3. Nation is still pitted against nation in the political arena, group against group and (within the nations) party against party, and man against man. The wise and the far-seeing, those prompted by a sane and unselfish commonsense, the idealist and the men and women of goodwill, are every-

where and are struggling to find a solution, to build a new world structure of law, order and peace, which will insure right human relations; but they are, in turn, a tiny minority in comparison to the vast multitude of human beings peopling our earth; their task is hard and from the point at which they must work, appears to them at times as presenting well-nigh insuperable difficulties.

Certain questions inevitably arise in the minds of the men of goodwill everywhere:

Can the Great Powers be trusted to function selflessly in the interests of the Little Powers and of humanity as a whole?

Can power politics and the various national imperialisms be forgotten and ended?

Can a world policy be devised which will insure justice for all, whether great or small?

Can world opinion be sufficiently strong in the interests of right human relations, that it can tie the hands of the sefishly aggressive, and open the door of opportunity to those who have as yet had little?

Is the hope of establishing an era of right human relations within nations as well as internationally, an impossible dream, a waste of time to consider, or an evidence only of wishful thinking?

Does the goal of right human relations, equal rights and opportunity for all men everywhere, provide an entirely possible goal for which all well-intentioned men can work with some hope of success?

What are the first steps which should be taken to promote such right endeavours, and to lay a secure foundation of world goodwill?

How can public opinion be sufficiently aroused so that the many steps to promote right human relations will be faced by legislators and politicians everywhere?

What should the minorities do in order to gain their just demands, without promoting more differences and feeding the fire of hatred?

How can we abolish the great lines of demarcation between races, nations and groups, and the cleavages that are to be found everywhere, working in such a manner that the "one humanity" emerges in the arena of world affairs?

How can we develop the consciousness that what is good for the part can also be good for the whole, and that the highest good of the unit within the whole guarantees the good of that whole?

These and many other questions arise and clamour for an answer. The answer comes in the form of a generally accepted platitude and is unfortunately in the nature of an anti-climax: *Establish right human relations by developing a spirit of goodwill.* Then and only then shall we have a world at peace and ready to move forward into a new and better era. Though a platitude is, in the majority of cases, the statement of a recognisable truth, it is difficult in this case to make people admit its feasibility. Nevertheless, because it is a truth, it is bound eventually to demonstrate as such, not only in the minds of a few people here and there, but on a large scale throughout the world. People are looking eagerly for the unexpected and the unusual, for an anticipated miracle and for God (whatever they mean in their own minds by that term) to take action, thus relieving them of responsibility and doing their work for them. (7-115/7)

4. The beauty of the present situation is that even in the smallest community a practical expression of what is needed on a worldwide scale, is offered to the inhabitants; differences in families, in churches, in municipalities, in cities, in nations, between races and internationally, all call for the same objective and for the same process of adjustment: *the establishing of right human relations.* The technique or method to bring this about remains everywhere the same: *the use of the spirit of goodwill.* (7-117/8)

5. Today men and women everywhere—in high places and in low, in every nation, community and group—are presenting a vision of right human relations which *must* constitute the standard for the future of mankind. Everywhere they are exposing the evils which must be eliminated, and they are educating ceaselessly in the principles of the New Age. It is these men who are of importance. In politics there are great and wise statesmen who are endeavouring to guide their people wisely, but have as yet too much with which to contend; of these Franklin D. Roosevelt was an outstanding modern example, for he gave of his best and died in the service of humanity. There are enlightened educators, writers and lecturers in every land who are seeking to show the people how *practical* is the ideal, how available the goodwill in mankind, and how easily applied are these ideals *when there are enough men and women of goodwill active in the world to force the issue.* This is the factor of importance. There are also scientists, physicians and agriculturists who have dedicated their lives to the betterment of human living; there are churchmen in all the faiths who follow sincerely the footsteps of the Christ (though they are not the leaders) and who repudiate the materialism which has ruined the churches; there are men and women

in their untold millions who see truly, think clearly and work hard in their communities to establish right human relations. (7-173/4)

(f) CHRIST AND RIGHT HUMAN RELATIONS

1. The phrase "right human relations" is one that is today being much discussed; it is being increasingly realised that it is a major human need, and the only hope of a peaceful and secure future. Wrong human relations have reached such a stage of difficulty that every phase of human life is in a state of chaotic turmoil; every aspect of daily living is involved —family life, communal living, business relations, and political contacts, governmental action and the habitual life of all peoples, including the entire field of international relations. Everywhere there is hate, competition, mal-adjustment, strife between parties, the vilest kind of muck raking and scandal making, deep distrust between men and nations, between capital and labour and among the many sects, churches and religions. The difference between a sect and a church is, after all, only one of degree and historical inception; it is one of interpretation, of fanatical adherence to some pet truth, and always—exclusiveness, which is contrary to Christian teaching. Nowhere is there peace today or understanding; only a small minority in relation to the Earth's population are struggling for those conditions which will lead to peaceful and happy relationships.

The strength of this fighting minority, struggling for peace and right relations, consists in the fact that the work they are attempting to do is in line with divine intention and purpose. Into this chaos of conflicting, competitive and fighting interests, Christ plans to reappear. I would ask you to contemplate the very real horror of what He has to face, and the necessity for some measure of order to be brought about in the world, for certain basic principles to be enunciated and partially, at least, accepted, before He can usefully work amongst men. If He were to come immediately, His voice would not be heard, for the noise of men's quarrelling is too great; if He sought to attract human attention, even through the prophesied sound of the trumpet (Matt. XXIV: 31), He would be classed simply as one who advertised himself; if He preached and taught, He would attract primarily those who think naturally in unison with His message, or the gullible and the credulous would flock to Him, as they do to all new teachers—no matter what they teach. The bulk of human beings are still too hungry, too devastated psychically, too bewildered and distressed and too unsure of their future, their freedom and their security to be in any condition to listen to Him. (Written about 1948).

He will not come, we may be sure, as a conquering hero, as the interpretations of the theological teachers have led man to believe, for that would certainly fail to identify Him and He would be simply classed as another military figure; of them we have had a plethora; He will not come as the Messiah of the Jews to save the so-called Holy Land and the city of Jerusalem for the Jews, because He belongs to the whole world, and no Jews nor any other people have special rights or unique privileges, or may claim Him as their own; He will not come to convert the "heathen" world for, in the eyes of the Christ and of His true disciples, no such world exists and the so-called heathen have demonstrated historically less of the evil of vicious conflict than has the militant Christian world. The history of the Christian nations and of the Christian church has been one of an aggressive militancy—the last thing desired by the Christ when He sought to establish the church on earth.

When He came before He said (and the words have been sadly misread): "I come not to bring peace, but a sword" (Matthew X: 34). This will be true especially during the early days of His advent. The sword which He wields, is the sword of Spirit; it is that sword which produces cleavage between a true spirituality and an habitual materialism. The major effect of His appearance will surely be to demonstrate in every land the effects of *a spirit of inclusiveness*—an inclusiveness which will be channelled or expressed through Him. All who seek right human relations will be gathered automatically to Him, whether they are in one of the great world religions or not; all who see no true or basic difference between religion and religion, or between man and man, or nation and nation, will rally around Him; Those who embody the spirit of exclusiveness and separativeness will stand automatically and equally revealed, and all men will know them for what they are. The cleaving sword of the spirit will—without wounding—bring revelation and indicate the first needed step towards human regeneration.

Standing as the focal point of the inner Triangle—of the Buddha, of the Spirit of Peace, and of the Avatar of Synthesis—the consequent outpouring potency of the Christ will be so great that the distinction between love and hate, between aggression and freedom, and between greed and sharing, will be made lucidly clear to the eyes and minds of all men and, therefore, the distinction between good and evil will be made equally clear. The invocative prayer, "From the point of love within the heart of God, let love stream forth into the hearts of men", will meet with fulfilment. Christ will let loose into the world of men the potency and

the distinctive energy of intuitive love. The results of the distribution of
this energy of love will be twofold:

i. Countless men and women in every land will form themselves into
groups for the promotion of goodwill and for the production of right
human relations. So great will be their numbers that from being a small
and relatively unimportant minority, they will be the largest and the
most influential force in the world. Through them, the New Group of
World Servers will be able to work successfully.

ii. This active energy of loving understanding, will mobilise a tremendous reaction against the potency of hate. To hate, to be separate,
and to be exclusive, will come to be regarded as the only sin, for it
will be recognised that all the sins—as listed and now regarded as
wrong—only stem from hate or from its product, the anti-social consciousness. Hate and its dependent consequences are the true sin against
the Holy Ghost, about which commentators have so long debated,
overlooking (in their silliness) the simplicity and the appropriateness
of the true definition.

The power of the hierarchical spiritual impact, focussed through Christ
and His working disciples, will be so great that the usefulness, the prac-
ticality and the naturalness of right human relations will become so evident that world affairs will rapidly be adjusted, and the new era of goodwill and of peace on earth will be inaugurated. The new culture and the
new civilisation will then be possible.

This is the picture of no optimistic, mystical and impossible event. It
is not based upon wishful thinking or upon a blind hope. Already today,
the disciples of the Christ are preaching the doctrine of right human relations; men and women of goodwill are endeavouring to show that only
through goodwill can true peace be brought about in the arena of international life. In the presentation of true "livingness" which the Christ will
demonstrate to the world of thinking men, there is necessarily no room
for exclusiveness or for separativeness, because that "life more abundantly" (which He seeks to channel to us) is a free and flowing current,
sweeping away obstructions and barriers, and establishing an unimpeded
circulation of truth and life itself—the essential quality of both being *love*.

All the world religions have posited the fact that God is Love essentially and that God is life essentially, as well as intelligence. That life
carries within itself the essential quality of the will of God, as well as the
love of God. Both are equally important, because that will is qualified by

love. Hitherto, men have known nothing of the factual nature of the quality of livingness, energised by love and will, except through a vague theoretical conception. The reappearance of Christ will establish the fact of this divine livingness; the work which He will accomplish—with the aid of His disciples—will demonstrate the love and the divine purpose which lie behind all phenomenal experience.

The establishing of right human relations is an aspect of the divine will for humanity, and the next facet of the divine expression to manifest itself in human affairs—individual, communal, national, and international. Nothing has ever finally impeded this divine expression, except the *time* factor, and that time factor is *determined by humanity* and is an expression of divine free will. The intended divine expression can move rapidly or slowly into manifestation, according as man decides; hitherto, man has decided upon a slow—a very slow—manifestation. It is here that the freedom of the human will shows itself. Because divinity is immanent or present in all forms, and therefore, in all human beings, that will *must* eventually be fulfilled; because of the tremendously material intention (esoterically speaking) of all forms at present, that Will has hitherto been retarded in its expression; it has *not* been the will of man to establish right human relations. Hence the discipline of war, the torture of the forms, and the misery in human living today.

These factors are bringing about a great and general transformation; the indications of this are easily to be seen by spiritually minded people. Such people are constantly saying (as Christ did in the Garden of Gethsemane), "Let the will of God be done". (Matthew XXVI: 39). They say it ignorantly and often hopelessly; nevertheless, it indicates a general process of spiritual re-orientation, of submission and of acquiescence. Christ demonstrated this *submission* when He said, "I came not to do my own will, but the will of Him Who sent me". (John VI: 38). He proved His *acquiescence* when He cried, "Father, not my will but Thine be done". Submission has in it the elements of conquest by circumstances and of a recognition which may not understand but which submits to that which is imposed. Acquiescence has in it the element of an understanding intelligence, and this marks a great step forward. Both admit the fact of a divine overshadowing will in the life of mankind today; both are preparatory to a recognition of Christ's work in bringing about right human relations. At present, the submission of mankind to the divine will is a negative submission; the true submission is a positive attitude of spiritual expectancy, leading eventually to a positive acquiescence.

A spiritual expectancy is also to be seen; it is part of the work of the

New Group of World Servers to intensify this. They have also to foster spiritual submission and intelligent acquiescence in the masses, who normally divide themselves into the two classes, expressing these two attitudes; these factors of submission, acquiescence and expectancy, are latent in every man. It is these three divine potentialities which will enable men to respond to the message of the Christ and, therefore, the selfless sacrifice, the understanding compromise and the comprehension of the many and diverse points of view (necessary to the establishing of right human relations) will be far easier to bring about.

We would all find it helpful to reflect upon what are the factors recognised in submission and acquiescence. In establishing right human relations, relinquishment, renunciation, submission to existent facts, and obedient acquiescence to divine law, are all involved. These are the things which Christ earlier demonstrated on Earth, and they are the things which He will help humanity to accept with enthusiasm and understanding. This will produce happiness. Happiness is a difficult lesson to learn; it is for mankind a totally new experience and Christ will have to teach men how to handle happiness correctly, to overcome the ancient habits of misery, and thus to know the meaning of true joy. Christ, however, is not coming simply to teach men the need for right human relations; He is coming to teach them how to establish it successfully themselves.   (8-108/15)

2. (Christ) will again appear and guide mankind into a civilisation and a state of consciousness in which right human relations and worldwide co-operation for the good of all will be the universal keynote. He will— through the New Group of World Servers and the men of goodwill— complete His association with the Will of God (His Father's business) in such a manner that the eternal will-to-good will be translated by humanity into goodwill and right relations. Then His task will be done; He will be free again to leave the world of men in the hands of that great spiritual Server Who will be the new Head of the Hierarchy, the Church Invisible. (13-609)

(g) RACIAL RELATIONS

1. There is no scientific and hitherto unknown mode of solving racial problems. It is finally a question of right thinking, decent behaviour, and simple kindness. The question will not be solved by inter-marriage, or by isolating groups for occupation of special areas, or by any man-made ideas of superiority or inferiority. Right human relations will come by a mutual recognition of mistakes, by sorrow for wrong action in the past,

and by restitution, if possible. It will come when nations can be educated to appreciate the good qualities of other nations, and to comprehend the part they play in the whole picture. It will be developed when the sense of racial superiority is killed; when racial differences and racial quarrels are relegated to the unholy past, and only a future of co-operation and of understanding is actively developed; it will make its presence felt when the living standards of right relation (sought by the enlightened people of every race) become the habitual attitude of the masses, and when it is regarded as contrary to the best interests of any nation to spread those ideas which tend to erect racial or national barriers, arouse hatreds, or foster differences and separation. Such a time will surely come. Humanity will master the problem of right human relations and attitudes. (13-195)

2. Peace must not be *imposed* by those who hate war. Peace must be a natural outcome and expression of the human spirit, and of a determination to change the world attitude into one of right human relations.

This is no impossible idealistic dream, but an immediate possibility, given the spirit of forgiveness and goodwill. . . .

It is not the imposition of any particular ideology upon the world, or its removal, which is of importance, but the establishing of those world conditions which will give all the nations adequate food, the necessities of life, and opportunity then to express themselves, and to make their unique contribution to the welfare of the whole family of nations.

The working details will have to be developed by all peoples in the closest collaboration. Men of vision, and not just politicians; world servers, and not just military leaders; humanitarians, and not just the rulers of nations, must determine these tremendous issues. As they do so they must be able to count upon the support of the men and women of goodwill in every land. (13-208/9)

(h) THE NEW WORLD ORDER

1. The men and women of goodwill must not be energised into activity with the note of sacrifice. . . . The clarion note of joy, through goodwill activity, must be sent out. Let the beauty of what can be, the glory of the vision and the spiritual, scientific and physical rebuilding of humanity be held before them, inspiring them to renewed effort.

Through the work earlier done all over the world by the men of vision and of goodwill, there exist today many thousands of people in Europe, America and elsewhere, who are waiting for the guidance which will start them into right activity. In every land the men and women of goodwill are to be found, ready to respond to a clear call and intelligent organisation in the service of reconstruction. Let them be found.

The message to be taught prior to any future peace, consists of the following three clear and practical truths:

i. That the error and mistakes of past centuries are the joint errors and mistakes of humanity as a whole. This recognition will lead to the establishing of *the principle of sharing,* so needed in the world today.

ii. That there are no problems and conditions which cannot be solved by the will-to-good. Goodwill nourishes the spirit of understanding and fosters the manifestation of *the principle of co-operation.* This co-operative spirit is the secret of all right human relations, and the enemy of competition.

iii. That there is blood relationship between men which, when recognised, dissolves all barriers and ends the spirit of separativeness and hate. The peace and happiness of each is the concern, therefore, of all. This develops *the principle of responsibility* and lays the foundation of right corporate action.

These are the basic beliefs of the men and women of goodwill, and provide the incentive to all service and action. These three practical and scientific truths embody the three basic facts and the initial acceptance of all world servers. They are contrary to no world position, subversive of no government or religious attitude, and are innate in the consciousness of all men, evoking immediate response. Their acceptance will "heal" international sores.

I call on all the men and women of goodwill in the world to study the principles of the new world order. I call upon them, as they fight for justice and the rights of the little nations and the future of the children of all nations, to begin to educate those whom they can reach, in right attitudes and in that foresighted vision which will make the mistakes of the past impossible in the future.

One basic divine attribute is not as yet as strong as it should be in humanity—the attribute of *forgiveness.* It is still associated with magnanimity. It is not seen to be essentially a condition of future relation between all nations, based upon a recognition of our common humanity. (13-206/7)

2. The new world order will facilitate the establishing of right human relations, based on justice, on the recognition of inherited rights, on opportunity for all—irrespective of race, colour or creed—on the suppression

of crime and selfishness through right education, and on the recognition of divine potentialities in man, as well as the recognition of a divine directing Intelligence in Whom man lives, and moves and has his being. (13-192)

3. The objective of those who are entrusted with the straightening out of the world, is not the imposition of democracy upon the entire world, or to force Christianity upon a world of diversified religions. It is surely to foster the best elements in any national government to which the people may subscribe, or which they intelligently endorse. Each nation should recognise that its form of government may be suited to it and quite unsuited to another nation; it should be taught that the function of each nation is the perfecting of its national life, rhythm and machinery, so that it can be an efficient co-partner with all other nations.

It is equally essential that the new world order should develop in humanity a sense of divinity and of relationship to God, yet with no emphasis upon racial theologies and separative creeds. The essentials of religious and political beliefs must be taught, and a new simplicity of life inculcated. Today, these are lost in the emphasis laid upon material possession, upon *things* and upon money. The problem of money will have to be faced; the problem of the distribution of wealth—whether natural or human—will need careful handling, and a compromise reached between those nations which possess unlimited resources and those who have few or none; the problem of the varying forms of national government must be faced with courage and insight; the restoration—psychological, spiritual and physical—of mankind must constitute a primary responsibility. The sense of security must be put on a firm basis—the basis of right relationship, and not the basis of force. Men must feel secure because they are seeking to develop international goodwill and can trust each other, and are not therefore dependent upon the strength of their armies and fleets.

The recognition of a spiritual Hierarchy, which is working through the New Group of World Servers, must steadily grow in some form or another. This will happen when the world statesmen and the rulers of the different nations and governing bodies—political and religious—are men of vision, spiritually motivated and selflessly inspired.

The future world order will be the effective expression of a fusion of the inner spiritual way of life, and the outer civilised and cultural way of acting; this is a definite possibility because humanity, in its upper brackets, has already developed the power to live in the intellectual and physical

worlds simultaneously. Many today are living in the spiritual world also.
Tomorrow there will be many more.   (13-192/3)

4. A new world order is possible, and there are certain steps which need
to be taken if the vision of this new world is to enter into the realm of
accomplished fact. Certain angles of the vision I can—with the greatest
brevity—point out to you; I can indicate the sign posts on the way to
the future world order. I shall find myself in the position of assuring you
at the same time that every step of that way will entail a fight, the over-
turning of that which is old and loved, and the destruction of that which
is inhuman, selfish and cruel; I shall have to impress upon you the prime
and initial necessity to overthrow the entrenched forces of aggression as
they function today through the medium of the totalitarian powers.

First, I would ask you all to ponder on the vision of this new world
order, preserving an open mind and realising that this new mode of living
hovers over humanity and will materialise when selfishness is defeated,
right human relations are correctly envisaged, and the ideal of this new
world order is divorced from all nationalistic concepts and aspirations.
It will not be an American world, or a French world, or a British world,
or a totalitarian world. It will be the outcome of the civilisation which
is passing and the culture which is the flower of that civilisation, but at
the same time it will be neither of them. It will be a human world,
based on right understanding of correct human relations, upon the recognition of equal educational opportunities for all men, for all races and
all nations, and upon the fundamental realisation that "God hath made
of one blood all peoples upon the earth". It will be a world in which
racial distinctions and national unities will be recognised as enriching the
whole, and as contributing to the significance of humanity. Such distinctions and nationalities will be preserved and cultured, not in a separative
isolation, but in the realisation that the many aspects of human unfoldment and differentiation produce one noble whole, and that all the parts
of this whole are interdependent. All will comprehend their relation to
each other in one progressive, synthetic, human endeavour, and the enterprise of united living will produce an interior work which will flower
forth in the production of a beauty and a richness which will distinguish
humanity as a whole. In this all will share, with wisdom and a planned
sufficiency, offering to the planetary life and to each other that which
they have to contribute. This will be made possible because the whole of
mankind will be recognised as the essential unit and as being of greater
spiritual importance than the part.

This is no idle and visionary dream. It is already happening. Embryonic movements toward this world synthesis are already being made. There is a dream of federation, of economic interdependence and of religious unity, plus social and national interrelation, which is rapidly taking form, first in the minds of men, and then in experiments. There is a tie of united purpose, felt by many in the political and economic fields, which is no wish fulfilment or fantasy, but indicative of an emerging reality. It is felt and recognised by thinkers everywhere. . . . It finds itself distorted and parodied in the concept of the superstate with which the dictators of the world, glamour their peoples. But the links are being forged which will draw down the vision and precipitate the pattern of things as they should be in this next world cycle.

When this vision of the new world order has been grasped by the men and women of goodwill throughout the nations, and has become part of the life and mind of every disciple and aspirant, then the next step will be to study the factors which are hindering its materialisation. For this a broad tolerance and an unprejudiced mind are essential, and these qualities are rare in the average student and the small town man. Past national mistakes must be faced; selfishness in the spheres of both capital and labour must be recognised; blindness, nationalistic ambitions, adherence to ancient territorial demands and assumed rights, inherited possessiveness, the refusal to relinquish past gains, disturbances in the religious and social areas of consciousness, uncertainties as to the realities of subjective and spiritual life, and the insincerities which are based on glamour and fear—all these factors are woven into the life pattern of every nation, without exception, and are exploited by the evil forces and evaded by the well-meaning but weak people of the world. These must all be seen in their true perspective. The eyes of the people who seek to work under the Forces of Light must be lifted from the world of effects into the realm of causes; there must be appreciation of the factors which have made and conditioned the modern world, and those predisposing factors must be recognised for what they are. This sizing up of the situation, and this recognition of blame and responsibility, must preface every attempt to bring down into active being the new world order.

The new world will not come as an answer to prayer, or by the passive wishful thinking and expectation of the peace-loving idealist and mystical visionary. They point the way and indicate the needed objective. It will come when the mystic and the man of vision awakens to the need of the hour and comes down from the world of dreams, of theories, and of words, into the hard arena of daily and public life. He must be willing to fight for that which he desires and knows to be good and true and right, and must stand firm against those who seek to distort the vision and to arrest its appearance, arming for battle so that final disarmament may be possible.

. . . The hindrances (which block the appearance of the future world order) appear to be many, but they can all be summed up in the one word, *Selfishness*—national, racial, political, religious and individual selfishness.

The practical aspect of the mode of elimination of the hindrances can also be simply stated. The vision will appear as fact on Earth when individuals willingly submerge their personal interests in the good of the group; when the group or groups merge their interests in the national good, when nations give up their selfish purposes and aim for international good, and when this international right relation is based upon the total good of humanity itself. Thus the individual can play his part in the bigger whole, and his help is needed, and thus the sense of individual futility is negated. To the most unimportant man in the most unimportant national unit, there comes the call for sacrifice and service to the group of which he is a part. Eventually humanity itself is thus swung—again as an integral unit—into the service of the Planetary Life.   (13-241/4)

(i) WORLD CITIZENSHIP

1. It is bridging work which now has to be done—bridging between what is today and what can be in the future. If during the coming years, we develop this technique of bridging the many cleavages found in the human family and in offsetting the racial hatreds and the separative attitudes of nations and people, we shall have succeeded in constructing a world in which war will be impossible and humanity will be realising itself as one human family and not as a fighting aggregate of many nations and peoples, competitively engaged in getting the best of each other and successfully fostering prejudices and hatred. This has, as we have seen, been the history of the past. Man has been developed from an isolated animal, prompted only by the instincts of self-preservation, eating and mating, through the stages of family life, tribal life and national life, to the point where today a still broader ideal is grasped by him—international unity, or the smooth functioning of the One Humanity.

This growing idealism is fighting its way into the forefront of the human consciousness in spite of all separative enmities. It is largely responsible for the present chaos and for the banding together of the United Nations. It has produced the conflicting ideologies which are seeking world expression; it has produced the dramatic emergence of national saviours (so-called), world prophets and world workers, idealists, opportunists, dictators and investigators, and humanitarians. These conflicting idealisms are a wholesome sign, whether we agree with them or not. They are definite reactions to the human demand—urgent and right—for better conditions, for more light and understanding, for greater co-operation, for security and peace and plenty in the place of terror, fear and starvation.

. . . It is difficult for modern man to conceive of a time when there will be no racial, national or separative religious consciousness present in human thinking. It was equally difficult for prehistoric man to conceive of a time when there would be national thinking. This is a good thing for us to bear in mind. The time when humanity will be able to think in universal terms still lies far ahead, but the fact that we can speak of it, desire it and plan for it is surely the guarantee that it is *not* impossible. Humanity has always progressed from stage to stage of enlightenment, and from glory to glory. We are today on our way to a far better civilisation than the world has ever known, and towards conditions which will ensure a much happier humanity and which will see the end of national differences, of class distinctions (whether based on an hereditary or a financial status) and which will ensure a fuller and richer life for everyone.

It will be obvious that very many decades must elapse before such a state of affairs will be actively present—but it will be decades and not centuries, if humanity can learn the lessons of the world war, if the reactionary and the conservative peoples in every nation can be prevented from swinging civilisation back on to the bad old lines. But a beginning can immediately be made. Simplicity should be our watchword, for it is simplicity which will kill our old materialistic way of living. *Co-operative goodwill* is surely the first idea to be presented to the masses and taught in our schools, thereby guaranteeing the new and better civilisation. *Loving understanding*, intelligently applied, should be the hallmark of the cultured and wiser groups, plus effort on their part to relate the world of meaning to the world of outer efforts—for the benefit of the masses. *World Citizenship* as an expression of both goodwill and understanding should be the goal of the enlightened everywhere, and the hallmark of the spiritual man. In these three, you have right relations established between education, religion and politics.   (7-63/5)

2. The time factor must govern as never before the activities of the men of goodwill and the work of those whose task it is to educate not only the children and the youth of the world, but also to train humanity in the major undertaking of right human relations and in the possibilities immediately ahead. The note to be struck and the word to be emphasised, is *humanity*. Only one dominant concept can today save the world from a looming economic fight to the death, can prevent the uprising again of the materialistic systems of the past, can stop the re-emerging of the old ideas and concepts, and can bring to an end the subtle control by the financial interests and the violent discontent of the masses. *A belief in human unity must be endorsed.* This unity must be grasped as something worth fighting and dying for; it must constitute the new foundation for all our political, religious and social reorganisation, and must provide the theme for our educational systems. Human unity, human understanding, human relationships, human fair play, and the essential oneness of all men— these are the only concepts upon which to construct the new world, through which to abolish competition and to bring to an end the exploitation of one section of humanity by another, and the hitherto unfair possession of the earth's wealth. As long as there are extremes of riches and poverty, men are falling short of their high destiny.

The kingdom of God can appear on earth, and this in the immediate future, but the members of this kingdom recognise neither rich nor poor, neither high nor low, neither labour nor capital, but only the children of the One Father, and the fact—natural and yet spiritual—that all men are brothers. Here lies the solution of the problem with which we are dealing. The spiritual Hierarchy of our planet recognises neither capital nor labour; it recognises only men and brothers. The solution is, therefore, education and still more education and the adaptation of the recognised trends of the times to the vision seen by the spiritually minded and by those who love their fellow men.   (7-83/4)

3. In every nation there are those who see a better vision of a better world, who are thinking and talking and planning *in terms of humanity,* and who realise that those who form the various groups—political, religious, educational and labour—are men and women and essentially, if unconsciously, brothers. They see the world whole and are working towards an inevitable unification; they recognise the problems of the nations, great and small, and the difficult situation in which the minorities today find themselves; they know that the use of force produces results which are not truly effective (for the cost is far too great) and are usually tran-

sient. They realise that the only true hope is an enlightened public opinion and that this must be the result of sound educational methods and just and exact propaganda.   (7-94)

4. Unity, peace and security will come through the recognition—intelligently assessed—of the evils which have led to the present world situation, and then through the taking of those wise, compassionate and understanding steps which will lead to the establishing of right human relations, to the substitution of co-operation for the present competitive system, and by the education of the masses in every land as to the nature of true goodwill, and its hitherto unused potency. This will mean the deflecting of untold millions of money into right educational systems, instead of their use by the forces of war and their conversion into armies, navies and armaments.

It is this that is spiritual; it is this that is of importance, and it is this for which all men must struggle. The spiritual Hierarchy of the planet is primarily interested in finding the men who will work along these lines. It is primarily interested in humanity, realising that the steps taken by humanity *in the immediate future* will condition the New Age and determine man's destiny. Will it be a destiny of annihilation, of a planetary war, of worldwide famine and pestilence, of nation rising against nation and of the complete collapse of all that makes life worth living? All this can happen unless basic changes are made and made with goodwill and loving understanding. Then, on the other hand, we can have a period (difficult but helpful because educative) of adjustment, of concession and of relinquishment; we can have a period of right recognition of shared opportunity, of a united effort to bring about right human relations, and of an educational process which will train the youth of all nations to function *as world citizens*, and not as nationalistic propagandists. What we need above all to see—as a result of spiritual maturity—is the abolition of those two principles which have wrought so much evil in the world, and which are summed up in the two words: Sovereignty and Nationalism.   (7-171/2)

(j)   WORLD UNITY

There is no counsel of perfection to give the world, or any solution which will carry immediate relief. To the spiritual leaders of the race certain lines of action seem right and to guarantee constructive attitudes:

1. The United Nations, through its Assembly and Committees, *must* be supported; there is as yet no other organisation to which man can hope-

fully look. Therefore, he must support the United Nations but, at the same time, let this group of world leaders know what is needed.

2. The general public in every nation *must* be educated in right human relations. Above all else, the children and the youth of the world must be taught goodwill to all men everywhere, irrespective of race or creed.

3. Time must be given for the needed adjustments and humanity must learn to be intelligently patient; humanity must face with courage and optimism the slow process of building the new civilisation.

4. An intelligent and co-operative public opinion must be developed in every land, and the doing of this constitutes a major spiritual duty. This will take much time but *if* the men of goodwill and *if* the spiritual people of the world will become genuinely active, *it can be done in twenty-five years.*

5. The world economic council (or whatever body represents the resources of the world) *must* free itself from fraudulent politics, capitalistic influence and its devious scheming; it *must* set the resources of the earth free for the use of humanity. This will be a lengthy task but it will be possible when world need is better appreciated. An enlightened public opinion will make the decisions of the economic council practical and possible. Sharing and co-operation *must* be taught instead of greed and competition.

6. There must be freedom to travel everywhere, in any direction and in any country; by means of this free intercourse, members of the human family may get to know each other and to appreciate each other; passports and visas should be discontinued because they are symbols of the great heresy of separateness.

7. The men of goodwill everywhere must be mobilised and set to work; it is upon their efforts that the future of humanity depends; they exist in their millions everywhere and—when organised and mobilised—represent a vast section of the thinking public.

It will be through the steady, consistent and organised work of the men of goodwill throughout the world that world unity will be brought about. At present, such men are only in process of organising and are apt to feel that the work to be done is so stupendous, and the forces arrayed against them are so great that their—at present—isolated efforts are useless to break down the barriers of greed and hate with which they are confronted. They realise that there is as yet no systemised spread of the principle of goodwill, which holds the solution to the world problem; they have as yet no idea of the numerical strength of those who are thinking as they do. They ask themselves the same questions which are agitating the minds of men everywhere: How can order be restored? How can there be fair distribution of the world's resources? How can the Four Freedoms become factual and not just beautiful dreams? How can true religion be resurrected and the ways of true spiritual living govern the hearts of men? How can a true prosperity be established which will be the result of unity, peace and plenty?

There is only one true way and there are indications that it is a way towards which many millions of people are turning. *Unity and right human relations—individual, communal, national and international—can be brought about by the united action of the men and women of goodwill in every country.*

These men and women of goodwill must be found and organised, and thus discover their numerical potency—for it is there. They must form a world group, standing for right human relations, and educating the public in the nature and power of goodwill. They will thus create a world public opinion which will be so forceful and so outspoken on the side of human welfare, that leaders, statesmen, politicians, businessmen and churchmen will be forced to listen and comply. Steadily and regularly, the general public must be taught an internationalism and a world unity which is based on simple goodwill and on co-operative interdependence.

This is no mystical and impractical programme; it does not work through the processes of exposing, undermining or attack; it emphasises the new politics, i.e. politics which are based upon the principle of bringing about right human relations. Between the exploited and the exploiting, the warmongers and the pacifists, the masses and the rulers, this group of men of goodwill will stand in their organised millions, taking no side, demonstrating no partisan spirit, fomenting no political or religious disturbance, and feeding no hatreds. They will not be a negative body, but a positive group, interpreting the meaning of right human relations, standing for the oneness of humanity and for practical, but not theoretical brotherhood. The propagation of these ideas by all available means and the spread of the principle of goodwill, will produce a powerful organised international group. Public opinion will be forced to recognise the potency of the movement; eventually the numerical strength of the men and women of goodwill in the world will be so great that they will influence world events. Their united voice will be heard on behalf of right human relations.

This movement is already gathering momentum. In many lands this plan for the formation of a group of people who are trained in goodwill and who possess clear insight into the principles which should govern human relations in world affairs, is already past the blueprint stage. The nucleus for this work is present today. Their functions might be summarised as follows:

1. To restore world confidence by letting it be known how much goodwill—organised and unorganised—there is in the world today.

2. To educate the masses in the principles and the practice of goodwill. The word "goodwill" is largely used at this time by all parties and groups, national and international.

3. To synthesise and co-ordinate into one functioning whole all the men and women of goodwill in the world who will recognise these principles as their *personal* directing ideal, and who will endeavour to apply them to current world or national events.

4. To create mailing lists in every country, of the men and women of goodwill who can be counted upon to stand for world unity, right human relations, and who will try—in their own lands—to reach others with this idea, through the medium of the press, the lecture platform and the radio. Eventually this world group should have its own newspaper or magazine, through means of which the educational process can be intensified and goodwill be found to be a universal principle and technique.

5. To provide in every country and eventually in every large city, a central bureau where information will be available concerning the activities of the men and women of goodwill all over the world; of those organisations, groups and parties who are also working along similar lines of international understanding and right human relations. Thus many will find those who will co-operate with them in their particular endeavour to promote world unity.

6. To work, as men and women of goodwill, with all groups who have a world programme which tends to heal world differences and national quarrels, and to end racial distinctions. When such groups are found to work constructively and are free from scurrilous attack or aggressive modes of action, and actuated by goodwill to all men, and are free from an aggressive nationalism and partisanship, then the co-operation of the men of goodwill can be offered and freely given.

It takes no great effort of the imagination to see that, if this work of spreading goodwill and educating public opinion in its potency is pursued, and if the men of goodwill can be discovered in all lands and organised, that . . . much good can be accomplished. Thousands can be gathered into the ranks of the men of goodwill. This is the initial task. The power of such a group, backed by public opinion, will be tremendous. They can accomplish phenomenal results.

How to use the weight of that goodwill and how to employ the will to establish right human relations, will grow gradually out of the work accomplished and meet the need of the world situation. The trained use of power on the side of goodwill and on behalf of right human relations, will be demonstrated as possible, and the present unhappy state of world affairs can be changed. This will be done, not through the usual warlike measures of the past, or the enforced will of some aggressive or wealthy group, but through the weight of a trained public opinion—an opinion which will be based on goodwill, on an intelligent understanding of the needs of humanity, on a determination to bring about right human relations, and on the recognition that *the problems with which humanity is today confronted can be solved through goodwill.* (7-176/81)

20. CONTROL OF SPEECH

1. It has been said that "the chief agency by which Nature's wheel is moved in a phenomenal direction, is sound", for the original sound or word sets in vibration the matter of which all forms are made and initiates that activity which characterises even the atom of substance.

The literature and all the scriptures of all the ancient nations and great religions bear testimony to the efficacy of sound in producing all that is tangible and visible. The Hindus say very beautifully that "the Great Singer built the worlds, and the Universe is His Song". This is another way of expressing the same idea. If this is realised and the science of this concept somewhat understood, the significance of our own words and the utterance of sound in speech, becomes almost a momentous happening.

Sound or speech and the use of words have been regarded by the ancient philosophers (and are increasingly so regarded by modern thinkers) as the highest agent used by man in moulding himself and his surroundings. Thought, speech and the resultant activity on the physical plane, complete the triplicity which make a man what he is, and place him where he is.

The purpose of all speech is to clothe thought and thus make our thoughts available for others. When we speak we evoke a thought and make it present, and we bring that which is concealed within us into audible expression. Speech reveals, and right speech can create a form of beneficent purpose, just as wrong speech can produce a form which has a malignant objective. Without realising this, however, ceaselessly and irresponsibly, day after day, we speak; we use words; we multiply sounds; and surround ourselves with form worlds of our own creation. Is it not essential, therefore, that before we speak we should think, thus remembering the injunction, "You must attain to knowledge, ere you can attain to speech"? Having thought, let us then choose the right words to express the right thought, attempting to give correct pronunciation, proper values, and true tonal quality to every word we utter.

Then will our spoken word create a thought-form which will embody the idea we have in our minds. Then too will our words carry no discord, but will add their quota to that great harmonising chord or unifying word which it is the function of mankind ultimately to utter. Wrong speech separates, and it is interesting to bear in mind that the word, the symbol of unity, is divine, whereas speech in its many diversifications is human.

As evolution proceeds, and the human family rises into its true position in the great plan of the universe, right and correct speech will be increasingly cultivated, because we shall think more before we utter words, or, as a great teacher has said, "through meditation we shall rectify the mistakes of wrong speech"; and the significance of word forms, true and correct sounds, and vocal quality will become ever more apparent. (4-142/4)

2. One of the greatest instruments for practical development lying in the hands of small and great, is the instrument of SPEECH. He who guards his words, and who only speaks with altruistic purpose, in order to carry the energy of Love through the medium of the tongue, is one who is mastering rapidly the initial steps to be taken in preparation for initiation. Speech is the most occult manifestation in existence; it is the means of creation and the vehicle for force. In the reservation of words, esoterically understood, lies the conservation of force; in the utilisation of words, justly chosen and spoken, lies the distribution of the love force of

the solar system—that force which preserves, strengthens, and stimulates. Only he who knows somewhat of these two aspects of speech can be trusted to stand before the Initiator and to carry out from that Presence certain sounds and secrets imparted to him under the pledge of silence.

The disciple must learn to be silent in the face of that which is evil. He must learn to be silent before the sufferings of the world, wasting no time in idle plaints and sorrowful demonstration, but lifting up the burden of the world; working, and wasting no energy in talk. Yet withal he should speak where encouragement is needed, using the tongue for constructive ends; expressing the love force of the world, as it may flow through him, where it will serve best to ease a load or lift a burden, remembering that as the race progresses, the love element between the sexes and its expression will be translated to a higher plane. Then, through the spoken word, and not through the physical plane expression as now, will come the realisation of that true love which unites those who are one in service and in aspiration. Then love between the units of the human family will take the form of the utilisation of speech for the purpose of creating on all planes, and the energy which now, in the majority, finds expression through the lower or generating centres, will be translated to the throat centre. This is as yet but a distant ideal, but even now some can vision that ideal, and seek—through united service, loving co-operation, and oneness in aspiration, thought, and endeavour—to give shape and form to it, even though inadequately.   (1-74/5)

3. Let the student inquire of himself whether the position he held mentally, and whether the words which he spoke on any particular occasion, were prompted by a desire to impose his will upon his hearers. This imposition of his will could be either right or wrong. When right, it would mean that he was speaking under the impulse of his spiritual will, that his words would be in line with soul purpose and intent, and would be governed by love and, therefore, would be constructive, helpful and healing. His attitude would be one of detachment, and he would have no desire to take prisoner the mind of his brother. But if his words were prompted by self-will and by the desire to impose *his* ideas upon other people and so to shine in their presence, or to force them to agree with his conclusions, his method would then be destructive, dominating, aggressive, argumentative, forceful, rude or irritable, according to his personality trends and inclinations.   (4-573)

4. Speaking symbolically, and without enlarging upon the significances, it might be stated that an Ashram has three circles (I refer not here to grades or ranks):

i. The circle of those who talk and who stand close to the outer door. Their voices may not penetrate too far and thus disturb the Ashram.

ii. The circle of those who know the law of silence, but find it hard. They stand within the central part and utter not a word. They know not yet the silence of the Ashram.

iii. The circle of those who live within the secret quiet place. They use not words and yet their sound goes forth, and when they speak—and speak they do—men listen.

This triple presentation of the balancing potencies of speech and of silence, are the comprehended effects of occult obedience—in itself a voluntary response to the power of the life of the Ashram, and to the mind and love of the Master of the Ashram. . . . Learn to know when to speak and when to be silent, remembering that the elimination of possessiveness and of self-reference will reduce speech to its spiritual essentials.   (6-550/1)

5. Let each of you gain that control of speech which has often been your goal but seldom your achievement, and remember that the most powerful factor in the control of speech is a loving heart. Wild and fearful talk, hateful gossip, cruel innuendo, suspicion, the ascribing of wrong and wicked motives to persons and peoples, and the divergences of attitude which have separated the many different nations in the world, are rampant today and have brought the world to its present distressing situation. It is so easy to drift into the same habits of speech and thought which we find around us, and to discover ourselves participating in attack and the spirit of hate. Guard yourselves strenuously against this and say nothing which could inflame hate and suspicion in connection with any race, any person, any group or any leaders of groups and nations. You will have to guard yourselves with care, so that even in defence of that which you may personally or nationally approve, you do not find yourselves full of hate and breaking the law of love—the only law which can truly save the world. Perhaps the key to your success along this line will be *the silence of a loving heart.*   (13-82)

21. CRITICISM

1. In the coming cycle I emphatically tell you that the true work will be carried forward (the work of spiritually welding the world into a synthesis, and the production of a recognised brotherhood of souls) only by those who refuse to be separative and whose words are watched so that no evil is spoken; these are the workers who see the divine in all and refuse to think evil and impute evil; they work with sealed lips; they deal not with their brothers' affairs, nor reveal that which concerns them; their lives are coloured by understanding and by love; their minds are characterised by a trained spiritual perception and that spiritual awareness which employs a keen intellect as the corollary of a loving spirit.

May I repeat in other words this theme, for its importance is vital and the effect of the work of these instruments on the world is immense. These men and women whose mission it is to inaugurate the New Age, have learned the secret of silence; they are animated ceaselessly by a spirit of inclusive love; their tongues lead them not astray into the field of ordinary criticism, and they permit no condemnation of others; they are animated by a spirit of protection. To them will be committed the work of fostering the life of the New Age. (4-631)

2. You have . . . a very critical mind; you are full of response to, and recognition of, the weaknesses and frailties of your family and associates. Let not this grow upon you, but let it cease, for it builds a barrier between you and them, and obstructs and hinders your service. (5-195)

3. It is yourself . . . whom you mainly criticise, but this can be as wrong and as unnecessary as criticising others. (5-198)

4. What matters it if each knows the weaknesses of his brother on the Path, and if all are aware of an individual's frailty? Are you yet so imperfect, and are you yet so unloving that knowledge need evoke criticism and resentment, instead of love and understanding? (5-301)

5. As yet you love not where you criticise. This you must learn to do, and that love will shed new light on that which you perceive, and you will learn to feel. Life will then open up before you in new rhythms of service and of usefulness. (5-558)

6. All "crises of criticism" must be most carefully avoided by all disciples if they want to bring about the needed rhythm. . . . There are times when criticism is unquestionably a recognition of fact. This means that a criti-

cising disciple has reached the point where his judgment is so based on love that it produces no *personality* effect in his own life or that of his fellow disciple. It is simply a loving recognition of limitation, and only becomes wrong when these undoubted facts are used to arouse criticism in the unqualified, and provide points for discussion.　(5-725)

7. We see in others what is in us, even when it is not there at all or to the same extent. Disciples need to learn the distinction between true analytical insight, and so-called criticism. A Master does not criticise the members of His Ashram. He seeks to analyse for them the points wherein they may hinder the usefulness of the service of the Ashram. There is a basic distinction between this constructive aid and the criticism which is based on a sense of personal superiority and a love of fault finding.　(5-729)

8. Group criticism, either voiced or strongly felt . . . can be based on many things, but is usually rooted in jealousy, thwarted ambition, or pride of individual intellect. Each member of any group, particularly those in the immediate circle of the leader or leaders, is prone to sit in judgment. The responsibility is not theirs; they know not the problems as they truly exist, and criticism is, therefore, easy. It should here be remembered that criticism is a virulent poison. It damages in every case eventually the one who criticises—owing to the fact of *voiced direction*—it hurts still more the one who is criticised. Where there is purity of motive, true love, and a large measure of detachment, the subtler bodies of the one who is under attack may remain immune, but the physical effects will be definite, and where there is any physical weakness or limitation, *there* will be found the localisation of the projected poison.

　. . . You might ask : What can a leader or a group of leaders do in these unfortunately normal and usual circumstances? Nothing, but continue in the work; retreat within themselves; speak the truth with love when occasion occurs; refuse to become bitter over the pain which the group occasions, and wait until the group members learn the lessons of co-operation, of silence, of loving appreciation, and a wise realisation and understanding of the problems with which all group leaders are faced in these difficult and individualistic days. That time will come.　(15-617/9)

22. THE SERVICE RENDERED BY HUMANITY

1. I would like also to point out the nature of the service humanity as a whole is rendering in the general plan of evolution. The rule under our consideration applies not only to the individual man, but to the pre-destined activity of the fourth Kingdom in Nature. Through his medita-tion, discipline and service, man fans into radiant light, illuminating the three worlds, that point of light which flickered into being at the time of his individualisation in past ages. This finds its reflection in the light in the head. Thus a rapport is set up, which permits not only of vibratory synchronisation but of a radiation and display of magnetic force, per-mitting of its recognition in the three worlds of a man's immediate en-vironment.

So it is with the human kingdom. As its illumination increases, as its light waxes more potent, its effect upon the sub-human kingdoms is ana-logous to that of the individual soul, its reflection, upon man in physical incarnation. I say analogous as a causative force, though not a correspon-dence in effects. Note this difference. Humanity is macrocosmic in relation to the sub-human states of consciousness, and this H.P.B. has well pointed out. The effect upon these lesser and more material states is primarily fourfold.

i. The stimulating of the spiritual aspect, expressing itself as the soul in all forms, such as the form of a mineral, a flower, or an animal. The positive aspect of energy in all these forms will wax stronger, pro-ducing radiation, for instance, increasingly in the mineral kingdom. In this lies a hint of the nature of the process that will set a term to our own planetary existence and eventually, to our solar system. In the vegetable kingdom, the effect will be the demonstration of increased beauty and diversity, and the evolution of new species with an objective impossible to explain to those not yet initiate. The production of nutritive forms which will serve the needs of the lesser devas and angels, will be one of the results.

In the animal kingdom the effect will be the elimination of pain and suffering and a return to the ideal conditions of the Garden of Eden. When man functions as a soul, he heals; he stimulates and vitalises; he trans-mits the spiritual forces of the universe, and all harmful emanations and all destructive forces find in the human kingdom a barrier. Evil and its effects are largely dependent upon humanity for a functioning channel. Humanity's function is to transmit and handle force. This is done in the early and ignorant stages destructively and with harmful results. Later when acting under the influence of the soul, force is rightly and wisely handled and good eventuates. True indeed it is that "the whole creation travaileth in pain until now, waiting for the manifestation of the sons of God".

ii. The bringing of light. Humanity is the planetary light bearer, transmitting the light of knowledge, of wisdom, and of understanding, and this in the esoteric sense. These three aspects of light carry three aspects of soul energy to the soul in all forms, through the medium of the anima mundi, the world soul. Physically speaking, this can be realised if we can appreciate the difference between our planetary illumination today and that of five hundred years ago—our brilliantly lit cities, our rural districts, shining through the night with their lighted streets and homes; our airways, outlined with their search-lights and fields of blazing globes; our oceans, dotted with their lighted ships, and increasingly our lighted airships will be seen, darting through the skies.

These are but the result of man's growing illumination. His knowledge aspect of light has brought this into being. Who shall say what will eventuate when the wisdom aspect predominates? When these are welded by understanding, the soul will control in the three worlds and in all kingdoms of nature.

iii. The transmission of energy. The clue to the significance of this can be grasped as a concept, though as yet it will fail of comprehension, in the realisation that the human kingdom acts upon and affects the three sub-human kingdoms. The downpouring spiritual Triangle and the up-raising matter Triangle meet point to point in humanity, when the point of balance can be found. In man's achievement and spiritualisation is the hope of the world. Mankind itself is the world saviour, of which all world Saviours have been but the symbol and the guarantee.

iv. The blending of the deva or angel evolution and the human. This is a mystery which will be solved as man arrives at the consciousness of his own solar Angel, only to discover that that too is also but a form of life which, having served its purpose, must be left behind. The angel or deva evolution is one of the great lines of force, contained in the divine expression and the solar Angels, the agnishvattas of the *The Secret Doctrine* and of *A Treatise on Cosmic Fire* belong—in their form aspect—to this line.

Thus humanity serves, and in the development of a conscious aptitude for service, in the growth of a conscious understanding of the individual part to be played in the working out of the plan and in the rendering of the personality subject to the soul, will come the steady progress of humanity towards its goal of world service. (4-98/101)

2. When men achieve illumination, intelligently precipitate the karmic quota of their time, and lift the subhuman kingdoms (with its reflex activity of lifting the Highest simultaneously), then they can and then they do share in the work of the Hierarchy.

That cycle of sharing has seemed for aeons too far away to be considered; when, however, humanity precipitated the war, they automatically and somewhat surprisingly brought the final achievement much nearer. The illumination of men's minds will rapidly follow. The process of lifting the subhuman kingdoms has been amazingly forwarded by science— the crowning accomplishment of which was the fission of the atom, and the penetration of the "spiritual interfering" aspect of the human spirit into the very depths of the mineral world. Ponder on this. (6-315)

3. Nothing which affects humanity or which stimulates it to a forward-moving activity, is without its inevitable effect upon the three lower kingdoms in nature. Forget not! Mankind is the macrocosm to this threefold lower microcosm. (6-327)

4. May I remind you of the occult statement that every living being or manifested life—from the planetary Logos down to the tiniest atom— either has been, is, or will be a man. This has reference to the past, to the present and to the future of every manifested life. Therefore, the fact of humanity and of that for which humanity stands, is probably the primary and major aspect of the divine Purpose. Pause and think about this statement. It is, therefore, the first clear fact which indicates the measure and the magnitude of a human being; and until two other facts are sequentially revealed to us, it will not be possible correctly to gauge the wider aspects of the Purpose of Sanat Kumara. Everything sub-human is slowly moving towards a definite human experience, it is also passing through the phase of human effort and consequent experience, or else it has moved out of that phase of limitation and—through initiation—is drafting human nature into a state of divinity (to use a most inadequate phrase).

The keynote, therefore, of the Lord of the World is HUMANITY, for it is the basis, the goal and the essential inner structure of all being. Humanity itself is the key to all evolutionary processes and to all correct understanding of the divine Plan, expressing in time and space the divine Purpose. Why He chose that this should be so, we know not; but it is a point to be accepted and remembered in all study of the Science of Impression, because it is the factor that makes relationship and contact possible, and it is also the source of all understanding. These are most difficult things to express and to enlarge upon, my brothers, and only the penetrating intuition can make these matters clearer to your avid and active intelligence.

You will note, therefore, that though we call one of the major centres HUMANITY, yet—in the last analysis—all the centres are constituted of lives progressing towards the human stage, of those units of life who are at the human stage, and those who have left that stage far behind, but who are endowed with all the faculties and all the knowledges wrought out into human expression in earlier planetary schemes or solar systems, or through our own definite and characteristic planetary life.

Because of this uniformity of experience, the art of contact, and the science of impression become entirely possible and normally effective. The great and omnipotent Lives in Shamballa can impress the omniscient Lives and lesser lives in the Hierarchy *because* They share a common humanity; the hierarchical Workers or Masters and Initiates can consequently impress humanity, because of a shared experience and understanding; then the lives that compose the human family present the goal to the sub-human kingdoms and can, and do, impress them because of basic instinctual tendencies which are expressed in the human group, but which are latent instinctual tendencies and potential assets in the three sub-human groups.

. . . The outstanding characteristic of humanity is intelligent sensitivity to impression. Ponder on this definite and emphatic statement. The work of science is, after all simply the development of the knowledge of substance and of form; this knowledge will make it possible for humanity eventually to act as the major impressing agent in relation to the three sub-human kingdoms in nature; that is humanity's primary responsibility. This work of relationship is practically the work of developing, or the mode of unfoldment, of human sensitivity. I refer here to sensitivity to impression from or by the Hierarchy.

The work done through the processes of initiation, is intended to fit disciples and initiates to receive impression from Shamballa; the initiate is essentially a blend of scientific and religious training; he has been reoriented to certain phases of divine existence which are not yet recognised by the average human being. I am endeavouring to make clear to you the basic synthesis underlying all manifested life upon our planet, and also the close interplay or relationship which forever exists and expresses itself through the supreme science of contact or of impression. (11-126/8)

5. Man's work is to raise the dead to life, to bring brotherhood into expression on the physical plane, and to transmit divine energy to a waiting world of forms. As the rays play their part with humanity and bring man forth into manifestation as he is in essence and reality, his work with the animal kingdom and with the other kingdoms will proceed steadily and inevitably. Scarcely knowing how or why, humanity will play its part in the work of building. The creative work will proceed and the Plan materialise. Man's work for the animal kingdom is to stimulate instinct until individualisation is possible. His work for the vegetable kingdom is to foster the perfume-producing faculty, and to adapt plant life to the myriad uses of man and of animals. Man's work with the mineral kingdom is to work alchemically and magically. With that process of transmutation and of subsequent revelation I cannot here deal. (14-267)

6. The *relation* of the human family to the divine scheme, as it exists, is that of bringing into close rapport the three higher kingdoms upon our planet and the three lower kingdoms of nature, thus acting as a clearing house for divine energy. The *service* humanity is to render is that of producing unity, harmony, and beauty in nature, through blending into one functioning, related unity the soul in all forms. This is achieved individually at first, then it takes place in group formation, and finally it demonstrates through an entire kingdom in nature. (15-363/4)

23. ENERGY

1. Energy is now regarded as all that IS; manifestation is the manifestation of a sea of energies, some of which are built into forms, others constitute the medium in which those forms live and move and have their being, and still others are in process of animating both the forms and their environing substantial media. It must also be remembered that forms exist within forms. . . . You, as you sit in your room, are a form within a form; that room is itself a form within a house, and that house (another form) is probably one of many similar houses, placed the one on top of another, or else side by side, and together composing a still larger form. Yet all these diverse forms are composed of tangible substance which—when co-ordinated and brought together by some recognised design or idea in the mind of some thinker—creates a material form. This tangible substance

is composed of living energies, vibrating in relation to each other, yet owning their own quality and their own qualified life.   (11-177/8)

2. The true educator should be working with energies in a world of energy; these energies are tinged and qualified by distinctive divine attributes, and each human being therefore can be regarded as an aggregate of energies, dominated by some one particular type of energy, which serves to make him distinctive among his fellows, and which produces the differences among human beings. If it is true that there are seven major types of energy qualifying all forms, and that these in their turn are subdivided into forty-nine types of qualified energy, the complexity of the problem emerges clearly. If it is true that all these distinctive energies play constantly upon energy-substance (spirit-matter), producing "the myriad forms which make up the form of God" (Bhagavad Gita, XI), and that each child is the micro-cosmical representation (at some stage of development) of the Macrocosm, the magnitude of the problem becomes evident, and the extent of our de-manded service will call forth to the utmost the powers which any human being can express at any given moment in time and space.   (12-24)

3. The basic approach for all who endeavour to grasp esotericism, or to teach esoteric students, is to lay the emphasis upon the world of ener-gies, and to recognise that behind all happenings in the world of pheno-mena (and by that I mean the three worlds of human evolution) exists the world of energies; these are of the greatest diversity and complexity, but all of them move and work under the Law of Cause and Effect. (12-60)

4. Energies *per se* are neither bad nor good. The Great White Lodge, our spiritual Hierarchy, and the Black Lodge, employ the same universal energies, but with different motives and objectives; both groups are groups of trained esotericists.   (12-61)

5. *The effect of the impact of energy is dependent upon the nature of the vehicle of response.* According to his equipment and the nature of his bodies, so will man react to the inflowing energies. This is a fundamental statement. It is a law and should be most carefully considered. The effects of a Master or initiate upon men are widely different, because each man brings to the impact of His vibration a type of physical body, an astral or emotional nature, and a mind, which are in each case different from all the others. The use each makes of the stimulating energy will be different; the focus of his consciousness is very different; his type of mind is quite

different; his centres, their activity and their internal organisation are different. And it is the same for groups, organisations and nations. (13-85)

6. Due to the effort of countless thousands of men and women everywhere, energies hitherto unable to penetrate deeper into substance than the hierarchical substance, and the levels of the higher mental plane, can now, for the first time, be successfully anchored on dense physical levels, or at least upon etheric levels. This is a fact and is far more important than you are perhaps able to appreciate. (13-659)

7. In all occult work one is occupied with energy—energy units, energy embodied in forms, energy streams in flow; these energies are made potent and embody our purpose through the use of thought; they follow along the well-defined thought currents of the group. (14-9)

8. Each form is a universe in itself, and all forms are alive, vibrating with divine activity. We use the word "energy" to express this activity, and beyond that we are as yet unable to pass. Energy is life, and energy is also death. Activity is to be sensed and known in the organic and in the inorganic—a vast series of atomic lives built up into a structure, and found to be in ceaseless motion. A vast series of living structures, built up into still greater and more inclusive forms, are all found again to be in equally ceaseless motion. These greater structures, in their turn, are found to be vibrant organisms, and so there unfolds before man's conscious vision nothing but life and activity, naught but motion and energy, and always a coherence, and ordered purpose, a growing synthesis, a Plan, and a *Will.* (14-195)

9. We have perhaps emphasised almost to the point of bewilderment the vast aggregation of impelling energies which play throughout our cosmos; individual man may well be stunned by a sense of his helplessness and his unique futility. But this is only due to the relatively undeveloped state of his "receiving apparatus". When thus bewildered let him remember that potentially he possesses the creative ability to build and gradually to develop a better mechanism of reception, which will enable him finally to be responsive to all impacts and to every type of divine energy. This capacity is indestructible and is itself a divine focus of energy which must and will without fail carry forward the good undertaken under the inspiration of the Great Architect of the Universe. He fashions all things to a divinely foreseen end, and in this sign—through His agents, Venus and Vulcan, typifying the form and the soul—will lead man from the unreal to the real. (16-403/4)

10. The use of energy may be along wrong lines, producing separation and trouble, or along right lines, leading to eventual harmony and understanding, but the energy is there and must make its effects in any case. As in the individual life, the results of the play of the life of the soul upon the form aspect, one or other of the rays will dominate and control. If the person or nation is spiritually oriented, the result of the energy impact will be good and will lead toward the working out of the divine Plan and thus be wholly constructive. Where personality force dominates, the effects will be destructive and hindering to the emergence of divine purpose. Nevertheless, even destructive force can and does finally work towards good, for the trend of the evolutionary force is unalterable. It can be slowed down or speeded up according to the purpose, aspiration and orientation of the entity (human or national); it can express soul purpose or personality selfishness, but the urge towards betterment will inevitably triumph.   (16-458/9)

11. Will you misunderstand when I say that disease is energy which is not functioning as desired or according to plan? Inpouring energies are brought into relation with forces, and good health, strong and adequate forms and vital activity result; the same inpouring energies can, however, be brought into relation with the same forces and a point of friction be set up, producing a diseased area, pain, suffering, and perhaps death. The energies and forces remain of the same essentially divine nature, but the relationship established has produced the problem. If this sentence is studied it will be obvious that a definition such as that can be used to cover all forms of difficulty, and that the ultimate producer of the situation (either good or evil) is the relationship aspect. This statement is of major importance in all your thinking.   (17-588)

(a)   CYCLIC NATURE OF ENERGY IMPULSES

1. The rhythmic nature of the soul's meditation must not be overlooked in the life of the aspirant. There is an ebb and flow in all nature, and in the tides of the ocean we have wonderful picturing of an eternal law. As the aspirant adjusts himself to the tides of the soul life he begins to realise that there is ever a flowing in, a vitalising and a stimulating, which is followed by a flowing out as sure and as inevitable as the immutable laws of force. This ebb and flow can be seen functioning in the processes of death and incarnation. It can be seen also over the entire process of a man's lives, for some lives can be seen to be apparently static and uneventful, slow and inert from the angle of the soul's experience, whilst others

are vibrant, full of experience and of growth. This should be remembered by all of you who are workers, when you are seeking to help others to live rightly. Are they on the ebb or are they being subjected to the flow of the soul energy? Are they passing through a period of temporary quiescence, preparatory to greater impulse or effort, so that the work to be done must be that of strengthening and stabilising in order to enable them to "stand in spiritual being", or are they being subjected to a cyclic inflow of forces? In this case the worker must seek to aid in the direction and utilisation of the energy which (if misdirected) will eventuate in wrecked lives but which, when wisely utilised, will produce a full and fruitful service.

The above thoughts can also be applied by the student of humanity to the great racial cycles and much of interest will be discovered. Again, and of more vital importance to us, these cyclic impulses in the life of the disciple are of a greater frequency and speed and forcefulness than in the life of the average man. They alternate with a distressing rapidity. The hill and valley experience of the mystic is but one way of expressing this ebb and flow. Sometimes the disciple is walking in the sunlight and at other times in the dark; sometimes he knows the joy of full communion and again all seems dull and sterile; his service is on occasion a fruitful and satisfying experience, and he seems to be able to really aid; at other times he feels that he has naught to offer and his service is arid and apparently without results. All is clear to him some days and he seems to stand on the mountain top looking out over a sunlit landscape, where all is clear to his vision. He knows and feels himself to be a son of God. Later, however, the clouds seem to descend and he is sure of nothing, and seems to know nothing. He walks in the sunlight and is almost overpowered by the brilliance and heat of the solar rays, and wonders how long this uneven experience and the violent alternation of these opposites is to go on. Once however that he grasps the fact that he is watching the effect of the cyclic impulses and the effect of the soul's meditation upon his form nature, the meaning becomes clearer and he realises that it is that form aspect which is failing in its response, and reacting to energy with unevenness. He then learns that once he can live in the soul consciousness and attain that "high altitude" (if I might so express it) at will, the fluctuations of the form life will not touch him. He then perceives the narrow-edged razor path which leads from the plane of physical life to the soul realm, and finds that when he can tread it with steadiness it leads him out of the ever changing world of the senses into the clear light of day and into the world of reality.

The form side of life then becomes to him simply a field for service and not a field for sensuous perception. Let the student ponder upon this last sentence. Let him aim to live as a soul. Then the cyclic impulses, emanating from the soul, are known to be impulses for which he himself is responsible and which he has sent forth; he then knows himself to be the initiating cause and is not subject to the effects.   (4-61/4)

2. The ebb and flow of daily life during a particular incarnation, will also demonstrate its interludes, and these the aspirant has to learn to recognise and to utilise. He has to register the distinction between intense outgoing activity, periods of withdrawal, and interludes wherein the outer life seems static and free from active interest. This he must do if he is to avail himself fully of the opportunity which life experience is intended to furnish. The whole of life is not concentrated in one furious continuous stretch of rushing forth to work, nor is it comprehended in one eternal siesta. It has normally its own rhythmic beat and vibration, and its own peculiar pulsation. Some lives change their rhythm and mode of activity every seven years; others alter every nine or eleven years. Still others work under shorter cycles, and have months of strenuous endeavour followed by months of apparent non-effort. Some people again are so sensitively organised that, in the midst of work, events and circumstances are so staged that they are forced into a temporary retirement wherein they assimilate the lessons learnt during the preceding period of work.

   Two groups of human beings work with apparently no physical plane ebb and flow, but manifest steadily an urge to work. These are people who are so little evolved and so low down (if one might thus express it) on the ladder of evolution, and so predominantly animal, that there is no mental reaction to circumstances, but simply a response to the call of physical needs, and the use of time for the satisfaction of desire. This never lets up, and therefore there is little that can be called cyclic in their expression. They include the unthinking toiler and the uncivilised man. Then there are those men and women who are on the opposite scale, and have climbed relatively high on the ladder of progress. These are so emancipated from the purely physical, and are so aware of the nature of desire, that they have learnt to preserve a continuous activity—based on discipline and service. They work consciously with cycles and understand somewhat their nature. They know the divine art of abstracting their consciousness into that of the soul in contemplation, and can control and wisely guide their work in the world of men. This is the lesson which all disciples are learning, and this is the high achievement of the initiates and trained workers of the race.   (4-514/5)

3. Cycles of realisation must inevitably be succeeded by periods of quiet unemotional growth and assimilation. During these months, the high moments may perhaps cease and the work will go on with no realised tensions and, consequently, with no moments of startling import. This is happily the case. A constant succession of spiritual enlightenments, and an unabated keying-up to high contacts, would eventually dull the instrument so that true recognitions would fade out. Ponder on this . . . and be grateful for the days of coming duty, of quiet living, of steadfast orientation towards the light, of silent communication with your soul, of study and of thought.   (5-323/4)

4. All life is cyclic, and this is a point which disciples are apt to forget and overlook; they then find themselves discouraged when the *intensity of feeling* leaves them. The initiate walks ever a straight course between the pairs of opposites, serene and unafraid.   (5-448)

5. The way of the aspirant climaxes at times, and might be described as a series of steady growth cycles, accentuated at intervals by definite periods of forced development, wherein one limitation after another is forcibly removed, by yourself. All limitations and hindrances have to go.   (5-598)

6. Under cyclic law there are periods of outgoing and of withdrawing, of progressing in service towards the periphery of activity, and also of a conscious abstraction of the consciousness from the outer circle and its centering again at the very heart of life.   (6-115)

(b)   ENERGY IN SERVICE

1. We will start with the premise that *"energy follows thought"*. This is the first and most fundamental, as well as the most ancient, premise of the esotericist. The second is related to the first, and will have a place in our considerations. It states that *"the eye, opened by thought, directs the energy in motion"*.

Disciples, during the early part of their training, are apt to regard energy as a pool or reservoir upon which they can learn to draw, thus appropriating a quota of that energy for their need, their service and their use. But energy is fluid and in motion; we live in a veritable sea of moving forces, qualified in countless ways, conditioned by countless minds, misdirected oft, directed wisely sometimes, yet all of them perforce finding place in the mind content of the One in Whom we live and move and have our being, and outside Whose range of influence naught can be. Disciples have, for aeons, been using the energies and forces found in the three

worlds for personality ends, and for the furthering of their major interests, whatever those may be. They have learnt somewhat to lay hold and
use a measure of soul energy, thereby enlightening their way, improving
their spiritual expression in the three worlds, and serving a little. They
are beginning to grasp the significance of intention and purpose, whilst
an inner programme is slowly conditioning their daily lives. There comes,
however, a point—a point which it is now your duty and privilege to
grasp—wherein another source of energy, of inspiration and of light can
be made available to disciples, and can be used for service. That is the
energy of the Forces of Light, originating in the Ashram and emanating
thence; you stand as yet upon the periphery of the Ashram but can avail
yourselves of these energies.   (6-132/3)

2. (The initiate has) to learn to distinguish between the various energies
he contacts. The initiate has to master the techniques of differentiating between :

   i. His own energy or energies, which have been generated as the result
   of his life experiences down the ages or centuries.

   ii. His ray energy which, rightly used, conditions his work with and for
   the Hierarchy.

   iii. The energy of the ashram of which he may avail himself in the
   process of carrying out activities—initiated by impression. In the early
   stages he calls this the energy of his Master, but learns later that it is—
   in reality—the energy generated by his Master's group, the ashram.

   iv. Hierarchical energy or the energy of certain associated ashrams or
   of the entire group of ashrams, the Hierarchy itself. The use of this
   highly qualified and most potent energy can only be employed when
   the disciple has earned the right to certain privileges and can be trusted
   to use the potencies correctly.

   v. The energy of the Head of the Hierarchy, or the Christ force, as it
   is sometimes called. This force imports into the usually available energies certain conditioning qualities which emanate from Shamballa, and
   are therefore related to the Will aspect. This type of force has not
   hitherto been available to working disciples, but is now available, having been released at the Wesak Festival of this year (1948). Even now
   it can be used only by highly trusted disciples, and usually by those
   only whose rays are the first Ray of Power and Will, or the second
   Ray of Love-Wisdom. These will be the rays of one or other of the

two major vehicles—that of the soul and that of the personality. There are naturally exceptions to this rule, and these exceptions will be increasingly numerous as time speeds by; but in the present time, first and second ray vehicles provide the line of least resistance.   (6-374/5)

3. Every initiate is himself a polarised point of precipitated energy; every initiate works from a known point of polarisation, and his main task is the precipitation of energy in order to energise, stimulate and create that which is needed in any immediate field of divine activity. Occult obedience is in reality the ability to work with these energies in relation to the Plan, even if only a tiny part of that Plan is known to the initiate. He becomes a part of a great energy distributing group.   (6-432)

4. Initiation is in fact a process wherein the initiate is taught how to work with energy, how to use the creative, attractive and dynamic energies in accordance with the hierarchical Plan, in order to bring about the precipitation of the planetary Purpose into the outer field of manifestation. (6-434)

(c) THE ETHERIC VEHICLE (The Vital Body)

1. Life itself, the training to be given in the future, the conclusions of science, and a new mode of civilisation, will all increasingly be focussed on this unique (etheric) substance, which is the true form to which all physical bodies in every kingdom in nature conform. Note that phraseology.
    . . . The etheric body exists in subtle etheric matter, and factually there is no true gap; there is simply the ignoring by humanity of an aspect of the physical body, which is of far more importance than is the dense physical vehicle. The consciousness of men today is physical-astral, and the factor of conditioning energies is ignored, overlooked, and—from the angle of consciousness—non-existent.
    One of the main obligations of occult students today, is to testify to the fact of the etheric body; modern science is already thus testifying because its researches have now landed it in the realm of energy. Electrotherapy, the growing recognition that man is electrical in nature, and the realisation that even the atom, in apparently inanimate objects, is a living vibrant entity, substantiate this occult point of view. Generally speaking, science has preceded esotericism in its recognition of energy as a dominant factor in all form expression. . . . The fact of all manifested forms being forms of energy, and that the true human form is no exception, is the gift of science to humanity and not the gift of occultism.   (11-139/40)

2. Here is a basic statement—one that is so basic that it governs and controls all thinking anent the etheric body:

The etheric body is primarily composed of the dominant energy or energies to which the man, the group, the nation, or the world reacts in any particular time cycle or world period.

If you are to understand clearly, it is essential that I lay down certain propositions anent the etheric body, which should govern all the student's thinking; if they do not, he will be approaching the truth from the wrong angle; this, modern science does not do. The limitation of modern science is its lack of vision; the hope of modern science is that it does recognise truth when proven. Truth in all circumstances is essential, and in this matter science gives a desirable lead, even though it ignores and despises occultism. Occult scientists handicap themselves either because of their presentation of the truth, or because of a false humility. Both are equally bad.

There are six major propositions which govern all consideration of the etheric body, and I would like to present them to students as a first step:

i. There is nothing in the manifested universe—solar, planetary, or the various kingdoms in nature—which does not possess an energy form, subtle and intangible yet substantial, which controls, governs, and conditions the outer physical body. This is the etheric body.

ii. This energy form—underlying the solar system, the planets, and all forms within their specific rings-pass-not—is itself conditioned and governed by the dominant solar or planetary energy which ceaselessly and without break in time, creates it, changes and qualifies it. The etheric body is subject to ceaseless change. This, being true of the Macrocosm, is equally true of man, the microcosm, and—through the agency of humanity—will eventually and mysteriously prove true of all the sub-human kingdoms in nature. Of this, the animal kingdom and the vegetable kingdom are already evidences.

iii. The etheric body is composed of interlocking and circulating lines of force, emanating from one or other, or from one or many, of the seven planes or areas of consciousness of our planetary Life.

iv. These lines of energy, and this close interlocking system of streams of force, are related to seven focal points or centres to be found within the etheric body. These centres are related, each of them, to certain types of incoming energy. When the energy reaching the etheric body is not related to a particular centre, then that centre remains quiescent and unawakened; when it is related and the centre is sensitive to its impact, then that centre becomes vibrant and receptive, and develops as a controlling factor in the life of the man on the physical plane.

v. The dense physical body, composed of atoms—each with its own individual life, light and activity—is held together by and is expressive of the energies which compose the etheric body. These, as will be apparent, are of two natures:

(a) The energies which form (through interlocked "lines of forceful energy") the underlying etheric body, as a whole and in relation to all physical forms. This form is qualified then by the *general* life and vitality of the plane on which the Dweller in the body functions, and therefore where his consciousness is normally focussed.

(b) The particularised or specialised energies by which the individual (at this particular point in evolution, through the circumstances of his daily life and his heredity) *chooses* to govern his daily activities.

vi. The etheric body has many centres of force, responsive to the manifold energies of our planetary Life, but we shall consider only the seven major centres which respond to the inflowing energies of the seven rays. All lesser centres are conditioned by the seven major centres; this is a point which students are apt to forget. It is here that knowledge of the egoic and of the personality rays is of prime usefulness.

It can be seen, therefore, how exceedingly important this subject of energy becomes, because it controls and makes the man what he is at any given moment, and likewise indicates the plane on which he should function, and the method whereby he should govern his environment, circumstances and relationships. If this is grasped by him, it will enable him to realise that he will have to shift his whole attention from the physical or the astral planes on to the etheric levels of awareness; his objective will then be to determine what energy should control his daily expression (or energies, if he is an advanced disciple). He will realise also that as his attitude, attainment and comprehension shifts to higher levels, his etheric body will be constantly changing and responding to the newer energies. These energies he will be *will-fully* bringing in; this is the right use of the word "will-full". (11-141/3)

3. According to the point in evolution will be the extent of the area which the etheric body covers beyond the outside of the physical body. It may extend for a few or many inches. (11-145)

4. Within the physical body, the network of the etheric body is to be found permeating every single part. It is peculiarly associated at this time with the nervous system, which is fed, nourished, controlled and galvanised by its etheric counterpart. This counterpart is present in millions of tiny streams or lines of energy, to which the Eastern occultist has given the name of "nadis". These nadis are the carriers of energy. (11-145)

5. The seven centres are *not* within the dense physical body. They exist *only* in etheric matter and in the etheric so-called aura, outside the physical body. (11-146)

6. The powerful effect of the inflow of energy, via the energy body, has itself automatically created these centres, or these reservoirs of force, these focal points of energy, which the spiritual man must learn to use, and through the means of which he can direct energy where needed. (11-146)

7. Each form (because it constitutes an aggregated area of substantial lives or atoms) is a centre within the etheric body, of the form of which it is a constituent part. It has, as the basis of its existence, a living dynamic point which integrates the form, and preserves it in essential being. This form or centre—large or small, a man or an atom of substance—is related to all other forms and expressing energies in the environing space, and is automatically receptive to some, and repudiates others through the process of non-recognition; it relays or transmits other energies, radiating from other forms, and it thus becomes in its turn, an impressing agent. You see, therefore, where differentiated truths approach each other and blend, forcing us to use the same terminologies in order to express the same factual truths or ideas. (11-179/80)

8. The etheric body . . . has one main objective. This is to vitalise and energise the physical body, and thus integrate it into the energy body of the Earth and of the solar system. It is a web of energy streams, of lines of force and of light. It constitutes part of the vast network of energies which underlies all forms, whether great or small (mirocosmic or macrocosmic). Along these lines of energy the cosmic forces flow, as the blood flows through the veins and arteries. This constant, individual—human, planetary and solar—circulation of life-forces through the etheric bodies of all forms, is the basis of all manifested life, and the expression of the essential non-separateness of all life. (17-2/3)

9. The etheric body is fundamentally the most important response apparatus which man possesses, producing not only the right functioning of

the five senses, and consequently providing five major points of contact with the tangible world, but it also enables a man to register sensitively the subtler worlds, and, when energised and controlled by the soul, the spiritual realms stand wide open also.   (17-83)

10. An understanding of what I have said, will lead the earnest student to a more practical application of his attitude to the centres, and also to a fixed endeavour to make his sphere of radiatory activity more useful to his fellow men. The reason for this will be that his attitude will express the quality of the subjective spirit and not the quality—hitherto rampant —of objective matter. Forget not that the etheric body is a material and substantial body, and is therefore an integral part of the physical plane; forget not that it is intended, first of all, to carry the energies of the emotional and of the mental plane in the unconscious experimental stage of incarnation; that it is also intended to carry the threefold energies of the soul in the stage of *consciously* gaining experience; and that also, as the antahkarana is built, it is intended to carry the energies of the Monad in the stage of consciously expressed divinity. See you, therefore, the beauty of the spiritual process, and the planned aid given to the sons of men at all stages of their return to the centre from whence they came? (11-176)

(d)   THE AWAKENING OF THE CENTRES

1. The question now arises : How can this awakening and co-ordination (of the centres) be brought about? What steps must be taken in order to produce this vitalisation and the eventual synthetic activity of the three centres? . . . So oft the aspirant is anxious to be told some new thing, and when he is told some old truth—so old and so familiar that it fails to call forth a registering response—he feels that the teacher has failed him, and so succumbs to a sense of futility and depression. . . . Let us enumerate (the requirements) in tabulated form, and then we will deal briefly with each point afterwards :

i. Character building, the first and essential requisite.

ii. Right motive.

iii. Service.

iv. Meditation.

v. A technical study of the science of the centres.

vi. Breathing exercises.

vii. Learning the technique of the Will.

viii. The development of the power to employ time.

ix. The arousing of the Kundalini fire.

. . . Do you appreciate the fact that if you were making full use of each piece of information given in the course of the training, and making it a fact in your experience, and were living out in your daily life the teaching so steadily imparted, you would be standing ere now before the Portal of Initiation? Do you realise that truth has to be wrought out in the texture of daily living before new truth can be safely imparted? . . .

Right Motive. . . . The question which the seeker now asks and which *he* only has the right to answer, is: What is the motive governing my aspiration and my endeavour? Why do I seek to build upon a true foundation? Why do I so diligently invoke my soul?

The development of right motive is a progressive effort, and constantly one shifts the focus of one's incentive when one discovers himself, as the Light shines ever more steadily upon one's way and constantly a newer and higher motive emerges. Again, let me illustrate: An aspirant in the early stages is practically always a devotee. To measure up to the standard set by a loved friend and teacher, he struggles and strives and gains ground. Later, this object of his devotion and ardent effort is superseded by devotion to one of the Great Ones, the Elder Brothers of the race. He bends all his powers and the forces of his nature to Their service. This incentive is, in its turn, surely and steadily superseded by a vital love for humanity, and love of one individual (be he ever so perfect) is lost sight of in love for the whole brotherhood of men. Unceasingly, as the soul takes more and more control of its instrument, and the soul nature steadily manifests, this too is superseded by love of the ideal, of the Plan and of the purposes underlying the universe itself. The man comes to know himself as naught but a channel through which spiritual agencies can work, and realises himself as a corporate part of the One Life. Then he sees even humanity as relative and fractional, and becomes immersed in the great Will.

Service. A study of right motive leads naturally to right service, and often parallels in its objective form, the motivating consciousness. From service to an individual as an expression of love, to the family, or to the nation, there grows service to a member of the Hierarchy, to a Master's group, and thence service to humanity. Eventually there is developed a consciousness of and service of the Plan, and a consecration to the underlying purpose of the Great Existence Who has brought all into being for the fulfilment of some specific objective.   (4-200/4)

2. It must be carefully borne in mind that the main task of the aspirant is the handling of energies, both in himself and in the world of physical phenomena and externalisation. This consequently involves an understanding of the centres and of their awakening. But understanding must come first, and the awakening at a much later date in the sequence of time. This awakening will fall into two stages:

First, there is the stage wherein, by the practice of a disciplined life and by the purification of the thought life, the seven centres are automatically brought into a right condition of rhythm, vitality and vibratory activity. This stage involves no danger, and there is no directed thought—in connection with the centres—permitted to the aspirant. By that I mean he is not allowed to concentrate his mind upon any one centre, nor may he seek to awaken or energise them. He must remain engrossed with the problem of purifying the bodies in which the centres are found, which are primarily the astral, etheric and physical bodies, remembering ever that the endocrine system and the seven major glands in particular, are the effectual externalisations of the seven major centres. In this stage the aspirant is working all around the centres, and is dealing with their environing matter and with the living substance which completely surrounds them. This is all that can be safely undertaken by the majority, and it is with this stage that the bulk of the aspirants in the world today are engaged and with which they must remain engaged for a long time to come.

Secondly, there is the stage wherein the centres, through the effective work of the earlier stage, become what is esoterically called "released within the prison house"; they can now become the subject (under proper direction by a teacher) of definite methods of awakening and of charging —the methods differing according to the ray (personality and egoic) of the aspirant. Hence the difficulty of the subject, and the impossibility of giving general and blanket rules. (4-587/8)

3. I would here like to point out two other matters, and so clarify the entire situation. There is much confusion on the subject of the centres, and much erroneous teaching, leading many astray and causing a great deal of misapprehension.

First I would state that no work, such as an effort to awaken the centres, should ever be undertaken whilst the aspirant is aware of definite impurities in his life, or when the physical body is in poor condition or is diseased. Neither should it be undertaken when the pressure of external circumstances is such that there is no place or opportunity for quiet and uninterrupted work. It is essential that for the immediate and focussed work on the centres, there should be the possibility of hours of seclusion and of freedom from interruption. This I cannot too strongly emphasise, and I do so in order to demonstrate to the eager student that at this period of our history there are few whose lives permit of this seclusion. This is, however, a most beneficent circumstance, and not one to be deplored. Only one in a thousand aspirants is at the stage where he should begin to work with the energy in the centres, and perhaps even this estimate is too optimistic. Better far that the aspirant serves and loves and works and disciplines himself, leaving his centres to develop and unfold more slowly and therefore more safely. Unfold they inevitably will, and the slower and safer method is (in the vast majority of cases) the more rapid. Premature unfoldment involves much loss of time, and carries with it often the seeds of prolonged trouble.   (4-589/90)

4. Work in connection with the centres is incidental to true spiritual development, and is or should be purely mechanical and automatic. The centres are physical, being aspects of the etheric body, and constructed of etheric matter, and their function is simply to express the energy which flows in from the astral body, or from the mind or from the soul (in three aspects).   (6-604)

5. I teach no mode of awakening the centres, because right impulse, steady reaction to higher impulsions and the practical recognition of the sources of inspiration, will automatically and safely swing the centres into needed and appropriate activity.   (10-261)

6. If the tuning up and awakening (of the centres) is forced, or is brought about by exercises of various kinds before the student is ready, and before the bodies are co-ordinated and developed, then the aspirant is headed towards disaster. Breathing exercises, or pranayama training should never be undertaken without expert guidance, and only after years of spiritual application, devotion and service; concentration upon the centres in the force body (with a view to their awakening) is ever to be avoided; it will cause over-stimulation and the opening of doors on to the astral plane, which the student may have difficulty in closing.   (13-18)

(e)   THE AURA

1. The aura of any form of life can be defined as the quality of a sphere of radiatory activity. Very little is as yet known about auras, and a great deal of nonsense has been written anent the matter. The aura is usually

spoken of in terms of colour and of light, due to the nature of the vision of the one who sees, and the apparatus of response which is in use. Two words only describe an aura from the point of view of occult knowledge, and they are "quality" and "sphere of influence". What the clairvoyant really contacts is an *impression* which the mind rapidly translates into the symbology of colour, whereas there is no colour present. Seeing an aura, as it is called, is in reality a state of awareness. That the seer may in all sincerity believe that he has registered a colour, a series of colours, or light, is entirely true in many cases, but what he has really recorded is the quality of a sphere of radiatory activity; this he does when his own individual sphere of radiatory activity is of the same nature and quality as that contacted. Most seers register the astral range of vibrations of a person or a group and this through the medium of their own astral body. The impact of a truth or of a mental concept and its recognition, is an expression of a similar contact, carried forward this time into the realm of the mind. (5-752)

2. The essential point to be grasped, is that sensitivity to impression is a normal and natural unfoldment, parallelling spiritual development. I gave you a clue to the entire process when I said that:

"Sensitivity to impression involves the engendering of a magnetic aura upon which the highest impressions can play."

I would have you give the deepest consideration to these words. As the disciple begins to demonstrate soul quality, and the second divine aspect takes possession of him, and controls and colours his entire life, automatically the higher sensitivity is developed; he attracts into his field of consciousness the outline, and later the details, of the hierarchical Plan; he becomes aware eventually of the planetary Purpose; all these impressions are not things which he must seek out and learn laboriously to ascertain, to hold and seize upon. They drop into his field of consciousness *because* he has created a magnetic aura which invokes them and brings them "into his mind". This magnetic aura begins to form itself from the first moment he makes a contact with his soul; it deepens and grows as those contacts increase in frequency and become eventually an habitual state of consciousness; then, at will and at all times, he is en rapport with his soul, the second divine aspect.

It is this aura which is in reality the reservoir of thought-substance upon which he can spiritually rely. This point of focus is upon the mental plane. He is no longer controlled by the astral nature; he is successfully constructing the antahkarana along which the higher impressions can flow; he learns not to dissipate this inflow, but to accumulate within the aura (with which he has surrounded himself) the knowledge and the wisdom which he realises his service to his fellow men requires. A disciple is a magnetic centre of light and knowledge just in so far as the magnetic aura is held by him in a state of receptivity. It is then constantly invocative of the higher range of impressions; it can be evoked and set into "distributing activity" by that which is lower and which is demanding aid. The disciple therefore, in due time, becomes a tiny or minute correspondence of the Hierarchy—invocative as it is to Shamballa, and easily evoked by human demand. These are points warranting careful consideration. They involve a primary recognition of points of tension, and their consequent expansion into magnetic auras or areas, capable of invocation and evocation.

These areas of sensitivity pass through three stages, upon which it is not my intention to enlarge:

i. Sensitivity to impression from other human beings. This sensitivity becomes of use in service *when* the needed magnetic aura has been engendered and is brought under scientific control.

ii. Sensitivity to group impression—the passage of ideas from group to group. The disciple can become a receptive agent within any group of which he is a part, and this ability indicates progress on his part.

iii. Sensitivity to hierarchical impressions, reaching the disciple via the antahkarana, and—later—from the Hierarchy as a whole, when he has attained some of the higher initiations. This indicates ability to register impression from Shamballa.

It would be of value if we now considered three points which are concerned with sensitivity to impression, with the construction of the resultant reservoir of thought, and with responsiveness to subsequent invocative appeals. These three points are:

i. Processes of Registration.

ii. Processes of Recording Interpretations.

iii. Processes of Resultant Invocative Response.

I would recall to your minds the knowledge that the aura, which each of you has created around the central nucleus of your incarnated self or soul, is a fragment of the over-shadowing soul which brought you into manifestation. This aura is (as you well know) composed of the emanations of the etheric body, and this in its turn embodies three types of energy for which you are individually responsible. These three types are (when added to the energy of prana, which composes the etheric vehicles):

i. The health aura. This is essentially physical.

ii. The astral aura, which is usually by far the most dominant factor, extensive and controlling.

iii. The mental aura, which is in most cases relatively small, but which develops rapidly once the disciple takes his own development *consciously* in hand, or once the polarisation of the personality is upon the mental plane. The time will eventually come when the mental aura will obliterate (if I may use such an inadequate term) the emotional or astral aura, and then the soul quality of love will create a substitute, so that the needed sensitivity does not entirely disappear, but is of a higher and far more acute nature.

In this threefold aura (or more correctly, fourfold, if you count the etheric vehicle) every individual lives and moves and has his being; it is this living, vital aura which is the recording agent of all impressions, both objective and subjective. It is this "agent of sensitive response" which the indwelling self has to control and use in order to register impression, or to direct etheric or mental impression out into the world of men. Astral impression is purely selfish and individual, and though it may affect a man's surroundings, is not directed as are the other energies registered. It is the aura which predominantly creates the effects which a person has upon his associates; it is not primarily his words which produce reactions, even though they are supposed to embody his reactions and his thinking, but which are, in reality, usually expressions of his emotional desires.

All of us, therefore, carry around with us a subjective mechanism which is a true and perfect picture of our peculiar point in evolution. It is the aura which a Master watches, and this is a factor of major importance in the life of a disciple. The light of the soul within the aura, and the condition of the various aspects of the aura, indicate whether or not the disciple is nearing the Path of Discipleship. As the emotional reactions lessen, and as the mental apparatus clarifies, the progress of the aspirant can be exactly noted. I would have you distinguish carefully between the astral and mental bodies, and that which emanate. The bodies (so called) are substantial in nature; the aura is essentially radiatory and extends from each substantial vehicle in every direction. This is a point which should be most carefully noted.

The problem of the aspirant as he "engenders" his magnetic aura, is himself to withdraw, and thus lessen the extent and the power of the astral aura, and extend and increase the potency of the mental aura. It should be remembered that the large majority of aspirants are definitely polarised in the astral nature, and that therefore their problem is to achieve a different polarisation, and to become focussed upon the mental plane. This takes time and vast effort. Eventually—as mentioned above —the radiation of the soul is substituted in place of the hitherto present emotional activity of the aspirant; this emanation is, in reality, a radiation from the love petals of the egoic lotus.   (11-95/9)

3. The "sphere of radiation" (aura) is a potent instrument in service, and its extent and purity of contact should be cultivated by the pledged disciple. There is true occult teaching in the statement in *The New Testament* that "the shadow of Peter passing by, *healed*". His aura was of such a nature that it had a beneficent effect wherever and whenever it touched or contacted those in his environment. The control of the Christ over His aura was such that "He knew when virtue had gone out of Him"—He knew, therefore, that healing energies had poured through one of His centres to a needy person or group of persons. It is the aura, and its potency of attraction, and its stability, which holds a group together, which also keeps an audience listening, and which makes an individual of importance along some definite line of approach to his fellow men. The "sphere of radiation" is easily determined by those who seek it out and who watch the effect of the radiation upon people in their community and environment. One highly emotional person, working through an overdeveloped and uncontrolled solar plexus centre, can wreck a home or an institution. I give this as an illustration. One radiant, creative life, consciously using the heart or the throat centres, can carry inspiration to hundreds. These are points well worth careful consideration. You must, however, bear in mind that these centres are brought into activity by the cultivation of certain major virtues, and *not* by meditation or concentration upon the centres. They are brought automatically into the needed radiatory condition by right living, high thinking, and loving activity. These virtues may seem to you dull and uninteresting, but they are most potent and scientifically effective in bringing the centres into the desired radiatory activity. When the task is done, and when all the centres are living spheres of outgoing, radiatory activity, they swing into each other's orbit, so that the initiate becomes a centre of living light, and *not* a composite of seven radiant centres. Think on this.   (11-174/5)

(f) RADIATION

1. You are in a position where you can be of much service to others. Your usefulness depends upon your ability to achieve a constant inner growth and progressive realisation, and your consequent capacity to meet all who seek your aid in a spirit of love, free from personal criticism and with intelligent reticence. . . . The intensification of the potency of your aura (your personality emanation), is most desirable, for it is through the right use of the aura that we stimulate others to renewed effort, or slow them down to less potent expression. This intensification is dependent upon the quality, potency and tempo of your subjective life.   (5-230)

2. Every disciple is a focal point of power to some degree. The more advanced the disciple, the greater the force or energy which will radiate from him; this necessarily presents situations which the lesser disciple has to handle. The true disciple never does this with intention. The theory (so prevalent among occult groups) that the leader or some senior working disciple must stage situations in order to develop the pupil, is contrary to occult law. The moment, however, you step into the range of the radiation of a Master or of any disciple senior to you, then things are bound to happen in your life. The radiation is effective when rightly received, registered, and consciously used to bring about the sensed and needed changes.   (5-740)

3. This whole question of spheres of influence is one upon which you need to ponder. It is closely related to the problem of the aura and its esoteric circumference; it concerns the "sound" of a disciple's life, and the nature and quality of the radiations which emanate from the "place where he stands". It is tied to the whole theme of orientation and of spiritual location, and to the magnetic effects of the at-one-ing of soul and personality. The problem of radiation and of magnetic influence, is apt to be viewed from the one-sided point of view of the disciple who considers the results of his radiation and of his magnetism upon those he contacts. There is however another point of view; these qualities—inevitable and inescapable—lie behind the entire theme of karma. They draw to the disciple that which can hinder him as well as aid him; his aura—which is a combination of radiations, energies and arranged forces—can repel the good or attract the bad, and vice versa; it can determine—through the contacts made and the relationships set up—the trend of the disciple's life. It is one of the main factors in the presentation of choices, and I would have you think on this.   (6-537/8)

4. The whole question of radiation and magnetism lies at the foundation of the hierarchical method of work. A disciple becomes spiritually magnetic; his radiation begins to make itself felt; this must inevitably be the case when head and heart are consciously related. Gradually that magnetism and that radiation make their presence felt in the disciple's environment, and evoke response from others. Not only so, but the magnetic-radiatory vibration attracts the attention of the Master, and the disciple finds his way into the Ashram along the line or the beam of his own radiatory activity, which has been akin to that of the Ashram. There, the intensified training he receives makes him still more spiritually efficient and "esoterically attractive" in the world of men. He continues with his task of gathering to him those whom he can help and who recognise him as their chosen helper and guide. Thus is an Ashram formed—each on its ray vibration, and each taking much time and lives of choice and of radiation.   (6-560)

24.   TELEPATHY

(a)   TELEPATHIC COMMUNICATION

1. This process of (telepathic) communication . . . has always been in operation among the adepts, the initiates and the senior disciples who are in physical plane bodies. Now the operation of this process is to be extended and steadily developed by the emerging group of mystics and world servers who constitute, in embryo, the world Saviour.   (11-6)

2. The strong desire to achieve success in telepathic work, and the fear of failure, are the surest ways to offset fruitful effort. In all such work as this, an attitude of non-attachment and a spirit of "don't care" are of real assistance. Experimenters along this line need to give more time and thought to the recognition of types of force. They need to realise that emotion and desire for anything on the part of the receiving agent, create streams of emanating energy which rebuff or repulse that which seeks to make contact, such as the directed thought of someone seeking rapport. When these streams are adequately strong, they act like a boomerang and return to the emanating centre, being attracted there by the power of the vibration which sent them forth. In this thought lies hid the cause of:

i. The failure on the part of the broadcasting or transmitting agent. Intense desire to make a satisfactory impression will attract the outgoing thought back again to the transmitter.

ii. The failure on the part of the receiving agent, whose own intense desire to be successful sends out such a stream of outgoing energy that the stream of incoming energy is met, blocked and driven back whence it came: or, if the receiver is aware of this and seeks to stem the tide of his desire, he frequently succeeds in surrounding himself with a wall of inhibited desire, through which naught can penetrate.   (11-10)

3. It is not my intention to give here the rules governing telepathic intercourse. Such intercourse is found between man and man, and groups and groups. The relationship is slowly and normally developed and requires no hastening. It is developing as the other senses of man and his apparatus of perception have developed. Humanity is, however, outstripping telepathic development in the rapid responsiveness of entire groups, and of human beings en masse, to group impression and to group impartation of ideas. The sudden response of groups and nations to mass ideologies, has been both unexpected and difficult to handle wisely and constructively. It was not anticipated by either Shamballa or the Hierarchy that mass impression would develop more quickly than that of individual sensitivity, but it has happened that way. The individual within a group and working within a group, is far more correctly sensitive than is the man struggling alone to render himself sensitive to impression.

One of the factors militating against personal telepathic development lies in the fact that the strong, potent and modern ascension of the spirit in man—as a whole—frequently offsets personality reactions, and telepathy is a personality matter, depending upon contact between mind and mind. The moment, however, that man *tries* to be telepathic, he is immediately swept into a vortex of abstract energies which condition him for spiritual impression far more than they fit him for personal relationships telepathically established.   (11-84/5)

(b) TELEPATHIC RAPPORT

The growth of telepathic rapport will bring in an era of universality and synthesis, with its qualities of recognised relationships and responsiveness. This will be, outstandingly, the glory of the Aquarian Age.

As the race achieves increasingly a mental polarisation through the developing attractive power of the mental principle, the use of language for the *conveying of thoughts between equals or of communicating with superiors* will fall into disuse. It will continue to be used in reaching the masses and those not functioning upon the mental plane. Already voiceless prayer and aspiration and worship are deemed of higher value than the pleadings and proclamations of voiced expression. It is for this stage in the unfoldment of the race for which preparation must be made, and the laws, techniques and process of telepathic communication must be made plain, so that they can be intelligently and theoretically understood.

Disciples must occupy themselves increasingly with right understanding, right designation and right definition of the new science of telepathy. Mental comprehension and mental sympathy will make true interplay possible, and this will bridge between the old way of understanding thought through the medium of the spoken or written word (embodying that thought as the individual thinker seeks to convey it), and the future stage of immediate response to thought, unlimited by speech or other medium of expression. Disciples will endeavour to work in both ways, and the medium of normal human relations and that of super-normal subjective relations, must be studied by them and expressed by them. In this way the time of bridging and the period of transition can be spanned. It will take about five hundred years for the race to become normally telepathic, and when I say normally, I mean *consciously*. (11-33/4)

(c) TELEPATHIC SENSITIVITY

1. The cultivation of sensitivity to telepathic impression is one of the most potent agencies in developing the coming use of the intuitive faculty.

The truly telepathic man is the man who is responsive to impressions coming to him from all forms of life in the three worlds, but he is also equally responsive to impressions coming to him from the world of souls and the world of the intuition. It is the development of the telepathic instinct which will eventually make a man a master in the three worlds, and also in the five worlds of human and super-human development. By a process of withdrawal (of occult abstraction) and of concentration upon the telepathic cult, the whole science of telepathy (as a seed of a future racial potency) can be developed and understood. This is a process now going forward, and it is going on in two ways: through the medium of telepathic groups and of telepathic people, and through the medium of exoteric scientific investigation. The building of the thought-form which will accustom the race to the idea of telepathic work, is proceeding apace, and the seed of this development is becoming very vital and powerful, and germinating with real rapidity. It is, in the last analysis, the seed of MAS-TERHOOD. (11-35/6)

2. The training given by the Masters in Their Ashrams to Their disciples, has one main objective: to increase, develop and enable them to utilise in service their inherent and innate sensitivity. . . . Our five senses have opened to all people five great realms from which impact comes, and we are so familiar with them all that our response is now automatic and, though registered, is not consciously so, unless there is a planned reason and direction intended. We all respond similarly and as automatically to emotional stimuli, and rapidly (very rapidly) the race is reaching out towards mental telepathy. Some few are beginning to work along the lines of spiritual telepathy. Few do more than register occasionally contacts emanating from a high source, and the result is usually also over-mixed with personality reactions.

Contact, with resultant impact from the soul, is also quite rapidly developing. (11-58)

3. You will have noticed that I have given no instruction as to the art of developing telepathic sensitivity. The reason is, as I have told you before, that this sensitivity should be, and always is, a normal unfoldment when the disciple is correctly oriented, completely dedicated and learning decentralisation. If it is a forced process, then the sensitivity developed is not normal and carries with it much difficulty and future danger. Where the disciple is concerned, release from the constant consideration of personal circumstances and problems, leads inevitably to a clear mental release; this then provides *those areas of free mental perception which make the higher sensitivity possible.* Gradually, as the disciple acquires true freedom of thought, and the power to be receptive to the impression of the abstract mind, he creates for himself a reservoir of thought which becomes available at need for the helping of other people, and for the necessities of his growing world service. Later, he becomes sensitive to impression from the Hierarchy. This is at first purely ashramic, but is later transformed into total hierarchical impression by the time the disciple is a Master; *the Plan is then the dynamic substance providing the content of the reservoir of thought upon which he can draw.* This is a statement of unique and unusual importance. Later still, he becomes sensitive to impression from Shamballa, and the quality of the Will which implements planetary Purpose is added to the content of his available knowledge. The point which I seek to make here, however, is the fact of the existence

of a growing reservoir of thought, which the disciple has created in response to the many varying impressions to which he is becoming increasingly sensitive; the ideas, concepts and spiritual objectives of which he is becoming aware, are steadily being formulated by him into thoughts with their appropriated thought-forms, and upon these he learns to draw as he seeks to serve his fellowmen. He finds himself in possession of a reservoir or pool of thought-substance which is the result of his own mental activity, of his innate receptivity, and which provides the material for teaching and the "fount of knowledge" upon which he can draw when he seeks to aid other people.   (11-94/5)

25. IMPRESSION

1. The method of work of the Hierarchy is that of *impression* upon the minds of Their disciples, of telepathic work carried on with the Master as broadcaster and the disciple as the recipient of impression and of energy. This reception of impression and energy has a dual effect:

i. It brings into activity the latent seeds of action and of habits (good or bad), thus producing revelation, purification, enrichment and usefulness.

ii. It vitalises and galvanises the personality into a right relation to the soul, to the environment, and to humanity.

It is necessary for you and for all disciples to grasp the correspondence to this hierarchical effort, and any effort which you may make in order to work as a group of individuals with groups or individuals. An appreciation of the power which you may let loose, of the dynamic effect which you may succeed in awakening in the subject of your directed thought, and of the impression which you may imprint in the mind and consciousness of the subject should incite you to a guarded purity of life (astral and physical), to a watchfulness over thoughts and ideas, and to a love which will safeguard you from all love of power. Thus you will preserve the integrity of those you seek to help and will be enabled to suggest, to strengthen and to teach subjectively, with no undue influence, no forcing, and no infringement of the liberty and spiritual franchise of the person concerned. A difficult task . . . but one to which you are equal, given due attention and obedience . . . as to motive, technique and method.   (11-40)

2. Among Themselves, the Masters do not deal with telepathy as a science warranting consideration, endeavour and impartation; They are concerned primarily with the *Science of Impression.* The term most often employed by Them is the esoteric equivalent of what the average person means when he says, "I have an impression". Impression is the subtlest reaction (more or less accurate) to the vibratory mental activity of some other mind or group of minds, of some whole, as its radiatory influence affects the unit or aggregate of units.

The first stage of correct telepathic reception is ever the registering of an impression; it is generally vague at the beginning, but as a thought, idea, purpose or intention of the sending agent concretises, it slips into the second stage, which appears as a definite thought-form; finally, that thought-form makes its impact upon the consciousness of the brain. (11-41)

3. Let us now deal with the . . . "Processes of Registration, of Recording Interpretations, and the Resultant Invocative Response." We must bear in mind always that I am stating general rules and that I am not dealing either with the ideal or with the undesirable; the *sources of impression* change as the disciple makes progress, though always the larger and the greater source will include all lesser sources.

The fact that a man is sensitive to hierarchical impression in his mental aura, will not prevent his being sensitive in his astral nature to the invocative and emotional call of human beings. The two together are most useful in effect, if the disciple sees to it that they are related. Forget this not, brother of mine. The *capacity to interpret* recorded impressions is likewise learnt as the mental aura develops under the influence of the "mind held steady in the light" of the soul; the disciple learns that all recorded truth is susceptible to many interpretations, and that these unfold with increasing clarity as he takes one initiation after another, and as he develops conscious responsiveness. The *ability to invoke* demonstrates from life to life, and involves the invocation of conscious response from the anima mundi, or from the subconscious soul of all things, as well as from the human consciousness and from the world of super-conscious contact.

This ability (to invoke) develops steadily as the aspirant treads the Path of Discipleship; it is frequently prefaced in the earlier stages by much confusion, much astral psychism, and frequent wrong interpretations. There is no need at this stage, however, for undue distress, because all that is needed is experience, and that experience is gained through experiment and its expression in daily life. In no case is the truism of learning through a system of trial and error proved more correct than it is in the life and experience of the accepting disciple. When he is an accepted disciple, the errors decrease in number, even though the trials (or the experimental use of the many varying energies) become more extensive and, therefore, cover a much wider range of activities.

The *Processes of Registration* are founded upon what I might call invocative approaches from a wide area of possible contacts. The disciple has to learn to distinguish between these many impacts upon his sensitive aura. In the early stages the majority of them are unconsciously registered, though the registration is acute and accurate; the goal, nevertheless, is *conscious* registration; this is brought about through the constant and steady holding of the attitude of the Observer. It is developed through the attainment of detachment—the detachment of the Observer, from all desires and longings which concern the separated self. It will therefore be obvious to you that the use of the word "observer" involves the concept of duality and, therefore, of separation. In this case, however, the motive prompting observation is not self-interest, but the determination to clarify the aura so that it can register only that which will be illuminating and related to the divine Plan, which will be to the benefit of humanity and, therefore, to the creation of a new server within the Ashrams of the Hierarchy.

The divisions made by certain psychologists of the consciousness of man into subconscious, conscious or self-conscious, and super-conscious, have a real measure of value here. It must be remembered, however, that the disciple, first of all, becomes a truly conscious unit of humanity and thus develops a true self-consciousness. This he arrives at by discriminating between the lower self and the higher self, and this renders his magnetic aura sensitive to an aspect of himself which has not hitherto been a controlling factor. From that achieved point he begins to register impressions with increasing clarity and accuracy. Usually, in the early stages, the one desire of the disciple is to register impressions from the Hierarchy; he much prefers that idea to the idea of registering impressions from his own soul or from the surrounding human factors, his fellow men, and the environment and the circumstances which they create. He longs for what may be called "vertical impression". This motive, being very largely self-centredness, turns the disciple introspectively in upon himself, and it is in this stage that many aspirants become prisoners, astrally speaking, because they register in their magnetic aura the many astrally motivated thought-forms of what they believe and hope "vertical impression" supposedly would convey. They contact with facility the astral counterparts of the higher worlds, which are reflected (and thereby distorted) into the astral plane; the world there registered is glamoured by wrong and selfish desires, and by the wishful thinking of well-meaning devotees. Upon this I need not enlarge. All disciples—at some point or another of their training—have to work through this phase of glamour; in so doing they clarify and intensify the magnetic aura and, simultaneously, clarify the surrounding astral world with which they are in contact. They learn also that the longing to register impressions from the Hierarchy *must* give place to the determination to place their magnetic aura at the disposal of humanity; they then learn to register human need and to understand thereby where help is possible, and their fellow men can be served. By means of this conscious registration of invocative appeals from the world of horizontal contacts, the magnetic aura of the disciple is cleared of the hindering and engrossing thought-forms, and from the aspirational desires and longings which have hitherto prevented right registration. The disciple then ceases to create them, and those which have been created die out, or atrophy for lack of attention.

Later on, when the accepting disciple becomes the accepted disciple, and is permitted to participate in ashramic activity, he adds the ability to register hierarchical impression; this however is only possible *after* he has learnt to register impression coming to him from his own soul (the vertical impression) and from the surrounding world of men (the horizontal impression). When he has taken certain important initiations, his magnetic aura will be capable of registering impression from the subhuman kingdoms in nature. Again, later on, when he is a Master of the Wisdom and, therefore, a full member of the fifth kingdom in nature, the world of hierarchical life and activity will be the world from which horizontal impression will be made upon his magnetic aura, and vertical impression will come from the higher levels of the Spiritual Triad and, still later, from Shamballa. Then the world of humanity will be to him what the sub-human kingdoms were when the fourth kingdom, the human, was the field of his registered horizontal impression. You have here the true significance of the Cross of humanity clearly revealed.

The fact of registration is no unusual phenomenon. Sensitive people are constantly being impressed from some level of consciousness or other, and are receptive to these impressions according to the level of consciousness upon which they normally function; mediums, for instance, are exceedingly prone to receive impressions from etheric or astral levels, as are the vast majority of astral psychics—and their name is legion. Impressions from mental levels (concrete, abstract, or of a more exalted nature) make their impress upon the minds of those who have attained a true measure of focus upon the mental plane. Scientists, mystics, mathematicians, occult students, aspirants and disciples, educators and humanitarians, and all who love their fellow men, are all susceptible to such impression, and one of the outstanding needs of the disciple is to develop adequate sensitivity to ashramic impression and contact. Then he moves out of the group of mental sensitives listed above.

The problem with which I now deal is far deeper and concerns the interpretation and the clear and correct recording of the impression, which is a far more difficult matter. The subject who is impressed must know the source of the impression; he must be able to relate it to some field of demanded information, correction, instruction, or energy distribution. He must be able to state clearly on what aspect of his recording mechanism (the mind, the astral body, the energy body, or the brain) the imparted and registered impression has made impact. One of the difficulties, for instance, facing the aspiring disciple and the earnest occult student, is to record directly *in the brain* impressions from the Spiritual Triad (and later from the Monad), via the antahkarana.

The impression must be a direct descent from mental levels to the brain, avoiding all contact with the astral body; only in so far as this direct descent is attained, will the recorded impression be devoid of error. It will not then be tinctured with any emotional complex whatsoever, for it is the astral level of consciousness which is the great distorter of essential truth. Impressions from the Ashram or from the Spiritual Triad (which are the only type of impressions with which I am here concerned) pass through three stages:

i. *The stage of mental recording.* The clarity and the accuracy of recording will be dependent upon the condition of the channel of reception, the antahkarana; in this recording, curiously enough, a certain *element of time* enters in. It is not time as you know it upon the physical plane, which is but the registration by the brain of passing "events"; it is the higher mental correspondence to time. Into this, I cannot here enter, as the theme is too abstruse; for time, in this connection, is related to distance, to descent, to focus, and to the power to record.

ii. *The stage of brain reception.* The accuracy of this reception will be dependent upon the quality of the physical brain cells, upon the polarisation of the thinking man in the head centre, and the freedom of the brain cells from all emotional impression. The difficulty lies here, that the receiving aspirant or the focussed thinker, is always aware emotionally of the descent of the higher impression and of the consequent clarification of the theme of his thought. This must, however, be recorded by a perfectly quiescent astral vehicle, and therefore you will see one of the main objectives of true meditation.

iii. *The stage of recognised interpretation.* This is an exceedingly difficult phase. Interpretation is dependent upon many factors: the educational background, the point reached in evolution, the mystical or the occult approach of the disciple to the centre of truth, his freedom from the lower psychism, his essential humility (which plays a major part in proper understanding), and his personality decentralisation. In fact, the character in its entirety is involved in this important matter of correct interpretation.

In this aspect of impression, the subject of SYMBOLS must necessarily be involved. All impressions must necessarily be translated and interpreted in symbols, in word forms or in pictorial representations; these the aspirant cannot avoid; and it is in the word forms (which are, needless to point out, in the nature of symbols) that he is apt to go astray. They are the media through which the registered impression is conveyed to the brain consciousness, i.e. to the physical plane awareness of the disciple, thus making possible his useful comprehension of abstract ideas or of those aspects of the Path which it is his duty to understand and teach.

There is no need for me to elaborate this theme. The true disciple is ever aware of the possibility of error, of the intervention of psychic intrusions and distortions; he knows well that true and effective interpretation of the imparted impression is dependent largely upon the purity of the receiving channel, and upon the freedom of his nature from all aspects of the lower psychism—a point often forgotten. A thick veil of concrete thought-forms can also distort the true interpretation, as can astral intervention; the teaching upon the Path and the spiritual impression can be interfered with by glamour from the astral plane, or by separative and concrete ideas emanating from mental levels. In this case it can be truly said that "the mind is the slayer of the real". There is a deep occult significance to the words "an open mind"; it is as essential to correct interpretation as is freedom from glamour and the psychic expressions to be found upon the astral plane. (11-100/7)

4. Your major task, as aspirants, is to cultivate the higher sensitivity; to render yourselves so pure and selfless that your minds remain undisturbed

by the happenings in the three worlds; to seek that attentive spiritual sense which will enable you to be impressed, and then to interpret correctly the impressions received.　(18-549)

26.　OCCULT BLINDNESS

1. Blindness is a prelude to initiation of no matter what degree. It is only at the last and highest initiation that the "tendency to blindness" comes to a complete end. In the early stages of evolution, blindess is natural, innate, unavoidable and impenetrable. For ages man walks in the dark. Then comes the stage wherein this normal blindness is a protection, but has also entered a phase wherein it can be overcome. Technically speaking, the blindness to which I have referred, is something different. From the moment when a human being catches the first, faint glimpse of the "something other" and sees himself in juxtaposition to that dimly sensed, distant reality, the blindness with which I have dealt is something *imposed by the soul* upon the hastening aspirant, so that the lessons of conscious experience, of discipleship, and later of initiation, may be correctly assimilated and expressed; by its means, the hurrying seeker is defended from making too rapid and superficial progress. It is depth and a profound "rootedness" (if I may coin such a word) for which the inner Teacher and later the Master looks, and "occult blindness", its need, its wise handling, and its final elimination, are part of the curriculum imposed upon the candidate. . . .

Blindness is therefore, esoterically speaking, the place of learning and is related to the eye, throat and heart doctrine. It is *not* related to the dim vision, the sensing of half truths and the gropings of the aspirant in the process of learning about himself, or as he visions the goal and seeks to walk the Path. That is a familiar condition and one to which beginners are subjected, and which they cannot avoid, for it is inherent in their natures. Occult blindness is spiritually induced, and "blacks out" the glory and the promised attainment and reward. The disciple is thrown back upon himself. All he can see is his problem, his tiny field of exprience, and his—to him—feeble and limited equipment. It is to this stage that the prophet Isaiah refers when he speaks of giving to the struggling aspirant "the treasures of darkness". The beauty of the immediate, the glory of the present opportunity, and the need to focus upon the task and service of the moment, are the rewards of moving forward into the apparently impenetrable darkness. For the initiate, this blindness is still more esoteric; there remains for him absolutely no light whatsoever—no earth light, nor any light within the three worlds at all. There is only blackness. To this the mystic has given the name "the dark night of the soul". (18-197/8)

2. The veils serve their purpose; blindness nurtures and protects, provided it is innate and natural, soul-imposed or spiritually engendered. If it is wilfully self-induced, if it provides an alibi for grasped knowledge, if it is assumed in order to avoid responsibility, then sin enters in and difficulty ensues. From this may all of you be protected. (18-200)

27. REVELATION

1. The entire objective of the initiation preparatory process is to bring revelation. You must ever bear in mind that that which is revealed is eternally present. There is, therefore, occult truth in the statement that there is "nothing new under the sun". All that is revealed upon the Path of Discipleship and of Initiation is forever there, but that which can perceive, reach out and include, has developed with the ages. Upon the Path of Discipleship, in the early stages, the eye of vision is the illumined mind. Upon the Path of Initiation, it is that of which the eye of the mind is the exteriorisation—the intuitional perception of the soul itself. But as evolution proceeds, that which is brought to the point of perceiving the existing verities, differs vastly as the centuries slip away. E'en the adept of the present is pronouncedly more perceptive and more accurately interpretive and his vision more penetrative than was the adept in Atlantean days, and the initiate who will achieve initiate perception during the coming Aquarian Age, will be greatly in advance of those who now function as the adepts of today. (6-252)

2. I have stated that initiation is essentially a process of revelation. For the disciple who is being prepared to take an initiation the emphasis is necessarily laid upon *recognition*—the intelligent recognition of what is to be revealed. This requires on his part a definite emergence from the world of glamour so that there can be a clear perception of the new vision; a new light is thrown upon old and well known truths so that their signi-

ficance is extraordinarily changed, and in that changing, the plan or purpose of Deity takes on an entirely fresh meaning. The inexperienced neophyte is constantly receiving revelations and recording what he regards as most unusual intuitions. All that is really happening, however, is that he is becoming aware of soul knowledge, whereas for the initiate the intuition is ever the revelation of the purpose of Shamballa and the working out, both from the short range and the long range angle, of the divine Plan.   (6-257/8)

3. As man the human being, man the disciple, and man the initiate gradually move onward on the stream of life, revelation comes step by step, moving from one great point of focus to another, until naught more remains to be revealed.   (6-293)

4. Every revelation has its place in a great series of revelations and enlightenments; the disciple has to find, within the form of the revelation, that which he must use in order to achieve the next destined point of attained revelation.   (6-308)

5. Once the initiate has penetrated to the point where revelation becomes possible, he automatically attains the needed fixation, concentration, poise, polarisation and focus, which will enable him to translate what has been revealed to him, in terms and symbols which will convey significance to the intelligentsia with whom all initiates principally work.
     . . . The most urgent and most difficult part of his task is correctly to apprehend the precipitating truth, information or revelation, and then to give it an equally correct *format* so that it can meet the immediate human need.   (6-312/3)

6. As a man progresses nearer and nearer to his goal, he finds himself beginning to realise that the entire technique of this unfoldment consists of a sequence of revelations which are induced by his recognition of subjective significances which are of a nature entirely different to the usual and apparent meanings. . . . My one effort today is to indicate the relation between initiation and revelation. The revelation—induced by right orientation and right thinking—is a part of the training of the initiate, and many thus in training delay their progress by not recognising the revelation when it tops the line of their spiritual horizon.   (6-318/9)

7. Revelation seldom breaks in all its completed beauty into the consciousness of the disciple; it is a gradual and steadily unfolding process.   (6-321)

8. Life for all men everywhere is full of revelation, recognised or unrecognised; it might be said that there is little else, though the majority of them are of small importance, except in their *combined sequence.* They might rather be regarded as creating or constituting a "field of revelation". (6-346)

9. In the initiatory process where the disciple is concerned, revelation is simply one way of expressing the constantly recurring effects of pressure forward and of vision. Throughout the entire evolutionary process, there is essentially nothing but a growing revelation. The two terms, Evolution and Revelation, go together. Any distinction lies within the field of revelation or—to word it otherwise—within the various planes of consciousness, and particularly that in which the revelation is taking place.

. . . Revelation is both formless and also within form, and the closer to realisation, the more subtle and devoid of form will be the revelation. . . . It can be a pictorial symbol or a subtle demonstration; it can be expressed only in words, or it can take the form of wordless recognition; it can be a goal or a future sensed possibility, but it can also be an incentive and the dynamic impulse of the initiate's life, because it is not distant but is a real aspect of his divine equipment. (6-367/8)

10. You talk of a series of initiations, but the Masters talk in terms of *a series of revelations,* and Their work with Their disciples is to prepare them for revelation. Bear in mind . . . that revelation is hard to take and to hold—a point oft overlooked. It is exhausting to the personality of the disciple, but it is of no service unless the personality recognises it; it is excessively stimulating and the initiate passes through three stages where a revelation is concerned: First comes the stage of ecstasy and of supreme recognition; then darkness follows, and almost despair when the revelation fades and the disciple finds that he must walk again in the ordinary light of the world; he knows now what he *is,* but it is at this point that his test lies, for he must proceed on that inner knowledge but dispense with the stimulation of revelation. Finally, he becomes so engrossed with his service, with aiding his fellow men, and with leading them towards *their* next revelation, that the excitement and the reaction are forgotten. He then discovers to his surprise that at any time and at will—if it serves his selfless interests—the revelation is forever his. Ponder on this. (6-389)

11. There is no initiation possible without a preceding revelation, and yet each initiation leads to a subsequent revelation. The objective of all initiation is a conferred revelation, yet no initiation is attained without an earlier self-engendered and not conferred revelation. (6-417)

12. The word "revelation" is one that has been greatly misused by mystics of the Church and of the great world religions; by them, its use is usually of a selfish nature, and the concept implied is that revelation is the due reward conceded to the mystic, because of his struggles and his deep search for God. Then, suddenly, God is revealed to him; suddenly the Angel speaks; suddenly his search seems ended, and reward in the form of a revelation is accorded him. This procedure and sequence of events has been the ordinary form for centuries and all the time the idea of God Transcendent dominated religious thought. But the revelation accorded is, in reality, related (until the sixth Initiation) to God Immanent, to God in form, to God in the human heart, and to that veiled and hidden supreme Reality which motivates all existence and which is for ever consciousness aware of itself. Revelation is a progress of penetration: first into the Mind, then into the Heart, and lastly into the Purpose of the One in Whom we live and move and have our being. (6-434/5)

13. The whole theme of revelation is the revelation of light, and that implies many different interpretations of the word "light"; it concerns the discovery of the lighted areas of being which otherwise remain unknown, and therefore hidden. We create light; we employ light; we discover greater lights which serve to reveal to us the Unknown God. It is the guiding light within us which eventually reveals those brighter lights which usher in the process of revelation. (6-436)

14. As the initiate proceeds on the Way (he) comes to the critical stage where "he recognises revelation". I would ask you to think carefully about these three words, because they involve the perception of some truths which are apt to be forgotten. For instance the truth that revelation is the revelation of *that which is ever present*; it is not in reality the revelation of something new and hitherto unknown. To put this in its simplest terms: the initiate discovers he can perceive more than he ever knew was existent or perceptible, but that he is only perceiving something that has always been there. The limitation he discovers, is in himself, and the Way of Revelation is through the discovery and the discarding of his own personal, or rather, individual limitations. (6-437)

15. The day is dawning when all religions will be regarded as emanating from one great spiritual source; all will be seen as unitedly providing the one root out of which the universal world religion will inevitably emerge. Then there will be neither Christian nor heathen, neither Jew nor Gentile, but simply one great body of believers, gathered out of all the current

religions. They will accept the same truths, not as theological concepts, but as essential to spiritual living; they will stand together on the same platform of brotherhood and of human relations; they will recognise divine sonship and will seek unitedly to co-operate with the divine Plan, as it is revealed to them by the spiritual leaders of the race, and as it indicates to them the next step to be taken on the Path of Approach to God. Such a *world religion* is no idle dream, but something which is definitely forming today.

A second emerging guide to the spiritual life, is the hope of *revelation*. Never before has man's need been greater and never has the surety of revelation been more certain; never has the spirit of man been more invocative of divine aid than it is today and, therefore, never before has a greater revelation been on its way. What that revelation will be, we cannot know. The revelation of the nature of God has been a slow unfolding process, paralleled by the evolutionary growth of the human consciousness. It is not for us to define or limit it with our concrete thinking, but to prepare for it, to unfold our intuitive perception, and to live in expectation of the revealing light. (7-140/1)

16. Another great Approach of divinity and another spiritual revelation are now possible. A new revelation is hovering over mankind and the One Who will bring it and implement it is drawing steadily nearer to us. What this great approach will bring to mankind, we do not yet know. It will surely bring us as definite results as did all the earlier revelations and the missions of Those Who came in response to humanity's earlier demands. The World War has purified mankind. A new heaven and earth are on their way. What does the orthodox theologian and churchman mean when he uses the words "a new heaven"? May these words not signify something entirely new and a new conception as to the world of spiritual realities? May not the Coming One bring us a new revelation as to the very nature of God Himself? Do we yet know all that can be known about God? If so, God is very limited. May it not be possible that our present ideas of God, as the Universal Mind, as Love and as Will may be enriched by some new idea or quality for which we have as yet no name or word, and of which we have no slightest understanding? Each of the three present concepts of divinity—of the Trinity—were entirely new when first sequentially presented to the mind or consciousness of man.

For some years now the spiritual Hierarchy of our planet has been drawing nearer to humanity, and its approach is responsible for the great concepts of freedom which are so close to the hearts of men everywhere.

The dream of brotherhood, of fellowship, of world co-operation and of peace, based on right human relations, is becoming clearer in our minds. We are also visioning a new and vital world religion, a universal faith which will have its roots in the past, but which will make clear the new dawning beauty and the coming vital revelation.   (8-148/9)

17.   I would point out that the two greatest revealing Agents Who have ever come to earth within the range of modern history, made the following simple revelations to humanity:

i. The cause of all human suffering is desire and personal selfishness. Give up desire and you will be free.

ii. There is a way of liberation and it leads to illumination.

iii. It profits man nothing to gain the whole world and lose his soul.

iv. Every human being is a Son of God.

v. There is a way of liberation and it is the way of love and sacrifice.

The lives of these Revealers were symbolic representations of that which They taught, and the rest of Their teaching is but an extension of Their central themes. Their contribution was an integral part of the general revelation of the ages which has led men from the primitive state of human existence to the complex state of modern civilisation. This general revelation can be called the Revelation of the Path which leads out of form to the Centre of all life; the purity of this revelation has been preserved down the ages by a small handful of disciples, initiates and true esotericists, who have always been present upon the Earth—defending the simplicity of that teaching, seeking for those who could respond to and recognise the germ or seed of truth, and training men to take Their place and to tread the way of intuitive perception. One of the major tasks of the Hierarchy is to seek for and find those who are sensitive to revelation, and whose minds are trained so that they can formulate the emerging truths in such a way that they reach the ears of the world thinkers, relatively unchanged. All revelation, however, when put into words and word forms, loses something of its divine clarity.

Much of the revelation of the past has come along the line of the religious impulse and, as the illusion has deepened and grown in time, the original simplicity (as it was conveyed by its Revealers) has been lost. All basic revelations are presented in the simplest forms. Accretion after accretion crept in; the minds of men made the teaching complex through their mental dissertations, until the great theological systems were built up, which we call, for instance, the Christian Church and the Buddhist system. Their Founders would have much difficulty in recognising the two or three fundamental and divine facts or truths which They sought to reveal and emphasise, so great is the mantle of illusion which has been thrown over the simple pronouncements of the Christ and of the Buddha. The vast cathedrals and the pompous ceremonies of the orthodox are far removed from the humble way of life of the Christ, the Master of all the Masters, and the Teacher alike of angels and of men, and from the simplicity of His present way of life as He watches and waits for the return of His people to the simple way of spiritual realisation.   (10-185/6)

18. Much of the true revelation since the time of Christ, has come to the world along the line of science. . . . The revelations of science, when basic and fundamental, are as divine as those of religion, but both have been prostituted to meet human demand. The era is close at hand when science will bend every effort to heal humanity's sores, and build a better and happier world.

The revelations of science, though focussed often through one man or woman, are more specifically the result of group endeavour and of trained group activity, than are the revelations of religion, so called. (10-187/8)

19. There is a little less illusion gathered around the revelations of science than has gathered around the revelations of what humanity calls the more definitely spiritual truths. One reason lies in the fact that the last great spiritual revelation, given by the Christ, was given two thousand years ago, and the development of man's mind, and his responsiveness to truth has grown greatly since that time. Again, the revelations of science are largely the result of group tension, eventually focussed in one intuitive recipient, and the revelation is thereby protected.   (10-189)

20. The Path of Evolution is in fact the path of recognitions, leading to revelation. . . . From light to light we pass, from revelation to revelation, until we pass out of the realm of light into the realm of life which is, as yet to us, pure darkness.   (10-205)

28. ILLUMINATION

1. By illumination I do not mean the light in the head. That is incidental and phenomenal, and many truly intuitive people are entirely unaware of this light. The light to which I refer is that which irradiates the Way. It is the "light of the intellect", which really means that which illumines the mind and which can reflect itself in that mental apparatus which is held "steady in the light". (10-3)

2. It is illumination that the majority of aspirants . . . must seek; and they must cultivate the power to use the mind as a reflector of soul light, turning it upon the levels of glamour, and therefore dissipating it. The difficulty, my brothers, is to do so when in the midst of the agonies and deceptions of glamour. It requires a quiet withdrawing in mind and thought and desire from the world in which the personality habitually works, and the centering of the consciousness in the world of the soul, there silently and patiently to await developments, knowing that the light will shine forth, and illumination eventually take place. (10-82)

3. The ordinary light of the ordinary man, which is similar to the headlights of a car and their self-sufficient blaze, serves only to intensify the problem and fails to penetrate into the mists and the fog. It simply throws it into relief so that its density and its deterring effects become the more apparent. The condition of fog is revealed—but that is all. So it is on the astral plane in relation to glamour; the light which is in man, self-induced and self-generated, fails ever to penetrate into or to dissipate the gloom and the foggy miasmic conditions. The only light which can dissipate the fogs of glamour and rid the life of its ill effects, is that of the soul, which—like a pure dispelling beam—possesses the curious and unique quality of revelation, of immediate dissipation, and of illumination. The revelation vouchsafed is different to that of the intuition, for it is the revelation of that which the glamour veils and hides, which is a revelation unique to the astral plane and conditioned by its laws. (10-139)

4. In defining *illumination* as the antithesis of glamour, it is obvious that my remarks must necessarily be limited to certain aspects of illumination and will only concern those directed forms of work and those presentations of the problem which will concern the use of light upon the astral plane . . . There are many other definitions possible, for the light of the soul is like an immense searchlight, the beams of which can be

turned in many directions, and focussed on many levels. We are, however, only concerned here with its specialised use.

Illumination and the light of knowledge can be regarded as synonymous terms, and many glamours can be dissipated and dispersed when subjected to the potency of the informative mind, for the mind is essentially the subduer of emotion through the presentation of fact. The problem is to induce the individual, or the race or nation, which is acting under the influence of glamour, to call in the mental power of assessing the situation, and subject it to a calm, cold scrutiny. Glamour and emotion play into each other's hands, and feeling runs so strong usually in relation to glamour, that it is impossible to bring in the light of knowledge with ease and effectiveness.

Illumination and perception of truth, are also synonymous terms, but it should be remembered that the truth in this case is not truth on the abstract planes, but concrete and knowable truth—truth which can be formulated and expressed in concrete form and terms. Where the light of truth is called in, glamour automatically disappears, even if only for a temporary period. But, again, difficulty arises because few people care to face the actual truth, for it involves eventually the abandonment of the beloved glamour, and the ability to recognise error and to admit mistakes, and this the false pride of the mind will not permit. Again, I would assure you that humility is one of the most potent factors in releasing the illuminating power of the mind, as it reflects and transmits the light of the soul. The determined facing of the factual life, and the stern recognition of truth—coldly, calmly and dispassionately—will greatly facilitate the calling in of the flood of illumination which will suffice to dispel glamour.   (10-144/5)

5. *The Technique of Light*. By means of this technique, the illumined mind assumes control over the astral or emotional body and dissipates glamour. When light pours in, glamour fades out. Illumination dominates and the vision of reality can be seen. This technique is related to Raja Yoga, and its goal is the second initiation; it produces ability to tread the Path of Discipleship, and enables the man to "live a life, enlightened by divinity". Illumination is the applied *power of transformation*.   (10-171/2)

29. THE INTUITION

1. The intuition is a growth, primarily, in sensitivity and in an inner response to the soul. This must be cultivated with care, and no attention should be paid to the factor of time. (5-595)

2. (The disciple) learns, finally, to substitute the intuition—with its swiftness and its infallibility—for the slow and laborious work of the mind, with its deviousness, its illusions, its errors, its dogmatisms and its separative thinking and cultures. (6-415)

3. That which is the opposite pole of illusion is, as you well know, the intuition. The intuition is that recognition of reality which becomes possible as glamour and illusion disappear. An intuitive reaction to truth will take place when—along a particular line of approach to truth—the disciple has succeeded in quieting the thought-form-making propensities of the mind, so that light can flow directly, and without any deviation, from the higher spiritual worlds. The intuition can begin to make its presence felt, when glamour no longer grips the lower man, and a man's low or high desires, interpreted emotionally or self-centredly, can no longer come between his brain consciousness and the soul. Fleeting moments of this high freedom come to all true aspirants at times, during their life struggle. They have then an intuitive flash of understanding. The outline of the future and the nature of truth sweeps momentarily through their consciousness, and life is never again exactly the same thing. They have had guarantee that all struggle is warranted and will evoke its adequate reward. (10-67)

4. The intuition is a higher power than is the mind, and is a faculty latent in the Spiritual Triad; it is the power of pure reason, an expression of the buddhic principle, and lies beyond the world of the ego and of form. Only when a man is an initiate can the exercise of the true intuition become normally possible. By that I mean that the intuition will then be as easily operative as is the mind principle in the case of an actively intelligent person. The intuition, however, will make its presence felt much earlier in extremity or on urgent demand. (10-81/2)

5. Let us now consider the intuition, which is the opposite of illusion, remembering that illusion imprisons a man upon the mental plane, and surrounds him entirely with man-made thought-forms, barring out escape into the higher realms of awareness or into that loving service which must be given in the lower worlds of conscious, manifested effort.

The major point I would seek to make here, is that the intuition is the source or the bestower of revelation. Through the intuition, progressive understanding of the ways of God in the world and on behalf of humanity, are revealed; through the intuition, the transcendence and the immanence of God is sequentially grasped, and man can enter into that pure knowledge, that inspired reason, which will enable him to comprehend not only the processes of nature in its fivefold divine expression, but also the underlying causes of these processes, proving them effects and not initiatory events; through the intuition man arrives at the experience of Kingdom of God, and discovers the nature, the type of lives and of phenomena, and the characteristics of the Sons of God as They come into manifestation. Through the intuition, some of the plans and purposes working out through the manifested created worlds, are brought to the attention, and he is shown in what way he and the rest of humanity can co-operate and hasten the divine purpose; through the intuition, the laws of the spiritual life, which are the laws governing God Himself, conditioning Shamballa, and guiding the Hierarchy, are brought to his notice progressively and as he proves capable of appreciating them and working them. (10-135/6)

6. *"The triple light of the Intuition"*. This light is formed by the blending of the light of the personal self, focussed in the mind, the light of the soul, focussed in the Angel, and the universal light which the Presence emits; this, when done with facility through concentration and long practice, will produce two results:

i. There will suddenly dawn upon the disciple's waiting mind (which still remains the agent of reception) the answer to his problem, the clue to what is needed to bring relief to humanity, the information desired which, when applied, will unlock some door in the realm of science, psychology or religion. This door, when opened, will bring relief or release to many. As before I have told you, the intuition is never concerned with individual problems or enquiries, as so many self-centred aspirants think. It is purely impersonal and only applicable to humanity in a synthetic sense.

ii. The "intruding agent of light" (as the *Old Commentary* calls these adventuring intuitives) is recognised as one to whom can be entrusted some revelation, some new impartation of truth, some significant expansion from a seed of truth already given to the race. He then sees a vision, hears a voice, registers a message, or—highest form of all—

he becomes a channel of power and light to the world, a conscious Embodiment of divinity, or a Custodian of a divine principle. These forms constitute true revelation, imparted or embodied; they are still rare, but will increasingly be developed in humanity.   (10-181/2)

7. The intuition is not a welling forth of love to people and, therefore, an understanding of them. Much that is called the intuition is recognition of similarities and the possession of a clear analytical mind. Intelligent people who have lived in the world for some time and who have experienced much, and who have contacted many other people, can usually sum up with facility the problems and dispositions of others, provided they are interested. This they must not, however, confound with the intuition.

The intuition has no relation to psychism, either higher or lower; the seeing of a vision, the hearing of the Voice of the Silence, a pleased reaction to teaching of any kind, does not infer the functioning of the intuition. It is not only the seeing of symbols, for that is a special sort of perception and the capacity to tune in on the Universal Mind upon that layer of Its activity which produced the pattern-forms on which all etheric bodies are based. It is not intelligent psychology, and a loving desire to help. That emanates from the interplay of a personality, governed by a strong soul orientation, and the group-conscious soul.

Intuition is the synthetic understanding which is the prerogative of the soul, and it only becomes possible when the soul, on its own level, is reaching in two directions: towards the Monad, and towards the integrated and, perhaps (even if only temporarily) co-ordinated and at-oned personality. It is the first indication of a deeply subjective unification which will find its consummation at the third initiation.

Intuition is a comprehensive grip of the principle of universality, and when it is functioning there is, momentarily at least, a complete loss of the sense of separateness. At its highest point, it is known as that Universal Love which has no relation to sentiment or to the affectional reaction, but is, predominantly, in the nature of an identification with all beings. Then is true compassion known; then does criticism become impossible; then only, is the divine germ seen as latent in all forms.

Intuition is light itself, and when it is functioning, the world is seen as light and the light bodies of all forms become gradually apparent. This brings with it the ability to contact the light centre in all forms, and thus again an essential relationship is established and the sense of superiority and separateness recedes into the background.   (10-2/3)

8. The intuition (as the philosopher understands it) is the ability to arrive at knowledge through the activity of some innate sense, apart from the reasoning or logical process. It comes into activity when the resources of the lower mind have been used, explored and exhausted. Then, and then only, the true intuition begins to function. It is the sense of synthesis, the ability to think in wholes, and to touch the world of causes. (16-516)

9. Something of the quality and the revelatory power of the intuition is known by all disciples; it constitutes at times (from its very rarity) a major "spiritual excitement". It produces effects and stimulation; it indicates future receptivity to dimly sensed truths, and is allied—if you could but realise it—with the entire phenomena of prevision. A registration of some aspect of intuitional understanding is an event of major importance in the life of the disciple who is beginning to tread the Path to the Hierarchy. It provides testimony, which he can recognise, of the existence of know-ledges, wisdom and significances, of which the intelligentsia of humanity are not yet aware; it guarantees to him the unfolding possibility of his own nature, a realisation of his divine connections, and the possibility of his ultimate highest spiritual attainment. (18-131)

30. SOUL AWARENESS

1. When humanity is assured of divinity and of immortality, and has en-tered into a state of knowledge as to the nature of the soul and of the king-dom in which that soul functions, its attitude to daily life and to current affairs will undergo such a transformation that we shall verily and indeed see the emergence of a new heaven and a new earth. Once the central en-tity within each human form is recognised and known for what it es-sentially is, and once its divine persistence is established, then we shall necessarily see the beginning of the reign of divine law on earth—a law imposed without friction and without rebellion. . . . When men, through meditation and group service, have developed an awareness of their own controlled and illumined minds, they will find themselves initiated into a consciousness of true being, and into a state of knowledge which will prove to them the fact of the soul, beyond all doubt or question-ing. (14-94/6)

2. When the consciousness of the soul, incarnate in a human form, arrives at a realisation of the futility of material *ambition,* it marks a high stage of personality integration, and precedes a period of change or a shift in *activity.* During this stage upon the Path of Return, the shift of the consciousness is away from the physical body altogether, into the etheric or vital body, and from thence into the astral body. There duality is sensed and the battle of the pairs of opposites takes place. The disciple makes his *appearance* as Arjuna. Only after the battle and only when Arjuna has made his fateful decisions, is it possible for him to make his approach upon the mental plane to the soul. This he does by:

i. Realising himself as a soul and not as a form. This involves a process of what is called "divine reflection", which works out in two ways. The soul now begins definitely to reject the form, and the man, through whom the soul is experiencing and expressing itself, is himself rejected by the world in which he lives.

ii. Discovering the group to which he belongs, blocking his way of approach until he discovers the way of approach by service.

iii. Identifying himself with his group upon his own ray, and so earning the right to make his approach, because he has learnt the lesson that "he travels not alone".

Then comes that peculiar stage of transcendent *aspiration,* wherein desire for individual experience is lost, and only the longing to function as a conscious part of the greater Whole remains.   (15-332)

31. MEDITATION

(a) WHAT IS MEDITATION?

You must learn to give a wider connotation to the word "meditation" than you have hitherto given. Concentrated thought is part of the planetary meditation; planning with care for the helping of the needy and pursuing all avenues of thinking to make that plan useful and effective, is meditation; laying oneself open to spiritual impression, and thus to co-operation with the Hierarchy, is meditation; in this enumeration of meditative possibilities I have not touched upon the major creative meditation which is responsible for the evolutionary process and the controlled moving forward of all the world of forms into greater glory and light.

The work hitherto done in (some) occult groups . . . has been nothing but the learning of a needed concentration. . . . The mystical type of meditation is of ancient formulation, and its use indicates the next step for the masses of men; the practice of mystical meditation is not that which should be followed by aspirants and disciples who seek to work in an Ashram in co-operation with the Plan and under the guidance of a Master.

Meditation only becomes effective creatively and on all the three planes in the three worlds, when the antahkarana is in process of construction. The worlds of the personality are the worlds of the third divine aspect and the creation of thought-forms therein (as usually carried forward by the concrete mind) is related to form, to the acquisition of that which is desired, and dedicated largely to the material values. But when a man is beginning to function as a soul-infused personality and is occupied with the task of rendering himself sensitive to the higher spiritual impression, then the creative work of the Spiritual Triad can be developed and a higher form of creative meditation can be employed. It is a form which each person has to find and discover for himself, because it must be the expression of his own spiritual understanding, initiated by a conscious construction or creation of the antahkarana and subject to impression from the Ashram with which he may be affiliated. (6-235/6)

(b) MEDITATION: OCCIDENTAL AND ORIENTAL

The occidental has in view the withdrawal of his consciousness to the heart at first, for already he works so much with the head centres. He works more by the use of collective forms and not individual mantrams; he does not work so much in isolation as his oriental brother, but has to find his centre of consciousness even in the noise and whirl of business life and in the throngs of great cities. He employs collective forms for the attainment of his ends, and the awakening of the heart centre shows itself in service. Hence the emphasis laid in the occident on the heart meditation and the subsequent life of service. (2-113)

(c) DANGERS OF MEDITATION

1. In the Aryan root-race, the attempt is being made to bridge the gap between the higher and the lower and, by centering the consciousness in the lower mind and later in the causal, to tap the higher until the down-

flow from that higher will be continuous. With most of the advanced students at present all that is felt is occasional flashes of illumination, but later will be felt a steady irradiation. Both methods carry their own dangers. In Atlantean days, meditation tended to over-stimulation of the emotions and although men touched great heights, yet they also touched great depths. Sex magic was unbelievably rampant. The solar plexus was apt to be over vivified, the triangles were not correctly followed, and the lower centres were caught in the reaction of the fire with dire results.

The dangers now are different. The development of mind carries with it the dangers of selfishness, of pride, of blind forgetfulness of the higher that it is the aim of the present method to offset. If the adepts of the dark path attained great powers in Atlantean days, they are still more dangerous now. Their control is much more widespread. Hence the emphasis laid on service, and on the steadying of the mind as an essential in the man who seeks to progress and to become a member of the Brotherhood of Light.   (2-111/2)

2. Meditation is dangerous and unprofitable to the man who enters upon it without the basis of a good character and of clean living. Meditation then becomes only a medium for the bringing in of energies which but serve to stimulate the undesirable aspects of his life, just as the fertilising of a garden full of weeds will produce a stupendous crop of them, and so crush out the weak and tiny flowers. Meditation is dangerous where there is wrong motive, such as desire for personal growth and for spiritual powers, for it produces, under these conditions only a strengthening of the shadows in the vale of illusion, and brings to full growth the serpent of pride, lurking in the valley of selfish desire. Meditation is dangerous when the desire to serve is lacking. Service is another word for the utilisation of soul force for the good of the group. Where this impulse is lacking, energy may pour into the bodies, but—lacking use and finding no outlet—will tend to over-stimulate the centres, and produce conditions disastrous to the neophyte. Assimilation and elimination are laws of the soul life as well as of the physical life, and when this simple law is disregarded, serious consequences will follow as inevitably as in the physical body.

. . . All work done by students must be done entirely in the head and from the head. There is the seat of the Will, or Spirit aspect, working through the soul.   (4-204/5)

3. Meditation involves the living of a one-pointed life always and every day. This perforce puts an undue strain on the brain cells, for it brings

quiescent cells into activity and awakens the brain consciousness to the light of the soul. This process of ordered meditation, when carried forward over a period of years and supplemented by meditative living and one-pointed service, will successfully arouse the entire system, and bring the lower man under the influence and control of the spiritual man; it will awaken also the centres of force in the etheric body, and stimulate into activity that mysterious stream of energy which sleeps at the base of the spinal column. When this process is carried forward with care and due safeguards, and under direction, and when the process is spread over a long period of time, there is little risk of danger, and the awakening will take place normally and under the law of being itself.

. . . I cannot impress too strongly upon aspirants in all occult schools, that the yoga for this transition period is the yoga of one-pointed intent, of directed purpose, of a constant practice of the Presence of God, and of ordered regular meditation carried forward systematically and steadily over years of effort.

When this is done with detachment and is paralleled by a life of loving service, the awakening of the centres and the raising of the sleeping fire of kundalini will go forward with safety and sanity, and the whole system will be brought to the requisite stage of "aliveness". I cannot too strongly advise students against the following of intensive meditation processes for hours at a time, or against practices which have for their objective the arousing of the fires of the body, the awakening of a particular centre, and the moving of the serpent fire. The general world stimulation is so great at this time, and the average aspirant is so sensitive and finely organised, that excessive meditation, a fanatical diet, the curtailing of hours of sleep, or undue interest in and emphasis upon psychic experience, will upset the mental balance and often do irretrievable harm. (13-18/9)

(d) VISUALISATION

1. The secret of all true meditation work in its earlier stages, is the power to visualise. This is the first stage to be mastered. Disciples should lay the emphasis upon this process; in it lies eventually the ability to use the creative powers of the imagination, plus mental energy, as a measure to further the ends of the Hierarchy and to carry out the Divine Plan. All the new processes in meditation techniques (for which the New Age may be responsible) must and will embody visualisation as a primary step for the following reasons:

i. Visualisation is the initial step in the demonstration of the occult law, that "energy follows thought". . . .

ii. The power to visualise is the form-building aspect of the creative imagination. . . . This process of energy direction can become a spiritual habit, if disciples would begin to do it slowly and gradually. . . .

iii. The power to visualise correctly is one definite mode of ascertaining truth or falsity. . . .

This visualising process and this use of the imagination, form the first two steps in the activity of thought-form building. It is with these self-created forms—embodying spiritual ideas and divine purpose—that the Masters work and hierarchical purpose takes shape. Therefore, my disciples, it is essential that you begin with deliberation and slowly to work in this manner, and to use the above information constructively and creatively. The need of the times is increasingly great and the utmost of work and of purpose is desired. (5-89/91)

2. See before you *a wheel of fire with seven spokes*. See it immediately before your eyes. Then, by an act of the creative imagination, see yourself as if you were that hub. From that central position, send out the seven streams of living love, radiating upon the world. When you do this, you serve and are, at the same time, completely protected This exercise can become instantaneous and effective. It generates a protective force, and at the same time makes you *a living centre of light and love*. (5-156)

(e) REALISATIONS RESULTING FROM MEDITATION

1. If the student but provides the right conditions, if he conforms to the necessary rules, if he aims always at regularity, at calmness, at that inner concentration that holds the mystery of the High Places, he will on certain occasions and with ever-increasing frequency awake to some definite realisations. These realisations will be the outer recognition of inner results, and will be the guarantee to him that he is on the right path. But I would here point out again that these results are only achieved after long practice, strenuous struggle, diligent disciplining of the threefold lower man, and consecrated service to the world. (2-281/2)

2. Always the calling forth of the response must be the work of the pupil, and the hour of that response depends upon the earnestness of his work, the consecration of his service, and his karmic liabilities. When he

merits certain response it will be demonstrated in his stars, and naught can hinder or delay. Equally, naught can really hasten, so the pupil need not waste time in doleful ponderings upon the lack of response. His is the part to obey the rules, to conform to the forms laid down, to ponder and wisely adhere to the prescribed instructions, and to definitely work and to ardently serve his fellow men. When he has done all this, when he has built the necessary vibrating material into his three lower bodies, when he has aligned them with the body egoic (even if only for a brief minute) suddenly he may see, suddenly he may hear, suddenly he may sense a vibration, and then forever he may say that faith is merged in sight, and aspiration has become recognition. (2-295)

3. Meditation is so oft regarded as the means for establishing soul contact. People oft forget, however, that this contact is brought about very frequently by an inner reflective attitude of mind, by a life given to service and selflessness, and by a determination to discipline the lower nature, so that it may become a true channel for the soul. When these three methods of development are fully expressed and become a life tendency or permanent habits, then meditation can be shifted into another category of usefulness and serve as a technique for the development of the intuition and for the solution of group problems. (5-349)

4. The disciple and the initiate are learning the technique (through meditation) whereby the Mind of God, the Universal Mind, or the thinking process of the planetary Logos, can be recorded and registered. For the majority, at present, the knowledge of the divine thought (as registered by disciples, as it works out in the emerging Plan, and as it gives livingness to life purpose) is reached through the Ashram. The Master imparts the nature of the Plan or the Purpose—according to the status of the initiate—and that is accepted by him under the Law of Free Occult Obedience. But the disciple or the initiate must not remain forever dependent upon the transmission of the divine thought to him by Those more advanced than he. He must learn to make his own contacts and to tap the "raincloud" for himself. He must—unaided—penetrate into the thinking processes (by permitted spiritual telepathy or impressibility) of Sanat Kumara. (6-154)

5. Your meditation should now be regarded by you as a process of penetration, carried forward as an act of service, with the intent to bring enlightenment to others. (6-313)

6. The future holds for each and all who duly strive, who unselfishly serve and occultly meditate, the promise of knowing Those Who already have full knowledge of the struggler. Therein lies the hope for the student of meditation; as he struggles, as he fails, as he perseveres, and as he laboriously reiterates from day to day the arduous task of concentration and of mind control, there stand on the inner side Those Who know him, and Who watch with eager sympathy the progress that he makes.   (2-258)

(f)   MEDITATION AND SERVICE

Man has to consider the particular *band of servers* to which he may be affiliated. Any man who is ready for occult meditation, must have demonstrated first for many lives his intelligent willingness to serve and to work among the sons of men. Unselfish service is the bedrock of the life of the occultist, and danger lurks when it exists not, and occult meditation carries a menace. Hence, the man must be an active worker in some part of the field of the world, and on the inner planes he must likewise be playing his part. Certain things will then have to be considered by the Teacher:

i. The group work a man is doing and how best he may be qualified to serve better in that group.

ii. The type of a man's work, and his relationship in that work to his associates—a very important occult factor—will be carefully weighed before a meditation is assigned, and certain types of meditation (perhaps desired by the man himself) may be withheld on account of their being unsuited to the work in hand, and because of their tendency to develop certain qualities which might handicap the server in his work. Those meditations which will increase ability to *serve* will ever be the aim. The greater aim includes, after all, the lesser.   (2-48/9)

32.   DISCIPLESHIP

1. A disciple is one who above all else, is pledged to do three things:

i. To serve humanity.

ii. To co-operate with the Plan of the Great Ones as he sees it, and as best he may.

iii. To develop the powers of the Ego, to expand his consciousness until he can function on the three planes in the three worlds, and in the causal body, and to follow the guidance of the higher self and not the dictates of his threefold lower manifestation.

A disciple is one who is beginning to comprehend group work, and to change his centre of activity from himself (as the pivot around which everything revolves) to the group centre.

A disciple is one who realises simultaneously the relative significance of each unit of consciousness, and also its vast importance. His sense of proportion is adjusted, and he sees things as they are; he sees people as they are; he sees himself as he inherently is, and seeks then to become that which he is.

A disciple realises the life or force side of nature, and to him the form makes no appeal. He works with force and through force; he recognises himself as a force centre within a greater centre, and his is the responsibility of directing the energy which may pour through him into channels through which the group can be benefited.

The disciple knows himself to be—to a greater or less degree—an outpost of the Master's consciousness, viewing the Master in a twofold sense:

i. As his own egoic consciousness.

ii. As the centre of his group; the force animating the units of the group and binding them into a homogeneous whole.

A disciple is one who is transferring his consciousness out of the personal into the impersonal, and during the transition stage much of difficulty and of suffering is necessarily endured. These difficulties arise from various causes:

i. The disciple's lower self, which rebels at being transmuted.

ii. A man's immediate group, friends, or family, who rebel at his growing impersonality. They do not like to be acknowledged as one with him on the life side, and yet separate from him where desires and interests lie. Yet the law holds good, and only in the essential life of the soul can true unity be cognised. In the discovery as to what is form, lies much of sorrow for the disciple, but the road leads to perfect union eventually.

The disciple is one who realises his responsibility to all units who come under his influence—a responsibility of co-operating with the plan of evolution as it exists for them, and thus to expand their consciousness and teach them the difference between the real and the unreal, between life and form. This he does most easily by a demonstration in his own life as to his goal, his object, and his centre of consciousness. (1-71/2)

2. Each and all has his place in the Plan, would he but qualify by doing the necessary work. That work should be :

An endeavour to recognise the Divine within each one. In this manner the true occult obedience, which is an essential in all occult training, will be fostered and developed, being not based, as is so often seen, on personality, but on that instinctive realisation of a Master, and the willing following that comes from the recognition of His powers, the purity of His life and aims, and the profundity of His knowledge.

An endeavour to think in group terms and clearly for oneself, not depending upon the word of others for clarification.

An endeavour to purify and refine all the bodies and make them more reliable servants.

An endeavour to equip throughout the mental vehicle, and to restore within it the facts upon which extended knowledge may be based.

If these things are done, great will be the day of opportunity. (2-309/10)

3. In the rigid disciplining of yourself comes eventual perfection. To the disciple naught is too small to undertake, for in the rigid adjustment of the details of the lower world life comes, at the end, attainment of the goal. The life of the disciple becomes not easier as the Gate is neared, but ever the watch must be more thorough, ever right action must be taken with no regard to result, and ever each body in all its aggregate of detail must be wrestled with and subjugated. Only in the thorough comprehension of the axiom "Know thyself" will come that understanding that enables man to wield the law and know the inner working of the system from the centre to the periphery. Struggle, strive, discipline, and rejoicingly serve, with no reward save the misunderstanding and the abuse of those who follow *after*—this is the role of the disciple. (2-310)

4. It is not the part of a coward, in these matters concerning the subjective life, to move with caution and with care; it is the part of discretion. The aspirant, therefore, has three things to do:

i. Purify, discipline and transmute his threefold lower nature.

ii. Develop knowledge of himself, and equip his mental body by good deeds and thought.

iii. Serve his race in utter self-abnegation.

In doing this he fulfils the law, he puts himself in the right condition for training, fits himself for the ultimate application of the Rod of Initiation, and thus minimises the danger that attends the awakening of the fire.   (3-162)

5. As the aspirant progresses, he not only balances the pairs of opposites, but the secret of his brother's heart becomes revealed to him. He becomes an acknowledged force in the world, and is recognised as one who can be depended upon to serve. Men turn to him for assistance and help along his recognised line, and he begins to sound forth his note so as to be heard not only in human but in deva ranks as well. This he does, at this stage, through the pen in literature, through the spoken word in lecturing and teaching, through music, painting and art. He reaches the hearts of men in some way or another, and becomes a helper and server of his race.

. . . At this stage also the aspirant's life becomes an "instrument of destruction" in the occult sense of the term. Wherever he goes, the force which flows through him from the higher planes, and from his own inner God, produces at times peculiar results upon his environment. It acts as a stimulator of both the good and the evil. The lunar Pitris who form the bodies of his brothers and his own body are likewise stimulated, their activity is increased, and their power greatly aggravated. This fact is used by Those Who work on the inner side to bring about certain desired ends. This it is also which oft times temporarily causes the downfall of advanced souls. They cannot stand the force pouring into them, or upon them, and through the temporary over-stimulation of their centres and vehicles they go astray. This can be seen working out in groups as well as in individuals. But, inversely, if the lunar Lords of the lower self have been earlier subjugated and brought under control, then the effect of the force and energy contacted is to stimulate the response of the physical brain consciousness and the head centres to egoic contact. Then the otherwise destructive force becomes a factor for good and helpful stimulation, and can be used by Those Who know how, to lead men on to further illumination.

All these stages have to work out on all the three lower planes and in the three bodies; this they do according to the particular Ray and subray. In this fashion the work of the disciple is carried forward, and his testing and training carried out until the two circles of petals are unfolded, and the third is organised. Thus he is brought, through right direction of energy and wise manipulation of force currents, to the Portal of Initiation, and graduates out of the Hall of Learning into the great Hall of Wisdom—that Hall wherein he gradually becomes "aware" of forces, and powers, latent in his own Ego and egoic group. It is the Hall wherein he gains the right to use the force of the egoic group, for he can now be trusted to wield it only for the helping of humanity. After the fourth Initiation, he becomes a sharer in, and can be trusted with some part of the energy of the planetary Logos and thus be enabled to carry forward the Plans of that Logos for evolution.   (3-865/7)

33.   REQUIREMENTS NEEDED BY ASPIRANTS

1. The group of Teachers with whom the average aspirants and pro-bationary disciples may be in touch on the mental plane, are but men of like passions but with a longer experience upon the path and a wiser control of themselves. They do not work with aspirants because They personally like or care for them, but because the need is great and They seek those whom They can train. The attitude of mind that They look for is that of teachableness and the ability to record and refrain from questioning until more is known. Then the aspirant is urged to question everything. May I remind you of the words of one Teacher who said, "Know us for sane and balanced men who teach as we taught on earth, not flattering our pupils but disciplining them. We lead them on, not forcing them forward by feeding their ambitions by promises of power, but giving them information and leading them to use it in their work, knowing that right use of knowledge leads to experience and achievement of the goal."

How often does one find a student more occupied with the Master and what He will do than he is with his own side of the question! And yet the fitting of himself for service and the equipping of himself for useful co-operation is, or should be, his main preoccupation.

Inquiry about the Master is more interesting than inquiry about the needed qualifications for discipleship. Interest for the data available in relation to the Adepts, is more potent than the steadfast investigation into limitations and disabilities which should engross the aspirant's attention. Curiosity as to the habits and methods of specific Masters and Their ways of handling Their disciples, is more prone to be displayed than patient application to right habits and ways of work in the life of the would-be disciple. All these matters are side issues and only handicap and limit, and one of the first things we advise one who would enter into communication with the Masters, is to take his eyes off those things which concern him not, focus his attention on the needed steps and stages which should demonstrate in his life, and eliminate those wasted moments, moods and thought periods which so often occupy the major part of his thought life.

When a Master seeks to find those fitted to be instructed and taught by Him, He looks for three things first of all. Unless these are present, no amount of devotion or aspiration, and no purity of life and mode of living suffices. It is essential that all aspirants should grasp these three factors, and so save themselves much distress of mind and wasted motion.

i. The Master looks for the light in the head.

ii. He investigates the karma of the aspirant.

iii. He notes his service in the world.

Unless there is an indication that the man is what is termed esoterically "a lighted lamp" it is useless for the Master to waste His time. The light in the head, when present, is indicative of :

(a) The functioning to a greater or less extent of the pineal gland, which is (as is well known) the seat of the soul and the organ of spiritual perception. It is in this gland that the first physiological changes take place, incident upon soul contact and this contact is brought about through definite work along meditation lines, mind control, and the inflow of spiritual force.

(b) The aligning of the man on the physical plane with his Ego, soul or higher self, on the mental plane and the subordination of the physical plane life and nature to the impress and control of the soul. This is covered sufficiently in the first two or three chapters of *Letters on Occult Meditation,* and these should be studied by aspirants.

(c) The downflow of force via the sutratma, magnetic cord, or thread from the soul to the brain via the mind body. The whole secret of spiritual vision, correct perception and right contact, lies in proper appreciation of the above statement, and therefore the *Yoga Sutras of Patanjali* are ever the text-book of disciples, initiates and adepts, for therein are found those rules and methods which bring the mind under control, stabilise the astral body and so develop and strengthen the thread (from the) soul that it can and does become a veritable channel of communication between the man and his ego. The light of illumination streams down into the brain cavity and throws into objectivity three fields of knowledge. This is often forgotten, and hence the undue stress and premature interpretations of the partially illuminated disciple or probationer.

The light first throws into relief and brings into the foreground of consciousness those thought-forms and entities which depict the lower life, and which (in their aggregate) form the Dweller on the Threshold.

Thus the first thing of which the aspirant becomes aware, is that which he knows to be undesirable and the revelation of his own unworthiness and limitations, and the undesirable constituents of his own aura burst on his vision. The darkness which is in him is intensified by the light which glimmers faintly from the centre of his being, and frequently he despairs of himself and descends into the depths of depression. All mystics bear witness to this and it is a period which must be lived through until the pure light of day drives all shadows and darkness away, and little by little the life is brightened and lightened until the sun in the head is shining in all its glory.

(d) Finally, the light in the head is indicative of the finding of the Path and there remains then for the man to study and understand the technique whereby the light is centralised, intensified, entered and eventually becomes that magnetic line (like unto a spider's thread) which can be followed back until the source of the lower manifestation is reached and the soul consciousness is entered. The above language is symbolic and yet vitally accurate, but is expressed thus in order to convey information to those who know, and protect those who as yet know not.

"The path of the just is as a shining Light" and yet at the same time a man has to become that path itself. He enters the light and becomes the light and functions then as a lamp set in a dark place, carrying illumination to others and lighting the way before them.

The next point that a Master has to consider before admitting a man into His group, is whether or not such a step is karmically possible, or whether there exist in a man's record those conditions which negate his admission in this life.

There are three main factors to be considered separately and in their relation to each other.

First, are there such karmic obligations in a man's present life as would render it impossible for him to function as a disciple? In this connection it must be carefully borne in mind that a man can become a disciple and merit the attention of a Master only when his life counts for something in the world of men, when he is an influence in his sphere, and when he is moulding and acting upon the minds and hearts of other men.

Until that is the case it is waste of a Master's time to personally deal with him, for he can be adequately helped in other ways and has, for instance, much knowledge from books and teachers which is as yet theory and not practice, and much experience to pass through under the guidance of his own Ego, the Master in his heart. When a man is a disciple he is one because he can be used for working out the Plan of the Hierarchy, and can be influenced to materialise those endeavours which are planned to enable humanity to make the needed forward steps. This involves (in his physical plane life) time and thought, right circumstance, and other considerations, and it is quite possible for a man to have reached the stage *from the character standpoint,* where he merits the recognition of a Master, and yet have obligations and duties to work through which would handicap him for active service in some particular life. This the Master has to consider and this a man's own Ego also considers.

The result quite frequently at this time is that (perhaps unconsciously to the physical brain) a man will shoulder a great amount of experience, and undertake the working out of an abnormal amount of responsibility in one particular life, in order to free himself for service and chelaship in a later life. He works then at the equipping of himself for the next life, and at the patient performance of duty in his home, his circle of friends, and his business. He realises that from the egoic standpoint, one life is but a short matter and soon gone, and that by study, intelligent activity, loving service, and patient endurance, he is working out of those conditions which are preventing his prompt acceptance in a Master's group.

A Master also studies the condition of an aspirant's physical body and of the subtler bodies to see whether in them are to be found states of consciousness which would hinder usefulness and act as obstacles. These conditions are likewise karmic and must be adjusted before his admission among other chelas becomes possible. A sick physical body, an astral body prone to moods, emotions and psychic delusions, and a mental body uncontrolled or ill-equipped, are all dangerous to the student unless straightened out and perfected. A chela is subjected constantly to the play of force coming to him from three main sources:

i. His own Ego,

ii. His Master,

iii. The group of co-disciples,

and unless he is strong, purified and controlled, these forces will serve but to stimulate undesirable conditions, to foster that which should be eliminated and to bring to the surface all the hidden weaknesses. That this has to be done inevitably is so, but much must be done along this line before admission into a group of disciples; otherwise much of the Master's valuable time will perforce be given to the elimination and nullifying of the effects of the chela's violent reactions on other chelas in the same group. It is better to wait and work gradually and intelligently oneself, than force one's way unprepared into lines of forces before one can handle either them or their consequences.

Another factor that an adept has to consider, is whether there are in incarnation those chelas with whom a man has to work and who are karmically linked to him by ancient ties and old familiarity in similar work.

Sometimes it may be deemed wiser for a man to wait a little while before being permitted to step off the physical path, until a life comes in which his own co-workers, keyed to his vibration, and accustomed to work with him, are also in physical bodies, for a Master's group is entered in service to be rendered and specific work to be done, and not because a man is to receive a cultural training which will make him an adept some day. Chelas train themselves and when ready for any work, a Master uses them. They develop themselves and work out their own salvation, and as step by step is taken, their particular Master lays more and more responsibility upon them. He will train them in service technique, and in vibratory response to the Plan, but they learn to control themselves and to fit themselves for service.

There are other karmic factors to be considered by a Master, but these are the three paramount ones and of the most importance for aspirants to consider now. They are specified so that no true and earnest worker need be depressed and discouraged if he has no conscious link with the Master and is unaware of any affiliation with an esoteric group of chelas. It may not be because he is not fit. It may simply be because his Ego has chosen this life to clear the decks for later action, to eliminate hindrances in one or other, or all of the three lower bodies, or to wait for that time when his admission may count the most.

The third factor, that of service, for which the Master looks, is one upon which the aspirant has the least to say, and may very probably misinterpret. Spiritual ambition, the desire to function as the centre of a group, the longing to hear oneself speaking, teaching, lecturing, or writing, are often wrongly interpreted by the aspirant as service. The Master looks not at a worker's worldly force or status, not at the numbers of people who are gathered around his personality, but at the motives which prompt his activity and at the effect of his influence upon his fellow men. True service is the spontaneous outflow of a loving heart and an intelligent mind; it is the result of being in the right place and staying there; it is produced by the inevitable inflow of spiritual force, and not by strenuous physical plane activity; it is the effect of a man's being what he truly is, a divine Son of God, and not by the studied effect of his words or deeds. A true server gathers around him those whom it is his duty to serve and aid by the force of his life and his spiritualised personality, and not by his claims or loud speaking. In self-forgetfulness he serves; in self-abnegation he walks the earth, and he gives no thought to the magnitude or the reverse of his accomplishment and has no preconceived ideas as to his own value or usefulness. He lives, serves, works and influences, asking nothing for the separated self.

When a Master sees this manifestation in a man's life, as the result of the awakening of the inner light and the adjustment of his karmic obligations, then He sounds out a note and waits to see if the man recognises his own group note. On this recognition, he is admitted into his own group of co-workers, and can stand in the presence of his Master. (4-182/9)

2. A few simple suggestions I will give you. These can be useful to all sincere aspirants:

i. In the ordered regulation of the life comes eventual synthesis and the right control of time, with all that eventuates therefrom.

ii. In the right elimination of that which is secondary, and in a sense of rightly adjusted proportion, comes that accuracy and one-pointedness which is the hallmark of the occultist.

iii. In the right aspiration at the appointed time, comes the necessary contact and the inspiration for the work that has to be done.

iv. In the steady adherence to *self-appointed* rules, comes the gradual refining of the instrument, and the perfecting of the vehicles that will be—to the Master—the medium of help among many little ones. (18-11)

34. WHAT IS A DISCIPLE?

1. (Man) has used (the form side) and has been dominated by it. He has also suffered from it and consequently in time revolted, through utter satiety, from all that pertains to the material world. Dissatisfaction, disgust, distaste, and a deep fatigue are characteristic very frequently of those who are on the verge of discipleship. For what is a disciple? He is one who seeks to learn a new rhythm, to enter a new field of experience, and to follow the steps of that advanced humanity who have trodden ahead of him the path, leading from darkness to light, from the unreal to the real. He has tasted the joys of life in the world of illusion and has learnt their powerlessness to satisfy and hold him. Now he is in a state of transition between the new and the old states of being. He is vibrating between the condition of soul awareness and form awareness. He is "seeing double".

His spiritual perception grows slowly and surely as the brain becomes capable of illumination from the soul, via the mind. As the intuition develops, the radius of awareness grows and new fields of knowledge unfold.

The first field of knowledge receiving illumination, might be described as comprising the totality of forms to be found in the three worlds of human endeavour, etheric, astral and mental. The would-be disciple, through this process, becomes aware of his lower nature and begins to realise the extent of his imprisonment and (as Patanjali puts it) "the modifications of the versatile psychic nature". The hindrances to achievement and the obstacles to progress are revealed to him and his problem becomes specific. Frequently then he reaches the position in which Arjuna found himself, confronted by enemies who are those of his own household, confused as to his duty and discouraged as he seeks to balance himself between the pairs of opposites. His prayer then should be the famous prayer of India, uttered by the heart, comprehended by the head, and supplemented by an ardent life of service to humanity.

Unveil to us the face of the true spiritual sun,
Hidden by a disk of golden light,
That we may know the truth and do our whole duty
as we journey to Thy sacred feet.

As he perseveres and struggles, surmounts his problems and brings his desires and thoughts under control, the second field of knowledge is revealed—knowledge of the self in the spiritual body, knowledge of the Ego as it expresses itself through the medium of the causal body, . . . and awareness of that source of spiritual energy which is the motivating impulse behind the lower manifestation. The "disk of golden light" is pierced; the true sun is seen; the path is found and the aspirant struggles forward into ever clearer light.

As the knowledge of the self and as the consciousness of that which the self sees, hears, knows and contacts is stabilised, the Master is found; His group of disciples is contacted; the plan for the immediate share of work he must assume is realised, and gradually worked out on the physical plane. Thus the activity of the lower natures decreases, and the man little by little enters into conscious contact with his Master and his group. But this follows upon the "lighting of the lamp"—the aligning of the lower and higher, and the downflow of illumination to the brain.

It is essential that these points should be grasped and studied by all aspirants so that they may take the needed steps and develop the desired awareness. Until this is done, the Master, no matter how willing He may be, is powerless, and can take no steps to admit a man to His group and thus take him into His auric influence, making him an outpost of His consciousness. Every step of the way has to be carved out by a man himself, and there is no short or easy road out of darkness into light. (4-58/60)

2. The problem of all disciples remains the same. This is to live simultaneously the acutely sensitive inner life of the Pilgrim upon the path of life, of a human being in the world of human events; to live the group life of the pledged disciple, and the mass life of humanity; to fulfil his own spiritual destiny, through the medium of a controlled personality and, at the same time, to participate fully in the life of humanity upon Earth—this is no easy task. (16-498)

35. STATUS OF DISCIPLES

The true initiate has never made the slightest claim, either privately or publicly, to be an initiate. It is against the occult law, and too many people of no particular spiritual focus or intellectual capacity make these claims, and consequent harm has ensued, thus lowering the idea of the Hierarchy and the nature of adeptship in the eyes of the watching public. . . . The word "disciple" is the legitimate and non-controversial word (as well as the truthful word) to be used for all grades of workers in the Hierarchy, from the probationary disciple, loosely affiliated with certain disciples in that Hierarchy, up to and including the Christ Himself, the Master of all the Masters, and the Teacher alike of Angels and of men. . . . The unwholesome curiosity as to status and title . . . is a blight on many occult groups, leading to the full tide of competition, jealousy, criticism and claim-making, which distinguishes the majority of the occult groups, which renders futile so many of their publications, and which hinders the general public from receiving the teaching in its purity and simplicity. Status and title, place and position, count for nothing. *It is the teaching that counts*—its truth and its intuitive appeal.   (5-781)

36. REQUIREMENTS OF THE DISCIPLE

1. Present day troubles are largely due to the lack of intuitive perception in the past, and this fault lies primarily among the mystics of the world and not so much among the lower aspirants. The trouble has not lain in lack of idealism or even in lack of intelligence and sincerity, it consists in the failure to sacrifice the personality at all times in order to make the intuitive realisation demonstrate its realities. *Compromise* has been permitted and in the occult world compromise is forbidden. When indulged in, it leads to disaster and sweeps away eventually, in ruin and storm, the personalities of those who so stoop. People have sought to adjust the truth to the hour, instead of adjusting the hour to the truth, and in diplomacy they have endeavoured to bring about as much of the reality as they deem wise. The Masters are looking out for those with clear vision, uncompromising adherence to the truth as sensed, and capacity to drive steadily forward toward the ideal. This entails the following factors:

164

i. A recognition of that ideal through meditation.

ii. Its application to the present through one-pointedness.

iii. Removal of the old and hindering thought-forms through self-sacrifice.

iv. A refusal to compromise, through clear vision.

v. A discrimination that enables the disciple always to distinguish between the acts of an individual and the individual himself.

vi. Realisation that, in the occult work, it is not permitted to interfere with personal karma any more than it is permitted to shield from the consequences of action. This entails therefore a refusal to interfere in anyone's business—that is, as regards the personality life, and yet involves a refusal to shirk the business of the larger cause. It is essential that the workers learn to discriminate between the factors which make for personal liberty and those which militate against group liberty.

A result to be brought about by the present opportunity to work, is the bringing in of the new cycle and the new group of participants. Workers in the new era will be drawn from all groups and the test of their choice depends largely upon the measure of impersonality with which they work and the strength of their inner contact with the soul. It is not easy for any of you, therefore, submerged as you are in the smoke and roar of battle, to judge results with accuracy or to judge people with perfect propriety. These things have to be dealt with on the inner planes and are noted by the watching guides of the race. I would like here briefly to point out a few of the things for which the Great Ones look.

They look to see whether the inner flame—the result of effort wisely to work and think and do—burns with increased brilliance; they note whether it remains hidden and dim through the whirl of astral currents and by thought-forms of personal antagonism, ambition and envy. As a result of world work some will be drawn into closer connection with the work of the Hierarchy, and others will be temporarily set back. Capacity to dominate the astral and to work from mental levels will largely count.

They look to see who can struggle and contend for principle with personalities, and yet keep the link of love intact. This counts perhaps more than men realise and a man who can stand for principle and yet love all human beings—refusing compromise and yet refusing hate—has something rare to offer in these days, and the Great Ones can use him. See to it, therefore all of you who work, that with clear vision, upright purpose and firm undeviating action, you forge ahead. See to it that you deal with patience and forbearance with those of your brothers who choose the lesser principle and the lesser right, who sacrifice the good of the group for their own personal ends or who use unworthy methods. Give to them love and care and a ready helping hand, for they will stumble on the way and sound the depth of the law. Stand ready then to lift them up and to offer to them opportunities for service, knowing that service is the great healer and teacher.

The Great Ones look to see the faculty of pliability and adaptibility working out, that faculty of adaptation that is one of the fundamental laws of species which nature so wonderfully demonstrates. The transference of this law to the inner planes and its working out in the new cycle of effort must be undertaken. This law of adaptation involves the appreciation of the need, the recognition of the new force coming in with the new cycle and the consequent bringing together in wide synthesis, of the need and of the force, regarding the personal self simply as a focal point for action and transmutation. It involves the transmutation of the five senses and their extension into the subtler planes so that sight, hearing, touch, taste and smell are welded into one synthetic co-operating whole, for use in the great work. On the physical plane, these tend to the unification of the personal life and to the adaptation of the physical world to the needs of the personal self. On the subtler planes they must be transmuted until they are adequate to the needs of the group of which the individual forms a fragmentary part. The ability to do this is one of the things that the Great Ones look for in those individuals whose privilege it may be to inaugurate the New Age.

Above all They look for an enlarged channel from the soul to the physical brain, via the mind. Such an enlarged channel indicates that a man can be used. One might almost express it by saying that They look for the perfecting of the antahkarana, that channel of communication between the soul consciousness and the brain, whose possessor is one whom the Masters can successfully use. They are guided in Their choice of workers by a man's personally achieved capacity and by his own hard won ability. When there is capacity, ability, and faculty, then the Great Ones joyfully employ him. The wrong angle has been at times over-emphasised, and the reverse of this taught. The Masters must not be sought because a man seeks capacity. They will be found when a man *has* capacity—capacity that makes him available for group work and that can be extended under careful instruction into the higher powers of the soul. Leadership in groups controlling the work of the New Age will grow out of the discipline of the individual, and leaders will be found among those who sense the inner issue. Leadership that endures does not come to those who strive for place and power, nor for those who have their eyes only on outward conditions and overlook the underlying causes. Leadership does not come to those who place the personal self and its position and power before the good of the group. It comes enduringly to those who seek nothing for the separated self, to those who lose themselves in the good of the whole.   (4-136/40)

2. No glamour, no illusion can long hold the man who has set himself the task of treading the razor-edged Path which leads through the wilderness, through the thick-set forest, through the deep waters of sorrow and distress, through the valley of sacrifice and over the mountains of vision to the gate of Deliverance. He may travel sometimes in the dark (and the illusion of darkness is very real); he may travel sometimes in a light so dazzling and bewildering that he can scarcely see the way ahead; he may know what it is to falter on the Path, and to drop under the fatigue of service and of strife; he may be temporarily sidetracked and wander down the bypaths of ambition, of self-interest and of material enchantment, but the lapse will be but brief. Nothing in heaven or hell, on earth or elsewhere can prevent the progress of the man who has awakened to the illusion, who has glimpsed the reality beyond the glamour of the astral plane, and who has heard, even if only once, the clarion call of his own soul.

The astral plane is also the Kurukshetra, both of humanity as a whole and of the individual human unit. It is the battleground whereon must be found the Waterloo of every aspirant. In some one life, there comes an emotional crisis in which decisive action is taken, and the disciple proves his control of his emotional nature. This may take the form of some great and vital test, covering a brief time but calling forth every resource of wisdom and of purity that the disciple possesses, or it may be a long and protracted emotional strain, carried over many years of living. But in the attaining of success and in the achievement of clear vision and right discernment (through right discrimination) the disciple testifies to his fitness for the second initiation.

. . . The outcome of good is inevitable. It is however a question of a slow or a rapid realisation and liberation from the great world illusion, and to this end every aspirant is begged to work strenuously and to lend his aid. Every man who liberates himself, who sees clearly, and who releases himself from the glamour of illusion, aids in the Great Work. (4-223/4)

3. I here appeal to all who read these words to reconsecrate themselves, and to recognise the opportunity they have of a united effort towards world usefulness.

It might be of use here if I expressed quite simply the requirements needed to bring about the manifestation of individual purpose or of group spiritual purpose. These can be summed up in three words:

i. Power.

ii. Detachment.

iii. Non-criticism.

So often simple words are used and because of their every day connotation their true significance and esoteric value are lost.

Let me give you a few thoughts anent each of these, with application only to the creative work of white magic.

Power is dependent for expression upon two factors:

(a) Singleness of purpose.

(b) Lack of impediments.

Students would be amazed if they could see their *motives* as we see them who guide on the subjective side of experience. Mixed motive is universal. Pure motive is rare and where it exists there is ever success and achievement. Such pure motive can be entirely selfish and personal, or unselfish and spiritual, and in between, where aspirants are concerned, mixed in varying degree. According, however, to the purity of intent and the singleness of purpose, so will be the potency.

The Master of all the Masters has said, "If thine eye be single, thy whole body shall be full of light". These words which He enunciated, give us a principle underlying all the creative work, and we can link up the idea which He clothed in words with the symbol I have earlier described in this Treatise. Power, light, vitality, and manifestation! Such is the true procedure.

It will be obvious, therefore, why the manifested unit, man, is urged to be vital in his search and to cultivate his aspiration. When that aspiration is strong enough, he is then urged to achieve the capacity to "hold his mind steady in the light". When he can do this, he will achieve power and possess that single eye which will redound to the glory of the indwelling divinity. Before, however, he has mastered this process of development, he may not be trusted with power. The procedure is as follows: The individual aspirant begins to manifest somewhat soul purpose in his life on the physical plane. He is transmuting desire into aspiration and that aspiration is vital and real. He is learning the meaning of light. When he has mastered the technique of meditation (and with this certain schools in existence at present are concerned) he can proceed to handle power, because he will have learned to function as a divine Thinker. He is now co-operative and is in touch with the divine Purpose.

As all true students know, however, the number of impediments is legion. Hindrances and obstacles abound. Singleness of purpose may occasionally be realised in high moments, but it does not abide with us always. There are the hindrances of physical nature, of heredity and environment, of character, of time and conditions, of world karma, as well as individual karma. What shall then be done? I have only one word to say and that is *persist*. Failure never prevents success. Difficulties develop the strength of the soul. The secret of success is ever to stand steady and to be impersonal.

The second requirement is *detachment*. The worker in white magic must hold himself free as much as he can from identifying himself with that which he has created or has attempted to create. The secret for all aspirants is to cultivate the attitude of the onlooker and of the silent watcher, and, may I emphasise the word *silent*. Much true magical work comes to naught because of the failure of the worker and builder in matter to keep silent. By premature speech and too much talk, he slays that which he has attempted to create, the child of his thought is still-born. All workers in the field of the world should recognise the need for silent detachment, and the work before every student who reads these Instructions must consist in cultivating a detached attitude. It is a mental detachment which enables the thinker to dwell ever in the high and secret place, and from that centre of peace calmly and powerfully to carry out the work he has set before himself. He works in the world of men; he loves and comforts and serves; he pays no attention to his personality likes and dislikes, or to his prejudices and attachments; he stands as a rock of strength and as a strong hand in the dark to all whom he contacts. The cultivation of a detached attitude personally, with the attached attitude spiritually, will cut at the very roots of a man's life; but it will render back a thousandfold for all that it cuts away.

Much has been written anent attachment and the need to develop detachment. May I beg all students in the urgency of the present situation, to leave off reading and thinking about it aspirationally and to begin to practise it and demonstrate it.

Non-criticism is the third requirement. What shall I say about that?

Why is it regarded as so essential a requirement? Because criticism (analysis and, consequently, separativeness) is the outstanding characteristic of mental types and also of all co-ordinated personalities. Because criticism is a potent factor in swinging mental and emotional substance into activity, and so making strong impress upon the brain cells and working out into words. Because in a sudden burst of critical thought, the entire personality can be galvanised into a potent co-ordination, but of a wrong kind and with disastrous results. Because criticism being a faculty of the lower mind, can hurt and wound, and no man can proceed upon the Way as long as wounds are made and pain is knowingly given. Because the work of white magic and the carrying out of hierarchical purpose, meets with basic hindrances in the relations existing between its workers and disciples. In the pressure of the present opportunity there is no time for criticism to exist between workers. They hinder each other and they hinder the work.

I have upon me at this time a sense of urgency. I urge upon all those who read these Instructions to forget their likes and their dislikes and to overlook the personality hindrances which inevitably exist in themselves and in all who work upon the physical plane, handicapped by the personality. I urge upon all workers the remembrance that the day of opportunity is with us and that it has its term. This present type of opportunity will not last forever. The pettiness of the human frictions, the failures to understand each other, the little faults which have their roots in personality and which are, after all, ephemeral, the ambitions and illusions must all go. If the workers would practise detachment, knowing that the Law works and that God's purposes must come to an ultimate conclusion, and if they would learn never to criticise in thought or word, the salvaging of the world would proceed apace and the new age of love and illumination would be ushered in.   (4-557/61)

4. Those who are in preparation for initiation, must learn to work consciously with glamour; they must work effectively with the presented truth, ignoring any pain or suffering or mental questioning which is incident to personality rebellion and limitation; they must cultivate that "divine indifference" to personal considerations which is the outstanding hallmark of the trained initiate.   (5-27)

5. You are not yet initiate, and you have faults, limitations, points of darkness, and much inertia, and at the same time self-satisfaction. The tendency to self-defence is strong in some of you, and this produces an unwillingness to recognise faults or even to admit, hypothetically, that

faults may be present. The tendency of self-deprecation is strong in others, and it produces that over-emphasis of the personality which is so detrimental to real progress. In these tendencies (which are so usual) there lies real danger for the would-be initiate. I warn you to watch for the indications of these conditions, and to assume an attitude of willingness to listen and to admit the possibility of failure in the one case, and of self-forgetfulness in the other. Look yourselves and life squarely in the face, and fearlessly see things as they are in truth. Do this not because it is I who am suggesting to you that a situation may be thus or so, but because you are willing to face up to facts, and are ready for unexpected discoveries about yourselves. One of the first lessons which a disciple needs to learn, is that where he thinks he is strongest and where he finds the most satisfaction, is very frequently the point of greatest danger and of weakness. Astral conditions are oft seen reversed; hence the glamour which often overcomes a disciple. (5-77)

6. The lessons to be learnt by all disciples (before they can work with power in the world) might be expressed as the need to gain discrimination between :

  i. Primary principles and secondary principles, or between two rights:

    (a) A greater and a lesser right.

    (b) That which is right for you but which may not be right for others.

  ii. Between one's personal dharma, obligation, and individual duties, and one's group responsibilities and relationships.

  iii. Between the needs which group work evidences and demands, and those of the individual.

  iv. Between essentials and non-essentials. (5-297)

7. Under the Law governing disciples, opportunities will inevitably arise which will enable you to adjust past conditions and any faulty handling. See that the dawning spirit of love irradiates your life, and pours through you to others, and see to it also that you render back to all, the love which you have received and will receive. (5-532)

8. Your insistence upon making the transition out of the lower into the higher life, and your pledge to your soul that you will recognise no impediment or handicap, has been noted. Assistance, therefore, will be given to you, and I shall be glad, through suggestion and watchful co-operation, to aid you on your way. I would remind you at this point also that

under the Laws of the New Age, such assistance is given only to those who have transcended selfish aspiration, and have lost sight of their own progress in the desire to serve. (5-551)

(a) SINCERITY

Constant study (of papers), and the apprehension by the ear and eye of statements anent the Ageless Wisdom, serve only to increase responsibility, or produce brain fatigue and staleness, with subsequent revolt from instruction. Only that which is brought into use in the life is of practical value and retains its livingness. Sincerity is the first thing for which those of us who teach inevitably look. (14-xvii)

(b) SENSITIVITY

1. The basic qualities for which we look are sensitivity, impersonality, psychic capacity, and mental polarisation. . . .

I have stated that the first requirement is *sensitivity*. What exactly is this? It does not mean primarily that you are a "sensitive soul"—this connotation of which usually means that you are thin-skinned, self-centred and always on the defensive! Rather do I refer to the capacity whereby you are enabled to expand your consciousness so that you become aware of ever-widening ranges of contact. I refer to the ability to be alive, alert, keen to recognise relationships, quick to react to need, mentally, emotionally and physically attentive to life, and rapidly developing the power to observe upon all three planes in the three worlds simultaneously. I am not interested in your personal relations where they concern your wrong personality sensitivity to depression, to self-pity, your defences, your so-called sensitivity to slights, to misunderstandings, your dislike of your environing conditions, your hurt pride, and qualities of this kind. These all cause you bewilderment and let loose in you the floodgates of compassion for yourself. But you do not need me to deal with them; of them you are well aware and can handle them *if you choose*. These faults are interesting only in so far as they affect the life of your group; they must be handled by you with care and with the open eye that senses danger from afar and seeks to avoid it.

The sensitivity which I want to see developed is alertness to soul contact, impressionability to the "voice of the Teacher", an aliveness to the impact of new ideas and to the delicacy of intuitional responsiveness. These are ever the hallmark of the true disciple. It is spiritual sensitivity which must be cultivated; this is only truly possible when you learn to work through the centres above the diaphragm, and to transmute solar plexus activity (which is so dominant in the average person), turning it into heart activity and the service of your fellow men. (5-47/8)

2. One of your great limitations is *over-sensitivity*. Your outer shell needs hardening; you must learn to tune out and to leave unrecognised that which might disturb your life of service. The proverb runs: "They say. What do they say? Let them say." For you this holds much truth. Disciples waste so much time in distress over the words, thoughts and deeds of other disciples, and thus time is lost that could be more constructively employed. . . . Remember . . . that all suffering along the lines of super-sensitivity indicates self-centredness. (5-563)

3. This growth in sensitivity is difficult to understand. The members of a Master's group and of His Ashram have to become increasingly sensitive —sensitive to the Master and to His pledged workers. You cannot be made sensitive or be rendered sensitive by some type of process or ordered training. Men and women *are* sensitive, only they do not know it, being so preoccupied with outer matters, with form life and objective things. Let me put it this way: What you say to yourself and to others—through your spoken words or your life—is so noisy that it is not easy to be what you are and to be recognised as a spiritual being. The Master is guided by what He knows of you in your quiet moments of aspiration, by what you have demonstrated for years to be your fixed life tendency, and by the manner in which you react at moments of crisis or tension. The task of the Master is to stimulate the disciple to be at all times what He knows him to be at his highest times. That is a simple and almost childish way of putting it, but it serves to express the general idea. A Master does this because the need of the world for decentralised, forward-looking, loving and intelligent workers is so great, particularly at this time. Many have reached the point where they may become sensitive if the loud assertions of personality are dimmed, and the light of the soul is permitted to pour through. Then the Master can be known and contacted. When you can get away from yourselves and your personal reactions, your own interpretations, and your personal demands, you will discover for yourselves how and in what manner the Master is seeking to impress you and the group with which you may be affiliated. You will become sensitive to that impression. You can then facilitate (as it is called) the activity of the Master by a profound and deep interest in the esoteric life, to the exclusion of your own and also of the Master's individuality. There are many

ways which can then be revealed, which will aid the interplay between you, the disciple, and the Master.   (5-710/1)

(c) PSYCHIC POWERS

1. The question of psychic powers is not so easy to explain. I do not refer to the lower psychic powers, which may or may not develop as time goes on and the need for them arises. I refer to the following capacities, inherent in the soul, which *must* be developed in all of you if you are to do your share in meeting world need, and work for the Hierarchy in the field of world service. Let us briefly enumerate them :

i. Intuitional response to ideas.

ii. Sensitiveness to the impression which some member of the Hierarchy may seek to make upon the mind of the disciple. It is for this reason that I am training you to utilise the Full Moon contact.

iii. Quick response to real need. You had not regarded this as one of the psychic powers, my brother, had you? I refer not here to a solar plexus reaction, but to heart knowledge. Ponder on this distinction.

iv. Right observation of reality upon the soul plane. This leads to right mental perception, to freedom from illusion and glamour, and to the illumination of the brain.

v. Correct manipulation of force, involving therefore, an understanding of the types and qualities of force, and their creative weaving into service upon the outer plane.

vi. A true comprehension of the time element, with its cyclic ebb and flow, and the right seasons for action—a most difficult psychic power to master, my brothers, but one which *can* be mastered through the use of patient waiting and the elimination of hurry.

All these powers, the disciple must eventually develop, but the process is necessarily slow.   (5-49/50)

2. The psychic life of a disciple is a definite part of his spiritual expression. It is only when it is uncontrolled, over-emphasised and over-estimated, that it is undesirable. It is a hindrance when it is misused or regarded as a substitute for other forms of divine expression. Then it produces that which is undesirable and immerses the disciple in the world of glamour and illusion. The psychic powers are valuable aids to service

when rightly developed and sanely used; they can be unfolded safely by the man who is mentally polarised and rightly oriented towards service. (5-111)

3. I have taught in my writings most clearly and definitely the undesirability of the lower psychic experiences. This has been done as the need to warn aspirants anent this matter is great. The difficulty is enhanced by the fact that lower psychics are not easily reached and warned, as they are ever determined that their clairvoyant and clairaudient powers are indicative of the advanced type of high spiritual unfoldment. Their minds are closed to all warnings and they function often behind a barrier of smug self-satisfaction. They forget that the aboriginal races and animals are all psychic, and register that which the more mental types fail to record. The rank and file of the people are inherently astral in their activities, their interpretations of phenomena, and their attitudes and focus. It is necessary then, to enforce the warnings and awaken the average psychic to the undesirability of his astral life.

Disciples, however, put no aspect of the divine manifestation outside their range of experience. They know that psychism in its lowest phases is a part of the divine expression, and is of an essentially higher nature than the purely physical processes of living in the body. A disciple cannot say that now, because he is a disciple, he will not be subject to this, that or the other experience. He has to be prepared for all experiences and to face the fact that eventually all disciples have to become psychics, both higher and lower, as was the Christ. The only safeguard for which he works, is to prevent the lower powers demonstrating until the higher psychic faculties are functioning; then the lower are controlled and operated (if I might so express it) from the level of the higher consciousness. . . .

The world today is entering a phase of extreme sensitivity. Disciples must train themselves to help. The shift of the consciousness of ordinary and mediocre individuals will be on to levels of conscious astralism, and the veil between the seen and the unseen will rapidly disappear. How can disciples be of service in that difficult period if they have no experience in the distinction and interpretation which must exist between aspects of phenomena? How can they rescue and safeguard others if they fear to enter into realms of life where the lower psychism rules? I am not asking you to cultivate psychic powers, but I do ask you to hold yourselves in *guarded readiness* to see and hear, interpreting it correctly, unblinded by prejudice and fear. The Path of Discipleship is not an easy one, but its compensations are adequate. Psychic sensitivity is involved in the understanding of this phase of discipleship.   (5-741/2)

4. How can the mystic avoid this error and confusion? How can he distinguish the real from the illusory? This constitutes an individual problem for every mystic, and there is no one profound and scientific rule whereby he can guide his reactions. The only rules which I can give you are so simple that those who are occupied at this time with teaching and proclaiming that which they have astrally contacted, may not like to follow them. The attitude of mind which will guard the mystic from astral delusion and error is:

i. The cultivation of a spirit of true humility. There is a spiritual arrogance which masks itself behind a cloak of humbleness and which is very prevalent at this time. It leads people to regard themselves as the chosen of the Hierarchy to save the world; it leads them to look upon themselves as the mouthpieces of the Masters or of the Christ; it tends to make them separative in their attitudes to other leaders and teachers, refusing to recognise the many aspects of the one work, and the many methods which the Mind of God has devised for reaching the masses.

ii. The refusal to accept any contact or message which has personality implications, or which sets its recipient apart, thus tending to the development of a Messiah complex. I like that phrase. It is simple and concise and illustrates dramatically the state of mind, and describes the assured nature of the consciousness of many of the present teachers of humanity. A true contact with the Hierarchy and the true accolade of service, carries with it the conviction of the existence of the many servers in the one Service, of the many messengers carrying the one message, of the many teachers of the many aspects of the one Truth, and of the many and various ways back to the Heart of God. When this all-embracing revelation accompanies the call to service, then the spirit of inclusiveness is developed, and the man can be sure that he is truly called to co-operate, and convinced of the reality of the vision.

iii. The freedom from emotional appeal. The true disciple and mystic is ever mentally polarised. His vision is free from the deluding reactions of the solar plexus centre. His vision awakens the heart centre and evokes the response of his personality energy (focussed in the ajna centre) and produces eventually a "centering in the place of light". This indicates the growing activity of the head centre. He may, later use controlled emotional appeal in dealing with the masses, but he himself seeks to remain free from all emotional control.

We are considering the unfoldment of the psychic powers, producing conditions in the subject which are regarded by the orthodox investigator as pathological in nature, or as indicating psychological trouble of a serious kind. However, we are today close to the time when the fact of there being modes of perception other than those of the physical senses, will be recognised, and the attitude of medicine and of the psychiatric and neurological sciences will undergo definite changes—much to the assistance and aid of humanity. (15-572/4)

5. Let us now consider how the abuse of the lower psychic powers may be arrested temporarily until such time as the initiate may seek to use them, in full consciousness and with full control.

The prime difficulty of the natural psychic and of the man who is born as a medium, is his inability intelligently to control the phenomena evidenced. Lack of control of the physical powers is deemed highly undesirable. Lack of psychic control should also be relegated to the same category. The medium is either in trance, or his psychic powers are brought into expression through the stimulation which comes from his contact with the group of sitters in the sceance room, or from a large audience. In other cases, he is all the time living on the borderland of consciousness between the physical and the psychic or astral planes. How can this be changed, provided the medium wishes for such a change, which is rare indeed. In three ways only:

i. By ceasing to be interested in the display of these powers, by refusing to use them any more, and by this means causing them gradually to die out. This leads to the closing of the solar plexus centre (and consequently of the open door to the lower levels of the astral plane) and the atrophying of that part of the inner mechanism which has made these powers possible.

ii. By the transference of the attention to the mystical life and to the expression of an intense aspiration towards the spiritual realities. This provides the new interest which eventually becomes dynamically expulsive of the old interests, and thus tends to shift the life-emphasis away from the lower levels of the astral plane to the higher levels. This also presupposes a tendency to spiritual orientation on the part of the psychic.

iii. By a course of intellectual training and of mental development which would, if persisted in for a sufficient length of time, automatically make the use of the lower powers impossible, because the shift of the flow of energy will be into the centres above the diaphragm. It is well known in psychic circles that mental training does bring to a close the psychic cycle. (15-585/6)

(d) ASTRAL POLARISATION

1. Just as long as a man identifies himself with his emotional body, just as long as he interprets life in terms of his moods and feelings, just as long as he reacts to desire, just so long will he have his moments of despair, of darkness, of doubt, of dire distress, and of depression. They are due to delusion, to the glamour of the astral plane, which distorts, reverses and deceives. There is no need to dwell on this. If there is one factor aspirants recognise, it is the need of freeing themselves from the Great Illusion. Arjuna knew this, yet succumbed to despair. Yet in his hour of need, Krishna failed him not, but laid down in the *Gita* the simple rules whereby depression and doubt can be overcome. They may be briefly summarised as follows :

i. Know thyself to be the undying One.

ii. Control thy mind, for through that mind the undying One can be known.

iii. Learn that the form is but the veil which hides the splendour of Divinity.

iv. Realise that the One Life pervades all forms so that there is no death, no distress, no separation.

v. Detach thyself therefore from the form side and come to Me, so dwelling in the place where Light and Life are found. Thus illusion ends.

It is his astral polarisation which lays a man open to his many emotional reactions and to waves of mass feeling of any kind. This is the cause of his being swept into that vortex of uncontrolled energy and misdirected emotional force which eventuates in a world war, a financial panic, a religious revival, or a lynching. It is this also that raises him to the heights of hilarity and of spurious happiness in which the "light deceptive" of the astral plane uncovers to him false sources of amusement, or the mass hilarity—owing to his sensitivity—sweeps him into that hysterical condition which finds its vent in unrestrained merriment and which is the opposite pole of unrestrained weeping. I refer not here to true merriment, nor the proper sense of humour, but to those hysterical outbreaks of hilarity which are so common among the rank and file of humanity and lead to reactions of fatigue.   (4-308/9)

2. The life of the disciple is ever a life of risks and dangers, entered into willingly and deliberately in the cause of spiritual unfoldment, and the service of humanity. But I would ask each of you to watch your emotional life and reactions with greatly increased care; I would ask you to watch particularly for the least outcropping of glamour. I would call your attention to the fact that the emergence of emotional conditions or of glamour in your life-expression, need not necessarily indicate failure. There is only failure if there is identification with these astral conditions, and a succumbing to old rhythms. The success of the meditation work assigned and regularly followed, may be proved to you by the appearance of these undesirable conditions; they must be then recognised for what they are, and evoke in you that "divine indifference" which permits the emotion or the glamour to die of attrition, because deprived of the "feeding-power" of the attention. The whole history of true emotional control is to be found in the sentence just given. The process of achieving this control, constitutes one of the most difficult periods in the life of the disciple, and quite one of the longest from the angle of time. For this you should be prepared. Particularly is it difficult at this time to triumph over emotion, because of the intense emotional condition of the entire human family, and the widespread fear and terror for which the energy of the Black Lodge of Adepts is responsible. This definitely complicates your problem and that of all disciples: it tends to foster a most potent glamour. So I beg of you to proceed with courage, joy, understanding, extreme caution and—at the same time—with speed.   (5-88/9)

(e) MENTAL POLARISATION

The quality of mental polarisation. What exactly is this power or quality? For you (at this time) it must express itself in two ways:

1. Through the life of meditation.

2. Through the control of the astral body.

Increasingly must your inner life be lived upon the mental plane. Steadily and without descent must the attitude of meditation be held—not for a few minutes each morning, or at specific moments throughout the day, but constantly, all day long. It infers a constant orientation to life and the handling of life from the angle of the soul. This does not refer to what is so often referred to as "turning one's back upon the world". The disciple faces the world, but he faces it from the level of the soul, looking clear-eyed upon the world of human affairs. "In the world, yet not of the world" is the right attitude—expressed for us by the Christ. Increasingly must the normal and powerful life of the emotional, astral, desire and glamorous nature be controlled and rendered quiescent by the life of the soul, functioning through the mind. The emotions which are normally self-centred and personal, must be transmuted into the realisations of universality and impersonality; the astral body must become the organ through which the love of the soul can pour; desire must give place to aspiration and that, in its turn, must be merged in the group life and the group good; glamour must give place to reality, and the pure light of the mind must pour into all dark places of the lower nature. These are the results of mental polarisation, and are brought about by definite meditation and the cultivation of the meditative attitude. (5-50/1)

(f) DETACHMENT

1. It is only in a spirit of real detachment that the best work of a disciple is done. The disciple comes to realise that because of this detachment he is (for the remainder of his life) simply a worker—one of a great army of hierarchical workers—with supposedly no personality inclinations, objectives, or wishes. There is for him nothing but constant work and constant association with other people. He may be a naturally isolated person, with a deep craving for solitude, but that matters not. It is the penalty he must pay for the opportunity to meet the need of the hour. (5-55)

2. You must develop the attentiveness of the One who looks on at life and at the life struggle of others. It is necessary for you to learn that when you can avoid identifying yourself so closely with people, refraining from suffering so consciously with them, you can be of greater service to them, and a finer friend and helper. Therefore, for you, *detachment* is an outstanding requirement and a quality to be cultivated. This is not the detachment of self-protection or of self-immunisation or of aloofness, but that soul detachment which works from soul levels and—seeing all life in the light which streams from the soul—regards everything from the standpoint of eternity. You will then see the real values involved, and the true perspectives of the picture. . . . You must see people truly and as they are—with their faults and their virtues, their divinity and their humanity.   (5-130)

3. You ought to acquire that inner, divine detachment which sees life in its true perspective. A man is thus left free and untouched by aught that may occur. The ideal attitude for you is that of the Onlooker who is in no way identified with aught that may happen on the physical and emotional planes, and whose mind is a limpid reflector of truth. This truth is intuitively perceived, because there are no violent mental reactions or emotional states of response; the vehicles of perception are quiet, and therefore there is nothing to offset correct attitude. When this state of consciousness is achieved, you will be able to teach with power, and at the same time possess that also which must be taught.   (5-146)

4. Your personality detachment must develop into a deeper attachment to the souls within the forms. Thus understanding grows. There is a vice of detachment as well as a vice of attachment, and the true servant of the Plan seeks the middle way.   (5-158)

5. Work with detachment and, because you are demanding nothing for the separated self, all things will therefore come to you.   (5-245)

6. You are learning the lesson of detachment with rapidity, and you are gradually standing free from the clinging hands of others. . . . The many acts of spiritual detachment lead eventually to the severing of that final thread which involves the death of all personality attachments. Then only those relationships are left which are upon soul levels. Your task is to learn to differentiate between such spiritual detachments and those enforced detachments which are undertaken on higher levels—of astral awareness. The problem of the disciple is to reach a point where he is not hindered or held back by any human being, and yet so to handle himself, as far as attitude is concerned, that he hurts no one in the process of withdrawal. The outer personality claims of attachment are oft so powerful that their clatter and their rattle prevent awareness of the golden thread which links us with another soul. Likewise, over-estimation of another person can act as a real hindrance. The chains must break, leaving only a golden thread between each soul — a golden thread which cannot break.   (5-311/2)

7. Forget not to love with detachment. . . . The ties through attachment over many years hold firm, and on the physical plane they must not, may not, be severed, but ever within yourself they must be completely snapped.   (5-383)

8. As you free yourself from the clinging chains of attachment to place or person, your intuitive perception will thereby be released, and you will

see in terms of reality and not in terms of form—no matter how high or purified.   (5-386)

9. Be attached to souls . . . but detached from personalities. Souls heal and aid each other's personalities. Personality relationships drain and devitalise.   (5-455)

10. The aim of each pledged and obligated disciple . . . must be to hold a subjective attitude of detached contact—an occult paradox!—and at the same time to carry forward the life of active service upon the physical plane.   (6-492)

(g)   IMPERSONALITY

1. Impersonality, particularly for high grade integrated people, is peculiarly difficult to achieve. There is a close relation between impersonality and detachment. Study this. Many cherished ideas, many hard won qualities, many carefully nurtured righteousnesses, and many powerfully formulated beliefs, militate against impersonality. It is hard for the disciple—during the process of his early training—to hold earnestly to his own ideals, and to pursue forcefully his own spiritual integration, and yet remain impersonally oriented towards other people. He seeks recognition of his struggle and achievement; he longs to have the light which he has kindled draw forth a reaction from others; he wants to be known as a disciple; he aches to show his power and his highly developed love nature, so that he may evoke admiration or, at least, challenge. But nothing happens. He is looked upon as no better than all the rest of his brothers. Life, therefore, proves dissatisfying.

These truths of self-analysis are seldom definitely faced or formulated by any of you and, therefore (because I seek to help you), I formulate them for you and face you with them. It is hard for intelligent men and women to see others closely associated with them dealing with life and problems from a totally different angle to their own—handling them in a weak or stupid way (from the angle of the disciple) and making apparently serious errors in judgment or technique. Yet, brother of old, why are you so sure that you are right, and that your point of view is necessarily correct? It may be that your slant on life and your interpretation of a situation needs readjustment, and that your motives and attitudes could be more elevated or purer. And even if they are—for you—the highest and the best that you can achieve at any given time, then pursue your way and leave your brother to pursue his. "Better a man's own dharma, than the dharma of another." Thus does the *Bhagavad-Gita* express this truth, telling the disciple to mind his own business.

This attitude of non-interference and the refusal to criticise, in no way prevents service to each other, or constructive group relations. It does not negate the expression of love or happy group co-operation. There is ever much opportunity for the practice of impersonality in all group relations. In every group there is usually one group member (and perhaps several) who constitute a problem to themselves and to their group brothers. Perhaps you yourself are such a one and know it not. Perhaps you know who, among your co-servers, provides a testing for his fellows. Perhaps you can see clearly what is the group weakness, and who it is that is keeping the group back from finer activity. That is well and good, provided that you continue to love and serve and to refrain from criticism. It is a wrong attitude to seek assiduously to straighten out your brother, to chide him or seek to impose your will on him, or your point of view, though it is always legitimate to express ideas and make suggestion. Groups of disciples are groups of free and independent souls who submerge their personal interests in service, and who seek that inner linking which will fuse the group into an instrument for the service of humanity and of the Hierarchy. Continue with your own soul discipline, and leave your brothers to continue theirs. (5-48/9)

2. You must also foster impersonality in those who work around you; this can only be accomplished as you yourself learn to be more impersonally personal. (5-266)

3. The Master looks for an effort on the part of the disciple to be impersonal in his dealings, both with Him and with his co-disciples; impersonality is the first step upon the road to spiritual love and understanding. The effort of most sincere disciples, is usually concentrated upon loving each other, and in this (to use an old simile) they put the "cart before the horse". Their effort should be to achieve, first of all, impersonality in their dealings for, when that has been achieved, criticism dies out and love can pour in.

The Master also looks for an effort upon the part of His disciples to work on a larger and more generous scale in connection with His work in the world of men; He leaves them free to work as they may choose, but He most certainly looks for the effort to take place along the lines of the specific activities which constitute His intention. To achieve this vital and strenuous effort, there must be the ability to focus upon the work and its needs and to develop the power to co-operate with those also engaged in similar work. This again involves impersonality and right focus. The Master is today looking for dedication to the needs of humanity in these days of human agony; this involves a sensitivity to world pain as it demonstrates from day to day in world affairs; it requires also a "divine indifference" to outer events in the life of the little self, and a sense of proportion which enables the disciple to see his little personal affairs—physical, emotional and mental—in terms of the whole. So again we arrive at *impersonality*—this time impersonality to a man's own creations.

. . . Impersonality has also to be developed in connection with the Master Himself. He is not occupied with making His group of disciples satisfied with themselves, their status or their service. He frequently lays the emphasis (in His few and rare contacts with His disciples) upon their failures and limitations. He does not only give them a steady flow of teaching and increased opportunity to serve. His work is primarily to help them detach themselves from the form aspect of life, and fit them to undergo certain great expansions of consciousness. (5-737/8)

4. Above all else, give love with impersonality and true understanding. It must not be the impersonality of a planned and forced achievement, but the impersonality of complete self-forgetfulness. The task is so vital that you and all your group brothers must lose sight of the little self in the need and opportunity of the moment. (6-603)

(h) DIVINE INDIFFERENCE

1. "With true divine indifference I shoulder every load that comes my way, for naught can touch my soul. To manifest this confidence, I dedicate myself." (5-523)

2. Those who are in preparation for initiation, must learn to work consciously with glamour; they must work effectively with the presented truth, ignoring any pain or suffering or mental questioning which is incident to personality rebellion and limitation; they must cultivate that "divine indifference" to personal considerations which is the outstanding hallmark of the trained initiate. (5-27)

3. You must learn to view what is said or suggested by any group brother, with a complete and carefully developed "divine indifference". Note the use of the word "divine", for it holds the clue to the needed attitude. It is a different thing to the indifference of not caring, or the indifference of a psychologically developed "way of escape" from that

which is not pleasant; nor is it the indifference of superiority. It is the indifference which accepts all that is offered, uses what is serviceable, learns what can be learnt, but is not held back by personality reactions. It is the normal attitude of the soul or self to the not-self. It is the negation of prejudice, of all narrow preconceived ideas, of all personality tradition, influence or background. It is the process of detachment from "the world, the flesh and the devil" of which *The New Testament* speaks. (5-59)

4. If I were asked to specify the outstanding fault of the majority of groups of disciples at this time, I would say that it is the expression of the wrong kind of indifference, leading to an almost immovable preoccupation with their personal ideas and undertakings. These militate against the group integration and tend to block the work.   (5-82/3)

5. You need to arrive at a point in group experience wherein you are not so intensely preoccupied with your own development, status and service; you all need to learn to decentralise yourselves so that the work to be done becomes the factor of main importance. When this is the case, then the intense self-interest with some aspect of the personality expression, some weakness of character, some dear objective, or some physical condition, will cease. You will find the cultivation of a "divine indifference" . . . of great assistance in forgetting the little self; this frequently looms so large (from habit) that it shuts out the higher self; it comes between the disciple and the Master and prevents contact with his co-disciples, thus negating effective service.   (5-97)

6. The soul stands free, unattached, unafraid, and is not controlled by that which exists in the three worlds. This is the true spiritual indifference.   (5-429)

7. The lessons of divine indifference, once mastered, release the soul to union with the One.   (5-225)

8. If you learnt that divine indifference which you need—indifference to yourself and to your personality interests, likes and dislikes, indifference to your cares, anxieties and successes. You would then be in a position, really to sense the importance of the work, the uniqueness of your opportunities at this time, and your really strategic position.   (5-661)

9. You are . . . on the path of the Christ, and in preparation for treading this path of aiding and salvaging humanity, you have to learn (through intense feeling) the futility of emotion and feeling as a means of salvaging

your brothers. You need to acquire that divine indifference which leaves the soul free to serve—untrammelled by personality reactions.   (6-460)

10. Endeavour, in the different circumstances of your life, to insulate yourself (for selfless purpose) from too close a contact with those in distress. Aid them; love them; but do not identify yourself with them. I speak of an astral insulation and not of a refusal to meet and contact suffering humanity upon the physical plane. I refer to an attitude assumed and held by the soul and mind in regard to the astral body, which enables you to express that divine indifference to feeling and to personal suffering as a result of that compassion which is the hallmark of the salvaging Elder Brothers of Humanity.   (6-461)

11. What is indifference? I wonder . . . if you understand the significance of this word "indifference"? It means in reality the achieving of a neutral attitude towards that which is regarded as the Not-self; it involves a repudiation of similarity; it marks the recognition of a basic distinction; it signifies refusal to be identified with anything save the spiritual reality as far as that is sensed and known at any given point in time and space. It is, therefore, a much stronger and vital thing than what is usually meant when the word is used. It is active repudiation without any concentration upon that which is repudiated.   (10-262)

(i) SERENITY

1. The disciple on the physical plane and the inner teacher (whether one of the Great Ones or the "Master within the Heart") need to know each other somewhat, and to accustom themselves to each other's vibration. Teachers on the inner planes have much to contend with owing to the slowness of the mental processes of students in physical bodies. But confidence and trust will set up the right vibration which will produce eventually accurate work. Lack of faith, of calmness, of application, and the presence of emotional unrest will hinder. Long patience those on the inner side need in dealing with all who must, for lack of other and better material, be utilised. Some physical injudiciousness may make the physical body non-receptive; some worry or care may cause the astral body to vibrate to a rhythm impossible for the right reception of the inner purpose; some prejudice, some criticism, some pride, may be present that will make the mental vehicle of no use. Aspirants to this difficult work must watch themselves with infinite care, and keep the inner serenity and peace and a mental pliability that will tend to make them of some use in the guarding and guidance of humanity.

The following rules might therefore be given:

i. It is essential that there should be an endeavour to arrive at absolute purity of motive.

ii. The ability to enter the silence of the high places will follow next. The stilling of the mind depends upon the law of rhythm. If you are vibrating in many directions and registering thoughts from all sides, this law will be unable to touch you. Balance and poise must be restored before equilibrium can be reached. . . . The silence that comes from the inner calm is the one to cultivate. Aspirants are urged to remember that the time will come when they too will form part of the group of teachers on the inner side of the veil. If then they have not learnt the silence that comes from strength and from knowledge, how will they bear the apparent lack of communication that they will then find exists between them and those on the outer side? Learn therefore, how to keep quiet or usefulness will be hampered by astral fretfulness when on the other side of death.

iii. Remember always that lack of calm in the daily life prevents the teachers on egoic levels from reaching you. Endeavour therefore to remain quiescent as life unrolls; work, toil, strive, aspire, and hold the inner calm. Withdraw steadily into interior work and so cultivate a responsiveness with the higher planes. A perfect steadiness of inner poise is what the Masters need in those whom They seek to use. It is an inner poise that holds to the vision, yet does its outer work on the physical plane with a concentrated physical brain attention which is in no way deviated by the inner receptiveness. It involves a dual activity.

iv. Learn to control thought. It is necessary to guard what you think. These are days when the race as a whole is becoming sensitive and telepathic and responsive to thought interplay. The time is approaching when thought will become public property, and others will sense what you think. Thought has, therefore, to be carefully guarded. Those who are contacting the higher truths and becoming sensitive to the Universal Mind, must protect some of their knowledge from the intrusion of other minds. Aspirants must learn to inhibit certain thoughts, and prevent certain knowledge from leaking out into the public consciousness when in contact with their fellow men.   (4-65/7)

2. I would point out that serenity and peace are not identical. Peace must ever be temporary and refers to the world of feeling and to conditions sus-

ceptible of disturbance. It is essential to progress, and an inevitable happening, that every step forward is marked by disturbances, by points of crisis and chaos, replaced later (when successfully handled) by periods of peace. But this peace is not serenity and a chela is only permitted to dwell within the Master's aura when *serenity has been substituted for peace.* Serenity signifies that deep calm, devoid of emotional disturbance, which distinguishes the disciple who is focussed in a "mind held steady in the light". The surface of his life may be (from the worldly angle) in a state of violent flux. All that he cherishes and holds dear in the three worlds may be crashing around him. But in spite of all, he stands firm, poised in soul consciousness, and the depths of his life remain undisturbed. This is not insensitivity or a forced autosuggestion, neither is it a capacity to exteriorise the consciousness in such a manner that individual events and happenings are ignored. *It is intensity of feeling transmuted into understanding.* When this has been attained, the chela has the right to live within the aura of the Master. There is nothing now in him which will require the Master to sidetrack His attention from vital efforts to the unimportant task of helping the disciple.   (5-750)

3. Learn that occult reticence which produces inner power and outer silence. Speak less and love more.   (5-237)

(j) HUMILITY

1. I would like also to point out with all the clarity and power at my disposal, the very deep necessity for humility and its constantly recurring expression. I refer not to an inferiority complex, but to that adjusted sense of right proportion which equips its possessor with a balanced point of view as to himself, his responsibilities and his life work. This, when present, will enable him to view himself dispassionately and his presented opportunities with equal dispassion. Undoubtedly all disciples, you among them, have speculated upon your status and standing upon the Path, and upon the status of your co-disciples. That is, after all, both natural and human. Some of you are too humble in the personal sense and not in the sense of true humility. By that I mean that you are so afraid of pride and bombast, and an over-estimation of your capacities, that you are untrue to the realities and belittle the power of your souls. . . . He needs to accept himself as he is, to be glad that there are those who guarantee to him the possibility of future unfoldment, because they have already achieved more than he has, and then to forget about himself as he accepts disciple-

ship, and finds himself so busy in true service that he has no time for ceaseless comparisons with others.

True humility is based on fact, on vision, and on time pressures. Here I give you a hint, and would ask you to think deeply on these three foundations of a major personality attitude, which must be held and demonstrated before each initiation. I would remind you that there must always be humility in the presence of true vision.   (5-95/6)

2. (The disciple) needs to cultivate that true humility which will force him to give all he has in selfless service, and then to forget that he has thus given of himself. He must have no thought of himself as a factor in the case. Only when detachment and humility are present, can a disciple really serve. Cultivate, therefore, these qualities and continue the giving of yourself in service.   (5-417)

3. Only a humble spirit, which is not occupied with the faults and failures of others, can prevent the injection of an attitude of criticism and judging.   (6-5)

(k) ESOTERIC SENSE

You ask me to define more clearly what I mean by the words "esoteric sense". I mean essentially the power to live and to function subjectively, to possess a constant inner contact with the soul and the world in which it is found, and this must work out subjectively through love, actively shown; through wisdom, steadily outpoured; and through that capacity to include and to identify oneself with all that breathes and feels, which is the outstanding characteristic of all truly functioning sons of God. I mean, therefore, an interiorly held attitude of mind which can orient itself at will in any direction. It can govern and control the emotional sensitiveness, not only of the disciple himself, but of all whom he may contact. By the strength of his silent thought, he can bring light and peace to all. Through that mental power, he can tune in on the world thought, and upon the realm of ideas, and can discriminate between and choose those mental agencies and those concepts which will enable him, as a worker under the Plan, to influence his environment, and to clothe the new ideals in that thought matter which will enable them to be more easily recognised in the world of ordinary everyday thinking and living. This attitude of mind will enable the disciple also to orient himself to the world of souls, and in that high place of inspiration and of light, discover his fellow-workers, communicate with them and—in union with them—collaborate in the working out of divine intentions.

This esoteric sense is the main need of the aspirant at this time of the world history. Until aspirants have somewhat grasped it and can use it, they can never form part of the New Group; they can never work as white magicians, and these Instructions will remain for them theoretical and mainly intellectual, instead of being practical and effective.

To cultivate this inner esoteric sense, meditation is needed, and continuous meditation, in the early stages of development. But as time elapses and a man grows spiritually, this daily meditation will perforce give way to a steady spiritual orientation, and then meditation, as now understood and needed, will no longer be required. The detachment between a man and his usable forms will be so complete, that he will live ever in the "seat of the Observer", and from that point and attitude will direct the activities of the mind and of the emotions and of the energies which make physical expression possible and useful.

The first stage in this development and culture of the esoteric sense consists in the holding of the attitude of constant detached observation. (4-603/4)

(1) PERSEVERANCE

1. Persevere without discouragement and with no undue pondering upon results achieved. You are not in a position rightly to gauge your own progress. Continue to serve and to work, and leave realisation with its results and effects to take place naturally without any forcing of the process. . . . Your physical brain is not yet in a condition wherein the inner activities can be accurately registered, but that is no indication that that activity is not great and right.   (5-309)

2. For years you have been working with steadfastness and with a certain amount of ebb and flow. When an aspirant for discipleship has worked with persistency for years, his life tendency becomes oriented towards the light, and this becomes a steady and fixed habit. This fact should prove a solace in moments of discouragement that all aspirants at times experience.   (5-382/3)

3. One of the major lessons which all disciples have to master before initiation becomes possible, is that of steady persistence in the face of all that seeks to produce difficulty.   (5-404)

4. Persistence is the hallmark of the pledged disciple.   (5-516)

(m) COURAGE

It takes courage to make spiritual decisions and to abide by them; it takes courage to adjust your lives—daily and in all relations—to the need of the hour and to the service of mankind; it takes courage to demonstrate to those around you that the present world catastrophe is of more importance to you than the petty affairs of your individual lives and your humdrum contacts; it takes courage to discard alibis which have prevented you from participating to date in the all-out effort which characterises today the activities of the Hierarchy; it takes courage to make sacrifices, to refuse time to non-essential activities, and to deal with the physical body as if it were free from all impediments; it takes courage to ignore frailties which may be present, the tiredness incident to a long life, the physical tendencies which handicap and limit your service, the sleeplessness which comes from world pressures or from a badly regulated life programme, and the nervousness and strain which are the common lot today; it takes courage to attack life on behalf of others, and to obliterate your own wishes in the emergency and need. (6-42/3)

(n) CAPACITY TO GIVE

1. What is (your) gift to the group? . . . The gift of a pure and unselfish spirit and a rare capacity to give. No greater gift can be yours—the driving urge to give selflessly, with no motive but that of pure and loving spirit (5-506)

2. You have so much to give. I refer not here to money, though that too must be included in the life offering of the disciple, at this time of world stress. I refer to greater and deeper gifts which you possess and are apt to refuse to recognise—a loving heart, a mind enriched by years of study and lives of service, and by a loyalty and a gift for friendship. (5-525)

3. There is a great law which can be embodied in the words "to those who give all, all is given". This is true of the individual disciple and of a Master's group. Most aspirants to discipleship today do not know or realise this law; they do not give freely and fully, either to the work of the Hierarchy or to those who need. Until they do, they limit their effectiveness and shut the door of supply, not only for themselves, but for the group with which they are affiliated in service. Herein lies responsibility. The clue to supply is personality harmlessness and the dedication of all individual resources to the service of the Great Ones, without restraint and spontaneously. When you, as a disciple, try to live harmlessly—in

thought and word and deed—when nothing is held back materially, emotionally or from the angle of time, when physical strength is so given and the gift of all resources is accompanied with happiness, then the disciple will have all that is needed to carry on his work, and the same is true of all working groups of servers. Such is the law. (5-692)

4. By holding man loses; by relinquishing, he gains; by seeking to grasp that which he has, it must and will inevitably disappear. (13-83)

37. EQUIPPING FOR SERVICE

1. One thing that is oft overlooked by the pupil when he enters upon the path of probation and starts meditation, is that the goal ahead for him is not primarily the completing of his own development, but his equipping for service to humanity. His own growth and development are necessarily incidental, but are not the goal. His immediate environment and his close associates on the physical plane, are his objectives in service, and if in the endeavour to attain certain qualifications and capacities he overlooks the groups to which he is affiliated, and neglects to serve wisely and spend himself loyally on their behalf, he runs the danger of crystallisation, falls under the spell of sinful pride, and mayhap even takes the first step toward the left-hand path. Unless inner growth finds expression in group service, the man treads a dangerous road. (2-115)

2. For all these troubles forms of meditation may be found which—if followed in time—will eventually dissipate them. The fundamental fact to be grasped here is that only when the pupil has an intelligent appreciation of the trouble or troubles affecting him, only when he has the ability to conscientiously follow the imparted formulas, and only when his object is unselfish, will he be trusted with these forms. When his object is to equip himself for service, when he aims only at the acquirement of healthy vehicles for the better carrying out of the Plan of the Great Ones, and when he desires not to escape disease for his own personal benefit, only then will the formulas work in connection with the egoic consciousness. The downflow of life from the God within, results in sound vehicles, so that it is only as the Personality becomes merged in the Ego, and the polarisation shifts from the lower to the higher, that the work becomes possible. (2-161)

3. Deepen your consecration and put first things first. Let nothing and no one stand between you, the vision, the Plan and your fellow disciples. (5-277)

4. When the personality is guided by the intuition and by clear thinking, and the life on the physical plane is given to the freely imposed rhythm of organised service, then power can be conferred, and definite usefulness be the result. (5-281)

5. What must we as a group do that we may be of service, and so constitute a good channel for the helping of humanity?

First of all, you must see to it that your attitude towards all teaching is that of willing service, with no thought of self. The growth in spiritual realisation and the lifting of humanity is that which is of moment, and not your own personal growth or development, nor your own satisfaction at receiving special and new information. You *will* grow, and your soul will take increasing hold upon its instrument, when your mind and effort are turned towards group service, and when your tongue is rendered harmless, through the inflow of love.

Secondly, let not your mind be occupied with idle speculations as to the identity of the teacher. What matters it who he is? Can you prove his identity in one way or another? And of what value is it to accept the statements of any fellow student who may claim to be informed on the matter, be he who he may? You cannot prove him right or wrong, and therefore it remains a waste of time which could well be given to more fruitful service, to closer study of the life-essentials, and to meditation. (14-111)

38. CONTROL OF THE MIND

You have to learn the control of the fluid, map-making, plan-formulating mind. . . . When a disciple first comes into a Master's group . . . the inflow of energy is so great, that the mind is frequently aroused to such an intense activity that it gets temporarily out of calm control. Too much is seen at once; too much is sensed and grasped; possibilities and plans, modes and methods of teaching and of service, and potentialities (hitherto unrealised) pour unhindered and simultaneously into the disciple's consciousness. When this takes place, there follows a period of

serious instability, of fluidity of thought and undertaking, of violent experimentation, and of what I might term a spiritual riot. This must eventually come to an end before the disciple can enter into his real service. . . .
A Master's group supports and protects the one who is passing through
the experience of over-stimulation. The protective work done in the Ashram of the Master, is something little realised by the average disciple.
Whilst this type of experience is going on, the outer group of a Master's
disciples proves of little service; it simply stimulates the mind, providing
outlets for the blind rioting consciousness.   (5-593/4)

39. PURIFICATION OF THE VEHICLES FOR SERVICE

1. The need arises these days for tested instruments. When Those Who
guide human evolution at this period cast Their eyes over the race in the
search for such instruments, They see few as yet ready for the service required. But likewise They see some who, with a certain amount of training will fill the need fairly adequately.

As evolution proceeds, the polarisation of the race changes. Men are
polarised now principally in their emotional bodies—the feelings, desires,
the concerns of the personality sway them. The emotional body is the
focal point for the personality. It acts as the clearing house for all that
concerns it, and as the junction of the lower and the higher. It is like a
busy railroad terminus, that receives cargo from all directions and empties
it into the great city of the personal physical plane life. Then, as progress
is made, the scene shifts higher, and the mental body becomes the focal
point. Later the causal body becomes the important unit, and later still
comes the ultimate sacrifice of even that, until the man stands bereft of all
that vibrates to the three worlds, and all is over as regards the personal
life—naught remains but the life of the Spirit, and the voluntary giving of
that life for the helping of the world.

In the speeding up of evolution, certain things have to be brought about
before the man can be used as a reliable instrument, true as tempered steel,
for the helping of the race. Forget not that, as a rule, a man (when
tested and tried) forms the best tool, because he comprehends utterly the
race consciousness, and because he enters into the problems of the day in
a manner more thorough than an Ego from an earlier period. Hence
the Masters desire to use those of you who live now to heal the wounds

of the present suffering generation. What then has to be done? The matter I now give contains nothing very unusual, but it does hold thought for consideration by any who may desire to help. . . . In preparing a soul for service the Guides of the race have to deal with each of the bodies:

The Training of the Physical Body

This involves certain definite requirements:

The building in of matter of the higher subplanes, and the elimination of the lower and coarser matter. This is needed because it is impossible for those with coarse bodies to contact high vibration. It is impossible for the Ego to transmit the higher knowledge and guidance through a coarse physical body. It is impossible for the loftier currents of thought to impact the little evolved physical brain. Hence the refinement of the physical body is an essential. It is effected in various ways, all of them reasonable and utilitarian.

By pure food. This involves a vegetarian diet, chosen with wise discrimination; it requires the eating of only those vegetables and fruits that vitalise. Careful judgment shown in the choice of food, wise refraining from too heavy eating, and a little pure good food, perfectly assimilated, are all that a disciple requires. You ask what foods? Milk, honey, whole wheat bread, all the vegetables that contact the sun, oranges (above all, oranges), bananas, raisins, nuts, some potatoes, unpolished rice, and may I again reiterate, just as much of all the above as to ensure activity.

By cleanliness. Much use of water, externally and internally, is vitally required.

By sleep. This should be always between the hours of ten in the evening and five in the morning, and as much as possible out of doors.

By sunshine. Contact with the sun should be much sought after, and the vitalisation that comes through its rays. The sun kills all germs and frees from disease.

When these four requirements are attended to adequately, a definite process of elimination proceeds, and in the course of a few years the whole physical body shifts its polarisation gradually up until ultimately you will have a body composed of atomic subplane matter. . . . This may take several incarnations, but it should be borne in mind that at each fresh incarnation a body is taken of the exact quality (if I may so put it) as the one previously discarded at death. Hence time is never lost in building.

Eventually two other methods will be available by which more rapid refining may be effected:

The use of coloured lights. These lights are played on the body of the disciple and effect a shaking-out process and a simultaneous stimulation of the atoms. This cannot be done till further information is given anent the Rays; when a man's ray is known, stimulation will come from the use of his own colour, a building-in will be brought about by the use of his complementary colour, and disintegration of unwanted matter will be brought about by the use of an antagonistic colour. This knowledge will later on be communicated to the great bodies that hold custody of the Mysteries, the Church and the Masons. Wait, for the time is not yet. When the Mysteries are restored some of this information will be in the hands of the two bodies I refer to.

The stimulation of music. Certain sounds shatter and break. Certain other sounds stimulate and attract. When the key of a man's life is known, when the sound he responds to is recognised, then comes the possibility of the utilisation of sound in refinement. All that is at present possible to those of you who seek to serve, is to attend to the above essentials and to seek contact with high vibration.

One more point I would like to give, and that is, that in the manipulation of electricity lies hid much that concerns the vivification of the bodies, especially just now of the etheric. The principal use the sun has, is the vitalising of the etheric. The heat of the sun is electrical force adapted to the need of the great average majority in all the kingdoms of nature. As progress is made an intensification of this force will be possible in individual cases. Herein lies one of the secrets of initiation. In the old days the Rod of Initiation acted actually as a conductor of this force to the centres of the initiate; it was so constructed that it answered this purpose. Now, on a higher turn of the spiral, just the same need and purpose are served, though the method of application necessarily differs, owing to the change in the polarisation of the race. The polarisation is now no longer physical, but is either emotional or mental. The method of application differs in all three, and hence the safeguarding of the secret. It holds the mystery hid.

The Refining of the Etheric

This coincides with that of the physical body. The method consists principally of living in the sunlight, in protection from cold, and in the assimilation of certain definite combinations of vitamins which before long will be given to the race. A combination of these vitamins will be formulated and made in tabloid form, with direct effect upon the etheric body. This will not be until that etheric vehicle is recognised by science, and definitely included in the training offered by the faculty of medicine. The study of etheric diseases—congestion and atrophy—will ere long be a recognised study, and will lead to definite treatments and formulas. As before said, all that you can now do in sensitising the dual physical, is to attend to the above rules, and allow time to bring about the remainder of the work.

The Refining of the Emotional Body

Here the method of procedure is different. The emotional body is simply a great reflector. It takes colour and movement from its surroundings. It receives the impress of every passing desire. It contacts every whim and fancy in its environment; every current sets it in motion; every sound causes it to vibrate unless the aspirant inhibits such a state of affairs and trains it to receive and register only those impressions which come from the intuitional level via the Higher Self, and therefore via the atomic plane. The aim of the aspirant should be to so train the emotional body, that it will become still and clear as a mirror, so that it may reflect perfectly. His aim should be to make it reflect only the causal body, to take on colour only in line with the great Law, and to move under definite direction and not just as blow the winds of thought, or rise the tides of desire. What words should describe the emotional body? The words: still, serene, unruffled, quiet, at rest, limpid and clear, of a quality mirrorlike, of surface even, a limpid reflector—one that accurately transmits the wishes, the desires, the aspirations of the Ego and not of the personality. How should this be accomplished? In several ways, some at the direction of the aspirant, and some at the direction of the Master:

1. By the constant watching of all desires, motives and wishes that cross the horizon daily, and by the subsequent emphasising of all those that are of a high order, and by the inhibition of the lower.

2. By a constant daily attempt to contact the Higher Self, and to reflect His wishes in the life. At first mistakes will be made, but little by little the building-in process proceeds, and the polarisation in the emotional body gradually shifts up each subplane until the atomic is reached.

3. By definite periods daily directed to the stilling of the emotional body. So much emphasis is laid in meditation on the stilling of the

mind, but it should be remembered that the stilling of the emotional nature is a step preliminary to the quieting of the mental; one succeeds the other and it is wise to begin at the bottom of the ladder. Each aspirant must discover for himself wherein he yields most easily to violent vibrations, such as fear, worry, personality desire of any kind, personality love of anything or anyone, discouragement, over-sensitiveness to public opinion; then he must overcome that vibration, by imposing on it a new rhythm, definitely eliminating and constructing.

4. By work done on the emotional body at night under the direction of more advanced egos, working under the guidance of a Master. Stimulation of vibration or the deadening of vibration follows on the application of certain colours and sounds. At this particular time two colours are being applied to many people for the specific purpose of keying up the throat and foremost head centre, namely, violet and gold.

Remember that the work is gradual, and as the polarisation shifts up, the moment of transition from one subplane to another is marked by certain tests applied at night; what one might term a series of small initiations that eventually will be consummated in the second great initiation, that marks the perfection of the control of the body of emotions. . . .

The Refinement of the Mental Body

This is the result of hard work and discrimination. It necessitates three things before the plane of the mental unit is achieved, and before the causal consciousness (the full consciousness of the Higher Self) is reached:

Clear thinking, not just on subjects wherein interest is aroused, but on all matters affecting the race. It involves the formulation of thought matter, and the capacity to define. It means the ability to make thought-forms out of thought matter, and to utilise those thought-forms for the helping of the public. He who does not think clearly, and who has an inchoate mental body, lives in a fog, and a man in a fog is but a blind leader of the blind.

The ability to still the mental body so that thoughts from abstract levels and from the intuitional planes can find a receptive sheet whereon they may inscribe themselves. This thought has been made clear in many books on concentration and meditation, and needs not my elucidation. It is the result of hard practice carried over many years.

A definite process brought about by the Master with the acquiescence of the disciple which welds into a permanent shape the hard won efforts and results of many years. At each initiation, the electrical or magnetic force applied has a stabilising effect. It renders durable the results achieved by the disciple. Like as a potter moulds and shapes the clay and then applies the fire that solidifies, so the aspirant shapes and moulds and builds, and prepares for the solidifying fire. Initiation marks a permanent attainment and the beginning of a new cycle of endeavour.

Above all two things should be emphasised:

1. A steady, unshaken perseverance, that recks not of time nor hindrance, but goes on. The capacity to persevere explains why the non-spectacular man so frequently attains initiation before the genius, and before the man who attracts more notice. The capacity to plod is much to be desired.

2. A progress that is made without undue self-analysis. Pull not yourselves up by the roots to see if there is growth. It takes precious time. Forget your own progress in conforming to the rules, and in the helping of others. When this is so, sudden illumination may come, and the realisation break upon you that the point has been reached when the Hierophant can demand your presence and bestow initiation upon you. You have, by hard work and sheer endeavour to conform to the Law and to love all, built into your bodies the material that makes it possible for you to stand in His Presence. The great Law of Attraction draws you to Him and naught can withstand the Law.   (2-333/41)

2. I have for some time watched you with concern, not because of any failure on your part, but because of the very real success of your spiritual effort. That sounds a paradoxical thing to say, does it not? But success can sometimes be bought at too high a price, and a special effort, leading to success which leaves the personality in a state of complete exhaustion, must in itself be considered a problem requiring solution. . . .

So great has been your determination to purify and cleanse your lower nature, that you have worn yourself out in the process; so great has been your introverted attention to the call of your soul, that your "normal outer-world hearing" (as it is esoterically called) has been dimmed. So great has been your determination to achieve the good way, that all the forces of your nature have been expended in the work of re-orientation, and now that the task has been done, it would appear . . . that there is nothing left in you wherewith to serve, by means of which to express the results of achievement, or to express that joy and peace which is the soul nature and of value to others.   (5-486/7)

3. The emphasis laid upon discipline, upon purification, upon hard, demanding work and upon relinquishing that which the personality holds dear, is a needed phase of occult development. This is generally and often sadly recognised. But—paralleling the period of pain and difficulty—is a compensatory activity of the soul which brings all life and circumstance into true perspective, and changes attitudes so completely that the recognition of adequate reward supersedes the realisation of pain. The Law of Sacrifice and the Law of Compensation are closely allied, but the first to become active in the life, and to become a recognised factor in daily living, is sacrifice. Compensation comes later into recognition.   (6-612)

4. These drastic physical disciplines are often attempted today by well-intentioned aspirants; they practise celibacy, strict vegetarianism, relaxation exercises, and many kinds of physical exercises, in the hope of bringing the body under control. These forms of discipline would be very good for the undeveloped and the lowest type of human being, but they are not the methods which should be employed by the average man or the practising aspirant. Concentration upon the physical body only serves to enhance its potency and to feed the appetites, and bring to the surface of consciousness that which should be securely secluded below the threshold of consciousness. The true aspirant should be occupied with emotional, not physical, control and with the effort to focus himself upon the mental plane, prior to achieving a stabilised contact with the soul.   (17-579)

40.   CARE OF THE PHYSICAL BODY

1. Fight not against disability or against what the world calls "old age". This is a thing you are very apt to do, and it is a normal reaction. Why not welcome Transition? Learn to glory in experience, which is the gift of wise old age, and look forward to the Great Adventure which confronts you. . . .

Pay not undue attention to the physical vehicle. Its preservation is of no moment and can—as in your case—become of too prominent importance. The time of your liberation is set by karmic law; this ever determines the demise of the real man within the body, but if the physical body is unduly nurtured, and if it becomes the recipient of undue care, it can hold that real man in prison in defiance of karmic law. That is a sorry spectacle to watch, for it means that the physical elemental is assuming power.   (6-696/7)

2. To sum up: The physical body is not a principle; it is not a main object of attention of the aspirant; it automatically responds to the slowly unfolding consciousness in all the kingdoms of nature; it constantly remains that which is worked upon and not that which has an innate influence of its own; it is not important in the active process, for it is a recipient and not that which initiates activity. That which is important is the unfolding consciousness, the response of the indwelling spiritual man to life, circumstances, events and environment. The physical body responds. When the physical body becomes, in error, the object of attention, retrogression is indicated; and this is why all profound attention to the physical disciplines, to vegetarianism, to diet and to fasting, and to the present modes of (so-called) mental and divine healing, are undesirable and not in line with the projected plan. Therefore, undue consideration and excessive emphasis upon the physical body is reactionary, and is like the worship of the golden calf by the children of Israel; it is reversion to that which at one time was of importance but today should be relegated to a minor position and below the threshold of consciousness. (17-613/4)

3. But, can one take life? I think not. Life IS. Naught in heaven or on earth can touch or affect it. This is a point oft forgotten. The rule as given to applicants consequently concerns their ability to accept and adhere to a self-imposed discipline. Through the means of that discipline, the control of the physical and astral natures are demonstrated by the applicant to *himself*, and the effect of the discipline is to reveal to him certain inevitable and basic weaknesses, such as control of the animal nature, the powerful imposition of desire, a sense of superiority, of pride and separativeness. His ability to sustain the discipline, and his appreciation of himself for so doing, plus a sense of superiority to those who are not so disciplined, are all indicative of essential weaknesses. His fanaticism, latent or expressed, emerges in his consciousness with clarity, and—when he is sincere—he is conscious of having brought about a measure of physical purity; but at the same time, he is left with the awareness that he perhaps may be starting with the outer and the obvious, when he should be beginning with the inner and with that which is not so easily contacted or expressed. This is a great and most important lesson. (18-125)

4. The true disciple does not need vegetarianism or any of the physical disciplines, for the reason that none of the fleshly appetites have any control over him. His problem lies elsewhere, and it is a waste of his time and energy to keep his eye focussed on "doing the right things physically", because he does them automatically and his spiritual *habits* offset all the lower physical tendencies; automatically these developed habits enable him to surmount the appeal of those desires which work out in the fulfilment of lower desire. No one is accepted into the circle of the Ashram . . . whose physical appetites are in any danger of controlling him. This is a statement of fact. This applies particularly and specifically to those preparing for the first initiation. Those preparing for the second initiation have to demonstrate their freedom from the slavery of ideas, from a fanatical reaction to any truth or spiritual leader, and from the control of their aspiration, which—through the intensity of its application—would sacrifice time, people and life itself to the call of the Initiator—or rather, to be correct, to what they believe to be His call.

. . . Some very sincere devotees and promising applicants are so preoccupied with form and its disciplining, that they have no real time to give to soul expansion. They are so interested in their reactions to their self-imposed discipline or to their capacity to conform, or their failure to accept the discipline, that the spiritual truths—seeking entrance into their hearts—fail to make such an entrance. Temperance in all things, the wise use of all sustaining forms, and self-forgetfulness, are the hallmark of the disciple, but not of the beginner.   (18-126/7)

5. Let me repeat: The physical disciplines are of value in the beginning stage, and impart a sense of proportion and an awareness of defects and of limitations. These have their place in time and space, and that is all. Once the world of the soul is entered, the disciple uses all forms wisely, with understanding of their purpose and with freedom from excess; he is not preoccupied with them, or fundamentally interested in them. His eyes are off himself and are fixed on the world of true values. He has no sense of self-interest, because a *group* awareness is rapidly superseding his individual consciousness.   (18-128)

41. DIET

1. It is known esoterically that the vegetable kingdom is the transmitter and the transformer of the vital pranic fluid to the other forms of life on our planet. . . . Those who seek to read the akashic records, or who endeavour to work upon the astral plane with impunity, and there to study the reflection of events in the astral light correctly, have perforce and without exception to be strict vegetarians. It is this ancient Atlantean lore which lies behind the vegetarian's insistence upon the necessity for a vegetarian diet, and which gives force and truth to this injunction. It is the failure to conform to this wise rule which has brought about the misinterpretations of the astral and akashic records by many of the psychics of the present time, and has given rise to the wild and incorrect reading of past lives. Only those who have been for ten years strict vegetarians, can work thus in what might be called the "record aspect of the astral light". When they add to their purified astral and physical bodies the light of reason and illumination of the focussed mind (which is very rarely found), then they become accurate interpreters of astral phenomena. Their link with the vegetable kingdom is then very close and unbreakable, and that link or binding chain will lead them through the door to the scene of their investigations. But unless the goal of a vegetarian diet is this field of service, the arguments for its following and for that form of diet are usually futile and of no real moment.   (14-241)

2. No set diet could be entirely correct for a group of people on differing rays, of different temperaments and equipment, and at various ages. Individuals are every one of them unlike on some points; they require to find out what it is that they, as individuals, need, in what manner their bodily requirements can best be met, and what type of substances can enable them best to serve. Each person must find this out for himself. There is no *group* diet. No enforced elimination of meat is required, or strict vegetarian diet compulsory. There are phases of life, and sometimes entire incarnations, wherein an aspirant subjects himself to a discipline of food, just as there may be other phases or an entire life wherein a strict celibacy is temporarily enforced. But there are other life cycles and incarnations wherein the disciple's interest and his service lie in other directions. There are later incarnations where there is no constant thought about the physical body, and a man works free of the diet complex, and lives without concentration upon the form life, eating that food which is

available and upon which he can best sustain his life efficiency. In preparation for certain initiations, a vegetable diet has in the past been deemed essential. But this may not always be the case, and many disciples prematurely regard themselves as in preparation for initiation.   (17-334)

42.   THE POWER TO HEAL

1. There is another great mind power which has to be unfolded. It is one which characterises all liberated souls, no matter what their ray. This is the power to heal. This work is as yet in embryo, and the group consciousness is as yet so young and unpolarised, that it is needless for me to enlarge upon the possibilities ahead. When man can be trained to be unselfishly and divinely magnetic and radio-active, then there will be poured out upon the world certain divine forces which will vivify and reconstruct, which will eliminate the evil and heal the sick. Hitherto the attempts of men in the field of medicine, of healing and of the various forms of therapy, have been the result of impulses to respond to these hovering forces, but that is all as yet.   (5-28)

2. All initiates of the Ageless Wisdom are necessarily healers, though all may not heal the physical body. The reason for this is that all souls that have achieved any measure of true liberation are transmitters of spiritual energy. This automatically affects some aspect of the mechanism which is used by the souls they contact.   (17-2)

3. I am not interested primarily in training individuals in order to make them more efficient healers. It is group healing at which I aim, and it is the work which is done in formation which interests me at this time. But no group of people can work as a unit unless they love and serve each other. The healing energy of the spiritual Hierarchy cannot flow through the group if there is disharmony and criticism. The first work, therefore, of any group of healers, is to establish themselves in love and to work towards group unity and understanding.   (17-6)

43. HEALING WORK

1. Healing need not necessarily be physical in its objective. The highest form of healing, at this time possible, is psychological. This, of course, produces physical results. When a healer can combine in himself both fields of activity, and produce that psychological synthesis and a consequent physical healing, then much, very much, can be done. (5-344)

2. The true healer . . . should be so centralised in the higher awareness, and subtly perceptive of the needs and condition of the person to be healed, that his reactions to the situation and to the needed help, will be automatic, intuitive, and consequently reliable. The true healer also correlates and uses all the various branches of the healing art—exoteric and esoteric, orthodox and experimental. He is not confined to one mode of service or to one scheme of presented healing. (5-353)

3. If a full review of the health of the world were to be undertaken and presented to the thinking public—taken in normal conditions and not in war time—the question arises whether there are one hundred thousand perfectly healthy people to be found, out of the billions now inhabiting the earth? I think not. If no actual and active disease is present, nevertheless the condition of the teeth, the hearing and the sight, leave frequently much to be desired; inherited tendencies and active predispositions cause grave concern, and to all this must be added psychological difficulty, mental diseases, and definite brain trouble. All this presents an appalling picture. Against the ills which it discloses, medicine is today battling; scientists are searching for alleviations and cures, and for sound and lasting methods of eradication; research students are investigating the latent germs, and health experts are seeking new ways to meet the onslaught of disease. Sanitation, compulsory inoculation, frequent inspection, pure food laws, legal requirements and better housing conditions, are all brought into this battle by the far-seeing humanitarian. Yet still disease is rampant; more hospitals are required, and the death rate soars.

To these practical agencies, Mental Science, New Thought, Unity and Christian Science offer their aid, and seek quite honestly to bring the power of the mind to bear upon the problem. At the present stage, these agencies and groups largely are in the hands of fanatics and devoted, unintelligent people; they refuse all compromise and seem unable to recognise that the knowledge accumulated by medicine and by those who work scientifically with the human body, is as God-given as their, as yet, unproved ideal. Later, the truths for which these groups stand, will be added to the work of the psychologist and the physician; when this has been done, we shall see a great improvement. When the work of the doctor and the surgeon in relation to the physical body is recognised as essential and good, when the analysis and conclusions of the psychologist supplement their work, and when the power of right thought comes likewise as an aid, then and only then, shall we enter upon a new era of well-being.

To the various categories of trouble must also be added a whole group of diseases which are more strictly mental in their effect—the cleavages, the insanities, the obsessions, the mental breaks, the aberrations and the hallucinations. To the various healing agencies mentioned above should be added the work undertaken by Members of the spiritual Hierarchy and Their disciples; it takes soul power and knowledge, plus the wisdom of the other healing groups, to produce health among people, to empty our sanatoriums, to rid humanity of the basic diseases, of lunacy and obsession, and to prevent crime. This is finally brought about by the right integration of the whole man, through a right comprehension of the nature of energy, and through a correct appreciation of the endocrine system, its glands and their subtle relationships.

At present there is little coherent and integrated work done *in unison* by the four groups:

i. Physicians and surgeons—orthodox and academic.

ii. Psychologists, neurologists and psychiatrists.

iii. Mental healers and New Thought workers, plus Unity thinkers and Christian Scientists.

iv. Trained disciples and those who work with the souls of men.

When these four groups can be brought into close relation, and can work together for the release of humanity from disease, we shall then arrive at an understanding of the true wonder of the human being. We shall some day have hospitals in which the four phases of this one medical and remedial work will proceed side by side and in the fullest co-operation. Neither group can do a complete task without the others; all are interdependent.

It is the inability of these groups to recognise the good in the other groups striving for the physical well-being of humanity, which makes it almost impossible for me to do more specific teaching and more direct talking on these matters. Have you any idea of the wall of antagonistic thinking and speech against which a new or pioneering idea has to batter itself? Have you ever seriously considered the aggregated and crystallised thought-forms with which all such new ideas (and shall I call them hierarchical proposals) have to contend? Do you appreciate the dead weight of preconceived and ancient determinations which have to be moved before the Hierarchy can cause a new and needed concept to penetrate into the consciousness of the average thinking (or again should I say, unthinking?) public?

The field of medicine is a most difficult field in which to work, for the subject is so intimate, and fears enter so strongly into the reactions of those who must be reached. The gulf between the old and established and new and the spiritually demanded, needs much long and careful bridging. A great deal of the difficulty is, curiously enough, to be found fostered by the newer schools of thought. Orthodox medicine is slow, and rightly slow, in adopting new techniques and methods; it is at times too slow, but the case of the new mode of treatment or diagnosis must be rightly proven and statistically proven, before it can be incorporated in the medical curriculum and method; the risks to the human subject are too great, and the good humanitarian physician will not make his patient the subject of experimentation. However, within the last few decades, medicine has advanced by leaps and bounds, the science of electricity and light therapy, and many other modern techniques and methods, have already been added to the various other sciences of which medicine avails itself. The demands of the intangible and the treatment of the nebulous—if such peculiar terms are in order—are being recognised increasingly, and are known to play an orthodox and recognised part in the newer approaches to disease.

The approach of the mental schools and cults, as they erroneously call themselves, has not proceeded so helpfully. This is largely their fault. Schools of thought, such as Mental Science, New Thought, Unity, Christian Science, Chiropractic enterprise, the efforts of the Naturopaths, and many others, hurt their cause, owing to the large claims which they make, and to their unceasing attacks upon orthodox medicine and other channels of proven helpfulness and upon the knowledge (acquired over centuries of experimentation) of the academic schools of medicine and surgery. They forget that many of their claims to success (and they are often irrefutable) can be classed under the general heading of faith cures and this can be done correctly or incorrectly. Such cures have long been recognised by the academic thinker, and known to be factual.

These cults, which are in fact the custodians of needed truths, need above everything else to change their approach and to learn the spiritual nature of compromise in these days of evolutionary unfoldment. Their ideas cannot come into full and desired usefulness apart from the already God-given knowledge which medicine down the ages has accumulated; they need also to keep a record of their numerous failures, as well as the successes which they loudly proclaim. I would here point out that these successes are in no way so numerous as those of orthodox medicine and of the beneficient work done by the clinics of our hospitals which—in spite of failures and often gross stupidity—greatly ameliorate the pains and ills of the masses of men. These cults omit to state, or even to recognise, that in cases of extreme illness or accident, the patient is physically unable to affirm or claim divine healing, and is dependent upon the work of some healer who works with no knowledge of the karma of the patient. Many of their so-called cures (and this is the case also with orthodox medicine) are cures because the hour of the end has not yet arrived for the patient, and he would have recovered in any case, though he often does so more rapidly, owing to the remedial measures of the trained physician.

In cases of serious accident, where the injured person will bleed, the cultist (no matter what his cult may be called) will perforce avail himself of the methods of the orthodox physician; he will apply a tourniquet, for instance, and take the measures which orthodox medicine enjoins, rather than stand by and see the injured person die because these methods are not used. When he is face to face with death, he will frequently turn to the tried and proved methods of help, and will usually call in a physician rather than be charged with murder.

All the above is said in no spirit of disparagement, but in an effort to prove that the many schools of thought—orthodox, academic, ancient, material, or spiritual, new, pioneering or mental—are interdependent; they need to be brought together into one great healing science. This will be a science which will heal the whole man and bring into play all the resources—physical, emotional, mental and spiritual—of which humanity is capable. Orthodox medicine is more open to co-operation with the newer cults than are the neophytes of the science of mental control of disease; they cannot, however, permit their patients to be turned into guinea pigs (is not that the term used in these cases, brother of mine?) for the satisfaction of the pioneering cultist, and the proving of his theories—no matter how correct when applied in conjunction with what has already been proved. The middle way of compromise and of mutual co-operation is ever the wisest, and this is a lesson much needed today in every department of human thinking.   (17-252/7)

4. No request for real aid must ever be refused. . . . A deaf ear must not be turned to trouble, either physical, mental or psychological. But I would call to your attention the fact that success in healing may not always mean release from disease and the so-called physical cure of the patient. It might simply involve, if physically successful, the postponement of the plan of the soul for the person. Success might mean the correction of wrong inner attitudes, of erroneous lines of thought, and at the same time leave the physical body as it was. It might mean the placing of the patient (through wise teaching and patience) en rapport with his soul and the consequent reorienting of the life to the eternal verities. It might consist in the proper preparation of the person for the tremendous purpose which we call Death, and thus bring about the relief of pain in this way. (17-352)

5. The healing of the physical body is not always the highest spiritual good; the over-estimation and serious, anxious care of the form life, of the physical vehicle, is *not* of major importance. (17-538)

6. Anyone can be a healer if he so chooses and is willing to conform to the requirements. The current idea that a person is a "born" healer, and therefore unique, in reality indicates only that it is one of his main directed interests. Therefore, because of this interest, his attention has been turned towards the healing art and consequently towards contact with patients; owing to the inevitable working of the law which governs thought, he discovers that energy follows his thought and flows through him to the patient. When he does this with deliberation, a healing will often follow. Any man or woman—given real interest and prompted by the incentive to serve—who thinks and loves, can be a healer, and it is time that people grasped that fact. (17-601)

44. THE EVOLVING FORM

1. All life is vibration and the result of vibration is form, dense or subtle, and ever subtler as ascension takes place. As the pulsating life progresses, its rate of vibration changes, and in this changing of vibration lies hid the secret of form-shattering and form-building. Forms are of four kinds in this era of the fourth round:

i. *The Form of the Personality,* that vehicle of physical, astral and mental matter, that provides the means of contact in the three worlds. It is built in each life, the key of the vibration being set up in the life preceding the present. That form proves adequate for the average man and serves him till death. The man who is entering on the occult path, starts with the vehicle provided, but during incarnation builds for himself ever a newer and better vehicle, and the more progressed he is the more consciously he works. Hence eventuates that constant turmoil and frequent ill-health of the beginner in the occult life. He senses the law, he realises the need of raising his key, and frequently he begins with mistakes. He starts to build anew his physical body by diet and discipline, instead of working from the inner outward. In the careful discipline of the mind and the manipulation of thought-matter and in transmutation of emotion comes the working-out on the physical plane. Add to the two above, physical plane purity as to food and manner of life, and in seven years' time the man has built for himself three new bodies around the permanent atoms.

ii. *The Form of the Environment.* This is really the evolutionary working out of the involutionary group soul. It relates to our contacts, not just exterior, but on the inner planes as well. In similarity of vibration comes coherency. When therefore a man raises his vibration and builds anew from the beginning, and alters consequently his key, it results in dissonance in his surroundings and subsequent discord. Therefore—under the law—there comes always to the striver after the Mysteries, and the manipulator of the law, a period of *aloneness* and of sorrow when no man stands by and isolation is his lot. In lesser degree this comes to all, and to the arhat (or initiate of the fourth degree) this complete isolation is a characteristic feature. He stands midway between life in the three worlds and that in the world of adepts. His vibration does not synchronise, prior to initiation, with the vibration of either group. Under the law he is alone. But this is only temporary. When the environment satisfies, then is the moment of anxiety; it indicates stagnation. The application of the law causes primary disruption.

iii. *The Form of the Devotee.* Yes, I mean just that word, for it expresses an abstract idea. Each person of every degree has his devotion, that for which he lives, that for which—in ignorance, in knowledge or in wisdom—he wields as much of the law as he can grasp. Purely physical may that devotion be, centred in flesh, in lust for gold, in possessions concrete. He bends all his energies to the search for the satisfaction of that concrete form, and thereby learns. Purely astral may be the aim of the devotee—love of wife or child, or family, pride of race, love of popularity, or lust of some kind—to them he devotes the whole of his energy, using the physical body to fulfil the desire of the astral.

Higher still may be the form of his devotion—love of art, or science or philosophy, the life religious, scientific, or artistic—to them he consecrates his energies, physical, astral and mental, and always the form is that of devotion. Always the vibration measures up to the goal, finds that goal, passes it and disintegrates. Pain enters into all shattering of the form and changing of the key. Many lives, for millennia of years, are spent under the lower vibrations. As evolution progresses, more rapid is the development, and the key changes from life to life, whereas in the earlier stages one key or tone might be sounded for several lives in their entirety. As a man nears the Path, the Probationary Path becomes strewn with many shattered forms, and from lesser cycle to lesser cycle he changes the key, often in one life heightening his vibration several times. See therefore how the life of all aspirants, if progressing with the desired rapidity, is one of constant movement, constant changes and differentiations, and continuous building and breaking, planning and seeing those plans disrupted. It is a life of ceaseless suffering, of frequent clashing with the environing circumstances, of numerous friendships made and transferred, of mutation ceaseless and consequent agony. Ideals are transcended only to be found to be stations on the road to higher; visions are seen, only to be replaced by others; dreams are dreamt only to be realised and discarded; friends are made, to be loved and left behind, and to follow later and more slowly the footsteps of the striving aspirant; and all the time the fourth form is being built.

iv. *The Form of the Causal Body*. This is the vehicle of the higher consciousness, the temple of the indwelling God, which seems of a beauty so rare and of a stability of so sure a nature that, when the final shattering comes of even that masterpiece of many lives, bitter indeed is the cup to drink, and unutterably bereft seems the unit of consciousness. Conscious then only of that innate Divine Spirit, conscious only of the Truth of the Godhead, realising profoundly and to the depths of his being the ephemeral nature of the form and of all forms, standing alone in the vortex of initiatory rites, bereft of all on which he may have leant (be it friend, Master, doctrine or environment), well may the Initiate cry out: "I am that I am, and there is naught else". Well may he then figuratively place his hand in that of his Father in Heaven, and hold the other out in blessing on the world of men, for only the hands that have let slip all within the three worlds, are free to carry the ultimate blessing to struggling humanity. Then he builds for himself a form such as he desires—a new form that is no longer subject to shattering, but suffices for his need, to be discarded or used as occasion warrants.

In these days you will need to ponder on this matter of the form, for with the entering in of a new ray, and the commencement of a new era, comes ever a period of much disruption until the forms that be have adapted themselves to the newer vibration. In that adaptation those who have cultivated pliability and adaptibility, or who have that for their personality ray, progress with less disruption than those more crystallised and fixed.

Particularly now should pliability and responsiveness of form be aimed at, for when He Whom we all adore comes, think you His vibration will not cause disruption if crystallisation is present? It was so before; it will be so again.

Cultivate responsiveness to the Great Ones, aim at mental expansion and keep learning. Think whenever possible in terms abstract or numerical, and by loving all, work at the plasticity of the astral body. In love of all that breathes comes capacity to vibrate universally, and in that astral pliability will come responsiveness to the vibration of the Great Lord. (4-262/5)

2. Each human life period sees a man taking a more evolved physical body of a greater responsiveness, tuned to a higher key, of more adequate refinement, and vibrating to a different measure. (17-421)

45. THE LIFE SPAN

The life span will eventually be shortened or lengthened at will by souls who consciously serve, and use the mechanism of the body as the instrument whereby the Plan is served. Frequently, today, lives are preserved in form—both in old age and in infancy—that could be well permitted liberation. They serve no useful purpose and cause much pain and suffering to forms which nature (left to herself) would not long use, and would extinguish. Note that word. Through our over-emphasis on the value of form life, and through the universal fear of death—that great transition which we must all face—and through our uncertainty as to the fact of immortality, and also through our deep attachment to form, we arrest the natural processes and hold the life, which is struggling to be free, confined to bodies quite unfitted to the purposes of the soul. Misunderstand me not. I desire to say naught that could place a premium on suicide. But I do say, and I say with emphasis, that the Law of Karma is oft set aside when forms are preserved in coherent expression which should be discarded, for they serve no useful purpose. This preservation is, in the majority of cases, enforced by the subject's group and not by the subject himself—frequently an unconscious invalid, an old person whose response apparatus of contact and response is imperfect, or a baby who is not normal. These cases constitute definite instances of an offsetting of the Law of Karma.   (17-350/1)

46. DEATH

1. As regards those who have passed into the light, whom you want to help, follow them with your love, remembering that they are still the same people, minus the outer limiting shroud or body. Serve them, but seek not that they should serve your need of them. Go to them, but seek not to bring them back to you.

It is physical plane life that is the purgatory, and life experience that is the school of drastic discipline. Let us not fear death, or that which lies beyond it. The wise disciple labours in the field of service, but looks forward steadily to the dawn of the "clear cold light" into which he will some day enter, and so close the chapter for a while upon the fever and the friction and the pain of earth existence.   (17-365)

2. Desire governs the process of death, as it also governs the processes of life experience. We say constantly that when the will-to-live is lacking, death is the inevitable result. . . .

You will note that I am here dealing with the theme of death as it makes its presence felt through disease or through old age. I am not referring to death as it comes through war or accident, through murder or through suicide. These causes of death, and other causes, come under a totally different directive process; they may not even involve the karma of a man or his individual destiny, as in the case of war. Then vast numbers of people are killed. This has nothing to do with the Law of Cause and Effect as a factor in the soul career of any individual. It is not an act of restitution, planned by a particular soul as it works out its individual destiny. Death, through the destructive processes of war, is under the directive and cyclic intention of the planetary Logos, working through the Council Chamber at Shamballa. (17-431)

3. Death releases the individualised life into a less cramped and confined existence, and eventually—when the death process has been applied to all the three vehicles in the three worlds—into the life of universality. This is a point of inexpressible bliss. (17-433)

4. Death appears frequently to be so purposeless; that is because the intention of the soul is not known; past development, through the process of incarnation, remains a hidden matter; ancient heredities and environments are ignored, and recognition of the voice of the soul is not yet generally developed. These are matters, however, which are on the verge of recognition; revelation is on its way, and for that I am laying the foundation. . . . Seek to arrive at a new slant upon the subject, and see law and purpose and the beauty of intention in what has hitherto been a terror and a major fear. (17-436)

5. I speak about Death as one who knows the matter from the outer world experience *and* the inner life expression: *There is no death.* There is, as you know, entrance into fuller life. There is freedom from the handicaps of the fleshly vehicle. The rending process so much dreaded, does not exist, except in the cases of violent and sudden death, and then the only true disagreeables are an instant and overwhelming sense of imminent peril and destruction and something closely approaching an electric shock. No more. For the unevolved, death is literally a sleep and a forgetting, for the mind is not sufficiently awakened to react, and the storehouse of memory is as yet practically empty. For the average good citizen, death is a continuance of the living process in his consciousness and a carrying forward of the interests and tendencies of the life. His consciousness and his sense of awareness are the same and unaltered. He does not sense much difference, is well taken care of, and oft is unaware that he has passed through the episode of death. For the wicked and cruelly selfish, for the criminal and for those few who live for the material side only, there eventuates that condition which we call "earth-bound". The links they have forged with earth and the earthward bias of all their desires, force them to remain close to the earth and their last setting in

the earth environment. They seek desperately, and by every possible means, to re-contact it and to re-enter. In a few cases, great personal love for those left behind, or the non-fulfilment of a recognised and urgent duty, holds the good and beautiful in a somewhat similar condition. For the aspirant, death is an immediate entrance into a sphere of service and of expression to which he is well accustomed, and which he at once recognises as not new. In his sleeping hours he has developed a field of active service and of learning. He now simply functions in it for the entire twenty-four hours (talking in terms of physical plane time) instead of for his usual few hours of earthly sleep.   (4-300/1), (17-446/7)

6. One of the factors governing incarnation is the presence of what is called the will-to-live; when that is to be found, and when it is powerful in man, he is strongly anchored upon the physical plane; when that is not strongly present or is withdrawn, the man dies. Life in the physical body is preserved, technically and occultly, under the impulse of the powerful will-to-be of the incarnated spiritual man.   (17-638)

47. THE UNFOLDING DISCIPLE

1. The various energies which play upon the human being and produce his unfoldment, constitute his field of experience. Those two words— unfoldment and experience—should ever be linked, for each produces the other. As one is subjected to experience in the form world, a paralleling unfoldment of consciousness is carried forward. As that unfoldment produces constant changes in realisation, and a consequent reorientation to a new state of awareness, it necessarily leads to new experience—experience of fresh phenomena, of new states of being, and of dimensional conditions hitherto unknown. Hence the frequent reaction of the disciple to the fact that for him, as yet, there is no point of peace. Peace was the objective of the Atlantean aspirant. Realisation is that of the Aryan disciple. He can never be static; he can never rest; he is constantly adjusting himself to new conditions; constantly learning to function therein, and then subsequently finding them pass away to give place, in their turn, to new. This goes on until the consciousness is stabilised in the Self, in the One. Then the initiate knows himself to be the onlooking Unity, watching the phenomenal phantasmagoria of life in form.

He passes from one sense of unity to a sense of duality, and from thence again into a higher unity. First, the Self identifies itself with the form aspect to such an extent that all duality disappears in the illusion that the Self is the form. We have then the form constituting apparently all that there is. This is followed by the stage wherein the indwelling Self begins to be aware of Itself as well as of the form, and we talk then in terms of the higher and the lower self; we speak of the self and its sheaths, and of the self and the not-self. This dualistic stage is that of the aspirant and of the disciple, up to the time of his training for the third initiation. He begins with a knowledge that he is a spiritual entity confined in form. His consciousness for a long period of time remains predominantly that of the form. Gradually this changes—so gradually that the aspirant learns the lesson of endurance (even to the point of enduring the not-self!) until there comes a life of balance, wherein neither preponderates. This produces in the man a state of apparent negativity and inertia, which may last for one life or two, and he seems to accomplish little in either direction. This is, for workers, a valuable hint in their dealings with people. Then the point of balance changes, and the soul appears to dominate from the standpoint of influence, and the entire consciousness aspect begins to shift into the higher of the two aspects. Duality however, still persists, for the man is sometimes identified with his soul and sometimes with his form nature; this is the stage wherein so many most earnest disciples are at this time to be found. Little by little however he becomes "absorbed" in the soul, and thus comes *en rapport* with all aspects of the soul in all forms, until the day dawns when he realises that there is nothing but soul, and then the higher state of unity supervenes.　(4-374/5)

2. The work of the Ibezhan adepts, and the mysteries of the Temple of Ibez, are still persisting, and are being carried on by the masters and adepts in physical incarnation throughout the world. They teach the meaning of the psyche, the ego, or the soul and of the human unit, so that the man may indeed be what he is, a God walking on earth, his lower nature (physical, astral and mental) completely controlled by the soul or the love aspect, and this not in theory, but in deed and truth.

When this is the case, the physical body will have no lure for the real man, the emotional nature and desire body will no longer lead astray, nor will the mind shut out that which is true and spiritual, but the God will use the three bodies as vehicles of service to the race. Then will the human kingdom be transcended and man pass into the spiritual kingdom, there to have further lessons, just as infant humanity, when passing out of the animal kingdom, was trained and taught its functions and work by the Ibezhan teachers.   (4-382)

3. All growth is cyclic and one progresses from step to step in spiral fashion, and this ever involves a retracing (apparently) of one's steps. This is, however, an illusion.   (5-108)

4. There is always in each disciple, at any given moment of his incarnated life, some one aspect of development which is of more importance than another.   (5-209)

5. In the work of the disciple, the time element counts not. Growth, deep rooted and established, is the goal, and growth, if sound and good, is slow.   (5-552)

6. The life of a disciple is a gradual but steady moving in towards the centre, and accepted disciples are definitely a part of the Hierarchy. The Hierarchy is a place of fusion of all souls upon the higher levels of the mental plane. Just in so far as a person comes under soul impression, then soul control and final identification with the soul, just so far does he move towards the centre of fusion. As your love for humanity increases and your interest in yourself decreases, so will you move towards that centre of light and love where the Masters stand in spiritual being.

   . . . The trained disciple is so preoccupied with the Plan, so infused with love for his fellow men, that his entire orientation is towards the service of the Plan and not towards his own individual progress, or towards the Master. The closer he gets to the centre and towards the Master, the less attention the Master pays him, and the less he is occupied with thinking about the Master. In the early stages, he perhaps necessarily thinks much about his relation to the Hierarchy, to the Master and to his own soul. In the intermediate stage, he is occupied with the achieving of a sense of proportion and a right inner adjustment, so that "he faces two ways, and each way sees the same vision". In the final stages when he is the disciple who is also the Master, his consciousness is absorbed into the will of the Creator; his attitude is one of unchanging love, and his work is that of irradiation—a radiation which evokes activity in others, initiates a response from his fellow men, and carries the Plan the next step forward in meeting the immediate need of humanity.   (5-682/3)

7. When (man) becomes the aspirant, and takes the first steps upon the path towards spiritual maturity, he begins to play a crucial role, which he maintains until he attains spiritual liberation, and himself becomes a mem-

ber of the Hierarchy, of the fifth or spiritual kingdom, through perfected service in the fourth or the human kingdom. (11-194)

8. Man might be defined as a unit of conscious life, swept into tangible expression through the discriminating love of God. Through his life experiences he is presented with innumerable choices, which gradually shift from the realm of the tangible into that of the intangible. As he attracts, or is attracted by the life of his environment, he becomes increasingly conscious of a series of shifting values, until he reaches that point in his development when the pull or the magnetic attraction of the subjective world, and the intangible mental and spiritual realities are more potent than the factors which have hitherto enticed him on. His sense of values is no longer determined by:

i. The satisfaction of his instinctual animal nature.

ii. The desires of a more emotional and sentimental kind which his astral body demands.

iii. The pull and pleasures of the mind nature, and of intellectual appetites.

He becomes potently attracted by his soul, and this produces a tremendous revolution in his entire life, regarding the word "revolution" in its true sense, as a complete turning around. This revolution is happening now, on such a universal scale in the lives of individuals in the world, that it is one of the main factors producing the present potency of experimental ideas in the world of modern times. The attractive power of the soul grows steadily, and the pull of the personality weakens as steadily. All this has been brought about by the process of experiment, leading to experience; by experience, leading to a wiser use of the powers of the personality; by a growing appreciation of a truer world of values and of reality, and by an effort on man's part to identify himself with the world of spiritual values and not with a world of material values. The world of meaning and of causes becomes gradually the world in which he finds happiness, and his selection of his major interests and the use to which he decides to put his time and powers, are finally conditioned by the truer spiritual values. He then is on the path of illumination. (14-339/40)

9. It must be borne in mind that the life of a personality falls into the following stages:

i. Its slow and gradual construction over a long period of time. For many cycles of incarnations, a man is not a personality. He is just a member of the mass.

ii. The conscious identification of the soul with the personality during this stage is practically non-existent. The aspect of the soul which is concealed within the sheaths, is for a long, long period dominated by the life of those sheaths, only making its presence felt through what is called "the voice of conscience". However, as time goes on, the active intelligent life of the person is gradually enhanced and co-ordinated by the energy which streams from the knowledge petals of the egoic lotus, or from the intelligent perceptive nature of the soul on its own plane. This produces eventually the integration of the three lower sheaths into one functioning whole. The man is then a personality.

iii. The personality life of the now co-ordinated individual persists for a large number of lives, and also falls into three phases :

(a) The phase of a dominant aggressive personality life, basically conditioned by its ray type, selfish in nature, and very individualistic.

(b) A transitional phase wherein a conflict rages between personality and soul. The soul begins to seek liberation from form life and yet— in the last analysis—the personality is dependent upon the life principle, conferred by the soul. Wording it otherwise, the conflict between the soul ray and the personality ray starts, and the war is on between two focussed aspects of energy. This conflict terminates at the third initiation.

(c) The control by the soul is the final phase, leading to the death and destruction of the personality. This death begins when the personality, the Dweller on the Threshold, stands before the Angel of the Presence. The light of the solar Angel then obliterates the light of matter.

The "control" phase is conditioned by the complete identification of the personality with the soul; this is a reversal of the previous identification of the soul with the personality. This also is what we mean when speaking of the integration of these two; the two are now one. It was of this phase that St. Paul was speaking when he referred (in Epistle to the Ephesians) to Christ making "out of two, one new man". It is primarily the phase of the final stages of the Probationary Path (where the work consciously begins) and its carrying forward to completion upon the Path of Discipleship. It is the stage of the practical and successful server; it is that wherein the entire focus and output of the life of the man is dedicated to the fulfilment of hierarchical intent. The man begins to work on and from levels not included in the three worlds of ordinary evolution, but which nevertheless have their effects and their planned objectives within those three worlds. (17-506/8)

10. To be static, to have attained all that can be attained, and to be at a complete standstill, would be utter death and, my brothers, there is no death. There is only progress from glory to glory, a moving forward from point to point on the Divine Way, and from revelation to revelation towards those points and revelations which are perhaps part of the Goal of God Himself.   (18-328)

48.   DUAL LIFE OF THE DISCIPLE

1. All right responsibilities must always be met by disciples. I refer to that inner, active, spiritual life which you should increasingly cultivate, and to that dual activity which every disciple has to follow simultaneously. This dual life embraces the world of inner relationships and of recognised subjective attitudes, but it also embraces the life of outer service and of those relationships which you have assumed as your physical plane dharma. Clear vision as to these outer relations in the world of professional activity, of friendships and of family relations, is a necessary requirement in treading the Path, and until a disciple sees these relations in their true and right proportions, his mind is frequently disturbed and his service handicapped. I give you here a hint. Every link that one makes on earth does not necessarily entail the recognition of a soul link. We make new and fresh links and start new lines of karma and of dharma. One of the first things that a disciple has to learn, is right judgment as to the relative soul age of his associates. He soon discovers that these vary. He learns then to recognise those whose wisdom and knowledge surpass his own, to co-operate with those who stand with him upon the Path, and to work for those whom he can help, but whose evolutionary status is not on an equality with his own. The ordered pattern of his life can then take on definite forms, and he can begin to work with intelligence.

These points you need to study, remembering that truth and clear vision are of greater value than blind loyalty and curtailed understanding. When grasped, they lead to increased happiness and to power in all relationships. A right sense of proportion does not necessarily involve criticism.   (5-307/8)

2. The disciple has . . . to master the process of carrying on a dual thinking process, wherein he is preserving a continuity of mental impression and a constant activity connected with daily living and service.   (6-134)

3. The trained intuitive or disciple lives ever the dual life of mundane activity and of intense and simultaneous spiritual reflection. This will be the outstanding characteristic of the Western disciple in contra-distinction to the Eastern disciple, who escapes from life into the silent places and away from the pressures of daily living and constant contact with others. The task of the Western disciple is much harder, but that which he will prove to himself and to the world as a whole, will be still higher. This is to be expected if the evolutionary process means anything. The Western races must move forward into spiritual supremacy, without obliterating the Eastern contribution, and the functioning of the Law of Rebirth holds the clue to this and demonstrates this necessity. The tide of life moves from East to West as moves the sun, and those who in past centuries struck the note of Eastern mysticism, must strike and are now striking the note of Western occultism.   (10-179/80)

49.   CHOICE OF PATH

What is that choice For the aspirant it is that between rapid and slow progress. For the disciple, accepted and loyal, it is the choice between methods of service. For the initiate it oft lies betwixt spiritual advancement and the arduous work of staying with the group and working out the Plan. For the Master it is the choice between the seven Paths, and it will therefore be apparent how much more strenuous and difficult is his problem.

All however prepares the aspirant for right choice through right discrimination, leading to right action, and made possible through practised dispassion. In this sentence is summed up the technique of the warrior upon the battlefield of the desire plane.

. . . Such is the path ahead of each and all who dare to tread it. Such is the opportunity offered to all students who have made their choice with dispassion, and are prompted by love and the desire to serve.   (4-230/2)

50.   RIGHT DECISION

1. You might ask . . . upon what a right decision should be based, and I would reply in the following terms:

i. On that which offers to you as spiritual opportunity, but which can be carried out without relinquishing right and inescapable obligations. I say *right* obligations, and not personality inclinations.

ii. On that which will give you a wider field of service, so that all your powers and gifts and acquired talents may be called into play, and give you that rounded out development which will equip you for your next life of activity.

iii. On that which can be done best by you and by no one else. Doors open and close, and the disciple in training has to cultivate that spiritual, instinctual response which will enable him to know through which door his soul desires him to pass.   (5-206)

2. Your line of development is service in the world. What line that service must take, is for you to know and decide, and the germ of your decision is already in your mind. I give no definite instructions at any time to govern a disciple's service. Not in this way do servers grow.   (5-292)

3. In the case of those who are pledged disciples . . . there is first of all *the crisis of opportunity* and its wise recognition. At some time every disciple is faced with some determining choice which leads eventually to the distinctive nature of his life service. This usually takes place between the ages of twenty-five and forty, usually around the age of thirty-five. I refer not here to the choice which every able bodied and sane man has to take when he determines his life work, his place of living and his life associates. I refer to a free choice made when these other lesser choices have been made. . . . This crisis of opportunity relates ever to life service. This is true in spite of karma or environing conditions. It is not a choice of the personality, based upon expedient or earthly motives, necessity or anything else. It is a choice based upon the relation of the soul to the personality and *only confronts disciples.*   (6-644)

4. How can I arrive at right decision? First of all by eliminating selfishness and arriving at that unconcern as to the happiness or the experience of the personality; secondly, by refusing to move hurriedly. The disciple has to learn that when he has arrived at right—and therefore for him irrevocable decision—that this very motive and decision start energy

working along the indicated lines and that, having decided, he now moves
slowly in the wake of that energy. There are deep significances in what
I am here telling you, and I beg you to strive to understand my meaning.
(6-737)

5. What is the criterion whereby a man may know which out of several
lines of activity is the right line to take? Is there, in other words, a revealing something which will enable a man unerringly to choose the right
action and go the right way? The question has no reference to a choice
existing between the path of spiritual endeavour and the way of the man
of the world. It refers to right action when faced with a choice.

There is no question but that a man is faced, in his progress, with
increasingly subtle distinctions. The crude discrimination between right
and wrong which occupies the child soul, is succeeded by the finer distinctions of right, or of more right, of high, or higher, and the moral or
spiritual values have to be faced with the most meticulous spiritual perception. In the stress and toil of life and in the constant pressure on each
one from those who constitute their group, the complexity of the problem is very great.

In solving such problems, certain broad discriminations can precede
the more subtle, and when these decisions have been made, the more
subtle can then take their place. The choice between selfish and unselfish
action is the most obvious one to follow upon the choice between right
and wrong, and is easily settled by the honest soul. A choice which
involves discrimination between individual benefit and group responsibility rapidly eliminates other factors, and is easy to the man who shoulders his just responsibility. Note the use of the words "just responsibility". We are considering the normal sane man, and not the over-con-
scientious morbid fanatic. There follows next the distinction between the
expedient, involving factors of physical plane relations of business and
finance, leading up to a consideration of the highest good for all parties
concerned. But having through this triple eliminative process arrived at a
certain position, cases arise where choice still remains in which neither
common sense nor logical, discerning reason seem to help. The desire is
only to do the right thing; the intent is to act in the highest possible way
and to take that line of action which will produce the best good of the
group apart from personal considerations altogether. Yet light upon the
path, which must be trodden, is not seen; the door which should be
entered is unrecognised and the man remains in the state of constant in-
decision. What, then, must be done? One of two things:

First the aspirant can follow his inclination and choose that line of action out of the residue of possible lines, which seems to him the wisest and the best. This involves belief in the working of the Law of Karma and also a demonstration of that firm decisiveness which is the best way in which his personality can learn to abide by the decisions of his own soul. It involves also the ability to go forward upon the grounds of the decision made, and so to abide by the results without forebodings or regrets.

Secondly, he can wait, resting back upon an inner sense of direction, knowing that in due time he will ascertain, through the closing of all doors but one, which is the way he should go. For there is only one open door through which such a man can go. Intuition is needed for its recognition. In the first case mistakes may be made, and the man thereby learns and is enriched; in the second case, mistakes are impossible and only right action can be taken.

It is obvious, therefore, that all resolves itself into an understanding of one's place upon the ladder of evolution. Only the highly advanced man can know the times and seasons and can adequately discern the subtle distinction between a psychic inclination and the intuition.

In considering these two ways of ultimate decision, let not the man who should use his common sense and take a line of action based upon the use of the concrete mind, practise the higher method of waiting for a door to open. He is expecting too much in the place where he is. He has to learn through right decision and right use of the mind to solve his problems. Through this method he will grow, for the roots of intuitive knowledge are laid deep within the soul and the soul, therefore, must be contacted before the intuition can work. One hint only can here be given : The intuition ever concerns itself with group activity and not with petty personal affairs. If you are still a man centered in the personality, recognise it, and with the equipment available, govern your actions. If you know yourself to be functioning as a soul and are lost in the interest of others, untrammelled by selfish desire, then your just obligation will be met, your responsibilities shouldered, your group work carried forward, and the way will unfold before you, whilst you do the next thing and fulfil the next duty. Out of duty, perfectly performed, will emerge those larger duties which we call world work; out of the carrying of family responsibilities will come that strengthening of our shoulders which will enable us to carry those of the larger group. What, then, is the criterion?

For the high grade aspirant, let me repeat, the choice of action depends upon a sound use of the lower mind, the employment of a sane commonsense and the forgetfulness of selfish comfort and personal ambition. This leads to the fulfilment of duty. For the disciple there will be the automatic and necessary carrying forward of all the above, plus the use of the intuition which will reveal the moment when wider group responsibilities can be justly shouldered and carried simultaneously with those of the smaller group. Ponder on this. The intuition reveals not the way ambition can be fed, nor the manner in which desire for selfish advancement can be gratified. (4-67/70)

6. It is relatively of no importance what you do. That which is of major importance is to register consciously and all the time, just exactly what you are doing. I would have you remember that right doing is the result of being. If your awareness of being is of a personality nature, so will be your activity. If your consciousness is focussed in spiritual being, your spontaneous, creative and active service will be consequently (followed) by radiation. I would have you ponder on this. . . . Be occupied with the problem of sensitive response, and not with the glamour of the work which you must do. Deal with causes and not with effects. The effects are inevitably effective. (5-135)

51. THE PROBATIONARY PATH

1. Whilst the man is on the Probationary Path he is taught principally to know himself, to ascertain his weaknesses and to correct them. He is taught to work as an invisible helper at first, and for several lives is generally kept at this kind of work. Later, as he makes progress, he may be moved to more selected work. He is taught the rudiments of the Divine Wisdom and is entered into the final grades in the Hall of Learning. He is known to a Master, and is in the care (for definite teaching) of one of the disciples of that Master, or, if of rare promise, of an initiate. (1-64)

2. The man stands on the Probationary Path. He is ignorant yet of what lies ahead, and is conscious only of wild and earnest aspiration and of innate divine longings. He is eager to make good, longing to *know,* and dreaming always of someone or something higher than himself. All this is backed by the profound conviction that in service to humanity will the dreamed-of goal be reached, will the vision become reality, the longing fructify into satisfaction, and aspiration be merged in sight. (2-36)

3. The probationer has to . . . equip himself emotionally and mentally, and to realise and prove that he has somewhat to impart to the group with which he is esoterically affiliated. Think upon this: too much emphasis is laid at times upon that which the pupil *will get* when he becomes an accepted disciple or probationer. I tell you here, in all earnestness, that he will not take these desired steps until he has somewhat *to give,* and something to add that will increase the beauty of the group, that will add to the available equipment that the Master seeks for the helping of the race, and that will increase the richness of the group colouring. This can be brought about in two ways that mutually interact:

i. By the definite equipping, through study and application, of the content of the emotional and mental bodies.

ii. By the utilisation of that equipment in service to the race on the physical plane, thereby demonstrating to the eyes of the watching Hierarchy that the pupil has somewhat to *give.* He must show that his one desire is to be a benefactor and to serve, rather than to grasp and acquire for himself. This life of acquisition for the purposes of giving must have for incentive the ideals touched in meditation, and for inspiration those downpourings from the higher mental levels and from the buddhic levels which are the result of occult meditation.   (2-269/70)

52. THE TREADING OF THE WAY

1. (The aspirant) is endeavouring to become a magical creator and to accomplish two things:

i. Recreate his instrument or mechanism of contact, so that the solar Angel has a vehicle, adequate for the expression of Reality. This involves, we noted, right type, quality, strength and speed.

ii. Build those subsidiary forms of expression in the outer world through which the embodied Energy, flowing through the recreated sheaths, can serve the world.

In the first case, the aspirant is dealing with himself, working within his own circumference, and thus learning to know himself, to change himself, and to rebuild his form aspect. In the other case, he is learning to be a server of the race, and to construct those forms of expression which will embody the new ideas, the emerging principles, and the new concepts which must govern and round out our racial progress.

Remember that no man is a disciple, in the Master's sense of the word, who is not a *pioneer*. A registered response to spiritual truth, a realised pleasure in forward-looking ideals, and a pleased acquiescence in the truths of the New Age, do not constitute discipleship. If it were so, the ranks of disciples would be rapidly filled, and this is sadly not the case. It is the ability to arrive at an understanding of the next realisations which lie ahead of the human mind, which marks the aspirant who stands at the threshold of accepted discipleship; it is the power, wrought out in the crucible of strenuous inner experience, to see the immediate vision and to grasp these concepts in which the mind must necessarily clothe it, which give a man the right to be a recognised worker with the Plan (recognised by the Great Ones, if not recognised by the world); it is the achievement of that spiritual orientation, held steadily—no matter what the outer disturbance in the physical plane life may be—that signifies to Those Who watch and seek for workers, that a man can be trusted to deal with some small aspect of Their undertaken work; it is the capacity to submerge and to lose sight of the personal lower self in the task of world guidance, under soul impulse, which lifts a man out of the ranks of the aspiring mystics into those of the practical, though mystically minded, occultists.

This is an intensely practical work, on which we are engaged; it is likewise of such proportions that it will occupy all of a man's attention and time, even his entire thought life, and will lead him to efficient expression in his personality task (imposed by karmic limitation and inherited tendency) and to a steadfast application of the creative and magical work. Discipleship is a synthesis of hard work, intellectual unfoldment, steady aspiration and spiritual orientation, plus the unusual qualities of positive harmlessness and the open eye, which sees at will into the world of reality.

Certain considerations should be brought to the notice of the disciple which—for the sake of clarity—we will tabulate. To become an adept it will be necessary for the disciple to:

i. Enquire the Way.

ii. Obey the inward impulses of the soul.

iii. Pay no attention to any wordly consideration.

iv. Live a life which is an example to others.

These four requirements may sound at the first superficial reading as easy of accomplishment, but if carefully studied, it will become apparent why an adept is a "rare efflorescence of a generation of enquirers". Let us take up each of these four points:

i. *Enquire the Way*

We are told by one of the Masters that a whole generation of enquirers may only produce one adept. Why should this be so? For two reasons:

First, the true enquirer is one who avails himself of the wisdom of his generation, who is the best product of his own period, and yet who remains unsatisfied and with the inner longing for wisdom unappeased. To him there appears to be something of more importance than knowledge, and something of greater moment than the accumulated experience of his own period and time. He recognises a step further on and seeks to take it in order to gain something to add to the quota already gained by his compeers. Nothing satisfies him until he finds the Way, and nothing appeases the desire at the centre of his being except that which is found in the house of his Father. He is what he is because he has tried all lesser ways and found them wanting, and has submitted to many guides, only to find them "blind leaders of the blind". Nothing is left to him but to become his own guide and find his own way home *alone.* In the loneliness which is the lot of every true disciple, are born that self-knowledge and self-reliance which will fit him in his turn to be a Master. This loneliness is not due to any separative spirit, but to the conditions of the Way itself. Aspirants must carefully bear this distinction in mind.

Secondly, the true enquirer is one whose courage is of that rare kind which enables its possessor to stand upright and to sound his own clear note in the very midst of the turmoil of the world. He is one who has the eye trained to see beyond the fogs and miasmas of the earth, to that centre of peace which presides over all earth's happenings, and that trained attentive ear which (having caught a whisper of the Voice of the Silence) is kept tuned to that high vibration and is thus deaf to all lesser alluring voices. This again brings loneliness, and produces that aloofness which all less evolved souls feel when in the presence of those who are forging ahead.

A paradoxical situation is brought about from the fact that the disciple is told to enquire the Way, and yet there is none to tell him. Those who know the Way may not speak, knowing that the Path is constructed by the aspirant as the spider spins its web out of the centre of his own being.

Thus only those souls flower forth into adepts in any specific generation who have "trodden the winepress of the wrath of God alone", or who (in other words) have worked out their karma alone, and who have intelligently taken up the task of treading the Path.

ii. *Obey the inward impulses of the soul*

Well do the teachers of the race instruct the budding initiate to practise discrimination and train him in the arduous task of distinguishing between :

(a) Instinct and intuition.

(b) Higher and lower mind.

(c) Desire and spiritual impulse.

(d) Selfish aspiration and divine incentive.

(e) The urge emanating from the lunar lords, and the unfoldment of the solar Lord.

It is no easy or flattering task to find oneself out, and to discover that perhaps even the service we have rendered and our longing to study and work, has had a basically selfish origin, and resting on a desire for liberation, or a distaste for the humdrum duties of everyday. He who seeks to obey the impulses of the soul has to cultivate an accuracy of summation, and a truthfulness with himself, which is rare indeed these days. Let him say to himself "I must to my own Self be true" and in the private moments of his life and in the secrecy of his own meditation, let him not gloss over one fault, nor excuse himself along a single line. Let him learn to diagnose his own words, deeds, and motives, and to call things by their true names. Only thus will he train himself in spiritual discrimination and learn to recognise truth in all things. Only thus will the reality be arrived at and the true Self be known.

iii. *Pay no consideration to the prudential considerations of worldly science and sagacity*

If the aspirant has need to cultivate a capacity to walk alone, if he has to develop the ability to be truthful in all things, he has likewise need to cultivate courage. It will be needful for him to run counter consistently to the world's opinion, and to the very best expression of that opinion, and this with frequency. He has to learn to do the right thing as he sees and knows it, irrespective of the opinion of earth's greatest and most quoted. He must depend upon himself and upon the conclusions he himself has come to in his moments of spiritual communion and illumination. It is here that so many aspirants fail. They do *not* do the very best they know; they fail to act in detail as their inner voice tells them; they leave undone certain things which they are prompted to do in their moments of meditation, and fail to speak the word which their spiritual mentor, the Self, urges them to speak. *It is in the aggregate of these un-accomplished details that the big failures are seen.*

There are no trifles in the life of the disciple, and an unspoken word, or unfulfilled action may prove the factor which is holding a man from initiation.

iv. *Live a life which is an example to others*

Is it necessary for me to enlarge upon this? It seems as if it should not be, and yet here again is where men fail. What after all is group service? Simply the life of example. He is the best exponent of the Ageless Wisdom who lives each day in the place where he is, the life of the disciple; he does not live it in the place where he thinks he should be. Perhaps after all the quality which produces the greatest number of failures among aspirants to adeptship, is cowardice. Men fail to make good where they are, because they find some reason which makes them think they should be elsewhere. Men run away, almost unrealising it, from difficulty, from inharmonious conditions, from places which involve problems, and from circumstances which call for action of a high sort, and which are staged to draw out the best that is in a man, provided he stays in them. They flee from themselves and from other people, instead of simply *living the life.*

The adept speaks no word which can hurt, harm or wound. Therefore he has had to learn the meaning of speech in the midst of life's turmoil. He wastes no time in self pity or self justification, for he knows the law has placed him where he is, and where best he can serve, and has learnt that difficulties are ever of a man's own making and the result of his own mental attitude. If the incentive to justify himself occurs, he recognises it as a temptation to be avoided. He realises that each word spoken, each deed undertaken, and every look and thought, has its effect for good or for evil upon the group.

Is it not apparent therefore why so few achieve and so many fail? (4-581/7)

2. Before me streams the Path of Light. I see the Way. Behind me lies the mountain path, with stones and cobbles on the way. Around me are

the thorns. My feet are tired. But straight ahead stretches the Lighted Way and on that Way I walk.   (6-648)

3. The signpost indicates the way to go; it does not reveal the goal. It is indicative but not conclusive. So with all truth up to the present time. (10-170)

4. The word "spiritual" does not refer to religious matters, so-called. All activity which drives the human being forward towards some form of development—physical, emotional, mental, intuitional, social—if it is in advance of his present state, is essentially spiritual in nature, and is indicative of the livingness of the inner divine entity. The spirit of man is undying; it for ever endures, progressing from point to point and stage to stage upon the Path of Evolution, unfolding steadily and sequentially the divine attributes and aspects.   (12-1)

5. What is it that we are endeavouring to do? We are treading the *Way of Release*, and on that way all drops from our hands; everything is taken away, and detachment from the world of phenomenal life and of individuality is inevitably forced upon us. We are treading the *Way of Loneliness,* and must learn eventually that we are essentially neither ego nor non-ego. Complete detachment and discrimination must finally lead us to a condition of such complete aloneness, that the horror of the great blackness will settle down upon us. But when that pall of blackness is lifted and the light again pours in, the disciple sees that all that was grasped and treasured, and then lost and removed, has been restored, but with this difference—that it no longer holds the life imprisoned by desire. We are treading the *Way that leads to the Mountain Top of Isolation,* and will find it full of terror. Upon that mountain top we must fight the final battle with the Dweller on the Threshold, only to find that that too is an illusion. That high point of isolation, and the battle itself, are only illusions and figments of unreality; they are the last strongholds of the ancient glamour, and the great heresy of separateness. Then we, the Beatific Ones, will eventually find ourselves merged with all that is, in love and understanding. The isolation, a necessary stage, is itself but an illusion. We are treading the *Way of Purification* and step by step all that we cherish is removed—lust for form life, desire for love, and the great glamour of hatred. These disappear and we stand purified and empty. The distress of emptiness is the immediate result; it grips us and we feel that the price of holiness is too high. But, standing on the Way suddenly the whole being is flooded with light and love, and the emptiness is seen as

constituting that through which light and love may flow to a needy world. The purified One can dwell then in that place where dwell the Blessed Lords, and from that place go forth to "illumine the world of men and of the deities." (14-34/5)

6. *Great is the Mystery of Those Who Blaze the Trail back to the Father's Home!* The word goes forth to all the sons of men, the Sons of God: Those who have reached the Portal of the Final Way must prove themselves, and in their proving teach and lift those who would follow in their steps.

Thus down the ages have the sons of men, who are the Sons of God, embodied in themselves the Light which shines, the Strength which lifts and serves, the Love that evermore endures. They walk the *Way* of purity, the *Way* into the innermost. We follow after. They served their time. We seek to do the same. (6-768)

53. THE IMMEDIATE GOAL FOR DISCIPLES

The immediate Goal for all aspiring disciples at this time can be seen to be as follows:

1. An achievement of clarity of thought as to their own personal and immediate problems, and primarily the problem as to their objective in service. This is to be done through meditation.

2. The development of sensitivity to the new impulses which are flooding the world at this time. This is to be brought about by loving all men more, and through love and understanding contacting them with greater facility. Love reveals.

3. The rendering of service with complete impersonality. This is done by eliminating personal ambition and love of power.

4. The refusal to pay attention to public opinion or to failure. This is done by application of strict attention to the voice of the soul, and by an endeavour to dwell ever in the secret place of the Most High. (4-635/6)

54. WORKING UNDER EXISTING CONDITIONS

1. Progress is made in spite of, and not because of, existing conditions. For disciples, such as those I am now going to attempt to teach, there is no retiring from the world. There is no condition of physical peace and of quiet wherein the soul may (not) be invoked. . . . The work has to go forward in clamour. The point of peace must be found in the midst of riot. Wisdom must be attained in the very midst of intellectual turmoil, and the work of co-operation with the Hierarchy on the inner side of life, must proceed amidst the devastating racket of modern life in the great cities. (5-6)

2. Your problem is not to get rid of difficulties, but simply to be in-different as to whether they exist or not. (5-659)

3. Most aspirants and disciples believe that they are bearing enough, and are tried to the limit of their capacity. This is not the case. The deeper sources of strength in them have not yet been evoked, and the tension under which they should act and live from day to day, is only as yet a feeble one—it is not all-exacting. Ponder on this last phrase. (6-243)

4. Be content with your duty and the immediate service which will lead you a step further upon the way to which you are ordained, and this way you can travel rapidly and with eager feet, or slowly and with lagging steps. (13-93)

55. STANDING ALONE

1. It is by standing *alone* that all disciples grow, and by feeling their way and discovering their own peculiar line of approach to the centre from which light streams out, and also by responding steadily and in realised loneliness to the call of duty and service. (5-186)

2. To work as a unit along your chosen line of service, has been your task. For all such souls, it is a problem to be faced when the time comes for their indentities to be merged in a group soul, and their personal iso-lation is thereby infringed and negated.

With you, however, this isolation is not the result of any separative tendency of the lower mind, for that is offset in you by your deep-seated love of the Masters and of humanity. It is the result of the essential loneliness which has beset your path, as it does the path of all disciples, and the development of that instinctive reticence which is an aspect of the necessary equipment of all who are struggling towards the Portal of Initiation. The vow of silence which all disciples take, must still be kept, but the power to share knowledge, experience, and the gains of illumination, must at the same time be cultivated; in the light which streams forth from the centre of Light, all that concerns the personality and service must stand revealed. All secrets must fade away, yet the revelations which come as one progresses along the Path, must be held in the secret chamber of the heart, where none may see them but those who share the same secrets. The reticence to be cultivated, is that of relationship with the group of Masters and the Hierarchy, plus the knowledges you share with those who walk shoulder to shoulder with you upon the Way. You withhold also, as dangerous, knowledge which you may have, from those who are not yet upon the Path of Discipleship. It is skill in action and in the distribution of information which must be developed. I mention this so that you may know the rightness of your attitude, but also in order that you may gather the fact that the present cycle of loneliness is still objectively true, but subjectively ended.   (5-211)

3. Your life has been relatively free up to this time, but the choosing of a comrade must and does in every case bring other issues and other values into being. Upon the planes of soul and mind, you still must stand alone, and if you grasp this from the very start, you will not find the complications of any great importance. . . . Remember . . . there can be equality in love and purpose (from the basic and the essential point of view), but not equality of inner understanding or of point achieved upon the Path. (5-277)

4. Your personal problem is enhanced and becomes exceedingly complex, because of the reactions of your immediate associates, and your strenuous endeavour to lift all that you possibly can off their shoulders. . . . Lift not too much, my brother. It is the right of their souls to learn the same lessons as you have had to learn, and an over-pitiful heart is not always the most helpful of possessions. A loving heart is always helpful. . . . Take not away from others this right to stand alone, by too great a display of that shielding love. . . . Let them stand up to the issues of the soul which are brought to their attention through the medium of the material lesson, and thus enable them to enter upon their next life better equipped to love,

to work and to live unselfishly. . . . True love has sometimes to stand aside and look on peacefully whilst others learn their lessons. . . . You think with clarity when the emotions of others do not overwhelm you, and sweep your astral body into unison with theirs. Refuse then to be overwhelmed, and regard not yourself as failing in some respect when others fail to meet the issues as they should. The reactions of others are not your responsibility. It is your responsibility to give them strength and detachment. Shoulder not, therefore, responsibilities which are not yours. This is one of the hardest lessons an initiate has to learn before he can be admitted as an active worker into the Hierarchy of Love. (5-404/5)

5. All that any disciple or aspirant has to do in relation to his fellow men, is to stimulate the light that is in them, leaving them free to walk in their own light and way upon the Path. (5-417)

6. A disciple, at your stage of development, . . . has to learn, first of all, to stand completely alone (though only apparently so and only for a temporary space of time), detached from contact with the Master. Sometimes even his own soul seems silent. But this is all illusion. Circumstances are staged to bring this condition about, and if they are not so staged by the disciple's own soul, then the Master acts to bring the circumstances about. The disciple must be thrown on his own resources. (5-593)

7. There comes a time in the training of any disciple when he *must* stand alone and feel sometimes that he has been deserted by his Master and by the other members of the Ashram. It is the higher and occult correspondence of the mystical experience of the true mystic, and to which he has given the name of "the dark night of the soul". All this is nevertheless only a part of the great illusion and has to be overcome and dissipated. When this victory has been achieved, and there has been evidenced the willingness to work alone and apparently with no ashramic direction— except a general knowledge of the Plan—then the disciple has demonstrated that he can be trusted; he becomes available for a higher rating and more responsibility can be placed upon him—if not in this life then in the next. (6-510)

8. Even the Hierarchy itself, with all its knowledge, visions and understanding, and with all its resources, cannot coerce and cannot forecast what mankind will do. It can and does stimulate to right action; it can and does indicate possibility and responsibility; it can and does send out its teachers and disciples to educate and lead the race; but at no point and in no situation does it command or assume control. It can and does bring

good out of evil, illuminating situations and indicating the solution of a
problem, and further than this the Hierarchy cannot go. If it assumed
authoritative control, a race of automatons would be developed and not
a race of responsible, self-directed, aspiring men. . . . At all costs man
must learn to stand and act alone.   (13-113)

56. LONELINESS

1. Remember that the lonely way is also the lighted way. Loneliness is
is an illusion which seeks to thwart the efforts of the server; it is a glamour
which can seriously impair true vision. That you may walk the *Way* in
peace and light, and that power in service may be yours, is the desire of
my heart for you.   (5-113)

2. Loneliness grows as the aspirant detaches himself from the world of
souls. There comes ever an interlude wherein the disciple senses an intense
seeming isolation, but it is only an illusion. You know that you are not
alone.   (5-419)

3. Loneliness . . . is one of the first things that indicates to a disciple
that he is being prepared for initiation. It will be apparent . . . that the
loneliness to which I refer is not that which is incident to those weaknesses of character which repel one's fellow men, to an aloof or disagreeable
nature, or to any form of self-interest which is so emphasised that it an-
tagonises other people. There is much loneliness in a disciple's life which
is entirely his own fault, and which is subject to cure if he employs the
right measure of self-discipline. With these he must deal himself, for they
concern the personality, and with your personalities I have no affair. I refer to the loneliness which comes when the accepting disciple becomes the
pledged disciple and steps out of a life of physical plane concentration, and
of identification with the forms of existence in the three worlds, and finds
himself in the midway place, between the world of outer affairs and the
inner world of meaning. His first reaction then is that he is alone; he has
broken with his past; he is hopeful but not sure of the future; the tangible
world to which he is accustomed must, he knows, be superseded by the
intangible world of values, involving a new sense of proportion, a new
range of values, and new responsibilities. This world he believes exists, and
he steps forward bravely and theoretically, but it remains for a while wholly

intangible; he finds few who think and feel as he does, and the mechanism of sure contact only exists within him in embryo. He is breaking loose from the mass consciousness with which he has been merged hitherto, but has not yet found his group, into which he will eventually be consciously absorbed. Therefore, he is lonely and feels deserted and bereft. . . . Such a sense of loneliness is only another form of self-consciousness, of undue self-interest, and (as you make progress upon the Path) you will find it disappearing. If you therefore feel lonely, you must learn to look upon it as a glamour or illusion and as a limitation which must be overcome. You must begin to act as if it were not. If only more disciples would learn the value of acting "as if". There is no time for any of you to be lonely these days, for there is no time for you to think about yourselves. (6-45/6)

4. Be not afraid of loneliness. The soul that cannot stand alone has naught to give. (6-755)

5. The revelation of a certain type of spiritual loneliness is one through which all disciples have to pass; it is a test of that occult detachment which every disciple has to master.

This solitariness has to be faced and understood, and it results in two realisations: first of all, a realisation of your exact point on the ladder of evolution, or on the Path; and secondly, an intuitive perception of the point in evolution of those we contact along the way of life. For quite a long time every disciple refuses to do either of these two things. A false humility, which in reality borders on a lack of truthfulness, keeps him from clear-eyed recognition of status—a recognition which necessarily involves more intelligence, and sounds out no call to pride. Few too dare trust themselves to see their fellow men as they really are, for fear of a critical spirit—so hard it is to develop the true practice of loving understanding which leads to the seeing of all people in truth, with their faults and their virtues, their pettiness and their grandeurs, and still to love them as before and even more.

This occult solitariness must be consciously developed by you, and not left to circumstances. It is a solitariness which rests on soul attainment and upon no spirit of separateness; it is a solitariness which boasts of many friends and many interruptions, but of these many, few—if any—are admitted to the point of sacred peace; it is a solitariness that shuts none out, but which withholds the secrets of the Ashram from those who seek to penetrate. It is, finally, a solitariness which opens wide the door into the Ashram.

. . . It will necessitate a conscious and definite withdrawal of yourself, and at the same time will lead to a still warmer expression of love upon the outer plane of life.

. . . It is wiser to cultivate the quality of spiritual solitude, than to have it forced upon you—as so often happens to so many.

. . . In this solitude there is no morbidness, there is no harsh withdrawing, and there is no aspect of separateness. There is only the "place where the disciple stands, detached and unafraid, and in that place of utter quiet the Master comes and solitude is not". (6-762/4)

57. ACCEPTED DISCIPLE

1. The . . . period, wherein a man is an accepted disciple, is perhaps one of the most difficult in a man's whole period of lives. It is made so in several ways:

He is definitely a part of the Master's group, and is within the consciousness of the Master at all times, being kept within His aura. This involves the steady holding of a high vibration. I would have you ponder on what the effect of this would be. To hold this vibration is at all times a difficult thing to do; it frequently involves an intensification of all that subsists within a man's nature, and may lead (especially at first) to curious demonstration. Yet, if ever a man is to be able to hold the force that is the result of the application of the Rod of Initiation, he has to demonstrate his ability to do so at an earlier stage, and be able to hold himself stably and to move steadily forward when subjected to the intensification of vibration that comes from the Master.

He has to discipline himself so that nothing can enter into his consciousness that could in any way harm the group to which he belongs, or be antagonistic to the Master's vibration. If I might so express it, so as to give you some conception of my meaning, when he first forms part of the group enclosed in the Master's aura, he is kept on the periphery of that aura until he has learnt to throw off automatically, and to reject immediately, every thought and desire unworthy of the Self and thus harmful to the group. Until he has learnt to do this he cannot advance into a closer relationship, but must remain where he can be automatically shut off. But gradually he purifies himself still more, gradually he develops group consciousness and thinks in group terms of service, gradually his aura takes on more and more the colouring of his Master's aura, till he *blends* and has earned the right to be gathered closer to his Master's Heart. Later I will explain the technical meaning of this phrase, when dealing with the work of the Master with the pupil. Suffice it to say, that as the term of "accepted disciple" progresses (and it varies in different cases) the disciple advances ever closer to the heart of the group, and finds his own place and functional activity in that body corporate. That is the secret: the finding of one's place—not so much one's place upon the ladder of evolution (for that is approximately known), but in *service*. This is of more importance than is realised, for it covers the period which, at the end, will definitely demonstrate which path a man will follow after the fifth initiation. (2-270/1)

2. There is much apprehension in people's minds as to how a Master lets an accepted disciple become aware that he is accepted. An impression is abroad that he is told so and that an interview is accorded wherein the Master accepts him and starts him to work. Such is not the case. The occult law holds good in discipleship as in initiation, and the man goes forward blindly. He hopes, but he does not know; he expects that it may be so, but no tangible assurance is given; from a study of himself and of the requirements, he arrives at the conclusion that perhaps he has reached the status of accepted disciple. He therefore acts on that assumption and with care he watches his acts, guards his words, and controls his thoughts so that no overt act, unnecessary word or unkind thought will break the rhythm which he believes has been set up. He proceeds with his work but intensifies his meditation; he searches his motives; he seeks to equip his mental body; he sets before himself the ideal of service and seeks ever to serve; and then (when he is so engrossed in the work on hand that he has forgotten himself), suddenly one day he sees the One Who has for so long seen him.

This may come in two ways: in full waking consciousness, or by the registering of the interview on the physical brain as it has been participated in during the hours of sleep. (4-169/70)

3. An accepted disciple is not in reality one who has been accepted by a Master for training. This is the distortion of a true idea which, in its progress from the mental plane to the physical, has achieved a complete reversal or distortion. An accepted disciple is one who:

i. Has accepted the fact of the Hierarchy, with the implications of loyalty and co-operation which that acceptance involves.

ii. Has accepted the fact that all souls are one, and who has, therefore, pledged himself to seek expression as a soul. The service to be rendered is the awakening and stimulation of all souls contacted.

iii. Has accepted the occult technique of service. His service to humanity determines all his activities, and subordinates his personality to the need of the time. Note that phrase. Cultivate insight and a fluid response to the *immediate need* and not a sensitive reaction to a distant goal.

iv. Has accepted the Plan, as indicated by the Teachers of the race. He seeks to understand the nature of that Plan and to facilitate its manifestation.

Other points (of a more individual nature) could be enumerated, but I would have you lay the emphasis upon the acceptances which have or should have motivated your attitude, and I would ask you not to emphasise so unduly in your private thoughts this idea of being "accepted by a Master". This thought and its teaching by many esoteric groups, has been productive of much error, much misunderstanding, much pain and much disillusionment.   (5-83)

4. All disciples who are being trained for that stage, called by the inappropriate name of "accepted disciple", are being taught to use their own magnetic vibration to gather to themselves those who will constitute their own group, those whom they can specifically help. This work they are being taught by being put into a position of trust in relation to their fellow men. . . . The Master accepts no one. He only recognises achieved capacity and ability, and then endeavours to use them for the furthering of the divine Plan.   (5-264/5)

5. Neither world disciples or accepted disciples are mystical visionaries or vague idealists, but men and women who are intelligently and practically seeking to make the ideal plan a factual experiment and success on earth. Such is the task in which all of you have the opportunity to help. Your ability to become world disciples eventually, is dependent upon your capacity to decentralise yourselves, and to forget your personalities. This forgetting involves not only your own personalities, but also the personalities of your fellow disciples and co-workers and of all you meet. It means also, that in the future you go forward into a greater measure of service, impelled thereto by the fire of love in your hearts for your fellow men.   (5-690)

6. Accepted disciples are in training for initiation. If, when they approach the Path of Discipleship, they fail to grasp this fact and to give the fullest co-operation, they postpone the time of that initiation. Their grasp of the fact will be demonstrated in the intensity of their proffered service. Planned service is one of the modes of the training. Disciples in the early stages of their work are apt to be primarily interested in themselves and in their own reactions and attitudes to the Master. The fact that they are working in a Master's group seems to them the fact of paramount importance. (5-693/4)

7. The term . . . of "Accepted Disciple" covers the stages of the first and second initiations; when a disciple has taken the third initiation, he is no longer technically an accepted disciple, even though he still remains in a Master's group until he has taken the fourth initiation. (5-728)

8. *Initiated disciples* have no interest in anything but the vision, the Plan and its direction and materialising upon earth. *Accepted disciples* are learning this, and in the meantime have to react to the vision in what I might call a second hand manner; they are occupied with the Plan and with the distribution of the forces which will materialise it. (5-731)

58.   SONSHIP TO THE MASTER

We now come to the time when the disciple moves on to the much coveted position of a "Son of the Master". He is then a part *consciously* and at all times of the Master's consciousness. The interplay between the Master and disciple is being rapidly perfected, and the disciple can now consciously and at will link up with the Master and ascertain His thoughts. He can enter into His plans, desires and will. This he has won by the right of familiarity of vibration, and because the shutting off process (necessitated earlier by discordant vibration) is practically superseded; the disciple has so purified himself that his thoughts and desires cause no disquietude to the Master, and no contrary vibration to the group. He has been tried and not been found wanting. His life of service in the world is more concentrated and perfected, and he is daily developing his power to give, and increasing his equipment. All this concerns his relationship to some Master and to some one group soul. It is not dependent upon his taking initiation. Initiation is a technical matter and can be expressed in terms of esoteric science. A man can take initiation and yet not be a "son of the Master". Discipleship is a personal relationship, governed by terms of karma and affiliation, and is not dependent upon a man's status in the Lodge. Keep this clear in your mind. Cases have been known when a man has acquired—through diligence—the technical requisites for initiation before becoming affiliated with any particular Master.

This later relationship of "son" to some Master, has a peculiar sweetness all its own, and carries with it certain privileges. The disciple can then lift some of the burden off his Master's shoulders, and relieve Him of some of His responsibilities, thereby setting Him free for more extended work. Hence the emphasis laid on *service, for it is only as a man serves that he advances.* It is the keynote of the vibration of the second abstract level. The Master at this period will confer with His "Son" and plan the work to be done upon their united point of view. In this way He will develop His pupil's discrimination and judgment, and lighten His own load along certain lines, thus setting Himself free for other important work.

The final period of those under discussion can have but little submitted about it. It covers the period when a man is mastering the final stages of the Path and is entering into closer and closer touch with his group and with the Hierarchy. He is not only vibrating in tune with his group and with his Master, but is beginning now to gather out his own people, and form a group himself. This group will be at first only on emotional and physical levels, and on the lower mental. After the fifth initiation he will enclose within his aura these groups and those on egoic levels who are his own. This in no way prevents his being one with his Master and group, but the method of interblending is one of the secrets of initiation.

All this, coupled with what has been earlier imparted, will give you some idea of the rights and powers acquired on the Probationary Path and on the Path of Initiation. The means of development are ever the same: occult meditation and service; the inner life of concentration and the outer life of practice; the inner ability to contact the higher, and the outer ability to express that faculty in terms of holy living; the inner irradiation from the Spirit, and the outer shining before men. (2-271/3)

59. MASTERS AND DISCIPLES

1. Throughout the world, disciples of these Masters have come into incarnation at this time, with the sole intent of participating in the activities and occupations and truth dissemination of the various churches, sciences, and philosophies, and thus producing within the organisation itself an expansion, a widening, and a disintegration where necessary, which might otherwise be impossible. It might be wise for occult students everywhere to recognise these facts, and to cultivate the ability to recognise the hierarchical vibration as it demonstrates through the medium of disciples in the most unlikely places and groups.

One point should here be stated in connection with the work of the Masters through Their disciples, and it is this. All the various schools of thought which are fostered by the energy of the Lodge are, in every case, founded by a disciple, or several disciples, and upon these disciples, and not upon the Master, lies responsibility for results and the consequent karma. The method of procedure is somewhat as follows: The Master reveals to a disciple the objective in view for an immediate little cycle, and suggests to him that such and such a development would be desirable. It is the work of the disciple to ascertain the best method for bringing about the desired results, and to formulate the plans whereby a certain percentage of success will be possible. Then he launches his scheme, founds his society or organisation, and disseminates the necessary teaching. Upon him rests the responsibility for choosing the right co-workers, for handing on the work to those best fitted, and for clothing the teaching in a presentable garb. All that the Master does is to look on with interest and sympathy at the endeavour, as long as it holds its initial high ideal and proceeds with pure altruism upon its way. The Master is not to blame should the disciple show lack of discrimination in the choice of co-workers, or evidence an inability to represent the truth. If he does well, and the work proceeds as desired, the Master will continue to pour His blessing upon the attempt. If he fails, or his successors turn from the original impulse, thus disseminating error of any kind, in His love and in His sympathy the Master will withdraw that blessing, withhold His energy, and thus cease from stimulating that which had better die. Forms may come and go, and the interest of the Master and His blessing pour through this or that channel; the work may proceed through one medium or another, but always the life force persists, shattering the form where it is inadequate, or utilising it when it suffices for the immediate need. (1-52/3)

2. Disciples and advanced Egos on the Probationary Path receive instruction at this particular time for two special purposes:

i. To test out their fitness for special work lying in the future, the type of that work being known only to the Guides of the race. They are tested for aptitude in community living with a view to drafting the suitable ones into the colony of the sixth sub-race. They are tested for various lines of work, many incomprehensible to us now, but which will become ordinary methods of development as time progresses. The Masters also test for those in whom the intuition has reached a point of development that indicates a beginning of the co-ordination of the buddhic vehicle, or—to be exact—has reached a point where molecules of the seventh sub-plane of the buddhic plane can be discerned in the aura of the Ego. When this is so They can go ahead with confidence in the work of instruction, knowing that certain imparted facts will be understood.

ii. Instruction is being given at this time to a special group of people who have come into incarnation at this critical period of the world's history. They have come in all at the same time, throughout the world, to do the work of *linking up the two planes, the physical and the astral, via the etheric.*

This sentence is for serious consideration, for it covers the work that a number of the newer generation have come to do. In this linking up of the two planes, people are required who are polarised in their mental bodies (or, if not polarised there, are nevertheless well rounded out and balanced) and can therefore work safely and with intelligence in this type of work. (1-66/7)

3. Part of my work is the steady search for aspirants of strong heart, fervent devotion and trained minds. . . . One lesson all aspirants need to learn and to learn early, and that is that concentration upon the personality of the Teacher, hoping for personal contact with Him, and constant visioning of that condition called "accepted chelaship", serves to postpone that contact and delay acceptance. Seek to equip your instrument, learn to function in quietness, fulfil your obligations and do your duty, develop restraint of speech and that calm poise that comes from an unselfish life motive, and forget the selfish satisfaction that might well up

in the heart when recognition of faithfulness comes from the watching Hierarchy. (4-129)

4. All this deeply esoteric work must only proceed under the direction of the skilled teacher. Platitudinously, the aspirant is told that "when the pupil is ready, the Master will appear". He then settles comfortably back and waits, or focusses his attention upon an attempt to attract the attention of some Master, having apparently settled in his mind that he is ready, or good enough. He naturally gives himself a spiritual prod at intervals, and attends spasmodically to the work of discipline and of purification. But steady and prolonged undeviating effort on the part of aspirants is rare indeed.

It is indeed true that at the right moment the Master will appear, but the right moment is contingent upon certain *self-induced* conditions. When the process of purification has become a life-long habit, when the aspirant can at will concentrate his consciousness in the head, when the light in the head shines forth and the centres are active, then the Master will take the man in hand. In the meantime he may have a vision of the Master, or he may see a thought-form of the Master, and may get much real good and inspiration from contact with the reflected reality, but it is not the Master and does *not* indicate the stage of accepted discipleship. Through the medium of the light of the soul, the soul can be known. Therefore seek the light of your own soul, and know that soul as your director. When soul contact is established, your own soul will, if I may so express it, introduce you to your Master. With all due reverence again may I add, that the Master waits not with eagerness to make your acquaintance. In the world of souls, your soul and His soul are allied, and know essential unity. But in the world of human affairs, and in the process of the great work, it should be remembered that when a Master takes an aspirant into His group of disciples, that aspirant is for a long time a liability and oft a hindrance. Students over-estimate themselves quite often, even when repudiating such an idea; subjectively they have a real liking for themselves and are frequently puzzled as to why the Great Ones give them no sign, nor indicate Their watching care. They will not and They need not, until such time as the aspirant has used to the full the knowledge which he has gained from lesser teachers, and from books and printed scriptures of the world. Students must attend to the immediate duty and prepare their mechanisms for service in the world, and should desist from wasting time and looking for a Master; they should achieve mastery where now they are defeated and in the life of service and of struggle they may then reach the point of such complete self-forgetfulness that the Master may find no hindrance in His approach to them. (4-594/5)

5. You will ever remember that Masters are made through the achieving of mastery, and not through obedience to any person. You will bear in mind that, I, your teacher, am not constantly aware of your physical condition or daily doings. I concern not myself with the affairs of the personality, and those misguided aspirants who claim that the Masters are forever telling them what to do, and are guiding them in their personal affairs, are still far from the grade of accepted discipleship. You will remember that the light will shine into a mind that is self-controlled and free from the mental dominance of another mind. (5-8)

6. Disciples should know that the Masters have three grades of workers. There are those doing the difficult work in the outer world. They materialise the forms through which the Hierarchy can express its intentions, and they make the human contacts. There are many such disciples, and they are doing this work from their own free choice and because they have realised the immediate and coming need of humanity, and have pledged themselves to serve. There are, secondly, those who act as links between the Elder Brothers of the race, the Masters of the Wisdom, Who embody the divine Plan, and the workers mentioned above. I do not say that they act as links between the disciple and his Master, for that is a direct relationship which none may touch, particularly in the more advanced stages. This second group of working disciples, however, act as intermediaries in the working out of the Plan in the world and they hold themselves in readiness to go anywhere when requested, thus aiding with their wisdom and experience and supplementing the capacities of the field workers, conferring with them. There are several such that are being sent expressly into the field at this time to hasten the work whenever possible and to increase the magnetic attraction of those centres through which the spiritual force of the New Age can flow.

This is all being done preparatory to a supreme effort which the Hierarchy of Masters plans to make. Should all of you in the field at this time work with complete surrender and devotion—giving all your time and interest to the cause—it may be possible to prepare the ground in such a manner that the coming effort of the Masters may prove adequate to the emergency.

The third group is that of the Masters Themselves and Their co-operating initiates. They work primarily upon the inner side. Their activities are confined largely to the mental plane and to the scientific use of thought. Thus they guide Their workers and helpers and influence and direct Their working disciples and the world disciples.

There is at this time an inner intention of blending the occidental and the oriental approaches to the ancient wisdom and to the Hierarchy. Co-operation and the mutual interchange of wisdom and of knowledge are essential if this is to be perfected. The objectives of both methods—the mystic and the occult—are the same.   (5-17/8)

7. The revelation of unity through the power of thought, is the glorious consummation of the work of the Brotherhood, and to this you do, as do all disciples, respond in your highest moments. It can, in a smaller way and according to the measure of your consecration, be your glory and your goal also if you hold the thought of *oneness,* of *service* and above all else *of love.*   (5-25)

8. Disciples come definitely into the aura of the Hierarchy. You are a disciple. Disciples evoke from us who are the teachers upon the inner side of life, many and diverse reactions. We look at some of you and feel that much time must elapse before we can fully trust you with our confidence; integration, wisdom and soul contact must first be induced. Others emerge into the Hierarchical Light and we know—as we study them—that though there is contact and knowledge, there is also ambition, violence and selfishness, and that these qualities must be offset and subdued before there can be freedom of action, both on our part and on theirs. Others again are lovely in themselves, with a high and sweet vibration, but they are weak and full of fear, sorrowful, or weighed down with care; they have to be taught the way of strength and of divine carelessness before their service can measure up to demand. Others again come into our sphere of influence who are integrated, wise, trustworthy, and with far more than the average capacity to serve and to prove useful. Their power to live, to influence and to serve is very great. Yet in some one part of their nature there is a weakness and their expression is limited.   (5-371)

9. It is the sign of real discipleship when a man works alone and apparently unaided, and seeks not to intrude his small affairs into the consciousness of his Master, realising as he does, the pressure of work upon the Great Ones.   (5-416)

10. In the intense preoccupation of our world work Those Who serve humanity have not the desire, nor have They the intention, to study the

details of a disciple's life or to intrude into his own personal affairs. All we are concerned with is to ascertain the growth of the inner light and the quality of his service. We look at both of these as they emerge into reality upon the physical plane. (5-491)

11. The disciple upon whom the Master can most confidently depend is the one who can—in periods of change—preserve that which is good and fundamental, while breaking away from the past, and add to it that which is of immediate service in the present. (5-681)

12. The disciples of the world are the intermediaries between the Hierarchy and Humanity. They are the product of *immediate* human endeavour; they set the pace for human unfoldment; they are therefore closely en rapport with the consciousness of the race of men. It is the quality of the new disciples, the rapidity with which men find their way into the ranks of the disciples, and the demand which the working disciples in the world make on behalf of humanity (which they *know*) that brings about the needed changes. (6-277)

13. The primary task of the Master is to aid the disciple to develop the intuition, and at the same time, keep the mental perception in an active and wholesome state. (6-280)

14. The Hierarchy has been pictured as a group of eager men, anxious to establish happy relations with humanity. In this, the Members of the Hierarchy are not primarily interested. The prime objective set before every Master of, or in, an Ashram, is to see the purposes of Sanat Kumara working out successfully through the medium of hierarchical endeavour. Their work lies with the advanced thinkers in the human family who are capable of grasping the Plan and of penetrating to the periphery of hierarchical influence. The Masters seek disciples among the world intelligentsia, but They do *not* seek for them among those who *constitutionally* join occult groups, and the ranks of the glamoured devotees who seek association with some Master. They seek for them among those who intelligently love their fellow men, and who are free from spiritual ambition and self-seeking. They never look for them among those who love the idea of being the sought and the beloved of the Masters. A man may have no practical knowledge of academic initiatory teaching, but—if loves his fellow men and is dedicated to their service and can use his mind on their behalf—he is probably nearer to initiation than the devotees of the occult schools. (6-429)

15. The task of any Master is only to bring to the attention of the man, working through the medium of a physical brain, that phase of the Ageless Wisdom which his own soul is seeking to have him register. (6-719)

16. The urgency of the time is great, and the Masters are exceedingly active and profoundly concerned at this time with the work of salvaging the world. They have not the time for personal work, except with Their own groups of accepted chelas, all of whom are active in the world work, or they would not be in the Master's group. Also They may work intermittently with small groups of probationers to whom They offer opportunity and give an occasional hint. Each of Them has a few, a very few, probationers in training, to take the place of chelas who pass on to initiation, but beyond these two groups, during this century, They do no personal work, leaving the many aspirants to the care of lesser initiates and chelas. Even Their work and Their personal chelas at this time are much restricted, and word has been sent out to the working disciples in the world to stand on their own feet, to use their own judgment and not handicap the Masters at this time of intense strain and danger by attracting Their attention needlessly. The world issues today are of such importance, and the opportunity before humanity is so great, and the Masters are so entirely occupied with world affairs, and with the dominant and prominent figures in high places in the nations, that the instruction of unimportant people in the various little occult groups and societies is temporarily suspended. The time is relatively so short in which to accomplish and carry out certain aspects of the Plan as entrusted to the Great Ones, that all true chelas are going about their work and endeavouring to solve their own problems without having to call on the Master's help, thus leaving Him free for more important work. The closer a disciple is to a Master, the more deeply he realises this fact, and the more he endeavours to fulfil his duty, learn his lessons, serve humanity, and lift some of the load of work off the shoulders of the Master.   (14-106)

17. The *main technique of the Hierarchy is that of conveying inspiration.* The Masters are not openly lecturing or teaching in the great cities of the world; They work entirely through Their disciples and initiates. It will, however, be possible for Them to appear increasingly among men, and evoke recognition, as the influence of Aquarius is more firmly established. The Masters in the meantime, must continue to work "within the silence of the universal Ashram", as it has been called, and from there They in-

spire Their workers, and these latter in their time and way, inspire the
New Group of World Servers.   (18-230)

60. OCCULT OBEDIENCE

1. I make suggestions based on experience in occult work. There is no
obligation to obey. We seek to train intelligent servers of the race, and
these are developed by self-initiated effort, freedom in action and discrimination in method, and not by unquestioning obedience, negative
acquiescence, and blind following. Let this not be forgotten. If any command may ever emanate from the subjective band of teachers of whom I
am a humble member, let it be to follow the dictates of your own soul
and the promptings of your higher self.   (4-103/4)

2. I will teach you. Whether or not you profit by the teaching is entirely
your own affair; that is something that the disciples of the New Age need
to learn. There is no such thing as occult obedience as usually taught
by the current occult schools. In the olden days in the East, the Master
exacted from His disciple that implicit obedience which actually made
the Master responsible, and placed upon His shoulders the destiny or the
karma of the disciple. That condition no longer holds good. The intellectual principle in the individual is now too much developed to warrant this
type of expectancy. Therefore, this condition no longer holds good. In the
coming New Age, the Master is responsible for the offering of opportunity
and for the right enunciation of the truth, but for no more than that. In
these more enlightened days, no such position is assumed by the teacher
as in the past, and I do not assume it. I shall with frankness speak. I know
my disciples, for no disciple is admitted into an Ashram without deep
consideration on the part of the teacher. I shall convey by hint and symbol
that which should be apprehended, and it will be noted and understood by
those among my disciples who have the opened inner ear, and true humility
of heart. If it is not recognised, time will pursue its onward course and
revelation will ultimately come. I exact therefore, no blind obedience. But,
however, if advice and suggestion are accepted, and you choose—*of your
own free will*—to follow my instructions, these instructions must be followed accurately. Also, there must be none of that constant looking for
results and for phenomena, which has deterred the course and the progress
of many would-be disciples.   (5-5)

3. What is this occult obedience which a Master is supposed to exact? Today, the Masters are dealing with the highly mental type of disciple, who believes in the freedom of the human will and consciousness and who resents the imposition of any so-called authority. The intellectual man will not accept any infringement of his freedom, and in this he is basically right. He objects to having to obey. This is today axiomatic. Out of this fundamental question, lesser ones arise which I would like to cite. Has the disciple to obey the slightest hint which the Master may give? Must every request and suggestion be accepted? Must all that a Master says be accepted as true and infallibly correct? Is the disciple wrong when he refuses (if he does) to recognise the Master's point of view and the statements He may make? Will the fact of Accepted Discipleship limit his freedom of opinion or choice, coerce his judgment, and make him simply a replica in thought of the Master's thought? These are questions of importance.

The obedience required is obedience to the Plan. It is *not* obedience to the Master, no matter what many old style occult schools may say. The obedience which is asked of you is based on your growing recognition of the Plan for humanity, as it emerges in your consciousness through the processes of meditation and through definite service, based upon a growing love of your fellow men.

The obedience demanded is that of the personality to the soul, as soul knowledge, soul light, and soul control become increasingly potent in the mind and brain reactions of the disciple. This whole problem of occult obedience would not arise at all if the rapport between soul and personality, or between the disciple and the Master, was complete and soundly established. The entire question is based upon the blindness and lack of knowledge of the disciple. As the rapport becomes more firmly established, no fundamental divergences of opinion can appear; the objectives before the disciple and the Master become identical, and the group life conditions the service rendered by both of them. It is, therefore, the limitations of the disciple which prompt the question, and his fear that too much may be asked of him by the Master and his soul. Is this not true, my brother? It is the holding on to your personality interpretations, wishes and ideas, which leads you to draw back from the word obedience. It is your liking for yourself and for your own point of view which—literally and factually—makes you afraid of a too prompt acquiescence in the known suggestions of the Master. I would have you remember that *suggestion* is all that a Master ever makes to a disciple, even though He may make a positive statement about human affairs. These statements may be entirely correct; the neophyte, however, is usually too blind or prejudiced by his own individual point of view to accept them. Obedience can only be rendered when there is a developed understanding and an inclusive vision; if that is lacking, the passing of time will adjust the matter. (5-686/7)

4. Have you ever realised that occult obedience—correctly understood and applied—is the royal route through the astral plane, particularly in connection with glamour and with sixth ray tendencies, to the very heart of the Hierarchy? People are apt to regard obedience as the carrying out of rules and orders, imposed upon them by some authoritative source. This, as you well know, is not the case in any true hierarchical training. Obedience, for the disciple, is a quick spiritual reaction to the Plan as it emanates from the Hierarchy, rapid and correct sensitive registration of the quality of the Ashram with which he may be affiliated, and a consequent and in time almost automatic undertaking (with speed) the required task. It is a task which the disciple assigns to himself and is *not* one ordered by the Master. The acceptance of the task is simply evidence that the disciple is an ashramic worker, pledged to the welfare of humanity. (6-586/7)

5. What is this occult obedience . . . about which we hear so much? Not what many occult groups make it out to be. It is not the control of an external organisation, dedicated to so-called occult work. It is not the imposed conditions of any teacher of any rank. It is not the exchange of the prison of one set of ideas for those of another set, with perhaps a larger range or import. A prison is a prison, whether it is a tiny cell or an isolated island of vast extent, from which escape is impossible.

The authority to which we, the teachers on the inner side, respond, is twofold in nature, and to it you are just beginning (as units in a group) to respond. To what do you respond? :

i. To the slowly emerging realisation of the "light beyond", using that phrase as a symbol. This light is different *in its appeal* to the individual. Yet it is ONE LIGHT. But its recognition reveals new laws, new responsibilities, new duties and obligations, and new relations to others. These constitute an authoritative control. None can escape this authority, but can disobey it in time and space and for a temporary period.

ii. To the authority of the *Rules of the Road* which are imposed upon one as one passes from the Path of Probation on to the Path of Discipleship. Yet it is ONE ROAD. Upon this "narrow, razor-edged path", one learns to walk with discipline and discretion and with the desire-lessness which one experiences in unison with one's fellow disciples. (10-49/50)

61. FREE WILL

1. These new types of groups will work together under the conscious guidance and suggestion of a member of the Great White Lodge. Note the word 'suggestion' my brothers. If these groups were subjected to the *authority* of such a member, then the objective of all the work undertaken would fail to materialise. An occult law would have been broken. Free, intelligent assistance is what we are asking from all our disciples today, and we leave them free to render it or not as they like, and in the manner which may seem best to them. I am your teacher. I make suggestion. I offer instruction. I indicate the way to the goal and to the field of service. I point out to you what we, the Teachers upon the inner side, seek to see accomplished. Temporarily and of your own free will, you have indicated your willingness to serve and to co-operate in my plans. Beyond thus indicating the way and the service, I will not go. It is for all of you, my disciples, to work out in joint collaboration and in the closest understanding the way that my suggestions and my hints should be utilised. I do not interfere.   (5-45/6)

2. It is wise for human beings to realise that mankind is free. Even the Hierarchy itself does not know which forces—those of good or those of evil—will ultimately prevail, because even if the forces of good triumph where the war is concerned, will they triumph where the peace is concerned? *Good* must ultimately triumph, but the Hierarchy does not know what the immediate future holds for humanity, because men determine their own destiny.   (5-74)

3. Divinity . . . awaits the expression of man's free will. . . .
    Therefore, another answer to the question posited is that the Christ and the spiritual Hierarchy never—no matter how great the need or important the incentive—infringe upon the divine right of men to make their own decisions, to exert their own free will, and to achieve freedom by fighting for freedom—individually, nationally and internationally. (8-164)

4. It is in this realm of *ideas* that humanity is not a free agent. This is an important point to note. Once an idea becomes an ideal, humanity can freely reject or accept it, but ideas come from a higher source and are *imposed* upon the racial mind, whether men want them or not. Upon the use made of these ideas (which are in the nature of divine emanations, embodying the divine plan for planetary progress) will depend the rapidity of humanity's progress or its retardation for lack of understanding. (9-7/8)

5. Negative, unintelligent mediumship and psychism reduces its exponent to the level of an automaton; it is dangerous and inadvisable because it deprives man of his free will and his positivity, and militates against his acting as a free intelligent human being. The man is not acting in these cases as a channel for his own soul, but is little better than an instinctual animal, if he is not literally an empty shell, which an obsessing entity can occupy and use.   (13-10)

6. I would reiterate, as I have in the past, that *it is humanity which determines its own fate*. Men have transcended the child stage and are now adult, though not mature. Maturity is achieved through self-engendered experience and decision, and for some time, we who seek to guide, have confined our efforts to reaching the intelligent people, impressing the spiritually minded, and in stimulating humanity to right action without encroaching upon man's growing expression of free will. So the outcome is unpredictable, though we may see a certain measure of inevitability in future happenings. But man is free to choose the way that he shall go, and much of the responsibility—for his choice rests upon the shoulders of the more instructed of the human family and upon those who have achieved some measure of vision.   (13-281)

7. The Hierarchy—because of the divine principle of free will in humanity —cannot foretell how men will act in times of crisis; the Hierarchy cannot enforce the good way of life against normal human desire, for this good way of action must come from out the very depths of human thinking and feeling, and must emerge as a free and non-supervised endeavour; the Hierarchy may not take those possible steps which will prevent men making mistakes, for it is through those mistakes that men learn "by the means of evil that good is best", as your great initiate-poet has expressed it. All that the Hierarchy can do is to present the needed teaching which will direct man's thinking along right lines, to point the way of true relationships, and at the same time demonstrate objectively the nature of the bad way.   (13-636)

8. It might be said that within the limits of the intelligent direction of the intelligent man there *is* free will, as far as activity in the human kingdom is concerned. Where no mind activity is present, and where there is no power to discriminate, to analyse and to choose, there is no free will. Within the vaster processes of the Plan, however, as it includes the entire planetary evolution, there is, for the tiny unit, man, no free will. He is subject, for instance, to what we call "acts of God", and before these he is helpless. He has no choice and no escape. Herein lies a hint upon the working of karma in the human kingdom; karma and intelligent responsibility are inextricably woven and interwoven. (15-29)

9. The great distinction between the human kingdom in the three worlds, and the other kingdoms in nature, is the factor of free will. In the matter of death, this free will has, in the last analysis, a definite relation to the soul; the will of the soul is either consciously or unconsciously followed, where the decision of death is concerned, and this idea carries with it many implications which students would do well to ponder. (17-248)

62. FREEDOM

1. Leave people free and seek not to influence them or to impose your ideas upon them. Your interpretation of them and of their need (no matter how close they may be to you) is not necessarily correct. Leave people free in all respects—with the freedom that you demand and expect for yourself. May I, in all love and tenderness, suggest that the ideas, methods, formulas, and ways of living, which seem right to you (and *are* right for you) may be entirely undesirable for others and that, if you force them on to others, their *souls* may remove them from your influence in the cause of freedom to expand. (5-245/6)

2. You are free, my brother. No one is seeking to hold you in this group. No one is seeking in any way to gain authority over you. No one wants you to work, or study or to serve, where your own soul does not prompt you to work and to express yourself. But remember that there is no freedom except in making free choice and in serving. The idea of freedom can itself constitute a prison. You can leave this particular group, but if you are to grow at all, you will find yourself inevitably within some other group for service. You can drop the responsibilities which you shouldered

when you joined this group, but you cannot escape the shouldering of other responsibilities. You can pass out of this group of brothers, as far as the outer plane linking is concerned, but you have already established links with them which cannot be broken by any personality activity or line of action, for they are soul links and must at some time be recognised. It is the service, the responsibility, and the group work which counts and lasts; the fluctuations and reactions of any personality can delay, but they cannot negate success.

Basically, fundamentally and essentially, you are pledged to the service of the Plan somewhere, somehow, some day. The fluctuations and indecisions and questionings of your personality do not matter in the long run and in the light of soul activity, but they do matter in time and space and temporarily, where your band of group brothers are concerned.

So feel free, my brother, but be quite sure that it is not a freedom demanded because group affiliation irks you. The more your soul grips your personality, the less you will be concerned with the problems of isolation and of freedom. Feel free, but be sure that it is not a freedom demanded because the steady discipline of occult training frets a temperament still essentially mystic. The more your soul grips you, the more your mind will awaken, and feeling (in the personal sense) fade out. Feel free, but be sure that it is not a freedom demanded because the sense of failure to organise your time and reduce your personality to rhythmic living, hurts your pride.   (5-288/9)

3. The necessity for an inner freedom, preserved inviolate, is for you an urgent one, but you are learning fast the lesson that freedom is a state of mind and not a condition of being.   (5-310)

4. The individual disciple, seeking initiation, is with deliberation and with his full and free consent merged into the group; he achieves this fusion by his own individual effort and is (throughout the entire process) an absolutely free agent, moving forward and becoming mentally inclusive, as rapidly or as slowly as he chooses. He determines the time and the event himself, without interference or obstruction from any outside source. (6-353)

5. Time and again, along the Road, he will revolt from control and will fall back into the glamour of his supposed freedom. There *is* freedom from control of the personality. There *is* freedom from the control of personalities. But there is never any freedom from the Law of Service, and from the constant interplay between man and man, and soul and soul. To stand

really free, is to stand in the clear unimpeded light of the soul, which is basically and intrinsically group consciousness.

Therefore, when one of you is beset by uncertainty and unrest, desiring and demanding to walk free, and that no authority be imposed upon you, see that you are not submitting to the glamour of a desire to be freed from your group impacts, and make sure that you are not seeking—as a sensitive soul—a way of escape. (10-48)

6. Freedom is the birthright of mankind, and free will is the highest of the divine characteristics. Freedom is misinterpreted and misused by many, owing to the point in evolution of the mass of humanity, but it is a fundamental, divine principle; and where principles are involved the Hierarchy knows no compromise. (13-429)

7. There has been much talk among esotericists (particularly in the Eastern presentation of the Path to Reality) anent liberation. The goal held before the neophyte is liberation, freedom, emancipation; this, by and large, is the keynote of life itself. The concept is a transitting out of the realm of the purely selfish, and of personal liberation, into something much wider and more important. This concept of liberation lies behind the modern use of the word "liberty" but is far wiser, better and deeper in its connotation. Liberty, in the minds of many, is freedom from the imposition of any man's rule, freedom to do as one wishes, to think as one determines, and to live as one chooses. This is as it should be, provided that one's wishes, choices, thoughts and desires are free from selfishness, and are dedicated to the good of the whole. This is, as yet, very seldom so.

Liberation is much more than all this; it is freedom from the past, freedom to move forward along certain predetermined lines (predetermined by the soul), freedom to express all the divinity of which one is capable as an individual, or which a nation can present to the world. (17-259/60

63. AGE OF THE DISCIPLE

1. We who teach, watch and guide the esoteric development of man, know that unless a certain measure of fusion is established by the time fifty-six years of age is attained, it is seldom established later. After that age, a man may hold to the point achieved, and foster his aspiration, but the dynamic submergence of the personality in the will and life of the soul, is rare after that time. When reached prior to the age of fifty-six, then subsequent growth and unfoldment on the Path of Discipleship is surely possible.   (5-596/7)

2. There are certain key points in all lives which are deciding and frequently releasing factors. A major one for all disciples occurs around the age of thirty-five, and still another at the age of forty-two. . . . Another key point comes ever at the age of fifty-six, and . . . the age of sixty-three will see another crisis.   (6-533)

3. The sixty-third year of your life, as in the life of all disciples, will be one of crisis and of supreme opportunity, and towards that point you should look and for it you should make preparation.   (6-636)

4. By the time a disciple reaches the age of forty-nine, his pathway of life service should be clearly defined.   (6-742)

5. It is interesting to observe that initiation is often taken (I might say it is usually taken) after passing the milestone of half a century. The reason is that if the disciple can produce the needed staying power and the required enthusiasm—by which I mean dynamic purpose—he can then be trusted to handle the powers conferred with wisdom, to display the needed poise, and to proceed upon his outward way with humility and caution. (6-761/2)

6. We have five points of crisis in the life of the individual. . . . The reflection of this fivefold experience in any individual life takes place in the following order in the life of the average intelligent aspirant, who responds to, and takes advantage of the civilisation and education of the present time :

i. Appropriation of the physical sheath.
This takes place between the fourth and seventh year, when the soul, hitherto overshadowing, takes possession of the physical vehicle.

ii. A crisis during adolescence, wherein the soul appropriates the astral vehicle. This crisis is not recognised by the general public, and is only

258

dimly sensed, from its evidenced temporary abnormalities, by the average psychologist. They do not recognise the cause but only the effects.

iii. A similar crisis between the twenty-first and twenty-fifth years, wherein the mind vehicle is appropriated. The man should then begin to respond to egoic influences, and in the case of the advanced man, he frequently does.

iv. A crisis between the thirty-fifth and forty-second years, wherein conscious contact with the soul is established; the threefold personality then begins to respond, as a unit, to soul impulse.

v. For the remaining years of life, there should be an increasingly strong relationship between the soul and its vehicles, leading—to another crisis between the fifty-sixth or the sixty-third years. According to that crisis will depend the future usefulness of the person, and whether the ego continues to use the vehicles on into old age, or whether there is a gradual withdrawal of the indwelling entity.   (15-52/3)

64. THE SANNYASIN

1. You are entering a phase in your life cycle in which you may become —if you so wish—the true sannyasin, the one who (freed from the more active tasks of the younger man who is starting out into the field of his life activity) can use the experience gained, the hard won knowledge assembled, and the wisdom garnered in active service of the Hierarchy and of humanity. You can now live for the sake of others, and find in our work the reward, interest and compensation, for all the struggle of the past. To serve has long been your aim, for you have loved your fellow men, and have struggled to retain this love for humanity in the face of disillusionment, disgust at the general world selfishness, and a tendency . . . to feel the futility of things and the uselessness of effort when confronting the present world debacle, and the weight of human pessimism. Against this you must struggle.   (5-136/7)

2. Your relation is with souls and not with temporary forms, and so you must live detached from personalities, serving them, but living ever in the consciousness of the soul—the true sannyasin.   (5-139)

3. The sannyasin, the one who—having tasted to the full of life experience —is now dedicated to the life of spiritual values and to their teaching to others. Ponder on this.   (5-204)

4. Mould your life upon the pattern of the sannyasin, and hold on to no physical plane attachments. If you do, they will fail you, and the pain in thus holding will hinder your feet as they stumble upon the Path. Walk free, my brother, and hold to nobody and hold no person to you in the bonds of attachment. Can you be a true sannyasin and stand in life alone or with only your brother disciples as comrades and friends? . . . Should you be able to see life's circumstances rebuilt around you, or see them crumble to nothingness with equal equanimity, then your field of service can enlarge. You will have no interest in the affairs of the little self. Seeing this, the many little selves will come to you for help.   (5-253/4)

5. You are . . . a pledged sannyasin. That carries with it joy, but responsibility; discipline, but realised gain. The work to be done by the sannyasin lies ever in the realm of increasing realisation. He has to become aware and conscious of each step that he takes and its result, of each motive that impels and its effect, and of each objective gained and its consequence. The fruits of discipline have to be clearly understood by him, without any attachment to the results of the work. This alert awareness must be fostered by you . . . A condition of increased sensitivity in yourself to yourself and to others must be increasingly developed. A conscious approach to the goal must be induced in you, so that you are ever aware of contact in two directions: you are aware of the inner subjective life and also aware of the outer objective world; this must be undertaken and developed by you as a synthetic, dual activity. Ponder on this.   (5-295)

6. There are . . . certain people who are outstandingly called to live the life of the sannyasin, the life of the one who—having fulfilled the duties of the scholar, of the householder, of the family man, and the business man—is now called to that attitude of life and that orientation to other purposes and goals, which we technically call that of the sannyasin, or the teaching disciple. In the olden times, such a man left his home and his business, and went out into the world, following the gleam, seeking the Master, and ever teaching as he went. Today, in the life of our Western civilisation, and under the dawning influence of the New Age, the call remains the same, but the disciple goes not out, leaving all the familiar scenes behind and negating outer usefulness. He remains where he is, continuing with the outer and physical fulfilment of his duty, but within a

Great change and a definite reorientation takes place. His attitude to life and affairs is basically altered. His whole inner life tendency becomes that of a *planned withdrawing*. He is passing through that stage upon the Way to which Patanjali refers in *The Yoga Sutras* under the term "right abstraction". It differs somewhat from the process called "detachment", because that process or motivated activity is applied primarily to the astral-emotional nature, to the desire life, whatever those attachments or desires may happen to be. This is a mental activity; it is an attitude of mind which affects primarily the entire life-attitude of the personality. It involves not only the detachment of the desire nature from that which is familiar, desired and appropriated from long habit, but it involves also a complete readjustment of the entire lower threefold man to the world of souls.

It is here that right habits and attitudes in life to the world of business, and of family relations, play their part, enabling the sannyasin to "continue on the upward way with heart detached and free", and yet to do so whilst performing right action, through right habit and right desire, to all with whom his lot is cast. To this difficult task your soul is now calling you. It constitutes your major life problem: To stand free whilst surrounded; to work in the subjective world, whilst active in the exterior world of affairs; to achieve true detachment whilst rendering to all that which is due. (5-313/4)

7. You are a sannyasin and as such must work towards an increasing release from ties of any kind, though (and herein lies a subtle distinction) not from release from environing conditions and responsibilities. What is required is an inner attitude of complete abandon to the will of your soul, which is the Will of God, as far as any individual is concerned. (5-391)

8. Be happy. Be happy as the sannyasin is happy who (through detachment from the little self and attachment to the greater Self in all) has left behind all that might hinder and hamper his service. Henceforth you belong not to yourself or to any earthly friend or claim. You belong to the servers of humanity and to us. (5-464)

9. Be a sannyasin—free, alone with God, your soul and Me. Then work and love. (6-755)

65. OLD AGE AND SERVICE

1. The choice with which you are confronted is not so much where you will work, but whether you have arrived at a high water mark in your developed life of service and can therefore go no further, or whether there are still to be found in you those springs of interest and those inner urges, which will enable you to reach outward and further into the life of the spirit. Such is oft the choice with which the disciple is faced, who reaches close to the three score years and ten of ordinary human enterprise. . . . The difficulty lies in the fact that, fundamentally, either decision is right. Few, however, face the choice consciously or intelligently or having made it, abide by the decision made. From the standpoint of the ordinary aspirant, the choice is relatively unimportant, because the time equation is of no great moment at this stage; a few years more or less are of no import in the eternity of soul reaction. Therefore, a decision to relax, to hold the point gained, but to refrain from further struggle, has in it no room for criticism. Remember this.

From the standpoint of the accepted disciple . . . there may be more to the choice than at first appears. It might be of service to you, and to all who may later read these instructions, if I dwelt for a moment upon the inevitable problem of the working disciple, upon the man who reaches the age which you have reached. Shall he rest back upon his laurels . . . or shall he—to use a biblical phrase—"gird his loins" anew and go forward with a fresh impetus and to a still higher summit of attainment? Shall he demonstrate the power of the seventh wave which will carry him forward much further upon the beach of life expression, or will the strong undertow of ordinary human frailty pull him back from renewed effort?

The reasons why a disciple must at least endeavour not to relax unduly and should push on in spite of fatigue (the fatigue of years of living), in spite of the increasing "creaking" of the human apparatus and the inevitable tendency which comes from constant service and constant contact with others, might be enumerated as follows:

i. He must endeavour to carry the rhythm of service and of fruitful living with him when—free of the physical body—he stands upon the other side of the veil. There must be no gap in that service.

ii. He must endeavour, as far as in him lies, to preserve the continuity of his consciousness as a *working* disciple, and should allow no gap to emerge between his present point of tension and that point of tension which supervenes after the death experience.

iii. He must endeavour to close the episode of this life experience so that it is apparent that he is a member of an Ashram; he must permit no break in the established relationship, or any cessation to the flow of ashramic life through him to the world of men. This activity, on account of the natural and normal deterioration of the physical vehicle as it grows older, is not so easy a task; it requires a definite concentration of effort, thus increasing the tension in which a disciple ever lives.

iv. For any disciple in my Ashram, the problem in this time of world crisis is peculiarly urgent, and this for the following reasons:

(a) My Ashram is the main affiliated Ashram with that of the Master K.H. To Him, my Master . . . is given the task, on a large scale, of world education along new lines. Through my Ashram, working under the inspiration of His, the newer esoteric presentation of truth is to be given out. The work that I have already done—through my books and through all the teaching which you have attempted to embody —is to render the teaching of the other and older esoteric schools and groups entirely exoteric. There is little left to them that is new; they must now link up with the sources which I represent, if their leaders are to present fresh and vital information to their students, or they must take what I have conveyed to the world, via A.A.B. and thus again reintegrate into the esoteric whole.

(b) Disciples in my Ashram have a dual responsibility to stand steady in a *preservation of realisation*—if I may use such a phrase. This steadiness must not be relaxed in any way as old age draws near, and it must not be permitted to disappear through the transition of death itself. It is through the unbroken conscious thinking of a welded group of disciples, that the Master of an Ashram works. It is not so much the active outer service of a group of disciples which is of major importance (though it has necessarily a vital purpose) as the coherent, integrated group thought which is so potent in effecting changes in the human consciousness.

(c) The peculiar problem of the present world crisis and the terrific readjustments in the human consciousness, incident to the inauguration of a new culture, civilisation and world religion, warrant my presenting the members of my Ashram . . . with the opportunity to preserve intact and free from all deterioration their "state of mind" throughout the remaining years of this life, through the process of dissolution, and on into the freedom of the other side of the veil. This preservation of conscious integrity is no easy task; it requires understanding and most deliberate effort.

I call you, therefore, my brother, to exactly this effort. The consequences to you will be a much harder life of service from now on; the results will be the carrying out of your plans for work with greatly intensified effort. (6-501/4)

2. There is a peculiar difficulty connected with the realisation that there are relatively only a few years ahead for the majority of the group. Here are four of the difficulties which prevent the sensible and happy realisation of the future transition :

i. The tendency to settle down and take the position that one has done the best one can and that that is all one can be expected to do. This renders the few remaining years simply an expression of habit and of established character, and prevents the undertaking of any new spiritual adventure.

ii. A recognition that one *has* reached one's high water mark for this life and nothing more can be expected. This may be true from the personality angle, but the soul remains eternally young and unsatisfied, knowing no static point.

iii. A preoccupation, growing year by year, with the *processes* of growing old, with its liabilities, its physical symptoms and ugliness, and its required (?) withdrawals. This is a usual and ordinary way of approaching one's declining years and the regular procedure with the great majority. See that it is not yours as the next decade elapses.

iv. The recognition that the soul, enjoying the full richness of life's garnered experience, is now free to serve. No new problems are tackled; no new disciplines are applied; but the disciple uses all that he has in the service of the Ashram, and that for the remainder of his life.

I am seeking to bring all these points to your consideration, for they embody choices which await you, and it is your right to know what they are. (6-637/8)

66. THE NEW GROUP OF WORLD SERVERS (N.G.W.S.)

(NOTE: This descriptive title is so frequently used in this chapter, that it has been decided to abbreviate it to N.G.W.S. *Compiler*.)

(a) CLASSIFICATION OF HUMANITY

The peoples of the world today are divided into four groups, from the angle of Those Who are seeking to guide humanity into the New Age. This is of course a wide generalisation, and there are many bridging groups between the four major divisions.

First, the Ignorant Masses: These, through poverty, lack of employment, illiteracy, hunger, distress and no leisure or means for cultural advantages, are in an inflamed condition. They are developed just enough to respond to the mental control and suggestion of slightly more advanced people. They can be easily regimented, influenced, standardised and swept into a collective activity by leaders of any school of thought which is clever enough and emotional enough to appeal to material desires, to love of country, and to hatred of those who possess more than they do. They can be controlled by fear, and thus aroused to action by emotional appeal.

Knowing no better and suffering so much, they are easily swept by the fires of hatred and fanaticism, and so they constitute one of the greatest and most innocent menaces of the present time. They are the playthings of the better informed, and are helpless in the hands of those who seek to use them for any purpose whatsoever. They can be reached most easily by emotional appeals and by promises, whereas ideas can make but little impact upon their consciousness, for they are not yet developed enough to do their own thinking. . . . The masses fight and die on the urge of inflammatory speeches, and seldom know what it is all about. Their condition *must* be bettered, but not through bloodshed and exploitation.

Secondly, the Middle Classes, so called, both higher and lower. These are the bulk of the nations, the bourgeoisie—intelligent, diligent, enquiring, narrow-minded, essentially religious, though frequently repudiating the forms of religion. They are torn and devastated by the economic conflict, and are, without exception, the most powerful element in any nation, because of their capacity to read, to discuss, to think, to spend money, and to take sides. They form the bulk of the partisans in the world, the fighters for a cause, and are formed into great groups, either for or against this, that, or the other party. They love to recognise and choose a leader, and are ready to die for a cause, and to make endless sacrifices for their ideals, based upon the ideas presented to them by their chosen leaders.

I am not differentiating the so-called aristocracy into a group, because that is entirely a class distinction, based largely on heredity and capital, and the modern adjustments in nations are rapidly fusing them into the large middle class. . . . Because of this levelling which is everywhere going on, the spiritual aristocracy can now emerge—an aristocracy based on a realisation of divine origin and goal, which knows no class distinction, no barriers in religion, and no separating differences. We are therefore dealing with *human divisions* and not *class distinctions*.

This second group is the most fruitful field from which the new leaders and organisers are being drawn. They constitute an intermediate group between the world thinkers, the intelligentsia, and the masses of men. In the last analysis, they are the determining factor in world affairs. . . .

Because of their intelligence, due to the improving educational facilities, the ability to read, and the impact of the new methods of propaganda, the press and the radio, they provide the most powerful group in the world in each nation, and it is to them that the leaders make their appeal, and it is their backing and their partisanship which is demanded, and which means success to any leader. They are the ones who have the controlling vote in national affairs. They are today swept by uncertainty, by questioning, by deep-seated fears, and by the desire to see justice done and the new order of things established. Above everything else they desire peace, stable economic conditions, and an orderly world. For this they are ready to fight, and are today fighting in every party, every group, and for every kind of political, nationalistic, religious, economic and social ideas. If they are not literally fighting, in the physical sense, they are fighting with words, speeches and books.

Thirdly, the Thinkers of the World: These are the intelligent and highly educated men and women, who sense ideas and formulate them into ideals. These people speak the words, write the articles and books, and utilise all the known methods to reach and educate the general public, and thus stir up the bourgeoisie to activity, and arouse through them the masses. Their function and the part they play is of supreme importance. From their ranks come those who are steadily influencing the trend of world affairs, sometimes for good and sometimes for selfish ends. They play upon the human mind as a musician plays upon his instrument, and the power of the press, of the radio, and of the public platforms is in their hands. Their responsibility is enormous. Some few, more perhaps than might appear, are working selflessly under the inspiration of the new era. They are dedicated to the amelioration of human conditions, and the betterment of world affairs along certain lines which seem to them (rightly or wrongly) to have in them the hope of the future, and the uplift of humanity. They are found in every government, party, society, and organisation, and in every Church and religious grouping. They constitute the most influential unit today, because it is through them that the large middle class is reached, swayed and organised for political, religious and social ends. Their ideas and utterances percolate down through the upper and middle classes, and finally reach the ears of the more advanced of the undeveloped masses.

Fourth, the New Group of World Servers: These are the people who are beginning to form a new social order in the world. They belong to no party or government, in the partisan sense. They recognise all parties, all creeds, and all social and economic organisations; they recognise all governments. They are found in all nations and all religious organisations, and are occupied with the formulation of the new social order. From the purely physical angle, they are not fighting either for the best in the old order or for the betterment of world conditions. They consider that the old methods of fighting and partisanship and attack, and the ancient techniques of party battle, have utterly failed, and that the means hitherto employed on all sides and by all parties and groups (fighting, violent partisanship of a leader or a cause, attacks on individuals whose ideas or manner of living is deemed detrimental to mankind), are out of date, having proved futile and unsuitable to bring in the desired condition of peace, economic plenty, and understanding. They are occupied with the task of inaugurating the new world order by forming throughout the world—in every nation, city and town—a grouping of people who belong to no party, take no sides either for or against, but who have as clear and definite a platform and as practical a programme as any other single party in the world today. They take their stand upon the essential divinity of man; their programme is founded upon goodwill, because it is a basic human characteristic. They are therefore organising the men of goodwill throughout the world at this time, outlining to them a definite programme, and laying down a platform upon which all men of goodwill can meet.

They state and believe that their initial appeal has been of such a nature, that given the assistance of the trained minds to be found in the third group outlined above, and given the needed financial assistance to do the required educational work and goodwill propaganda, they can so

change the world (through the sole agency of the men of goodwill) that—
without war, without arousing hatred between men, and without attacking any cause, or giving partisanship to any cause—the new order can be
firmly established upon earth.   (15-632/7)

(b) HISTORICAL BACKGROUND

About the year A.D. 1400, the Hierarchy of Masters was faced with a
difficult situation. As far as the work of the second ray was concerned
(which had to do with the impartation of spiritual truth) there had come
to be what I might call a complete exteriorisation of that truth. The
activity of the first ray had also brought about an intense differentiation
and crystallisation among the nations and governments of the world.
These two conditions of concrete orthodoxy, and political differences,
persisted for many generations, and are still manifesting. Today we have
a similar condition, both in the world of religion and in that of politics.
This is true, whether one is considering India or America, China or Germany, or whether one is studying the history of Buddhism with its many
sects, Protestantism with its myriads of warring groups, or the
many schools of philosophy in the orient or occident. The condition is
widespread, and the public consciousness tremendously diversified, but
this state of affairs marks the summation of the period of separativeness,
and the end before so many centuries, of this intense distinctiveness of
thought.

After noting and watching this trend of affairs for another one hundred
years, the Elder Brothers of the race called a conclave of all departments,
about the year A.D. 1500. Their object was to determine how the urge to
integration, which is essentially the keynote of our universal order, could
be hastened, and what steps could be taken to produce that synthesis and
unification in the world of thought, which would make possible the manifestation of the purpose of the divine Life which had brought all into
being. When the world of thought is unified, then the outer world will fall
into a synthetic order. It should be remembered here that the Masters
think in large terms and work in the wider cycles of evolutionary endeavour. The tiny and temporary cycles, the small ebb and flow of the cosmic processes, do not engage Their attention in the first instance.

At this conclave They had three things to do:

1. To view the divine Plan on as large a scale as possible, and refresh
Their minds with the vision.

2. To note what influences or energies were available for use in the large endeavour to which They were pledged.

3. To train the men and women who were then probationers, chelas and initiates, so that in due time They could have a satisfactory band of assistants on whom They could in future centuries rely.

They had in connection with these aspirants, two problems:

1. They had to deal with the failure on the part of even the most advanced disciples to preserve continuity of consciousness, a failure even now manifested by even initiates.

2. The Masters found the minds and brains of chelas curiously insensitive to the higher contacts, and this again is a condition which still prevails. The chelas, then as now, possessed aspiration, a desire to serve humanity, devotion and occasionally a fair mental equipment, but that telepathic sensitivity, that instinctive response to hierarchical vibration, and that freedom from the lower psychism, which are the needed prerequisites to intensive intelligent work, were singularly lacking. For that matter, they are still distressingly so. Telepathic sensitivity is decidedly on the increase as a result of world conditions and the evolutionary trend, and this is (for the workers on the inner plane) a most encouraging sign, but love of psychic phenomena and failure to differentiate between the vibrations of the various grades of hierarchical workers, still greatly hinder the work.

The Plan. You might here ask, and rightly so: What is this Plan? When I speak of the Plan, I do not mean such a general one as the plan of evolution, or the plan for humanity which we call by the somewhat unmeaning term of soul unfoldment. These two aspects of the scheme for our planet are taken for granted, and are but modes, processes and means to a specific end. The Plan as at present sensed, and for which the Masters are steadily working, might be defined as follows: It is the production of a subjective synthesis in humanity, and of a telepathic interplay which will eventually annihilate time. It will make available to every man all past achievements and knowledges, it will reveal to man the true significance of his mind and brain, and make him the master of that equipment, and will make him therefore omnipresent and eventually open the door to omniscience. This next development of the Plan will produce in man an understanding—intelligent and co-operative—of the divine purpose for which the One in Whom we live and move and have our being, has deemed it wise to submit to incarnation. Think not that I can tell of the Plan as it truly is. It is not possible for any man, below the grade of initiate of the third degree, to glimpse it, and far less understand it. The development of the mechanism whereby a disciple may be *en rapport* with Those responsible for the working out of the Plans, and the capacity to know (and not just dimly sense) that tiny aspect of the whole which is the immediate step ahead, and with which co-operation is possible, that can be achieved by all disciples and should be held as the goal before all aspirants. With the exception of probationary disciples who are not as yet sufficiently stable in their endeavour, all can therefore strive towards achieving continuity of consciousness, and at awakening that inner light which, when seen and intelligently used, will serve to reveal other aspects of the Plan and specially that one to which the illumined knower can respond and usefully serve.

To bring this about, has been the objective of all training given during the past 400 years, and from this fact you can vision the utter patience of the Knowers of the race. They work slowly and with deliberation, free from any sense of speed, towards Their objective, but—and herein lies the immediate interest of what I have to communicate—They do have a time limit. This is based upon the Law of Cycles. It concerns the operation of certain periods of opportunity, which necessarily have their term. . . .

Looking ahead, during the conclave to which I have made reference, the assembled Servers of the race noted the future coming in of the Aquarian age, with its distinctive energies, and its amazing opportunities. These They noted and They sought to prepare man for that period which would approximate 2500 years, and which could if duly utilised, bring about unification, consciously and intelligently, of mankind, and so produce the manifestation of what I prefer to call "scientific brotherhood" in contradistinction to the sentimental connotation of the term now so prevalent.

It appeared to Them at that time, that it would be necessary to do two things before the coming potencies of the Aquarian age could profitably be employed. First of all, humanity must have its consciousness elevated to the mental plane; it must be expanded so that it included not only the world of emotion and of feeling, but also that of the intellect. The minds of men must be made widely and generally active, and the entire level of human intelligence must be raised. It was necessary, secondly, that something should be done to break down the barriers of separateness, of isolation and of prejudice which were keeping men apart from each other and which They foresaw would increasingly do so. Cycle by cycle, men were becoming more and more wrapped up in their own selves—satis-faction and exclusiveness, and racial pride. The result of this would lead inevitably to wide cleavages and the erection of world barriers between nation and nation, and between race and race.

This determination of the members of the Hierarchy to train the minds of men more rapidly and to build towards a more synthetic unity, brought them to a decision which involved the formation of group units, and brought about the emergence of those groups of workers and thinkers who, through their activities, have so largely governed and moulded our world for the past three or four centuries. We have therefore, dating from this conclave, the inauguration of definite and specific group work along clearly defined lines, with each group standing for some peculiar present-ation of truth, and for some aspect of the knowledge of reality.

These groups fall generally into four major divisions; cultural, politi-cal, religious, and scientific. In more modern times three other groups have definitely emerged; they are the philosophical, the psychological, and the financial groups. Philosophers have, of course, always been with us, but they have been for the most part isolated units who have founded schools characterised by partisanship and separativeness. Now there are no outstanding figures as in the past, but groups who represent certain ideas. It is of profound importance that the work of these seven groups of thinkers be recognised as part of the hierarchical programme, designed to produce a certain situation, to bring about certain preparatory con-ditions, and as playing a definite part in the work of world evolution as far as humanity is concerned.

Under the influence of the different rays as they cycled in and out of activity, little groups of men emerged, played their part *in group form-ation*, and disappeared, often unaware of their inherent synthesis and of their co-workers. As can be seen in any intelligent historical retrospect, the work that they did for the race, and their contribution to the pageant of the progress of mankind, stands out with clarity. I have not the time to take this procession of groups, each custodian of a special contribution, and trace for you the work they did or the subjective impulses under which they worked. I can but indicate the trend of their endeavour, and leave to some illumined student of history the delineation of the golden thread of their spiritual work as they raised the mental standard of the race and put man *en rapport* with the world in which he lived, opening his eyes not only to the nature of matter and of form, but also to the hidden depths of his own being. Through their activities we now have a humanity in close relation, though not at-one, and a humanity characterised by three things:

1. An amazing interrelation and intercommunication, of which the radio, the press, modern transportation, and the telephone and telegraph are the servants.

2. A wide-spread philanthropic enterprise, and the growth of the sense of responsibility for one's brother, which was totally unknown in the year 1500. Movements such as the Red Cross, educational foundations, hospitals, and the present economic relief measures to be found in every country, are its exoteric manifestations.

3. A division of the entire human family, consciously or unconsciously, into two basic groups: first, those who stand for the old order of things, who are reactionary, and separative. They represent separative nationalism, boundaries, servitude, and servile obedience; they exemplify religious sectarianism and dependence upon authority. They are against all modern innovations and progress. Secondly, those who vision a unified world wherein love of God means love of one's neighbour, and where the motives underlying all religious, political and educational activities, are characterised by a world consciousness and the Welfare of the entire body and not of the part.

The unification to which the forward looking people aspire, does not involve the neglect of any part, but it does involve the care and nurture of each part in order that it may contribute to the well being of the entire organism. It involves, for instance, the right government and proper development of every national unit so that it can adequately perform its international duties, and thus form part of a world brotherhood of nations. This concept does not even involve the formation of a world state, but it does involve the development of a universal public consciousness which realises the unity of the whole, and thus produces the determination that each must be for all and all for each, as it has been said. Only in this way can there be brought about an international synthesis which will be characterised by political and national unselfishness. This universal state of mind will not again inevitably involve the founding of a world of universal religion. It requires simply the recognition that all formulations of truth and of belief are only partial in time and space, and are temporarily suited to the temperaments and conditions of the age and race. Those who favour some particular approach to the truth will nevertheless achieve the realisation that other approaches and other modes of expression and terminologies, and other ways of defining deity, can be equally correct and in themselves constitute aspects of a truth which is greater and vaster than man's present equipment can grasp and express. Even the Great Ones Themselves but dimly sense reality, and though They are aware of deeper underlying purposes than are Their chelas, yet even They see not the ultimate goal. They too are forced to use such unmeaning terms in Their teaching as Absolute Reality, and Ultimate Realisation.

Hence, during the past three centuries, group after group has appeared and played its part, and we today reap the benefit of their accomplishment. Under the cultural group for instance, we find emerging the poets of the Elizabethan age, and the musicians of Germany and of the Victorian era. Groups of artists are likewise to be found, giving us the famous schools which are the glory of Europe. Two famous groups, one cultural and the other political, also played their parts, the one producing the Renaissance and the other bringing about the French Revolution. The effects of their work are still to be felt, for the modern humanistic movement with its emphasis upon the past, which is completed in the present, and its search for the roots of man's equipment in the earlier trends, harks back to the Renaissance. Revolution and the determination to fight for the divine rights of man, find their prime inaugurating influence and impetus in the revolution in France. Revolt, the formation of political parties, the class warfare which is so rampant today, and the splitting of every country into warring political groups, though sporadic always, have become universal during the past two hundred years, and are all the results of the group activity started by the Masters. Men have grown thereby and have learnt how to think, and even though they may think wrongly, and may initiate disastrous experiments, the ultimate good is inevitable and unavoidable. Temporary discomforts, passing depressions, war and bloodshed, penury and vice, may lead the unthinking into the depths of pessimism. But those who know and who sense the inner guiding hand of the Hierarchy, are aware that the heart of humanity is sound and that out of the present chaos, and perhaps largely because of it, there will emerge those competent to deal with the situation and adequate to the task of unification and synthesis. This period has been occultly called the "age of restoration of what has been broken by the fall". The time has come when the separate parts can be reunited and the whole stand together again in its earlier perfection.

The religious groups have likewise been many—so many that their enumeration is hopeless. We have the groups of Catholic mystics, who are the glory of the occident, there are also the protesting Lutherans,

Calvinists and Methodists, the Pilgrim Fathers—those sour and earnest men—the Huguenot and Moravian martyrs, and the thousands of modern sects in every group. These have all served their purpose, and have led man to the point of revolt and away from acquiescence in authority. They have driven man to the stage of thinking for himself by the force of their unique example. They stood for freedom and the personal right to know.

These latter groups have acted largely under the influence of the sixth and second rays. The cultural emerged under that of the fourth ray, whilst the first ray has impelled the political activities which have brought such changes in the nations. Under the fifth and third ray impulses, groups of scientific investigators have arisen, working with the forces and energies that constitute the divine Life, dealing with the outer garment of God, searching from without towards the within, and demonstrating to man his essential unity with all creation and his relationship, intrinsic and vital, with all forms of life. The names of the individuals in any group are legion and of relatively no importance. It is the group and its interrelated work that counts. It is interesting to note that in the scientific group, the underlying unity is particularly noticeable, for its members are singularly free from sectarianism and selfish competition. This cannot be said of the religious and political groups.

In relation to the many nations and the myriads of men on earth, these moulding groups under the various divisions, are few in number. Their personnel, their contribution to the growth of human expression, and their place in the Plan, can quite easily be traced. The point to be emphasised is that they have all been motivated from the inner subjective side of life; they have come forth under a divine urge and with a specific work to accomplish; they have all been composed in the primary stage of disciples and initiates of the lesser degrees; they have all been subjectively guided step by step by their own souls, which have, in their turn, been co-operating consciously with the Hierarchy of Knowers. This has been the case even when the individual man has been totally unaware himself of his place in the group and that group's divine mission. Let it be remembered also that *there has not been a single failure,* though again and again the individual has not been cognisant of success. The mark of these workers is that they build for posterity. That those who have followed them have failed, and that those who have responded to this work have not been true to the ideal, is disastrously true, but the initial group has uniformly achieved. This surely negates pessimism and demonstrates the exceeding potency of the subjective activity.

The three groups to which I earlier referred, require a word of comment. Their work is curiously different to that of other groups and their ranks are recruited from all the ray groups, though the members of the third group (that of the financiers) are found primarily upon the seventh ray, that of ceremonial organisation. In the order of their emergence, they are the groups of philosophers, psychologists and business men.

The group of philosophers of more modern date, are already powerfully moulding thought, whilst the ancient schools of Asiatic philosophers are just beginning to influence western ideas. Through analysis, correlation and synthesis, the thought power of man is developed and the abstract mind can be unified with the concrete. Through their work therefore, that interesting sensitivity of man, with its three outstanding characteristics of instinct, intellect and intuition, is brought to a condition of intelligent co-ordination. Instinct relates man to the animal world, intellect unites him to his fellow men, whilst the intuition reveals to him the life of divinity. All these three are the subject matter of philosophical investigation, for the theme of the philosophers is the nature of reality and the means of knowledge.

The two most modern groups are the psychologists, who work under the Delphic injunction "Man, know thyself", and the financiers who are the custodians of the means whereby man can live upon the physical plane. These two groups necessarily, and in spite of apparent divergencies and differences, are more synthetic in their foundational aspects, than any of the others. One group concerns itself with mankind, with the varying types of humanity, the mechanism employed, and man's urges, characteristics, and with the purpose—apparent or hidden—of his being. The other group controls and orders the means whereby he exists, controlling all that can be converted into energy, and constituting a dictatorship over all modes of intercourse, commerce and exchange. They control the multiplicity of form-objects which modern man regards as essential to his mode of life. Money, as I have before said, is only crystallised energy or vitality—what the oriental student calls "pranic energy". It is a concretisation of etheric force. It is therefore vital energy externalised, and this form of energy is under the direction of the financial group. They are the latest group in point of date, and their work (it should be borne in mind) is most definitely planned by the Hierarchy. They are bringing about effects upon the earth which are most far reaching.

Now that centuries have elapsed since the conclave in the sixteenth century, these external groups have played their part and performed most notable service. The results achieved have reached a stage where they are internationally effective, and their influence is not confined to one nation or race. The Hierarchy is now faced with another situation, which requires careful handling. They must gather up and weld together the various threads of influencing energy, and the differing trends of thought power which the work of the groups since the year 1500 has produced. They have also now to offset some of the effects which are tending towards a further differentiation. This must inevitably be so when force is brought into contact with the material world. Initial impulses have in them the potency both for good and evil. As long as the form remains of secondary importance and relatively negligible, we call it good. Then the idea and not its expression controls. As time elapses and the energy of the thought makes its impact upon matter, and lesser minds seize upon the particular type of energy, or are vitalised by it, then evil begins to make its presence felt. This finally demonstrates as selfishness, separateness, pride and those characteristics which have produced so much harm in the world.   (4-401/13)

(c) BIRTH OF THE NEW GROUP OF WORLD SERVERS

1. We are passing through an intermediate stage of chaos and of questioning, of rebellion and consequent apparent licence. The methods of science—investigation and analysis, comparison and deduction —are being applied to religious belief. The history of religions, the foundations of doctrine, the origin of ideas, and the growth of the God idea, are being subjected to research and study. This leads to much disputation; to the rejection of old established ideas as to God, the soul, man and his destiny. . . . Out of the medley of ideas, theories, speculations, religions, churches, cults, sects and organisations, two main lines of thought are emerging—one doomed eventually to die out, the other to strengthen and grow until it, in its turn, gives birth to that (for us) ultimate formulation of truth which will suffice for the next age and carry man to a high pinnacle of the Temple and to the Mount of Initiation. These two lines are :

   i. Those who look back to the past, who hang on to the old ways, the ancient theologies, and the reactionary rejection methods of finding truth. These are the people who recognise authority, whether that of a prophet, a bible or a theology. These are those who prefer obedience to imposed authority to the self-imposed guidance of an enlightened soul. These are the followers of a Church and a government, who are distinguished by a pure devotion and love, but refuse recognition to the divine intelligence with which they are gifted. Their devotion, their love of God, their strict but misguided conscience, their intolerance mark them out as devotees, but they are blinded by their own devotion and their growth is limited by their fanaticism. They belong mostly to the older generation and the hope for them lies in their devotion and the fact that evolution itself will carry them forward into the second group.

To this first group is committed the work of crystallisation which will result in the complete destruction of the old form; to them is given the task of defining the old truths so that the mind of the race will be clarified, that non-essentials and essentials will be recognised for what they are, and fundamental ideas so contrasted with the formulation of dogmas, that that which is basic will be seen, and the secondary and unimportant beliefs therefore rejected, for only the basic and causative will be of value in the coming age.

ii. The second group is as yet a very small minority, but a steadily growing one. It is that inner group of lovers of God, the intellectual mystics, the knowers of reality who belong to no one religion or organisation, but who regard themselves as members of the Church universal and as "members one of another". They are gathered out of every nation, race and people; they are of every colour and school of thought, yet they speak the same language, learn by the same symbols, tread the same path, have rejected the same non-essentials, and have isolated the same body of essential beliefs. They recognise each other; they accord equal devotion to the spiritual leaders of all races, and use each other's Bibles with equal freedom. They form the subjective background of the new world; they constitute the spiritual nucleus of the coming world religion; they are the unifying principle which will eventually save the world.

In the past we have had world Saviours—Sons of God who have enunciated a world message and brought an increase of light to peoples. Now, in the fulness of time, and through the work of evolution, there is emerging a group who perhaps will bring salvation to the world, and who—embodying the group ideas and demonstrating the group nature, manifesting in a small way the true significance of the body of Christ, and giving to the world a picture of the true nature of a spiritual organism—will so stimulate and energise the thoughts and souls of men, that the New Age will be ushered in by an outpouring of love, knowledge and harmony of God Himself.

Religions in the past have been founded by a great soul, by an Avatar, by an outstanding spiritual personality, and the stamp of their lives and words and teaching has been set upon the race and has persisted for many centuries. What will be the effect of the message of a group Avatar? What will be the potency of the work of a group of knowers of God, enunciating truth and banded together subjectively in the great work of saving the world? What will be the effect of the mission of a group of world Saviours, not as Christs, but all knowers of God in some degree, who supplement each other's efforts, reinforce each other's message, and constitute an organism through which the spiritual energy and principle of spiritual life can make their presence felt in the world?

Such a body now exists with its members in every land. Relatively they are few and far between, but steadily their numbers are increasing and increasingly their message will be felt. In them is vested a spirit of construction; they are the builders of the New Age; to them is given the work of preserving the spirit of truth, and the reorganising of the thoughts of men so that the racial mind is controlled and brought into that meditative and reflective condition which will permit it to recognise the next unfoldment of divinity. (4-327/30)

2. About seventeen years ago (about 1916: *Compiler*) the Masters met and came to a momentous decision. Just as it had been decided at the earlier conclave (A.D. 1500) to gather out of the inchoate masses of men, groups of workers along various lines, and set them the task of elevating humanity and expanding the human consciousness, so now it was felt wise to gather out of the many groups, a group which should contain (as does the Hierarchy itself) men of all races, of all types and tendencies. (4-413)

3. If it is true that there is being gathered together in the background of our present world-state a group of mystics who are distinguished by knowledge, vision, and a power to work on mental levels, unseen and unrecognised by men, it could also be noted that this band is not confined to the strictly religious types. Men and women in every branch of human thought are found among this group, including scientists and philosophers. (4-331)

4. If we look on, as can Those on the inner side, and if we were in a position to contrast the "light" of humanity as it is today with what it was two or three hundred years ago, we would recognise that enormous strides had been made. This is evidenced by the fact that the emergence of a band of "conditioning souls", under the name of the N.G.W.S., has been possible since 1925. (15-261)

(d) ORGANISATION OF THE N.G.W.S.

1. We have spoken often of the integrating group of knowers who are beginning to function upon earth, gathered together in loose formation, and held by the inner spiritual tie, and not by any outer organisation. (4-398)

2. It is a group that has no exoteric organisation of any kind, no head-quarters, no publicity, no group name. It is a band of obedient workers and servers of the WORD—obedient to their own souls and to group need. All true servers everywhere therefore belong to this group, whether their line of service is cultural, political, scientific, religious, philoso-phical, psychological or financial. They constitute part of the inner group of workers for humanity, and of the world mystics, whether they know it or not. They will be thus recognised by their fellow group members when contacted in the casual ways of world intercourse. (4-414)

3. The growth of the group and of its ideas will be slow and sure. The group exists already. It has not to be formed and organised, and there is therefore for none of you the assuming of any sense of responsibility nor the organising of any activity designed to lure these disciples, who have chosen thus to work subjectively, into publicity. Such are not the methods approved by the Elder Brothers of the race, nor is it the way that They Themselves work.

Know each of you for yourselves whether you stand for the new posi-tion, the new attitude towards work, and for the subjective method. De-cide once and for all whether you prefer to work in the old exoteric ambi-tious manner, building and vitalising an organisation, and so producing all the mechanism which goes with such a method of work. Remember that such groups are still greatly needed and are useful. It is not yet the New Age, and the little ones must not be left exposed to the new forces, nor turned out bereft of the nursery to which they naturally belong.

Should the new mode of work appeal to you, see to it that the person-ality is subordinated, that the life of meditation is kept paramount in im-portance, that sensitivity to the subjective realm is cultivated, and any necessary outer activities are handled from within outwards. Avoid a purely mystical introspection or its opposite extreme, an over-emphasised organising spirit, remembering that a life of truly occult meditation must inevitably produce outer happenings, but that these objective results are produced by an inner growth and not by an outer activity. An ancient Scripture teaches this truth in the following terms:

When the sun progresses into the mansion of the serving man, the way of life takes the place of the way of work. Then the tree of life grows until its branches shelter all the sons of men. The building of the Temple and the carrying of the stones cease. The growing trees are seen; the buildings disappear. Let the sun pass into its appointed place, and in this day and generation attend ye to the roots of growth.

Little groups will spring up here and there whose members respond to the new note and whose growth into the world group will be watched over by one or more working disciples. But these latter do not organise the groups; they grow as a man in this place and another in that place, awakens to the new vision, or comes into incarnation in order to take his place in the work and bring in the new era. These groups will demonstrate no sense of separateness; they will be unaware of personal or of group ambition; they will recognise their unity with all that exists, and will stand before the world as examples of pure living, constructive building, creative activity subordinated to the general purpose, beauty and inclusiveness. Perhaps in the early stages of integration, the words friendliness and co-operativeness best describe them. They are not interested in dogmas or doctrines, and have no shibboleths. Their outstanding characteristic will be an individual and group freedom from a critical spirit. This non-criticism will not grow out of an inability to see error, or failure to measure up to an idea; falsity, impurity and weakness will be recognised for what they are, but when noted will only serve to evoke a loving helpfulness.

Little by little these groups will come to know each other and to meet with one another at set times and places. They will come to these mutual conferences with no desire to impress one another, and with no thought of relative numerical strength; they will demonstrate no ambition to increase their ranks. How should they, when they know themselves all to be members of the one World Group? They have no teaching to give of a doctrinal nature, and will not seek to demonstrate learning. They will meet solely to discuss modes of world helpfulness, the formation of a platform so universal and composed of such basic truths, that it can be presented under all the varying methods and utilise the many terminologies. They will endeavour to employ each other's terms, and to familiarise themselves with each other's approach to reality and symbology.

Little by little also the special contribution and note of each group will be recognised, and where a need exists for just that special approach and the particular note or method of interpretation in any part of the world, there will be an immediate and united impulse to facilitate the work that that special group could do in that place.

These groups, with the one subjective group of conscious living souls behind them, will be too busy with world service and interests to waste time on trifling non-essentials. They will not have the time to play around with group names and insignia and badges and the technicalities of fraternities when they meet together. World needs, world opportunities, and the rapid development of the consciousness of mankind, and the initiation of humanity into the spiritual realities, will so engross their attention, that they will have no interest in purely physical plane arrangements, nor in laying the emphasis upon their own personal growth. They will be well aware that response to world need in service and the life of focussed meditation, will promote their growth. Their eyes are not upon themselves, upon their own good characters, or upon their individual accomplishments. (4-425/7)

4. One of the characteristics, distinguishing the group of world servers and knowers, is that the outer organisation which holds them integrated, is practically non-existent. They are *held together by an inner structure of thought* and by a telepathic medium of interrelation. The Great Ones, Whom we all seek to serve, are thus linked, and can—at the slightest need and with the least expenditure of force—get *en rapport* with each other. They are all tuned to a particular vibration. (11-1)

5. The outer organisation is of importance in so far as it leads to the skillful use of opportunity and money, but the organisation is again only a means to an end. The organisation of the N.G.W.S. is not possible. They must ever remain unorganised and unlabelled, free to work as they individually see fit. It is the organisation of the available resources to which we refer, so that the Plan may be promoted, the ideals become practical, and the work be carried intelligently forward. (15-667)

(e) CHARACTERISTICS OF THE N.G.W.S.

1. Today, in the world, another great moment of crisis has arrived. I refer not to the present world condition, but to the state of the human consciousness. Mind has arrived at a functioning power, personalities are co-ordinated. The three aspects of man are being blended; another formation or precipitation from the Hierarchy of adepts has become possible. On the physical plane, without any exoteric organisation, ceremonials, or outer form, there is integrating—silently, steadily and powerfully—a

group of men and women who will supersede eventually the previous hierarchical effort. They will supersede all churches, all groups, and all organisations, and will eventually constitute that oligarchy of elect souls who will govern and guide the world.

They are being gathered out of every nation, but are gathered and chosen, not by the watching Hierarchy or by any Master, but by the power of their response to the spiritual opportunity, tide and note. They are emerging out of every group and church and party, and will therefore be truly representative. This they do, not from the pull of their own ambition and prideful schemes, but through the very selflessness of their service. They are finding their way to the top in every department of human knowledge, not because of the clamour they make about their own ideas, discoveries and theories, but because they are so inclusive in their outlook and so wide in their interpretation of truth that they see the hand of God in all happenings, His imprint upon all forms and His note sounding forth through every channel of communication between the subjective reality and the objective outer form. They are of all races; they speak all languages; they embrace all religions, all sciences and all philosophies. Their characteristics are synthesis, inclusiveness, intellectuality and fine mental development. They own to no creed, save the creed of Brotherhood, based on the one Life. They recognise no authority, save that of their own souls, and no master save the group they seek to serve, and humanity whom they deeply love. They have no barriers set up around themselves, but are governed by a wide tolerance, and a sane mentality and sense of proportion. They look with open eyes upon the world of men, and recognise those whom they can lift and to whom they can stand as the Great Ones stand—lifting, teaching and helping. They recognise their peers and equals, and know each other when they meet and stand shoulder to shoulder with their fellow workers in the work of salvaging humanity. It does not matter if their terminologies differ, their interpretations of symbols and scriptures vary, or their words are few or many. They see their group members in all fields—political, scientific, religious and economic—and give to them the sign of recognition and the hand of a brother. They recognise likewise Those who have passed ahead of them upon the ladder of evolution and hail them Teacher, and seek to learn from Them that which They are so eager to impart.   (4-399/401)

2. The members of the N.G.W.S.—e'en when they work without mental realisation . . .—are nevertheless working "under impression", as it is called. Their main duty, and the duty to which their souls call them, is

to preserve an inner sensitivity. This they do in the majority of cases, and . . . their intense interest in their work makes them one-pointed and dedicated to their task. Therefore, all personality reactions are subordinated to the work in hand, and the lower man presents no impediments to that impression.   (5-159)

3. The N.G.W.S. (is) constituted today of two bodies of people:

i. Those who are aware of the Plan, are subject to and sensitive to hierarchical impression, and dedicated to the task of bringing about the desired fusion or group at-one-ment. These are the consecrated servers of the world who are free from all taint of separativeness, full of love to all men, and eager for the spread of understanding goodwill. They correspond to the "consecrated loving heart".

ii. A small minority who have emerged out of the N.G.W.S. and who can (in every country) function in group formation if they choose, and so bring about the fusion for which the N.G.W.S. is working and for which the point of tension in humanity and in the Hierarchy predisposes and has prepared the hearts of men. Their opportunity and responsibility is great, because they know the Plan, they are in touch with the guiding teachers on the inner side—and are sensitive to the higher impression. They correspond to the points of illumination, and so to the "illumined minds". . . .   (13-96/7)

4. The N.G.W.S. is not a new organisation which is forming in the world. It is simply a loose linking together of all men of constructive peace aims and goodwill, who lay the emphasis upon the prior need of establishing right human relations before any lasting peace is possible. This group in no way interferes with the allegiance and loyalties of any man. It is a banding together of all who seek to express *the spirit of Christ* and are free from the spirit of hatred and revenge. The challenge of this group to the world is to drop all antagonisms and antipathies, all hatred and racial differences, and attempt to live in terms of the one family, the one Life, and the one humanity.

The N.G.W.S. believes that (through the agency of goodwill) the new world order can be firmly established on Earth.   (13-205/6)

5. The strength of the N.G.W.S. lies in three factors:

i. They occupy a midway position between the masses of men and the inner subjective world government.

ii. They draw their membership (if such an inadequate word can be used) from all classes—the aristocracy, the intelligentsia, the bourgeoisie, higher and lower, and the upper layer of the proletariat.

iii. They are closely interrelated, and in constant contact and rapport with each other, through unity of objective, definiteness of method, and uniformity in technique and goodwill.   (15-638/9)

6. Partisanship, fighting for or against, and party spirit, distinguish the modern world of men. With these activities, which lead to separation and division and strife, the N.G.W.S. have no time or interest. They stand for those attitudes which will eventually produce a third party, free from political and religious hatreds. As yet they are unknown, unrealised, and relatively powerless to make a definite impression on world thought. If, however, there is skill in action and adherence to the principles of harmonious co-operation, they can, in a very few years, demonstrate real power and influence.

The work can then swing into its second cycle of pronounced and definite influence. This will be possible only if those who have this vision will make every effort and every possible sacrifice of time and money, to bring it about. Between the exploited and the exploiting, the warlike and the pacifist, the masses and the rulers, this group will stand, taking no sides, demonstrating no partisan spirit, fomenting no political or religious disturbance, and feeding no hatreds, either of individuals, nations or races. They will stand as the interpreters of right human relations, for the basic oneness of humanity, for *practical* brotherhood, for positive harmlessness in speech and writing, and for that inner synthesis of objectives which recognises the value of the individual and at the same time the significance of group work. The propagation of these ideas, and the spread of the principles of goodwill will produce this third group in world affairs.

In a few year's time, if the work is carried forward along these lines, public opinion will be forced to recognise the potency of this movement towards peace, international understanding, and mutual goodwill.   (15-675)

(f) REQUIREMENTS FOR MEMBERSHIP

1. The personnel of the group is known only to the Elder Brothers of the race, and no register of names is kept, and there are only three main requirements :

i. A certain amount of at-one-ment between the soul and its mechanism is essential, and that inner triplicity, usually dormant in the majority, of soul-mind-brain must be in alignment and active.

ii. The brain has to be telepathically sensitive in two directions and at will. It must be aware of the world of souls and also of the world of men.

iii. There must also exist a capacity for abstract or synthetic thought. This will enable a man to leap over racial and religious barriers. When this is present also, there is an assured belief in the continuity of life and its correlation to the life after death.

To sum up the situation, it must be noted that the groups in the past have stood for certain aspects of truth, and have demonstrated certain ray characteristics. The new group will express all the aspects and have in it members on all rays. The majority of the workers in the many groups have carried forward certain details of the Plan, and added their quota of energy to the forward urge of humanity, but they have for the most part done this without any true understanding of what they were accomplishing, and without any real comprehension of that body-soul relationship, which leads to really intelligent work, unless we except a few prominent mystics such as Meister Eckhart. They have been primarily groups of personalities, with that added touch of genius which indicates a certain contact with the soul. The group that is now in process of formation, is composed of those who are aware of the fact of the soul, and have established a soul intercourse that is real and lasting; they look upon the mind, emotions and body nature as simply an equipment whereby human contacts can be established, and their work, as they see it, is to be carried forward through the medium of this equipment, acting under the direction of the soul. They are therefore living souls, working through personalities, and not personalities actuated by occasional soul impulses. The members of the many groups were all somewhat one-sided, and their talents ran along some specific line. They demonstrated a capacity to write as Shakespeare, to paint like a Da Vinci, to produce musical masterpieces like a Beethoven, or to bring about world changes like Napoleon. But the new type of group worker is a rounded out individual, with a capacity to do almost anything to which he sets his hand, but with a basic impulse to work on thought levels more than on the physical plane. He is therefore of use to the Hierarchy, as he can be used in a variety of ways, for his flexibility and experience, and his stability of contact can be all subordinated to the group requirements.

The true exponent of this new group type will of course not appear for many decades. He will be a true Aquarian with a universal touch, an intense sensitivity, a highly organised mental apparatus, an astral equipment which is primarily responsive to the higher spiritual vibrations, a powerful and controlled energy body, and a sound physical body, though not robust in the ordinary use of the term. (4-414/6)

2. You ask me: What keeps a man from becoming a member of such a group? I tell you with emphasis that four things only keep a man from affiliation:

First: An unco-ordinated personality. This involves necessarily an untrained mind and a feeble intellect.

Second: A sense of separateness, of distinction, and of being set apart or different from one's fellow men.

Third: The possession of a creed. No matter how good a formula of beliefs it may be, it inevitably produces exclusiveness. It bars some out.

Fourth: Pride and ambition.

You ask again: How shall I qualify? The rules are simple, and are three in number. First, learn to practise harmlessness; then desire nothing for the separated self, and thirdly, look for the sign of divinity in all. Three simple rules, but very hard to accomplish.

Behind this group of mystics, which includes thinkers in every department of human thought (let me reiterate the word *thinkers*) and of human knowledge, stands the Hierarchy of Masters, and in between these two groups stand also a band of teachers, of whom I am one. These act as intermediaries and as transmitters of energy. May I repeat and beg you to attend, that this group which is slowly forming is gathered out of every imaginable group of thinking and intelligent men. As yet, and this may surprise a few, there are not very many occultists (so-called) among them. This is due to the fact that the occultists are numerically few in relation to the masses of humanity, and also to their tendency to be sectarian, exclusive and self-righteous. Selfless humanitarian workers are there; political leaders and economists and scientific workers in the world's laboratories are also there; churchmen and religious adherents from all the world religions are there, and the practical mystics and a few occultists. The true occultist is rare. (4-430/1)

3. This great and spiritual grouping of servers is, on the physical plane, only very loosely linked. On the astral plane the linking is stronger and is

based upon love of humanity; on the mental plane the major linking takes place, from the angle of the three worlds as a whole. It will be apparent, therefore, that certain developments must have taken place in the individual before he can consciously become a functioning member of the N.G.W.S., which is the principal group at this time definitely working under the Law of Group Progress .

i. He must have the heart centre awakened, and be so outgoing in his "behaviour" that the heart is rapidly linked up with the heart centres of at least eight other people. Groups of nine awakened aspirants can then be occultly absorbed in the heart centre of the planetary Logos. Through it, His life can flow and the group members can contribute their quota of energy to the life influences circulating throughout His body. The above piece of information is only of interest to those who are spiritually awakened, and will mean little or nothing to those who are asleep.

ii The head centre must also be in process of awakening, and the ability to "hold the mind steady in the light" must be somewhat developed.

iii. Some forms of creative activity must likewise be found and the server must be active along some humanitarian, artistic, literary, philosophic or scientific lines.

All this involves personality integration and alignment and that magnetic, attractive appeal which is distinctive of all disciples in some form or another. In this way, from the standpoint of esotericism, certain great triangles of energy will be found in the individual, and consequently increasingly in humanity.   (15-197/8)

4. A man's political and religious affiliations can be strongly held and inspire his true loyalty, and yet need in no way prevent his being an active part of the N.G.W.S. They need not deter him from being actively on the side of world goodwill or provide a barrier to that spiritual sensitivity which makes him susceptible to the higher inner spiritual impression.

The servants of the spiritual Hierarchy, and the world disciples, are found in every nation; they are loyal to that nation's ideology or political trend of thought or government; the members of the N.G.W.S. embrace every political creed and recognise the authority of every imaginable religion. Men and women of goodwill can be discovered functioning in every group, no matter what its ideology or creed or belief. The Hierarchy does not look for co-operation in any one school of thought, political creed, or national government. It finds them in all, and co-operates with all. This I have frequently said, yet you find it difficult to believe, so convinced are many of you that your peculiar belief and your particular acceptance of truth is the best undoubtedly and the most true. It may be for you, but not for your brother of another persuasion, nation or religion.   (15-739/40)

(g) MEMBERSHIP

1. Members of the N.G.W.S. are gathered from all branches of human enterprise, of which organised religion is only one. There are scientists who, repudiating violently the unproven, yet are giving all they have of scientific ability and knowledge to the service of humanity—each in his chosen scientific field; there are men of financial stature, who regard money as a responsibility to be dispensed wisely in the service of others, yet the mystical or occult terminology may mean nothing whatsoever to them; there are educators, preoccupied with wise formulations of knowledge and with an encyclopedic understanding of garnered wisdom of the ages, which they seek to utilise in fitting the younger generation to live beautifully, constructively and creatively; there are churchmen and religious leaders (in some one or other of the world religions) who are not tied or handicapped by the form; the spirit of light is in them, and they intelligently love their fellow men. All of these people, if they are members of the N.G.W.S., must inevitably be reflecting thinkers, must have creative objectives, must be truly intelligent, and must have added *expanding* love to their intelligence.

These men and women have a dual relationship: to the rest of humanity whom they seek to serve, and also to the Hierarchy, via some Ashram— an Ashram which is the source of their inspiration and of their creative efforts to think and to work.

The accepted disciple in this group work, is in conscious rapport with both planetary centres (that of Humanity and that of the Hierarchy) and their creative thinking largely conditions the group. Many, however, in this group are conscious of their relation to humanity and of their planned service, but are totally unaware of the unseen source of their inspiration. This matters not, for—if their motive is pure, their intelligence keen and their meditational capacity adequate—they receive the inspiration and develop the intuition in any case. It is those in the N.G.W.S. who can and do meditate, who are the real agents of the relation existing between the Hierarchy and Humanity. Such a relation has, of course, always existed, and always there have been many mystics and a few occultists who have served as channels of relationship; today, the group is newly organised, and the task of invocation and evocation is for the first time in history evenly balanced, or is upon what you might call a fifty-fifty basis.

Again, the N.G.W.S. is composed of widely diverse men and women, gathered out of all nations, holding many different points of view, and following the many different professions and ideologies; it is therefore more truly representative of humanity and more truly potent than ever before.

When the work of the Invocation reaches a high stage of development, and the climaxing year of 1952 is over, it will then be wise to bring to the attention of the general public, and on a worldwide scale, the factual nature of the N.G.W.S.

... The N.G.W.S. is composed of the following groups:

i. Initiates and disciples who are consciously a part of the Great White Lodge.

ii. Aspirants and lesser disciples who are affiliated with the Hierarchy, but who do not usually possess that continuity of consciousness which will come later.

iii. Those upon the Probationary Path who are not yet affiliated with the Hierarchy; they are, however, subject to hierarchical impression and are determined to serve their fellow men.

iv. An increasing number of people who respond to the idealism and the purpose of the N.G.W.S. and who will rapidly join the group.

The main requirement is *Meditation* but—as you know—it is not necessarily the set meditation of occult schools and churches; membership in the group, however, requires the development of the reflective spirit along some line of human understanding; it requires also the power to focus attention upon that which can serve humanity, and a compassionate recognition of human need. The unthinking man or woman, or those engrossed entirely in business, political and family ties, cannot form a part of the N.G.W.S., because the group demands a definite measure of decentralisation; to this, habits of meditation rapidly contribute. (6-202/5)

2. Members of the N.G.W.S. stand for the following ideals:

i. They believe in an inner world government and in an emerging evolutionary Plan. They can see its signs down the ages. That they may express the significance of this inner world government and of the planetary Hierarchy in varying terms, is inevitable. That they may regard it from the peculiar angle of their own tradition and schooling, is also inevitable but unimportant. That which is of importance is that they are in touch with the centre of energy which is attempting to guide human affairs; they know something of the detail of the immediate Plan, and to the furtherance of this they are bending all their energies.

ii. They are steadily cultivating an international spirit of goodwill and to this they consecrate every effort. They avoid all points of dissension, regarding them as incidental to the point in evolution which the race has reached, and they are convinced of the inevitable change for the better which is on its way. They emphasise the point of common endeavour and seek to interpret to the public the trend of the present world efforts as these begin the work of swinging the world on to new paths and producing in the minds of the people new and better ideals.

iii. They seek to teach also the fact that the many national, religious, and social experiments are only modes of expansion, ways of growth, and needed lessons. They seek to point out that the effects of these will be twofold. First, they will demonstrate the usefulness of those lines of thought and consequent methods which will eventually bring about the release of mankind from its present limitations and distress. These experiments are not lost effort. They have a definite place and purpose. Second, they will demonstrate the recognition of those methods and techniques in government and religion which are undesirable, because they spread the virus of hatred, breed class and racial distinctions, and are consequently detrimental to world understanding, international goodwill, and spiritual amity.

There is no thinking man today in prominent position who does not in his highest moments appreciate the necessity for world peace, international order, and religious understanding—all leading in the last analysis to economic stability.   (15-658/9)

3. For the members of the N.G.W.S. and for the men and women of goodwill, the Hierarchy of spiritual Leaders have laid down the following rules:

i. That they must aim at achieving peaceful relationships with, and harmonious acquiescence in, as well as co-operation with the government or state to which they owe allegiance or loyalty. This does not mean endorsing all policies and lines of activity undertaken by such governments, but it does mean the refraining from all that could cause difficulty. There is always scope for much constructive activity within any governmental policy or regime, and it is to these constructive and peaceful enterprises that the servers of the Great Ones and for humanity will direct their attention.

ii. They must refrain from all interference in the affairs of any political or religious group.

iii. They must endeavour to express *practical* goodwill in the environment where their lot may be cast.

iv. They must strive after harmlessness in speech and in life in relation to their family, community, nation or group of nations. This means a consistent policy of non-attack. No leader or nation or race must be attacked or defamed.

This is a matter of practical import, and is not at all an easy thing to attain. It lays the foundation for the rapid formation and definite emergences of the N.G.W.S. and for the discovery and organising of the men of goodwill throughout the world, wherever they may be found. The spiritual Hierarchy cannot work through people whose tongues are critical, whose ideas and attitudes are separative, and who are violently partisan in their beliefs and comments. This is a statement of fact. I seek to have you train yourselves in such right activity, beginning with your own lives and your personal expression in the world.   (15-747/8)

(h) THE GROUP SYMBOL

The group is and will be kept entirely subjective. Its members are linked telepathically, or they recognise each other through the quality of the work they are doing in the outer world, and the inclusiveness of the note they sound. It is inspired from above by the souls of its members and the Great Ones, and is energised into activity by the need of humanity itself. It is composed of living conscious souls, working through co-ordinated personalities. Its symbol is a golden triangle, enclosing an even-armed cross with one diamond at the apex of the triangle. This symbol is never produced in form at all. It shines above the heads of all who are in the group, and cannot be seen by anyone (not even a clairvoyant) except a group member, and then only if—for purposes of work—his recognition needs stimulation. The motto of the group is *The Glory of The One.*

More I may not tell you now, but this will give you some idea of the reality of the work that is going on. It may serve as an incentive to fresh effort on the part of all working to equip themselves for selfless service. (4-431)

(i) UNITING THE MEN OF GOODWILL

1. This spirit of goodwill is present in millions, and it evokes a sense of responsibility. This is the first indication in the race that man is divine. It is upon this steadily growing goodwill that the N.G.W.S. is counting, and which it is their intention to utilise. It is found in the membership of every group which exists for world betterment, and constitutes an unused power which has never yet been organised into a whole, as the loyalty and effort of the individual man of goodwill has hitherto been given to his organisation or endeavour. It is the intention of the N.G.W.S. not to interfere with this loyalty or to arrest any activity, but to gather into one organised whole all these people, without creating a new organisation or sidetracking any of them from the work they have already undertaken.

The N.G.W.S. is already a functioning, active group. Every man and woman in every country in both hemispheres, who is working to heal the breaches between people, to evoke the sense of brotherhood, to foster the sense of mutual interrelation, and who sees no racial, national or religious barriers, is a member of the N.G.W.S., even if he has never heard of it in these terms.

. . . The members of the N.G.W.S. are not a band of impractical mystics. They know exactly what they seek to do, and their plans are laid in such a manner that—without upsetting any existing situation—they are discovering and bringing together the men of goodwill all over the world. Their united demand is that these men of goodwill should stand together in complete understanding, and thus constitute a slowly growing body of people whose interest is shown on behalf of humanity and not primarily on behalf of their own immediate environment. The larger interest will not, however, prevent them from being good citizens of the country where their destiny has cast them. They will conform to and accept the situation in which they find themselves, but will (in that situation and under that government or religious order) work for goodwill, for the breaking down of barriers, and for world peace. They will avoid all attack of existing regimes and personalities; they will keep the laws of the land in which they have to live, but they will cultivate the spirit of non-hatred, utilising every opportunity to emphasise the brotherhood of nations, the unity of faith, and our economic interdependence. They will endeavour to speak no word and do no act which can separate and breed dislike.

These are broad generalities, governing the conduct of the men of goodwill who seek to co-operate with the work being done by the N.G.W.S. As they learn effective co-operation and achieve steadiness in the right attitudes to their fellow men, they are gradually absorbed into the ranks of the New Group, not through a process of formal affiliation, for no such process exists (there being no formal organisation) but through the development of the necessary qualities and characteristics. It is of value to reiterate at this point that *the N.G.W.S. is not an organisation.* It has no headquarters, but only units of service throughout the world; it has no president or lists of officers; it has only servers in every country, who are occupied simply with the task of discovering the men of goodwill. This is the immediate task. These men of goodwill must be found and trained in the doctrine of non-separateness, and educated in the principles of co-operation and the characteristics of the new social order, which is essentially a subjective re-alignment, resulting in pronounced changes brought about through the weight of a world opinion, based on a goodwill which knows no national or racial barriers or religious differences. Year by year there should develop much active work and much dissemination of the teachings upon universal goodwill, so that it changes from a beautiful sentiment and becomes the practical application of goodwill by action in the affairs of everyday life, in every country throughout the world.

. . . The next task to which the N.G.W.S. will consecrate their efforts, will be to eliminate the fear in the world. This can be done and will take place when the men and women of goodwill awake to the fact of the wealth of goodwill there is in every land. There are millions of these men of goodwill in the world; they have been increasing steadily in numbers as a result of the agony of the world war, but feeling isolated and alone, they have been impotent and futile. They have felt separated, useless and unimportant. As individuals they are. As part of a great world movement, with a spiritual basis and expressive of the essential divinity in man, they are not. The massed power of goodwill, a thing which has remained hitherto unorganised, will be found to be irresistible. (15-642/5)

2. Loosely knit together by mutual understanding and similarity of objective, the members of the N.G.W.S. stand, whether they are con-

scious or unconscious of each other or the group, as it is here described. In every country they are found and actively are working. Through them the men of goodwill are being discovered. Their names and addresses are being noted and collected into mailing lists. Their capacity, whatever it may be, to serve their fellow men, will be also noted when possible, and utilised if desired. Thus through the men of goodwill everywhere, the principle of goodwill can be nurtured and developed in every country, and eventually turned to practical use. These people will constitute a new body of practical thinkers in every nation, who will be no menace to any government, nor will they work against the established order. They will throw themselves into those movements and undertake those activities which can in no way foster hatred, spread enmity, or cause division among their fellow men. To this group, no government or church can object.   (15-648)

(j) THEIR MISSION

1. This group (N.G.W.S.) has a specific mission, and some of the facts about it might be stated as follows :

It is first of all an attempt at an externalisation of the Hierarchy upon the physical plane, or a small working replica of this essentially subjective body. Its members are all in physical bodies, but must work entirely subjectively, thus utilising the inner sensitive apparatus and the intuition. It is to be composed of men and women of all nations and ages, but each one must be spiritually oriented, all must be conscious servers, all must be mentally polarised and alert, and all must be inclusive.

One of the essential conditions imposed upon the personnel of this group is that they must be willing to work without recognition, on the subjective levels. They must work behind the scenes as do the Great Ones. Its members therefore must be free from all taint of ambition, and from all pride of race and of accomplishment. They must be also sensitively aware of their fellow men and of their thoughts and conditioning environment.

. . . This group gives to the word "spiritual" a wide significance; they believe it to mean an inclusive endeavour towards human betterment, uplift and understanding; they give it the connotation of tolerance, international synthetic communion, religious inclusiveness, and all trends of thought which concern the esoteric development of the human being.

It is a group therefore without a terminology or Bible of any kind; it has no creed nor any dogmatic formulations of truth. The motivating

impulse of each and all, is love of God as it works out in love for one's
fellow man. They know the true meaning of brotherhood, without distinction of race. Their lives are lives of willing service, rendered with
utter selflessness and without any reservations.   (4-413/4)

2. An instruction upon the N.G.W.S was sent out and given wide distribution by means of the pamphlet entitled *The Next Three Years*. This
signalised the anchoring—if I might so call it—of the N.G.W.S. upon the
physical plane. They are now in active existence. The group is slowly
integrating and slowly making its influence felt in the primary work of
educating public opinion—the only potent means of work and of far
more potency and ultimate value, than any legislation or emphasis upon
authority.

Growing out of the integration of this New Group, there is being
formed in the world that "bridge of souls and servers" which will make
possible the merging of the inner subjective Hierarchy of souls and the
outer world of humanity. This will constitute an actual fusion or blending, and will mark the initiation of the human family through the
achievement of its foremost pioneering members. This is the true "marriage in the Heavens" of which mystical Christianity speaks, and the result of this fusion will be the manifestation of the fifth kingdom in
nature, the Kingdom of God. In the past history of the race, a great
event occurred, which brought into manifestation the fourth kingdom in
nature, the human kingdom. We stand now on the verge of a similar but
still more momentous event—the appearance of the fifth kingdom, as a
result of the planned activity of the N.G.W.S., working in collaboration
with the Hierarchy of perfected souls, and under the guidance of the
Christ Himself. This will usher in the New Age wherein five kingdoms in
nature will be recognised as existing side by side upon earth.   (5-31/2)

3. From the United States of America, the teaching must go out. But
Europe is the field for the educating of the world in the ideas of a true
world unity, and for the wise presentation of the Plan. From that conti-
nent can the inspiration go forth to the East and to the West.

Go forward into this work with sure courage and with no sense of pressure. Blend the wise methods of the present organisations with the vision
of the newer types of work. This is a spiritual work in which you are engaged, and it has educational objectives which have for their goal the dissemination of those principles which must govern world-living and world
attitudes during the coming New Age. In the presentation of the work
which the N.G.W.S. can do, certain definite and immediate possible pro-

grammes can be indicated, such as the educating of public opinion in the principle of non-separativeness. But to do this, much meditation and much clear thinking will be involved. . . . The technique to be followed, and the method employed to arouse interest and to evoke the needed support, are for Western disciples and workers to decide and not for me, your Oriental brother. I can but stimulate your soul to clarity of perception, to wise vision, to true understanding and to right planning. The rest of the work, and the materialising of the project, lies in your hands and with those who respond to the ideas presented. (5-161/2)

4. The function of the N.G.W.S. is dynamically to "force" the energy of the will-to-good into the world; the average man and woman, responding unconsciously, will express goodwill. (6-38)

5. The N.G.W.S. (seek) to prepare humanity for the reappearance of the Christ. That preparatory work is the major incentive lying back of all that I do, and was the prime reason for the formation of the group in the early part of the century. Pioneers of this group appeared in the nineteenth century but the organisation, as it now exists, is of relatively modern days.

. . . It is necessary for you all to get a wider vision of the enterprise which this group has undertaken, or else the meditation work which you will do will hinder and not help. The task of the group of World Servers is *not* the spreading of esoteric or occult information. In preparing the world of men for the reappearance of the Christ, the needs of all the many grades in the social order must be met; world groups of every description have to be contacted. Much of the work to be done, therefore, will be purely economic and will concern the right feeding and the development of a true security for millions who—for many lives—will not be interested in matters esoteric. The reform of the churches of the many world religions, is another aspect of the same work, requiring no occult information but the introduction of commonsense and progressive ideas into theology, and the shift of the ecclesiastical emphasis from material values to spiritual. The political regimes of the world need orienting to each other; it has never been the divine plan that all nations and races should conform to some standard political ideology, or be reduced to a uniform general form of government. Nations differ; they have different cultures and traditions; they can function adequately under varying and distinctive governments; nevertheless, they can at the same time attain a unity of purpose, based upon a genuine desire for the true welfare and progress of all men everywhere.

In all these spheres of human thought and activity, the N.G.W.S. are playing a prominent part. At the very heart of that worldwide group are those who are in the Ashram of the Masters—as are some of you—or on the periphery or within the sphere of influence of these Ashrams. Their task is largely a meditative one, carried on in order to influence the minds of those members of the group who are not yet in touch with any Ashram; they work thus from humanitarian, interested and basically ray reasons, and all such members are more or less under the control of their soul ray; this affects most definitely the varying fields of service. These are the areas of thought within the human family wherein the preparation for the coming of the Christ must be carried forward; but this activity is not, as a rule, associated with the esoteric angle or approach to truth, but strictly with the angle of the betterment of human relationships. The Christ Himself (two thousand years ago) tried to demonstrate this mode of helpful activity; he kept the esoteric teaching for the few, who could approach understanding, but He dealt with the masses from the angle of commonsense and physical plane helpfulness. Have this ever in mind. (6-231/3)

6. The bringing together of all the agents of goodwill (who are responsive to the energy of the divine will-to-good) constitutes the major objective of the N.G.W.S. and always has been. Their work can now be constructively and creatively intensified through the association of the Avatar of Synthesis with the Christ. Their task is to usher in the New Age; in that New Age, the five Kingdoms in Nature will begin to function as one creative whole. Their work falls into the following parts, functions or activities:

i. The production of a human synthesis or unity, which will lead to an universal recognition of the *one humanity,* brought about through right human relations.

ii. The establishing of right relations with the subhuman kingdoms in nature, leading to the universal recognition that there is *One World.*

iii. The anchoring of the Kingdom of God, the spiritual Hierarchy of our planet, in open expression on Earth, thus leading to the universal recognition that the *sons of men are one.* (8-78)

7. The Science of Contact governs relations within our *entire* planetary life and includes, for instance, the rapport being established between humanity and the domesticated animals. These animals are to their own

kingdom what the N.G.W.S. is to humanity. The N.G.W.S. is the linking bridge and the mode of communication between the Hierarchy (the fifth kingdom) and Humanity (the fourth kingdom) under *the present* divine Plan; the domesticated animals fulfil, therefore, an analogous function between Humanity (the fourth kingdom) and the animal kingdom (the third). These analogies are often fertile fields for illumination   (11-68)

8. (Their goal is) of providing a centre of light within the world of men. Let this never be forgotten, and let the N.G.W.S. realise its mission, and recognise the demands of humanity upon it. What are these demands? Let me enumerate them, and then let me ask you to take them in all simplicity and act upon them :

   i. To receive and transmit illumination from the kingdom of souls.

   ii. To receive inspiration from the Hierarchy, and go forth consequently to inspire.

   iii. To hold the vision of the Plan before the eyes of men, for "where there is no vision, the people perish".

   iv. To act as an intermediate group between the Hierarchy and humanity, receiving light and power, and then using both of these, under the inspiration of love, to build the new world of tomorrow.

   v. To toil in Pisces, illumined by Taurus, and responsive in degree to the Aquarian impulse coming from the Hierarchy.

These objectives are not only individual objectives, but the goal for the entire group. All who respond to the life-giving force of Taurus, can and will work in the N.G.W.S., even though they have no occult knowledge and have never heard of their co-workers under that name. Forget this not.   (18-232/3)

(k) ACTIVITIES AND TECHNIQUES

1. The aims and ideals of the N.G.W.S. must also be presented constantly and clearly to the thinking public. The form in which this must be done, and the medium used, is for the associated servers to decide. Attention should be called to those activities which are obviously in line with the Plan, and the work and the programmes of the World Servers, wherever they are found and located, must be made known and aided. To do this, we need to combine wise and deliberate action with speed, owing to the urgency of the crisis. Those whose function it is to co-operate and help

will appear, but our spiritual perception must be alert to recognise them. . . .

By means of right inner activity and wise leadership, the N.G.W.S. will respond increasingly to the presented new ideas, and will grow in strength, optimism, inner relation and interplay. They will and should become a strong united body in the outer world. . . .

The N.G.W.S. has the immediate task of achieving power in moulding men's ideas to the needed changes of thought and the new technique of work all over the world. To do this, there must be the explanation of the ideas which lie behind the group, and a clear statement of those parts of the Plan which are of immediate application. There must be a steady emphasis upon the reality of that which is inner and subjective (the world of real values) and upon the dynamic power of ideas as they control, and can be shown to control, all that is happening in every disturbed nation today. *What is going on in the world today is the working out of ideas.* As to the technique to be employed, certain contrasts might be touched upon.

All nations at this time are engrossed with the imposition of some idea, or group of ideas, upon their peoples. This seems to the leaders, no matter how enlightened they may be, to necessitate force in some form or another, and to call for drastic coercion. This must necessarily be the case where the time factor is misinterpreted. The immediate good of the people as a whole is felt by the leaders far to outweigh any temporary happenings to individuals and smaller groups. In the work of the N.G.W.S., this time element will be better understood and the work must be carried forward with as much rapidity as possible, yet without any coercion, mental or physical. The laying of right foundations, and the promulgation of right principles, is of tremendous importance and must be ensured, but there must be no undue emphasis laid upon the regimenting of men's thoughts within a given time. With care, with prevision, with forethought and with skill, must the ground be laid and the arguments given for the fostering of goodwill and the growth and spread of brotherhood on an international scale.

Theoretically, the ideal of brotherhood has been presented by many organisations, by many fraternities and many theosophical bodies; but those who have promulgated the idea of brotherhood in these various organisations, are themselves too separative and sectarian to carry forward the work constructively. . . . The materialising of these ideas, which have hitherto remained theoretical, is the prime function of the N.G.W.S. They have to remove the whole theory from the realm of sentiment, of idealism, and of mystical aspiration, and must bring the question, as a concrete demonstrated factor, before the public.

They must place the emphasis upon the expression of goodwill and the fulfilment of the law of love, and not upon affiliation with organisations, with their labels and their doctrines. The N.G.W.S. must keep itself free of all these, for otherwise the work will crash upon the ancient rocks of doctrine and of organisation. The members of the New Group must remain loosely linked together by their mutual goodwill and the unanimity of their objectives, expressed irrespective of national boundaries, racial distinctions and religious prejudices. It must throw the weight of its influence behind all movements, which are struggling to overcome differences, and which express similar aims. Its members will sponsor, aid and foster many endeavours which work toward international understanding and synthesis, and express those religious interpretations which teach the spirit of unity.

The power which the N.G.W.S. will eventually wield, will be drawn from two sources: *First,* from that inner centre or subjective world government, whose members are responsible for the spread of those ideals and ideas which have led humanity onwards from age to age. This inner centre has always existed and the great leaders of the race, in every field, have been connected with it. . . . The members of this government may be alive in physical bodies, or discarnate. . . . These great souls are primarily distinguished by the fact that they know no mental limitation, and their inclusiveness is such that for them there are no racial distinctions, nor any religious differences.

The *second* source from which the N.G.W.S. will draw its power, will be from men of goodwill in the world at any given time. They will be able to swing into activity at any moment such a weight of thought and such a momentous public opinion, that they will eventually be in a position definitely to affect world affairs. One of their functions will be to bring in touch with each other, men of similar ideals and also to direct and further their efforts.

Knowledge of these ideals will be spread everywhere in the face of opposition and distrust; these truths must be expressed in every possible language and by every available means, and every available person must be utilised to circulate them. No effort should be spared at the present time and for the next few years. This work must first of all be undertaken through the medium of the printed page and later, when trained people are available, through the medium of the spoken word.

There must be synthesis of effort and the elimination of unnecessary and personal aspects of the work.

Members of the N.G.W.S. learn mostly through the ear, and through that careful attention which comes from an inner attitude of constant *listening.* They are unfolding that spiritual perception which is latent but unused in the average man. . . . This attitude of listening and a subsequent prompt readjustment to the inner, received commands, is characteristic of the N.G.W.S.   (15-660/5)

2. It would be of value at this time to indicate three of the functions of this New Group, so that there may be a clear picture of the work that must be accomplished during the next few years. This work is intended:

i. To produce a balancing of the forces present in the world today, and responsible for the widespread unrest and chaos, so that it will be possible for the race to swing back to a point of equilibrium.

ii. To act as the interpreters of the new attitudes and the new activities which must eventually govern men in the coming New Age.

iii. To bring about the eventual synthesis and unification of the men of goodwill and of understanding, into one coherent body. The many who are working in isolated fashion in the various fields of human endeavour (political, religious, scientific and economic), must be brought into touch with each other, and thus made to realise their essential unity.

The major objective and aim of all who are associated with the N.G.W.S. is to bring order out of chaos, and to resolve the widely separative issues of modern life into some kind of stability. Men would then have time to make the needed readjustments, to think through to a few vital conclusions, and to bring about a period of relative quiet in which to order the newer ways of living, so that the wider issues may be perceived and developed.   (15-668/9)

3. As regards the required united work, I can but indicate the following lines of activity, and it is for you to follow them, if you will, or make it possible for others to do so:

i. Discover the men and women of goodwill. These you will not recognise if you are full of racial, national or religious prejudice.

ii. Put these people in touch with the Units of Service in the countries where you live.

iii. Educate them in the following ideas:

(a) The principles of goodwill and the medium and methods of their true expression in the daily life.

(b) The necessity of their being active and practical and consistent workers in the spread of goodwill in the world.

(c) The usefulness of building up live mailing lists (I think you call it) of those who see life from the angle of the spiritual values, and who seek to build for the future.

iv. The authorities of any and every nation should be kept in touch with your activities, so that they are aware of all that you are seeking to do, and can therefore, realise that there is nothing subversive in the planned activities, and nothing that has in it the seeds of trouble for any ruler or national government.

v. Keep constantly in touch with the Units of Service, and use care in choosing those who represent the work you have undertaken.

vi. Let the meditation groups be carefully handled and have about them nothing that could be regarded as secret, or might bring them under suspicion of being secret organisations. This they are not. This non-secrecy must be emphasised in connection with all the work.

vii. As far as the use of the press and the radio is concerned, go forward as actively and earnestly as possible. . . . Upon these two lay the emphasis, for by them the majority of human beings are reached.

viii. Let each Wesak Full Moon be a period of intensive effort, preceded by personal preparation and purification, and lay the force of the emphasis upon:

(a) The producing of sensitivity to the inner spiritual impression, emanating from the Hierarchy and the Group.

(b) The achieving of an intelligent appreciation of the steps to be taken during the coming twelve months, and the laying of careful plans so that they may indeed materialise.

(c) The correct distribution of your time and resources so that you do become an active worker in the cause of goodwill.

(d) The effort to co-operate with all that is being done along these lines, which entails the discovery of all groups and persons working with similar objectives.

(e) The submergence of your temporary interests in the good of the whole, and through love of humanity.

I will say no more at this time. I have sought to indicate that which should be possible. If my suggestions are followed, and if the work is carried forward diligently, there is every indication that the work of the Hierarchy and of the Christ will be tremendously expedited. The need and the opportunity call for right understanding, and they demand also a joyful co-operation and the sacrifice of yourselves and of your time and money, in the attempt to make our work possible.   (15-748/50)

(1)   DANGERS TO BE AVOIDED BY THE GROUP

It must not be forgotten that many people of many races and religious views, form a part, consciously or unconsciously, of this group. Some of them are so close to the Plan that their clarity of vision and their understanding is very real. They know. They need to be very sure, however, as to their right action from the angle of time. Skill in action is their main problem and not accuracy of perception. Others are not so close to the Plan and only know it in a vague and general way. They are consecrated and dedicated souls, but personal ambition and national and religious prejudices, still govern their minds, their reactions and their habits of speech. They sometimes resent the fact that others of different race, tradition and religious sentiment may be as close to the Plan and the Custodians of the Plan as they are. They question the authority of individuals in the N.G.W.S., and sometimes work towards the undoing of disciples in the same field as their own. This must not be. There is no time today for such trifling things as personal prestige, or for the emphasising of one organisation at the expense of another, or for the assumed priority of this or the other teaching. These are the things that do not matter, but which do hinder. What is of importance at this time is the unified stand which can be made by the men of goodwill in the world during the next few years, in order to turn the tide in human affairs, avert possible catastrophe and bring in the era of unity, peace and plenty. Personal ambitions have to go. Personal desire, self defence, or self-assertiveness have no place in the ranks of the N.G.W.S. How can goodwill be fostered in the world, if those who profess it are fighting amongst themselves? How can the Plan of the Great Ones make progress and the leadership of the world pass into the hands of those who have a definitely spiritual objective, if they are quarreling over place, position, and precedence? Personalities do not count and only souls have power.

Let all of us, therefore, who belong to the N.G.W.S. or who respond to their message of goodwill, sacrifice our personal differences, our petty interpretations, and our selfish ambitions upon the altar of world service and friendships. Thus we can offer to the Custodians of the Plan an instrument which They can freely use.

Another danger may arise if undue emphasis is laid upon the organisation aspect of the N.G.W.S. It must never be forgotten that there is here no ordinary organisation, such as is usually found in the world. The group is an organism, not an organisation. It is not a propaganda group, as that term is usually understood. It is not interested in politics, religion or place. Its work is the educating of the human being and the expanding of the human consciousness, so that the newer and truer ideas may be grasped. Its function is the spreading of the message of international goodwill and religious unity. The members of the N.G.W.S. are primarily interpreters. That they may have high place and position, that they may be powerful and influential people, that they may work through the spoken and the printed word, that they may employ every possible means which brains and money can use in their endeavour, and that they may evidence the highest skill in action, will be true if things progress as desired; but all these things are to be regarded as simply a means to an end—the production of worldwide goodwill, of intelligent and loving understanding and unity, peace and plenty.   (15-365/7)

(m) TRAINING OF SERVERS

1. This program (of training workers) will require patience and much co-operative work. The members of the N.G.W.S. must be discovered through their reaction to these ideals; they must be trained in the new policies, and educated in the technique of right thought, non-aggressive action, and the elimination of antagonisms of every kind; they must be taught the manner by which these basic ideals of world unity, economic synthesis and religious co-operation are to be expressed and attained. The law of *Love,* expressed *intelligently,* must be applied to all human relationships.

This work of educating the men and women of goodwill in the world must be proceeded with as rapidly as possible. The work must, however, be carried on with no infringement of harmony. There must be no interference with national preferences and programs, and no belittling of national governments, no matter what they may be. No political activity should be carried on in the name of the N.G.W.S. Such action would continue the old methods and perpetuate the old hatreds. There must be no attack upon any party or group, and no criticism of any leader or national activity. Such old methods have long been tried, and have failed to bring peace on earth. The members of the N.G.W.S., and those associated with them, stand for no party, neither for nor against any group or form of control. This is their imperative position. For attack or counter-attack they have not the time, energy or money. Yet their attitude is not one of "passive non-resistance". They are at work balancing world forces, and fostering the growth of that group of men who stand for goodwill, understanding and brotherhood. (15-674)

2. No idle pacifism will be taught. It is no mystical dream which waits for God to take action, and which relies on the future to straighten things out. It is no impractical idea, incapable of application. It is the plan for the development of a group of people, gathered out of every nation, who are trained in the spirit of goodwill, and who possess such a clear insight into the principles that should govern human relations in world affairs, that they can work with power in the field of human peace and under-standing. It is a systematised process of education. By its means, men and women everywhere are to be trained to live as exponents of goodwill in every department of life, and the power of intelligent goodwill to ad-just difficulties in every department of human affairs is unbelievably potent. But as yet, that growing spirit of goodwill has not been intelligently de-veloped, applied, and systematised. Thousands of men and women are ready today throughout the world to be trained, and to be brought into co-operation with each other, so that there can eventually be unity of effort in the cause of peace and harmonious relations. The N.G.W.S. seeks to dis-cover these people, and unify them into a coherent group. (15-676)

3. The men and women of goodwill who are willing to listen, to consider and to work, must be found and contacted in every country. . . . These men and women of goodwill should be subjected to an intensive training. This should be carried forward through printed pamphlets, personal con-tact, and correspondence; through lectures and discussions and eventually, if possible, through the medium of some periodical which will literally be the organ of the N.G.W.S. It will carry information as to the activi-ties which foster goodwill, international understanding, world education and scientific achievement.

At the end of that period there should be enough people in the world who are alive to these principles and to the opportunity, so that they can begin to make a definite impact upon the public consciousness. In this way the contacting of the true intelligentsia of the world will proceed with increased rapidity. The education of these thinkers should be carried on by the World Servers in conformity with the following rules:

i. No word must be spoken or written which could be construed as evidencing partisanship, or as an attack upon any ruler, any form of government, or any national activity. "Hatred ceaseth not by hatred; hatred ceaseth by love."

ii. Nothing must be published in any pamphlet, newspaper, circular or letter which could evoke antagonism from any government, any political party, any economic strategist, or any religious organisation. Only principles of universal application must be expressed, and no partisanship is permitted.

iii. No race or nation must be regarded (either in the spoken or written word) as of greater importance essentially than any other race or nation. Humanity as a whole must be emphasised. Yet those who think otherwise than this must not be subjected to attack. Racial hatreds, religious differences, and national ambitions, are to be ignored by this balancing third group, the N.G.W.S.

iv. Members of the N.G.W.S. are never to identify themselves with any political, religious or social propaganda. Such propaganda is separative in its effects, and breeds divisions and hatreds. . . .

v. *Units of Service* in all nations must be built up steadily. A number of such units already exists. Their objectives are as follows:

(a) To educate the people in their nation in service, in kindly effort, and in non-aggressive action. A *positive harmlessness* will be inculcated, which in no way negates intense, intelligent activity, and the propagation of those ideals which lead to mutual understanding, and eventually to unity, peace and plenty.

(b) To provide in every country, and eventually in every city, a central bureau where information will be available concerning the activities of men and women of goodwill all over the world. . . .

(c) To bring together the members of the N.G.W.S. and those associated with them, through similarity of ideas and vision. . . .

(d) To list and investigate the work and the ideals of all groups which purport to have an international program which tends to heal world differences and national quarrels, to work for a better understanding between the races, and to harmonise religious distinctions and class wars. . . .

vi. No secrecy must ever be permitted in the work of the N.G.W.S. Secret societies are organisations ever open to attack and suspicion. . . . Members of the N.G.W.S. must be encouraged to seek out those in high places in government circles and church, and enlighten them as to the objectives of the group.

. . . The initial concepts must be carried forward in their essential purity; the process of thus educating the public must go forward with diligence and tact, and wisdom must be cultivated in order to avoid all antagonism, all criticism and all hatred. The power of such a group, working in such a fashion, will be tremendous. They can accomplish phenomenal results. This is no idle promise, but it is contingent upon the preservation of the initial concepts and the steady practice of goodwill. (15-679/83)

4. It is in the N.G.W.S. that the training of the needed disciples for the Ashrams of the Masters takes place at this time in world history. This is a new hierarchical venture. In this group also accepted disciples learn to work in the same manner as does the Hierarchy. The Hierarchy works within the field of the world of human living; the New Group provides a similar field for the new disciple. It is towards that group also that initiates in the various Ashrams converge at times, in order to study the calibre and quality of the disciples who are engaged in world salvage, for it is through these disciples that the Hierarchy carries out its plans. Initiates do their main work upon mental levels and from behind the scenes, and because of this their potency is great; this is particularly so with those who have taken the third initiation. A certain percentage of them are, however, active out in the world of daily living. (18-230)

5. Not only has the individual approach to the Hierarchy been superseded by a group approach, but it is now found to be possible to make a certain measure of the training, objective and exoteric. Hence the establishment of the N.G.W.S. This is primarily a group which, while working on the outer plane of daily, physical living, yet preserves a close ashramic integration; it thus provides a field of service for accepted disciples who are seeking a service-expression, and it also provides a rallying point for all determined aspirants, where they can be tried out and where their motives and persistence can be tested, prior to direct acceptance. This is something new, for it shifts the responsibility of preparing aspirants for accepted discipleship onto the shoulders of the pledged disciple, and away from the immediate attention of the accepting Master. He is thus freed for other fields of service. (18-239/40)

(n) THE PRESENT SITUATION

1. What then is the present situation in connection with the integrating group of mystics? Let me be somewhat (more) explicit.

In every European country, in the United States of America, and in parts of Asia and South Africa, are to be found certain disciples, usually unrecognised by the world at large, who are *thinking truth*. Let me call your attention to that phrase. The most important workers in this new group, and those who are closest to the Great Ones, are those whose daily thought-life is oriented by the new ideal. That this thought-life of theirs may work out in definite exoteric activities may be true, but they are first of all and always those who live in and work from the "high and secret place". Their influence is wielded silently and quietly and they lay no emphasis upon their personalities, upon their own views and ideas, or upon their methods of carrying forward the work. They possess a full realisation of their own limitations, but are not handicapped thereby, but proceed to think through into objective manifestation that aspect of the vision which it is their mission to vivify into form. They are necessarily cultured and widely read, for in these difficult transitional times, they have to cultivate a world grasp of conditions and possess a general idea of what is going on in the different countries. They possess in truth no nationality in the sense that they regard their country and their political affiliations as of paramount importance. They are equipped to organise, slowly and steadily, that public opinion which will eventually divorce man from religious sectarianism, national exclusiveness, and racial biases.

One by one, here and there, they are being gathered out and are gathering to them those who are free from the limitations of past political, religious and cultural theories. They, the members of the one group, are organising these forward looking souls into groups which are destined to bring in the new era of peace and of goodwill. These latter, who are being influenced by the group members, are as yet only a few thousands among the millions of men, and out of the four hundred accepted disciples working in the world at this time (about 1934: *Compiler*), only about 156 are equipped by their thought activity to form part of this slowly forming group. These constitute the nucleus of what will be some day a dominant force. During the next twenty-five years their influence will become potent enough to attract political attention, provided those of you who have seen the vision of a *powerful subjective body of thinking Souls* can speak the needed words, and outline those concepts which will hasten the work of integration, and put the units in this group in touch with one another. Do your utmost to see that this is done and make this the message and keynote of the work you all do wherever you are.   (4-416/8)

2. The pronounced contrast in ideas—as, for instance, the contrast between totalitarianism and the democratic freedom of thought (does such democratic freedom really exist, my brother?)—is forcing men to think, to reflect, to question and to meditate. The world is thereby greatly enriched, and the whole human family is transiting out of a pronounced cycle of karma yoga into the required cycle of raja yoga, from unthinking activity into a period of illumined mind control. It is a mental illumination which is brought about by the meditative and the reflective activity of humanity as a whole, and this is carried forward under the guidance of the N.G.W.S., working under hierarchical impression.   (6-219)

3. The key of humanity's trouble (focussing as it has in the economic difficulties of the past two hundred years and in the theological impasse of the orthodox churches) has been to take and not give, to accept and not share, to grasp and not to distribute. This has involved the breaking of a law which has placed humanity in a position of positive guilt. War is the dire penalty which mankind has had to pay for this great sin of separateness. Impressions from the Hierarchy have been received, distorted, misapplied and misinterpreted, and the task of the N.G.W.S. is to offset this evil.

. . . Men do not live up to what they already know; they fail to make practical their information; they short circuit the light; they do not discipline themselves; greedy desire and unlawful ambition control and not the inner knowledge.   (7-7)

4. Humanity is sick and awaiting healing. The healing will be brought about through the medium of the N.G.W.S. and by the men of goodwill, aided by the Hierarchy, from which planetary centre the healing energies will be drawn.   (17-663)

5. What should be the work of the immediate present? Let me outline the programme as far as I can.

The first thing to be done is to strengthen the ties and establish firmly the link between yourselves and all those whom you recognise as possible working disciples in the new group. To do this, acquaint yourselves with the work of the leaders of groups in the various countries of the world—such as Switzerland, the United States, Holland, Germany and Great Britain. From their reaction to the vision of this new age type of work you can then make a temporary decision. Watch them at their work.

Note the emphasis laid by them upon personalities. If personal ambition seems to govern their activities, if their position is one of a determination to work in the group of mystics because of its novelty, or because it gives them a certain standing or because it intrigues their imagination or gives them scope for gathering people around them, then proceed no further, but—preserving silence—leave time and the law to correct their attitude.

Secondly, be receptive towards those who seek you out and seem to vibrate to the same note. When I say you, I mean the group to which you all subjectively belong. They will come if you work with decision and sound out the note of unity so clearly that they are in no doubt as to your motives and your disinterested activity. Some of the 156 who form the present ($\pm$1934) nucleus, will be known to you and will work in unison with you, though maybe not in your peculiar field of action.

The picture to be held before your eyes is that of a vast network of groups, working along the many possible lines, but having at their heart or behind them—working silently, and persistently influencing through soul contact—one or more members of the new, slowly emerging group. These focal points through which the Hierarchy is now seeking to work, stand together telepathically, and exoterically they must work in the completest understanding, preserving always an attitude of non-interference, and leaving each worker free to teach his own group as he sees fit. The terms used, the methods employed, the types reached, the truths taught, the discipline of life demonstrated, concern no one but the working disciple.

The members of this group of New Age workers will, however, possess certain general characteristics. They will impose no enforced dogmas of any kind, and will lay no emphasis upon any doctrine or authorities. They are not interested in having any personal authority, nor do they rest back upon traditional authority, whether religious, scientific, cultural or any other form of imposed truth. Modes of approach to reality will be recognised, and each will be free to choose his own. No discipline will be imposed by these workers upon those who seek to co-operate with them. The ideas of any one person or leader as to how the units in his particular sphere of activity should live and work, should meditate and eat, will be regarded as of no practical value. The members of this new group, work esoterically with souls, and deal not with the details of the personality lives of the aspirants they seek to inspire.

This is a basic rule and will serve to eliminate many worthy aspirants from this group of world servers now in process of forming. The tendency to impose one's own point of view indicates a lack of understanding and it will rule many out. (4-418/9)

(o) USHERING IN THE NEW AGE

The future is of great promise, provided man can learn the lessons of the present which have been clearly presented to him; he must accept them and understand clearly the nature of his problem and of the crisis with its many ramifications and various implications.

. . . The slow and careful formation of the N.G.W.S. is indicative of the crisis. They are overseeing or ushering in the New Age, and are present at the birth pangs of the new civilisation and the coming into manifestation of a new race, a new culture, and a new world outlook. The work is necessarily slow, and those of you who are immersed in the problems and pains, find it hard to view the future with assurance, or to interpret the present with clarity. (12-44/5)

(p) THE FUTURE OF THE GROUP

1. As regards the future of this world group of which we have been speaking, much depends upon two things :

First, it is necessary for all those isolated disciples working in every country in the world, to become aware of one another, and then to enter into telepathic rapport. This may seem to you to be a wonderful but impractical vision. I assure you that this is not so. The work of establishing this rapport may indeed be slow, but it is an inevitable effect of the growing sensitivity of all the souls who are working in the field of the world. The first indication of it is that instinctive recognition of those who constitute part of this group when they meet and contact each other in the ways of world intercourse. There comes to them an immediate flashing forth of the light, an instantaneous electrical interplay, a sudden sensing of a similarity of vision and of objective, or a vital opportunity to aid in and to co-operate with each other in the work in which it is realised that all are interested.

Working disciples everywhere, when they meet each other, will know at once that their work is identical, and will advise with each other as to where co-operation and supplementary endeavour may be possible. In about thirty years the interrelation between the units in this group (scattered as they may be all over the world) will be so close, that daily they will meet each other at a set time and in the secret place.

. . . The *second* requirement which will establish relation between the working disciples in this group, is the capacity to preserve a constant and sequential recollection of both the inner and the outer life. We call it *continuity of consciousness*, and by this we mean the power to be fully aware of all happenings in all spheres and departments of man's being during the entire twenty-four hours of the day. As yet this is far from being the case. There is no real awareness of existence during the hours of sleep. The dream life as related, is as full of illusion as any of the more definitely lower psychic experiences. The slowly growing interest in dreams from the standpoint of psychology and the investigation of their probable source, are the first weak attempts towards establishing the awareness on a really scientific basis. There is as yet no conscious registering of mental activity during such times, for instance, as when the emotional body holds the centre of the stage. With what is the mind occupied during a long period of emotional upset? It has, we know, its own life and its laws. Again, what are the activities of the soul when the personality is occupied exclusively with its own affairs? Is it impossible for you to vision a time when the development of consciousness will have reached the stage where there will be a sentient reaction in all the departments of man's nature, and all of it recorded by the brain? Already men are aware both of physical plane activity and emotional aliveness simultaneously. That is for the majority a common and ordinary condition. Where two activities can be registered at once, why not three and even four? Such is the future ahead of the race, and the disciples, actively employed, will be the first to express and demonstrate this extended consciouness.

Thus telepathic interplay and extended sentiency must be developed and are also closely interlinked with each other.

I have therefore pointed out the immediate future development of the *individual* disciple. What lies ahead in the immediate future for the *group*?

First of all, a preliminary period of emergence into the public consciousness, and thus of making its presence felt. This will be done through the steady communication of the new ideals and the constant emphasis laid upon the essential oneness of all humanity. It will be the result of the uniformity and inclusiveness of the note sounded by one here and another there. During this stage there must be no hurried work and no precipitate action of any kind. The growth of the group and of its ideas will be slow and sure.   (4-421/5)

2. Later, as a result of their telepathic relationship and their united conferences, there may emerge certain esoteric groups and schools for de-

velopment, in order more rapidly to equip them for world service. In these schools modes of meditation, the intensification of vibration and the laws of the universe will be taught, and the right use of colour and of sound. But all will be subordinated to the idea of service and the uplift of humanity. Also the schools referred to in *Letters on Occult Meditation* will gradually come into being.   (4-427/8)

(q) CREATIVE WORK

What . . . is the creative work confronting the Ashrams in the Hierarchy and the members of the N.G.W.S., working creatively under the inspiration and the impression of the Hierarchy? It falls into two parts:

1. The work of bringing order out of chaos.

2. The task of preparing the way for the reappearance of the Christ.

There is much that must be done to change conditions, institute new values, and produce the bringing in of an entirely new civilisation—a civilisation which will permit the externalisation of the Ashrams, or of the Hierarchy, and a restitution, therefore, of hierarchical or spiritual control as it was known in old Atlantean days, only this time on a much higher turn of the spiral, and with the intelligent co-operation also and the wise assistance of humanity, which was a factor lacking in the earlier civilisation. Once this has been dealt with in the reflective, concentrated meditation of the individual aspirant, in the united reflection and meditation of the many spiritually inclined groups in the world today, and once the N.G.W.S. and the Hierarchy are working in the closest kind of co-operation, then the visualisation and the projection of the *intended* civilisation will have reached a definite and a most important *point of precipitation.* Then, the invocative appeal of the united Hierarchy and N.G.W.S. will be so potent that it will evoke a response from humanity and a cycle of organisation, of planning and of effective expression will follow. Reflection, meditation and visualisation will give place to scientific *thinking* (which is essentially meditation) and to the needed physical plane activity. (6-218/9)

(r) CYCLIC RHYTHM OF THE NEW GROUP WORK

All creative processes proceed with a cyclic rhythm. The rhythm set by the N.G.W.S. is a three year cycle, and to this rhythm you will find yourself conforming. The end of one such cycle came in May, 1936. . . . Have these dates carefully in mind, and thus lay your plans for the future. Thus will you be working with the law and along the lines of least resistance. Make each three year cycle conform to the rhythm of creation. In the first year, lay your emphasis upon the activity of the manifesting principle, using that which appears and with which you have to work. In the second year, let the clarity and the quality of the note to be sounded by the manifesting form, appear and be heard. In the third year, behind the form and expressing itself through the quality, let the livingness and the work of the indwelling life emerge for all to see. Bear this in mind as you consolidate the work. The keynote of the first year's work is consolidation, that of the second year must be expansion, whilst the keynote of the third year must be the making of a definite impact upon the public consciousness, by the sounding and the emphasising of some one clear note. If this cyclic measure is kept thus in mind, no serious mistakes will be made. . . . The N.G.W.S. must work in these three year cycles, and the foundation of cyclic attainment must be laid. This cyclic rhythm will release from strain, and yet enable the workers in the Group to feel that there is no failure. It is impossible to do good work where a sense of failure or lack of attainment is found.   (5-165)

(s) THE PLAN FOR HUMANITY

1. The first thing to be grasped is that there is a Plan for humanity, and that this Plan has always existed. It has worked out through the evolutionary developments of the past ages, and also through that special impetus which has been given it from time to time by the great intuitives and teachers of the races. Today there are a sufficient number of men and women in the world, adequately developed, so that they can contact it and work in connection with it. It is becoming more a matter of group recognition than of intuitive revelation. Secondly, it is to be noted that there is upon our planet a group of men and women belonging to every nation, who are definitely upon the Path of Discipleship, and because of their status, they are all of them as definitely serving the race. They are subjectively welded together into a body, which we have called the N.G. W.S., for lack of a better name. Their characteristics are well known, for many have made a careful study of this group for two or three years, and many also form a part of it.

   . . . It is encouraging for us to observe, that the N.G.W.S. working in connection with the rapidly emerging Plan of the Great Ones, has been vitally increased in numbers during the past few years, and there is a much closer inner welding than heretofore. The group will be found divided into two parts:

i. An inner nucleus, composed of those active servers who know themselves to be disciples, is consciously in touch with the Plan, and is strenuously working at its development.

ii. Those who have responded to the vision as it has been presented to them by that inner nucleus, and have ranged themselves definitely on the side of the Plan. They are, therefore, men and women of goodwill.

Connected with these two groups, there is a steadily growing public, which is becoming increasingly responsive to the new ideas. They have expressed their interest and are eager to see the Plan materialise in proper form on earth. The diverse needs of all these groups must be met, and this is the definite problem of all who are working in conscious collaboration with the Hierarchy.   (15-649/51)

2. *Objectives of the Plan*: The statement has been made that Those Who constitute the inner government of the world, or the so-called planetary Hierarchy, are working to facilitate the entry of the new ideals and aims into the consciousness of the race. These new ideals and aims are characteristics of the New Age. This statement is of importance, because it indicates that the effort now on foot is in line with the evolutionary development going on upon our planet. It is therefore assured of ultimate success. The work that the N.G.W.S. is endeavouring to do is intended to hasten that process, and so avert a long period of distress and disorder. Whether this effort succeeds or not, the final aim is assured, but it can be hastened if men will only appreciate fairly the situation with which they are immediately faced, and take the necessary steps to change the present condition.

The new Plan of the Great Ones is, therefore, in the last analysis, simply an extension of the Plan as it has always existed. No changes in the basic idea are involved. The success of the present endeavour is contingent upon the availability of the forces which stand for progressive righteousness and the ability of the disciples of the world to act in unison, and so to influence public opinion, that there can be a world wide change in human attitudes, but the members of the N.G.W.S. must refrain from dissipating their efforts in secondary activities. For these latter, there will be time, once the main objective has been reached. The immediate objectives of the Plan might be stated as follows:

i. *To raise the level of the human consciousness,* so that intelligent thinking men and women will be consciously in touch with the world of ideas and the realm of intuitive perception. This means that they will be oriented towards reality. . . . This is no picture of an immediate Utopia. The modification of the present situation, even in a small measure, is a Herculean task, and will strain the resources of the N.G.W.S. to the utmost.

ii. The second objective of Those Who are working out the Plan, is the *clarifying of the international situation.* It is necessary that each nation should realise two things :

First, the importance of attending to its own business and its own internal problems, which are those of beautifying the national life, by the production of order, stabilisation, and above all, freedom. Each nation must internally adjust itself to peace. This must be done, not by the armed force of some powerful group, but by the wise consideration of the needs of the entire people, excepting no part of the national life.

Second, the prime importance of each nation realising its responsibility to all other nations, and the interrelation of all parts of the life of our world. . . .

iii. The third objective is *the growth of the group idea,* with a consequent general emphasis upon group good, group understanding, group interrelation, and group goodwill. These four are the ideals of that subjective group, working on the physical plane, which we call the N.G.W.S.

If these ideals can be materialised, this New Group provides a nucleus for that future world group which will gradually knit together all men in the cause of true brotherhood. . . .

This group will provide an international unit, made up of intelligent men of goodwill, which must inevitably control world destiny and bring about world peace, and thus organise the new world order. They will do this without the use of the old political machines, the violent propaganda, and the organised force which are characteristic of the old world order. Their method is the method of education; they will mould public opinion and foster natural goodwill and national, religious, and economic interdependence. What they are really attempting to do is to awaken into fuller activity an aspect of human nature which is always present, but which has hitherto been subordinated to selfish or ambitious ends. Human beings are innately kind when their minds are not distorted and their

vision impaired by the false teaching of any selfish interest, political propaganda and racial or religious difficulties.

. . . These aims will be achieved, not by propaganda backed by force,
but by example, backed by sacrifice and love. Another important objective
of the Plan, which will materialise later when world conditions are bettered, is the emergence into physical plane activity of that group of souls of
Whom the N.G.W.S. are the outer representatives. This appearance can
be called (in Christian phraseology) the second coming of Christ with
His Disciples, or it can be called the manifestation of the planetary Hierarchy, or the appearance of the Masters of the Wisdom, Who will restore
upon earth the ancient mysteries and institute again the order of Initiation.

Such is a broad and general idea of the objectives of the Plan and the
aim of its Custodians. Each phase of it constitutes a field of active service, and all men of goodwill everywhere and the members of the
N.G.W.S. find their place in one or another of its departments. The members of this group are in reality an intermediate group, between the Custodians of the Plan, as they express the mind and purpose of God, and the
intelligent public. They constitute the "brain trust" of the planet, for they
are definitely wrestling with the problem of unrest and distress in the economic, political and religious fields. Through them the Plan must work
out, and if they work with the desired selflessness and wisdom, and if they
demonstrate adequate skill in action, they will eventually achieve much
power. It will, however, be power based upon an intelligent goodwill,
upon a right understanding of brotherhood, and upon a determination to
bring about the good of the whole body and not the good of certain sec-
tions of the national life, or of certain nations at the expense of other sec-
tions and other nations. Hence, my constant emphasis upon the necessity
of thinking *in terms of goodwill to the whole.*   (15-652/9)

(t) IMPRESSING THE PLAN

1. The Hierarchy is the Custodian of that aspect of the cyclic, planetary
Purpose which is called the *Plan*; this covers such relatively brief periods
as civilisations—where humanity is concerned. In relation to Shamballa,
the intermediate group of meditating, creative Workers is called into activity in order to receive impression of the immediate, desired hierarchical
activity, to transmit the needed energies from Shamballa to the united
Ashrams and thus, esoterically, "inform" the Hierarchy of that which
merits immediate attention.

Again, upon a lower level of the evolutionary spiral, the Hierarchy in its turn impresses the N.G.W.S. with the Plan to be at once applied to the helping of humanity. This group is the major creative agent in the three worlds for the remainder of this cycle of planetary experience. This has not always been the case. Humanity can now intelligently work with the presented Plan, and this for the first time in human history. I would have you note this. Men can now do their little share in bringing the divine Purpose into manifestation, because they have now unfolded the needed mental capacity. The control and the creative development of the three lower kingdoms in nature is slowly being taken out of the hands of the deva evolution (hitherto responsible) and placed under the supervision of mankind; as it is said in the ancient Archives of the Masters:

> Eventually, the solar Lords, through manas (the mind) will control the lunar lords of elemental substance, and not alone their own, but that which looks to them for aid. Thus will redemption come to all through man, and thus the glory of the Lord of Life be seen.   (6-223/4)

2. All that we are able to recognise of the Purpose, is the hierarchical Plan, and this only disciples and advanced aspirants can judge and recognise. This Plan is based upon knowledge of divine guidance in the Past, the recognition of progress out of that Past into the Present, plus the effort to become sensitive to the right emergence of that Plan (embodying ever an aspect of the Purpose) in the immediate Future. The Purpose is related to the Past, the Present and the Future; the Agents of the Plan are impressed from Shamballa, via the Nirmanakayas; the process is then repeated, and advanced humanity become the recipients, the sensitive recipients, of the Plan as transmitted to them by the impressing Agents, the Masters, working through the N.G.W.S. This group is the lower correspondence of the Nirmanakayas, the recipients of impression from Shamballa. See you, therefore, the beauty and the synthesis, the interdependence and the co-operative interplay which is demonstrated right through the chain of Hierarchy, from the very highest Agent to the very lowest recipient of divine impression.   (11-121/2)

3. Behind . . . humanity stand Those Whose privilege and right it is to watch over human evolution and to guide the destinies of men. This They carry forward, not through an enforced control which infringes upon the free will of the human spirit, but through the implanting of ideas in the minds of the world thinkers, and the evocation of the human

consciousness, so that these ideas receive due recognition and become in time the controlling factors in human life. They train the members of the N.G.WS. in the task of changing ideas into ideals. These become in time the desired objectives of the thinkers, and are by them taught to the great middle class, and thus worked up into world forms of government and religion, forming the basis of the new social order, into which the masses are patiently incorporated.   (15-638)

4. The workers on the inner side, and the disciples who are responsible for the working out of the Plan, have made great efforts to reach and stimulate the N.G.W.S. They have been successful. Such success is in no way dependent upon any recognition of the Hierarchy on the part of the Servers. Where that exists it is a help, but it is dependent upon receptivity to spiritual impression, which means responsiveness to the new ideas which are expressive of the spirit of fusion, of synthesis, of understanding, and of co-operative goodwill. Look out for such people and work with them. Do not hold the prevalent attitude that they must work with you. It is for us, who perhaps know a little bit more about the Plan than they do, to do the moving forward. It is for us to evidence intelligent understanding, and to set the needed example by submerging our own ideas and personal desires in the good of the whole.

There must be on our part, if we react to all this, the reorientation of our entire lives for the next few years, to the urgency of the things to be done. This will necessarily involve the readjustment of our lives to the new impulses; it will entail the elimination of the non-essentials so that we can find time for the task; it will mean the cultivation of that spiritual sensitivity which will render us aware of the impressions and impulses coming from the inner side of life, and will make us quick also to recognise our brothers who are pledged to the same life of goodwill and who are awake—as we are—to the urgency of human need, and the immediacy of the day of opportunity; it will require the development in all of the spirit of silence, for silence is the best method whereby spiritual force is both generated and stored for us; and it will bring about the training of ourselves to see clearly the issues involved in any situation (personal, national or international) and then enable us to bring to bear upon it the interpretative light of expressed goodwill.   (15-746/7)

(u) EXPRESSING OF GROUP LOVE

1. Only a few, here and there, really grasp the vision of the future and realise what is going on, seeing truly the beauty of the emerging Plan. It

is with these few that the Members of the Hierarchy can work, because they (even when lacking understanding) bear no ill-will or hatred to others. Love is a great unifier and interpreter.

This energy of love is primarily concentrated (for purposes of hierarchical activity) in the N.G.W.S. This group has been chosen by the Hierarchy as its main channel of expression. This group, composed as it is of all world disciples and all working initiates, finds its representatives in every group of idealists and servers, and in every body of people who express human thought, particularly in the realm of human betterment and uplift. Through them, the potency of love-wisdom can express itself. These people are frequently misunderstood, for the love which they express differs widely from the sentimental, affectionate personal interest of the average worker. They are occupied mainly with the interests and the good of the whole group with which they may be associated; they are not primarily concerned with the petty interests of the individual—occupied with his little problems and concerns. This brings such a server under the criticism of the individual, and with this criticism they must learn to live, and to it they must pay no attention. True group love is of more importance than personal relationships, though those are met as need (note, I say, *need*) arises. Disciples learn to grasp the need of group love and to amend their ways in conformity with group good, but it is not easy for the self-interested individual to grasp the difference. Through the medium of those disciples who have learned the distinction between the petty concerns of the individual, plus his interest in himself, and the necessities and urgencies of group work and love, the Hierarchy can work and so bring about the needed world changes, which are primarily *changes in consciousness.*   (9-20/1)

2. Discover the members of the N.G.W.S. whenever possible, and strengthen their hands. Look for them in every nation and expressing many lines of thought and points of view. Remember always that in doctrine and dogma, and in technique and methods, they may differ widely from you, but in love of their fellow men, in practical goodwill and in devotion to the establishing of right human relations they stand with you, they are your equals, and can probably teach you much.   (13-641)

(v) STAGE OF DEVELOPMENT OF THE DISCIPLE

1. The problem consists in ascertaining upon which step of the ladder and in which phase one finds oneself at any particular time. Behind each human being stretches a long series of lives, and some are now headed

towards the stage of dominant selfish personality expression and are making themselves individuals in full conscious awareness. This is, for them, as much a step forward as is discipleship for all of you. Others are already personalities and are beginning to experiment with the energy flowing through them, and to gather around themselves those people who vibrate to their note and for whom they definitely have a message. Hence the myriads of small groups all over the world, working in every known field of human expression. Others have passed beyond that stage, and are becoming decentralised from the personality expression in the three worlds of human life, and are motivated by an energy which is the higher aspect of the personality energy. No longer do they work and plan to express their personalities and to make their individual impact upon the world, or to gather magnetically around themselves a group of people who look up to them, and thus feed the springs of their pride and ambition and who make them both influential and important. They are beginning to see things in a newer and truer perspective. In the light of the Whole, the light of the little self fades out, just as the light that is inherent in every atom of the body is gathered together and obliterated in the light of the soul when that blazes forth in all its glory.

When this stage of selflessness, of service, of subordination to the One Self, and of sacrifice to the group becomes the objective, a man has reached the point where he can be received into that group of world mystics and knowers and group workers which is the physical plane reflection of the planetary Hierarchy.   (4-397/8)

2. One of the main teachings which can be seen most clearly in all instructions of a truly esoteric character, concerns the *attitude* of the student of the occult. He is supposed to be dealing with things subjective and esoteric; he aims to be a worker in white magic. As such, he must assume and consistently hold the position of the Observer, detached from the mechanism of observation and contact; he must recognise himself as essentially a spiritual entity, different in nature, objectives and methods of working, from the bodies which he considers it wise to occupy temporarily and to employ. He must realise his unity and lines of contact with all similar workers, and thus arrive at a conscious awareness of his position in the spiritual hierarchy of Beings.

So much misinformation has been spread abroad, and so much emphasis has been unwisely laid upon status and position in the so-called hierarchy of souls, that sane and balanced disciples now seek to turn their thoughts elsewhere, and to eliminate as far as may be all thought of grades and spheres of activity. It is possible, in the swing of the pendulum, to swing too far in the opposite direction and to discount these stages of activity. Do not misunderstand me however; I do not suggest that an attempt be made to place people and to decide where they stand upon the evolutionary ladder. This has been most foolishly done in the past, with much dishonour to the subject, so much so that, in the minds of the public, the whole matter has fallen under disrepute. If these stages are regarded sanely for what they are—states of extended consciousness, and grades of responsibility—then the danger of personality reaction to the terms "accepted disciple, initiate, adept, master", would be negligible and much trouble would be eliminated. It must ever be remembered that individual status is rigidly kept to one-self, and the point of evolution (which may be truthfully recognised as lying ahead of that of the average citizen) will be demonstrated by a life of active unselfish service, and by the manifestation of an illumined vision which is ahead of the racial idea.

In the gathering together in the world at this time of the New Group of World Workers, true caution must be preserved. Each worker is responsible for himself and his service and for no one else. It is wise to gauge and approximate the evolutionary status, not upon claims made, but upon work accomplished and the love and wisdom shown. Judgment should be based upon an evidenced knowledge of the Plan as it works out in the wise formulation of the next step ahead for the human race; upon a *manifested esoteric sense,* and upon an influence or an auric power which is wide, constructive and inclusive.   (4-601/3)

3. Conscious incorporation in the (N.G.W.S.) necessitates the cessation of personality life, and brings out the subordination of the little self to the work of the whole. These words are easily written and read; they embody, however, the task of all disciples at this time. Where this incentive and realisation are lacking, the disciple is still a long way from his goal. (15-73)

(w) THE EXTERNALISATION OF THE HIERARCHY

1. Humanity at this time is passing through a cycle of excessive activity. For the first time in human history this activity embraces mankind on a large scale in the entire three aspects of the personality consciousness. The physical bodies, the emotional and mental states of consciousness, are all in a condition of potent upheaval. This unified triple activity is increased

by a cycle of equally intense planetary activity, due to the coming in of a new age, the passing of the sun into a new sign in the Zodiac, and the preparation consequently going on to fit man to work easily with the new forces and energies playing upon him. At the centre of human life, the integrating group of New World Servers must meet therefore a very real need. Their work must primarily be to keep such a close link with the soul of humanity—made up of all souls on their own level of being—through their own organised soul activity, that there will always be those who can "work in the interludes" and so keep the Plan progressing, and the vision before the eyes of those who cannot as yet themselves enter into the high and secret place. They have, as I oft times have said, to learn to work subjectively, and this they must do in order to preserve—in this cycle of activity and exoteric expression—the power, latent in all, to withdraw into the centre. They constitute the door, speaking symbolically. Capacities and powers can die out for lack of use; the power of divine abstraction and the faculty to find what has been called the "golden path which leads to the clear pool and from thence to the Temple of Retreat" must not be lost. This is the first work of the Group of World Mystics, and they must keep the path open and the way clear of obstructions. Otherwise white magic might temporarily die out and the selfish purposes of the form nature assume undue control. This dire event happened in Atlantean days and the then group of workers had to withdraw from all external activity and "abstract the divine mysteries, hiding them away from the curious and the unworthy".

Now a new attempt is being made to free the "prisoners of the planet". The Hierarchy, through the Group of World Servers now in process of formation, is seeking to externalise itself, and to restore the mysteries to humanity to whom they truly belong. If the attempt is to succeed, it is basically necessary that all of you who have sensed the vision or seen a part of the intended Plan, should re-dedicate yourselves to the service of humanity, should pledge yourselves to the work of aiding to the utmost of your ability (ponder those words and search out their significance) all world servers, and should sacrifice your time and give of your money, to further the endeavour of the Great Ones. Rest not, above all, from your meditation work; keep the inner link; think truth at all times. The need and the opportunity are great and all possible helpers are being called to the forefront of the battle. All can be used in some way, if the true nature of sacrifice is grasped, if skill in action is developed, and if work without attachment is the effort of each and all of you. (4-520/1)

2. (Another) move by the Hierarchy would be the impressing of the minds of enlightened men everywhere by spiritual ideas embodying the new truths, by the "descent" (if I may so call it) of the new concepts which will govern human living, and by the overshadowing of all world disciples and the N.G.W.S. by the Christ Himself. This planned move of the Hierarchy is progressing well; men and women everywhere and in every department of life, are enunciating those new truths which should in the future guide human living; they are building those new organisations, movements and groups—large or small—which will familiarise the mass of men with the reality of the need and the mode of meeting it. This they are doing because they are driven thereto by the warmth of their hearts and by their loving response to human distress; without formulating it thus to themselves, they are, nevertheless, working to bring into visibility the Kingdom of God on Earth. No denial of these facts is possible, in view of the multiplicity of organisations, books and speeches.   (8-48)

3. Great Forces, under potent spiritual Leadership, are standing ready to precipitate themselves into this world of chaos, of confusion, of aspiration, of hope and of bewilderment. These groups of energies are ready for focussing and distribution by the Hierarchy, and that Hierarchy under its Great Leader, the Christ, is closer to mankind than ever before in human history. The N.G.W.S. are also standing attentive to direction in every country in the world, united in their idealism, in their humanitarian objectives, in their sensitivity to spiritual impression, in their united, subjective purpose, in their love of their fellow men, and in their dedication to selfless service. The men and women of goodwill are also to be found everywhere, ready to be guided into constructive activity, and to be the agents, gradually trained and educated, for the establishing of that which has never yet before truly existed—*right human relations*.   (8-95)

(x) PREPARING FOR THE REAPPEARANCE OF THE CHRIST

1. We have considered the need of preparation for the coming of the Christ, and some of the basic requirements which will arise as people brace themselves for the needed activity, including the raising of the necessary finances to carry forward the preparatory work. The individual worker has, first of all, to decide if his incentive and spiritual expectancy is adequate to the task ahead. Only that is of importance which provides a needed momentum for action, and only that worker will be equal to the task, who has a vision of sufficient clarity to enable him to work with understanding and sincerity. He must discover that it *is* possible for

him to play his part in the furthering of the divine Plan. The fact of Christ and the genuine possibility of His reappearance, must become important motivating factors in his consciousness. He looks around for those with whom he may work, and who have the same spiritual objectives as he has. In this way and in due time, he finds that there exists on Earth a well or-ganised and integrated group to which can be given the name of the New Group of World Servers. He finds that they are everywhere, and are func-tioning in every country and in all the organised religious groups and all other groups, dedicated to the well-being of humanity and to preparing the way for the return of the Christ.

This is primarily a group which, while working on the outer plane of daily, physical living, yet preserves a close, inner, spiritual integration with the centre of energy from which it can draw all that is needed for active, spiritual work. The group provides a field of service for all who are seeking service-expression; it also provides a rallying point for all who are willing to be tried out, and a place where their motives and per-sistence can be tested, prior to a steady unfoldment of spiritual oppor-tunity. He is thus freed for ever enlarging areas of service.

The N.G.W.S. provides essentially a training ground and a field of experience for those who hope to grow in spiritual stature, and to fit themselves to be the active, directed disciples of the Christ. The appear-ance of this group on Earth at this time, is one of the indications of the success of the evolutionary process, as applied to humanity. This method of work—the use of human beings as agents to carry forward the work of salvation and of world uplift—was initiated by the Christ Himself; He worked with men very frequently through others, reaching humanity through the medium of His twelve Apostles, regarding Paul as substituting for Judas Iscariot. The Buddha tried the same system, but the relation of His group was, in the first instance, to Him and not so much to the world of men. Christ sent His Apostles out into the world to feed the sheep, to seek, to guide and to become "fishers of men". The relation of the disciples of the Christ was only secondary to their Master but primarily to a demanding world; that attitude still controls the Hierarchy, yet with no loss of devotion to the Christ. What the Buddha had instituted sym-bolically and in embryo, became factual and existent under the demands of the Piscean Age.

In the age into which we are now emerging, the Aquarian Age, this mode of group work will reach a very high point of development, and the world will be saved and reconstructed *by groups* far more than by in-dividuals. In the past we have had World Saviours—Sons of God Who have given to men a message which brought an increase of light to the people. Now, in the fullness of time, and through the processes of evolution, there is emerging a group who will bring salvation to the world, and who (embodying groups, ideas, and emphasising the true meaning of the Church of Christ) will so stimulate and energise the minds and souls of men, that the New Age will be ushered in by an outpouring of the Love, Knowledge, and Harmony of God Himself, as well as by the reappearance of the Christ in Whom all these three faculties of divinity will be embodied.

. . . For the last ten years, this N.G.W.S. has been reorganised and revitalised; the knowledge of its existence is spreading all over the world. It is today a group of men and women of every nation and race, and of all religious organisations and humanitarian movements, who are fundamentally oriented towards the Kingdom of God, or who are in process of thus orienting themselves. They are disciples of the Christ, working consciously and frequently unconsciously for His reappearance; they are spiritual aspirants, seeking to serve and make real the Kingdom of God on Earth; they are men of goodwill and intelligence who are trying to increase understanding and right human relations among men. This group is divided into two major divisions:

i. A group composed of the disciples of the Christ who are consciously working with His plans, and of those who, instructed by them, are consciously and voluntarily co-operating. In this latter category we can find ourselves if we so desire, and if we are willing to make the necessary sacrifices.

ii. A group composed of aspirants and world conscious men and women, who are working unconsciously under the guidance of the spiritual Hierarchy. There are many such, particularly in high places today, who are fulfilling the part of destroyers of the old form, or of builders of the new. They are not conscious of any inner synthetic plan, but are selflessly occupied in meeting world need as best they may, with playing parts of importance in national dramas, or with working persistently in the field of education.

The first group is in touch with the spiritual Hierarchy to some extent, and to a large extent where true disciples are concerned; its members work under spiritual inspiration. The second group is in close touch with the masses of men; it works more definitely under the inspiration of ideas. The first group is occupied with the Plan of the Christ as far as its members can grasp its essentiality, whilst the second group works with the new concepts and hopes which are emerging in the consciousness of mankind, as men begin subjectively and often unconsciously to respond to the preparations for the coming of the Christ. Steadily and as a result of the work of the N.G.W.S., humanity is awakening to the possibilities ahead.

The awakening of the intelligentsia in all countries to the recognition of *humanity* is a prelude to the establishment of brotherhood. The unity of the human family is recognised by man, but before that unity can take form in constructive measures, it is essential that more and more of the thinking men and women throughout the world should break down the mental barriers existing between races, nations and types; it is essential that the N.G.W.S. should itself repeat in the outer world that type of activity which the Hierarchy expressed when it developed and materialised the N.G.W.S. Through the impression and expression of certain ideas, men everywhere must be brought to the understanding of the fundamental ideals which will govern the New Age. This is the major task of the N.G.W.S.

As we study and learn to recognise the N.G.W.S. in all its branches and spheres of activity—scattered all over the world and embracing true and earnest workers and humanitarian people in every nation, every religion, and every organisation of humanitarian intent—we shall awaken to the realisation that there is on Earth today a body of men and women whose numbers and range of activities are entirely adequate to bring about the changes which will enable the Christ to walk again amongst us. This will come about if they care enough, are ready enough to make the needed sacrifices, and are willing to sink their national, religious and organisational differences in the carrying out of those forms of service which will reconstruct the world. They must educate the race of men in a few simple and basic essentials and familiarise humanity with the thought of the reappearance of the Christ and the externalisation of the Kingdom of God. Their work will be largely to summarise and make effective the work of the two Sons of God : the Buddha and the Christ.

The success of the work of the N.G.W.S. is inevitable; they have made much headway during the past ten years (published 1948 : *Compiler*); the inner integration of that part of the group which works in close touch with Christ and the spiritual Hierarchy is such that the outer success is guaranteed. They provide a channel through which the light, love and power of the Kingdom of God can reach the more exoteric workers.

Therefore, let us realise that all spiritually inclined men and women, all who seek and work for the establishing of right human relations, all who practise goodwill and truly endeavour to love their fellow men, are an integral part of the N.G.W.S. and that their major task at this time is to prepare a way for the reappearance of the Christ.

Let me emphatically here state that the major method with which we can concern ourselves, and the most potent instrument in the hands of the spiritual Hierarchy, is the spreading of goodwill and its fusion into a united and working potency. I prefer that expression to the words "the organisation of goodwill". Goodwill is today a dream, a theory, and a negative force. It should be developed into a fact, a functioning ideal, and a positive energy. This is our work, and again we are called to co-operate. (8-180/6)

2. The early signs of (the Christ's) approach, with His disciples, can already be discerned by those who note and rightly interpret the signs of the times. There is (among these signs) the coming together spiritually of those who love their fellow men. This is in reality the organising of the outer physical army of the Lord—an army which has no weapons but those of love, of right speech, and right human relations. This unknown organisation has proceeded with phenomenal speed during the aftermath of the war, because humanity is sick of hate and controversy.

The general staff of the Christ is already active in the form of the N.G.W.S.; they are as potent a body of forerunners as has ever preceded a great world Figure into the arena of mankind's living. Their work and influence is already seen and felt in every land, and nothing can destroy that which they have accomplished.   (8-44) and (13-598)

(y) CONCLUSION

1. The various plans under consideration for the furthering and growth of the N.G.W.S., should and will go steadily forward. The ideas briefly outlined above, should be worked out in detail. People must be trained to work for the expansion of these ideas. The general public must be educated as to the aims and objectives of the New Group. Meditation groups should be formed, dedicated to the work of contacting the vision and of drawing in the needed wisdom and power. The Great Invocation should be increasingly used, and daily and hourly must the Invocation be sent forth. The gist of that which is here set forth, should be rearranged and readapted for the use of the general public, for it is only through constant reiteration that men learn, and these things must be said again and again before the real work of the N.G.W.S. can make itself felt.

The function of the N.G.W.S. is to balance the forces leading to disintegration and destruction by embodying in itself the forces of integration and construction. The New Group will eventually offset the tendency (so prevalent at this time) towards racial hatreds, and the teaching given out will tend to negate the present ideas which are powerful in producing the current cleavages and barriers among men, thus causing separation and war. Where there is an appearance of a group or groups, expressing ideas which potently emphasise one angle of public opinion and one aspect of life, there must inevitably appear, under the law of balance, that which will offset it. At the present point in the history of the race, the groups which foster the spirit of cleavage and which build up barriers to impede the free spirit of man, have appeared first. They do their needed work, for they too are included in the Plan. Then, under the law, there must appear the group or groups which embody those ideas which lead to integration and constructive building. They will swing the world on to a higher turn of the spiral; they will heal the breaches, break down the barriers, and end the cleavages.   (15-667/8)

2. The task before the N.G.W.S. is great, but it is not an impossible task. It is engrossing but as it constitutes an imposed life pattern, it can be worked out in every aspect of a man or woman's daily life. We are now called to serve intensively *for a period of years,* to abnormal living, and to the shouldering of a responsibility about which we have known for several years, but which we have not shouldered. Our interest has been powerfully evoked, but not demonstrated as it might have been. The demand for co-operation has been clearly sounded from the inner side, and by the leaders and workers in the N.G.W.S. We have responded with some aid, but not with sacrifice; we have given some assistance, but it has been the minimum and not the possible maximum (except in a few cases, whose assistance has been whole hearted and recognised). We have been told that the members of the N.G.W.S. are working in every land to spread goodwill, world understanding, and religious unity. The idea has been reassuring and we have rested back upon their efforts—the efforts of a hard pressed few.   (15-732)

3. I make no further appeal for your help. I have been endeavouring to educate you in the new ideals and in the work of the N.G.W.S. The responsibility for right action and for the effort to reach the public, rests upon the aspirants and disciples of the world who read my words. There is nothing that I, personally, can do. It is your *time* (and all of you, without exception, can give some) for which Christ and humanity are today cal-

ling. It is your activity and skill in reaching those you can reach for which we make demand. It is your money that is needed to enable us to reach the interested public. It is your meditation and intense inner co-operation which will construct that channel through which the spirit of peace can work, and the forces of Light enter. *The Hierarchy waits.* It has done all that is possible from the angle of Its opportunity. The Christ stands in patient silence, attentive to the effort that will make His work materialise on earth, and enable Him to consummate the effort He made 2 000 years ago in Palestine. The Buddha hovers over the planet, ready to play His part if the opportunity is offered to him by mankind. I beg you to note what I here have said. Everything now depends upon the right action of the men of goodwill.   (15-750/1)

4. The new world will be built upon the ruins of the old. The new structure will rise. Men of goodwill everywhere, under the guidance of the N.G.W.S., will organise themselves into battalions of life, and their first major task must be the development of right human relations, through the education of the masses. This means the paralleling development of an enlightened public opinion, which is (speaking esoterically) right response to the sound which conveys the will of God to the ears of the attentive. Then humanity will indeed move outward from the desert, leave the seas behind, and know that God is Fire.   (18-88)

67.   THE SERVING HIERARCHY

1. The Brotherhood is a community of souls who are swept by the desire to serve, urged by a spontaneous impulse to love, illumined by one pure Light, devotedly fused and blended into groups of serving Minds, and energised by One Life. Its Members are organised to further the Plan which They consciously contact, and with which They deliberately cooperate.   (5-23)

2. The Hierarchy of Illumined Minds is a group Whose telepathic powers enable Them to be sensitive to the mind currents and to register the thoughts of Those Who personify the Mind of God, the Universal Mind, and to register the thought-forms of Those Who are as far beyond the Hierarchy of Masters as They, in Their turn, are beyond the disciples of the world.

Those Lives Who carry out the ideas of the Divine Mind, exist in Their graded orders, and with the detail of Their groupings we are not concerned, except with the fact that the planetary Brotherhood is in telepathic rapport with Those Who are responsible for the planetary conditions in the solar system, with the Great Council, therefore, at Shamballa. They are also in immediate telepathic rapport with each other. The slowly manifesting powers of the radio and the sensitive workings of the perfecting radio mechanisms and of television, are but the response in physical matter of the perfected telepathic powers and television of the minds of the Masters of the Wisdom. Forget not, that such powers are inherent in all men.

The inner group of Masters with Whom I am associated, work telepathically also with Their disciples and the disciples with each other in lesser degree.   (5-24)

3. The production of the outer form on earth, through the medium of books, of esoteric schools and the educating of public opinion, has been committed to a group of us who form a part of the inner world government—disciples and initiates—and to this group, I play the part of secretary and of organising contact man—if I may use words which will mean something to your ears, versed as you are in physical plane organisation work; they mean little or nothing to us, versed as we are in the work of producing living organisms. This group to which I refer, is composed of two oriental initiates (of whom I am one) and of five occidental initiates.   (5-33)

4. There are many in the Hierarchy at this time, who have refused further opportunity of progress, in order to stay with and help the sons of men.   (5-290)

5. The group of a Master is a focus of power, built up by the Master in three ways :

i. By the potency of His Own thought life, evoked by His response to the united hierarchical purpose, and a growing ability to respond to Shamballa.

ii. By His ability to integrate the centre of power (His group for which He has made Himself responsible) into the immediate activity of the Hierarchy.

iii. By His wisdom in His choice of collaborators. His group of disciples will be effective in world service and useful to His Superiors, just in so far as He employs judgment in gathering together the men and women whom He is preparing for initiation.

. . . A Master can be greatly hindered or aided in His work for humanity by His choice of disciples.   (5-684/5)

6. The Hierarchy is essentially the group of the Lord of the World; it is His Ashram. In this statement lies the enunciation of a relatively new truth as far as human knowledge is concerned. Before the Hierarchy can work more openly and with fuller recognition by mankind, there must be the elimination of all hate and all sense of separateness, and the evocation of goodwill and right human relation as the result of the activities of all disciples.   (5-685)

7. The New Age will bring in eventually a civilisation and a culture which will be utterly different to anything hitherto known. I would remind you here that all civilisations and cultures are externalisations—modified, qualified and adapted to racial and national needs—of the potent, vibrating and planned activity of the world of initiates and disciples who constitute the Hierarchy of the time. Their plans, Their thinking and Their living potency pour out ceaselessly, and affect the consciousness of Their disciples; these latter step down the inflowing energies so that the thinkers and idealists can grasp these new emerging truths more accurately. Eventually the truths thus grasped change the consciousness of humanity as a whole and raise it—if you like that phrase; thus modes of daily living, civilised methods of conduct and cultural developments eventuate. All this is traceable to the group of initiates upon the inner side, who thus serve their fellow men and carry forward, consciously and with intent, the Law of Evolution.   (6-271)

8. The work or the radiatory activity of the Hierarchy is today more potent than at any time in human history. The Masters and Their disciples (under the guidance of the World Teacher of that period) were physically present on earth in early Atlantean times, and the radiation emanating from Them was protective, guarding and nurturing. Later, the Hierarchy withdrew into a subjective expression, and humanity was—under the Law of Evolution—left to its own devices, thus to learn the Way and tread the Path of Return through individual experiment and experience. The Masters (in this long interim) have not come forth to contact humanity on any large or group scale; many of Their senior disciples have, however, emerged at varying intervals and when needed; the World Teacher has

also come forth to sound the key or note for each new civilisation and to express the results of the passing civilisation. Men have had, therefore, to find their way alone to the Hierarchy; in silence that Hierarchy has waited, until the number of "enlightened souls" was so great that their invocative appeal, and their magnetic radiation reached a potency which could not be denied; the balance of equilibrium, attained between the Kingdom of God on Earth and the Kingdom of God in Heaven (to use Christian phraseology), became such that the "Gates of Return" could be opened and free intercourse established between the fourth and the fifth kingdoms in nature. The gates (and I am still speaking in symbols) are already opening, and soon will stand wide open to admit the passing of the "Son of Man, the perfected Son of God", back to the place—our Earth—where He earlier demonstrated perfect love and service. But—as you know—this time He will not come alone, but will bring with Him the Heads of certain of the Ashrams, as well as a trained group of initiates and disciples.

These happenings are taking place *today* before the eyes of all men, even though much that is going on remains totally unrecognised over vast areas of the world of thought and by many millions of men. However . . . there are enough initiates and disciples working upon the physical plane at this time to ensure a recognition so extensive that the steady, consistent arousing of human expectation is guaranteed. Ponder on this, and learn to recognise on every side the signs of human anticipation, and the pronounced indication of the approach of the Hierarchy.   (6-409/10)

9. The future ahead of my workers and the work to be done, which will emanate from my Ashram, is one of great activity. The plans are outlined and the work assigned is clearly proposed. I receive my instructions from a "joint committee" of the spiritual leaders behind the world scene; They are the senior members of the Hierarchy, working under the Christ. They arrive at Their decisions after due consultation with senior workers, such as myself—Masters and initiates above the third initiation. Thus the work becomes fused and blended, and the entire Hierarchy, at a time of crisis such as the present, is swung into one unified activity. From that point of focussed intention, each then proceeds to carry out the Plan, via Their Ashram, and thus the work makes its impact upon the outer world.   (6-501)

10. The Hierarchy itself is the result of human activity and aspiration; it has been created by humanity. Its members are human beings who have lived, suffered, achieved, failed, attained success, endured death and

passed through the experience of resurrection. They are the same in nature as are those who struggle today with the processes of disintegration, but who—nevertheless—have in them the seed of resurrection. All states of consciousness are known to Them and They have mastered all of them; They have mastered them as men, thus guaranteeing to humanity the same ultimate achievement. We are apt to look upon the members of the Hierarchy as different radically from humanity, forgetting that the Hierarchy is a community of successful men, Who earlier submitted Themselves to the purificatory fires of daily living, working out their own salvation as men and women of affairs, as business men, as husbands and wives, farmers and rulers, and that they know life, therefore, in all its phases and gradation. They have surmounted the experiences of life; Their great Master is the Christ; They have passed through the initiations of the new birth, the baptism, the transfiguration, the final crucifixion and the resurrection. But They still are men and differ from the Christ only in the fact that He, the first of our humanity to attain divinity, the Eldest in a great family of brothers (as St. Paul expresses it), the Master of the Masters, and the Teacher of angels and of men, was deemed so pure, so holy and so enlightened, that He was permitted to embody for us the great cosmic principle of love; He thus revealed to us, for the first time, the nature of the heart of God.

These perfected men, therefore, exist; They are more than men because the divine spirit in them registers all stages of consciousness and awareness—subhuman, human and superhuman. This inclusive development enables them to work with men, to contact humanity at need, and to know how to lead us forward to the phases of resurrection. (13-472/3)

11. What is it that you all can do? . . . Teach the law of evolution and its inevitable corollary, perfected men. Men must be taught that Great Souls exist, and exist entirely to serve Their fellow men. The public must be familiarised with Their names and attributes, with Their work and purpose, and men must be told that They are coming forth for the salvation of the world. (13-515)

12. For millions of years, as a result of the triumph of evil in those days, the Hierarchy has stood in silence behind world events, occupied with the following work—a work which will eventually be carried on exoterically instead of esoterically :

i. The Hierarchy stands as a wall between humanity and excessive evil. Forget not that as humanity is thus protected, that protection extends also to all the subhuman kingdoms, of which the fourth kingdom, the human, is the Macrocosm. The excessive evil, emanating from cosmic sources, requires the trained skill of the Hierarchy and the fiat of Shamballa to prevent it flooding over disastrously.

ii. The Hierarchy works constantly at the task of awakening the consciousness aspect in all forms, so that it is awakened, expanded and intelligently employed.

iii. The Hierarchy directs world events, as far as mankind will permit (for the free will and free decision of mankind may not be ignored), so that the unfolding consciousness may express itself through developing and adequate social, political, religious and economic world forms. They give direction; They throw a light; They impress those who are in contact with Them, and through the inflow of ideas and through revelation They definitely influence the tide of human affairs.

iv. The Hierarchy directs and controls, more than is realised, the unfolding cyclic cultures and their resultant civilisations. These can then provide adequate forms, temporarily useful for the emerging soul of humanity. The format of cultures and civilisations receives special attention.

v. The Hierarchy receives and transmits energies and consequent forces from Shamballa, with resultant effects within the Hierarchy itself, and also with effects upon humanity and upon the soul of all things to be found in all kingdoms.

vi. The Hierarchy receives that esoteric "Fire of God" which brings to an end cycles, ideologies, organisations and civilisations, when the due and right time comes. This They do in order to make place for that which is better and which will prove adequate and not limiting to the awakening consciousness and the emerging life.

vii. The Hierarchy prepares men for initiation by:

(a) Receiving them into the Ashrams of the Masters.

(b) Offering Their disciples opportunity to serve in relation to the emerging Plan.

(c) Inaugurating through the means of the disciples of the period those new presentations of the training needed for initiation. Each *major* cycle receives new forms of the same ancient, yet basic, teaching. This present one is such a cycle, and much of my own work is in connection with this.

All of these activities and functions of the Hierarchy are well known to many of you theoretically, and to some at first hand—which is a good and useful thing to recognise. These activities have all been carried on "behind the veil" and are, of course, only a very small part of the total work of the Hierarchy. Much of it would be entirely incomprehensible to you. However, if the disciples of this modern world, and the initiates, can measure up to their present and presented opportunity, it should be possible for all of this, not only to be carried forward in the full light of day, but with the co-operation and the understanding acceptance of the intelligent people everywhere, and also with the devoted acquiescence (though blind acceptance) of the man in the street.   (13-519/20)

13. What in the last analysis, is this Hierarchy? It is a great salvaging corps of dedicated, liberated Units of Life, working in group formation with all forms and lives in all kingdoms, and with all souls particularly. As the Hierarchy so works, Its emphasis is solely on the *consciousness aspect* of all forms; Its present agency of salvage and of service is the mind, as it expresses Itself through the minds of all humanitarians, all aspirants, all disciples (of all rays and degrees) and of all initiates; the Hierarchy also can express Itself through the medium of thought currents and ideas and through them impose Its hierarchical concepts upon the embryonic minds of the general and average public; and It also directs the educational work of all nations, so that the undeveloped masses can become—in due turn —the intelligent general public.   (13-526)

14. Today, as never before, the Hierarchy stands as a "mediating trans- mitter" between :

i. Humanity and the Will of God. The revelation of the true significance and purpose of that Will as it stands behind all world events, is needed now as never before. This can come through a closer relation between the Hierarchy and Humanity.

ii. Humanity and its karma, for it is equally essential that the laws for the transmutation of karma into active present good are clearly grasped.

iii. Humanity and cosmic evil, focussed for many millennia of years in what has been called the Black Lodge. Speculation anent this Lodge and its activities is both fruitless and dangerous.   (16-445)

15. A Master has no personality at all. His divine nature is all that He has. The form through which He works (if He is working through and living in a physical vehicle), is a created image, the product of a focussed will

and the creative imagination; it is not the product of desire, as in the case of a human being. This is an important distinction and one which warrants careful thinking. . . . They no longer respond to the ancient call of the reincarnating soul, which again and again has gathered to itself the lives which it has touched and coloured by its quality in the past. The soul and the causal body no longer exist by the time the fourth initiation is undergone. What is left is the Monad and the thread, the antahkarana, which it has spun out of its own life and consciousness down the ages, and which it can *focus at will* upon the physical plane, where it can create a body of pure substance and radiant light for all that the Master may require. This will be a perfect body, utterly adapted to the need, the plan and the purpose of the Master. None of the lesser lives (as we understand the term) form part of it, for they can only be summoned by desire. In the Master there is no desire left, and this is the thought held before the disciple. (18-101)

16. The Hierarchy stands at the midway point:

i. Throwing all its weight on the side of that which is new, spiritual and desirable.

ii. Adapting itself simultaneously to new conditions and new emerging factors.

iii. Standing like a wall of steel, unshatterable and immovable between humanity and the forces of evil.

This has been an epoch of crisis, and the great moment for which the Hierarchy has been preparing ever since it was founded upon the Earth. Slowly down the ages, men have been trained and prepared for initiation; they have taken then their place within the ranks of the Hierarchy and have—later—passed into the higher centre, Shamballa. (18-236)

17. The Hierarchy pursues its own line of spiritual unfoldment as a paralleling activity to its services on Earth in connection with planetary evolution. Men are so apt to regard their own lives and destiny, and the unfoldment of the human consciousness, as the factor of only and paramount importance upon Earth and in the evolutionary processes of the planet. These conditions *are* of importance, but they are not the only factors of importance, nor does humanity stand alone and isolated. Humanity occupies a midway point between the subhuman and the superhuman kingdoms, and each of these groups of evolving lives has its own important destiny—important to all contained within the group ring-pass-not.

They have their own chosen and differing modes, methods and ways of achievement. Just as individual man has to learn the art of science of relationship to other men and to his environment, so humanity *as a whole* has to learn its relationship to that which lies above and beyond mankind, and with that which is below and left behind. This involves a sense of proportion which can be attained only by the mind principle in man.   (18-333)

18. There is no pain or agony for the Master Who has attained liberation. The Masters have each and all renounced that which is material; They have been lifted out of the three worlds by Their Own effort; They have detached Themselves from all hindrances; They have left hell behind, and the term "spirits that are in prison" no longer applies to Them. This They have done for no selfish purpose. In the early days of the Probationary Path, selfish aspiration is foremost in the consciousness of the aspirant; however, as he treads the path, and likewise the Path of Discipleship, he leaves all such motives behind (a minor renunciation) and his one aim, in seeking liberation and freedom from the three worlds, is to aid and help humanity. This dedication to service is the mark of the Hierarchy.   (18-703)

68.   EXTERNALISATION OF THE HIERARCHY

1. Two things must be realised as the interested student considers this event of externalisation :

i. The senior Members of the Hierarchy will not at first be the ones who will make the needed approach. Under Their direction and Their close supervision, this approach will be made—in the early stages—by initiates of and under the degree of the third initiation, and also by those disciples who will be chosen and designated to implement Their efforts, and so will work under Their direction. It is only in the later stages, and when the time has come for the return into recognised physical expression of the Christ, leading to the definite restoration of the Mysteries, that certain of the senior Members of the Hierarchy will appear and take outer and recognisable physical control of world affairs. The time for this will be dependent necessarily upon the success of the steps taken by the members of the Hierarchy who are not so advanced.

ii. Members of the Hierarchy, whether working in the early stages or later when the true externalisation takes place, will work as members of the human family and not as proclaimed members of the Kingdom of God or of souls, known to us as the Hierarchy; they will appear in office of some kind or another; they will be the current politicians, business men, financiers, religious teachers or churchmen; they will be scientists and philosophers, college professors and educators; they will be the mayors of cities and the custodians of all public ethical movements. The spiritual forcefulness of their lives, their clear, pure wisdom, the sanity and the modern acceptableness of their proposed measures in any department in which they choose to function, will be so convincing that little impediment will be set in the way of their undertakings.   (13-570/1)

2. The preparatory work of externalisation falls into three phases or stages, as far as relation to mankind is concerned:

First. The present stage in which a few isolated disciples and initiates, scattered all over the world, are doing the important task of destruction, plus the enunciation of principles. They are preparing the way for the first organised body of disciples and initiates who—coming from certain Ashrams—will proceed with the next phase of the work.

Second. The stage of the first real externalisation upon a large and organised scale will succeed upon the above endeavours. These disciples and initiates will be the real Builders of the new world, of the new civilisation; they will assume leadership in most countries and take high office in all departments of human life. This they will do by the free choice of the people and by virtue of their advanced and proven merit. By this means, gradually the Hierarchy will take over the control upon the physical plane—subjectively as well as objectively—of the direction of human affairs. This direction will be in virtue of their known and approved capacity, and will not involve the imposition of any hierarchical control or authority; it will simply signify the free recognition by free people, of certain spiritual qualities and effective activities which they believe signify that these men are adequate to the demanded job, and whom they therefore choose as directing agents in the new and coming world. Freedom of choice under the authority of a spiritual livingness which demonstrates competency, will be distinctive of the attitude of the general public. Men will be put into high office and into positions of power not because they are disciples or initiates, but because they are wise and intelligent servants of the public, with an internal awareness, a deeply religious and inclusive consciousness, and a well-trained mind with an obedient brain.

This stage of hierarchical appearance is dependent upon the effective service of the first group of isolated and hardworking disciples who are the senior members of the New Group of World Servers, and who are today working among the sons of men. This second group will take over from them, and theirs will be the task of instituting a more unified preparation for the return of the Christ. The first group prepare humanity for the possibility; the second group definitely prepare for the return itself. They will build for a future which will arise out of the wreckage they will remove; they will instill certain basic concepts anent right human relations into men's minds. Their immediate group work, when they are coming into power and recognition, will consist of a sweetening and a clarification of the political situation and the presentation of those ideas which will eventually lead to a fusion of those principles which govern a democracy and which also condition the hierarchical method—which is somewhat different; this effort will produce a third political situation which will not be entirely dependent upon the choices of an unintelligent public, or on the control which the hierarchical technique evidently involves. The mode of this new type of political guidance will later appear.

This second group will implement the new religion; by the time they come into control, the old theological activities will have been completely broken; Judaism will be fast disappearing; Buddhism will be spreading and becoming increasingly dogmatic; Christianity will be in a state of chaotic divisions and upheavals. When this takes place and the situation is acute enough, the Master Jesus will take certain initial steps towards reassuming control of His Church; the Buddha will send two trained disciples to reform Buddhism; other steps will also be taken in this department of religions and education, over which the Christ rules, and He will move to restore the ancient spiritual landmarks, to eliminate that which is non-essential, and to reorganise the entire religious field—again in preparation for the restoration of the Mysteries. These Mysteries, when restored, will unify all faiths.

Groups of spiritually-minded financiers, who are conscious members of an Ashram, will take hold of the world economic situation and bring about great and needed changes. All these activities, built upon the preparatory work of the first group, are also preparatory in nature.

Third. The stage wherein Christ and the Masters of the Wisdom can make public appearance, and begin to work publicly, openly and outwardly in the world of men. The time of Their coming will be dependent upon the success of the work undertaken by the first two groups; it is not possible for me to prophesy anent this matter. So many factors are involved : the earnest work of the two groups, the readiness and the willingness of mankind to learn, the rapidity with which the forces of restoration and of resurrection can rehabilitate the world, the responsiveness of advanced humanitarians and intelligentsia to the opportunity to rebuild, to recreate and to recognise the factors which the new culture and the new civilisation will demand. Even the Hierarchy Itself, with all Its sources of information, does not know how long this will take, but They are ready to move at any time.   (13-571/4)

3. As a result of the cleansing of the Earth through the medium of the world war (1914-1945), and through the suffering to which humanity has been subjected (with a consequent purifying effect which will demonstrate later), it will be possible for the Hierarchy to externalise itself and function openly upon the physical plane. This will indicate a return to the situation which existed in Atlantean days, when (using Biblical symbolism) God Himself walked among men—divinity was present in physical form, because the Members of the Hierarchy were guiding and directing the affairs of humanity as far as innate free will permitted. On a higher turn of the spiral, this again will happen. The Masters will walk openly among men.   (18-330)

4. The Hierarchy is itself also at a point of spiritual crisis. Its initiates stand before the Door which leads to the Way of the Higher Evolution, and the entire personnel of the Hierarchy waits to make a united move forward, paralleling—on its own level—the move forward which humanity is also destined to make.

But, my brothers, here is the point of interest. Under the great law of synthetic expression (called by us the Law of Synthesis, the law governing the first divine aspect) the Hierarchy must move forward in such a manner that the effort must encompass the physical plane, as well as the higher planes. The activity engineered must cover the three worlds of human evolution as well as the three worlds of the Spiritual Triad. Forget not the overlapping of these two worlds which takes place upon the mental plane and warrants the well known phrase "the five worlds of superhuman evolution". Hence, therefore, the necessity for the externalisation of the Hierarchy, and the demonstration of Their united ability to work from the physical plane up to the highest, in order to move unitedly through this Door on to the Way. Speaking symbolically, this externalisation is for the Members of the Hierarchy an act of sacrificial service, but it is also a symbolic gesture. The Hierarchy incarnates on Earth again, and for the first time since its last incarnation in Atlantean days. It is, however, a group incarnation and not the incarnation of individual Members. This is probably a subtle point too difficult for you to grasp.

The externalisation of the Hierarchy, therefore, and the restoration of the Mysteries, are not something done for humanity, or simply carried out because men have earned a closer contact, have the right to some reward or are now so spiritual that the Hierarchy can have a good and useful time helping them. The picture is entirely different. What looms with such importance in the consciousness of men, is in reality, quite secondary in relation to the hierarchical crisis which we are considering. This reappearance upon the physical plane and the consequent life of service (involving factors of profound significance to men), are an expression of the inherent spiritual impulse which is impelling hierarchical action in two directions, but involving one unified movement, embracing all the five planes of superhuman evolution, and necessitating a group recapitulation of incarnated process.

The Hierarchy has its own life and its own goals and objectives, its own evolutionary rhythm, and its own spiritual expansions; these are not the same as those of the human kingdom.   (18-334/5)

69. A MASTER'S ASHRAM

1. It might be valuable if I endeavoured to define an Ashram to you and so leave you with a clear idea of the difference between a Master's particular group, and the many outer groups which, though working under His inspiration and upon the Plan, are not definitely and technically His Ashram.

An Ashram is a subjective fusion of individuals and not of personalities, gathered together for service purposes. It is a blending of individual activity into one whole—a whole which is united on objective and vision, but which may (and frequently does) have differing methods and techniques. The work of the Ashram is essentially the presentation to the world of those service purposes which are carried forward as seems best to the individual disciples, under the "impression of the Master" and with the co-operation of His group. A group of disciples is not pledged to do the same type of work in the same way and at the same time. They are pledged to work under the inspiration of their soul, as their souls may direct and dictate, strengthened by contact with the Master and with each other. They are related to each other through identity of vision and of vibration, plus mutual respect and complete freedom—particularly the latter.

As you ponder on this, I would ask you to realise that an Ashram is not a group of people, working under the tutelage of some Master. This is an important point to remember. It is—as said earlier—a magnetic point of tension, a fusion of energies, directed towards a common centre, and involving two magnetic factors:

i. *A united urge towards group formation upon the mental plane.* This is the higher correspondence to the herd instinct of the animal world and of the world of men, but is of a spiritual nature and quite differently motivated. The lower herd instinct is motivated largely by the instinct of self-preservation; the higher by the recognition of the immortal nature of the soul, and by the instinct to serve, even with the sacrifice of oneself. The law of "death unto life" controls. When the magnetic pull of the group is adequately strong, then comes the death of the personality life. Until, therefore, the group of disciples in all its parts expresses this outgoing sacrificial urge, it is not an Ashram.

ii. *The magnetic pull of the positive centre at the very heart of the group;* that means the magnetic pull of the Master. As you well know, theoretically at least, at the centre of the Ashram stands ever the Master, or else an initiate or a world disciple. His task is to blend and fuse the energies, tendered and proffered by the group (under the urge to serve) and to indicate the field of service. The mode of this instinctual activity is called occult obedience, and this is voluntarily rendered and unitedly followed. When any group—working in this way under a Master— is moved by one spiritual impulse, and functions through one firm organisation (like electrons around the positive nucleus in an atom), the potency of the group will become immediately effective and not before.

I would at this point indicate to you that the so-called inner Ashram is to the outer group, what the soul and its vision is to the individual disciple, working in his personality vehicles. *It is the place of interior resort.*

Disciples can, therefore, grasp their growth towards fusion as an Ashram (in process of physical exteriorisation) by the development of their spiritual recognition of the inner group potency, and their facility to contact the Master—both as individuals or in group formation. (5-703)

2. No one is integrated into an Ashram, until he has pierced beyond the confines of the purely personal levels of awareness; until he is sensitive to the ray and quality of the Master of the Ashram, and until he is normally soul conscious.   (5-704)

3. The necessity of daily living, the many and diverse family contacts, the resentments against life and its impacts, a dislike of criticism and of being misunderstood, the many problems of character, the pressures of psychic unfoldment, and the pettinesses of circumstance, frequently loom so large that awareness of the Ashram and its life is only an occasional inspiration, instead of a fixed habit of life.   (5-704)

4. Disciples in an Ashram are primarily occupied with world affairs. As a group they are pledged to world work; as individuals they are learning so to work.   (5-705)

5. All of you need to become so sensitive to the quality of my Ashram, and so preoccupied with the opportunity to serve which confronts every disciple these days, that your own personal development, your unique problem (so regarded by you) and your reactions, should be forgotten.   (6-69)

6. (The Master) has gathered (His disciples) together in order to further the ends of His Ashramic enterprise; He has *not* gathered them together in order to teach them or to prepare them for initiation, as has hitherto been taught. Aspirants and disciples *prepare themselves* for the processes of initiation by becoming initiated into the mysteries of divinity *through discipline, meditation and service.* . . . It would be of value to you if you considered the factors which hold an Ashram together and which establish its unity. The major ones, and those which you can understand, are as follows:

i. The most important capacity of a Master of an Ashram is that He has earned the right to communicate directly with the Council at Shamballa, and thus to ascertain at first hand the immediate evolutionary task which the Hierarchy is undertaking. He is not called Master by the initiates in His Ashram; He is regarded as the Custodian of the Plan, and this is based on His ability to "face the greater Light which shines in Shamballa". It is the Plan which gives the keynote to the activities of any Ashram at any particular time, during any particular cycle.

ii. This unanimity of purpose produces a very close subjective relationship, and each member of the Ashram is occupied with making his fullest possible contribution to the task in hand. Personalities do not en-

ter in. . . . The joint undertaking and the united adhering to the desired and arranged cyclic technique binds all members of the Ashram
into one synthetic whole; there is therefore no possible controversy or
any emphasis upon individual ideas, because no personality vibratory
quality can penetrate in the periphery or the aura of an Ashram.

iii. The planning and the assignment of tasks connected with the enterprise in hand, is carried forward through the medium of an ashramic, reflective meditation, initiated by the Custodian of the Plan. "The
Master of an Ashram does not say: "Do this" or "Do that". Together,
in unison and in deep reflection the plans unfold, and each disciple and
initiate *sees* occultly where he is needed and where—at any given
moment—he must place his co-operative energy. Note my wording
here. The members of an Ashram, however, do not sit down for a joint
meditation. One of the qualities, developed through ashramic contact,
is the ability to live always within the field of intuitive perception—a
field which has been created, or a sphere of energy which has been generated, by the united purpose, the combined planning and the concentrated energy of the Hierarchy. . . . The ashramic reflective meditation
is an integral part of the constantly developing perception of the dis-
ciple-initiate, and it (in its turn) is a part of the whole hierarchical reflective meditation. This latter is based upon inspiration (in the occult
sense) from Shamballa. The moment a disciple can share in this constant unremitting meditation or reflection without its interfering with his
service and his other lines of thought, he becomes what is called "a disciple who shall no more go out".

iv. Another factor productive of group unity and synchronous preci-
sion in working, is the complete freedom of the Ashram from any spirit
of criticism. There is no tendency among its personnel to be critical,
and no interest whatsoever in the outer, personal lives of the members,
should they be amongst those functioning in the three worlds. Criticism,
as seen among men, simply is a mode of emphasising the lower self,
and deflects the attitude to the material aspects of a person's life. There
is necessarily clear vision among the members of an Ashram; they know
each other's capacities and limitations, and they know, therefore, where
they can complement each other and together create and present a perfect team in world service. . . .   (6-104/6)

7. Disciples in an Ashram are of no political persuasion and own to no
nationalistic bias. This is not an easy thing for them to achieve at once,

but the group consciousness gradually assumes control, and with it the disciple's ability to think and work with the group in terms of the Plan. (6-361)

8. The value to the Ashram of a trained and functioning disciple lies in his ability to "see with the Ashram" that activity which is required, and the technique and mode of bringing about still another development within the eternal Plan; to this must be added the disciple's understanding of the civilisation and the culture of which he is a part, and a comprehension of the field in which his endeavour must lie. Being a functioning human being and a part of the great panorama of life, he can interpret to the Ashram what he sees of extended evil, what he notes of humanity's striving towards the good, and the "revealing voice" of the speechless masses; his suggestions as to the immediate mode of turning the hierarchical ideas into ordinary human ideals, are of importance to the Master of his Ashram. His value in this aspect of the hierarchical work is that he is *not* a Master, that he is necessarily closer in touch with the daily life of ordinary human beings, and that the field of his activities is with personalities, whereas the Masters and the senior initiates work with souls. When a disciple is a truly soul-infused personality, he can give to the Master most valuable assistance. (6-391)

9. The further a disciple penetrates into the Ashram, the less need he finds for contact with the Master; he comes to realise the extent of the Master's responsibilities and arrives at a juster value of his own relative unimportance. He then submits himself to "the sustaining aura of the Ashram".
. . . Disciples have to learn to turn their spiritual habits into instinctual responsiveness; this is the higher correspondence to the instinctual animal reactions with which we are familiar. When this has been achieved, the disciple can then depend upon himself automatically to do or say the right thing; more important still, the Master can count upon him, knowing that he can be depended upon. He is then "permitted to move throughout the Ashram without impediment, and all the Plan is safe with him". This is what I want you to aim at in your remaining years, so that you will (in your next life) from childhood, express the way of the disciple. (6-555/6)

10. Disciples need to regard the Ashram more definitely as a place of *spiritual enveloping,* if I may use so peculiar a phrase. They need to regard it as a circle of protection, remembering that if their consciousness can escape into the Ashram, they are in a place of complete security

where naught can reach or hurt them. Neither pain nor anxiety can over-whelm the man who dwells in the consciousness of eternity; this sense of the eternal, coupled with the realisation of essential unity, marks all dwellers in an Ashram. . . . This place is a reality and not a dream or a figment of wishful thinking; it is a sphere of focussed awareness where the minds, the love, the aspiration and the spiritual consciousness of many meet, and meet in truth.   (6-652)

11. An Ashram exists for work and not primarily for training of disciples. That training is necessarily given, but *the prime object of an Ashram is to accomplish a particular phase of work.*   (6-676)

12. An Ashram is a place of quietly confident, regulated effort. The Plan and the immediate service-activity are known, and disciples and initiates—each aware of his task and equipment—proceed to carry out the phase of the One Work which is theirs. Each senses its relationship to the phases of the work undertaken by his group brothers; it is in learning to see the picture whole (as the Master ever sees it) that confidence and security are developed.   (6-720)

13. An Ashram is ever in a state of constant flux and movement. Dis-ciples are passing out of it to form their own Ashrams or to take up a specific place in another Ashram as they meet the requirements of more advanced stages. They are shifting from one degree to another; they are moving forward steadily from the periphery to the centre, from the outer ring-pass-not to the lighted dynamic centre. As they move forward, pre-serving ever the close inner unity, place is made for new disciples—to be admitted and trained for service.

Part of the service rendered by members of an Ashram, is to make way for new aspirants. This they do by hastening their own progress and moving forward. When disciples take one of the final initiations, or when they are admitted to a higher and more potent Ashram, vacancies occur which are always promptly filled. The occult law which governs all pro-gress in an Ashram is sometimes called the Law of Fulfilment. By this is meant the full compliance of a disciple with the service demands upon the outer plane. When his service is as full and as effective as he can render it, then—under a condition which is in the nature of a group occult paradox—his outer effectiveness produces an inner effectiveness. You have all been taught (though theoretically for the most part) that inner effectiveness produces illumined and potent service. Now learn the re-verse side of this truth.   (6-742/3)

14. An Ashram is an emanating source of hierarchical impression upon the world. Its "impulsive energies" and its inciting forces, are directed toward *the expansion of the human consciousness,* through the magnetic lives of the group members as they carry on their duties, obligations and responsibilities in the outer world; it is aided also by the steady vibratory activity of the members of the Ashram who are not in physical incarnation, and by the united clear thinking and convinced awareness of the entire Ashram. Beginners, such as are most aspirants (though not all), are usually engrossed with the fact of the Ashram. Trained disciples are engrossed with the work to be done, and the Ashram—as an Ashram—plays little part in their thinking; they are so preoccupied with the task ahead, and with the need of humanity and of those to be served, that they seldom think of the Ashram or of the Master at its centre. They are part of the ashramic consciousness. . . .

The members of the Ashram constitute *a united channel for the new energies* which are, at this time, entering the world; these energies pour dynamically through the Ashram, out into the world of men; they stream with potency through the Master at the heart of the Ashram; they move with "luminous speed" throughout the inner circle; they are stepped down by those who constitute the outer circle, and this is right and good; they are delayed by the beginner and the new disciple from breaking forth into the world of men, and this is not so good. They are delayed because the new disciple has turned his back upon the world of men, and his eyes are fastened upon the inner goal, and not upon the outer service; they remain fixed upon the Master and His senior disciples and workers, and not upon the mass of human need.   (11-194/5)

15. An Ashram has in it disciples and initiates at all points of evolutionary development, and of all grades and degrees; these all work together in perfect unison, and yet—*within* their differentiated ranks, for each degree stands alone yet united with all the others—with their own established rapport, their coded telepathic interplay, and a shared occult secrecy and silence which guard the secrets and knowledges of one grade from another, and from the unready. Similarly, when an aspirant, seeking upon the physical plane to find those who will share with him the mystery of his next immediate step or demonstrated expansion, discovers his own group, he will find that it has in it those who have not reached his particular point of wisdom, and those also who have already left him far behind. He will be drawn into a vortex of force and a field of service simultaneously. Ponder on this statement. He will learn, therefore, the

lessons required by one who is to work in an Ashram and will know how to handle himself with those who may not yet share with him the secrets which he already knows, and with those who have penetrated deeper into the Mysteries than he has.   (18-346)

70.   DISCIPLES PREPARING FOR THE NEW AGE

1. At the present stage of preparation, the task of the disciple who is charged with laying the foundation for the New Age methods, and with the labour of getting ready for the first group of Ashram members, is hard indeed. He stands for so much that is deemed visionary and impossible; the difficulties which confront him seem impossible; he teaches truths whose first effect is necessarily destructive, because he endeavours to rid humanity of old forms of religious, economic and political doctrine; his impersonality—which recognises faults as well as virtues—enrages many, and often those from whom he had expected understanding and a true impartiality; his failure to be impressed or attentive to old rites and ceremonies, to ancient and obsolete but precious ideas, and his constant warfare on conditioning glamours and illusions, meet in these early stages, with little encouragement. He works frequently alone and usually with little recognition, and lacks time for his own personal hierarchical contacts; he is not necessarily connected with any so-called esoteric groups and—if he is—his task is that much harder; only advanced disciples, with a full and conscious constant contact with their particular Ashram, are able to work in this way. Occult bodies and esoteric groups are, at this time, the most glamoured of any of the world groups; the work of any disciple in such groups is bound, in the early stages, to be destructive. . . . The members who are true and sound, broadminded and sane, and rightly oriented and dedicated, will find their way into esoteric bodies which are free from dogmatism and doctrines, and which are recipients of hierarchical life.   (13-571)

2. The disciples sent out from the various Ashrams do not arrive on earth conscious of a high mission, or knowing well the nature of the task to which they have been subjectively assigned. In the case of certain disciples who will be of special world prominence, and who are of initiate rank, they may attain to a conviction of mission (if I may call it so) in

their extreme youth, and thus be oriented towards their life task from the very start; that conviction will grow and deepen and clarify as the years go by. But it must be remembered that the majority of disciples will not so react. They will come into incarnation with certain gifts and innate talents and with certain firmly rooted ideas, endowed with irrevocable ideals and a brain which is responsive to a well-developed mind. They will, normally and through natural trends and predilections, find their way into that field of human activity wherein they are intended to work and in which they are to bring about certain basic changes in line with hierarchical intent. This hierarchical intent will usually be unknown to them (though this may not always be the case), but the work to be done will seem to them impelling and necessary and something which they must do at all costs. They will find their way into politics, into the educational movements and into science; they will work as humanitarians, as social workers and in the field of finance, but they will follow these lines of activity through natural inclination and not because they are being "obedient" to instruction from some Master. They will be successful in their endeavour because the potency of the Hierarchy will be behind them, and there is much that the inner Ashram can accomplish for its outer working disciples in the way of opening doors, implementing efforts and arranging contacts and other facilities; this is all done, however, without any evidence of the inner impulsion. Recognition of the inner effort will be dependent upon the status in the Ashram of the disciple. When the disciple is a very advanced one, he may become aware of his high mission and know it to be no fanatical and self-initiated intention, but a definite task undertaken in response to ashramic planning. Such cases will usually be the exception and not the rule, particularly in the early stages. Such hierarchical workers will gather around them lesser disciples who will work along the same lines, through community of interest but not through recognition of similar instructions—a very different thing. In the one case, the consciousness of mission is developed through periods of definite planning with the Ashram and in consultation with the Master or His senior workers. In the more usual case, the disciple reacts and works in response to impression, being at this stage totally unaware from whence the impression comes; he regards it as an activity of his own mind, acting as a directing agent in all the planned activities, the life theme and purpose which are his service dynamic.

One major characteristic is, however, present in all these working disciples and aspirants; this is a wide humanitarianism and a determination to aid in the cause of human welfare. One interesting distinction will later emerge and condition the New Age in contra-distinction to past and present methods. Disciples and aspirants will not be dedicated to purely humanitarian and welfare work. That will be a motive and not an objective in work. They will not give up their days and efforts solely to the relief of human necessity. All phases of human living—politics, finance and science, as well as religion—will be recognised to be their immediate and spectacular task, but the motivation in the future will not be primarily business success or personality ambition, but the impulse to subordinate these to the general effort and to aid humanity as a whole, with a long range vision.

It is this growing spirit of humanitarianism which will lie behind all movements towards world socialisation in the various nations. This movement is symptomatic of a change in the orientation of man's thinking, and therein lies its major value. It is not indicative of a new technique of government in reality, and this peculiar phase of it is ephemeral; it is at the same time foundational to the new world order which will emerge out of all these experiments which human thinking is at this time evolving.

These are the things which will be in the consciousness of disciples commissioned by the Hierarchy to bring about the needed changes and the new orientation, and not any recognition of Masters and Their orders or of any hierarchical and ashramic background.

Whilst in incarnation, such disciples stand free to serve one-pointedly and wholeheartedly that section or phase of human effort in which their lot and life-trend appear to cast them. They may be quite unconscious of any spiritual objective (so-called today) except the recognition that they love their fellowmen; this love will condition all they do and will motivate their every effort.

From the standpoint of the Master, they can be reached, impressed and directed, and most definitely they are so reached; from their own standpoint they are simply busy, energetic people, gifted with a good mind, profoundly interested in their chosen life task, and proving themselves capable of effective work along some particular line, able to influence and direct others in similar activity, and definitely bringing about changes in the branch of human endeavour with which they are concerned, thus lifting underlying principles on to higher levels. This is straight hierarchical work. It affects on broad lines the consciousness of humanity.

These disciples may be conscious that their effort and their thinking are part of a forward-moving evolutionary endeavour; to that extent they are mission conscious, but the value of this attitude is that it relates them, in consciousness, to many others, similarly motivated and conscious of a similar vision. It is of course wise to remember that all such disciples are pronounced ray types and are integrated personalities in the highest sense of the word. They will work on earth as high grade personalities, under the impact of strong motives which emanate from the soul in response to impression from the Ashram, but of this, in their physical brains, they know nothing and care less. Part of their effectiveness in service is due to the fact that they are not preoccupied with soul contact and with the idea of academic service. Their eyes are on the job to be done, their hearts are with their fellow men, and their heads are busy with methods, techniques and practices which will raise the entire level of endeavour in their chosen field. Hence their inevitable success.

Disciples who are intensely interested in personal responsiveness to the soul, who work diligently at the problem of soul contact, who are busy with the art of serving consciously, and who make service a goal, who are keenly alive to the fact of the Ashram and to the Master, will *not* be asked to do this work of preparing for the externalisation of the Hierarchy. Advanced disciples who are stabilised in the Ashram, and who are so used to the Master that He assumes in their consciousness no undue prominence, can be trusted to work along right lines in the world and do the work of preparation. They cannot be sidetracked or deflected from one-pointed attention to the task in hand by any soul call or urge; hence they are free to do the intended work.

The situation, therefore, in relation to the consciousness of disciples in the intensely difficult, though interesting, period with which humanity is faced, could be summed up in the following statements:

i. The disciple is not motivated by any desire to externalise the Hierarchy or to see the Ashram with which he is affiliated, functioning physically on the outer plane. He may be totally unaware of this hierarchical intention. If he is aware of this underlying purpose, it is entirely secondary in his consciousness. The good of humanity and a stabilised spiritual future for mankind, are his major life incentives.

ii. The disciple is strictly humanitarian in his outlook. He works for the One Humanity and though aware possibly that he is affiliated with the Hierarchy, his loyalties, his service and his life intention are directed entirely to the cause of human betterment. In this attitude he is coming to resemble the Masters Whose life directive is not hierarchical possibilities, but adherence to the purposes of Shamballa, in action, in relationships, and to the Plan for all living units in the three worlds.

iii. The intuition of the disciple is alert and active; the new ideas and the vital fresh concepts are foremost in his mind. He almost automatically repudiates the reactionary and conservative thinking of the past and—without fanaticism and undue emphasis—he lives, talks and instructs along the new lines of right human relations.

iv. The disciple, occupied with hierarchical plans for the future, has a completely open mind as regards the growth of true psychic powers. He deplores and represses all negative conditions and forms of thinking as he contacts them in his environment, but he encourages the growth of all forms of higher sensory perception which expand the human consciousness and enrich its content.

v. According to his hierarchical status, he will become increasingly a channel of power in the world. His own ashramic life will deepen as his world service develops. The statement in the Bible (or rather injunction) to "take root downward and bear fruit upward" has for him a deeply occult significance.

I am not here touching upon the growth of a disciple *as a disciple,* or on his individual progress on the Path; I am considering the type of consciousness with which he faces the task which confronts him. Unless he fulfils within himself the requirements enumerated in this section of our study, he will not be one of the workers in this interlude between the old age and the new.   (13-582/7)

71.   SERVICE AS APPROACH TO THE GREAT ONES

1. The effective use of invocation is dependent upon the point of spiritual development of the one who seeks the aid of true prayer and invocation. One thing which should be grasped anent all these Great Lives, is that what is commonly called "worship" is abhorred by Them. Worship, the power to adore and the sense of awe (which is one of the highest aspects of fear) are *not* desired by Them. Such attitudes are emotional in origin and based upon the sense of duality, and therefore upon feeling. These Lives are embodiments of service, and can be reached by true servers

with the appeal of service. Bear this in mind. As man progresses upon the Path he forgets worship; he loses all sense of fear, and adoration fails to engross his attention. All these attitudes are obliterated by the realisation of an overpowering love and its consequent interplay and tendency to increase identification. (13-268)

2. (Christ) works through His Masters and Their groups, and thereby greatly intensifies His efforts. He can and will work through all groups just in so far as they fit themselves for planned service, for the distribution of love, and come into conscious alignment with the great potency of the inner groups. . . . (The Kingdom of God) exists, and is not a place of disciplines or golden harps and peopled by unintelligent fanatics, but a field of service and a place where every man has full scope for the exercise of his divinity in human service. (13-604)

72. CHANNELS FOR SERVICE

1. You seek to be a channel and you long adequately to serve. This I *know*. Be willing, therefore, to let the "forces of light" enact their will within your life, e'en though you awaken with surprise to unknown and unrealised aspects of yourself—both good and not so good. (5-231)

2. Keep humble, sensitive to others and unmoved by circumstance. . . . The key to all success is to realise that you are only a channel. (5-502)

3. To be truly effective . . . you must cultivate the attitude of being only a clear unobstructed channel, and you must not block that channel with *your* ideas, *your* plans and *your* physical plane activities. (6-443)

73. LIGHT BEARERS

1. It is indeed and in truth from glory to glory that we go. The past glory of individualisation must fade away in that of initiation. The glory of the slowly emerging self-consciousness must be lost in sight of the wonder of the group consciousness of the race, and this the foremost thinkers and workers today most ardently desire. The glory that can be seen faintly shining in humanity, and the dim light which flickers within the human form, must give place to the radiance which is the glory of the developed son of God. Only a little effort is needed, and the demonstration of a steady staying power, to enable those who are now on the physical plane of experience to evidence the radiant light, and to establish upon the earth a great station of light which will illumine the whole of human thought. Always there have been isolated light bearers, down the ages. Now the group light bearer will shortly be seen. Then shall we see the rest of the human family (who respond not yet to the Christ impulse) having their progress facilitated towards the path of probation. The work will still be slow, and much remains yet to be done; but if all the aspirants of the world and all the disciples at work in the world today, will submerge their personal interests in the task immediately ahead, we shall have what I might pictorially call the opening of a great station of light on earth, and the founding of a power house which will greatly hasten the evolution and elevation of humanity, and the unfoldment of the human consciousness. (14-314/5)

2. The world of men today is full of those who have taken one or other of the initiations, and there are great disciples, from all the rays, working on the physical plane as senior workers for humanity under the Hierarchy; there will be many more during the next one hundred years. (Written in 1949). Some of these do not know their particular hierarchical status in their physical brains, having deliberately relinquished this knowledge in order to do certain work. That which I here write is intended—during the next forty years—to find its way into their hands, with the deliberate intent of bringing to the surface of their brain consciousness, who and what they are in truth. This is a part of the programme planned by the Hierarchy, prior to the externalisation of the Ashrams. The Masters feel that these senior disciples and initiates (being on the spot) should soon begin to work with more authority. This does not mean that they will assert their spiritual identity and claim initiate status. This they could not do on

355

account of their point on the ladder of spiritual evolution. But—knowing who they are from the angle of the Hierarchy, and what is expected of them—they will strengthen their work, bring in more energy, and point the way with greater clarity. Their wisdom will be recognised as well as their compassion, but they themselves will recede into the background; they may even appear to be less active outwardly, and so be misjudged, but their spiritual influence will be growing; they care not what others think about them. They recognise also the mistaken views of all the modern religions anent the Christ; some may even be persecuted in their homes, or by those they seek to help. None of this will matter to them. Their way is clear and their term of service is known to them.   (18-707/8)

74. THE JOY OF SERVICE

1. Happy the disciple who can bring the vision nearer still to humanity, and work it into existence on the physical plane. Remember this, that the materialisation of any aspect of the vision on the physical plane, is never the work of one man. Only when it has been sensed by the many, only when they have worked at its material form, can their united efforts draw it into outer manifestation. Thus you see the value of educating public opinion; it brings the many helpers to the aid of the few visionaries. Always the Law holds good—in descent, differentiation. The two or three sense the Plan intuitively; then the rhythm they set up with their thought sweeps the mental plane matter into activity; thinkers seize hold of the idea. This is a hard thing to learn and difficult to do, but the reward is great.

To those who wrestle, strive, and hold on, the joy is doubled when the materialisation comes. The joy of contrast will be yours, for knowing the past of darkness you will revel in the light of fruition; the joy of tried and tested companionship will be yours, for years will have proved to you who are your chosen associates, and in community of suffering will come the strengthened link; the joy of peace after victory will be yours, for to the tired warrior the fruits of achievement and rest are doubly sweet; the joy of participation in the Masters' Plan will be yours, and all is well that associates you closely with Them; the joy of having helped to solace a needy world, of having brought light to darkened souls, of having healed in some measure the open sore of the world's distress, will be yours, and in the consciousness of days well spent, and in the gratitude of salvaged souls, comes the deepest joy of all—the joy a Master knows when He is instrumental in lifting a brother up a little higher on the ladder. This is the joy that is set before you all—and not so very far ahead it lies. So work, not *for* joy but *towards* it; not for reward, but from the inner need to help; not for gratitude, but from the urge that comes from having seen the vision and realisation of the part you have to play in bringing that vision down to earth.

It is helpful to differentiate between happiness, joy and bliss:

First, *happiness,* which has its seat in the emotions, and is a personality reaction.

Second, *joy,* which is a quality of the soul and is realised in the mind, when alignment takes place.

Third, *bliss,* which is the nature of the Spirit and about which speculation is fruitless until the soul realises its oneness with the Father. This realisation follows upon an earlier stage wherein the personal self is at-oned with the soul. Therefore speculation and analysis as to the nature of bliss is profitless to the average man whose metaphors and terminologies must perforce be personal and related to the world of senses. Does the aspirant refer to his happiness or joy? If he refers to the latter, it must come as the effect of group consciousness, of group solidarity, of oneness with all beings, and may not be interpreted in terms of happiness after all. Happiness comes when the personality is meeting with those conditions which satisfy it in one part or other of its lower nature; it comes when there is a sense of physical well being, of contentment with one's environment or surrounding personalities, or of satisfaction with one's mental opportunities and contacts. Happiness is the goal of the separated self.

When, however, we seek to live as souls, the contentment of the lower man is discounted, and we find joy in our group relationships and in bringing about those conditions which lead to the better expression of the souls of those we contact. This bringing of joy to others in order to produce conditions in which they may better express themselves, may have a physical effect, as we seek to better their material conditions, or an emotional effect, as our presence brings to them peace and uplift, or an intellectual result as we stimulate them to clarity of thought and understanding. But the effect upon ourselves is joy, for our action has been selfless and non-accuisitive, and not dependent upon the aspirant's circumstance or worldly state. Much happiness is necessarily foregone when ill-health makes its pressure felt, as the environment is difficult, and the "accumulated karma of many births" presses down, or as the troubles of the family, nation or race weigh upon the sensitive personality. The happiness of

youth or the self-centred contentment of the selfish insulated person
(hiding himself behind the shield of his protective desires) must not be
confounded with joy.

It is a platitude as well as an occult paradox to say that in the midst of
profound personality distress and unhappiness, the joy of the soul may
be known and felt. Such however is the case, and it is for this the student
must aim. Some people are happy because they shut their eyes to truth, or
are self-hypnotised, hiding themselves within a shell of illusion. But the
aspirant has frequently reached the stage wherein his eyes are wide open;
he has learnt to speak truth to himself, and has built up no separating
wall between himself and others. He is awake and alive; he is sensitive
and frequently suffering. He wonders why apparently, what the world
calls happiness and peace have left him, and asks what is to be the outcome.   (4-368/71)

2. I call you to *cultivated* joyousness, which will end in releasing you to
fuller service.   (5-138)

3. Ponder on joy, happiness, gaiety and bliss; these release the channels
of the inner life and reach—in a wide circle—many kinds of men. They
heal and cleanse the physical body, and help you do your work with little
effort, a proper sense of values, and a detachment which is based on love
and not isolation.   (5-170)

4. *Happiness* is the result of achieved personality desire; *joy* is the expression of the soul's surety, whilst *bliss* is the consummation which the
monad bestows upon the initiate.   (5-181)

5. You are experienced in the Way and even though your physical body
is no longer young, the remainder of your life expression holds much
for you, if the coming years are taken joyously and with high expectancy.   (5-383)

6. You can train yourself to build in that quality of joy which is the characteristic of a personality which is consciously anchored in the soul realm.
(5-398)

7. Joy is the quality which grows out of self-realisation.   (5-399)

8. Aim at demonstrating happiness. Be joyous in your work and service. Be not so intense, but go happily along the lighted Way.   (5-408)

9. Be joyful, for joy lets in the light, and where there is joy there is little
room for glamour and misunderstanding.   (5-461)

10. Be happy. Learn to feel joy—a joy which is based on the knowledge that humanity has always triumphed and passed onward and forward in spite of apparent failures, and the destruction of past civilisations; a joy, which is founded upon the unshakable belief that all men are souls, and that "points of crisis" are factors which are of proven usefulness in calling in the power of that soul, both in the individual man, in a race, or in humanity as a whole; a joy which is related to the bliss which characterises the soul on its own level, whereon the form aspects of manifestation do not dominate. Ponder on these thoughts and remember you are grounded in the centre of your Being and can, therefore, see the world truly and with no limited vision; you can stand unperturbed, knowing the end from the beginning and realising that love will triumph. (5-471)

75. THE LIFE OF SERVICE

1. I seek to give you today, in closing this series, something of general use. I wish to speak to you anent service and its perfect rendering. What I give you in this connection may be of vital use. Remember always that material gain in knowledge for the individual causes stagnation, obstruction, indigestion and pain, if not passed on with wise discrimination. Food absorbed by the human body, if not assimilated and passed through the system, causes just the above conditions. The analogy is correct. Much tuition comes to many these days, but it is for the use of a needy world, and not for their own exclusive benefit.

In rendering service three things are of moment:

i. The motive.

ii. The method.

iii. The attitude following action.

With wrong motives and methods I deal not. To you they are known. I indicate the right, and by adjustment of the life of service to my indications comes correction and inspiration. A life of much service opens up to many these days; see, all of you, that it commences right. A right beginning is liable to eventuate in continuous correctness, and helps much in the endeavour. Where failure follows in such a case, all that is needed is a readjustment. In failure where the beginning has been at fault (an inevitable failure), the need is for the renewal of the inner springs of action.

i. *The motives for service*

These motives are threefold in the order of their importance :

(a) A realisation of God's Plan of evolution, a sensing of the world's dire need, an apprehension of the immediate point of world attainment, and a consequent throwing of the total of one's resources into the furtherance of that end.

(b) A definite personal goal of achievement, some great ideal—such as holiness of character—that calls forth the soul's best endeavour; or a realisation of the reality of the Masters of the Wisdom, and a strong inner determination to love, serve and reach Them at all costs. When you have this intellectual grip of God's Plan, coupled with the strong desire to serve the Great Ones, in physical plane activities will come the working out.

(c) A realisation next of one's innate or acquired capacities and fitting of those capacities to the appreciated need. Service is of many kinds, and he who wisely renders it, who seeks to find his particular sphere, and who, finding it, gives effort gladly for the benefit of the whole, is the man whose own development proceeds steadily. But nevertheless the aim of personal progress remains secondary.

ii. *The methods of service*

These are many and varied. I can but indicate the ones of paramount importance.

First and foremost comes, as I have often inculcated, the faculty of *discrimination.* He who considers that he can attempt all things, who balks not at aught that happens his way, who rushes wildly in where wiser ones refrain, who considers he has capacity for that which arises, who brings zeal but no brains on this problem of service, but dissipates force; he renders oft destructive action, he wastes the time of wiser and greater ones in the correcting of his well meant mistakes, and he serves no end but his own desires. The reward of good intention may be his, but it is frequently offset by the results of foolish action. He serves with discrimination who realises wisely his own niche, great or small, in the general scheme; who calculates soberly his mental and intellectual capacity, his emotional calibre and his physical assets, and then with the sum of the whole applies himself to fill the niche.

He serves with discrimination who judges with the aid of his Higher Self and the Master what is the nature and the measure of the problem to be solved, and is not guided by the well meant, though often ill-judged suggestions, requests and demands of his fellow servers.

He serves with discrimination who brings a realisation of *time* into action, and comprehending that each day contains but twenty-four hours, and that his capacity contains but the expenditure of just so much force and no more, wisely adjusts his capacity and the time available to each other.

Next follows *a wise control of the physical vehicle*. A good server causes the Master no anxiety from physical causes, and may be trusted so to guard and husband his physical strength, that he is always available for the carrying out of the Master's requests. He does not fail from physical disability. He sees that his lower vehicle gets sufficient rest, and adequate sleep. He rises early and retires at a seemly hour. He relaxes whenever possible; he eats wholesome and suitable food and refrains from heavy eating. A little food, well chosen and well masticated, is far better than a heavy meal. The human race eats these days, as a rule, four times as much as is required. He ceases from work when (through accident or the recurrence of inherited physical disability) his body reacts against action and cries out for attention. He then seeks rest, sleep, dietary precautions, and necessary medical attention. He obeys all wise instruction, giving time for his recovery.

The next step is a steady *care and control of the emotional body*. This is the most difficult of the vehicles to tend, as is well known. No excessive emotion is permitted, though strong currents of love for all that breathe are allowed to sweep through. Love, being the law of the system, is constructive and stabilising, and carries all on in line with the law. No fear or worry or care shake the emotional body of the aspiring servant of all. He cultivates serenity, stability, and a sense of secure dependence on God's law. A joyous confidence characterises his habitual attitude. He harbours no jealousy, no cloudy grey depression, and no greed or self-pity, but—realising that all men are brothers and that all that is exists for all—he proceeds calmly on his way.

Then ensues *the development of his mental vehicle*. In the control of the emotional body the server takes the attitude of elimination. His aim is to train the emotional body that it becomes devoid of colour, has a still vibration, and is clear and white, limpid as a pool on a still summer's day. In fitting the mental body for service, the worker strives at the opposite of elimination; he seeks to build in information, to supply knowledge and facts, to train it intellectually and scientifically so that it may prove, as time goes on, a stable foundation for the divine wisdom. Wisdom supersedes knowledge, yet requires knowledge as a preliminary step. You must remember that the server passes through the Hall of Learning prior to entering the Hall of Wisdom. In training the mind body he seeks therefore orderly acquisition of knowledge, a supply of that which may be lacking, a sequential grasp of the innate mental faculty accumulated in previous lives, and lastly, a steadying of the lower mind so that the higher may dominate and the creative faculty of thought may be projected through the stillness. From the Silence of the Absolute was projected the universe. From darkness issued light, from the subjective emanated the objective. The negative stillness of the emotional body makes it receptive from above. The positive stillness of the mental body leads to the higher inspiration.

Having sought to control and wisely use his personality in its three departments, the lover of humanity seeks *perfection in action.* No magnificent dreams of martyrdom and the glorious yet ephemeral chimeras of spectacular service engross his attention, but the instant application of all his powers to the next duty, is the line of his endeavour. He knows that perfection in the foreground of his life and in the details of his environing work will cause accuracy in the background too, and result in a whole picture of rare beauty. Life progresses by small steps, but each step, taken at the right time, and each moment wisely occupied, leads to long distance covered and a life well spent. Those Who guide the human family test out all applicants for service in the small detail of everyday life, and he who shews a record of faithful action in the apparently non-essential will be moved into a sphere of greater moment. How, in an emergency or crisis, can they depend on someone who in everyday matters does slovenly and ill-judged work?

A further method of service shews itself in *adaptability.* This involves a readiness to retire when other or more important people are sent to fill the niche he may be occupying, or (inversely) an ability to step out of office into work of greater importance, when some less competent worker can do his work with equal facility and good judgment. It is the part of wisdom in all who serve, neither to rate themselves too highly nor to underrate themselves. Bad work results when the non-efficient fill a post, but it is equally a loss of time and power when skilled workers hold positions where their skill has not full scope and where less well equipped men and women would do as well. Be ready, therefore, all ye who serve, to stay a lifetime in office non-spectacular and seemingly unimportant, for such may be your destiny and the place you best may serve; but be equally ready to step on to work of more apparent value when the Master's word goes forth, and when circumstances—and not the server's planning—indicate that the time is come. Ponder this last sentence.

iii. *The attitude following action*

What should this attitude be? Utter dispassion, utter self-forgetfulness, and utter occupation with the next step to be taken. The perfect server is he who does to the utmost of his ability what he believes to be the Master's will, and the work to be done by him in co-operation with God's Plan. Then, having done his part, he passes on to a continuance of the work, and cares not for the result of his action. He knows that wiser eyes than his see the end from the beginning; that insight, deeper and more loving than his, is weighing up the fruit of his service; and that judgment, more profound than his, is testing the force and extent of the vibration set up, and is adjusting that force according to the motive. He does not suffer from pride over what he has done, nor from undue depression over lack of accomplishment. At all times he does his very best, and wastes not time in backward contemplation, but steadily presses forward to the accomplishment of the next duty. Brooding over past deeds, and casting the mind back over old achievement, is in the nature of involution, and the servant seeks to work with the law of evolution. This is an important thing to note. The wise server, after action, pays no attention to what his fellow servants say, provided his superiors (either incarnating men and women, or the Great Ones Themselves) prove content or silent; he cares not if the result is not that which he anticipated, provided that he faithfully did the highest thing he knew; he cares not if reproach and reproof assail him, provided his inner self remains calm and non-accusing; he cares not if he loses friends, relatives, children, the popularity once enjoyed, and the approbation of his environing associates, provided his inner sense of contact with Those Who guide and lead remains unbroken; he cares not if he seems to work in the dark and is conscious of little result from his labours, provided the inner light increases and his conscience has naught to say.

To sum it all up:

The *motive* may be epitomised in these few words: The sacrifice of the personal self for the good of the One Self.

The *method* may also be shortly put: Wise control of the personality, and discrimination in work and time.

The *resultant attitude* will be: Complete dispassion, and a growing love of the unseen and the real.

All this will be consummated through steady application to occult Meditation.   (2-343/9)

2. You have served from a rigid sense of duty, but you must now learn to serve with the loving spontaneity which carries all before it. . . . There may also come into your life (as it does into the life of all true servers) an interlude or cycle of experience which may temporarily negate your present cycle of influence, but this should only be preparatory to a greater power in service.   (5-113)

3. You have to lose sight of the far-off spiritual possibility in the service of the hour.   (5-124)

4. Your field of service is growing, which is ever the reward of service rendered.   (5-206)

5. Choose not the subjects of your service, but serve all who seek your aid. Seek them not yourself.   (5-253)

6. Seek the way of selfless service, and all is well.   (5-291)

7. You belong to the work to be done and not to yourself. This is true of all disciples of all degrees, probationary, accepted and initiated. You are needed in the pressure of the coming work, and you must keep the instrument in good condition.   (5-292)

8. Go forward my brother, looking not behind but with your eyes fixed in steadfastness upon the Way of a world Server. It is a hard way, with many ups and downs, and many steep hills and valleys of shadow, but there is rest and shade in the valley and sunshine on the hills.   (5-375)

9. Some people . . . are so constituted that they become servers and centres of light publicly before their fellow men. Their influence and their power are great. Others work (*with equal power*) from a quiet centre of relative retirement, and they wield, if I may again repeat myself, an equal force. . . . Put your strength and light behind that of the workers who serve the Hierarchy upon the open battlefield of life.   (5-434)

10. A more intense inner life, and a more vital life of service are, I know, your ideals, but the one is dependent upon the other.   (5-535)

11. The success of all large undertakings is based on the little things, the minor tasks, faithfully fulfilled, of the disciple who is free from personal ambition.   (5-614)

12. You must be prepared for tests and difficulties until you have proved yourself; these seldom come the expected way. One of your major safeguards is ever . . . to adhere to and carry forward the next duty, and to concentrate upon that which has been undertaken. Avoid that which lies outside the periphery of the work, regarding anything else as a sidetrack. (5-618)

13. Day by day link up with your soul; day by day pledge yourself to the work to be undertaken; day by day seek a deepened relation with me, with my Ashram, and with your group brothers; day by day investigate your service as rendered up to date in the searchlight of the soul, and then, my brother, with my aid and blessing go forward, recognised by us as one of our spiritual assets. Work to bring the light of love and of spiritual orientation to those whom you are called to serve. . . . Lean on your soul.   (6-500)

14. One point I seek to emphasise to you at this time, is the need for you to recognise more definitely that *the way into the inner sanctum is the way of outer service.* This service must not be motivated by the exigencies of the period, or by financial considerations, or the behests of the personality. It may or may not include the place where your outer work is being done; it may necessitate a change in your setting and circumstances, but the disciple—if true to his soul and the Ashram—serves his fellow men *as an esotericist* as well as a humanitarian and a psychologist. (6-636)

15. Students need to remember that devotion to the Path or to the Master is not enough. The Great Ones are looking for *intelligent* co-operators and workers more than They are looking for devotion to Their Personalities, and a student who is walking independently in the light of his own soul is regarded by Them as a more dependable instrument than a devoted fanatic. The light of his soul will reveal to the earnest aspirant the unity underlying all groups, and enable him to eliminate the poison of intolerance which taints and hinders so many; it will cause him to recognise the spiritual fundamentals which guide the steps of humanity; it will force him to overlook the intolerance and the fanaticism and separativeness which characterise the small mind and the beginner upon the Path, and help him so to love them that they will begin to see more truly and enlarge their horizon; it will enable him to estimate truly the esoteric value of service, and teach him above all to practise that *harmlessness* which is the outstanding quality of every Son of God. A harmlessness that speaks no word

that can damage another person, that thinks no thought which could poison or produce misunderstanding, and which does no action which could hurt the least of his brethren—this is the main virtue which will enable the esoteric student to tread with safety the difficult path of development. Where the emphasis is laid upon service to one's fellow men and the trend of the life force is outward to the world, then there is freedom from danger, and the aspirant can safely meditate and aspire and work. His motive is pure, and he is seeking to decentralise his personality and shift the focus of his attention away from himself to the group. Thus the life of the soul can pour through him, and express itself as love of all beings. He knows himself to be a part of a whole and the life of that whole can flow through him consciously, leading him to a realisation of brotherhood and of his oneness in relation to all manifested lives. (13-19/20)

16. Disciples learn to work with the Plan by *working*; they learn to discover the inner expanding consciousness of humanity by the development of an increasing sensitivity to it; and they find their co-workers in the Plan by the old and tried method of trial and error. The less evolved the disciple and worker, the larger the number of trials and the greater the number of errors.   (13-332)

76. DANGERS IN THE LIFE OF SERVICE

1. It might be pointed out that there are three main points of danger in the life of service. I am not here dealing with the individual training of the disciple, but with his life of service, and with the activities in which he is engaged as a worker. His temperament, equipment of characteristics (physical, emotional, and mental) do have a potent effect on his environment and on the people he seeks to help, and also his family background, his world training, and his speech.

The *first* point of danger is his physical condition. On this I cannot enlarge beyond begging all disciples to act with wisdom, to give themselves sufficient sleep, right food (which must vary for each individual), and those surroundings, if possible, which will enable them to work with the greatest facility. The penalty for the infringing of these suggestions works out in lack of power in service and in the growing thraldom of the physical body. Where the physical body is in poor condition, the disciple has to add the liabilities incident upon the bringing in of force which he finds himself unable to handle.

The *second* point of danger is to be found in the astral illusion in which all humanity lives, and its power to glamour even experienced workers. ... Only mental control, plus true spiritual perception, will suffice to pierce this illusory astral miasma, and reveal to the man that he is a spiritual entity in incarnation, and in touch—through his mind—with the Universal Mind. The penalty which overtakes the disciple who persistently permits himself to be glamoured, is obvious. His vision becomes fogged and misty and he "loses the sense of touch" as it is called in the Old Commentaries. He wanders "down the lanes of life and misses that straight highway which will lead him to his goal".

The *third* danger (and one that is very prevalent at this time) is that of mental pride and consequent inability to work in group formation. The penalty for this is often a temporary success and an enforced working with a group, which has been devitalised of its best elements and which has in it only those people who feed the personality of the head of the group. Because of the emphasis upon his own ideas and his own methods of working, a disciple finds that his group lacks those factors and those people who would have rounded it out, who would have balanced his endeavour, and given to his undertaking those qualities which he himself lacks. This is, in itself, a sufficient punishment, and quickly brings the honest disciple to his senses. Let a disciple who is intelligent, honest and basically true, so err, and in time he will awaken to the fact that the group he has gathered around him, are moulded by him or he is moulded by them; they are oft embodiments of himself and repeat him. The law works rapidly in the case of a disciple, and thus adjustments are speedily made. (4-636/8)

2. Let not the glamour of attainment of your service goals . . . blind your eyes to the need for further and constant training. The disciple oft becomes absorbed in the work to be done to such an extent, that he forgets that the outer life of service will become arid and full of personality, unless it is paralleled by a growing sensitivity to the impulses of the soul. That soul is love and understanding. Cease not to work at the problem of true spiritual perception, and be not so occupied with the task of service that you neglect the lessons which you yourself must learn. Live as you teach, and keep your values clear. You have done good and faithful service and

helped many. Take help yourself without unduly emphasising in your own consciousness your own need.   (5-261)

3. You do not keep your line of service clear. You wander into too many other fields of service which are not yours, and where you are not wanted. (5-612)

4. You are sensitive to the Plan, but occupied with your own plans and believe that your plans are part of the Plan.   (5-613)

77. SERVICE TO INDIVIDUALS

1. The purpose of all training which I have given you and all my disciples, is to produce a greater capacity to service. I would like to see you doing some definite service in relation to your fellow men. . . . I refer to that service which a disciple renders when he approaches every human being as a soul.

This type of service involves the recognition of one's own capacity, the intensification of one's ability to love one's fellow men, the power to draw others to one with the request—spoken or implied—for spiritual help, and then the power to work with the person and give him right help in the right way. This, in its turn, involves an inner brooding upon the quality and the need of the one to be served. This subjective process must precede all outer work; upon the strength and the persistence of it depends the success of the attempt to help. This process of inner, brooding reflection is oft omitted through enthusiasm and self-confidence. When, however, it has been accomplished, and the server stands ready to help, then he can depend upon the needy one and circumstance to indicate to him the next step. I would have you reflect deeply upon this, and I would have you begin—in a new and fresh way—to endeavour to bring light to individuals with a pure, disinterested selflessness. I would have you work with discrimination, with purity of motive, and with an effort to eliminate all personality reactions, for it is upon the rock of the personality that many well intentioned servers wreck their work.

. . . Only one other suggestion would I give. Keep yourself out of the picture altogether, and your private affairs, your personal likes and dislikes, entirely eliminated.   (5-484/5)

2. Your duty lies in the daily releasing of steady illumined love, free from all criticism. It is not your duty to aid your brother to become a better occultist and disciple. That is his concern, his soul's concern, and mine. (6-131)

3. Be not unduly concerned at the plight of those you love. Trust their own souls and know that they, alone, must learn the needed lessons. (6-655)

78. MOTIVES FOR SERVICE

1. These are days when many adjustments and changes are being wrought in the world of men. In the resulting confusion, individuals are appreciating the necessity for the uniting of their forces and for co-operation in their efforts, and the need for group work is more apparent than ever before. These are days, therefore, wherein quietness and confidence must be your strength, and wherein the only safeguard lies in a close searching of all underlying motives. As seen on the surface, many apparently diverse principles emerge and the surge of battle appears to go, first one way and then another. As seen on the inner side, the emerging factors are simpler. The contest leads primarily to a testing of motives, and through this testing it is made apparent (to the watching Guides) who, in every group, are capable of clear thinking, accurate discrimination, patient endurance, and an ability to proceed along the probationary path toward the portal of initiation, untrammelled and undisturbed in their inner life by the upheavals on the surface. Could you but see it, the unrest and difficulty everywhere is producing a good which far outweighs the seeming evil. Souls are finding themselves and learning dependence upon the inner Ruler. When all outward props fail and when all the apparent authorities differ in the solution proffered, then souls are thrown back upon themselves and learn to seek within. This inner contact with the higher self is becoming apparent in gradually unfolding degree, and leads to that self-reliance and inward calm which is based upon the rule of the inner God and which, therefore, makes a man an instrument for service in the world. (4-129/30)

2. Evil itself is but an illusion, for it is the use that is made of motive and opportunity by personality separativeness and selfishness which con-

stitutes evil. From right motive and the same circumstances good may emerge.   (5-241/2)

3. I seek to see you less committed to the attitude of the devotee, and more impersonal, more free to serve for the sake of service and not to serve because of your devotion to a teacher, a cause or a belief.   (5-562)

4. I am seeking here to divorce your minds from the *idée fixe* that the initiate works because he knows. I would reverse the statement and say he knows because he works. There is no point of attainment at which the Initiator says to the initiate: Now you know, and therefore you can work. Rather it is: Now you serve and work, and in so doing you are embarked upon a new and difficult voyage of discovery; you will discover reality progressively and arrive at whole areas of expression, because you serve. Resulting from this service, certain powers and energies will manifest, and your ability to use them will indicate to you, to your fellow initiates, and to the world that you are a worker, fully conscious upon the inner side of life.   (6-282)

79.   LOVING SERVICE

1. A kind heart is of potent use in our service, provided that it is kept in place by a wise head, and does not assume the form of a glamour. That then makes it a definite and hindering weakness. We need today disciples who are capable of seeing people truly; able to see them as they are, and yet to love them and serve them just the same. . . . When the radiation is the radiation of love, the resultant words and actions can be stern without hurting. . . . A loving radiation and an intelligent assessment (or do I mean appraisement . . . ?) of those you seek to aid, will render you more effective in service to your fellow men than anything else.   (5-382)

2.   I tread the lighted Way into the hearts of men. I serve my brother and his need. Those whom I, the little self, love not, I serve with joy because I love to serve.   (5-481)

3. With a tender heart of love and pity, serve all you meet, knowing that "each heart hides its own bitterness". This constitutes your major lesson on the Path at this time . . . the lesson of utter self-forgetfulness. Forget the past and all that it brought to you of pain and of joy; forget the per-

sonal self and all that it has to give or what it withholds; forget that which you said or has been said anent you and your ways, and seek simply to serve. Serve with a joyous heart and equilibrium. (5-562/3)

4. Let the light and radiance of the soul illumine your service, and let your intellect not prove to be the dominating factor. Let spontaneous love and not a cultivated kindness condition your relations with your fellow men. (6-656)

80. SELFLESS SERVICE

1. You render to yourself too much service, too much thought, too much care and too many things. Your service should become horizontal and expandingly inclusive. (5-568)

2. The way of considered unselfishness lies open to you—a way you never yet have gone. By that I mean . . . that you have never served with a completely sacrificial spirit. You have done kind things and made small sacrifices, but you have never yet served as a soul—possessing nothing and asking nothing for the separated self. This is your lesson in the coming year—the lesson of a life given to service, to distribution, to out-going, to self-forgetting, to the life of full surrender, of discipline and of relinquishment. (5-570)

3. When you have forced yourself out of your picture, and have learnt to be silent as to yourself and what you think, and feel, and do . . . the rich-ness of the contribution you will have to give will be so great, that your field of service and your power to co-operate with the Hierarchy, will be greatly expanded. (5-655)

4. The task of the Master is to evoke from His disciples such a depth of consecrated love, and such a realisation of today's opportunity, that the personality aspects of their lives will fade out in their consciousness, and their main preoccupation will be: What must be my service at this time? What are the non-essential things in my life to which I should pay no attention? What is the task to be done? Who are the people I can help? Which aspects of the Master's work should I endeavour to give the most help at this time? These questions must all meet with a balanced, intel-ligent and non-fanatical response and answer. (5-693)

5. Many are still too preoccupied with what *they* are attempting to do, with their own development and with their own capacity or non-capacity to help; but at the same time they are inadequately handling the problem of self-effacement and complete dedication to their fellow men. "What can I *do*?" is of less importance to them than "What am I learning, and is the Master satisfied with me?" I shall be satisfied with you when you have forgotten both yourself and me in your strenuous service for mankind.   (6-24)

6. The beginner and newcomer in the Ashram, new in his service (from the angle of his present life experience if not from the angle of the soul), new in his registering of a sense of power, which relation to the Ashram always conveys, and new in his joyous reaction to the recognition given him by those to whom he seeks to give help, speaks increasingly of "*my* work, *my* group, *my* teaching, *my* people, *my* plans", and in so doing stabilises himself in his chosen field of service. This is a temporary phase, oft unrecognised by the disciple, though annoying to those who hear. As he proceeds in the spiritual life, and intensifies his understanding of the Master, as he enters more deeply into the life of the Ashram and into the aura of his Master, and as his vision grows—revealing possibilities of service and the limitations of his equipment, plus a divine indifference—he drops the possessiveness of his approach to service, and regards all that he does as his response to the life of the Ashram, as his contribution to the work of the Ashram, and thus eventually comes to the point where he himself fades out of his own picture and from the centre of his work, and only the need to be met and the power of the Ashram to meet that need remain.

This marks a definite step forward, and it is this attitude of selflessness and this capacity to be a channel for the power, the love, the knowledge and the life of the Ashram, which constitute in the last analysis what is meant by occult obedience.   (6-549/50)

7. Release for humanity will come when the so-called good people of the world give up their pet theories and their beloved ideals, and grasp the essential fact that entry into the Kingdom of Heaven and into the New Age will take place when mankind is truly loved and selflessly served, and when the true, divine purpose is seen and humanity is found to be one indivisible whole. Then petty nationalisms, religious differences and selfish idealisms (for that is what they often are, as most people are idealists because they seek to save their own souls) are subordinated to human need, human good and the future happiness of the whole.   (13-255)

8. As the individual aspirants lose sight of self in service, and as they arrive at the stage of indifference to personality claims and happenings, they learn to cherish a spirit of confidence, of joy and of love, deep and lasting, for each other; they learn to work together wholeheartedly for the helping of the world and the assistance of the Hierarchy. (15-117)

9. If you will note your own present attitudes and actions, you will discover that primarily (I might add almost necessarily) they centre around yourselves, your own recognitions, your own grasp of truth, and your own progress upon the Path. But—as you achieve initiate status—self-interest declines until it disappears and, as an ancient Word has it, "only God is left"; only that remains in consciousness which is THAT, which is beauty, goodness and truth; which is not form but quality, which is that which lies behind the form, and that which indicates destiny, soul, place, and status. Ponder on these words, for they convey to you where (as evolution goes on) you will later lay the emphasis. (18-293)

81.   SCOPE OF SERVICE

1. A disciple is known by his influence upon his environment, and an initiate by the wide scope of his world service. How does it happen then that a few of you (not all) are not distinguished by such service and are of relatively small importance in world affairs? Several things could explain this. First of all, a disciple may be called to work off certain karmic relationships, to fulfil certain obligations of very ancient origin, and thus "clear the decks" for more complete and uninterrupted service to humanity at a later date. This occurs quite frequently between the first and second initiations. Sometimes a disciple may be doing effective service upon the inner planes, and on a large scale, and yet there may be no evidence of this upon the physical plane, except in the beauty of a life lived. Others may be learning certain techniques of psychological relationships and of energy distribution, and may have dedicated some particular life to the acquiring of these esoteric sciences. One life is but a short moment in the long cycle of the soul. The true disciple will never fall back on the reasons given above as alibis for lack of effort. I would remind you that world influence alone does not always imply discipleship.

There are many groups—well known and magnetic—which have at their centre some dominant personality who is not necessarily a disciple.

. . . You need to arrive at a point in group experience wherein you are not so intensely preoccupied with your own development, status and service; you all need to learn to decentralise yourselves so that the work to be done becomes the factor of main importance. When this is the case, then the intense self-interest with some aspect of the personality expression, some weakness of character, some dear objective, or some physical condition, will cease. You will find the cultivation of a "divine indifference" . . . of great assistance in forgetting the little self; this frequently looms so large (from habit) that it shuts out the higher self; it comes between the disciple and the Master, and prevents contact with his co-disciples, thus negating effective service.   (5-96/7)

2. Where there is a recognition of principles, of impartiality in service, and pure intelligent goodwill, then give freely of your time and help. Hold out the hand of fellowship. Where there is life, and the type of seed is one, then the same flower will appear throughout the world in all lands. Naught can alter the expression of the type and genius of the manifestation. Bear this in mind.   (5-165/6)

3. Through the power of *your* soul you must awaken *their* souls into *selfless* activity. You can touch them dynamically, and then never again will their orientation be purely personal. The task of re-orienting people can be yours. Some people work with groups and, through the inclusiveness of their auras and the potency of their souls, they sweep large numbers of people into a higher aspirational attitude and into a deeper spiritual tide. Others have the duty of finding the advanced men and women of the world, the individuals who stand at the portal of discipleship—but blindly, knowing not where they are or why. They then, through their dynamic soul potency, call into living activity the soul imprisoned in these waiting personalities. Such is your task—to teach and vivify. (5-324/5)

4. How seldom do those who have the time and the leisure serve as do those who have no time or leisure!   (5-543)

5. It is for you to find the way to serve and to gain the needed sense of proportion, the necessary realisation as to the basic essentials of the spiritual life, and the tested discrimination and discerning faculty which will indicate to you the manner, the time and the mode of your service. (5-544)

6. You will ask what your service is to be. That, my brother, will grow out of your meditation. It is not for me to tell you what activity your personality must follow; it is your own soul which must do so. . . . As far as in you lies, stand firmly in your endeavour to aid the New Group of World Servers. That should be the prime effort for many years to come of all true aspirants. (5-574)

7. Let not the beauty of that which might be done lead you to forget that which has been begun; otherwise you may land yourself in the world of illusion and consequent futility. (5-578)

8. Let simplicity be your guide, and one-pointed love your major objective. Choose a field of service which has its defined limits—for all disciples are limited and cannot cover a planetary range in their thoughts. Then work—mentally and physically—within these limits. The completion of some self-appointed task within the field of karmic limitations and of environment, where your destiny has cast you, is all that is required of you. . . . Let your service lie within the field of contact where you find yourself, and reach not out over the entire planet. Is there any greater or more important matter than to fulfil your task and carry it to completion before you pass over to the other side, and to do it in the place where you are and with your chosen comrades? (5-582), (17-372)

9. It is not possible for the individual disciple in any Ashram to co-operate in all phases of the Master's work, and it is not possible for you, for instance, to co-operate in every phase of the work in my Ashram. . . . But it is possible for you to choose some phase of that plan and give it your paramount attention. . . . These activities can—if adequately and strongly carried forward—aid in the esoteric work of the world and the exoteric rehabilitation of right human relations. (6-138)

10. Let humanity constitute your field of service, and may it be said of you that you knew the spiritual facts and were a dynamic part of these spiritual events; may it not be said of you that you knew these things, and did nothing about them and failed to exert yourself. Let not time slip by as you *work*. (18-760)

82. MONEY IN SERVICE

1. The aspirant has an appreciation of the occult value of money in service. He seeks nothing for himself, save that which may equip him for the work to be done, and he looks upon money, and that which money can purchase, as something which is to be used for others and a means to bring about the fruition of the Master's plans as he senses those plans. The occult significance of money is little appreciated, yet one of the greatest tests as to the position of a man upon the probationary path, is that which concerns his attitude to and his handling of that which all men seek in order to gratify desire. Only he who desires naught for himself can be a recipient of financial bounty, and a dispenser of the riches of the universe. In other cases where riches increase, they bring with them naught but sorrow and distress, discontent and misuse. (3-866), (1-75)

2. Just as money has been in the past the instrument of men's selfishness, now it must be the instrument of their goodwill. (5-166)

3. This whole question of money is one of the greatest difficulty at this time, and also one of the utmost simplicity. The difficulty is due to the wrong thought which, for generations, has been brought to bear upon the problem, leading to wrong attitudes, even among the most devoted disciples. The attitude of humanity to money has been coloured by greed, by grasping for the lower self, by jealousy, by material desire, and by the heart-breaking need for it which—in its turn—is the result of these wrong attitudes. These wrong attitudes lead to the disastrous economic conditions which we find all around us. They are effects of causes which are initiated by man himself. In the regeneration of money, and in the changing of man's attitude to it, will eventually come world release. If this cannot take place, then some dire condition will arise; money (as we know it) will vanish off the earth, and the situation will have to be met in some other way. Let us hope that this will not be needed, but that it will be possible to change the thought of humanity where money is concerned, so that it will be regarded as a great spiritual asset, as a definite spiritual responsibility, and as a means to real world work. The custodians of money will then shoulder their responsibility without fear and with due understanding. At present, they hold on to it through fear of the future and distrust of each other. The key to the right expenditure of money, and to its correct use, can be summed up in the following statement, to which I would ask all of you to pay attention :

As money has in the past ministered to personal and family need, so in the future it must minister to group and world need. Each unit has, in the past, attempted to act as a magnet and to attract to itself that which will meet what it regards as its need—using personal activity and labour, if of no influence or education, and financial manipulation where that was possible. Groups in the future must act as magnets; they must see to it that they are animated by a spirit of love. I give you a thought here which is capable of much expansion. *Need, love and magnetic power, are the three things which—consciously or unconsciously—attract money.* But they must all manifest at once. The need in the past has not always been real, though it has been *felt* (such is the world glamour and illusion). The love has been selfish and unreal; the demand for things material, has been for that which is not necessary to health or happiness. The magnetic force utilised has been, therefore, wrongly motivated, and this process—carried forward over so long a time—has led to the present dire financial situation in the world.

By the transmutation of these factors, and the expression of their higher correspondences—through right love, right thought or meditation and right technique—the financial requirements of the new groups and of the New Group of World Servers *will* be found. I would suggest that an elaboration of these ideas should be disseminated among all whom you know who could help. I would ask you to ponder much on these ideas for, in the education of the intelligent world servers, this question of money and of right attitudes towards money, and right meditation upon money, must be boldly faced. The emphasis laid by certain groups on meditation for the raising of funds (usually for personal use or for the selfish ends of their own particular organisation or group) has been based upon this emerging concept of the *group use* of money. Being, however, selfishly and personally interested, the money was thought of in relation to the individual and not in relation to the group. This attitude must and will be changed.

One thing more I would ask of you . . . and of the group who read my words. Money is the manifestation of energy. All energy can be applied in differing ways, being in itself an impersonal and blind force. It can be selfishly or unselfishly used. That, in itself, constitutes the main difference. Motive and creative thought determine the magnetic power of any individual, group or centre. Determine your motive; see that your group ideal and group love are dominant; use skill in action; this will involve right preliminary meditation, plus correct thinking; then you will find that that which you need will be forthcoming. (5-271/3)

4. That powerful physical concretisation of energy which we call "money", is proving a topic of the most definite concentration; it is being most carefully considered, and the minds of thinking financiers and of wealthy humanitarian persons and philanthropists, will be gradually led forward from a strictly philanthropic activity to an activity which is impulsed and brought into expression by spiritual insight, and by *a recognition of the claims of Christ* (no matter by what name He may be called in the East or in the West) upon the financial reservoir of the world. This is a hard thing to bring about, for the subtle energies of the inner worlds take much time in producing their effects upon the objective, tangible plane of divine manifestation. Money is not yet used divinely, but it will be. (6-221)

5. It is useless . . . to meditate along lines which will aid in preparing the world for the coming of the Hierarchy and for the reappearance of the Christ *unless,* again, that preparation is an integral part of your own constant daily endeavour, and is not just simply wishful thinking and the formulation of a hopeful theory anent the future of humanity. It is useless for you to meditate in order to reorient money, for instance, towards spiritual work (and by "spiritual work" I do not here refer to the work of the churches and of the world religions) unless all the monies which *you* individually have to handle, are dedicated to right usage, the fulfilment of your right obligations and the covering of your karmic responsibilities, plus the constant recognition of the relation of all money to the spiritual future of the race and the requirements of the hierarchical Plan. There must always be, in your consciousness, a recognition of the needs of all men, and this must be true of all spiritually-minded people, of all true esotericists, and of the religiously inclined man whose heart and understanding are more divinely inclusive than are the hearts of the average followers of any religious doctrine, enunciated by the theologians of any faith.

It *must* be realised that money is the energy which can set in motion and make possible the activities of the New Group of World Servers— no matter what their colour, caste or Church. Money does not yet lie in their hands. Their need for it is great. Millions are needed to spread the required knowledge of the hierarchical Plan; millions are needed to further the work of men of goodwill; millions are needed to educate the masses in the fact that He for Whom all men wait is on His way back to ordinary visibility. The billions which are spent at present on luxuries, on expensive and unnecessary objects of desire, the billions (and, my brother, it is billions, as world statistics show) which go towards the purchase of candy, liquor, tobacco, jewellery and expensive furs, the millions which go in the violent search for excitement and for ceaseless nightly pleasure and, finally, the billions which go the way of armed conflict in all nations, *must* be deflected towards those expenditures which will make the plans of the Hierarchy possible, which will aid humanity in its search for the new, spiritual and free way, and which will therefore bring into being the new civilisation. Billions are required to overcome the materialism which has dominated mankind for untold aeons; billions are also needed to bring about the reconstruction of human affairs and thus purify and beautify our modern world to such an extent that the Christ can appear among men; through the wise expenditure of the financial resources of the world in the many fields of human betterment and uplift, the Christ will be enabled to "see of the travail of His soul and be satisfied". (6-224/6)

6. "O Thou in Whom we live and move and have our being, the Power that can make all things new, turn to spiritual purposes the money in the world; touch the hearts of men everywhere so that they may give to the work of the Hierarchy that which has hitherto been given to material satisfaction. The New Group of World Servers needs money in large quantities. I ask that the needed vast sums may be made available. May this potent energy of Thine be in the hands of the Forces of Light."

(From: *Reflective Meditation on Attracting Money for Hierarchical Purposes.* 6-228/31)

7. The dominating words in our newspapers, over our radios, and in all our discussions, are based upon the financial structure of human economy: banking interests, salaries, national debts, reparations, cartels and trusts, finance, taxation—these are the words which control our planning, arouse our jealousies, feed our hatreds or our dislike of other nations, and set us one against the other. *The love of money is the root of all evil.*

There are, however, large numbers of people whose lives are not dominated by the love of money and who can normally think in terms of the higher values. They are the hope of the future but are individually imprisoned in the system which, spiritually, *must* end. Though they do not love money, they need it and must have it; the tentacles of the business world surround them; they too must work and earn the wherewithal to live; the work they seek to do to aid humanity cannot be done without the required funds. (7-80)

8. *Lack of Financial Support for the Work of the Christ*

This is perhaps the major difficulty, and it appears to many at times to be an insuperable one. It involves the problem of true financial trusteeship and the deflection of adequate sums of money into channels which will definitely aid in the work of preparation for the return of the Christ. It is closely tied up with the problem of right human relations.

The problem is, therefore, a peculiarly hard one, for the spiritual workers of the world have not only to train people *to give* (according to their means) but, in many cases, they have—first of all—to provide them with a motive so magnetic in its appeal that they must perforce give. They have also to provide the trust, foundation or organisation through which the given money may be administered. This presents them with a most impressively difficult task. The impasse which at present exists, is not based only upon the novelty of raising funds in preparation for the return of the Christ, but it is based also upon the trained selfishness of the majority who own the world's wealth, and who—even if they do give —do so because it fosters prestige and indicates financial success. Necessarily, there are exceptions to this, but they are relatively few.

Generalising, therefore, and over-simplifying the subject, we can assume that money finds its way into four main channels of expenditure:

i. Into the myriad homes in the world in the form of wages, salaries, or inherited wealth. . . .

ii. Into great capitalistic systems and monopolies which are found as towering structures in most lands. . . .

iii. Into the churches and religious groups throughout the world. . . .

The fact remains that had the directing agencies (through whose hands the money of the world is channelled) any true vision of the spiritual realities, of the one humanity and the one world, and had their objective been the stimulation of right human relations, the mass of men everywhere would be responding to a future possibility very different from the present one; we would not be faced as we are today with the expenditures—running into countless billions—necessitated by the need to restore *physically,* not only the physical bodies of countless millions of men, but entire cities, transportation systems and centres responsible for the reorganisation of human living.

Equally, it can be said that if the spiritual values and the spiritual responsibilities attached to money (in large quantities or small) had been properly appreciated and taught in homes and schools, we would not have had the appalling statistics of the money spent, prior to the war in every country in the world (and spent today in the Western Hemisphere) on candy, liquor, cigarettes, recreation, unnecessary clothes and luxuries. These statistics run into hundreds of millions of dollars every year. A fraction of this money, necessitating the minimum of sacrifice, would enable the disciples of the Christ, and the New Group of World Servers to prepare the way for His coming, and to educate the minds and hearts of men in every land in right human relations.

Money—as with all else in human living—has been tainted by selfishness and grabbed for selfish individual or national ends. Of this, the World War (1914-45) is the proof, for, although there was much talk of "saving the world for democracy" and "fighting a war to end war", the main motive was self-protection and self-preservation, the hope of gain and the satisfaction of ancient hatreds, and the regaining of territory. The years which have elapsed since the war, have proved this to be so. The United Nations is unfortunately perforce occupied with rapacious demands from all sides, with the angling of the nations for position and power, and for the possession of the natural resources of the earth—coal, oil, etc., and also with the underground activities of the great Powers and of the capitalists which they create.

Yet all the time, the one humanity—no matter what the place of residence, what the colour of the skin, or what the religious belief—is clamouring for peace, justice and a sense of security. This, the right use of money and a realisation on the part of many of their financial responsibility (a responsibility based on the spiritual values) would rapidly give them. With the exception of a few great far-sighted philanthropists and of a mere handful of enlightened statesmen, churchmen and educators, this sense of financial responsibility is to be found nowhere.

The time has now come when money must be revaluated and its usefulness channelled into new directions. The voice of the people must prevail, but it must be a people educated in the true values, in the significances of a right culture, and in the need for right human relations. It is, therefore, essentially a question of right education and correct training in world citizenship—a thing that has not yet been undertaken. . . .

Thus the story goes—each nation fighting for itself, and all rating each other in terms of resources and finance. In the meantime, humanity starves, remains uneducated, and is brought up on false values and the wrong use of money. Until these things are in process of being righted, the return of the Christ is not possible.

In the face of this disturbing financial situation—what is the answer to the problem? There are men and women to be found in every land, every government, every church and religion, and every educational foundation, who have the answer. What hope is there for them and for the work with which they have been entrusted? How can the people of the world, the men of goodwill and of spiritual vision help? Is there anything they can do to change the thinking of the world in regard to money, thus deflecting it into channels where it will be more correctly used? The answer must be found.

There are two groups who can do much: those already using the financial resources of the world, if they will catch the new vision and also see the handwriting on the wall which is bringing the old order down in destruction, and secondly, the mass of the good, kindly people in all classes and spheres of influence.

Men of goodwill and of spiritual inclination must reject the thought of their relative uselessness, insignificance and futility, and realise that now (in the critical and crucial moment that has come) they *can* work potently. The Forces of Evil *are* defeated, though not yet "sealed" behind the door where humanity can put them, and which the New Testament foretold would happen. Evil is seeking every avenue available for a new approach, but—and this we can say with confidence and insistence—the little people of the world, enlightened and selfless in their viewpoint, *exist in sufficient numbers to make their power felt*—if they will. There are millions of spiritually minded men and women in every country who, when they come to the point of approaching in mass formation this question of money, can *permanently re-channel it*. There are writers and thinkers in all lands who can add their powerful help, and who will, if correctly approached. There are esoteric students and devoted church people to whom appeal can be made for aid in preparing the way for the return of Christ, particularly if the aid required is the expenditure of money and time for the establishing of right human relations and the growth and spread of goodwill.

A great campaign to raise money is not demanded, but the selfless work of thousands of apparently unimportant people is required. I would say that the most needed quality is *courage*; it takes courage to put aside diffidence, shyness and the dislike of presenting a point of view, particularly a point of view connected with money. It is here that the majority fail. It is relatively easy today to raise money for the Red Cross, for hospitals and for educational institutions. It is exceedingly difficult to raise money for the spread of goodwill, or to secure the right use of money for forward looking ideas, such as the return of the Christ. Therefore, I say that *the first prerequisite is Courage.*

The second requirement for the workers of the Christ is to make those sacrifices and arrangements which will enable them to give to the limit of their capacity; there must not be simply a trained ability to present the subject but each worker must practise what he preaches. If, for instance, the millions of people who love the Christ and seek to serve His cause, gave at least a tiny sum of money each year, there would be adequate funds for His work; the needed trusts and spiritually-minded trustees would then automatically appear. The difficulty is not with the organising of the money and work; it lies with the seeming inability of people to give. For one reason or another, they give little or nothing, even when interested in such a cause as that of the return of Christ; fear of the future or the love of purchasing, or the desire to give presents, or failure to realise that many small sums mount up into very large sums—all these things militate against financial generosity, and the reason always seems adequate. Therefore, *the second prerequisite is for everyone to give as they can.*

Thirdly, the metaphysical schools and the esoteric groups have given much thought to this business of directing money into channels which appeal to them. The question is often asked: Why do the Unity Schools of thought, the Christian Science Church, and many New Thought movements always manage to accumulate the required funds, whilst other groups, and particularly the esoteric groups, do not? Why do truly spiritual workers seem unable to materialise what they need? The answer is a simple one. Those groups and workers who are the closest to the spiritual ideal, are as a house divided against itself. Their main interest is on abstract, spiritual levels, and they have not apparently grasped the fact that the physical plane, when motivated from the spiritual levels, is of equal importance. The large metaphysical schools are focussed on making a *material demonstration,* and so great is their emphasis and so one-pointed is their approach, that they get what they demand; they have to learn that the demand and its answer must be the result of spiritual purpose, and that that which is demanded must not be for the use of the separated self, or for a separative organisation or church. In the New Age which is upon us, prior to the return of the Christ, the demand for financial support must be for the bringing about of right human relations and goodwill, and not for the growth of any particular organisation. The organisations so demanding, must work with the minimum of overhead and central plant, and the workers for the minimum yet reasonable salary.

Not many such organisations exist today, but the few now functioning can set an example which will be rapidly followed, as the desire for the return of Christ grows. Therefore, *the third prerequisite is the service of the one humanity.*

The *fourth prerequisite must be the careful presentation of the cause* for which the financial support is required. People may have the courage to speak, but an intelligent presentation is of equal importance. The major point to be emphasised in the preparatory work for the return of Christ, is the establishing of right human relations. This has already been started by men of goodwill all over the world, under their many names.

We come now to the *fifth prerequisite*: *a vital and sure belief in humanity as a whole.* There must be no pessimism as to the future of mankind, or distress over the reappearance of the old order. "The good, the true and the beautiful" is on its way, and for it mankind is responsible, and not some outer divine intervention. Humanity is sound and rapidly awakening. We are passing through the stage where everything is being proclaimed from the housetops—as Christ stated would be the case—and as we listen to, or read the flood of filth, crime, and sensual pleasure or luxury buying, we are apt to be discouraged; it is wise to remember that it is wholesome for all this to come to the surface and for us all to know about it. It is like the psychological cleansing of the subconscious to which individuals submit themselves; it presages the inauguration of a new and better day.

There is work to do and the men of goodwill, of spiritual instinct, and of truly Christian training must do it. They must inaugurate the era of the use of money for the spiritual Hierarchy, and carry that need into the realms of invocation. Invocation is the highest type of prayer there is, and a new form of divine appeal which a knowledge of meditation has now made possible.

There is naught to add in the way of an appeal for funds, courage or understanding. If the courage of the Christ, as He faces return to this physical, outer world, if the need of humanity for right human relations and the sacrificing work of the disciples of the Christ are not enough to fire you and to energise you and those whom you can reach, there is nothing that can be said which will be of any use. (8-171/80), (13-623/31)

9. Money has been deflected into entirely material ends, even in its philanthropic objectives. The most spiritual use now to be found in the world is the application of money to the purposes of education. When it is turned away from the construction of the form side and the bringing

about solely of material well-being of humanity, and deflected from its present channels into truly spiritual foundations, much good will be done, the philanthropic ends and the educational objectives will not suffer, and a step forward will be made. This time is not yet, but the spiritualising of money and its massing in quantities for the work of the Great Ones, the Disciples of the Christ, is part of a much needed world service and can now make a satisfactory beginning; but it must be carried forward with spiritual insight, right technique and true understanding. Purity of motive and selflessness are taken for granted.   (13-61)

10. Money is the consolidation of the loving, living energy of divinity, and the greater the realisation and expression of love, the freer will be the inflow of that which is needed to carry forward the work. You are working with the energy of love and not with the energy of desire, the reflection or distortion of love. I think if you will ponder on this, you will see the way more clearly.   (13-335)

83.   CREATIVE SERVICE

One of the major sciences of the coming age will be built around the active rendering of service. We have used the word "Science" because service as a spiritual quality, will rapidly be recognised as the phenomenal expression of an inner reality, and along the line of a right understanding of service will come much revelation as to the nature of the soul. Service is a method of producing phenomenal outer and tangible results upon the physical plane; I call your attention to this as an evidence of its creative quality. By right of this creative quality, service will eventually be regarded as a world science. It is a creative urge, a creative impulse, a creative momentous energy. This creativity of service has already been vaguely recognised in the world of human affairs under varying names, such as the science of vocational training. Recognition of the impetus coming from a right understanding of social relations and their study, is not lacking. Much is also being studied along this same line in connection with criminology and the right handling of the youth of any nation and national group.   (15-130)

84. LIMITATIONS

1. At this time there are three qualities predominating in the planetary form—fear, expectancy and a climaxing desire (in the human family) for material possession. Note the word "climaxing". The summation of human desire for material happiness has been reached, and the peak of that desire has been passed; thus mankind has achieved and surmounted much. But the rhythm of the ages is strong.

These three qualities have to be grasped and discounted by the aspirant as he seeks to serve from mental levels. In the place of fear he must substitute that peace which is the prerogative of those who live always in the Light of the Eternal; in the place of questioning expectancy he must substitute that placid yet active, assurance of the ultimate objective which comes from a vision of the Plan and his contact with other disciples and later with the Master. Desire for material possession must be superseded by aspiration for those possessions which are the joy of the soul—*wisdom, love* and *power to serve*. Peace, assurance and right aspiration! These three words, when understood and experienced in the life of every day, will bring about that right "condition of the waters" which will ensure the survival of every thought-form, rightly engendered in meditation by the man, functioning as a soul.   (4-161/2)

2. With many people physical conditions impair their work, for their attention becomes focussed on the undesirable physical situation; disciples, however, often have a curious capacity to continue with their work no matter what may be happening to them physically. The physical brain can be so much the reflector of the mental life, that he will remain essentially unaffected by any outer conditions. The disciple learns to live with his physical liabilities under adverse conditions, and his work maintains its usual high level.

The emotional problem may be the hardest. But only the disciple can handle his own self-pity and free himself from the inner emotional storm in which he finds himself living. . . . When will disciples learn that the attitude which involves a certain "don't care" reaction and a form of indifference is one of the quickest ways by which to release the Self from personality claims? This is not the "don't care" spirit which will affect the disciple's attitude to other people. It is the attitude of the integrated, thinking personality of the disciple towards the astral or emotional body. It leads him to assume the position that not one single thing which produces any reaction of pain or distress in the emotional body, matters in the very least. These reactions are simply recognised, lived through, tolerated and not permitted to produce angry limitation. All disciples would do well to ponder what I have just said. The whole process is based on a deep-seated belief in the persistence of the immortal Being within the forms of soul and personality. (5-56/7)

3. The problem that has to be faced by all who have passed through the fires of Renunciation who are walking the way of humility whilst conscious of the grandeur of the soul, and who are, at the same time, far from young in years, is that of facing the last decade or so of life with understanding, and with no fear of physical limitations. So many in the final years of life, live, think and act in such a manner that the soul withdraws its attention. Thus only the personality remains. To all of you who have passed the half century, I would say: Face the future with the same joy as in youth, yet with an added usefulness, knowing that the wisdom of experience is yours, the power to understand is yours, and that no physical limitation can prevent a soul from useful expression and service. I would remind you of something which is oft forgotten: It is far easier for the soul to express itself through an older experienced body, than through one that is young and inexperienced, provided that there is no pride and no desired selfishness, but only longing to love and serve. (5-465/6)

4. One's limitations, physical and otherwise, look unduly large; one's faults are exaggerated in one's consciousness, though not so oft in expression; the extent of the service needed and demanded by the soul appears so great that the disciple at times refuses co-operation for fear of failure or from undue consciousness of himself; excuses for non-service or for only partial service are easily found and appropriated; postponement of all-out help today plus complete dedication to human need, is easily condoned on the basis of health, time, home limitations, fear of one kind or another, age, or a belief that this life is preparatory to full service in the next; alibis are easy to discover. (6-43)

5. The disciple has to take himself as he is at any given time, with any given equipment, and under any given circumstances; then he proceeds to subordinate himself, his affairs and his time to the need of the hour, particularly during a phase of group, national or world crisis. When he does this within his own consciousness, and is therefore thinking along lines of the true values, he will discover that his own private affairs are taken care of, his capacities are increased, and his limitations are forgotten. (6-44)

6. Every disciple has to achieve complete freedom from racial limitations, and to break down certain separative barriers, otherwise they remain and hinder.   (6-602)

7. Death and limitation are synonymous terms. When the consciousness is focussed in form and identified entirely with the principle of limitation, it regards freedom from form life as death; but, as evolution proceeds, the consciousness shifts increasingly into the realm of that which is transcendent, or into the world of the abstract, i.e. into that which is abstracted from form and focussed in itself. This, by the way, is a definition of meditation from the angle of goal and achievement.   (16-615)

85.   IRRITATION

Irritation is exceedingly prevalent these days of nervous tension, and it most definitely imperils progress and retards the steps of the disciple upon the Way. It can produce dangerous group tension if present in any of you, and this induced group tension can interfere with the free play of the power and light which you are supposed to use even when the other group members remain unconscious of the emanating source. Irritation definitely generates a poison which locates itself in the region of the stomach and of the solar plexus. Irritation is a disease, if I might use that word, of the solar plexus centre, and it is definitely contagious to an almost alarming extent. So . . . watch yourselves with care, and remember that just in so far as you can live in the head and in the heart, you will end the disease of imperil and aid in the transference of the forces of the solar plexus into the heart centre.   (10-151/2)

86. POINTS OF TENSION

1. Your major need is for an intensification of your inner spiritual aspiration. You need to work more definitely from what might be called a point of tension. . . . It is intensity of purpose which will change you from the plodding, fairly satisfactory aspirant into the disciple whose heart and mind are aflame. Perhaps, however, you prefer to go forward steadily, with no group effort, making your work for me and for the group an ordered part of the daily life, which you can adjust pretty much as you like, and in which the life of the spirit receives its reasonable share, in which the service aspect is not neglected, and your life presentation is neatly balanced and carried forward without much real strain. When this is the case, it may be your personality choice or your soul decision for a specific life, but it means that you are *not* the disciple, with everything subordinated to the life of discipleship.

I would like here to point out two things to you.

First: If you can so change your tension that you are driven by the life of the spirit, it will entail a galvanic upheaval in your inner life. For this, are you prepared? *Secondly*: It will not produce any outer change in your environing relationships. Your outer obligations and interests must continue to be met, but I am talking to you in terms of inner orientations, dynamic inner decisions, and an interior organising for service and for sacrifice. Perhaps you prefer the slower and easier way? If that is so it is entirely your own affair and you are still on your way. You are still a constructive and useful person. I am simply here facing you with one of the crises which come in the life of all disciples, wherein choices have to be made that are determining for a cycle, *but for a cycle only*. It is preeminently a question of speed and of organising for speed. This means eliminating the non-essential and concentrating on the essentials—the inner essentials, as they concern the soul and its relation to the personality, and the outer ones as they concern you and your environment.   (5-538/9), (18-496/7)

2. Intensity, or working from a point of tension, brings in the flood-tide of revelation, and it is then possible for a disciple to learn in one short day what might otherwise take months and even years to learn. *Tension when focussed rightly, is the great releasing power.* So many disciples focus tension wrongly and release energy in the wrong direction and (if I might so inadequately express it) from the wrong location. Right tension is

389

brought about first by correct orientation; this necessitates a true sense of values and freedom from those minor preoccupations which produce extension instead of tension. If you are (to give a very usual illustration) preoccupied with your physical condition, you will not experience the tension which will make you a magnetic centre of power and love; if you are preoccupied with the failures of other people, or with their ideas about you, you will again fail to experience the tension which releases. You would find it of value to discover where your "extensions" are and then retreat inward to the point of tension from which you can consciously and effectively direct soul energy.

This is the true esoteric work. The majority of disciples are not even 60 per cent effective, because their points of tension are scattered all over the personality and are not focussed where the point of individual tension should be. Each has to discover that point of spiritual tension for himself. The reason that disciples are not sensitive to the Master, to the life of the Ashram, and to each other, is that they are extended and not tense; they are working and living on the periphery of consciousness and not at the centre. Their service, therefore, is partial; their concentration is weak and they are overwhelmed by inertia, by lack of interest in others, and by many preoccupations with the form side of life. (5-734/5)

3. Most disciples are *not* working from a point of spiritual tension, but from a point of personality focus—a step forward indeed from that of the average unthinking person, but one to which they cling unduly long. As long as a man is focussed in his personality, the point of spiritual tension will evade him. He will be driven by personality aspiration and not by ashramic force, and this focus in form will lead to trouble, both to the individual aspirant and to his group. Spiritual tension as a result of complete dedication of the personality to the service of humanity stimulates and empowers but does not evoke the lower life of the personal self. (5-745)

4. What must the disciple do whilst the point of tension is dominating him and his fellow men? The answer is a simple one. Let each disciple and all groups of disciples develop the ability to think sanely, with right orientation and a broad point of view; let them think truly, evading no issues, but preserving always a calm, dispassionate and loving understanding; let them demonstrate in their environment the qualities which will establish right human relations, and show on a small scale the behaviour which will some day characterise enlightened humanity; let them not be discouraged, but let them hold firmly to the conviction of the inevitable spiritual destiny

of humanity; let them realise *practically* that "the souls of men are one" and learn to look beyond the immediate outer seeming, to the inner (and sometimes remote) spiritual consciousness; let them *know* that the present world conflict will be terminated. (18-638)

87. POINTS OF CRISIS

1. See to it that in the inner life there is potency and dynamic impulse, e'en when the outer life seems moulded to a pattern. It is a needed pattern, because it makes your service possible. The moment a man sets his hand to the plough and starts upon his ploughing, from that moment, until he has completed his task he remains internally free but outwardly bound.

But climaxing moments are of importance and the pursuit of an even tenor is not usually good for a disciple, if overlong perpetuated. . . . It is good for the aspirant who is working upon the control of the emotional body and the attaining of astral equilibrium. It is not so good for the pledged disciple whose career should have in it—as did the career of the Christ—the valley and the mountaintop experience, and the cave experience also, with its loneliness and its period of introspective culture.

. . . Create not these crises for yourself. They are not of a physical nature, nor need they be emotional. But they should be mental and of the soul. If these crises occur within the astral body, they produce a contraction—which is incident to selfish concentration, to that pain or pleasure which comes when there is the satisfaction or the negation of that which is demanded, emotionally or sentiently. Is this not so, my brother? But the crises of the soul are expansions, registered by the inflow of love and light. They are mentally recognised crises of inclusiveness. These lead one on and prepare one for the later more vast expansions which we call initiations. It is these expansive crises in the various aspects of your nature, which I ask that you watch and register and record during the coming year. Note in which body or vehicle of experience they occur. Note, too, your reaction to them and their after effect in your personal life and in your service. You will find this of major interest. (5-228/9)

2. All periods of strain are but preparatory to the handling of still more work with increased efficiency and speed. (5-264)

3. True accomplishment involves a life of steady radiance, and stable uniform activity; but . . . in this activity and general accomplishment there must come—as the years go by—what I might call *crises of achievement*. There must be culminating moments when the uniform activity climaxes into hours of dynamic crisis. Then one cycle of work ends in some direction or another, and a new cycle of activity commences in the same place and within the limits of the same general endeavour; this is conciously recognised as a new beginning. Unless such moments of crisis occur, the life simmers down to a general dead level and (even if useful) offers not the chance for an extreme effort with its consequent need to draw upon the full resources of the soul.   (5-268/9)

4. These periods of upheaval and rearrangement come at times—sometimes soul induced and sometimes as personality events. They must be lived through, the veiled lessons learnt and the possible expansion of consciousness induced. We facilitate or hinder these expansions by the moves we make; we hasten or delay our growth by our enacted decisions. The true disciple, however, proceeds upon his way *at any cost* and naught can arrest his progress on the Path.   (5-276)

5. You are all living on the verge of new happenings, of increased opportunities, fresh complexities, and of definite spiritual crises. . . . *We grow by the presentation of moments of crisis*. Face such times with detachment, with deep inner comprehension and consecration, and with illumined understanding, and swerve not from your basic objective to serve the race of men, the Plan and Us. Such is the appeal I make to all my disciples.   (5-338)

6. A disciple makes his own crises, and where life is devoid of crisis (at your stage of development) it means the disciple is standing still. It means that his work is of such a kind that it makes no impact on his surroundings and his associates. It therefore, has no value. For you the necessity is to stand in your circle of life as a quiet centre, but let it be the quiet which is achieved by the mastering of turmoil and not the quiet of a stagnant pool.   (5-534)

7. We are living in a time of spiritual crisis. When a human crisis and a spiritual crisis coincide, there comes one of the major periods of opportunity and decision in general human affairs; hence the extreme gravity of the present moment.   (6-428)

8. Crises . . . can be objective or subjective; they can take place on the physical plane, and are then not of such great significance from the spiritual

angle, even though they cause much suffering and pain to the personality; they can emerge into consciousness on the emotional or the mental planes and they then present opportunity for action, but mostly for action connected with the personality; or they can be the result of soul intent, registered by the personality and recorded in the brain. They are then of supreme importance but very frequently remain unrecognised, unless the disciple is very alert and constantly aware of the cyclic flow of spiritual energy. (6-637)

9. In the life of every disciple, particularly of those who face certain great expansions of consciousness, a *point of crisis* will come about. In that point of crisis, decisions are voluntarily or involuntarily made; having made them, the disciple then stands at a *point of tension*, with the decision behind him and the next step to be taken becoming clearer to his mental perception, and influencing his attitude of the future. When the work is done in the period of tension, then there comes what we might call the *point of emergence.* This is both an emergence from and also an emergence into a field of experience.   (8-68)

10. Shirk not these crises, hard and difficult though they may appear to be. Difficult they are. Forget not that the habit of confronting crises is a long-established one within the consciousness of humanity. Man has the "habit of crisis", if I may so call it. They are only the points of examination as to strength, purpose, purity and motive and the intent of the soul. They evoke confidence when surmounted and produce greatly expanded vision. They foster compassion and understanding, for the pain and inner conflict they have engendered is never forgotten for they draw upon the resources of the heart. They release the light of wisdom within the field of knowledge and the world is thereby enriched.   (16-477)

88.   LOSING TIME FOR SERVICE

I will admit you into a piece of personal history and one which is quite ordinary in the life of a disciple. It may serve to carry its lesson and its warning. Several lives ago, my Master saw in me a weakness. It was one of which I was quite unaware, and it was in fact a quality which I regarded as a strength and which I hugged to myself as a virtue. I was then a young man, anxious to help my Master and humanity, but in the last analysis, I was very keen about myself as an aspirant and very pleased with myself— cloaking this satisfaction under the garb of a reiterated humility. The Master poured into me His strength and energy, and so stimulated me that what I thought was a virtue and what I had denied and repudiated as a vice, proved my undoing. I symbolically crashed to earth through the very weight of my weakness. You might well ask what this weakness was? It was my love for my Master which was my undoing. He pointed out to me after the failure, that my love for Him was in reality based upon pride in myself, and a profound satisfaction with myself as an aspirant and a disciple. This I violently denied and was grieved that He should so misunderstand me. I proved Him to be right, eventually, through a life of failure and the depth of my egotism. I learnt through that failure, but I lost much time from the standpoint of useful service. I found that I was really serving myself and not humanity. From similar mistakes I seek to save you, for time is a great factor in service. For the masses of humanity, time is not of very great importance, but for the servers of the race, it matters much. Lose not time, therefore, in undue self-analysis, self-depreciation or self-defence. Go forward with discrimination where your unfoldment is concerned, and with love and understanding, where your group is concerned. Where I, your teacher, am concerned, give to my words the attention which is due, and endeavour to co-operate with me. I shall then some day have the joy of welcoming you to the "Secret Place" where all true servers and initiates must eventually meet and unite.   (5-77/8)

89. MASTER OF TIME

1. Be the ruler of your time and make the hours of each day your servants, exacting from each hour its full quota of work or rest, without the sense of undue pressure or rush. When the time problem is solved by you, you will enter into a greatly increased usefulness.   (5-281)

2. (Organise) your time so that you get out of each day its full quota of inspiration, mental work, and physical plane activity. Thus you will impose upon yourself that discipline which will not negate or inhibit your efforts, but which will produce the maximum of results with the minimum of effort. Ponder on this.   (5-286)

90. THE FUTURE

1. Look not so much into the future with speculation or with foreboding, nor even with hope, which is but a form of optimistic speculation. Live today as your soul dictates and the future will round out itself in fruitful service. . . . Relax and rest back on the strength which is in you and which surrounds you.   (5-385)

2. Face the future with joy and know that it holds for you renewed opportunity and later a readjustment of your time and interests which will permit you the leisure for deepened understanding and an increased usefulness in service.   (5-401)

3. Live not so utterly within yourself, but forget yourself. The past lies behind you. The future will be of your own making. . . . There is no present moment, but each coming second determines simultaneously the future and expresses the past. The past works out through the medium of the very qualities you demonstrate; the future sows the seeds of further good or evil.   (5-474)

4. Regard all that has happened to you as special training, what might be called "Basic training", in order that your future initiate service may be carried out according to plan. That service is the choice of your soul. It is not imposed upon you by me or by the will of the Ashram, or by any other factor save your soul.   (6-665)

5. I urge you to face the future with strength, to free your minds from all vestiges of doubt, and to *know* (in your own life and for the race) that the forces of materialism and cruelty will *not* triumph. Again I say to you, *the Hierarchy stands.* Go forward with assurance. (13-337)

6. I have been working with A.A.B. as my amanuensis since November 1919. During that period the world has seen great and significant changes and one of the most significant has been the growth—the phenomenal growth—of spiritual perception. This shows itself in the fact that, in spite of the world catastrophe, in spite of the rampant horror and evil which is stalking our planet, and in spite of human pain, terror, suspense and uncertainty, there are today (1942) two factors present in the human consciousness: the vision of a better future, and a fixed unalterable determination to make that vision *fact* in human experience. This better world is to be a world in which the spiritual values will control, viewing those values as that which is good and right for the whole of humanity, and not simply as religious and theological interpretations. Spiritual perception has become inclusive, and now concerns the physical plane as well as the metaphysical.

It is not perhaps easy for you to realise the importance of this development which—again in the face of all contending forces—has enabled men to recognise that the Kingdom of God must function on Earth; that it must be externalised and that it need not be some distant point of wishful thinking, but should condition man's daily life and control all his planning for the future. For this, men are today working and fighting. They call the vision by many names: better world conditions, the new world order, world reconstruction, the new civilisation, brotherhood, fellowship, world federation, international understanding—it matters not. It is the theme of betterment, of universal welfare, of general security, of widespread opportunity, irrespective of race, colour or creed. This is the factor of importance. The underlying purposes of God are working out. (13-338/9)

7. The training of the public consciousness must therefore go steadily forward, and thus we shall lay the foundation for the later changes. . . . The coming three generations (written about 1935) in which I include the present one of boys and girls, will bring into incarnation a group of people who will be well equipped to lead humanity out of the present impasse. This fact warrants remembrance, and is often forgotten. There are always those at every epoch in human history who are able to solve the problems which arise, and who are sent in for that very purpose. The sex problem, in the last analysis, is a temporary one, little as you may think

it today, and it grows out of a basic mistake—out of the prostitution of man's God-given faculties to selfish physical ends, instead of their consecration to divine purposes. Man has been swept and carried off his feet by his instinctual animal nature, and only a clear and clean mental understanding of the real nature of this problem will be strong enough to carry him forward into the New Age and into the world of right motive and right action. Man has to learn and deeply grasp the fact that the main purpose of sex is not the satisfaction of appetites, but the providing of physical bodies through which life may express itself. (14-298/9)

8. The day will come, in the experience of humanity, when men will look back at the pre-war centuries and wonder at their blindness and be shocked at their selfish and materialistic past. The future will shine with an added glory and, though difficulties and problems incident to world adjustment and the new relationships between the spiritual man and his material environment will be found, the future will prove itself as the best yet unrolled. Difficulties will be found on all planes up until the last initiation, but the *destructiveness* of the life process will never again be so potent. The reason for this is that humanity is most definitely emerging from the thraldom of matter and in such cases destruction parallels the impact of the descending spirit upon opposing matter. Ponder on this statement. (16-500)

91.   THE LAW OF REBIRTH

1. All souls incarnate and reincarnate under the Law of Rebirth. Hence each life is not only a recapitulation of life experience, but an assuming of ancient obligations, a recovery of old relations, an opportunity for the paying of old indebtedness, a chance to make restitution and progress, an awakening of deep-seated qualities, the recognition of old friends and enemies, the solution of revolting injustices, and the explanation of that which conditions the man and makes him what he is. Such is the law which is crying now for universal recognition, and which, when understood by thinking people, will do much to solve the problems of sex and marriage.

Why will this be so? Because when this law is admitted as a governing intellectual principle, all men will tread more carefully the path of life, and will proceed with greater caution to fulfil their family and group obligations. They will know full well that "whatsoever a man soweth, that will he also reap", and that he will reap it here and now, and not in some mystical and mythical heaven or hell; he will have to make his adjustments in the life of everyday upon earth, which provides an adequate heaven and a more than adequate hell. The spreading of this doctrine of rebirth, its scientific recognition and proving, is fast going forward. (14-300/1)

2. Advanced souls, and those whose intellectual capacity is rapidly developing, come back with great rapidity, owing to their sensitive response to the pull of obligations, interests and responsibilities already established upon the physical plane. . . .

Man reincarnates under no time urge. He incarnates under the demands of karmic liability, under the pull of that which he, as a soul, has initiated, and because of a sensed need to fulfil instituted obligations; he incarnates also from a sense of responsibility and to meet requirements which an earlier breaking of the laws governing right human relations have imposed upon him. When these requirements, soul necessities, experiences and responsibilities have all been met, he enters permanently "into the clear cold light of love and life" and no longer needs (as far as he himself is concerned) the nursery stage of soul experience on earth. He is free from karmic impositions in the three worlds, but is still under the impulse of karmic necessity, which exacts from him the last possible ounce of service that he is in a position to render to those still under the Law of Karmic Liability. (17-403/5)

3. An incarnation is a definitely determined period (from the angle of the soul) wherein *Experiment, Experience* and *Expression* are the keynotes in each incarnation. Each successive incarnation continues the experiment, deepens the experience and relates the expression more closely to the latent unfolding divinity. (18-337)

92. FACTORS GOVERNING INCARNATIONS FOR SERVICE

1. The factors governing the appearance in incarnation of a disciple, are as follows:

First, his desire to work off karma rapidly and so liberate himself for service. The Ego impresses this desire upon the disciple during incarnation, and thus obviates any counter desire on his part for the bliss of devachan, or even for work on the astral plane. The whole objective, therefore, of the disciple after death is to get rid of his subtler bodies, and acquire new ones. There is no desire for a period of rest, and as desire is the governing factor in this system of desire, and particularly in this planetary scheme, if it exists not, there is no incentive to fulfilment. The man, therefore, absents himself from the physical plane for a very brief time, and is driven by his Ego into a physical body with great rapidity.

Second, to work out some piece of service under direction of his Master. This will involve some adjustments and occasionally the temporary arresting of his karma. These adjustments are made by the Master with the concurrence of the disciple, and are only possible in the case of an accepted disciple of some standing. It does not mean that karma is set aside, but only that certain forces are kept in abeyance until a designated group work has been accomplished.

Third, a disciple will return into incarnation occasionally so as to fit into the plan of a greater than himself. When a messenger of the Great Lodge needs a vehicle through which to express Himself, and cannot use a physical body Himself, owing to the rarity of its substance, He will utilise the body of a disciple. We have an instance of this in the manner the Christ used the body of the initiate Jesus, taking possession of it at the time of the Baptism. Again, when a message has to be given out to the world during some recurring cycle, a disciple of high position in a Master's group will appear in physical incarnation, and be "overshadowed" or "inspired" (in the technically occult sense) by some teacher greater than he.

Fourth, a disciple may, through lack of rounded development, be very far advanced along certain lines, but lack what is called the full intensification of a particular principle. He may, therefore, decide (with the full concurrence of his Ego and of his Master) to *take a series of rapidly recurring incarnations* with the intention of working specifically at bringing a certain quality, or series of qualities, to a point of higher vibratory content, thus completing the rounding of his sphere of manifestation. This accounts for the peculiar, yet powerful, people who are met at times; they are so one-pointed and apparently so unbalanced that their sole attention is given to one line of development only, so much so that the other lines are hardly apparent. Yet their influence seems great, and out of all proportion to their *superficial* worth. A realisation of these factors will deter the wise student from hasty judgments, and from rapid conclusions concerning his fellow men.

Occasionally a variation of this reason for rapid and immediate incarnation is seen when an initiate (who has nearly completed his cycle) appears in incarnation to express almost entirely one perfected principle. This he does for the good of a particular group which—though engaged in work for humanity—is failing somewhat in its objective through the lack of a particular quality, or stream of force. When this becomes apparent on the inner side, some advanced disciple puts the energy of that particular quality at the disposal of the Hierarchy, and is sent forth to *balance* that group, and frequently to do so for a period of rapidly succeeding lives.

These are a few of the causes governing the periodic manifestation of those who are grouped in the hierarchical records as "the aligned points of fire". They are distinguished by the energy flowing through them, by the magnetic quality of their work, by their powerful group effects, and by their physical plane realisation of the Plan.   (3-1149/51)

2. Much help can also come to you if you will remember that there are certain lives in which the development of the equipment is the major goal. Then come later lives in which the prepared equipment is used.   (5-148)

93.   INCARNATING SOULS AFFECTING CIVILISATION

The majority of the souls in the human family come into incarnation in obedience to the urge or the desire to experience, and the magnetic pull of the physical plane is the final determining factor. They are, as souls, oriented towards earth life. Increasingly, awakening souls, or those who are (occultly speaking) "coming to themselves", enter into physical life experience only dimly aware of another and higher "pull". They are, therefore, without as true an orientation to the physical plane as are the bulk of their fellow men. These awakening souls are the ones who can at times be influenced to retard or delay their entry into physical life, in order to effect a conditioning of the processes of civilisation. Or again, they can be prevailed upon to hasten their entrance into life so as to be available as agents for such a conditioning process. This process is not carried forward by them through any emphasised or intelligently appreciated activity, but is naturally brought about by the simple effect of their living in the world and there pursuing their life objectives. They thus condition their surroundings by the beauty, the power or the influence of their lives, and are themselves frequently quite unconscious of the effect that they are having. It will be apparent therefore, that the needed changes in our civilisation can be brought about rapidly or slowly, according to the number of those who are living as *souls in training*.   (15-260)

94. KARMA

1. I would call your attention to the subject of karma. There comes ever in the life of a disciple and in the soul's experience some one particular life wherein the Law of Cause and Effect assumes importance in the consciousness. From that life and that moment, the disciple begins to deal with karma, consciously and definitely. He learns to recognise it when events and happenings come which require understanding and which evoke questioning; he begins to study the quality of his radiation as a karmic agent, and therefore he becomes the maker and constructor, in a new and important sense, of his own destiny and future. His reactions to life and circumstances cease to be simply emotional in nature, and become deliberately dictated by conscious observation; they then have in them a significant quality of preparation which is absent from the life of the average man.   (6-538)

2. As to *Karma*, what a man has made he can unmake. This is oft forgotten. Karma is not a hard and fast rule. It is changeable, according to man's attitude and desire. It is the presenting of the opportunity to change; this grows out of past activities, and these rightly met and correctly handled, lay the foundation for future happiness and progress. . . . Karma is not all that is bad and evil. Men make it so through their stupidities.   (13-255).

3. Everything that is happening in the world today and which is so potently affecting humanity—things of beauty and of horror, modes of

living and civilisation and culture, prejudices and likings, scientific attainment and artistic expression, and the many ways in which humanity throughout the planet colours existence—are aspects of effects initiated somewhere, on some level, at some time by human beings, both individually and en masse.

Karma is therefore that which Man—the Heavenly Man in Whom we live, humanity as a whole, mankind in groups, as nations, and individual man—has instituted, carried forward, endorsed, omitted to do, or has done, right through the ages until the present moment. Today the harvest is ripe and mankind is reaping what it has sown, preparatory to a fresh ploughing in the springtime of the New Age, with a fresh sowing of the seed which will (let us pray and hope) produce a better harvest. (17-262/3)

4. All these stages:

    i. elementary group karma—of the primitive man,

    ii. individual karma of the self-conscious developing man,

    iii. karma, related to the life of the disciple,

    iv. hierarchical karma,

must be added to the well known *Karma of Retribution,* with which the disciple is already familiar; to it must also be added national and racial karma, plus the educational karma which all disciples bring upon themselves when they are desirous of entering an Ashram to prepare for initiation.

There is also the *Karma of Reward* in contra-distinction to that of *Retribution*; this is a type of karma oft forgotten, but one which will become better known in the coming world cycle. Humanity has worked off much evil karma, and the karma based on causes later to be initiated, will not generate such dire effects as that of the past. Not all karma is bad, in spite of what man thinks. Much of it is necessarily punitive and distressing, owing to humanity's ignorance and low stage of development. When karmic retribution becomes acute and terrible, as it is in today's appalling world experience, it indicates that humanity has reached a point where consequences can be meted out on a large scale and with justice. Very little suffering is attached to karma where there is ignorance, leading to irresponsibility and complete lack of thought, and there is attached to affairs but little true sense of guilt. There may be unhappy conditions and distressing circumstances, but the ability to respond to such conditions with commensurate pain is lacking; there is little mental reaction to the processes of karmic retribution. This should be borne in mind. The Aryan race is now, however, so developed mentally and on a large scale, that karma is truly horrible and agonising, and can express itself through world conditions. At the same time, the present widespread distress indicates the extent and success of human unfoldment, and is a most hopeful and promising sign. In this idea, you have the clue as to why the good, the holy and the saintful servers of the race carry—in this world cycle—such a heavy load of karmic ill. (17-290/1)

5. Karma has always been interpreted in terms of disaster, and consequences that are painful, of error, of penalty, and of evil happenings, both for the individual and for the group. Yet, such is the beauty of human nature, and much that is done is of such a fine quality, and so selfless and so happily oriented, that the evil is frequently offset by the good. There is everywhere, little as it may be realised, an abundance of good karma of a potency (under the same Law) equal to that which is regarded as bad. Of this small mention is ever made. This good karma brings into activity forces which may work out as healing energies in any specific case. Upon these energies for good, which have been earned and *are* operating, the healer can always count. . . . Ponder upon it. (17-349)

6. Will you be astonished also if I state that under the Law it is quite possible to "interfere with karma"? The great Laws can be transcended and frequently have been in the past, and increasingly will be in the future. . . . The energy of faith can set in motion superior energies, which can negate or retard disease. The whole subject of faith, and its vital significance and potency, is as little understood as is the Law of Karma. This is a tremendous subject, and I cannot further enlarge upon it. But I have said enough to offer you food for thought. (17-350)

95. KNOWLEDGE

1. *"The initiate knows, because he works"* . . . The entire story of evolution is covered in these few words. The Christ put it in other words when He said "If any man shall do His will, he shall know"; under the occult law, doing ever precedes knowledge because knowledge is gained through experiment and experience. The disciple or aspirant works always in the dark, particularly in the early stages of his unfoldment, following a deep

and hidden instinct towards right activity. By that hard and persistent performance of duty, under the pressure of conscience at first, under the impulse of his awakening soul, and under the influences of the Master, he moves forward from darkness to light; he discovers that obedience to his spiritual instincts leads him inevitably into the realm of knowledge, and that knowledge—when acquired—is transformed eventually into wisdom. He then becomes a Master and walks no longer in the dark.

Aspirants usually bitterly resent the many cycles of darkness through which they seem to go; they complain of the difficulty of working in the dark and of seeing no light anywhere; they forget that the ability to work in the dark or in the light is all one inherent capacity. The reason for this is that the soul knows nothing but *being,* and light and dark are—to the soul—one and the same thing. Above everything else, knowledge comes through conscious experiment, and where there is no experimental activity, no experience can be gained. Knowledge is the reward of both these factors—a knowledge which is not theoretical but which is proven, factual, and the intelligent result of hard work; it is also the result of frequent distress (rightly handled) and of spiritual anticipation.

The above is true of the life and work of the individual aspirant as he tackles the problem of his own lower nature, and prepares for the stage of becoming a soul-infused personality; it is true also of the working disciple, seeking knowledge and wisdom as he works out the hierarchical Plan as best he can. He must perforce experiment and gain practical experience; he must learn the meaning of both success and failure, and the knowledge which can be gained thereby. Knowledge comes at first through the struggle to move forward into greater and clearer light; then it comes as the aspirant (seeking soul expression) learns to forget himself in the need of others as they demand whatever light and knowledge he may possess; wisdom takes the place of knowledge when, in the transmuting fires of struggle, pain and hard work, the aspirant transforms himself into the working disciple and is gradually absorbed into the ranks of the Hierarchy. (6-393/5)

2. Knowledge when given, must be used; it must be made of practical application in the daily life. Upon all of you who read these words, as they come fresh from my heart, my mind and lips, rests a duty of doing three things, which *I give to you in the order of their importance*:

i. The moulding of your daily lives upon the basis of the imparted truth if it is to you indeed a truth. It is perhaps to you simply interesting, a fascinating side line of study; perhaps it is something which it pleases you to get because of its novelty, and because it is a little different from the general run of teaching; perhaps it pleases you to get these instructions a little ahead of the rest of humanity. All these reactions are of small importance, being those of the personality. They are perhaps the most probable reactions for the majority. If there is nothing deeper in your reaction than those I have mentioned, then these teachings are not for you, for the responsibility upon your shoulders is thereby very great; but if you are attempting, no matter in how small a way, to apply the truth as you see it to your own life, then they are for you.

ii. The building of that structure of thought which will embody this newer teaching. You can—if you desire—help construct the thought-form of the New Age teaching. You do this, above all, by your thought; by your practical application of any truth, which you may have understood, to your personal life at any cost; by your sacrifice and your service to your fellow men, and by the constant dissemination of any knowledge which you may possess.

iii. Distribution of the teaching over a long period of time. Have you done anything along this line, thus shouldering your responsibility? (15-711/2)

96. RESPONSIBILITY

1. Relinquish that close attention to the lives of those around you, which is the easy way of working for all who are second ray disciples. Their sense of responsibility is so great and their desire to shelter and to guard so strong, that they unduly cherish those who are linked to them by karmic obligation, and whose lives touch theirs in the life of every day. Go your own way with strength and silence, and do that which your soul demands. Let not the lesser voices of the loved and near deflect you from your progress upon the path of service. You belong now to the world, and not to a handful of your fellow men. (5-140/1)

2. The *sense of responsibility* shines forth in flickering flames from every soul which has sought and found alignment. Fan those flames into a steady fire in every soul you meet. Ponder on this. (5-167)

3. No one achieves anything of reality by the laying down of any assumed responsibility. (5-395)

4. The usefulness of disciples to those who are linked karmically to them, and for whom they feel—rightly or wrongly—a sense of responsibility, shifts from stage to stage with growth. One's physical care for one's loved ones may and must persist in some measure, though a mother's care for a child cannot persist into adult years. There may be a responsibility which one chooses to shoulder (again rightly or wrongly), but it must not offset or undermine any responsibility which it should be theirs to shoulder. One's mental assistance should be always available, but it should not be given when one's mind is bewildered by fogs of questioning and doubt, or when there is a spirit of criticism. One's *spiritual responsibility* is, curiously enough, usually the last to be recognised; and action taken on that recognition is equally slow. Yet, in the last analysis, it is by far the most important, for one's spiritual influence can be lasting and carry with it releasing power to those we love, whereas the other responsibilities—being those of personality relationships—always carry with them glamour and that which is not of the kingdom of the spirit.

For the remaining years of your life lay the emphasis upon your spiritual responsibilities, and your *spiritual effect* upon all you contact, or with whom your lot is cast. Work ever along the line of soul contact, leading to soul release and to the soul activity of those you love, and e'en of those you may not love! Thus you will begin to work on and from spiritual levels, and your potency as a worker will silently increase. This will in no way negate your right usefulness on planes other and lower than the spiritual.   (5-518/9)

5. The difference between your attitude now and your attitude thirty years ago, is that then you did not realise what it was all about, and now you do. Then you had, in reality, no responsibility for you did not know the nature of the task to be done. But, *through soul contact*, you do know now what the problem is, and your responsibility to do something definite is, consequently, heavy.

. . . You have no responsibility for your children and never had since they reached maturity and the right to live their own lives. You have earned the right to your own soul's freedom and expression.   (5-524)

6. Begin, my brothers, to do your own work, leaving others to shoulder their assigned responsibilities, and waste no time in interfering in any phase of work which does not call for your attention.   (6-89)

7. Revelation brings responsibility, and oft times danger. Men, as individuals, can grasp certain of these truths of initiation and use them for

themselves with impunity, but their revelation to the unready might involve
serious risks.   (6-316)

8. The sense of responsibility is *the first* and the outstanding characteristic
of the soul. In so far, therefore, as a disciple is in contact with the soul
and is becoming a soul-infused personality, and is consequently under
soul direction, so far will he undertake the task presented to him.   (6-390)

97. SACRIFICE

1. The sense of sacrifice is faintly seen in every soul that loves the Plan.
Teach them that sacrifice must touch the depths of giving, and not call
forth that which upon the surface lies or that which can be known. The
unseen sacrifice must go with that which can be seen. Teach this.   (5-167)

2. Group work involves sacrifice, and oft the doing of that which might
not be preferred, and which might not—from the personality angle—be
the easier way out and the easier activity.   (5-290)

3. *The idea of self-sacrifice.* This idea has lately shifted from the individual and his sacrifice, to the group presentation. The good of the whole
is now held theoretically to be of such paramount importance that the
group must gladly sacrifice the individual or group of individuals. Such
idealists are apt to forget that the only true sacrifice is that which is self-
initiated, and that when it is an enforced sacrifice (imposed by the more
powerful and superior person or group) it is apt to be, in the last analysis,
the coercion of the individual and his enforced submission to a stronger
will.   (12-120/1)

4. Death, as the human consciousness understands it, pain and sorrow,
loss and disaster, joy and distress, are only such because man, as yet,
identifies himself with the life of the form and not with the life and consciousness of the soul. . . . The moment a man identifies himself with his
soul and not with his form, then he understands the meaning of the Law
of Sacrifice; he is spontaneously governed by it, and he is one who will
with deliberate intent *choose to die.* But there is no pain, no sorrow, and
no real death involved.   (15-94)

5. This urge to sacrifice, to relinquish this for that, to choose one way or
line of conduct and thus sacrifice another way, to lose in order eventually

to gain—such is the underlying story of evolution. This needs psychological understanding. It is the governing principle of life itself, and runs like a golden pattern of beauty through the dark materials of which human history is constructed. When this urge to sacrifice in order to win, gain or salvage that which is deemed desirable is understood, then the whole clue to man's unfoldment will stand revealed. This tendency or urge is something different to desire, as desire is academically understood and studied today. What it really connotes is the emergence of that which is most divine in man. It is an aspect of desire, but it is the dynamic, active side and not the feeling, sensuous side. It is the predominant characteristic of Deity.   (15-97)

6. Under the Law of Sacrifice these three rules might be interpreted thus:

i. Relinquish or sacrifice the age-old tendency to criticise and adjust another's work, and thus preserve the inner group integrity. More plans for service have gone astray and more workers have been hindered by criticism than by any other major factor.

ii. Relinquish or sacrifice the sense of responsibility for the actions of others, and particularly of disciples. See that your own activity measures up to theirs, and in the joy of struggle and on the way of service, the differences will disappear and the general good will be achieved.

iii. Relinquish the pride of mind which sees its way and its interpretations to be correct and true, and others' false and wrong. This is the way of separation. Adhere to the way of integration which is of the soul and not of the mind.

. . . It is essential that the disciples shall learn to sacrifice the non-essential in order that the work may go forward. Little as one may realise it, the many techniques and methods and ways, are secondary to the major world need. There are many ways and many points of view, and many experiments and many efforts—abortive and successful, and all of them come and go. But humanity remains. All of them are in evidence of the multiplicity of minds, and of experiences, but the goal remains. Difference is ever of the personality. When this Law of Sacrifice governs the mind, it will inevitably lead all disciples to relinquish the personal in favour of the universal and of the soul, that knows no separation, no difference. Then no pride, nor a short and myopic perspective, nor love of interference (so dear to many people), nor misunderstanding of motive will hinder their co-operation with each other as disciples, nor their service to the world.   (15-108/9)

98. PAIN AND SUFFERING

1. A word about pain might be in place here, though I have naught of an abstruse nature to communicate anent the evolution of the human hierarchy through the medium of pain. The devas do not suffer pain as does mankind. Their rate of rhythm is steadier although in line with the Law. They learn through application to the work of building and through incorporation into the form of that which is built. They grow through appreciation of and joy in the forms built, and the work accomplished. The devas build and humanity breaks, and through the shattering of the forms man learns through discontent. Thus is acquiescence in the work of the greater Builders achieved. Pain is that upward struggle through matter which lands a man at the feet of the Logos; pain is the following of the line of the greatest resistance, and thereby reaching the summit of the mountain; pain is the smashing of the form and the reaching of the inner fire; pain is the cold of isolation which leads to the warmth of the central sun; pain is the burning in the furnace in order finally to know the coolness of the water of life; pain is the journeying into the far country, resulting in the welcome to the Father's Home; pain is the illusion of the Father's disowning, which drives the prodigal straight to the Father's heart; pain is the cross of utter loss, that renders back the riches of the eternal bounty; pain is the whip that drives the struggling builder to carry to utter perfection the building of the Temple.

The uses of pain are many, and they lead the human soul out of darkness into light, out of bondage into liberation, out of agony into peace. That peace, that light and that liberation, with the ordered harmony of the cosmos, are for all the sons of men. (4-531/3), (5-676/7)

2. Only in the stress of circumstances can the full power of the soul be evoked. Such is the law. (5-181)

3. The difficulties and the trials which the disciple experiences upon the Way are, as you have discovered, only relative; they are oft offset by the pouring in of a sense of inner release. The compensations on the Way are not so often considered as are the difficulties. In the human being there is ever a tendency towards sorrow and suffering which has eventually to be negated; this tendency is one of the problems which the Hierarchy has to face, as it seeks strenuously, at this time, to lift mankind out of the morass in which it finds itself. This "tendency to misery", founded as it is on an attitude of mind, is of such ancient habit that it seems inconceivable to

man that a different point of view and a totally different reaction to life affairs could ever be possible.   (5-400)

4. (Difficult) times are growing times, and serve to train the disciple. The deeper the capacity for usefulness and the deeper the inner conservation, the more severe will oft be the disciplining. . . . Two planks of the raft on which the disciple eventually makes his escape, can be called *service* and *patience.* By a close attention to the needs of his fellow men, and by means of that uncomplaining endurance which is the hall mark of the disciple, he brings to an end the time of difficulty, and emerges thence freer, richer and more useful. There come times in the life of every true aspirant, when he simply continues to persevere, no matter how disinclined he may feel and no matter how acute may be the inner turmoil. (5-418/9)

5. One of the outstanding characteristics of the pledged disciple is that he learns to stand steady and unmoving, no matter what may be happening to him or around him. . . . There is appalling suffering everywhere. Physically and emotionally, people throughout the world are handling the maximum of pain. The accepted disciple, however, is suffering also mentally, and to this must be added his capacity to identify himself with the whole; his trained imagination also presents special difficulty, for he can include possibilities which others may not envisage, and his sweep and grasp of the Plan is presumably greater; he is also endeavouring to apply the knowledge of this Plan to the immediate environing situation, and is strenuously attempting to understand and at the same time to interpret to others, no matter what he may be undergoing in his own personal life.   (6-643/4)

6. (Realise) that, in the light of the eternal verities, all pain is but temporary, all trouble and struggle ephemeral, and that we have passed oft this way before upon the unhappy little planet of suffering which we call the Earth. *We come to know that we shall not pass this way so oft again. . . .*

Just as there are days in a year which seem to stand out because of their darkness, and to be overcharged with blackness and agony, so there are lives which equally so stand out in a cycle of lives, because of the varied experiences which they convey, the bitter piling up of pain and distress, and the handling of an accumulation of unhappy and oft agonising karma. But, my brother, all lives are not like this, and the fact that your present life has been for years so hard is the guarantee that you have worked off much karma, that you stand infinitely freer, and are less handicapped. The fruits of all this suffering you will reap as you enter your next incarnation.

So be of good cheer, and look forward and out towards a future of service and of joy, and this because you have endeavoured to live selflessly and to carry your load bravely, and because your life and deeds, and your entire career, have helped so many.

I would remind you that pain, when it is lived out mentally for others, is the worst kind of pain. This you know. But I would remind you that the capacity so to do and so to identify yourself with pain that is not specifically your own, is something that all disciples have to master, because it is one of the first steps towards shouldering world pain and the agony of the human family, thus becoming a participant in the "fellowship of Christ's sufferings" and a lifter of world burdens. We work and live on a planet of pain. Until a man is an initiate of high degree he cannot even begin to sense the reasons why this is so; he must perforce then take refuge in the trite platitudes, that suffering humanity has evolved to account for things as they are. None of these in any way approximate the true reasons, or give any real insight into the problem. Men must wait for understanding until they can no longer be hurt or limited by the pain of others. This follows when we have learnt to handle our own pain. Then, and only then, can they begin to lift the burden of humanity as a whole and do their responsible share in lightening it.

We come again here to those contradictory and beautiful words: Isolated Unity. When one is isolated from form attachments and when one is freed for identification with the life aspect, then one can know the true meaning of unity, then one is released from pain and one is free to release others also.   (6-649/50)

7. *The idea of the value of sorrow and of pain.* In the process of teaching the race the necessary quality of *detachment,* in order that its desire and plans shall no longer be oriented to form living, the Guides of the race have emphasised the idea of the virtues of sorrow and the educational value of pain. These virtues are real, but the emphasis has been overdone by the lesser teachers of the race, so that the racial attitude today is one of sorrowful and fearful expectancy, and a feeble hope that some reward (in a desirable and usually material form, such as the heaven of the various world religions) may eventuate after death, and thus compensate for all that has been undergone during life. The races today are steeped in misery and an unhappy psychological acquiescence in sorrow and pain.

The clear light of love must sweep away all this, and joy will be the keynote of the coming New Age. (12-120)

8. The "sharp shears of sorrow must separate the real from the unreal; the lash of pain must awaken the sleepy soul to exquisite life; the wrenching away of the roots of life from the soil of selfish desire must be undergone, and then the man stands free". So runs the *Old Commentary* in one of its more mystical stanzas. (18-499)

9. *Great is the Mystery of Pain*

The word went forth to all the sons of men, the Sons of God: Learn through the struggle of earth life to choose the way that is better—then the best. Evade not pain. Seek not the easiest way, which is not to be found. Tread then the *Way* which leads through sorrow, pain and dire distress to that High Place from which you come—the Place where God walks with the sons of men, who are the Sons of God. Before the august Presence, all pain shall disappear; sorrow shall fade away, and death shall triumph not. Beauty and goodness and the strength of God irradiate the face of men. (6-767)

99. GLAMOUR AND ILLUSION

(a) GLAMOUR

1. *Glamour of Fatigue.* Let not the glamour of fatigue and of disappointment over world conditions lead to abortive work. . . . Fight it by nonrecognition and by complete absorption in the immediate task; I refer to a wise absorption which neglects no due physical care, nor due time for relaxation. The work goes forward in the world along the correct, indicated inner lines. The disciple who has achieved a measure of sensitivity to the Whole, must learn to discriminate between aspects of that whole. . . . Learn to register with equal sensitivity the mass of the world idealisms and aspiring thought; then the glamour of fatigue and of innate disgust will give place to a keen interest and understanding of the glamour-free disciple. (5-170)

2. Glamour is not dispelled by paying close attention to it. It disappears by the power of clear and steadfast meditation, and the freeing of oneself from self attention. (5-358)

3. Glamour is the powerful enemy of all who tread the Path of Disciple-ship. . . . Disciples who live on mental levels are freer from glamour than are those whose polarisation is more purely emotional. Therefore, one of the first things we seek to teach all of you is to work, live and think in freedom from the astral plane. . . .

Glamour is, of course, such a subtle thing that it ever masquerades as the truth. It is powerful because it finds its point of entry into a disciple's consciousness through those states of mind and those habits of thought, which are so familiar that their appearance is automatic and constitutes an almost unconscious manifestation. There are (for the average disciple) three main attitudes of mind and of feeling, which predispose him to being glamoured:

i. *Self-pity.* To this all disciples are prone. Their lives are necessarily difficult and they are more sensitive than the average. They are also being constantly tried and tested in this particular direction. Self-pity is a powerful and deluding force; it exaggerates every condition and isolates a person in the centre of his own life, and the dramatic situations evoked in his own thoughts. . . .

ii. *A spirit of criticism.* This induces more states of glamour than any other one factor; and here, who shall say he is immune? When harm-lessness and kindness in thought and word are practised, and automatic-ally become a part of a disciple's daily life expression, then glamour will end. . . .

iii. *Suspicion.* The most poisonous of all weaknesses is this glamour; it is usually the most false and—even when well founded—is still capable of poisoning the very roots of being, of distorting all attitudes to life, and of bringing into activity the creative imagination as its potent servant. Suspicion ever lies, but lies with such apparent truth that it seems only correct and reasonable. . . . Give not way to suspicion; but be careful not to cast it away from you into the hidden depths of your-self, whence again it must inevitably raise its head. End its power in your life by doing three things:

(a) By assuming more definitely the attitude of the Onlooker, who sees all people and happenings through the light of love and from the angle of the eternal values.

(b) By leaving everybody free to live their own lives and to shoulder their own responsibilities, knowing that they are souls and are being led towards the light. Simply give them love and understanding.

(c) By the fullness of your own life of service, which leaves you no time for the moments and hours of suspicion which blight so many lives.

These three things, if persisted in and practised, will do more to release you from glamour than any other one thing.   (5-510/3)

4. Avoid at least one glamour, and that is the glamour that it is your task to shoulder all responsibilities and make all final decisions. Leave people . . . the opportunity which you yourself so much welcome, of learning the needed lessons. Seek not unduly to lift and shield, for the shielding mother-complex is in itself a glamour.   (6-643)

5. The disciple is the victim and, let us hope, the dissipator of both glamour and illusion, and hence the complexity of his problem and the subtlety of his difficulties. He must bear in mind also (for his strengthening and cheer), that every bit of glamour dissipated and every illusion recognised and overcome, "clears the way" for those who follow after, and makes easier the path of his fellow disciples. This is par excellence, the Great Service, and it is to this aspect of it that I call your attention. Hence my attempts in these instructions to clarify the issue.   (10-44)

6. A deep distrust of one's reactions to life and circumstance, when such reactions awaken and call forth *criticism, separativeness* or *pride,* is of value. The qualities enumerated above, are definitely breeders of glamour. They are occultly "the glamorous characteristics". Ponder on this. If a man can free himself from these three characteristics, he is well on the way to the relinquishing and the dissipation of all glamour. I am choosing my words with care in an effort to arrest your attention.

. . . It is the soul itself which dispels illusion, through the use of the faculty of the intuition. It is the illumined mind which dissipates glamour.   (10-82/3)

7. Glamour can always be found where there exists:

i. *Criticism,* when careful analysis would show that no criticism is really warranted.

ii. *Criticism,* where there is no personal responsibility involved. By that I mean, where it is not the place or the duty of the man to criticise.

iii. *Pride* in achievement or satisfaction that one is a disciple.

iv. Any sense of superiority or *separative* tendency.   (10-84)

(b) THE GLAMOUR OF MATERIALITY

The glamour of materiality is the cause of all the present world distress, for what we call the economic problem is simply the result of this particular glamour. . . . That which will meet a need that is vital and real, ever exists within the divine plan. That which is unnecessary to the right expression of divinity and to a full and rich life, can be gained and possessed, but only through the loss of the more real and the negation of the essential.

Students, however, need to remember that that which is necessary varies according to the stage of evolution which has been reached by an individual. For some people, for instance, the possession of that which is material, may be as great a spiritual experience and as potent a teacher in life expression as the more elevated and less material requirements of the mystic or hermit. We are rated as regards action and point of view, by our place upon the ladder of evolution. We are rated really by our point of view and not by our demand upon life. The spiritually minded man and the man who has set his feet upon the Path of Probation, and who fails to attempt the expression of that which he believes, will be judged as caustically and pay as high a price as does the pure materialist—the man whose desires centre around substantial effects. Bear this in mind and sit not in the seat of the judge or the scornful.

Today the glamour of materiality is lessening perceptibly. The peoples of the world are entering the wilderness experience, and will find in the wilderness how little is required for full living, true experience and real happiness. The gluttonous desire for possessions is not regarded as so reputable a desire as formerly, and a desire for riches is not producing the clutching hands as earlier in racial history. Things and possessions are slipping out of the hands which have hitherto tightly held them, and only when men stand with empty hands and a realised new standard of values, do they again acquire the right to own and to possess. When desire is absent, and the man seeks nothing for the separated self, the responsibility of material wealth can again be handed back to man, but his point of view will then be free from that particular glamour, and the fogs of astral desire will be lessened. Illusion in many forms may still hold sway, but the glamour of materiality will be gone. It is the first destined to disappear. . . .

. . . The Guides of the Race have felt the necessity of standing by whilst the forces set up by man himself proceed to strip him and thus release him to walk in the wilderness. There, in what is called straitened circumstances, he can readjust his life and change his way of living, thus discovering that freedom from material things carries with it its own beauty and reward, its own joy and glory. Thus he is liberated to live the life of the mind. (10-75/6)

(c) THE GLAMOUR OF IDEALISM

Ideals must go as they are now formulated, because we are entering into a New Age wherein all things will become new. They can safely be relinquished when their place is taken by a real soul love for humanity—inclusive, sane and practical. Ideals are formulations by the human mind. The Hierarchy has no ideals. The Hierarchy is simply the channel for pure love, and where love exists there is no danger of harshness, of cruelty, of misunderstanding, of evasion of facts, or of harmfulness. Much also that many regard as harmless is definitely harmful in its general effects. Ideals, as usually held, feed pride, lead to stubbornness, and engender a separative superiority; they produce impractical attitudes and negative activities. The one who thus holds them frequently serves only in the limited field, conditioned by his chosen work and coloured by his idealism. He excludes the *Whole* and thinks in terms of the past and as he wants to think. There is no real understanding of an opposing idealism and often no real attempt to comprehend its basis. His emphasis upon his own ideals (in his own consciousness even when not imposed on others) prevents understanding, and he is so busy up-holding them and defending them (oft again to himself), and being conditioned by them, that the larger human issues escape his attention. He settles down within the limits of his own beliefs. This makes him immediately a theologian, and his usefulness then rapidly evaporates, except in the intimate circle of his fellow idealists. As time goes on, crystallisation takes place. A "crystal barrier" is set up between the personality and the soul. The soul is seen but its influence is insulated. But—because there is a vision of the soul still persisting—the disciple is deeply satisfied. The crystallisation eventually affects all aspects of the nature. Emotions settle into "grooves of crystal"; the mind becomes set and brittle. The physical body crystallises also and gets old rapidly because there is no free flow of life.

One thing only will prevent this happening: Loving understanding and a consequent sacrifice of the life to humanity *as a whole*. The greatest good of the greatest number becomes his life theme, and to this the whole man is subordinated. (6-530/1)

(d) THE ILLUSION OF POWER

The Illusion of Power is perhaps one of the first and most serious tests which comes to an aspirant. It is also one of the best examples of this "great mistake", and I therefore bring it to your attention as being one against which I beg you most carefully to guard yourself. It is rare indeed for any disciple to escape the effects of this error of illusion, for it is, curiously, based upon right success and right motive. Hence the specious nature of the problem. It might be expressed thus :

An aspirant succeeds in contacting his soul or ego through right effort. Through meditation, good intention, and correct technique, plus the desire to serve and to love, he achieves alignment. He becomes then aware of the results of his successful work. His mind is illumined. A sense of power flows through his vehicles. He is, temporarily at least, made aware of the Plan. The need of the world and the capacity of the soul to meet that need, flood his consciousness. His dedication, consecration and right purpose enhance the directed inflow of spiritual energy. He knows. He loves. He seeks to serve, and does all three more or less successfully. The result of all this is that he becomes more engrossed with the sense of power, and with the part he is to play in aiding humanity, than he is with the realisation of a due and proper sense of proportion and of spiritual values. He over-estimates his experience and himself. Instead of redoubling his efforts and thus establishing a closer contact with the kingdom of souls, and loving all beings more deeply, he begins to call attention to himself, to the mission he is to develop, and to the confidence that the Master and even the planetary Logos apparently have in him. He talks about himself; he gestures and attracts notice, demanding recognition. As he does so, his alignment is steadily impaired; his contact lessens, and he joins the ranks of the many who have succumbed to the illusion of sensed power.

This form of illusion is becoming increasingly prevalent among disciples and those who have taken the first two initiations. There are today many people in the world who have taken the first initiation in a previous life. At some period in the present life cycle, recurring and recapitulating as it does the events of an earlier development, they again reach a point in their realisation which they earlier reached. The significance of their attainment pours in upon them, and the sense of their responsibility and knowledge. Again they over-estimate themselves, regarding their missions and themselves as unique among the sons of men, and their esoteric and subjective demand for recognition enters in and spoils what might otherwise have been fruitful service. Any emphasis upon the personality can distort most easily the pure light of the soul as it seeks to pour through the lower self. Any effort to call attention to the mission or task which the personality has undertaken, detracts from that mission, and handicaps the man in his task; it leads to the deferring of its fulfilment until such time when the disciple can be naught but a channel through which love can pour, and light can shine. This pouring through and shining forth, has to be a spontaneous happening, and contain no self-reference. (10-52/3)

(e) OVERCOMING THE DWELLER

"How can I overcome this Dweller and yet at the same time refuse to concentrate upon myself and my problems? This I am told by you not to do, and yet the Dweller is the sum-total of all personality holds and defects, all potencies—emotional, mental and physical—which limit my expression as a soul. What can I therefore do?"

My answer would be: You must first of all accept the fact of the Dweller, and then relegate that Dweller to its rightful place as part of the Great Illusion, the great phantasmagoria of existence and as an integral part of the life of the three worlds. You must then proceed upon your planned life of service (What definite plan or plans have you, my brother?) and act as if the Dweller existed not, thus freeing yourself from all personality influence in due time, and leaving your mind free for the task in hand. I could perhaps word it another way. When your interest in hierarchical work and the programme of the Ashram with which you are connected, is adequately strong, it will then dominate all your actions, and all your thoughts (waking or sleeping); you will then find that the grip of the Dweller will be broken, that its *life* has been destroyed by the force of attrition, and its *form* destroyed in the fires of sacrifice. (6-47/8)

100. SUCCESS

1. The walls of difficulty must go down, and success must follow effort—the united pressure of determined souls pushing through to victory in spite of real odds. This united and definite effort must be carried forward without discouragement or questioning—with due attention to the time factor, and with a sense of urgency. This will negate all lost motion, and will permit no opportunity to slide. There are, my brother, many who will give their co-operation but who, at this time, sidetrack their co-operation, owing to fear or to the over-emphasis of non-essentials. I refer here to those men of goodwill who are today aware of the urgency of the Master's work but still hold back assistance in full measure. There are those also who do not realise the urgency, and are unaware of the immediacy of the Plan or even that there is a Plan. They, however, when faced with the issue, will give.

. . . One-pointed, directed effort can achieve results in spite of world conditions, misrepresentations by those who do not understand, and the failure of responsive interest on the part of one's disciples—throughout the world or close at hand.

Brace yourself, therefore, and with the other members of my group, push through. Stand steady and do not be so seriously troubled as to the progress of the work which seems not yet to move as rapidly as desired. When the movement does come, it will be rapid. . . .   (5-166/7)

2. Were you so free, you would not suffer so much over people or over the frustration which always comes—and always will—until the disciple no longer cares for success or non-success, for appreciation or for non-appreciation. Ponder on this, and search your heart more closely.   (5-262)

3. The wise disciple regards all outer expression on the physical plane of experience as *achievement*. There is no essential failure. At this stage in the life of the disciple, there may be a failing to meet the requirements with perfection; there may come cycles of aridity and of a seemingly static condition; there may be times wherein the sense of futility is deep and real. But none of these will be lasting. The grip of the soul upon its instrument, the personality, is too strong for these cycles to be more than transient episodes.   (5-267)

101. FAILURE

1. Recognise failure—if it is there—but then with a face lifted to the light, and a smile upon your lips, turn your back upon such failure and go with steadfastness forward. (5-366)

2. It is not easy for disciples or initiates to identify themselves with weakness or with failure, and yet that must be done. They constitute just as much a part of the expression of humanity, as does strength or success, and there can be no separation in attitude, or failure in identification. Disciples have to learn to identify themselves with the whole. (5-450)

3. One thought only will I give you to repeat whene'er you are discouraged, tired or weak :

> At the centre of all love I stand, and naught can touch me here, and from that centre I shall go forth to love and serve. (5-527)

4. You have as yet done no service that will carry over into the future, because it has been done at a sacrifice of yourself, that has involved the sacrifice of your time, your personal interests, and your personal desires, based upon your personal qualities. You have looked on at the service of others, and wondered why and how they chose to serve in the various ways they did; you have suggested service to others and have at times made it possible for them to serve; you have talked to groups on service, and yet with no results adequate to the force expended. Why has this been so? Because all the time you were not giving of yourself in love, but only of that which was exterior to yourself. (5-585)

5. The only regret that is justifiable is based on failure to learn the lessons of failure. (5-604)

6. Service frequently runs contrary to much that one would like to see accomplished and to much that has been planned by servers; we know that service means endless disappointment, ceaseless struggle, hard knocks, apparent unaccountable failure—and all because *as yet* the spiritual strength of humanity is not commensurate to the material pull. (5-620)

7. Failures, where they may be found, need not persist, for the group love can offset them all; personality weaknesses, mistakes and faults are overlooked and forgotten in the urgency of human need; they do not even penetrate into the Ashram. I would ask you to remember this, and with

humility in your hearts, persistence in your efforts, and love to all men, pass on your way.   (6-110)

8. Aspiring disciples are far more conscious of the failings and the personality attributes of others than are the more advanced disciples in the Ashrams. The advanced disciple may be—and is—well aware of the failings, failures and undesirable qualities of others with whom he is associated, but his critical mind is not the determining factor, as it is with most of the less developed. He is far more conditioned by the aspirations, the effort and the fixed intention than by the personality angle. He gauges the soul's grip upon the lower self, primarily from the angle of the stability of its hold; his treatment of the aspirant is therefore based upon that recognition, and not upon any analysis of the aspirant's lack of development. This is a point of immense importance, for it is this type of consideration which governs the Masters when They are choosing and training a group for initiation. The Master is not occupied with the temporary faults, but with the soul grip and intention, and with the aspirant's *habitual* response to soul energy, when that energy is applied.

. . . The Masters think in terms of cycles and not in terms of an individual life; as you cannot yet do that, except theoretically, it is not possible for you to understand. The experience, the failures and the achievements of the disciples in my Ashram are seen by me, for instance, in terms of one thousand year cycles. What you may have done in this life, unless of outstanding significance, is in all probability quite unknown to me; if I choose to know, I can do so, and I do so in those cases where the results of some activity have repercussions upon my Ashram or upon a large proportion of the group of disciples.

Let me put it this way: the petty selfishness and the silly little vanities and the irritations which disturb you, the unkind words you may speak of or to others, and the withholding of love, or the fact of wrong emphasis in your daily life, are *not* noted by me or by any Master. They are the affair of your own soul; the results affect your family, friend, or communal group, and are none of Our business. Yet those are the things which you notice in others and which affect your judgment, evoking like or dislike, praise or blame, but inevitably putting you—as an individual—upon the judgment seat. There no Master sits. When Christ said: "Judge not and ye shall not be judged", He indicated a state of mind where understanding so controls that the aspirant no longer praises or blames; because of this general attitude within his mental approach to people, he is then free to become a full member of an Ashram.   (6-333/5)

9. The Master neither sees nor notices the small failures, the moments of distress or disturbance, or the personality frictions which (from the angle of the observing disciple) seem to mar the picture. At intervals—rare at first but more frequent when the service rendered attains greater importance—the Master makes Himself aware of the general progress, the growth of the general structure of service which the disciple is creating, and the extension of his light in the world. It amuses us at times to note that some disciples (particularly those trained in the earlier, personality-tainted groups) believe the Masters pry into their daily lives, know their petty faults and silly little failures, and are fully aware of all they think and do. We wonder sometimes where they think the Masters find the time, and why They should be so interested in habits of thought and action and speech, which the disciple is rapidly overcoming.

We are only interested in the good which any individual may be demonstrating.   (6-456)

10. You will note that I am not preoccupied with your mistakes or failures. These are inevitable and are relatively unimportant, because a disciple at your point of development is ever aware of them, and can be trusted to take the needed steps toward adjustment.   (6-756)

11. You did fail, my brother. But why stay overwhelmed by failure for year after year and remain with your eyes concentrated on the lower self that failed? All have failed and will again along some line. E'en the Masters fail at times to pass through one or other of the highest initiations at Their first attempt and—from the hierarchical angle—that connotes failure. But the failure is scarce recognised; the effort is made to register what caused the failure.   (6-732)

102.   RECOGNITION

1. I would like to point out to the student that, having with steadfastness gone forward, he will discover that the exoteric and esoteric linking of the outer schools and inner school, or rank of knowers of truth, is so close, that not one earnest student goes totally unrecognised. In the press of the work and in the burden and toil of the day's labours, it is an encouragement to know that there are those who watch, and that every loving deed, every aspiring thought and every unselfish reaction, is noted and known.

Bear in mind, however, that it comes to the recognition of the Helpers through the increased vibration of the aspirant, and not through a specific knowledge of the deed accomplished or the thought sent out. Those who teach are occupied with principles of truth, with vibratory rates, and with the quality of the light to be seen. They are not aware of, nor have They the time to consider specific deeds, words and conditions, and the sooner students grasp this and put out of their minds any hope of contacting a phenomenal individual whom they call a Master, with so much leisure, of such developed powers that He can occupy Himself with their trivial affairs in time and space, the more rapidly will they progress.

Where, however, there is steady growth, an application to occult principles so that definite changes are produced in the bodies used, and an increasing radiatory light, it is known and recorded, and the aspirant is rewarded by increased opportunity to serve his fellow men. They do not reward by recommendation, by patting on the head, or by expressing their pleasure in words. They are occupied in making knowers and masters out of everyday men and women by:

i. Teaching them how to know themselves.

ii. Setting them free from authority by awakening interest and enquiry in their minds, and then indicating (not more than that) the direction in which the answer should be sought.

iii. Giving them those conditions which will force them to stand on their own feet and rely on their own souls, and not on any human being, be he a beloved friend, teacher, or a Master of the Wisdom.   (4-638/9)

2. The outer recognition of the inner status (as well as of inner states of consciousness, which is another name for the same thing) must come ever from within the disciple's own nature; we, the teachers, are only permitted to put the seal of recognition upon the fact afterwards.   (5-108/9)

3. It is of real value to a disciple at times to summarise achievement, and to accept it. A new cycle always eventuates from such a moment of recognition and conclusion.   (5-348)

4. I know that you do not ask for recognition, but that is ever accorded by us, the teachers on the inner side, when duly merited. I can, therefore, tell you that your work is recognised.   (5-362)

5. Humility must always accompany a spiritual self-respect, which forbids a disciple to stand anywhere upon the Path except in his rightful

place. The fact is that discipleship warrants recognition. There is no false pride in knowing that one is a disciple. . . . Recognition of status, however, is purely a personal matter; it should be faced and accepted, and then followed by *silence*. (5-562)

6. Look life in the face . . . and be ready to recognise and admit error; be equally ready, however, to perceive where success has crowned your effort and glorified your way; learn also to look for your failures, where the outside world may see only success or some kind of achievement. (5-641)

7. The Master recognises those who recognise the Plan and are trying (with full or with qualified dedication) to help bring it about. He then stimulates them as a group, because they have identity of vision and dedication; this enables them, under that stimulation and inspiration, to become more effective in the chosen (self-chosen) lines of service. I would have you, therefore, ponder carefully upon the following recognitions:

   i. The recognition of the vision.

   ii. The recognition of the Plan, for vision and Plan are not the same.

   iii. The recognition which the Master accords to a group of dedicated aspirants when He accepts them as His disciples.

   iv. Your recognition of the Master's ideas as goals to future endeavour.

   v. Your recognition of each other as souls and servers.

When these recognitions are properly understood, there will then be eventual recognition, by the Hierarchy, of a group of disciples who can be used as a channel through which spiritual energy, light and love can be poured into a needy and agonising world. The group will then be endowed with power to serve, but it will not be power given to it by the Master. It will be a potency which it has engendered itself. This power which disciples wield, comes as a response to a life rightly lived and love fully given. (5-691/2)

8. The initiate, on his tiny scale, likewise has to learn to work behind the scenes, unknown and unrecognised and unacclaimed; he must sacrifice his identity in the identity of the Ashram and its workers, and later in the identity of his working disciples, out in the world of daily life. He institutes the needed activities, and brings about the required changes, but he receives no reward, save the reward of souls salvaged, lives rebuilt and humanity led onward upon the Path of Return. (6-288)

9. The . . . quality which must be utterly rooted out and destroyed, is that of all reaction towards recognition, whether that recognition is accorded by the world of men, by other disciples, or by the Master. The ability to work without any token of recognition, to see others claim the reward of action taken, and even to be unaware that the results of the good initiated by the individual disciple or his group are claimed by others, are the hallmarks of the hierarchical worker. The Masters get no recognition for the work done by Their disciples, though They initiated the original impulse and have given both guidance and direction; the disciple carries out the Plan; he shoulders the responsibility; he pays the price, either good or bad, or the karmic results of instituted activity, and he is the one who gains the recognition of the crowd. But—until the disciple seeks *no* recognition, until he fails to think in terms of results, and is unaware of the reaction of the world to his work as an individual disciple—he has yet far to go in order to gain the higher initiations. The entire problem becomes increasingly difficult when an entire ashramic group is concerned, for the recognition of the group service seems little to ask from the world which is served; nevertheless, such a demand and such an expectation delay the complete absorption of the group into the inner Ashram.   (18-211/2)

103.   RELAXATION AND RECREATION

1. Conserve your strength and remember that right relaxation is just as much a part of the service you can render as the strenuous, unremitting work which leads to *enforced* and perhaps inconvenient interludes of gaining physical strength. The steady, unbroken, inner push, carried forward through right organisation of the outer factors of time and physical strength, is essential. It is not possible, unless there is a balanced life of service, of recreation and again of service.   (5-164)

2. Watch your physical strength somewhat, and live not at so high a tension. Relax a little during the coming months, and foster those lighter moments of relaxation which give to your soul opportunity to attend to its own affairs upon its own high level. Then it can return in greater force and with a more potent vibration to its habitation—the threefold personality. This the disciple is apt to forget in the intensity of his longing for soul contact, for illumination and realisation, and for conscious contact

with his Master. That contact, remember, when once established upon the Path of Discipleship, is never broken. Stand, therefore, upon this belief, and relax and play at times.   (5-218)

104. CONSCIOUSNESS

(a) THE INDWELLING CONSCIOUSNESS

1. One point you all need to grasp is that the progressing disciple does not move into new fields or areas of awareness, like a steady marching forward from one plane to another (as the visual symbols of the theosophical literature would indicate). What must be grasped is that *all that IS is ever present*. What we are concerned with is the constant awakening to that which eternally IS, and to what is ever present in the environment, but of which the subject is unaware, owing to short-sightedness. The aim must be to overcome the undue concentration upon the foreground of daily life which characterises most people, the intense preoccupation with the interior states or moods of the lower self which characterises the spiritually minded people and the aspirants, and the imperviousness or lack of sensitivity which characterises the mass of men. The Kingdom of God is present on Earth today and forever has been, but only a few, relatively speaking, are aware of its signs and manifestations. The world of subtle phenomena (called formless, because unlike the physical phenomena with which we are so familiar) is ever with us, and can be seen and contacted and proved as a field for experiment and experience and activity, if the mechanism of perception is developed as it surely can be.

The sounds and sights of the heavenly world (as the mystics call it) are as clearly perceived by the higher initiate, as are the sights and sounds of the physical plane as you contact it in your daily round of duties. The world of energies, with its streams of directed force and its centres of concentrated light, are likewise present, and the eye of the see-er can see it, just as the eye of the mental clairvoyant can see the geometrical pattern which thoughts assume upon the mental plane, or as the lower psychic can contact the glamours, the illusions and delusions of the astral world. The subjective realm is vitally more real than is the objective, once it is entered and known. It is simply (how simple to some and how insuperably difficult to others, apparently!) a question of the acceptance, first of all, of its existence, the development of a mechanism of contact, the cultivation of the ability to use this mechanism at will, and then *inspired interpretation.*

It might be said that consciousness itself, which is the goal—on this planet—of all the evolutionary process, is simply the demonstrated result of the Science of Contact. It is likewise the goal in some form or other, and at some stage or other, of all planetary existences within the solar system itself. The unfoldment of this conscious response is, in reality, the growth of the sensitive awareness of the planetary Logos HIMSELF. The human mechanism and its ability to respond to its environment (as science well knows) has been developed in response to an inner urge, present in every human being and in all forms of life, and to the "pull" and magnetic effect of the surrounding environment. Step by step, the forms of life upon the physical plane, down through the ages, have unfolded one sense after another; one form of sensitive response after another becomes possible as the mechanism is produced, until the human being can receive impressions from the physical plane and rightly interpret them; can respond to the emotional contacts of the astral plane, and succumb to them or surmount them; and can become telepathic to the world of the mental plane, thus sharing—physically, emotionally and mentally—in the life and contacts of the three worlds which constitute his environment, and in which he is submerged whilst in incarnation. What he gets out of this life of constant impression, is largely dependent upon his power to invoke his environment and draw from it (in evocative response) what he needs in all the various departments of his being. This, in its turn, forces him—whether he likes it or not—to produce an effect upon other people; this can be far more potent for good or evil, and from the telepathic angle, than he likes to think or can conceive.   (11-53/5)

2. Each point of life within a centre has its own sphere of radiation, or its own extending field of influence; this field is necessarily dependent upon the type and the nature of the indwelling Consciousness. It is this magnetic interplay between the many vast centres of energy in space which is the basis of all astronomical relationships—between universes, solar systems and planets. Bear in mind, however, that it is the CONSCIOUS-NESS aspect which renders the form magnetic, receptive, repudiating and transmitting; this consciousness differs according to the nature of the entity which informs or works through a centre, great or small. Bear in mind also that the life which pours through all centres, and which animates the whole of space, is *the life of an Entity*; it is, therefore, the same life in all forms, limited in time and space by the intention, the wish, the

form and the quality of the indwelling Consciousness; the types of consciousness are many and diverse, yet life remains ever the same and indivisible, for it is the ONE LIFE.   (11-180)

(b)   EXPANDING CONSCIOUSNESS

1. Every expansion of consciousness, resulting in increased scope of service, is to be taken at a cost, and for this you will have to be prepared. (5-245)

2. Each expansion of consciousness is preceded by a period of testing in some one of the three bodies, and in some aspect of the lower nature. . . . Such tests produce an inner unfoldment which may be more apparent to those who teach than to yourself. This testing and its results constitute a responsibility, and open up avenues of approach to the central reality of the soul, hitherto not employed.   (5-545)

3. I would remind you of the Law which states that "we grow through the medium of our recognitions". A recognition, when it is seen as an aspect or fractional part of a greater whole, is the seed of a major expansion of consciousness. A stabilised expansion of consciousness connotes initiation. This is an occult statement of major importance.   (5-740)

4. The objective of each aspirant is to expand his consciousness to include that which lies beyond himself, to attain to the more elevated states of consciousness in the life of the group and of humanity, and to integrate himself consciously into the Hierarchy, eventually into Shamballa, and occultly to "*know*" God in His many phases of all-inclusive extension and perfection.   (5-766)

5. In the total evolution of the spiritual man through physical incarnation during untold hundreds of lives, the entire process is simply one of expanding consciousness, and of attaining—sequentially and stage by stage—an ever more inclusive awareness.   (6-194)

6. The disciple, when he becomes an accepted disciple (and this through the Lodge's recognition of his pledge to his own soul), arrives at a definite and factual recognition of the Hierarchy. His suppositions, his desires, his aspirational wish-life, his theories, or whatever you may choose to call his reaching out and up towards divinity, give place to clear knowledge of the liberated group of souls. This happens not through the occurrence of convincing phenomena, but through an inflow of the intuition. He undergoes, therefore, an expansion of consciousness which may or may not be

registered in the brain. Every step of the way from that point of recognition onward has to be consciously achieved, and must involve a conscious recognition of a series of expansions. These expansions are not initiation. Have that clearly in your mind. The initiation lying immediately ahead is simply the effect of the recognition. They might be called "stabilising points of crisis", in which the "occasional becomes the constant and the intended becomes the intentional". Ponder on these words.   (6-247)

7. The life of the initiate is one of constant registration of new knowledge which must be transmuted into practical wisdom, of occult facts which must take intelligent place in the life-service of the initiate, and of new inclusions of areas of consciousness; these latter must become the normal field of experience and of expression; they then become the ground for further expansion.   (6-307)

8. The point in consciousness is not necessarily identical with the point in evolution. A high point in evolution can be reached unconsciously and the disciple is frequently not truly aware of what IS. He has to become consciously aware of his exact point of attainment *before* he can really know what the next step is which he must consciously take.   (6-414)

9. (The realisation of many aspirants) is often bigger than the present equipment of brain cells warrants. Therefore, knowledge and registered expansion of consciousness is temporarily withheld until a better physical vehicle is available. I mention this because some suffer from discouragement when, after years of work and the achievement of old age, they find themselves registering a static condition, or what they deem to be static. There is no need for such feeling, but there is need for care and the progression of the interior work, e'en when the external recording is apparently lacking.   (6-488)

10. It is the expansion of consciousness and the production of increased sensitivity and perceptive awareness, which is the goal of all divine and hierarchical effort. The goal is not for betterment of material conditions. These will automatically follow when the sense of awareness is steadily unfolded. The future of humanity is determined by its aspiration and ability to respond to the idealism which is today flooding the world.   (12-103)

11. The psychics of the world are increasing greatly in number, and the growing sensitivity of the race to impression is a cause of rejoicing and of danger. All over the world aspirants are registering contacts hitherto

unknown, are seeing a phenomenal world usually hidden to them, and are generally becoming aware of an expansion of consciousness. They are registering a world of phenomena—often astral, sometimes mental, and occasionally egoic—which does initiate them into a new dimension of consciousness, and into a different state of being. This expansion of consciousness serves both to encourage them in their endeavour and to complicate the way of the aspirant.   (14-97)

12. The objective of all training given to the disciple, is to shift his conscious awareness from the point where he is, to levels which are higher than those in the three worlds of definitely human evolution; the intention is to teach him to function on those planes of conscious contact which are as yet so subjective that he only accepts them as existent in theory. The trained initiate knows that they have to become his natural habitat, and that eventually he has to relegate the ordinary and normal human experience to the three worlds of daily expression. These become eventually the worlds that exist below the threshold of consciousness; they are relegated to the realm of the subconscious—recoverable consciously, if necessary for right service of humanity, but as much below the threshold of consciousness as are the ordinary emotional reactions of the average man. These are always recoverable (as modern psycho-analysis has demonstrated) and can become capable of expression and of formulation into conditioning concepts—thus actuating mental perception if deemed of adequate importance. However, it should be borne in mind that the greater part of the emotional life of the disciple must become increasingly subconscious, just as the physical plane life of the normal healthy human being is entirely automatic and thus subconscious. When the disciple has striven to expand his consciousness, when he has learnt to stabilise his consciousness in the Spiritual Triad, then he becomes part of a great and constant hierarchical effort, which strives upwards towards the "Place of Clear Electric Light", to which the clear cold light of the reason is the first key to the first door.   (18-138/9)

(c) CONTINUITY OF CONSCIOUSNESS

I would ask you, as life proceeds and you face eventually and inevitably the discarding of the vehicle, to hold increasingly on to your knowledge of the Hierarchy, and thus to pass over to the other side with complete dedication to the hierarchical Plan. This is not simply a suggestion on my part; it is an attempt on my part to call to your attention the concept of a spiritual continuity of knowledge and of a rightly oriented attitude. Thus time will not be lost; you can—if you so choose, each and all of you—attain a true continuity of consciousness. (6-101) [See also Section 66 (p) (1) on page 311.]

(d) LIMITATION AND IMPRISONMENT

1. With the problem of limitation is closely linked that of liberation. Into the prison house of form enter all that live; some enter consciously and some unconsciously, and this we call birth, appearance, incarnation, manifestation. Immediately there sweeps into activity another law, or the working out of an active principle which we call the Law of Cycles. This is the principle of periodic appearance—a beneficent operation of the love-wisdom of innate divinity, for it produces that sequence of the states of consciousness which we term Time. This produces therefore in the world field of awareness a gradual and slow growth towards self-expression, self-appreciation, and self-realisation. (4-533/4)

2. Let it be remembered always that each field of awareness in its boundaries constitutes a prison, and that the objective of all work of liberation is to release the consciousness and expand its field of contacts. Where there are boundaries of any kind, where a field of influence is circumscribed, and where the radius of contact is limited, there you have a prison. Ponder on this statement for it holds much of truth. Where there is an apprehension of a vision and of a wide unconquered territory of contacts, then there will inevitably be a sense of imprisonment and of cramping. Where there is realisation of worlds to conquer, of truths to be learnt, of conquests to be made, of desires to be achieved, of knowledges to be mastered, there you will have a festering sense of limitation, goading on the aspirant to renewed effort, and driving the living entity on along the path of evolution.

Instinct, governing the vegetable and animal kingdoms, develops into intellect in the human family. Later intellect merges into intuition and intuition into illumination. When the superhuman consciousness is evoked, these two—intuition and illumination—take the place of instinct and of intelligence.

Illumination—what does that lead to? Straight to the summit of achievement, to the fulfilment of cyclic destiny, to the emergence of the radiant glory, to wisdom, power, God consciousness. These words however mean but little or nothing in comparison with a Reality which can only be sensed by any human being when his intuition is awakened and his mind illumined. (4-535)

(e) SERVING BY RELEASING THE PRISONERS

Grasping these facts anent imprisonment how, to be practical, can a man become a releasing agent for the "prisoners of the planet"? What can humanity as a whole achieve along this line? What can the individual do?

The task of humanity falls primarily into three divisions of labour. Three groups of prisoners can be released, and will eventually find their way out of their prison house through the instrumentality of man. Already human beings are working in all three fields:

1. Prisoners within the human form. This involves working with one's fellow man.

2. Prisoners within the animal kingdom, and already much is being done in this field.

3. Prisoners within the forms of the vegetable world. A beginning has been made here.

Much work is being accomplished by man for men, and through the agency of scientific, religious and educational endeavour, the human consciousness is steadily expanding, until one by one the Sons of God are breaking through their limitations into the world of souls. In the retrospect of history, the picture of the emerging prisoner, Man, can be seen in clear delineation. Little by little he has mastered the planetary boundaries; little by little he has grown from the stage of cave man to that of a Shakespeare, a Newton, a Leonardo da Vinci, an Einstein, a St. Francis of Assisi, to a Christ and a Buddha. The capacity of man to achieve in any field of human expression, seems practically unlimited, and if the past few thousand years have seen such a stupendous growth, what shall we see in the next five thousand years? If prehistoric man, little more than an animal, has grown into the genius, what unfoldment is not possible as more and more of innate divinity makes its presence felt? The superman is with us. What will the world manifest when *all* mankind is tending towards a concrete manifestation of superhuman powers?

Man's consciousness is being released in varying directions and dimensions. It is expanding into the world of spiritual realities and beginning to embrace the fifth or spiritual kingdom, the kingdom of souls. It is interpenetrating, through scientific research, the world of superhuman endeavour, and investigating the many aspects of the Form of God, and of the forms that constitute the Form.

In touching upon the work of humanity in releasing the prisoners in the vegetable and animal kingdom, I want to point out two things, both of profound importance:

First, in order to release the "prisoners of the planet" that come under the title of *subhuman,* man has to work under the influence of the *intuition*; when working to release his fellow men he has to know the meaning of *Illumination.*

When the true nature of *Service* is comprehended, it will be found that it is an aspect of that divine energy which works always under the destroyer aspect, for it destroys the forms in order to release. Service is a manifestation of the Principle of Liberation, and of this principle, death and service, constitute two aspects. Service saves, liberates and releases on various levels, the imprisoned consciousness. The same statements can be made of death. But unless service can be rendered from an intuitive understanding of all the facts in the case, interpreted intelligently, and applied in a spirit of love upon the physical plane, it fails to fulfil its mission adequately.

When the factor of spiritual illumination enters into that service, you have those transcendent Lights which have illumined the way of humanity, and have acted like search-lights, thrown out into the great ocean of consciousness, revealing to man the Path he can and must go.

I would like to point out another thing. I have given no specific rules for releasing the prisoners of the planet. I have made no classification of the prisons and their prisoners, nor of the methods of work nor of techniques of release.

I urge only upon each and all who read these Instructions the necessity for renewed effort to fit themselves for service by a conscious and deliberate effort to develop the intuition and to achieve illumination. Every human being who reaches the goal of light and wisdom, automatically has a field of influence which extends both up and down, and which reaches both inwards to the source of light and outwards into the "fields of darkness". When he has thus attained he will become a conscious centre of life-giving force, and will be so without effort. He will stimulate, energise and vivify to fresh efforts all lives that he contacts, be they his fellow aspirants, or an animal, or a flower. He will act as a transmitter of light in the darkness. He will dispel the glamour around him and let in the radiance of reality.

When large numbers of the sons of men can so act, then the human family will enter upon its destined work of planetary service. Its mission is to act as a bridge between the world of spirit and the world of material

forms. All grades of matter meet in man, and all the states of consciousness are possible to him. Mankind can work in all directions and lift the
subhuman kingdom into heaven and bring heaven down to earth.
(4-535/8)

105. TRAINING

(a) TRAINING OF DISCIPLES

1. Only as the man becomes *intuitive* does he become of use in a Master's
group, and I commend to all aspirants that they most carefully study the
meaning and significance of the intuition. When it is beginning to function, then the disciple can pass from the stage of probation to that of
acceptance in a Master's group.

You might ask here how this can be known or ascertained by the probationer.

A great deal of training is given to a probationer without his really
recognising it consciously. Fault tendencies are indicated to him as he
seeks with sincerity to train himself for service, and the analysis of motive
when truthfully undertaken, serves amazingly to lift the would-be disciple
out of the astral or emotional world into that of the mind. It is in the
mental world that the Masters are first contacted, and there They must
be sought.

But the time has come when the Light in the head is not only present,
but can be somewhat used. The karma of the aspirant is such that it
becomes possible for him, through strenuously applied effort, to handle
his life in such a way that he can not only fulfil his karma and carry out
his obligations, but has sufficient determination to enable him to handle
the problems and obligations of discipleship also. His service to others is
carried out with the right motive, and is beginning to count and make its
power felt, and he is losing sight of his own interests in those of others.
When this occurs certain esoteric happenings take place.

The Master confers with some of His senior disciples as to the advis-
ability of admitting the aspirant within the group aura, and of blending his
vibration with that of the group. Then, if decision is arrived at, for the
space of two years a senior disciple acts as the intermediary betwixt the
Master and the newly accepted aspirant. He works with the new disciple,

stepping down (if I so might express it) the vibration of the Master so as to accustom the disciple's bodies to the higher increased rate. He impresses the disciple's mind, via his Ego, with the group plans and ideals, and he watches his reaction to life's occurrences and opportunities. He practically assumes, protem, the duties and position of Master.

All this time the aspirant remains in ignorace of what has happened and is unaware of his subjective contacts. He, however, recognises in himself three things:

Increased Mental Activity

This at first will give him trouble, and he will feel as if he were losing in mind control instead of gaining it, but this is only a temporary condition and gradually he will assume command.

Increased Responsiveness to Ideas, and increased capacity to vision the Plan of the Hierarchy. This will make him, in the early stages fanatical to a degree. He will be continually swept off his feet with new ideals, new "isms", new modes of living, new dreams for race betterment. He will take up one cult after another as they seem to make possible the coming millennium. But after a time he regains poise, and purpose assumes control of his life. He works at his own job, and carries forward his contribution to the activity of the whole, to the best of his ability.

Increased Psychic Sensitiveness

This is both an indication of growth and at the same time a test. He is apt to be taken in by the allurements of the psychic powers; he will be tempted to side-track his efforts from specialised service to the race, into the exploitation of the psychic powers, and their use for self-assertion. The aspirant has to grow in all parts of his nature, but until he can function as the soul, the psyche, consciously and with the use of co-operative intelligence, the lower powers must be quiescent. They can only be safely used by advanced disciples and initiates. They are weapons and instruments of service to be then used in the three worlds by those who are still tied by the Law of Rebirth to those worlds. Those who have passed through the great Liberation and have "occultly crossed the bridge" have no need to employ the powers inherent in the lower sheaths. They can use the infallible knowledge of the intuition, and the illumination of the principle of Light.   (4-167/9)

2. The training of the New Age, and the coming technique to use in fitting disciples for their work, is *through service to achievement,* with the emphasis upon the service and not upon achievement. Your work in

the world, and your work in my group of disciples, is your mode of future inner development. To your group of students you bring what mental power you have, and develop it thereby; to the group you bring your intuitional capacity, and by constant use it also grows. You are thereby led forward, and the group contribution to other groups is deepened. (5-292)

3. The Master does not train a group of men and women to be good and obedient disciples, carrying out His wishes and working out His purposes. He is training them eventually to take initiation and become Masters themselves, and He never loses sight of this objective. You, as disciples, have therefore to learn to handle force and to draw energies into the destined area of service, and this is a fact you must constantly have in mind.   (5-691)

4. As you extend your power to grasp the needed lessons, and learn to train your minds to think in ever wider and more abstract terms, you draw from me a correspondingly adequate instruction. The limitation to the imparted truth lies on your side and not on mine.   (6-11)

5. One of the most needed things for all disciples is to apply the teaching I may give to the idea of promoting and increasing their world service, thus rendering practical and effective in the world the teaching received, and the stimulation to which they have been subjected.   (6-12)

6. I have told you that changes are imminent in the training of the initiates of the future, and that the techniques of developing a disciple's consciousness will be different to those used in the past. They will not be the same as those hitherto employed in the East. These have motivated the teaching along this line which has gone out in the West. This does not mean that the earlier methods were not correct and right. It means that the intelligent grasp of the disciple and the initiate is now so advanced (relatively speaking) that the old methods would no more apply than do the simple sums in arithmetic, set in grammar school, aid the progress of the college graduate.   (6-276)

7. The world is full of teaching and of books able to inspire and help all true seekers after spiritual knowledge. The last fifty years have seen much teaching given out and much esoteric training given to the world and available now to all who earnestly seek it. Aspirants have much to work upon and much theory to render into practice, and this leaves the Masters free for more important work.   (14-107)

8. This Science of Meditation and the conscious building of the antahka-rana, will be the first two preliminary stages in the esoteric curriculum. Today, the true teaching of meditation and the construction of the bridge of light between the Triad and the personality, are the most advanced teaching given anywhere.

Humanity is, however, ready for exceedingly rapid development, and this readiness will demonstrate increasingly in the postwar period (written 1943: *Compiler*), and for it the disciples of the world must make ready. Two factors will bring this about: the first is the tremendous stimulation which the war, its demands and its consequences have given to the human consciousness, and secondly, the coming in of very advanced souls ever since the year 1925. These souls will be ready to give the needed training and instruction when the right time comes, having brought it over with them when they came into incarnation, and knowing normally and natural-ly what the modern esoteric student is struggling to grasp and under-stand.   (18-122/3)

(b) TRAINING OF STUDENTS

1. This Rule (Four) warrants the closest consideration and study. Rightly understood and rightly studied, it would lead each aspirant out of the phenomenal world into the kingdom of the soul. Its instructions, if carried out, would lead the soul back again into the phenomenal world as the cre-ating force in soul magic and as the manipulator and dominating factor of, and through, the medium of the form.

In the training of the occidental student, blind unquestioning *obedience* is never asked. Suggestions are made as to method and as to a technique which has proved effective for thousands of years and with many disciples. Some rules as to breathing, as to helpful process and as to practical living on the physical plane will be imparted, but in the training of the new type of disciple during the coming age, it is the will of the watching Gurus and Rishis that they be left freer than has heretofore been the case. This may mean a slightly slower development at the beginning but will result, it is hoped, in a more rapid unfoldment during the later stages upon the Path of Initiation.

Therefore, students are urged to go forward during their period of train-ing with courage and with joy, knowing that they are members of a band of disciples, knowing that they are not alone but that the strength of the band is theirs, the knowledge of the band is theirs too as they de-velop the capacity to apprehend it—and knowing also that the love and wisdom and understanding of the watching Elder Brothers are back of every aspiring Son of God, e'en though apparently (and wisely) he is left to wrestle through to the light in the strength of his own omnipotent soul   (4-152/3)

2. At present you are not working along New Age lines, for your work is along the old lines—of superior teachers, gathering their groups around *them*, of mystery where there is no mystery, because there is no mystery in esoteric teaching, and this is a lesson which you sorely need to learn, and of criticism (openly critical) of the student, which is sadly lacking in love. No New Age teacher gathers a group around himself, exacting their loyalty and obedience, nor does he shut the door to other aspects of truth, as you have done. He offers the teaching, and regards himself as only a student.   (6-528)

(c)   RULES OF LIFE FOR THE YOUNG ASPIRANT

The young and promising aspirants must be sought out and carefully inculcated with the trend of the new ideals. They must be taught to look for the divine and the good in all—both people and circumstances. Breadth of vision must be developed and that wide horizon pointed out which will enable the aspirants to live through this transitional period which is now with us, so that when they reach middle life they will stand as pillars of strength in the new world. Do not narrow them down to the ancient disciplines, and teach them not to lay emphasis upon diet, celibacy, times and seasons, and so distract their attention away from the newer and sacred art of being and the wonder of living as a soul.

Forget not that when a man is living as a soul and his entire personality is therefore subordinated to that soul, unselfish purpose, purity of life, conformity to law and the setting of a true example of spiritual living will normally and automatically follow. Food, for instance, is frequently a matter of climatic expediency and of taste, and that food is desirable which keeps the physical body in condition to serve the race. Again, a divine son of God can surely function as freely and as effectively when in the married state as in the celibate; he will, however, brook no prostitution of the powers of the body to the grosser satisfactions, nor will he offend against established custom, nor lower the standard which the world has set for its highest and best. The issues have been confused and the emphasis has been too often laid upon the physical acts and not upon the life of the actor. When the attention is fixed upon the soul, the physical plane life will be rightly handled. It will be realised that there is greater hindrance to the growth of the man in spiritual being, through a critical attitude or a state of self satisfaction, than by the eating of meat.

Two rules of life activity must be taught the young aspirant:

He must be taught to focus on constructive activity, and to refrain from pulling down the old order of living. He must be set to building for the future, and to thinking along the new lines. He must be warned not to waste time in attacking that which is undesirable, but must instead bend all his energies to creating the new temple of the Lord through which the glory may be manifested. In this way public attention will gradually be focussed upon the new and beautiful, and the old established creations will fall into decay for lack of attention, and so disappear.

He must be taught also that partisanship is in no way a sign of spiritual development. He will not therefore use the words *anti* this or *pro* that. Such terms automatically breed hatred and attack, and effort to resist change. They put the user on the defensive. Every class of human beings is a group of brothers. Catholics, Jews, Gentiles, occidentals and orientals, are all the sons of God.   (4-419/21)

106. TEACHING

1. Use the knowledge which you have to emphasise the facts of which you are sure. Take your stand upon the basic certainties, and remember, that in the synthesis of the apparently contradictory complexities, there will come eventually enlightenment. . . . In occult training, the old adage remains profoundly true, that "a little knowledge is a dangerous thing". The Path leading to omniscience is one of pitfalls and of difficulties. Has it ever struck you what complexities the Great Ones face as They deal with a constantly changing humanity? Principles remain eternally the same. But techniques and methods of presentation alter with each cycle, because the receiving equipment of man steadily alters and improves. This improvement does not necessarily mean an easier type of pupil; it often means the reverse. The Teacher has not only to impart the old truth in a new way, but has often to offset the established habits of thought and the impatience of a too eager mind.   (5-347)

2. Constant reading, and consciousness of instructions and teaching which are *not* carried through into action upon the outer plane, simply present

a way of escape from reality. Unless a Master's instructions meet with an experimental response, they loosen the ashramic tie, and eventually the disciple slips into an interlude (sometimes of great length and involving several lives) of drifting, of reading and thinking and not working, of the pleasure of attention without the pain of accomplishment.   (6-39)

3. Transmit the teaching to those you serve, but be not occupied or interested in the sources or origins of this teaching. *They matter not.* Nevertheless, the responsibility of the teacher rests upon you. The teacher should be so occupied with the need of the taught and with the clarification of the truth as it is given to him, in terms that they can comprehend, that he cannot be sidetracked through undue interest in the origin of the revelation.   (6-493)

4. The true teacher must deal in truth and in sincerity with all seekers. His time (in so far as he is held by the time equation on the physical plane) is too valuable to waste in social politeness or in refraining from making critical comment where a good purpose would be served. He must depend thoroughly upon the sincerity of those whom he teaches. Nevertheless, criticism and the pointing out of faults and errors does not always prove helpful; it may but increase responsibility, evoke antagonism or unbelief, or produce depression—three of the most undesirable results of the use of the critical faculty.

By stimulating their interest, by producing a subjective synthesis in the group he is teaching, and by fanning the flame of their spiritual aspiration, the group may arrive at a right discrimination as to their joint quality and necessities, and thus they will render the ordinary faultfinding attitude of the teacher unnecessary.

Those upon the teaching ray will learn to teach by teaching. There is no surer method, provided it is accompanied by a deep love, personal yet at the same time impersonal, for those who are to be taught. Above everything else, I would enjoin upon you the inculcation of the group spirit, for that is the first expression of true love. Two points only would I make :

First of all, in teaching children up to fourteen years of age, it is necessary to bear in mind that they are emotionally focussed. They need to *feel*, and rightly to feel beauty, strength and wisdom. They must not be expected to rationalise before that time, even if they show evidence of the power so to do. After fourteen years, and during adolescence, their normal mental response to truth should be drawn out and counted upon to deal with presented problems. Even if it is not there, an effort should be made to evoke it.

Secondly, an attempt should be made to approximate the child's place upon the ladder of evolution, by a study of his background, his physical equipment, the nature of his response apparatus with its varied reactions, and his major interests. This enquiry sets up a subjective rapport with the child, which is far more potent in its results than would be months and months of strenuously used words in the effort to convey an idea. (12-13/4)

5. What is taught should matter. The aspects of truth which I present to your consideration should count; the measure of help which I can give and the spiritual and mental stimulation to recognise spiritual truth should be the subject of your effort. The sole authority is the teaching, and not the teacher; upon the rock of authority many schools have foundered. There is but one authority—each man's own immortal soul, and that is the only authority which should be recognised.

... We are training men to live as souls and not as children to be nursed and cared for in a protected nursery run by rules and orders. . . . In the light of your own intuition and illumined mind (developed and brought to usefulness through meditation) take that aspect of the teaching which suits and aids you, and interpret it in the light of your own need and growth.

The days of *personality* contact, of *personality* attention and of personal messages are over, and have been over for quite a while, save in the vale of illusion, on the astral plane. This is a hard message, but no true disciple will misunderstand. From the depths of his own experience and struggle he knows it to be so. It is the group of Masters, the Hierarchy as a whole, that is of moment, and its interaction with humanity; it is the Masters' group of disciples that counts, and its relation to probationary disciples on the physical plane, who are seen by the group as existing in group formation all over the world, no matter where its units may be; it is the body of teaching that can be made available, and its effect upon the collective mind of the thinkers of the race, that is of vital importance; it is the interplay between the subjective group of world workers and—on the outer plane of objectivity—the lovers of humanity which seems to us, the teachers, to be of supreme importance. The satisfying of individual aspiration, the meeting of the desire of the probationers, and the feeding of spiritual ambition, appeal to us not at all. The times are too serious, and the crisis too acute.

It is of course a fact that there are today groups of aspirants receiving definite instruction, and disciples being subjected to definite training. But it must be remembered (in spite of all statements by the devotees of the world to the contrary) that no training is given in these cases as to the handling of the details of the personality life; the specific problems of health, finance and family concerns, are not dealt with nor considered; nor is comfort given or time taken to reassure or satisfy the unstable personality. Training aspirants as to the technique of spiritual growth *is* undertaken; correction of the hidden factors producing emotional conditions may be suggested; meditations may be arranged in order to bring about certain results; but no personality work is attempted. Disciples handle their own personalities. In the pressure of world work, the Masters are finding Themselves with less and less time to give even to Their disciples. How then do those who are not in the ranks of accepted disciples expect the Master to have the time to deal with their little affairs? (14-111/4)

6. It may be profitable to provide material whereby the mental bodies of the students can grow, and wherein they can find sustenance and the means to develop. Few people can evolve from within themselves the thoughts and ideas which should lead them on in the realisation of truth; and those of us, therefore, who are responsible for the teaching of the race, must perforce provide that which is required. Also, in so doing, we work for the coming generation of enquirers, knowing full well that the advanced teaching of today, and the new ideas which influence the pioneers of humanity, become the inspiration of the thinking public in the succeeding generation, and the theology, in due time, of that which follows them. The beliefs and knowledges of the esotericists of today (of the real spiritual esotericists, not of the so-called esoteric groups) are resolved into the formulas of faith of their successors, and become eventually identified with religious beliefs and organisations. (14-232)

7. If you will have patience and will be willing to learn by absorption more than by analysis, you will later discover that you know much—intuitively and discriminately. (17-308)

107. TRANSMISSION OF TEACHINGS

1. I would like to point out certain factors and methods which should be borne in mind in connection with *inspirational writing* and mediumship, and which have a bearing on the writing of such books as *The Secret Doctrine*, the Scriptures of the world, and those transmitted volumes which potently affect the thought of the race. The interpretation of the process arises from many causes; the status of the writers can be over-estimated or not sufficiently appreciated; terms used by the transmitter, being dependent upon his educational status, may also be incorrect or give rise to misinterpretation. It is necessary, therefore, that some understanding of the process should be found.

Some transmitters work entirely on astral levels, and their work is necessarily part of the great illusion. They are unconscious mediums and are unable to check the source from whence the teachings come; if they claim to know that source, they are frequently in error. Some receive teaching from discarnate entities of no higher evolution, and frequently of lower, than themselves. Some are simply abstracting the content of their own subconsciousnesses, and hence we have the beautiful platitudes, couched on Christian phraseology, and tinctured by the mystical writings of the past, which litter the desks of disciples, working consciously on the physical plane.

Some work only on mental levels, learning, through telepathy, that which the Elder Brothers of the race and their own souls have to impart. They tap the sources of knowledge stored in the egoic consciousness. They become aware of the knowledge stored up in the brains of disciples on the same ray as themselves. Some of them, being outposts of the Master's consciousness, become also cognisant of His thought. Some use several of the methods, either consciously or unconsciously. When they work consciously, it is then possible for them to correlate the teaching given and, under the Law of Correspondences and through the use of symbols (which they see through mental clairvoyance), to ascertain the accuracy of their teaching. Those who work unconsciously (I refer not to astral psychics), can use only trust and discrimination until they are further evolved. They must accept nothing that contradicts facts imparted through the Lodge's great Messengers, and they must be ready to superimpose upon the modicum of knowledge which they possess, a further structure of greater extent.

Each generation now should produce its *seers*. I like the word spelt "seeers", for to see is to know. The fault of all of you is that you see not; you perceive an angle, a point of vision, a partial aspect of the great fabric of truth, but all that lies hidden behind is occult to your three dimensional vision. It is necessary for those who want to act as true transmitters and intermediaries between the Knowers of the race and the "little ones" that they keep their eyes on the horizon and seek thus to extend their vision; that they hold steadily the inner realisation that they already have and seek to increase its scope; that they hold on to the truth that all things are headed towards the revelation, and that the form matters not. They must seek pre-eminently to be dependable instruments, unswayed by passing storms. They must endeavour to remain free from depression, no matter what occurs; liberated from discouragement; with a keen sense of proportion; a right judgment in all things; a regulated life; a disciplined physical body and a whole-hearted devotion to humanity. When these qualities are present, the Masters can begin to use Their destined workers; where they are absent, other instruments must be found.

Some people learn at night and regularly bring over into their physical brain consciousness the facts they need to know and the teachings they should transmit. Many methods are tried, suited to the nature of the aspirant or chela. Some have brains that act telepathically as transmitters. I deal with the safer and rarer methods which utilise the mental vehicle as the intermediary between the soul and the brain, or between the teacher and the disciple. Methods of communication on the astral level, such as the ouija board, the planchette pencil, automatic writing, the direct voice, and statements made by the temporarily obsessed medium, are not utilised as a rule by chelas, though the direct voice has had its use at times. The higher mental methods are more advanced and surer—even if rarer.

The true transmitters from the higher egoic levels to the physical plane, proceed in one or other of the following ways:

i. *They write from personal knowledge*, and therefore employ their concrete minds at the task of stating this knowledge in terms that will reveal the truth to those that have eyes to see, and yet will conceal that which is dangerous from the curious and the blind. This is a hard task to accomplish, for the concrete mind expresses the abstract most inadequately and, in the task of embodying the truth in words, much of the true significance is lost.

ii. *They write because they are inspired*. Because of their physical equipment, their purity of life, their singleness of purpose, their devotion to humanity, and the very karma of service itself, they have developed the capacity to touch the higher sources from which pure truth, or symbolic truth, flows. They can tap thought currents that have been set in motion by that great band of Contemplators, called Nirmanakayas, or those definite, specialised thought currents originated by one of the great staff of teachers. Their brains, being receptive transmitters, enable them to express these contacted thoughts on paper—the accuracy of the transmission being dependent upon the receptivity of the instrument (that is, the mind and the brain) of the transmitter. In these cases, the form of words and the sentences are largely left to the writer. Therefore, the appropriateness of the terms used and the correctness of the phraseology, will depend upon his mental equipment, his educational advantages, the extent of his vocabulary and his inherent capacity to understand the nature and quality of the imparted thought and ideas.

iii. *They write because of the development of the inner hearing.* Their work is largely stenographic, yet is also partially dependent upon their standard of development and their education. A certain definite unfoldment of the centres, coupled with karmic availability, constitutes the basis of choice by the teacher on the subtler planes who seeks to impart a definite instruction and a specialised line of thought. The responsibility as to accuracy is therefore divided between the one who imparts the teaching and the transmitting agent. The physical plane agent must be carefully chosen and the accuracy of the imparted information, as expressed on the physical plane, will depend upon his willingness to be used, his positive mental polarisation, and his freedom from astralism. To this must be added the fact that the better educated a man may be the wider his range of knowledge and scope of world interests, the easier it will be for the teacher on the inner side to render, through his agency, the knowledge to be imparted. Frequently the dictated data may be entirely foreign to the receiver. He *must* have a certain amount, therefore, of education, and be himself a profound seeker of truth before he will be chosen to be the recipient of teachings that are intended for the general public or for esoteric use. Above everything else, he must have learnt through meditation to focus himself on the mental plane. Similarity of vibration and of interests hold the clue to the choice of a transmitter. Note that I say; similarity of vibration and of interests and not equality of vibration and of interests.

This form of work might be divided into three methods: There is *first* the *higher clairaudience* that speaks directly from mind to mind. This is not exactly telepathy, but a form of direct hearing. The teacher will speak to the disciple as person to person. A conversation is therefore carried on entirely on mental levels with the higher faculties as the focussing point. The use of the head centres is involved and they must both be vivified before this method can be employed. In the astral body the centres corresponding to the physical, have to be awakened before astral psychism is possible. The work that I refer to here involves a corresponding vivification in the mental body counterparts.

Secondly, we have *telepathic communication*. This is the registry in the physical brain consciousness of information imparted:

(a) Direct from Master to pupil; from disciple to disciple; from student to student.

(b) From Master or disciple to the ego and thence to the personality, via the atomic sub-planes. You will note therefore that only those in whose bodies atomic sub-plane matter is found, can work this way. Safety and accuracy lie in this equipment.

(c) From ego to ego via the causal body and transmitted direct according to the preceding method or stored up to work through gradually and at need.

Thirdly, we have *inspiration*. This involves another aspect of development. Inspiration is analogous to mediumship, but is entirely egoic. It utilises the mind as the medium of transmission to the brain of that which the soul knows. Mediumship usually describes the process when confined entirely to the astral levels. On the egoic plane this involves inspiration. Ponder on this explanation for it explains much. Mediumship is dangerous. Why is this so? Because the mental body is not involved and so the soul is not in control. The medium is an unconscious instrument, he is not himself the controlling factor; he is controlled. Frequently also the discarnate entities who employ this method of communication, utilising the brain or voice apparatus of the medium, are not highly evolved, and are quite incapable of employing mental plane methods.

Some people combine the method of inspiration and of receiving instruction along various lines and, when this is the case, great accuracy of transmission is found. Occasionally again, as in the case of H.P.B. you have deep knowledge, ability to be inspired and mental clairaudience combined. When this is the case, you have a rare and useful instrument for the aiding of humanity.

Inspiration originates on the higher levels; it presupposes a very high point in evolution, for it involves the egoic consciousness and necessitates the use of atomic matter, thus opening up a wide range of communicators. It spells safety. It should be remembered that the soul is always good; it may lack knowledge in the three worlds, and in this way be deficient; but it harbours no evil. Inspiration is always safe, whereas mediumship is always to be avoided. Inspiration may involve telepathy, for the person inspiring may do three things:

(a) He may use the brain of the appointed channel, throwing thoughts into it.

(b) He may occupy his disciple's body, the latter standing aside, consciously, in his subtler bodies, but surrendering his physical body.

(c) A third method is one of a temporary fusing, if I may so call it—an intermingling, when the user and the used alternate or supplement, as needed, to do the appointed work. I cannot explain more clearly.

iv. *They write what they see.* This method is not of such a high order. You will note that in the first case you have wisdom or availability on buddhic or intuitional levels; in the second case you have transmission from the causal body, from the higher mental levels; in the third case you have sufficient development to enable the aspirant to receive dictation. In the fourth case, you have the ability to read in the astral light but frequently no ability to differentiate between that which is past, that which is, and that which will be. Therefore you have illusion and inaccuracy. This is a method, however, sometimes used but—unless directly used under stimulation applied by a Master—it is liable to be most misleading, as is its corollary, astral clairaudience. It is the method of mental clairvoyance, and requires a trained interpreting mind, which is rare indeed to find.

In all these cases that I have cited, error may creep in owing to physical limitation and the handicap of words, but in the case of those who write from personal knowledge, the errors in expression will be of no real moment, whilst in the second and third cases the errors will be dependent upon the point in evolution of the transmitting agent. If, however, he couples intelligence, devotion and service, with his capacity to receive and hear, he will soon correct the errors himself and his understanding will grow.

Later two new methods will be employed which will facilitate the transmission of truth from the inner side to the outer plane. Precipitated writing will be given to those who can be trusted, but the time is not yet for its general use. It will be necessary to wait until the work of the esoteric schools has reached a more definite phase of development. Conditions as yet are not appropriate, but humanity is urged to be ready and open-minded and prepared for this development. Later will come the power to materialise thought-forms. People will come into incarnation who will have the ability temporarily to create and vitalise these thought-forms, and so enable the general public to see them. The time, however, is not yet. There is too much fear, and not enough experience of truth in the world. More knowledge must be acquired as to the nature of thought and of matter, and this must be followed experimentally by those with acute trained minds, a high rate of vibration, and bodies built of the finest matter. The attainment of this will involve discipline, pain, self-abnegation and abstinence. See you to it.   (4-174/82)

2. *Inspired Writing*

One of the interesting things that is happening, and one of the factors which will serve eventually in the work of demonstrating the fact of the soul, is the mass of communications, inspired writings, and telepathic dictations which is flooding the world today. As you know, the spiritualistic movement is producing a vast amount of this inspired or pseudo-inspired literature, some of it of the very highest order and unquestionably the work of highly evolved disciples, and some of it most mediocre in quality. The various theosophical societies have been the recipients of similar communications, and they are found in every occult group. True communications are frequently of deep spiritual value, and contain much teaching and help for the aspirant. Students of the times would do well to remember that it is the teaching that is of moment, not the supposed source; by their intrinsic value alone these writings and communications must be judged. These communications emanate in the majority of instances from the soul plane, and the recipient or the communicator (the intermediary of the scribe) is either inspired by his own soul, or has tapped the thought level and knowledge of the ray group to which his soul belongs. He tunes in on a reservoir of thought, and his mind and brain translate these thoughts into words and phrases.

In a lesser number of cases, the man who is receiving a dictation or writing is in telepathic rapport with some more advanced disciple than himself, and his mind is being impressed by some chela in his group. This chela, who is closer to the Master than he is, passes on to him some of the knowledge that he has absorbed through being able to live within the Master's aura. But the Master is not concerned in the process; it lies between the chela and the aspirant. In these cases the receiver of the communication is often misled, and thinks that the Master Himself is dictating to him, whereas in reality he has—through a more advanced chela than himself—tuned in on the Master's thought atmosphere.

None of the Masters of the sixth initiation (such as the Masters M. and K.H.) are at this time working through dictation with Their disciples. They are too much engrossed with world problems, and with the work of watching over the destinies of the prominent world figures in the various nations, to have any opportunity to dictate teaching to any particular disciple in some small field of activity and upon subjects of which sufficient is already known to enable the disciple to go ahead alone and unaided. Two of the Masters are working telepathically and through dictation with several accepted disciples, and Their effort is to inspire these disciples, who are active in world work, to greater usefulness in the Plan. They are working in this way in order to impress a few of the prominent thinkers in the field of science and of social welfare with the needed knowledge which will enable them to make the right moves in the emergence of the race into greater freedom. But I know of no others, in this particular generation, who are so doing, for They have delegated much of this work to Their initiates and disciples. The bulk of the communicators today (working through aspirants on the physical plane) are active working chelas of accepted degree who (living as they do in the thought aura of the Master and His group) are steadily endeavouring to reach all kinds of people, all over the world, in all groups. Hence the increasing flood of communications, of inspired writings and of personal messages and teaching.

When you add to the above the equally large flood of communications which emanate from the transmitters' own souls, and from the realm of the subconscious, you have accounted for the mass of the material going out now. In all this there is need for deep thankfulness at the growing responsiveness and sensitivity of man. (14-107/9)

3. The training of the aspirant, the indicating to him of possible trends and lines of evolution, and the definition of the underlying purpose, is all that it is wise to impart at the present stage in which the average aspirant finds himself. This has been attempted in these Instructions, and there has been given also some new teaching anent the emotional vehicle. In the next century, when man's equipment is better developed, and when a truer meaning of group activity is available, it will be possible to convey more information, but the time is not yet. All that is possible for me is to grope for those feeble words which will somewhat clothe the thought. As they clothe it they limit it, and I am guilty of creating new prisoners who must ultimately be released. All books are prison houses of ideas, and only when speech and writing are superseded by telepathic communication, and by intuitive interplay, will the plan and the technique of its ex-

pression be grasped in clearer fashion. I talk in symbols; I manipulate words in order to create a certain impression; I construct a thought-form which, when dynamic enough, can impress the brain of a transmitting agent, such as yourself. But, as I do so, I know well how much must be left unrelated, and how seldom it is possible to do more than point out a cosmology, macrocosmic or microcosmic, which will suffice to convey a temporary picture of divine reality.

. . . But how can the whole be comprehended by the part? How can the entire Plan be noted by a soul which sees as yet but a tiny fraction of the structure? Bear this steadily in mind as you study and ponder these Instructions, and remember that, in the light of the future knowledge of humanity, all that is here conveyed is like a fifth reader in grammar school to the text books utilised by a college professor. It will serve however to graduate the aspirant out of the Hall of Learning into the Hall of Wisdom, if he uses the information given.

Learn to be telepathic and intuitive. Then these forms of words and these ideas, clothed in form, will not be needed. You can then stand face to face with naked truth, and live and work in the terrain of *ideas* and not in the world of *forms*.   (4-523/4)

4. The teaching which I have given out has been intermediate in nature, just as that given by H.P.B., under my instruction, was preparatory. The teaching planned by the Hierarchy to precede and condition the New Age, the Aquarian Age, falls into three categories :

i. Preparatory, given 1875-90 . . . written down by H.P.B.

ii. Intermediate, given 1919-49 . . . written down by A.A.B.

iii. Revelatory, emerging after 1975 . . . to be given on a worldwide scale via the radio.

In the next century, and early in the century, an initiate will appear and will carry on this teaching. It will be under the same "impression", for my task is not yet completed, and this series of bridging treatises between the material knowledge of man and the science of the initiates, has still another phase to run.   (18-255)

108. ESOTERIC STUDIES

1. In the work of the present moment must the future possible developments be forgotten. . . . Working without attachment to results, is a hard lesson for all disciples to learn, but one well worth while. (5-105)

2. Waste not time in anxiety as to the phenomenal achievement. That *must* inevitably come if the fiery aspiration of each of you, and the power to persist is steadfastly nurtured. (5-107)

3. There are many paradoxes in what I am here giving you, and apparently some contradictions where orthodox occultism is concerned, but that is ever the case as the teaching expands in content, and the earlier all-inclusive facts are seen to be minor aspects of still greater facts. You can see, therefore, the significance and the importance of the dictum in *The Secret Doctrine* that the Hierarchy and all in the Council Chamber of Sanat Kumara (or Shamballa) have invariably passed through the human stage of evolution, for only human beings can perfectly blend and express life-reason, and only human intellect can consciously create what is needed in order to bring the needed stages of manifested life into being. (11-66)

4. The great hindrance to the work of the majority of the esoteric schools at this time, is their sense of separateness and their intolerance of other schools and methods. . . . There is no basic difference in teaching, even if the terminology used may vary, the technique of work is fundamentally identical. If the work of the Great Ones is to go forward as desired in these days of stress and of world need, it is imperative that these various groups should begin to recognise their real unity in goal, guidance and technique, and that their leaders should realise that it is fear of other leaders, and the desire that their group should be numerically the most important, which prompts the frequent use of the words, "This is a different discipline", or "Their work is not the same as ours". It is this attitude which is hindering the true growth of spiritual life and understanding among the many students gathered into the many outer organisations. At this time, the "great heresy of separateness" taints them. The leaders and members talk in terms of "our" and "your", of this "discipline" and that, and of this method being right (usually their own) and the other method which may be right, but is probably doubtful, if not positively wrong. Each regards their own group as specifically pledged to them and to their mode of instruction, and threaten their members with dire results if they co-operate

with the membership of other groups. Instead, they should recognise that all students in analogous schools, and working under the same spiritual impulses are members of the *one school* and are linked together in a basic subjective unity. The time must come when these various (and at present) separative esoteric bodies will have to proclaim their identity, when the leaders and workers and secretaries will meet with each other and learn to know and understand each other. Some day this recognition and understanding will bring them to the point where they will endeavour to supplement each other's efforts, exchange ideas with each other, and so in truth and in deed constitute one great college of esotericism in the world, with varying classes and grades, but all occupied with the work of training aspirants and preparing them for discipleship, or superintending the work of disciples as they prepare themselves to take initiation. Then will cease the present attempts to hinder each other's work by comparison of methods and of techniques, by criticism and defamation, by warning and the cult of fear, and the insistence of exclusiveness. It is these attitudes and methods which at this time are hindering the entrance of the pure light of truth.   (13-16/7)

109. EDUCATION

1. Modern education has been primarily competitive, nationalistic and, therefore, separative. It has trained the child to regard the material values as of major importance, to believe that his particular nation is also of major importance, and that every other nation is secondary; it has fed pride and fostered the belief that he, his group and his nation, are infinitely superior to other people and peoples. He is taught consequently to be a one-sided person, with his world values wrongly adjusted and his attitudes to life distinguished by bias and prejudice.

. . . The general level of world information is high, but usually biassed, influenced either by national or religious prejudices, serving thus to make a man a citizen of his own country but not a human being with world relations. World citizenship is not emphasised.   (12-38/9)

2. In the field of education united action is essential. Surely a basic unity of objectives should govern the educational systems of the nations, even though uniformity of method and of technique may not be possible. Differences of language, of background and of culture, will and should al-

ways exist; they constitute the beautiful tapestry of human living down the ages. But much that has hitherto militated against right human relations must and should be eliminated.

In the teaching of history, for instance, are we to revert to the bad old ways wherein each nation glorifies itself at the expense frequently of other nations, in which facts are systematically garbled, in which the pivotal points in history are the various wars down the ages—a history, therefore, of aggression, of the rise of a material and selfish civilisation and one which had the nationalistic and, therefore, separative spirit, which has fostered racial hatred and stimulated national prides? . . . Greed, ambition, cruelty and pride are the keynotes of our teaching of history and geography.

These wars, aggression and thefts, which have distinguished every great nation without exception, are facts and cannot be denied. Surely, however, the lessons of the evils which they wrought (culminating in the war 1914-45) can be pointed out, and the ancient causes of present day prejudices and dislikes can be shown and their futility emphasised. Is it not possible to build our theory of history upon the great and good ideas which have conditioned the nations and made them what they are, and emphasise the creativity which has distinguished all of them? Can we not present more effectively the great cultural epochs which—suddenly appearing in some one nation—enriched the entire world, and gave to humanity its literature, its art and its vision?

. . . The world itself is a great fusing pot, out of which the One Humanity is emerging. This necessitates a drastic change in our methods of presenting history and geography. Science has always been universal. Great art and literature have always belonged to the world. It is upon these facts that the education to be given to the children of the world must be built—upon our similarities, our creative achievements, our spiritual idealisms, and our points of contact. Unless this is done, the wounds of the nations will never be healed, and the barriers which have existed for centuries, will never be removed.

The educators who face the present world opportunity, should see to it that a sound foundation is laid for the coming civilisation; they must undertake that it is general and universal in scope, truthful in its presentation, and constructive in its approach. . . . They must lay an emphatic importance upon those great moments in human history wherein man's divinity flamed forth, and indicated new ways of thinking, new modes of human planning, and thus changed for all time the trend of human affairs. . . .

Two major ideas should be taught to the children of every country. They are: *The value of the individual and the fact of the one humanity.* . . . The value of the individual, and the existence of that whole we call *Humanity,* are most closely related. This needs emphasising. These two principles, when properly taught and understood, will lead to the intensive culture of the individual and then to his recognition of his responsibility as an integral part of the whole body of humanity.   (12-45/8)

3. The college or the university should in reality be the correspondence in the field of education, to the world of the Hierarchy; it should be the custodian of those methods, techniques and systems of thought and of life which *will relate a human being to the world of souls,* to the Kingdom of God, and not only to other human beings upon the physical plane; not only to the world of phenomena, but also to the inner world of values and quality.

Again I repeat, this fitting of a man for citizenship in the Kingdom of God is not essentially a religious activity, to be handled by the exponents of the great world religions. It should be the task of the higher education, giving purpose and significance to all that has to be done. If this seems idealistic and impossible to you, let me assure you that by the time the Aquarian Age is in full flower, this will be the assured and recognised objective of the educators of that time.   (12-49)

4. It should be remembered (and this is being more widely recognised) that the quality of the young children now coming into incarnation, is steadily getting better and higher. They are in many cases abnormally intelligent, and what you (in your technical parlance) call their I.Q., is frequently phenomenally high. This will be increasingly the case, until young people of fourteen will have the equipment and intelligence of the brilliant college men and women of today.   (12-50)

5. We might say that:

The *first* effort of education to civilise the child, will be to train and rightly direct his instincts.

The *second* obligation upon the educators will be to bring about this true culture, by training him to use his intellect rightly.

The *third* duty of education will be to evoke and to develop the intuition.

When these three are developed and functioning, you will have a civilised, cultured and spiritually awakened human being. A man will then be instinctively correct, intellectually sound, and intuitively aware.

His soul, his mind, and his brain will be functioning as they should, and in right relation to each other, thus again producing co-ordination and correct alignment.   (12-50)

6. The whole goal of the future and of the present effort, is to bring humanity to the point where it—occultly speaking—"enters into light". The entire trend of the present urge forward, which can be noted so distinctly in the race, is to enable the race to acquire knowledge, to transmute it into wisdom by the aid of the understanding, and thus to become "fully enlightened". *Enlightenment is the major goal of education.*   (12-52)

7. The keynote of the new education is essentially right interpretation of life, past and present, and its relation to the future of mankind; the keynote of the new religion must and should be right approach to God, transcendent in nature and immanent in man, whilst the keynote of the new science of politics and of government will be right human relations, and for both of these, education must prepare the child.   (12-57)

8. The output of men's thoughts in writing and in speech, embodying that which is old, that which is new and modern, and that which is superficial and relatively worthless, is so vast today that it is impossible to register it, and the lifetime of a book is brief. To crown all, there is a definite effort to bring the resources of education within the reach of every man upon the planet. This eventually will be done, and the intended type of education will accomplish the following things, thus laying the ground for the future unfoldment of the higher and better education :

i. Make available to the average citizen what has "come to light" in the past.

ii. Evoke interest in the new sciences and knowledge which are coming to light in the present.

iii. Develop the memory and the power to recognise that which is presented to the mind.

iv. Correlate the past with the present.

v. Train citizens in the rights and nature of possession, with the attention to the processes of enjoyment and right use of the material and intellectual gifts of life, and their relation to the group.

vi. Indicate, after due study, the right vocation.

vii. Teach the methods whereby the co-ordination of the Personality can be brought about.

All this will turn the man out into the arena of life with a certain amount of knowledge of what has been discovered in the past, and what is his intellectual heritage; with a certain amount of mental activity, which can be developed and trained if the man himself so desires it and brings it about by the right handling of himself in relation to his environment; with certain mental ideals, dreams and speculations, which can be transmuted into valuable assets if the man is dowered with persistence, if his imaginative faculties have not been dulled by an unbalanced, enforced curriculum, and if he has been fortunate enough to have a wise teacher and some understanding senior friends. (12-58/9)

9. One of our immediate educational objectives must be the elimination of the competitive spirit, and the substitution of the co-operative consciousness. Here the question at once arises: How can one achieve this and at the same time bring about a high level of individual attainment? Is not competition a major spur to all endeavour? This has hitherto been so, but it need not be.

Today the average child is, for the first five or six years of his life, the victim of his parents' ignorance or selfishness, or lack of interest. . . .

The damage done to children in the plastic and pliable years, is often irremediable, and is responsible for much of the pain and suffering in later life. What then can be done? What, apart from the more technical approaches outlined by me in earlier parts of this instruction, should be the effort on the part of parents and educators?

First, and above everything else, the effort should be made to provide an atmosphere wherein certain qualities can flourish and emerge:

i. *An atmosphere of love,* wherein fear is cast out and the child realises he has no cause for timidity, shyness or caution, and one in which he receives courteous treatment at the hands of others, and is expected also to render equally courteous treatment in return. This is rare indeed to find in schoolrooms, or in homes for that matter. This atmosphere of love is not an emotional, sentimental form of love, but is based upon a realisation of the potentialities of the child as an individual, on a sense of true responsibility, freedom from prejudice, racial antagonisms, and above everything else, *upon compassionate tenderness.* This compassionate tenderness is founded on the recognition of the difficulty of living, upon sensitivity to the child's normally affectionate response, and upon a knowledge that love always draws forth what is best in child and man.

ii. *An atmosphere of patience,* wherein the child can become, normally and naturally, a seeker after the light of knowledge; wherein he is sure of always meeting with a quick response to enquiry, and a careful reply to all questions, and wherein there is never the sense of speed or hurry. ... This impatience on the part of those upon whom they are so pathetically dependent, sows in them the *seeds of irritation,* and more lives are ruined by irritation than can be counted.

iii. *An atmosphere of ordered activity,* wherein the child can learn the first rudiments of responsibility. The children who are coming into incarnation at this time, and who can profit by the new type of education, are necessarily on the very verge of soul consciousness. One of the first indications of such soul contact, is a rapidly developing sense of responsibility. This should be carefully borne in mind, for the shouldering of small duties and the sharing of responsibility (which is always concerned with some form of group relation) is a potent factor in determining a child's character and future vocation.

iv. *An atmosphere of understanding,* wherein a child is always sure that the *reasons* and motives for his actions will be recognised, and that those who are his older associates will always comprehend the nature of his motivating impulses, even though they may not always approve of what he has done or of his activities. ...

It is the older generation who foster in the child an early and most unnecessary sense of guilt, of sinfulness and of wrong doing. So much emphasis is laid upon petty little things that are not really wrong, but are annoying to the parent or teacher, that a true sense of wrong (which is the recognition of failure to preserve right relations with the group) gets overlaid and is not recognised for what it is. The many small and petty sins, imposed upon children by the constant reiteration of "No", by the use of the word "naughty", and based largely on parental failure to understand and occupy the child, are of no real moment. If these aspects of the child's life are rightly handled, then the truly wrong things, the infringements upon the rights of others, the encroachments of individual desire upon group requirements and conditions, and the hurting or damaging of others in order to achieve personal gain, will emerge in right perspective and at the right time. Then the voice of conscience (which is the whisper of the soul) will not be deadened, and the child will not become anti-social. He only becomes anti-social when he has not met with understanding, and therefore does not understand, or when circumstances demand too much of him.   (12-74/8)

110. GROUP ASPECTS

(a) THE LAW OF GROUP LIFE

1. Our group relations must be seen and acknowledged. Not only must a man fulfil in love his family and national obligations, but he must think in the wider terms of humanity itself, and so bring the Law of Brotherhood into expression. Brotherhood is a group quality. The young people who are now coming in will come into life equipped with a much deeper sense of the group, and with their group awareness much more fully developed than is now the case. They will solve their problems, including the sex problem, by asking themselves when situations arise of a difficult nature: Will this action of mine tend to the group good? Will the group be hurt or suffer if I do thus and so? Will this benefit the group and produce group progress, group integration, and group unity? Action which fails to measure up to the group requirements will then automatically be discarded. In the deciding of problems, the individual and the unit will slowly learn to subordinate the personal good and the personal pleasure to group conditions and group requirements. . . . An understanding of the Law of Rebirth, a goodwill towards all men, working out as harmlessness, and a desire for group goodwill, will gradually become determining factors in the racial consciousness, and our civilisation will adjust itself in time to these new conditions.   (14-302/3)

2. All the varying aspects of the life of God are interdependent, and not one proceeds onward into fuller realisation without benefitting the entire group.   (18-11)

(b) CHOOSING THE RIGHT WORKERS

1. The task of finding the right people and of inspiring them, is your immediate task. . . . You are in training as a wielder of men, and a guide of aspirants in the building work of the New Age upon which the Great Ones are now engaged. You must learn discrimination and understanding and right choice—through experiment, through failure and through success. All men are souls. Yes, my brother, but all men are not yet ready for disinterested service. Right judgment is a needed quality for you when considering people. For the work which you seek to vitalise, look not for the sweet, the gentle, the kind and tender, because so many very good people are oft unintelligent and lazy. Look for those strong souls who,

responding to the need of humanity and reacting to the impulse of love, are yet capable of thinking in strong terms, are vital in their planning, consecutive in their activity, and who waste no time in beautiful visionary dreams. The visionary mystic senses the ideal, but (using not his mind) makes no compromise between the wonderful ideas, which may materialise in a far distant future, and the present period of hard necessity. Look for those who may not resemble you in their second ray background, but who give you of their confidence and love because they recognise your wisdom, realise your inner link with the Hierarchy, and lean on your experience and soul strength. Attract not to yourself for the work you seek to do, the sweet and feeble, the weak, well-meaning, gently ineffectual person. *Look for the strong souls through whom you must learn to work.* Look for those who can co-operate with the Plan.

Look also for your co-workers outside the ranks of the psychologically distressed and the abnormal people. . . . You must refrain from welding them into any structure which you may build for the Great Ones. They are not yet ready, and would constitute poor stones in the building, and weak links in your work. You must build for the future.

. . . Symbolically I say to you: Look for those who have blended head and heart, and above whose foreheads shines the mystic symbol of the *builder.*

That you may integrate more freely and more fully in the work of the Great White Lodge, and enter into a closer fellowship and relationship with the builders of the New Age, is the earnest wish and prayer of your friend, your brother, and your teacher. (5-144/5)

2. When you can stand with greater firmness in spiritual being, and when you can work more definitely and consciously with the soul aspect, and less engrossingly with the personality, your life will simplify, and certain of your unique personality problems will disappear. Then, and only then, will your soul call to you those who can be your true co-operators.

One hint I will here give you: Look not for those who are *potential* spiritually, but who are not yet expressive, but look for those mature souls who do not need your help, but who seek your collaboration as you seek theirs. You have sought for your collaborators among those you help, but there you will not find them.

. . . One of the difficult things for humble aspirants to grasp, is that peculiar moment in their life history when they *must* shift into the realm of discriminating work. This fits them to work as we, the teachers upon the inner side, have learned to work. We work not with all who would demand our aid, but leave the "lesser lights" to be handled by our disciples and the lesser teachers. We confine ourselves to training those stronger souls, those more potent people whose lives can be "focussed in radiance" and whose response and effort warrant our endeavour. There are many gathered around you, my brother, to whom you have given much strength and teaching, and whose tendency is to confuse acquiescence in your teaching and acceptance of your strength, for the more difficult task of achieving divine self-confidence and innate, not borrowed, strength. Let such people *go* and—standing as a radiant centre of magnetic force—draw to yourself co-operators in the Plan, and not consumers of your energy. Go through the lists of those you have sought to help, and relinquish them to their own souls. Mind not their criticism, but dedicate yourself to more important work—a work which will appear when you have freed yourself from the clinging hands of well-meaning but weak-minded aspirants. Then, around the star which is your soul, will be many "shining points". There have been times when I have been hard put to it to find you, because of the obscuration brought about by those who surround and well nigh smother you as they cling to you. Stand free. . . .   (5-154/5)

(c)   GROUP TRAINING

The entire technique of training disciples for initiation, and of absorbing them into the various Ashrams which constitute the great Ashram of the Lord of the World, has been altered. The Masters are no longer concerned with an individual, here and there, who endeavours to go forward on the Path, who evidences capacity, and who is apparently ready for what has been called "the evocation of the initiate consciousness". It is becoming obvious to the Hierarchy that with the arrival of the Aquarian Age, group preparation, group initiation and group acceptance, must and will supersede the older methods. These older methods, built around the direct relationship between a Master and a disciple, reached their highest point of usefulness early in the Piscean Age.   (18-239)

(d)   GROUP INTEGRITY

1. The spiritual thought, resulting in magical work of one brother of pure intent, is of far greater potency than that of many brothers who follow the tendencies of the personality. Though every true aspirant, as he grasps the magnitude of the Plan and surveys the forces arrayed against him, may be overcome by the apparent futility of his effort, and the seeming smallness of the part he plays, let him remember that there is a steadily growing

group of those similar to him, and that this is a group effort. Under the Law, the Great Ones work through Their disciples in all countries, and never before have there been so many endeavouring to fit themselves for this function of being "Transmitters of the Purpose", and never before has there existed such a strong inner integrity and subjective relation between workers in all fields in all parts of the world. For the first time in history is there a coherent group for the Masters to use. Heretofore, there have been lonely, isolated workers, or tiny detached groups, and this has greatly hampered the work. Now this is changed.

I want to charge you all to realise this and to work to substantiate this group integrity, and to develop the power to recognise all such workers everywhere, under any name or organisation, and to co-operate with them when so recognised. This is no easy thing to do. It presupposes the following:

i. An inner sensitiveness to the Plan.

ii. An ability to recognise principles, governing conduct and administration.

iii. A capacity to overlook the non-essentials and to emphasise the essentials.

iv. A submergence of personal ambition and interest in the furthering of the group ideals.

v. A steady preservation of the inner contact through meditation and the overlooking and non-emphasis of personality reactions.

These are the basic prerequisites and should receive the attention of workers and students in all groups.

It would be of value if each student would link up every day at five o'clock, by an act of the will, with this rapidly integrating group of servers, mystics and brothers. To this end it might be wise to commit to memory the following brief dedication to be said silently at that hour, with the attention focussed in the head:

May the Power of the One Life pour through the group of all true servers.

May the Love of the One Soul characterise the lives of all who seek to aid the Great Ones.

May I fulfil my part in the One Work through self-forgetfulness, harmlessness, and right speech.

Then carry the thought forward from the rapidly forming group of world-servers to the Great Ones who stand back of our world evolution.

This can be done in a few seconds of time wherever one may be and in whatever company, and will not only aid in the magical work of the forces of light, but will serve to stabilise the individual, to increase his group consciousness, and to teach him the process of carrying forward interior subjective activities in the face of, and in spite of, outer exoteric functioning. (4-260/1)

2. There exist upon Earth, in every nation, men and women who (in some form or another) recognise the spiritual Hierarchy of the planet, who have a quality of non-separateness, definitely present or else rapidly developing, and who are gathered together in no limiting organisation, but primarily by their trend of thought and the habit of their activity. They constitute a group who are subjectively, spiritually, practically and openly creating a new form of human relationship. This new relation results in mutual understanding and a mental co-operation which recognises no barriers or national limitations. On the inner side of spiritual incentive and endeavour, they work today as one group; on the outer side of world affairs, they may not be aware of each other physically, or arrive at any open contact, yet they are animated by the same principles and are carrying forward—in all nations and in every great department of human thinking and planning—a similar work. (13-633/4)

3. (The New Group of World Servers) offer a practical expression of an existent unity, based upon oneness of motive, of recognition, of orientation (towards the spiritual world and towards the service of humanity), of methods and of ideas; and all this in spite of the fact that the physical plane relationship is usually non-existent and outer organisation and recognition lack. The unity is subjective, and for that reason is impervious to every taint of separateness. (18-299)

(e) BONDS OF SERVICE

1. Become more definitely a radiant centre of magnetic life, fusing the people with whom you may work through love and understanding. That is a hard and difficult task, for it means bringing together in the bonds of service many elements which might not otherwise fuse and blend. This involves an understanding, an analysis of human beings, and a slow and patient work. As your work may grow and its boundaries extend, you will be faced increasingly with the perplexities and difficulties incident

upon human relationships. These must be handled with impersonality, love and silence. Seek to integrate others into the service of
humanity by yourself standing in spiritual being and radiating love and
wisdom. . . . "Live on the mountain top and walk there with your
brothers. Keep the vision clear above the fogs of earth". (5-277)

2. No esoteric group is soundly handled and correctly motivated, unless
the spiritual energies which are available to it, and the knowledge and the
wisdom unfolded, find expression in definite service. (6-89)

(f) GROWTH THROUGH SHARING

1. The cycle now being inaugurated in the world is that of "Growth
through Sharing", and advanced humanity can now share the work, the
responsibility, and the trained reticence of the Hierarchy, whilst paralleling this and simultaneously, the mass of men are learning the lessons of
economic sharing; and, my brothers, in this lies the sole hope of the world.
   Every initiation to which disciples are admitted permits this closer occult sharing in the hierarchical life. This involves, for advanced humanity,
a noticeable increase in vitality and in vital tension and potency. Its reflection among the masses is shown in the constant demand for speed and in
the enormous speeding up of the life of mankind in every department of
living. This speeding up synchronises with the increasing readiness of disciples everywhere for initiation—according to their status and developed
ability.
   The difference . . . between the past and the present readiness lies in the
fact that in the past this readiness was a purely individual matter; today
it is something which is closely related to a man's group, and the individual aspect is of secondary importance. As time and speed increase in
importance for the masses of men, the disciple (ready for initiation) regards his personal advancement upon the Path as of far less importance
than his developed capacity to serve his fellow men, serving them through
the group with which he may be affiliated and to which he may be drawn.
For the disciple facing the first two initiations, this group will be some
exoteric body of men who claim his allegiance, and in which he learns
group co-operation and methods of working; for the more advanced disciple, it is the Ashram and direct service under the instigation of some
Master. (6-316/7)

2. Sharing is associated with that which is of value, which should be shared
if justice is to be demonstrated, and basically, with those values which are

life-giving. The sharing to which I am here referring is the sharing in all reactions, of all attitudes, of all types of wisdom, of all problems and difficulties and limitations, so that they become constructive in the group sense and cease to be destructive.   (6-328). See also (6-328/33)

(g) DISCIPLE AND GROUP RELATIONSHIPS

1. Perhaps I could here give some indications of the groups on the various planes to which a man is assigned. These groups are many and diverse, and at different periods of a man's life may change and differ, as he works out from under the obligating karma that governs the affiliations. Let us remember too that as a man enlarges his capacity to serve, he at the same time increases the size and number of the groups he contacts, till he reaches a point in some later incarnation when the world itself is his sphere of service and the multitude those whom he assists. He has to serve in a threefold manner before he is permitted to change his line of action and pass on to other work—planetary, systemic or cosmic.

i. He serves first *through activity,* through the use of his intelligence, using the high faculties of mind and the product of his genius to aid the sons of men. He builds slowly great powers of intellect and in the building overcomes the snare of pride. He takes then, that active intelligence of his and lays it at the feet of collective humanity, giving of his best for the helping of the race.

ii. He serves *through love,* becoming, as time elapses, one of the saviours of men, spending his life and giving of his all through perfect love of his brothers. A life then comes when the utmost sacrifice is made and in love he dies that others may live.

iii. He serves then *through power.* Proved in the furnace to have no thought save the good of all around, he is trusted with the power that follows from active love, intelligently applied. He works with the law, and bends all his will to make the power of the law felt in the threefold realms of death.

In all these three branches of service you will notice that the faculty of working with groups is one of paramount importance. These groups are diverse, as before I have said, and vary on different planes. Let us briefly enumerate them :

i. *On the physical plane.* The following groups will be found :

(a) His family group . . .

(b) His associates and friends . . .

(c) His associated band of servers . . .

ii. *On the emotional plane . . .*

iii. *On the mental plane . . .*

. . . As you will see, I have not specified certain dangers attacking any particular body. It is not possible to cover the subject thus. In later days, when occult meditation is more comprehended and the matter scientifically studied, students will prepare the necessary data and treatises covering the entire subject as far as then may be. I sound, however, a note of warning, I indicate the way, the teachers on the inner side seldom do more. We aim at developing thinkers and men of clear vision, capable of logical reasoning. To do this we teach men to develop themselves, to do their own thinking, reason out their own problems, and build their own characters. Such is the Path.   (2-115/9)

2. Every disciple has to learn to subordinate his own ideas of personal growth to the group requirements, for—in order to have a co-ordinated group, functioning as a serviceable unit—some disciples will have to hasten their progress in certain directions, and others will have to slow down theirs temporarily to the pace of the majority. This will happen automatically, if the group identity is the dominant factor in the thoughts of each disciple, and desire for personal growth and for spiritual satisfaction is relegated to a secondary place. The groups within each Ashram are intended to work together eventually, just as the various departments of some great organisation work together effectively as a unit. They must function smoothly and intelligently. This will be possible when the individual members in the groups and the individual groups lose sight of their own identities in an effort to make this experiment of the Hierarchy successful. The feelings, reactions, wishes and successes of the individual most emphatically do not count. Only that is regarded as of moment which will further group effort and enrich the group consciousness. Only that, for instance, attracts my attention, which brings more spiritual power to my group of disciples, or which increases its light or dims its radiance. You need to remember that I look at my groups of disciples always subjectively and *as a group.* It is the total radiance which I see; it is the united rhythm which I note, and the united tone and colour; it is the sound they collectively emit which I hear. May I reiterate that in one sense your individualities are of no interest or moment to me, except in so far as you raise or lower the group vibration. As personalities, you matter not to

us, the teachers on the inner side. As souls you are of vital moment. Each disciple in the group of any Master may have many weaknesses and limitations. These act as hindrances to others in the group. But, as souls, such disciples *are* somewhat awakened and alive, and have achieved a certain measure of alignment. So it is with all of you in my group. As souls I cherish you, and seek to aid and lift, to expand and enlighten.

I would like here to emphasise one point as we consider the individual in the group and his group relations. Watch with care your thoughts anent each other, and kill out at once all suspicion, all criticism, and seek to hold each other unwaveringly in the light of love. You have no idea of the potency of such an effort, or of its power to release each other's bonds, and to lift the group to an exceedingly high place.   (5-10)

3. No group can be used in world service that is not working in perfect accord, and this harmony must be attained *as a group*. It must be brought about, not through the process whereby people withdraw within themselves and thus inhibit that which upsets group equilibrium, but by the process of loving self-forgetfulness.   (5-194/5)

4. In the life of every aspirant, there comes a life wherein he finds the group to which he belongs. I refer to the inner group of disciples and the outer group of servers with whom he can and must co-operate. When these two discoveries synchronise (which is not always the case), much time is saved, and the opportunity is great.   (5-225)

5. The effect of the work you have been doing with the group . . . has been to feed *your* devotional nature, to emphasise *your* development, *your* training, *your* work, *your* need, and what is thought of *you*. None of it has been of any value to this group of disciples to whom you had pledged yourself or to your associates in service. . . . It has indeed produced a separating effect between yourself, your group and your surroundings.   (5-239)

6. All gained quality of any kind must be regarded by the individual as a group asset and not as a personal achievement. This requires emphasising and involves clear thinking and detachment on the part of group members. All true recognition calls for these qualities.   (5-280)

7. Not idly have you all been brought together into this close relation with each other. Therefore, give to each other more freely, but without criticism and enquiry; love and steady each other as you go through the needed fusing and testing.   (5-397)

8. Frequently disciples handicap themselves because, not having learnt to forget their personalities, they have an attitude of deep concern over demonstrated past failures and a consciousness of very real inadequacy. They become over-preoccupied with the personnel of the group and not with the group soul. You, as disciples, are too preoccupied with the inter-personality relationship, and are not sufficiently focussed upon the group-soul and upon the Master, the centre and the focal point of energy of the group. If you would reject all criticism, if you cultivate the joy of relationship, and seek ever to participate together in whatever spiritual blessing may be outpoured for the helping of the world, if you seek to contact the Master as a group, if you are in a position to know your group, and if you tune out all anxiety as to success or non-success in the apportioned service, you would greatly aid in the task with which the Master of any group is confronted. The needed fusion can always take place among disciples when they meet on the level of the soul and when the service to be rendered is the dominant factor, and not so much the *how* of rendering it; for this each disciple is independently responsible. (5-690/1)

(h) GROUP CONSCIOUSNESS

One of the ideas which a disciple should learn . . . is that he *is* already a part of the Hierarchy, whilst at the same time he is part of struggling, unhappy humanity. Therefore, he is not alone or isolated; he is a part of the Hierarchy because he has "entered with his group": this is a fact, even if he fails to comprehend the full implications of that phrase. At the same time, he learns that only in so far as he has developed group consciousness, and is beginning to function as "one absorbed within the group" can he truly pass into a closer and more vitally contributory relation to the Ashram to which he belongs. (6-358/9)

(i) TELEPATHIC SENSITIVITY

1. The need for telepathic sensitivity in every group composed of disciples, is based upon three necessities; I would like you to understand this more clearly:

i. The cultivation of an inter-relation of a telepathic nature upon the mental plane is essential. This has always been an established fact or condition in the case of a Master and His disciple, and between the senior disciples in any group of accepted disciples. The time has now

come when this group quality must—for the sake of a needy world—
be developed by disciples of lesser attainment in the group.

ii. This telepathic unfoldment will lead to a greater sensitivity to others.
This is the secret of a Master's work, and the factor which enables him
to work through His disciples, using them as outposts of His consciousness. To do this with exactitude, He must be able to know their condition (mental, psychical and physical) when He chooses so to know. He
can thus discover whether they are available or not for any specific
service, whether they can be safely used or not, and whether their sensitivity is such and their interpretation of what they sense is of sufficient
accuracy, so that they will respond intelligently to the need. Have I not
had to study all of you this way? Think this out and ponder upon the
implications.

iii. This telepathic sensitivity will also lead to the new science of intercommunication which, in the New Age, will reach general use and comprehension. Of this condition, the radio is the outer physical symbol.
(5-63)

2. It is through telepathy that ideas have been disseminated in the world,
by the process of mentally impressing the mind of some disciple or sensitive person. It is then their task to find and direct the mind and activities
of those individuals whose task is not only to be responsive to this impression, but to bring it out into the consciousness of the world thinkers.
(5-63/4)

3. How can this collective impressing go on and yet leave a man free?
Because it will be kept clear of all directed will-force; all that workers and
disciples in my groups will seek to do, is to impress certain minds with
the outlines or suggestions as to the Plan; these ideas will deal particularly
with the concept that separation is a thing of the past, and that unity is
the goal of the immediate future; that hatred is retro-active and undesirable, and that goodwill is the touchstone which will transform the world.

How then can you keep your minds free from your own interpretations? By achieving that poised and positive negativity on the part of the
two lower aspects of the personality—the astral body and the brain as
well as the etheric brain; these determine the reactions of the lower centres,
particularly of the solar plexus centre. The mind will then be left free to
fulfil three functions:

i. That of soul contact; this will result in illumination and a working
knowledge of the immediate aspects of the Plan.

ii. That of thought formulation and thought-form creation. Then a clear thought-form can be constructed with definiteness, and it can be positively directed.

iii. That of working on mental levels with your group brothers so that your thought-form is a part of their thought-form and you can, therefore, unitedly produce a living, embodied form which can be directed as I may determine.

Another question might here arise: Are there any specific and brief rules which should be obeyed? The following might be given, but I would remind you that it is what you *are* that counts in this work more powerfully than anything else. The controlling factor is *harmlessness* in thought and word; the practise of this, with proper observation, will greatly help all of you. Next comes a *refusal to think unkindly* or with criticism; this is essential in connection with those whose minds you seek to impress. *Silence,* complete and unbroken as to what you are doing, is also a vital factor; the utterance of words in connection with this most subtle and confidential work (or even discussion of the work with a fellow-disciple) can shatter the delicate thought-form which you are attempting to build. It can render the work of weeks abortive. A *balanced attitude* in relation to those in power throughout the world, must also be cultivated; they need above all else the inspiration which can be brought to them from the Hierarchy.

I would ask you, therefore, to practise purging the content of your minds of all critical and unkind thoughts, so that you can achieve an attitude of divine indifference to the ephemeral and fleeting personalities, and to the chaos everywhere to be seen, and so endeavour to tune in on the attitude of the Hierarchy. This involves the emphasis of the consciousness aspect and the careful observation of all that goes on beneath the surface-awakening, arousing and stimulating to a pronounced mental activity, the hitherto unconscious masses. The events which are happening in every country, are bringing this about with much rapidity; humanity is coming alive and its consciousness is awakening to the subjective values. The Hierarchy is sore beset to meet humanity's emerging need of guidance. The sensitivity of the human race (as the result of economic insufficiency, of war, anxiety and pain) is becoming so acute, that we who work on the inner side, must hasten to impress sensitive, awakening psychics, with the right impression. Hence our effort to create these groups, and to use people like yourselves, who are (theoretically) harmless, but actually full of prejudice and hasty judgments. We have to use the material which lies to hand, and are greatly handicapped at all times. (5-65/6)

(j) GROUP WORK

1. As birds fly together to summer realms, so souls unite in flight. Passing through the gate, they thus alight before the throne of God.

   Thus wrote an unknown saint of the Church, who travelled not alone. (5-291)

2. What should disciples in a Master's group look for as evidence of successful group work? First and foremost, as you well know, group integrity and cohesion. Nothing can be done without this. The subjective linking of the disciples with each other in their own group, and the linking of the group with other groups occupied with special work within the Ashram, and the emergence (as a result of this) of a group and an ashramic consciousness, are vital objectives. It is hoped that this will also eventuate in a telepathic interplay which will bring potent results and successful outer work. From these activities will emerge a group circulation of energy, which will be of service in world salvage. Each of you should remember that purity of body, control of the emotions and stability of mind are fundamental necessities, and should be daily the attempted achievement. Again and again, I come back to these prime character requirements and—tiresome as the reiteration may be—I urge upon you the cultivation of these qualities. I would like to remind you also that you are adult and mature men and women, who need not specific statements as to faults and characteristics. I seek only to make suggestion as to trends of thought. Note here the word *suggestion,* for that is all I seek to give. The disciple must be left free to follow a suggestion or a hint as seems wise to him. This entire work might be termed an experiment in esoteric commonsense and in willingness to accept suggestion. It is a trial of the intuition and a test in discrimination. This work to which I have called you, is also an experiment in impersonality, in willingness to work and learn, in freedom to choose or reject, in observation and in techniques. All have their value. (5-15/6)

3. As individuals, you may be of small importance; as units in the group which I am preparing and training for definite service in future lives even more than in this, you are of sufficient moment to warrant my interest. A group is no more powerful than its weakest link, and a group suffers esoterically and as a whole, and its power is definitely curtailed when one

member fails to measure up to opportunity, or recedes into the glamours of the personality. This you have seen happen. As individuals I seek to help you, but *only* with a view to your group integration, to your group influence and understanding, and your group love, plus the strength which you can each bring to the whole.

I, therefore, appeal to you, as a group, for an intensification of your group love, purpose and service, so that the inner, subjective integration may proceed apace.   (5-75)

4. In the New Age, which is upon us, all true work is *group work,* with the individual subordinated to the group good.   (5-343)

5. You will usually find . . . that it is easy to gather around you many little people, of relatively futile accomplishment (from the angle of world service) but that the finer minds have no time for such acquiescence; they proceed upon their way, leaving you to follow after and to catch up with them eventually.   (5-587)

6. Let me remind those I reach through these books, that the main result I look for is one of *group* co-operation and understanding, and not that of individual benefit. By studying and reading with care, a group interplay is set up, the group becomes more closely integrated, the units in it more closely linked together, and as a group more closely blended in the unfolding Plan of the Great Ones. We are building and planning for the future and for humanity, and not for the personal unfoldment of any particular aspirant. The individual growth is of no tremendous significance. The formation and development of a band of pledged aspirants, trained to work together and to respond in unison to a teaching, is of real moment to those of us who are responsible for the training and for the preparation of the group of world disciples who will function with freedom and power in a later cycle. You see a tiny portion of the Plan. We see the Plan as it unfolds for a series of lives ahead, and we are today seeking those who can be taught to work in group formation and who can constitute one of the active units in the vast happenings that lie ahead, connected with that two-thirds of humanity who will stand upon the Path at the close of the age, and with that one-third who will be held over for later unfoldment. We are training men and women everywhere so that they can be sensitive to the Plan, sensitive to their group vibration, and thus able to co-operate intelligently with the unfolding purpose. It is a mistake to think that the Plan is to train aspirants to be sensitive to the

vibration of a Master or to the Hierarchy. That is but incidental and of minor importance.

It is for the purpose of training aspirants so that group awareness may be developed, that these books have been written. Recognise clearly that you *personally* do not count, but that the *group* most surely does. Teaching is not given only in order to train you or to provide you with opportunity. All life is opportunity, and individual reaction to opportunity is one of the factors which indicate soul growth. For this, the training school of the world itself suffices. (14-xvii/iii)

7. The soul has to relinquish also the sense of responsibility for that which other disciples may do. . . . Each personality pursues its own course, must shoulder its own responsibilities, work out its own dharma, and fulfil its own karma, and so answer for itself to its Lord and Master, the Soul. . . . Only as servers co-operate from the standpoint of an inner subjective linking, can a united work be carried forward.

. . . Not as yet is the vision seen with a sufficient clarity by the many servers, to make them work with perfect unanimity of purpose and objective, of technique and method, or complete understanding and oneness of approach. That fluid, perfect co-operation lies as yet in the future. The establishing of an inner contact and relationship, based on a realised oneness of purpose and soul love, is magnificently possible, and for this all disciples must struggle and strive. On the outer plane, owing to the separative mind during this age and time, a complete accord on detail, on method, and on interpretation of principles, is not possible. But—the inner relationships and co-operation *must* be established and developed, in spite of the outer divergences of opinion. When the inner link is held in love, and when disciples relinquish the sense of authority over each other, and of responsibility for each other's activities, and at the same time stand shoulder to shoulder in the One Work, then the differences, the divergences, and the points of disagreement, will automatically be overcome.

There are three rules which are important to disciples at this time:

First, see to it that you permit no rift to appear in the inner relation in which you stand to each other. The integrity of the inner band of servers must be preserved intact.

Secondly, pursue your own duty and task, shoulder your own responsibility, and then leave your fellow disciples to do the same, free from the impact of your thought and criticism. The ways and means are many; the points of view vary with every personality. The principle of work is love for all men and service to the race, preserving at the same time a deeper inner love for those with whom you are destined to work. Each soul grows into the way of light through service rendered, through experience gained, through mistakes made, and through lessons learnt. That necessarily must be personal and individual. But the work itself is one. The Path is one. The love is one. The goal is one. These are the points that matter.

Thirdly, preserve ever in work the attitude of mind which must grow out of the two rules above, faithfully followed. Your point of view and consciousness are your own, and therefore, are for you right. Not necessarily is that which seems so clear to you and of such vital importance to you, of the same value or importance to your brothers. (15-106/7)

8. The group can be, and frequently is, responsive to the "bright centre", Shamballa, where the initiate by himself, and in his own essential identity, cannot so respond. The individual must be protected by the group from the terrific potencies which emanate from Shamballa. These must be stepped down for him by the process of distribution, so that their impact is not focussed in any one or all of his centres, but is shared by all the group members. Here is the clue to the significance of group work. One of its major functions, esoterically speaking, is to absorb, share, circulate, and then distribute energy. (18-68)

(k) LEADERSHIP

1. Know for what they are those who are in high position, guiding humanity, and whose responsibility it is to lead humanity out of slavery into freedom. Aid them with love, because they are where they are through their individual destiny and the guidance of their souls. . . .

The accepting of facts is one of the first duties of a disciple. In the task of aiding humanity, as a part of the Master's group or Ashram, the fact that there are men and women placed in positions of power, to carry out the divine Plan, is one of the first to be faced. This must be done uncritically, avoiding constant recognition of their limitations, with an understanding of their problem, with realisation of the call of their souls to yours, and the pouring upon them of a constant stream of "loving understanding". They are more advanced disciples than you are—little as this may be realised. They are—consciously or unconsciously—under the "impression" of the Masters; there is little that the average disciple can do for them in moulding their thought or in shaping their decisions. I refer of course to *the leaders of the Forces of Light* upon the outer physical plane. But disciples and aspirants can surround them with a guarding wall of light and love; they can refrain from handicapping them with thoughts of criticism which can swell the tide of criticism which the worldly minded pour out upon them. (5-706)

2. Leaders have to learn to stand alone, and can ever do so if they love enough. (6-704)

3. What are the lessons which all true leaders have to learn?

It might be of service to you if I put one or two before you—very briefly, so that you can (if truly in earnest to serve your fellow men, as I believe you are) begin to master them, to understand their need and to apply them to yourself with a view to fuller and more useful service.

The first is the *lesson of vision.* What are your goals? What is the spiritual incentive which will be and is strong enough to hold you steady to the purpose and true to the objective? No one can formulate the vision for you; it is your own personality problem, and upon the strength of the vision and the beauty of the picture which you paint with your imagination, will depend much that you do and become.

The second lesson is the *development of a right sense of proportion.* This, when truly developed and correctly applied, will enable you to walk humbly on the Way. No true leader can be anything but humble, for he realises the magnitude of his task; he appreciates the limitations of his contribution (in the light of the vision) and the need for constant self-development, and the cultivation of the spirit of steady inner spiritual learning, if he is ever to make his proper contribution. Therefore, keep learning; keep dissatisfied with yourself and your attainment, not in any morbid sense, but so that the principle of growth and of pushing forward, may be fostered in you. We help others through our own effort to attain; this means clear thinking, humility and constant adjustment.

The third lesson is the *development of the spirit of synthesis.* This enables you to include all within the range of your influence and also to be included within the range of influence of those greater than yourself. Thus is the chain of the Hierarchy established. . . .

Another lesson which in reality grows out of the above, is the *avoidance of the spirit of criticism,* for criticism leads to barriers and loss of time. Learn to distinguish the spirit of criticism from the ability to analyse and make practical application of analysis. Learn to analyse life, circumstances and people from the angle of the work, and not from the angle of your personality point of view; analyse also from the angle of the Ashram, and not from the angle of the executive or the schoolmaster upon the physical plane. (6-704/5)

4. Can your imagination picture to you your reaction when—because you are the leader—you have to shoulder all the blame for any failure, even when not personally responsible; you have to accept without retaliation the attacks of those you are trying to help, who expect too much from you, who force you to live in the blaze of public opinion; what will you do when your chosen workers fail to understand, or prove disloyal or criticise without warrant, or pit their ambition against you, and willfully refuse to see your point of view, and talk about you among other people and whip up resentments against you—resentments which are probably without foundation? These are not the kind of things that your personality easily accepts, and your creative imagination had better begin dealing with these problems so that the emerging principles of conduct may stand clear before you. Have you the inner grace of heart to admit error and weakness or to say that you made a mistake in technique or method of approach, in judgment or in speech, should need arise to heal a breach and in the interests of the work?   (6-707)

(1) NEW AGE GROUPS

1. To those of us who are working on the inner side, the workers in the world fall into three groups :

i. Those, few and far between, who are true Aquarians. These work under real difficulties, for their vision is beyond the grasp of the majority, and they meet often lack of understanding, frequent disappointment in their fellow workers, and much loneliness.

ii. Those who are straight Pisceans. These work with much greater facility and find a more rapid response from those around them. Their work is more doctrinal, less inclusive and coloured by the spirit of separation. They include the mass of world workers in all the various departments of human thought and welfare.

iii. Those Pisceans who are enough developed to respond to the Aquarian message, but who—as yet—cannot trust themselves to employ the real Aquarian methods of work and message.

For instance, they have in the political field, a sense of internationalism, but they cannot apply it when it comes to the understanding of others. They think they have a universal consciousness, but when it comes to a test, they discriminate and eliminate. They constitute a much smaller group than the true Pisceans, and are doing good work and filling a much needed place. The problem they present however to the Aquarian worker, lies in the fact that though they respond to the ideal and regard themselves as of the New Age, they are not truly so. They see a bit of the vision and have grasped the theory, but cannot express it in action.

Thus we have these three groups doing much needed work and reaching through their united undertakings the mass of people and fulfilling thus their dharma. One group works necessarily under the glamour of public opinion. The intermediate group has a most difficult task to perform, for where there is no clear vision the voice of their chosen environment and the voice of the inner group of world Knowers, are often in conflict, and they are pulled hither and thither as they respond first to one and then to the other. The group of those who respond more fully to the incoming Aquarian vibration, register the voices of the leaders of the other two groups, but the voice of the guiding Masters and the voice of the group of world Masters, serve to guide them unerringly forward. (4-632/3)

2. The seventh ray will bring to the consciousness of the coming initiates the concept of group service and sacrifice. This will inaugurate the age of the "divine service". The vision of the giving of the individual in sacrifice and service, within the group and to the group ideal, will be the goal of the masses of advanced thinkers in the New Age, whilst for the rest of humanity, brotherhood will be the keynote of their endeavour. These words have a wider connotation and significance than the thinkers of today can know and understand. (14-361)

(m) THE KINGDOM OF GOD ON EARTH

1. It is of importance that you realise that today something new is happening. There is the emergence of a new kingdom in nature, the fifth kingdom; this is the Kingdom of God on earth, or the kingdom of souls. It is precipitating on earth and will be composed of those who are becoming group-conscious, and who can work in group formation. This will be possible, because these people will have achieved a self-initiated perfection (even if relative in nature) and will be identified with certain group expansions of consciousness. It will also be because they have arrived at love of their fellow men, just as they have loved themselves in the past. Think on this with clarity, my brothers, and grasp if you can, the full significance of this last sentence.

Their work will largely be to summarise and make effective the work of those two great Sons of God, the Buddha and the Christ. As you know, One of Them brought *illumination* to the world and embodied the principle of Wisdom, and the Other brought *love* to the world and embodied in Himself a great cosmic principle—the principle of Love. How can the effectiveness of Their work be brought about? The process will follow three lines:

i. Individual effort, made by the individual disciple, using the technique of detachment, of dispassion and discrimination, which the Buddha taught.

ii. Group initiation, made possible by the self-initiated effort of individual disciples, following out the injunctions of the Christ, and leading to a complete subordination of the personality and of the unit to group interest and group good.

iii. Group endeavour, carried forward as a group, to love all beings and to apprehend and understand the true significance of the Aquarian technique of group love and work.   (5-3/4)

2. Christ taught also that the Kingdom of God was on Earth and told us to seek that Kingdom first and let all things be of secondary importance for its sake. That Kingdom has ever been with us, composed of all those who down the ages, have sought spiritual goals, liberated themselves from the limitations of the physical body, emotional controls and the obstructive mind. Its citizens are those who today (unknown to the majority) live in physical bodies, work for the welfare of humanity, use love instead of emotion as their general technique, and compose that great body of "illumined Minds" which guides the destiny of the world. The Kingdom of God is not something which will descend on Earth when man is good enough! It is something which is functioning efficiently today and demanding recognition. It is an organised body which is already evoking recognition from those people who do seek first the Kingdom of God, and discover thereby that the Kingdom they seek is already here. Christ and His disciples are known by many to be physically present on Earth, and the Kingdom which They rule, with its laws and modes of activity, is familiar to many and has been throughout the centuries.

Christ is the world Healer and Saviour. He works because He is the embodied soul of all Reality. He works today, as He worked in Palestine two thousand years ago, through groups. There He worked through the three beloved disciples, through the twelve apostles, through the chosen seventy, and the interested five hundred. . . . Now He works through His Masters and Their groups, and thereby greatly intensifies His efforts. He can and will work through all groups just insofar as they fit themselves for planned service, for the distribution of love, and come into conscious alignment with the great potency of the inner groups.

Those groups who have always proclaimed the physical Presence of the Christ, have so distorted the teaching by dogmatic assertions on unimportant details and by ridiculous claims that they have evoked little recognition of the underlying truth, nor have they portrayed a kingdom which is attractive. That Kingdom exists, but is not a place of disciplines or golden harps, peopled by unintelligent fanatics, but a field of service and a place where every man has full scope for the exercise of his divinity in human service. (8-50/1)

111. INITIATION

(a) RULES FOR APPLICANTS FOR INITIATION

Rule 1

Let the disciple search within the heart's deep cave. If there the fire burns bright, warming his brother yet heating not himself, the hour has come for making application to stand before the door.

When love for all beings, irrespective of who they may be, is beginning to be a realised fact in the heart of a disciple, and yet nevertheless love for himself exists not, then comes the indication that he is nearing the Portal of Initiation, and may make the necessary preliminary pledges. These are necessitated before his Master hands in his name as a candidate for initiation. If he cares not for the suffering and pain of the lower self, if it is immaterial to him whether happiness comes his way or not, if the sole purpose of his life is to serve and save the world, and if his brother's need is for him of greater moment than his own, then is the fire of love irradiating his being, and the world can warm itself at his feet. This love has to be a practical, tested manifestation, and not just a theory, nor simply an impractical ideal and a pleasing sentiment. It is something that has grown in the trials and tests of life, so that the primary impulse of the life is towards self-sacrifice and the immolation of the lower nature. (1-192/3)

Rule 2

When application has been made in triple form, then let the disciple withdraw that application, and forget it has been made.

Herein lies one of the initial tests. The disciple's attitude of mind must be that he cares not whether he takes initiation or not. Selfish motive must not enter in. Only those applications which reach the Master through the energy engendered through pure altruistic motive, are transmitted by Him to the recording angel of the Hierarchy; only those disciples who seek initiation because of the added power to help and bless that it confers, will find a response to their plea. Those careless of initiation receive not the occult accolade, and those anxious, through selfishness or curiosity, to participate in the mysteries, enter not the door but remain knocking outside. Those who are keen to serve, those who are weighed down with a sense of world need, and the personal responsibility thereby awakened, and who have fulfilled the law, knock and meet with response, and make application which meets with recognition. They are the ones who send forth a cry for added power to aid, which penetrates the ear of Those Who silently wait. (1-193/4)

(b) PREPARING FOR INITIATION

1. (The disciple) finds his soul through the fusion of soul and personality; he finds his group through the absorption of this fusing soul-form with a Master's group, and finally he is absorbed into the Master's Ashram. . . .

When the new structure of the coming world order is taking shape, the process will be speeded up considerably; this will not, however, be for a hundred years, which is but a brief moment in the eternal history of humanity. From synthesis to synthesis the life of God passes. First the synthesis of the atomic lives into ever more perfect forms, until the three kingdoms of nature appear; then the synthesis in consciousness, enabling the human being to enter into the larger awareness of the Whole, and finally to enter into that mysterious event which is the result of the effect of all preceding development and to which we give the name of Identification. From the first identification, which is the higher correspondence of the stage of individualisation, progressive absorption into ever larger wholes takes place, and each time the Word goes forth: Accepted as a group.

Have I succeeded in giving you a somewhat wider vision of the significance of initiation in these brief expositions? Do you see more clearly the growing beauty of the Whole, and the goodness of the Purpose, and

the wisdom of the Plan? Do you realise more deeply that beauty, goodness and wisdom are not qualities, as their inadequate nomenclature would
imply, but are great facts in manifestation? Do you grasp the truth that
they are not descriptive of Deity, but are the names of Lives of a potency
and activity of which men can as yet know nothing?

Some understanding of this must slowly seep into the mind and consciousness of each disciple, as that mind becomes irradiated by soul light
in the earlier stages, and later responds to the impact of energy coming
from the Spiritual Triad. Only when this is visioned, even if not understood, will the realisation come to the struggling disciple, that the words:

*Withdraw not now your application. You could not if you would; but
add to it three great demands and forward move* are a living command
conditioning him, whether he will or not. The inability to withdraw from
the position taken, is one of the first true results of hearing the Word
spoken after passing the two tests. There is an inevitability in living the
life of the Spirit, which is at once its horror and its joy. I mean just that.
The symbol or first expression of this (for all in the three worlds is
but the symbol of an inner reality) is the driving urge to betterment which
is the outstanding characteristic of the human animal. From discontent to
discontent he passes, driven by an inner something which constantly reveals to him an enticing vision of that which is more desirable than his
present state and experience. At first this is interpreted by him in terms of
material welfare; then this divine discontent drives him into a phase of
the struggle which is emotional in nature; he craves emotional satisfaction and later intellectual pursuits. All the time this struggle to attain
something ever on ahead creates the instruments of attainment, gradually perfecting them until the threefold personality is ready for a vision of
the soul. From that point of tension the urge and the struggle become
more acute . . . and he steps upon the Path.

Once he is an accepted disciple, and has definitely undertaken the work
in preparation for initiation, there is for him no turning back. He could
not if he would, and the Ashram protects him.   (18-58/60)

2. As the intellect of man develops, the requirements for initiation become more drastic and exacting, and the initiate therefore becomes of a
distinctly higher order. The Master today is infinitely wiser and more full
of love, and more "occultly reasonable" than was the Master in Atlantean
times.   (18-388)

3. The Ashram has its own objectives, intentions and inner techniques,
which are unconnected with the disciple's life and his service in the three

worlds. The work of the disciple in preparation for initiation is not basically concerned with his daily world service, though there would be no initiation for him if that life of service were lacking. His life of service is, in reality, an expression of the particular initiation for which he is being prepared. This is a theme too vast for us to consider here, but it is an idea upon which you could well ponder. (18-547)

(c) INITIATION

1. After a longer or shorter period of time the disciple stands at the Portal of Initiation. We must remember that as one approaches this portal and draws nearer to the Master, it is, as says "Light on the Path", with the feet bathed in the blood of the heart. Each step up is ever through the sacrifice of all that the heart holds dear on one plane or another, and always must this sacrifice be voluntary. He who treads the Probationary Path and the Path of Holiness is he who has counted the cost, whose sense of values has been readjusted, and who therefore judges not as judges the man of the world. He is the man who is attempting to take the "kingdom by violence", and in the attempt is prepared for the consequent suffering. He is the man who counts all things but loss if he may but win the goal, and who, in the struggle for mastery of the lower self by the higher, is willing to sacrifice even unto death. (1-82)

2. Initiation does not simply enhance and deepen the soul quality; it does not simply enable the personality to express soul powers, and thus emphasise and draw out the best that is in the disciple and his service, but it makes available to him, progressively, forces and energies of which he has had no previous knowledge and which he must learn to use as an initiate of a certain degree upon the Lighted Way. It reveals to him worlds of being hitherto unsuspected and unrecognised, with which he must learn to co-operate, and it integrates him more definitely into the "lighted area" of our planetary life, bringing fresh revelation and vision, but making the unlighted area dark indeed. (6-666)

3. Initiation has been so frequently presented as being a ceremony, that I have felt it necessary to offset strenuously that erroneous significance. If, however, you are to comprehend that which I have to say, you will have to call in what measures of enlightened understanding you may possess.

Initiation is only a ceremony in so far that there comes a climaxing point in the initiatory process, in which the disciple's consciousness becomes dramatically aware of the personnel of the Hierarchy and of his own position in relation to it. This realisation he symbolises to himself—successively and on an increasingly large scale—as a great rhythmic ceremonial of progressive revelation in which he, as a candidate, is the centre of the hierarchical stage. This is definitely so (from the ceremonial angle) in the first two initiations, and in relation to the Christ as the Initiator. . . . The ceremonial aspect is due to the thought-form making capacity of the disciple. (18-530/1)

4. The initiatory process is in reality the result of the activity of three energies :

i. The energy generated by the disciple as he seeks to serve humanity.

ii. The energy made available to the disciple as he succeeds in building the antahkarana.

iii. The energy of the hierarchical Ashram into which he is being "absorbed" or integrated.

It is these three energies, each with its own mode of expression, and each producing its own specific results, which implement or engineer the initiatory process; these energies are evoked by the disciple himself, and their increasing strength and revelatory capacity depend largely upon the disciple's determination, purpose and will, his persistence and spiritual integrity. (18-534/5)

5. Periods of search, periods of pain, periods of detachment, periods of revelation, producing points of fusion, points of tension and points of energy projection—such is the story of the Path of Initiation.

Initiation is in truth the name given to the revelation or new vision which ever draws the disciple onward into greater light; it is not something conferred upon him or given to him. It is a process of *light* recognition and of *light* utilisation in order to enter into ever clearer light. Progress from a dimly lighted area in the divine manifestation, into one of supernal glory, is the story of the Path of Evolution. (18-538)

6. It is the recognition of the varying "lights" upon the Lighted Way that signifies readiness for initiation. The initiate enters into light in a peculiar sense; it permeates his nature according to his development at any point in time and space; it enables him to contact and see the hitherto unseen, and on the basis of the newly acquired knowledge, to direct his steps still further.

I am not here speaking in symbols. Each initiation dims the light already acquired and used, and then immerses the initiate in a higher light. Each initiation enables the disciple to perceive an area of divine consciousness hitherto unknown but which, when the disciple has familiarised himself with it and with its unique phenomena, vibratory quality and inter-relations, becomes for him a normal field of experience and activity. . . . Again duality enters into his mental perception, for he is now aware of the lighted area from which he comes to the point of tension or of initiation; through the initiatory process he discovers a new and more brilliantly lighted area, into which he may now enter. This involves no leaving of the former field of activity in which he has worked and lived; it simply means that new fields of responsibility and of opportunity confront him because he is—through his own effort—able to see more light, to walk in a greater light, to prove more adequately than heretofore his capacities within the greatly increased area of possibility.   (18-539/40)

7. Initiation is (in its simplest definition) an understanding of the Way, for understanding is a revealing energy which permits you to achieve. Initiation is a growth in experience and the attainment thereby of a point of tension. Holding that point of tension, the initiate sees that which lies ahead. *Initiation permits a progressive entry into the mind of the creating Logos.* This last definition is perhaps one of the most important I have ever given. Ponder on my words.   (18-557)

8. No disciple can pass through the initiatory experience unless he *is* a soul-infused individual and is consciously aware on soul levels of the various happenings, possibilities, undertakings and implications.

. . . It is wise to note that an initiation is in reality a crisis, a climaxing event, and is only truly brought about when the disciple has learnt patience, endurance and sagacity in emerging from the many preceding and less important crises. An initiation is a culminating episode, made possible because of the self-inspired discipline to which the disciple has forced himself to conform.

. . . Little has been said anent the . . . truth that initiation admits a man into some area or level of the divine consciousness—into a plane or rather a state of being hitherto regarded as sealed and closed.   (18-662)

(d) GROUP INITIATION

It dawns on the initiate, as he proceeds from one initiation to another, that each time he moves forward on the Path or penetrates into the heart of the Mysteries in company with those who are as he is, who share with him the same point in evolution, and who are working with him towards the same goal, that he is not alone; that it is a joint effort that is being made. This is in fact the keynote of an Ashram, conditioning its formation. It is composed of disciples and initiates at various stages of initiate-unfoldment, who have arrived at their point of ashramic consciousness *together*, and who will proceed *together* until they arrive at that complete liberation which comes when the cosmic physical plane drops below the threshold of consciousness or of sensitive awareness, and no longer holds any point of interest for the initiate.

. . . Spiritual selfishness has led the average esoteric student to appropriate initiation, and to make it personal and individual. Yet one of the prime prerequisites for initiation is a clear and concise recognition of one's own group, not through a process of wishful thinking, but through factual co-operation and work upon the physical plane. I said *group*, my brother, and not organisation, for they are two very different things.

Have carefully in mind, therefore, the fact of group initiation, and forego the process of considered thought anent *your* preparation for initiation. Some groups are being prepared for initiation in which the following factors control—as far as the individual is concerned:

1. A group of men and women whose souls are on some one ray, are gathered together subjectively by a Master on the same ray, for group training.

2. Opportunity is given to such people to contact on the physical plane some of those who are thus subjectively linked, and thus mutually convey a sense of group solidarity. The subjective relationship is assured by an objective contact. Recognition is therefore a preliminary test of initiation, and this should be remembered.

3. Such people, thus being trained and related, are from the angle of the initiation to be taken, at the same point in evolution. They are taking the same initiation and are being subjected to the same tests and difficulties. These tests and difficulties are due to the fact of the personality ray, which may be (and usually is) quite different to the soul ray. It is the personality ray which works to prevent contact, to mislead in recognition, to retard progress, and to misinterpret information. As long as a disciple in training is focussed in his personality, group initiation will not be possible for him, his recognition of co-aspirants will be fleeting and rapidly disturbed by the critical lower mind, and a wall of thought-forms, created by the personality, anent the group members, will be

thrown up and prevent a united moving forward through the Door of Initiation.

4. Group initiation cannot be achieved by a group in training until the members, as a group, have developed their particular "spiritual enterprise". It is the law of the spirit that the disciple must appear before the Initiator empty-handed, but that in group formation the group members unitedly contribute something to the enrichment of the Ashram. This may take the form of some considered project in line with the Plan, whereby they testify to their comprehension of that Plan, and demonstrate to the initiate-company in which they find themselves, and those senior disciples to whose contact they are to be admitted, that they have already proven their fitness for acceptance, and have proven it along the line of service. It has to be a group enterprise, a group service and a group contribution. The specific contribution of the individual does not appear.

This thought of group initiation must be remembered, for it will colour all that I will seek to convey to your minds, and will hasten the day of your own acceptance.

No one is admitted (through the processes of initiation) into the Ashram of the Christ (the Hierarchy) until such time as he is beginning to think and live in terms of group relationships and group activities. Some well-meaning aspirants interpret the group idea as the instruction to them that they should make an effort to form groups—their own group or groups. This is not the idea as it is presented in the Aquarian Age, so close today; it *was* the mode of approach during the Piscean Age, now passed. Today, the entire approach is totally different. No man today is expected to stand at the centre of his little world and work to become the focal point for a group. His task now is to discover the group of aspirants with which he should affiliate himself, and with whom he must travel upon the Path of Initiation—a very different matter, and a far more difficult one.   (18-342/4)

(e) THE INITIATE

1. *Occult Memory*. The initiate finally becomes aware increasingly of the growth of that inner recollection, or "occult memory", which concerns the work of the Hierarchy and primarily his share in the general Plan. When the initiate, who occultly recalls, in his waking consciousness, a ceremonial fact, finds all these manifestations of increased growth and

486486

486486

486486486486486486

486486486

486486

conscious realisation *in himself,* then the truth of his inner assurance is proven and substantiated to him.

It must be remembered that this inner substantiation is of no value to anyone but the initiate. He has to prove himself to the outer world through his life of service and the work accomplished, and thereby call forth from all his environing associates a recognition that will show itself in a sanctified emulation and a strenuous effort to tread the same path, actuated ever by the same motive—that of service and brotherhood, not self-aggrandisement and selfish acquirement. It should also be remembered that if the above is true in connection with the work, it is still more true in connection with the initiate himself. *Initiation is a strictly personal matter with a universal application.* It rests upon his inner attainment. The initiate will know for himself when the event occurs and needs no one to tell him of it. The expansion of consciousness called initiation, must include the physical brain or it is of no value. As those lesser expansions of consciousness which we undergo normally every day, and call "learning" something or other, have reference to the apprehension by the physical brain of an imparted fact or apprehended circumstance, so with the greater expansions which are the outcome of the many lesser.

At the same time, it is quite possible for men to be functioning on the physical plane and to be actively employed in world service, who have no recollection of having undergone the initiatory process, yet who, nevertheless, may have taken the first or second initiation in a previous or earlier life. This is the result, simply, of a lack of "bridging" from one life to another, or it may be the outcome of a definite decision by the Ego. A man may be able better to work off certain karma and to carry out certain work for the Lodge if he is free from occult occupation and mystic introspection during the period of any one earth life. There are many such amongst the sons of men at this time, who have previously taken the first initiation, and a few who have taken the second, but who are nevertheless quite unaware of it, yet their centres and nervous organisation carry proof to those who have the inner vision. If initiation is taken for the first time in any life, the recollection of it extends to the physical brain.

Curiosity, or even ordinary good living, never brought a man to the Portal of Initiation. Curiosity, by arousing a strong vibration in a man's lower nature, only serves to swing him away from, instead of towards the goal he is interested in; whilst ordinary good living, when not furthered by a life of utter sacrifice for others, and by a reticence, humility, and disinterestedness of a very unusual kind, may serve to build good vehicles which will be of use in another incarnation, but will not serve to break down those barriers, outer and inner, and overcome those opposing forces and energies which stand between a "good" man and the ceremony of initiation.

The Path of Discipleship is a difficult one to tread, and the Path of Initiation harder still; an initiate is but a battle-scarred warrior, the victor in many a hard-won fight; he speaks not of his achievements, for he is too busy with the great work in hand; he makes no reference to himself or to all that he has accomplished, save to deprecate the littleness of what has been done. Nevertheless, to the world he is ever a man of large influence, the wielder of spiritual power, the embodier of ideals, the worker for humanity, who unfailingly brings results which succeeding generations will recognise. He is one who, in spite of all this great achievement, is seldom understood by his own generation. He is frequently the butt of men's tongues, and frequently all that he does is misinterpreted; he lays his all— time, money, influence, reputation, and all that the world considers worth while—upon the altar of altruistic service, and frequently offers his life as a final gift, only to find that those whom he has served throw his gift back to him, scorn his renunciation, and label him with unsavoury names. But the initiate cares not, for his is the privilege to see somewhat into the future, and therefore he realises that the force he has generated will in due course of time bring to fulfilment the Plan; he knows also that his name and effort are noted in the archives of the Lodge, and that the "Silent Watcher" over the affairs of men has taken notice. (1-101/4)

2. The initiate will find, when he returns from the ceremony, and takes up his work in the world, that the stimulation received will bring about in his bodies a period of great activity, and also of strife. This strife, persisted in to the point of victory, will result in his taking out of his body undesirable matter, and building in new and better material; he will find that his powers for service are enormously increased, and his nervous energy intensified, so that he can draw upon reserves of force in service hitherto unsuspected. He will find, also, that the response of the physical brain to the voice of the higher Self, and its receptivity to the higher and subtler impressions, is greatly furthered. Eventually, through the work accomplished, he will succeed in eliminating all matter of a sub-atomic character, and will then build bodies of substance of the highest sub-plane on each plane; he will become aware that all his energies can be consciously and constructively controlled, that he knows the real meaning of continuity of consciousness, and can function simultaneously on the three planes with full inner realisation. (1-135)

3. The mark of the initiate is his lack of interest in himself, in his own unfoldment and his own personal fate, and all aspirants who become accepted disciples, have to master the technique of disinterestedness. Their eyes have also to be lifted away from the group of workers and from the hierarchy which they constitute, and to be fixed on wider horizons and vaster realms of activity.   (14-xxi)

4. *Dual the moving forward. The Door is left behind. That is a happening of the past.*

The first point which should be noted is that we have here the definition of an initiate. He is one who, in his twofold nature (soul and personality), moves forward. No longer is his point of tension that of the personality. He has fused and blended two divine aspects in himself, and they now constitute one integrated unit. This fusion produces its own point of tension. He has moved forward through the door. A point of tension again ensues in which a Word goes forth in response to the invocative cry of the new initiate. A Word is returned to him: Accepted as a group. Then he, with the group of which he is now a recognised part, moves forward. For the initiate (as I have earlier pointed out) the past is left behind: "Let there be no recollection"; the present embodies a point of tension; the future indicates a moving forward from that point of tension as a result of its effective action. The door closes behind the initiate, who is now an accepted member of his group, and as the *Old Commentary* puts it, "its sound in closing informs the watching world that the initiate has passed into a secret place, and that to reach him in the real sense, they too must pass that door". This conveys the thought of individual self-initiation, to which all must be subjected, and indicates also the loneliness of the initiate as he moves forward. He does not yet understand all that his group as a whole grasps; he is himself not understood by those on the other side of the door. He has sensed for some time the group with which he is now affiliated, and is becoming increasingly aware of their spiritual impersonality, which seems to him to be almost a form of aloofness, and which in no way feeds in him those elements which are of a personality nature; he therefore suffers. Those left behind as a part of his old life, in no way comprehend his basic (even if undeveloped) impersonality. This attitude of theirs evokes in him, when sensed, a resentment and a criticism which he realises is not right, but which at this stage he seems unable to avoid, whilst those he criticises endeavour to tear him down or (at the least) to make him feel despised and uncomfortable.

In the early stages he takes refuge from those left behind, by withdrawing himself and by much unnecessary and almost obstrusive silence. He learns to penetrate into the consciousness of his new group, by strenuously endeavouring to develop their capacity for spiritual impersonality. He knows it is something which he must achieve and—as he achieves it—he discovers that his impersonality is not based on indifference or upon preoccupation, as he had thought, but upon a deep understanding, upon a dynamic focus on world service, upon a sense of proportion, and upon a detachment which makes true help possible. Thus the door and the past are left behind. St. Paul attempted to express this idea when he said! "Forgetting the things which are behind, press forward towards the prize of your high calling in Christ". I would ask your attention to the word "calling".   (18-71/3)

(f) FIRST INITIATION (Birth)

1. At the first initiation, that of the birth of the Christ, the *heart centre* is the one usually vivified, with the aim in view of the more effective controlling of the astral vehicle, and the rendering of greater service to humanity. After this initiation the initiate is taught principally the facts of the astral plane; he has to stabilise his emotional vehicle and learn to work on the astral plane with the same facility and ease as he does on the physical plane: he is brought in contact with the astral devas; he learns to control the astral elementals; he must function with facility on the lower subplanes, and the value and quality of his work on the physical plane becomes of increased worth. He passes, at this initiation, out of the Hall of Learning into the Hall of Wisdom. At this time, emphasis is consistently laid on his astral development, although his mental equipment grows steadily.

Many lives may intervene between the first initiation and the second. A long period of many incarnations may elapse before the control of the astral body is perfected, and the initiate is ready for the next step.   (1-84)

2. In a group of disciples . . . the large majority have already taken the first initiation, and are being prepared for one of the later initiations. There is nothing surprising in this statement, or any particular cause for elation or for pleasure. An immense number of the world aspirants evidence— through their aliveness to the spiritual issues, through the intensity of their aspiration, and through their struggles to be good, self-sacrificing and wise —that the life of the indwelling Christ is most definitely moving in them and *is* present in their hearts. The initiation of "spiritual fixation upon the physical plane" (as the birth at Bethlehem, the first initiation, is sometimes

called), has already been undergone by thousands, and they are sincerely
and definitely moving forward upon the Way. I would remind you here
that many, many lives can elapse between the first initiation and the second
—long, long interludes of silent and almost unapparent growth. You are
in no way unique or far ahead of the senior world aspirants. In that lies
cause for encouragement and humility. It is naturally *not* my intention to
state who is being prepared for any particular initiation. *That is a matter
for each of you to discover for himself.* It is a matter of interior orientation and not a matter of outside information.   (5-94/5)

3. It is seldom realised that hundreds of thousands of people in every
land have taken, or are preparing to take, the first initiation. . . . Humanity, the world disciple, is now ready for this. Indications of the accuracy
of the above statement can be seen in the re-orientation of people everywhere to things spiritual, their interest in human good and human welfare,
the perseverence they show in their search for light and their longing and
desire for a true peace, based on right human relations, implemented by
goodwill.   (9-149)

4. Many thousands of people in the world today have taken the first initiation, and are oriented towards the spiritual life and the service of their
fellow men; their lives, however, frequently leave much to be desired, and
the soul is obviously *not* in constant control; a great struggle is still being
waged to achieve purification on all three levels. The lives of these initiates
are faulty and their inexperience great, and a major attempt is instituted
in this particular cycle to achieve soul fusion. When that is attained, then
the third initiation (the first, hierarchically speaking) is taken.   (18-385)

5. The first initiation might be regarded as the goal and the reward of
the *mystical experience*; it is fundamentally not an occult experience in
the true sense of the term, for it is seldom accurately realised or consciously prepared for, as is the case of the later initiations, and this is why the
first two initiations are not considered major initiations. . . . The mystical
Way leads to the first initiation. Having achieved its purpose, it is then
renounced, and the "lighted Way" of occultism is then followed, leading
to the lighted areas of the higher states of consciousness.   (18-666)

6. The first initiation marks the beginning of a totally new life and mode
of living; it marks the commencement of a new manner of thinking and
of conscious perception. . . . The "new man" has to learn to walk, to talk,
and to create; the consciousness is now, however, being focussed elsewhere.
This leads to much pain and suffering until the definite choice is made,

a new dedication to service is vouchsafed, and the initiate is ready to undergo the Baptism Initiation.

. . . (It can be assumed) that all those who truly love their fellow men, who are interested in the esoteric teaching, and who seek to discipline themselves in order to attain greater beauty of life, are initiate and have undergone the first initiation.   (18-667)

(g)   SECOND INITIATION (Baptism)

1. Once the second initiation is taken the progress will be rapid, the third and fourth following probably in the same life, or the succeeding.

The second initiation forms the *crisis* in the control of the astral body. Just as, at the first initiation, the control of the dense physical has been demonstrated. The sacrifice and death of desire has been the goal of endeavour. Desire itself has been dominated by the Ego, and only that is longed for which is good for the whole, and in the line of the will of the Ego, and of the Master. The astral elemental is controlled, the emotional body becomes pure and limpid, and the lower nature is rapidly dying. At this time the Ego grips afresh the two lower vehicles and bends them to his will. The aspiration and longing to serve, love, and progress become so strong, that rapid development is usually to be seen. This accounts for the fact that this initiation and the third, frequently (though not invariably) follow each other in one single life. At this period of the world's history such stimulus has been given to evolution that aspiring souls—sensing the dire and crying need of humanity—are sacrificing all in order to meet that need.

Again, we must not make the mistake of thinking that all this follows in the same invariable consecutive steps and stages. Much is done in simultaneous unison, for the labour to control is slow and hard, but in the interim between the first three initiations some definite point in the evolution of each of the three lower vehicles has to be attained and held, before the further expansion of the channel can be safely permitted. Many of us are working on all the three bodies now, as we tread the Probationary Path.

At this initiation, should the ordinary course be followed, (which again is not at all certain) *the throat centre* is vivified. This causes a capacity to turn to account in the Master's service, and for the helping of man, the attainments of the lower mind. It imparts the ability to give forth and utter that which is helpful, possibly in the spoken word, but *surely* in service of some kind. A vision is accorded of the world's need, and a further portion of the Plan shown. The work, then, to be done prior to the taking of the third initiation, is the complete submerging of the personal point of view in the need of the whole. It entails the complete domination of the concrete mind by the Ego.   (1-84/6)

2. The second initiation is closely related to the Hierarchy as a planetary centre, and to the activity of the second ray. This initiation will produce in the initiate a growing sense of relationships, of a basic unity with all that breathes, and a recognition of the One Life which will lead eventually to that state of expressed brotherhood which it is the goal of the Aquarian Age to bring into being.   (9-138)

3. The disciple is learning to discipline his lower nature and to achieve a measure of mastery over his physical inclinations; he thus releases physical energy and brings order into his life. This takes a very long time and may cover a cycle of many incarnations. . . . He discovers that his emotional nature, his lower psychic faculties, his astral development, and the potency of glamour, are now all arrayed against him.

. . . He discovers that he lives in a chaos of emotional reactions and of conditioning glamours. He slowly begins to realise that in order to take the second initiation, he must demonstrate emotional control; he realises also that he must have some knowledge of those spiritual energies which will dissipate glamour, plus an understanding of the technique whereby illumination from the mind—as the transmitting agent of the light of the soul—can dispel these glamours and thus "clarify the atmosphere", in the technical sense.

I might emphasise that as yet no initiate demonstrates complete control during the intermediate period between any initiation and the next higher initiation; the intermediate period is regarded as "a cycle of perfecting". That which is being left behind and subordinated to the higher realisation is slowly dominated by energies which are to be released into the consciousness of the initiate at the initiation for which he is being prepared. This interim period is always one of great difficulty. . . .

The initiatory process between the first and the second initiations, is for many the worst time of distress, difficulty, realisation of problems, and the constant effort to "clear himself" (as it is occultly called), to which the disciple is at any time subjected.   (18-576/7)

4. Facing (the initiate who has taken the second initiation) is a great transition from an emotional aspirational focus to an intelligent, thinking focus. He has, theoretically at least, cast off the control of the astral body and nature; much still remains to be done; old desires, ancient astral reac-

tions and habitual emotions are still powerful, but he has developed a new attitude to them, and a new perspective to the astral body. . . . He is now negative to their appeal and positive to the higher demanding focus. That which he now loves and longs for, desires and plans for, lies in another and higher dimension. He has, through his willingness to pass through the second initiation, struck the first blow at his innate selfishness, and has demonstrated his determination to think in wider and more inclusive terms. The group begins to mean more to him than himself.

. . . At the second initiation, he is granted a vision of a higher focus, and his place in the larger whole begins slowly to reveal itself. A new creativity and a new focus become his immediate goals, and for him life can never again be the same. The old physical attitudes and desire may still at times assume control; selfishness may continue to play a potent part in his life expression, but—underlying these, and subordinating them—will be found a deep dissatisfaction about things as they are, and an agonising realisation of failure. It is at this point that the disciple begins to learn the uses of failure, and to know certain fundamental distinctions between that which is natural and objective, and that which is supernatural and subjective.

. . . Realise that no one "takes" initiation and passes through these crises, without a previous demonstration of a wide usefulness and of a trained intelligent capacity. This may not be the case where the first initiation is concerned, but where the second initiation is involved, there must ever be the background of a useful, dedicated life and an expressed determination to enter the field of *world* service. There must also be humility, and a voiced realisation of the divinity in all men. (18-677/9)

5. Freedom is the keynote of the individual who is facing the second initiation, and its aftermath—preparation for the third initiation. Freedom is the keynote for the world disciple today, and it is freedom to live, freedom to think, and freedom to know and plan, which humanity demands at this time. (18-684)

(h) THIRD INITIATION (Transfiguration)

1. After the second initiation the teaching shifts up a plane. The initiate learns to control his mental vehicle; he develops the capacity to manipulate thought matter, and learns the laws of creative thought building. He functions freely on the four lower sub-planes of the mental plane, and before the third initiation he must—consciously or unconsciously—be complete master of the four lower sub-planes in the three planes of the three

worlds. His knowledge of the microcosm becomes profound, and he has mastered theoretically and practically, in great measure, the laws of his nature, hence his ability experimentally to master on the four lower sub-planes of the physical, astral, and mental planes. The last fact is of interest. The control of the three higher sub-planes is not yet complete, and here is one of the explanations as to the failures and mistakes of initiates. Their mastery of matter in the three higher sub-planes is not yet perfect; these yet remain to be dominated.

At the third initiation, termed sometimes the Transfiguration, the entire personality is flooded with light from above. It is only after this initiation that the Monad is definitely guiding the Ego, pouring His divine life ever more into the prepared and cleansed channel. . . .

Again, a vision is accorded of what lies ahead; the initiate is in a position at all times to recognise the other members of the Great White Lodge, and his psychic faculties are stimulated by the vivification of the *head centres.* It is not necessary nor advisable to develop the synthetic faculties, or clairaudience and clairvoyance, until after this initiation. The aim of all development is the awakening of the spiritual intuition; when this has been done, when the physical body is pure, the astral stable and steady, and the mental body controlled, then the initiate can safely wield and wisely use the psychic faculties for the helping of the race. Not only can he use these faculties, but he is able now to create and vivify thought-forms that are clear and well-defined, pulsating with the spirit of service and not controlled by lower mind or desire. These thought-forms will not be (as is the case with those created by the mass of men) disjointed, unconnected, and uncorrelated, but will attain a fair measure of synthesis. Hard and ceaseless must the work be before this can be done, but when the desire nature has been stabilised and purified, then the control of the mind-body comes more easily. Hence the path of the devotee is easier in some ways than that of the intellectual man, for he has learnt the measures of purified desire, and progresses by the requisite stages.

The personality has now reached a point where its vibrations are of a very high order, the matter in all three bodies relatively pure, and its apprehension of the work to be done in the microcosm, and the share to be taken in the work of the macrocosm is very advanced.　(3-86/8)

2. Aspirants and disciples should remember that after the third initiation, *the effects* of the initiation which they may be undergoing are not confined simply to the individual initiate, but that henceforth at all the later initiations, he becomes the transmitter of the energy which will pour through him

with increasing potency at each application of the Rod. He acts primarily as an agent for the transmission, for the stepping down and for the consequent safe distribution of energy to the masses. Each time a disciple achieves an initiation and stands before the Initiator, he becomes simply an instrument whereby the planetary Logos can reach humanity, and bring to men fresh life and energy. The work done prior to, and at the third initiation, is purely preparatory to this type of service required from an "energy transmitter". (18-689)

3. This third initiation is in reality the first of the major initiations. . . .

The first two initiations—regarded simply as initiations of the threshold—are experiences which have prepared the body of the initiate for the reception of the terrific voltage of this third initiation. This voltage is passed through the body of the initiate under the direction of the planetary Logos, before Whom the initiate stands for the first time. (18-687)

(i) FOURTH INITIATION (Crucifixion)

1. Before the fourth initiation can be taken, the work of training is intensified, and the hastening and accumulation of knowledge has to be unbelievably rapid. The initiate has frequent access to the library of occult books, and after this initiation he can contact not only the Master with Whom he is linked and with Whom he has worked consciously for a long time, but he can contact and assist (in measure) the Chohans, the Bodhisattva, and the Manu.

He has also to grasp the laws of the three lower planes intellectually, and likewise wield them for the aiding of the scheme of evolution. He studies the cosmic plans and has to master the charts; he becomes versed in occult technicalities and develops fourth dimensional vision, if he has not already done so. He learns to direct the activities of the building devas, and at the same time, he works continually at the development of his spiritual nature. He begins rapidly to co-ordinate the buddhic vehicle, and in its co-ordination he develops the power of synthesis, at first in small measure, and gradually in fuller detail.

By the time the fourth initiation is taken, the initiate has mastered perfectly the fifth sub-plane, and is therefore adept—to use a technical phrase—on the five lower sub-planes of the physical, astral, and mental planes, and is well on the way to master the sixth. His buddhic vehicle can function on the two lower sub-planes of the buddhic plane.

The life of the man who takes the fourth initiation, or the Crucifixion, is usually one of great sacrifice and suffering. It is the life of the man who

makes the Great Renunciation, and even exoterically it is seen to be strenuous, hard, and painful. He has laid all, even his perfected personality,
upon the altar of sacrifice, and stands bereft of all. All is renounced, friends,
money, reputation, character, standing in the world, family, and even life
itself.   (1-88/9)

2. This initiation of Renunciation is of supreme importance to humanity
and to the individual initiate. . . . First of all, this great act of renunciation
marks the moment when the disciple has nothing in him which relates him
to the three worlds of human evolution. His contact with those worlds in
the future will be purely voluntary and for purposes of service.   (18-696)

112. DARK FORCES

1. No danger need be feared from (the Brothers of Darkness). It is only as
discipleship is approached and a man stands out ahead of his fellows as
an instrument of the White Brotherhood, that he attracts the attention of
those who seek to withstand. When through application to meditation,
and power and activity in service, a man has developed his vehicles to a
point of real achievement, then his vibrations set in motion matter of a
specific kind, and he learns to work with that matter, to manipulate the
fluids, and to control the builders. In so doing he encroaches on the domain
of those who work with the forces of involution and thus he may bring
attack upon himself. This attack may be directed against any of his three
vehicles and may be of different kinds. Let me briefly point out some of the
methods employed against a disciple . . . :

i. Definite attack on the physical body. All kinds of means are employed to hinder the usefulness of the disciple through disease or the crip-
pling of his physical body. Not all accidents are the result of karma, for
the disciple has usually surmounted a good deal of that type of karma, and
is thus comparatively free from that source of hindrance in active work.

ii. Glamour is another method used, or the casting over the disciple of a
cloud of emotional or mental matter which suffices to hide the real, and
to temporarily obscure that which is true. The study of cases wherein
glamour has been employed, is exceedingly revealing and demonstrates
how hard it is for even an advanced disciple always to discriminate be-

tween the real and the false. Glamour may be either on the emotional or mental levels, but is usually on the former. One form employed is to cast over the disciple the shadows of the thought of weakness or discouragement or criticism, to which he may at intervals give way. Thus cast, they loom in undue proportion and the unwary disciple, not realising that he is but seeing the gigantic outlines of his own momentary and passing thoughts, gives way to discouragement, aye even to despair, and becomes of little use to the Great Ones. Another form is to throw into his mental aura suggestions and ideas purporting to come from his own Master but which are but subtle suggestions that hinder and help not. It takes a wise disciple always to discriminate between the voice of his real Teacher and the false whispers of the masquerading one, and even high initiates have been temporarily misled.

Many and subtle are the means used to deceive and thereby curtail the effective output of the worker in the field of the world. Wisely therefore have all aspirants been enjoined to study and work at the development of *viveka* or that discrimination which safeguards from deception. If this quality is laboriously built in and cultivated in all events, big and little in the daily life, the risks of being led astray will be nullified.

iii. A third method frequently employed is to envelop the disciple in a thick cloud of darkness, to surround him with an impenetrable night and fog through which he stumbles and often falls. It may take the form of a black cloud of emotional matter, of some dark emotion that seems to imperil all stable vibration and plunges the bewildered student into a blackness of despair; he feels that all is departing from him; he is a prey to varied and dismal emotions; he dreams himself forsaken of all; he considers that all past effort has been futile and that naught remains but to die. At such times he needs much the gift of *viveka,* and to earnestly weigh up and calmly reason out the matter. He should at these times remind himself that the darkness hides naught from the God within, and that the stable centre of consciousness remains there, untouched by aught that may betide. He should persevere until the end—the end of what? The end of the enveloping cloud, the point where it merges itself into sunlight; he should pass through its length and out into the daylight, realising that nothing can at any time reach to and hurt the inner consciousness. God is within, no matter what transpires without. We are so apt to look out at environing circumstances, whether physical, astral or mental, and to forget that the inmost centre of the heart hides our points of contact with the universal Logos.

iv. Finally (for I cannot touch on all the methods used), the means employed may be to cast a mental darkness over the disciple. The darkness may be intellectual, and is consequently still more difficult to penetrate, for in this case the power of the Ego *must* be called in, whereas in the former frequently the calm reasoning of the lower mind may suffice to dispel the trouble. Here, in this specific case, the disciple will be wise if he not only attempts to call his Ego or Higher Self for the dispelling of the cloud, but calls likewise upon his Teacher, or even upon the Master, for the assistance that They can give.

These are but a few of the dangers encircling the aspirant, and I hint at them solely for the purpose of warning and guidance, and not to cause alarm.   (2-131/3)

2. *Safeguards Against the Dark Brothers.* Oft too the Dark Brother masquerades as an agent of the light, oft he poses as a messenger of the gods, but for your assurance I would say that he who acts under the guidance of the Ego will have clear vision, and will escape deception.

At this time their power is ofttimes mighty. Why? Because so much exists as yet in the personalities of all men that respond to their vibration, and so it is easy for them to affect the bodies of men. So few of the races, comparatively speaking, have as yet built in the higher vibration that responds to the keynote of the Brotherhood of Light, who move practically entirely on the two highest levels (or the atomic and sub-atomic sub-planes) of the mental, emotional and physical planes. When moving on these sub-planes the attacks of elementals on lower planes may be felt but effect no harm, hence the necessity of pure living and controlled pure emotions and elevated thought.

You will notice that I said that the power of the Dark Brotherhood is dominant apparently on the physical and emotional planes. Not so is it on the mental, which is the plane on which the Brothers of the Light work. Mighty dark magicians may be located on the lower mental levels, but on the higher, the White Lodge dominates, the three higher sub-planes being the levels that They beg the evolving sons of men to seek; it is Their region, to which all must strive and aspire. The Dark Brother impresses his will on human beings (if analogous vibration exists) and on the elemental kingdoms of involution. The Brothers of Light plead, as pleaded the Man of Sorrows, for an erring humanity to rise upward to the light. The Dark Brother retards progress and shapes all to his own ends; the Brother of Light bends every effort to the hastening of evolution and—foregoing all that might be His as the price of achievement—stays amid the fogs, the strife, the evil and the hatred of the period if, in so doing, He may by all means aid some, and (lifting them up out of the darkness of earth) set their feet upon the Mount, and enable them to surmount the Cross.

And now what methods may be employed to safeguard the worker in the field of the world? What can be done to ensure his safety in the present strife and in the greater strife of the coming centuries?

i. A realisation that purity of all the vehicles is the prime essential. If a Dark Brother gains control over any man, it but shows that that man has in his life some weak spot. The door whereby entrance is effected must be opened by the man himself; the opening whereby malignant force can be poured in, must be caused by the occupant of the vehicles. Therefore the need of scrupulous cleanliness of the physical body, of clean steady emotion permitted in the emotional body, and of purity of thought in the mental body. When this is so, co-ordination will be present in the lower vehicles, and the indwelling Thinker himself permits no entrance.

ii. The elimination of all fear. The forces of evolution vibrate more rapidly than those of involution and in this fact lies a recognisable security. Fear causes weakness; weakness causes a disintegration; the weak spot breaks and a gap appears, and through that gap evil force may enter. The factor of entrance is the fear of the man himself, who opens thus the door.

iii. A standing firm and unmoved, no matter what occurs. Your feet may be bathed in the mud of earth, but your head may be bathed in the sunshine of the higher regions. Recognition of the filth of earth involves not contamination.

iv. A recognition of the use of commonsense and the application of this commonsense to the matter in hand. Sleep much and, in sleeping, learn to render the body positive; keep busy on the emotional plane and achieve the inner calm. Do naught to overtire the body physical, and play whenever possible. In hours of relaxation comes the adjustment that obviates later tension.   (2-136/8)

3. Those disciples who work today in the world and do so *consciously* in order to aid the Christ and His mission, come within the protecting aura with which the Head of the Hierarchy at all times surrounds certain work undertaken by the Hierarchy in connection with our planet. This work of preparation for His coming is curiously fraught with danger, because of the immense and constant antagonism it arouses (and is arousing increasingly) in the opposing forces of evil. The main attack of these forces is upon disciples, and particularly those in a position and at the point in

evolution where they can act with potency, and greatly help in the task of reaching others. . . . This does not mean that you will be free from attack and—because you are a disciple—attack on all three bodies simultaneously, but it means that such attack will arouse in you no fear. Remember always . . . that it is fear that permits the entry of wrong potencies, and that such an attack may not be aimed at your weakest point, but preferably at your strongest; it is there where disciples are often caught unawares and thus suffer a temporary setback.   (6-748/9)

4. Evil or wrong exists only when the emphasis is retained in the wrong aspect from the point of view of the unfoldment attained, or when that which has been used and developed to the necessary point, holds the life or consciousness too long. Hence the beneficent nature of death.

The Forces of Darkness are powerful energies, working to preserve that which is ancient and material; hence they are pre-eminently the forces of crystallisation, of form preservation, of the attractiveness of matter, and of the lure of that which is existent in the form life of the three worlds. They consequently block deliberately the inflow of that which is new and life-giving; they work to prevent the understanding of that which is of the New Age; they endeavour to preserve that which is familiar and old, to counteract the effects of the oncoming culture and civilisation, to bring blindness to the peoples and to feed steadily the existing fires of hate, of separateness, of criticism and of cruelty. These forces, as far as the intelligent peoples of the world are concerned, work insiduously and cloak their effort in fair words, leading even disciples to express hatred of persons and ideologies, fostering the hidden seeds of hatred found in many human beings. They fan to fury the fear and hate of the world in an effort to preserve that which is old, and make the unknown appear undesirable, and they hold back the forces of evolution and of progress for their own ends. These ends are as inscrutable to you as are the plans of the Ruler of Shamballa.

These are forces which it is well for you to recognise as existing, but there is little that you, as individuals or as groups can do about them beyond seeing to it that there is nothing in you which could make you—unimportant as you are—a focal point for their efforts or an agent for the distribution of their peculiar type of energy—the energy of focussed and directed hate, of separation, of fear and pride. With them we who are connected directly with the Hierarchy have to deal, but you can aid more than you know through the regulation of thoughts and ideas, through the cultivation of a loving spirit, and through the general use of the Great Invocation.   (13-75/6)

113. THE WHITE MAGICIAN

1. Above all, will the emphasis be laid upon the fact that the white magician is he who utilises all power and knowledge in the service of the race. His inner development must be expressed in terms of service before he is permitted to pass on into the advanced school.   (2-331)

2. What constitutes the equipment needed by a white magician? I would say one thing: All students realise that certain requirements must be met if a man is to be entrusted with any measure of understanding of the technique of the Great Work. I take it for granted, however, that the *character* qualifications are not those to which our question refers. All aspirants know, and down the ages have been taught, that a clean mind and a pure heart, love of truth, and a life of service and unselfishness, are prime requisites, and where they are lacking, naught avails and none of the great secrets can be imparted.   (4-543)

3. The white magician works with the forces of nature and swings them back into control of advanced humanity. This can already be seen working out through the activity of the scientists which the latter end of the last century, and this twentieth century, have produced. That much of their magical work has been turned into selfish channels by the tendency of this materialistic age, and that many of their wise and true discoveries in the realm of energy are today adapted to ends which serve man's hatred or love of self, is equally true. But this in no way militates against the wonder of their achievements. When the motive is transmuted from pure scientific interest to love of the divine revelation, and when service to the race is the determining force, then we shall see the true white magic. Hence therefore the need to turn the mystic into the occultist, and to train the modern aspirant in right motive, mind control and brotherly love—all of which must and will express themselves through harmlessness.   (14-359)

114. MANTRAMS

1. I am a messenger of Light. I am a pilgrim on the way of love. I do not walk alone, but know myself as one with all great souls, and one with them in service. Their strength is mine. This strength I claim. My strength is theirs and this I freely give. A soul, I walk on earth. I represent the ONE.   (5-140)

2. I know the Law, and towards the goal I strive. Naught shall arrest my progress on the Way. Each tiny life within my form responds. My soul has sounded forth that call, and clearer day by day it sounds. The glamour holds me not. The Path of Light streams clear ahead. My plea goes forth to reach the hearts of men. I seek, I try to serve your need. Give me your hand and tread the Path with me.   (5-265)

3. I strive towards understanding.
   Let wisdom take the place of knowledge in my life.   (6-140)

4. I strive towards co-operation.
   Let the Master of my life, the soul, and likewise the One
   I seek to serve, throw light through me on others.   (6-140)

5. In the centre of the Will of God I stand.
   Naught shall deflect my will from His.
   I implement that will by love.
   I turn towards the field of service.
   I, the Triangle divine, work out that Will
   Within the square, and serve my fellow men.   (6-141)

6. I am one with my group of brothers, and all that I have is theirs. May the love which is in my soul pour forth to them. May the strength which is in me lift and aid them. May the thoughts which my soul creates reach and encourage them.   (6-245)

7. There is a certain esoteric mantram which embodies . . . the attitude of the disciple who is striving, in co-operative endeavour with others, to link hierarchical intent with human aspiration, and thus bring humanity nearer to its goal. The intent of the Hierarchy is to increase men's *capacity for freedom* in order to function effectively with that "life more abundantly" which the Christ will bring, and which demands that the spirit of man be free—free to approach divinity and free also to choose the Way of that approach. The mantram bears the name . . .

502

The Affirmation of the Disciple

I am a point of light within a greater Light.
I am a strand of loving energy within the stream of Love divine.
I am a point of sacrificial Fire, focussed within the fiery Will of God.
    And thus I stand.

I am a way by which men may achieve.
I am a source of strength, enabling them to stand.
I am a beam of light, shining upon their way.
    And thus I stand.

And standing thus, revolve
And tread this way the ways of men,
And know the ways of God.
    And thus I stand.

This . . . is the best I can do with words and phrases as I attempt to transcribe into language words so ancient that they antedate Sanskrit and Senza. But the meaning is clear, and that is the point of importance. (6-175) and (11-197)

8. The sons of men are one, and I am one with them. I seek to love not hate; I seek to serve and not exact due service. I seek to heal, not hurt.
    Let pain bring due reward of light and love. Let the soul control the outer form, and life, and all events, and bring to light the love which underlies the happenings of the time. Let vision come and insight; let the future stand revealed. Let inner union demonstrate, and outer cleavages be gone. Let love prevail. Let all men love.

These words may seem inadequate, but said with power and an understanding of their significance, and with the potency of the mind and heart behind them, they can prove unbelievably potent in the life of the one who says them. They will produce also an effect in his environment, and the accumulated effects in the world, as you spread the knowledge of the formula, will be great and effective. It will change attitudes, enlighten the vision and lead the aspirant to fuller service and to a wider co-operation based upon sacrifice.   (13-142), (6-147)

9.   We know, O Lord of Life and Love,
                    about the need;
                Touch our hearts anew with love,
                    that we too may love and give.   (13-154)

115. THE PILGRIM

1. *The Rules of the Road*

i. The Road is trodden in the full light of day, thrown upon the Path by Those Who know and lead. Naught can then be hidden, and at each turn upon that Road a man must face himself.

ii. Upon the Road the hidden stands revealed. Each sees and knows the villainy of each. And yet there is, with that great revelation, no turning back, no spurning of each other, no shakiness upon the Road. The Road goes forward into day.

iii. Upon that Road one wanders not alone. There is no rush, no hurry. And yet there is no time to lose. Each pilgrim, knowing this, presses his footsteps forward, and finds himself surrounded by his fellow men. Some move ahead; he follows after. Some move behind; he sets the pace. He travels *not* alone.

iv. Three things the Pilgrim must avoid. The wearing of a hood, a veil which hides his face from others; the carrying of a water pot which only holds enough for his own wants; the shouldering of a staff without a crook to hold.

v. Each Pilgrim on the Road must carry with him what he needs; a pot of fire, to warm his fellow men; a lamp, to cast its rays upon his heart and shew his fellow men the nature of his hidden life; a purse of gold, which he scatters not upon the Road, but shares with others; a sealed vase, wherein he carries all his aspiration to cast before the feet of Him Who waits to greet him at the gate—a sealed vase.

vi. The Pilgrim, as he walks upon the Road, must have the open ear, the giving hand, the silent tongue, the chastened heart, the golden voice, the rapid foot, and the open eye which sees the light. He knows he travels not alone.   (5-583/4), (10-50/1)

2. *The Cup of Karma*: Until the cup has once been used, filled, drained, and seen as naught, it cannot safely hold within that which is later given.

But when to utter emptiness the Pilgrim drains the cup, then to the world in torment now he turns. With cup in hand (drained once, filled again, and refused to selfish need) he tends the need of struggling men who tread the way with him. The draught of love, of sacred fire, of cool, health-giving stream, he lifts not towards himself, but holds it forth to

504

others. Upon the road of weary man, he becomes a Lord of Power—power gained through work accomplished, power reached through conscious will. Through the cup of Karma drained, he gains the right to serve.

Look on, O Pilgrim, to the goal. See shining far ahead the glory that envelops and the light that naught can dim. Seize on the cup and swiftly drain, delay not for the pain. The empty cup, the steady hand, the firm and strong endeavour, lead to a moment's agony and thence to radiant life. (18-762/3)

3. *The Listening Pilgrim*: He who is silent, quiet and calm within, who sees all by means of light divine and is not led by light reflected within the threefold spheres, is he who will shortly hear. From out the environing ether will strike a note upon his ear, unlike the tones that sound within the world terrestrial.

Listen, O Pilgrim, for when that sound strikes in colourful vibration upon the inner sense, know that a point has been achieved marking a great transition.

Watch then, O Pilgrim, for the coming of that hour. With purified endeavour mount nearer to that Sound. Know when its tone steals through the misty dawn, or in the mellow sunlight strikes soft upon the ear, that soon the inner hearing will become expanded feeling and will give place to sight and perfect comprehension.

Know when the music of the spheres comes to you note by note, in misty dawn or sunny noon, at cool of eve, or sounding through the deep of night, that in their rhythmic tone lies secret revelation. (18-763)

116. AN ESOTERICAL CATECHISM

(From Archive XIII of the Masters' Records)

1. *What part, O Pilgrim on the Way, play you within this scheme? How will you enter into peace? How stand before your Lord?*

I play my part with stern resolve, with earnest aspiration; I look above, I help below; I dream not, nor I rest; I toil; I serve; I reap; I pray; I am the cross; I am the Way; I tread upon the work I do; I mount upon my slain self; I kill desire, and I strive, forgetting all reward. I forego peace; I forfeit rest, and in the stress of pain I lose myself and find Myself and enter into peace.   (1-212/3)

2. *What dost thou see, O disciple on the Path?*

Naught but myself, O Master of my life.

Look closer at thyself, and speak again. What seest thou?

A point of light which waxes and which wanes, and makes the darkness darker.

Look with intense desire towards the dark, and when the light shines forth grasp opportunity. What now appears?

A horrid sight, O Master of my life. I like it not. It is not true. I am not this or that. This evil selfish thing, it is not me. I am not this.

Turn on the light with will and power and fierce desire, and then recount the vision that may come. What seest thou?

Beyond the dark, revealed to me by means of light, I see a radiant form which beckons me. What is this Being, standing gracious in the dark and in the light? Is it and can it be my Self?

What dawns upon thy sight as thou standest on the Way, O worn and tired disciple, yet triumphant in the light?

A radiant shining form which is my Self, my soul. A dark and sombre figure, yet old and wise, experienced and sad. This is my self, my lower self, my ancient tried appearance upon the ways of earth. These two stand face to face, and in between, the burning ground. . . . They move and merge. . . . The Path comes to an end. The Way stretches before. Sight is attained, and in the light reality appears.

What canst thou now reveal, O Server on the Way?

Revelation comes through me, O Lord of Life. I see it not.

Why canst thou see it not? What hinders apprehension?

Naught hinders me. I seek not sight for I have seen. My task is revelation. I seek naught for myself.

What comes thy way for revelation? What hast thou to reveal?

Only that which has for aeons long existed, and has for aye been here. The Oneness of the Presence; the area of love; the living, loving, wise, inclusive One, enfolding all and being all, and leaving naught outside.

To whom must come this revelation, O Server of the world of living things?

To all enfolded in the living, loving Presence; to those who all unknown to them maintain that Presence and for ever shall endure—as doth that Presence.

And who are those who live within that Presence but know it not?

They are myself and thou, and still they are myself and still are all I meet. It is the one in every form who think mayhap that form is all; who living thus in time and space, see not the light of life within the form, who hide within, behind the veils, between the four and five (*the four kingdoms in nature and the Kingdom of God. A.A.B.*) and see naught else. To them I must reveal the truth.

How will you do this hardest of all tasks, O triumphing disciple?

By letting it be seen I am myself the truth; by living as a fragment of that Presence and seeing all its parts. And thus is revelation brought into the four and by the fifth. (18-302/3)

117. SOME WORDS OF CHEER

1. It is only as the disciple is willing to relinquish all in the service of the Great One, and to hold naught back, that liberation is achieved, and the body of desire becomes transmuted into the body of the higher intuition. It is the serving perfectly each day—with no thought or calculation about the future—that brings a man to the position of the perfect Server. And, may I suggest one thing? All care and anxiety is based primarily on selfish motive. You fear further pain, you shrink from further sad experience. It is not thus that the goal is reached; it is reached by the path of renunciation. Perhaps it may mean the renunciation of joy, or the renunciation of good reputation, or the renunciation of friends, and the renunciation of all that the heart clings to. I say *perhaps*; I say not, it is so. I but seek to point out to you that if that is the way you are to reach your goal, then for you it is the perfect way. Aught that brings you rapidly to Their Presence and to Their Lotus Feet, is by you to be desired and eagerly welcomed.

Cultivate daily, therefore, that supreme desire that seeks solely the commendation of the inner Guide and Teacher, and the egoic response to good action dispassionately performed.

Should bereavement come your way, smile through it all; it will end in a rich reward and the return of all that has been lost. Should scorn and despisings be your lot, smile still, for only the look of commendation that comes from the Master is the one to seek. Should lying tongues take action, fear not, but forge ahead. A lie is a thing of earth and can be left behind as a thing too vile to be touched. The single eye, the unalloyed desire, the consecrated purpose, and the ear that turns in deafness to all earth's noise

—such is the aim for the disciple. I say no more, I but desire that you do not dissipate needless force in vain imaginings, feverish speculations and troubled expectations.   (2-43/4)

2. All who work and struggle for the good of humanity under the direction of the Hierarchy, take heart and renew your courage. The Hierarchy not only *stands* (as oft I have told you), but It is approaching daily and yearly closer to humanity. The power of the focussed, spiritual unity of the Hierarchy can be felt today in many ways; it is largely responsible for the patient effort of all humanitarian workers and of all who vision unity in the face of great odds, and in spite of the fatigued lethargy and the pessimism which conditions, too hard for human endurance, have imposed upon men's minds. The Hierarchy stands and works. The Masters are working according to Plan—a Plan which is founded in the past history of the race and can there be traced; a Plan which necessitated, because of human selfishness, the drastic horror of the war (1914-45); a Plan which today can and will bridge the gulf which now exists between the unsatisfactory, selfish and material past and that new future which will demonstrate a large measure of world unity, and which will steadily and with skill in action substitute the spiritual values for those which have hitherto held sway.

The guarantee of this is the developing intelligence of men everywhere fighting blindly for freedom and for understanding, and receiving ever the inner assurance, knowledge and aid of Those Who are working out (as always) those situations and conditions wherein mankind can best arrive at divine expression.   (13-672/3)

3. Be of good cheer, for there is no true defeat of the human spirit; there is no final extinction of the divine in man, for divinity ever rises triumphant from the darkest pit of hell. There is need, however, to overcome the inertia of the material nature in response to human need, individually and by the nations not engrossed with the essentials of the situation. This shows signs of happening. There is no power on Earth which can prevent the advance of man towards his destined goal, and no combination of powers can hold him back.   (16-532/3)

118. CONCLUSION

1. *Dedication to the Service of Humanity*

I close with an appeal to all who read these instructions to rally their forces, to renew their vows of dedication to the service of humanity, to subordinate their own ideas and wishes to the group good, to take their eyes off themselves and fix them anew upon the vision, to guard their tongues from idle speech and criticism, from gossip and innuendo, and to read and study so that the work may go intelligently forward. Let all students make up their minds in this day of emergency and of rapid unfolding opportunity to sacrifice all they have to the helping of humanity. Now is the need and the demand. The urgency of the hour is upon us, and I call upon all of you whom I am seeking to help, to join the strenuous Effort of the Great Ones. They are working day and night in an effort to relieve humanity and to offset those evils and disasters which are immanent in the present situation. I offer to you opportunity, and I tell you that you are needed—even the very least of you. I assure you that groups of students, working in unison and with deep and unfaltering love for each other, can achieve significant results.

That each of you may so work, and that each of you may lose sight of self in the realisation of world need, is my earnest prayer and deepest aspiration. (4-639/40)

2. *Talks to Disciples*

Above all, I would say: Seek to recover the fervour of your earlier, spiritual aspiration and self-discipline. If you have never lost it (though many disciples have) seek to force that energy of inspiration to work out in an effective display of definite action upon the physical plane. How, you ask, my brothers? By increasing the radiance of your light in the world through love and meditation, so that others may turn to you as to a beacon light in the dark night of life which seems in this century to have descended upon humanity; seek to love more than you have ever believed was possible, so that others—frozen and chilled by life circumstance and the present horror of human existence—may turn to you for warmth and comforting. What I, and all who are affiliated with the Hierarchy, seek to do at this time of desperate crisis, is to find those who are dependable points of living energy, and through them pour out the love, the strength and the light which the world needs and must have if this

509

storm is to be weathered. I ask you to render this service to me and to humanity. I ask nothing spectacular; it will, however, require a strenuous effort of your souls if you are to respond adequately; I ask nothing impossible; I would remind you that the apathy of the physical body and brain, the inertia of the feeling nature, and the sense of futility of the mind when confronted with large issues, will seem to hinder you.

Again I point the Way to you, and again I wait. Will you intensify your inner life and achieve the power which will enable you to live simultaneously as an efficient human being and a living, loving soul? It is the establishing of the continuity of this dual process which is your main need at this time; it will lead to fusion, personality co-ordination, and a greatly increased efficiency. Many disciples are not young, and the settled habit of thought and of the feeling life is not easy to disrupt. They *must*, however, be disrupted and you must feel no resentment. The rhythms of the personality are stabilised and constitute your line of least resistance. You must cut athwart these, thus forming the cross of life, and existence will then take on added difficulty. The results will be new rhythms of beauty.

To those who are standing in the blaze of pain (and their numbers are legion), of agony, anxiety and distress—seeing it on every hand and attempting to stand steady in the midst of it all—I say: That which appears is not always that which truly is; that which rends and disrupts the personality life is frequently the agent of release, if rightly apprehended; that which will emerge when the Forces of Light have penetrated the world darkness, will demonstrate the nature of the undying human spirit. To all of you I say: My love surrounds you, and the aura of the Ashram of which I am the centre, stands like a great defending wall around you and around all who are battling for the right. *See that you battle.* You can then, if you will, sense this loving protection. Each day, if you will, you can put yourself *en rapport* with your Master. We are not blind or uncaring. We know, however, that there are worse evils than death and pain. We know that this is the hour of humanity's greatest opportunity, and that if men can pass triumphantly through this and (by the strength of their own souls) surmount this very present evil, then the evolution of humanity will be hastened beyond all that was believed possible. It will constitute a release, self-achieved and self-initiated. This means as much in the life of mankind as it means in the life of the individual disciple. That chance and that opportunity must *not* be taken from man; the gained spiritual and eternal values are of far greater importance than his temporary agony.

Little as you may realise it as you think of us in our so-called safe retreats, the capacity of identification with all that is involved in world pain today, and the sensitivity of Those connected with the Hierarchy to the unhappy condition of humanity, makes Their task of standing-by one of supreme spiritual agony. They understand, for *They are one with all men.* This involves a far greater comprehension than you can grasp, and one which can only be adequately expressed in the word "identification". They need the staunch support of all Their disciples, the steadfast love, the loyal attitude, the unquestioning response to human need, which will enable Them to carry more easily the heavy burden which human karma has laid upon Them and *which They carry voluntarily.*

Will you give this? Will you aid Our work in every possible way, both as personalities, dedicated to service, and as souls who walk the lighted Way? The need of humanity for love and light, the need of the Hierarchy for channels, and for those who will work under direction upon the earth, can call forth all that you have to give, and can evoke your soul (the only true reward that the disciple seeks) in power and love. This will happen to you, if you will forget the little self.

That your knowledge may be transmuted into wisdom, and the eye of vision control your living processes and all your undertakings, is the desire (deep within my heart) for each and all of you.   (5-99/102)

3. "The key is found; and with the pressure of the hands in service of the light, and with a beating heart of love, the key is turned. The door swings open wide.

"With hasty feet, the one who hastens towards the light, enters the door and waits. He holds the door ajar for those who follow after. He thus, in action, waits.

"A voice sounds forth: My brother, close the door, for each must turn the key with his own hand, and each must enter through that door alone.

"The blazing light within the Temple of the Lord is not for all at the same moment or hour of the day. Each knows his hour. Your hour is now. So, brother, close the door. Remember, those behind know not the door has opened, or the door has closed. They see it not. Rest on that thought, my brother, and passing through the door, close it with care, and enter upon another stage upon the Way—alone and not alone."   (5-313), (18-766/7)

4. I am giving you here certain needed hints, and much upon which to ponder. I give you of my time and of my love, of my interest and my understanding. Let us together *serve.*   (6-59)

5. Let love play its part in all your lives and all your interrelations, as it must and does in the Hierarchy; look upon the Ashram to which you are affiliated as a miniature Hierarchy, and model your efforts upon what you have learned anent the Hierarchy; count all things but loss unless they are productive along the line of service to humanity, and become increasingly factual in your attitude to all disciples and to the Hierarchy. The coming cycle is momentous in its offering of opportunity, and I would have you—again as individuals and as a group—measure up to this chance. Fix your eyes on human need and your hand in mine (if I may speak thus to you in symbols) and go forward with me to greater influence and deeper usefulness.   (6-110)

6. And so they stand—Humanity and the Hierarchy. And so you stand, my brother, personality and soul, with freedom to go forward into the light if you so determine, or to remain static and unprogressive, learning nothing and getting nowhere; you are equally free to return to identification with the Dweller, negating thus the influence of the Angel, refusing imminent opportunity and postponing—until a much later cycle —your determining choice. This is true of you and of Humanity as a whole. Will humanity's third ray materialistic personality dominate the present situation, or will its soul of love prove the most powerful factor, taking hold of the personality and its little issues, leading it to discriminate rightly and to recognise the true values, and thus bring in the age of soul or hierarchical control? Time alone will show.   (10-160)

7. I call you to prayer and to meditation, for both are needed today, fusing as they do the emotional and mental bodies into one aspiring whole. I call you to discipline, for that is the meaning of fasting, and to the constant effort to live at the highest possible point all the time; this is so often a dream but not often a fact. Today, in the hour of the world's need, aspirants and disciples who are willing to make at least consistent, persistent effort are needed by humanity and the Hierarchy.

My brothers, I have presented the picture; I have held before you for years the vision of opportunity, service and discipleship. I have outlined to you the mechanism of service which already is in existence and which can be galvanised into activity and world usefulness. I leave the matter in your hands, asking you to remember that the united interest, love, service and money of the many is far more potent than even the consecrated effort of the two or three. No one is futile or useless, unless he chooses so to be. . . . There must be steadiness, selflessness and silence, plus courage and confidence—confidence in the strength of your own souls, confidence in the watching Hierarchy and confidence in the Plan. (13-353/4)

8. *Your spiritual goal is the establishing of the Kingdom of God.* One of the first steps towards this is to prepare men's minds to accept the *fact* that the reappearance of the Christ is imminent. You must tell men everywhere that the Masters and Their groups of disciples are actively working to bring order out of chaos. You must tell them that there IS a Plan, and that nothing can possibly arrest the working out of that Plan. You must tell them that the Hierarchy stands, and that It has stood for thousands of years, and is the expression of the accumulated wisdom of the ages. You must tell them above all else that God is love, that the Hierarchy is love, and that the Christ is coming because He loves humanity.

This is the message which you must give at this time. And with this responsibility I leave you. *Work,* my brothers. (13-701)

9. The moment of greatest development is oft the moment of greatest pain. . . . To those of you who have the inner sight and intuitive comprehension, comes the opportunity to aid that apprehension and to lead a despairing world—deep cast into darkness and distress—one step nearer to the light. The work you have to do is to take the knowledge which is yours and adjust its application to the world's need, so that recognition of the truth may be rapid. In the heart of every man lies hid the flower of the intuition. On that you can depend, and no eternal or cosmic fact, clothed in a suitable form, will fail to receive its need of recognition and understanding. (18-11)

10. The major keynote of every single planetary initiation, even to the very highest, is RELATIONSHIP. What other qualities may be revealed to the Initiate on other Paths we know not, but the goal of all endeavour upon our planet, is right relations between man and man, and between man and God, between all expressions of divine life, from the tiniest atom up and on into infinity.

From the standpoint of our planetary evolution, there is naught but love, naught but goodwill and the will-to-good. This exists already, and its true manifestation is nearer today than at any time in planetary history.

From stage to stage, from crisis to crisis, from point to point, and from centre to centre, the life of God progresses, leaving greater beauty behind it as it moves through one form after another, and from kingdom to kingdom. One attainment leads to another; out of the lower kingdoms man has emerged, and (as a result of human struggle) the Kingdom of God will also appear. The bringing in of that Kingdom is all that truly concerns humanity today, and all living processes in mankind are bent towards preparing each individual human being to pass into that Kingdom. The knowledge that there may be greater manifestations than even the Kingdom of God may be inspiring, but that is all. The manifestation of the Kingdom of God on Earth, the preparing of the Way for its great Inaugurator, the Christ, the making possible the externalisation of the Hierarchy upon Earth, give us each and all a fully adequate task and something for which to live and work, to dream and to aspire.

. . . May light and love and power shine upon your ways, and may you in due time and with as little delay as possible, stand before the Initiator and join the ranks of Those Who—actively and consciously—love Their fellow men, work as constructive and regenerative Energies, and forever —SERVE.

I sign myself . . . as the Master *Djwhal Khul.*

THE TIBETAN   (18-737/8)

I have already given you more than you can understand, but not more than you can begin slowly to study and eventually to comprehend. (6-366)